CHAMPIONS ALL!

*Champions of
the Football League
1888/89 to 1991/92
and the Premier League
1992/93 to 2006/07*

Tony Brown

A *SoccerData* Publication

Published in Great Britain by Tony Brown,
4 Adrian Close, Beeston, Nottingham NG9 6FL.
Telephone 0115 973 6086. E-mail soccer@innotts.co.uk
www.soccerdata.com
Limited edition, published 2007

© Tony Brown, 2007

All rights reserved. No part of this publication may be reproduced, stored in a retrieval system, or transmitted in any form, or by any means, electronic, mechanical, photocopying, recording or otherwise without the prior permission in writing of the Copyright holders, nor be otherwise circulated in any form or binding or cover other than in which it is published and without a similar condition including this condition being imposed on the subsequent publisher.

The cover design is by Bob Budd.

Printed and bound by the Cromwell Press, Trowbridge, Wiltshire

ISBN 978-1-905891-02-3

Published in a limited edition

of 400 copies, of which this is

number 97

and signed by the author:

Celebrating ten years

of the SoccerData imprint.

THE AUTHOR'S INTRODUCTION

This is a personal account of 108 Championship winners, from 1888/89 to 2006/07. The book includes the Football League champions to 1992 and the Premier League champions from 1993 onwards.

I saw my first game at Nottingham Forest's City Ground in 1955, so it is with a slight sense of unease that I realize I could have seen 53 of these championship teams; nearly half. I'm suddenly aware of my age! Of course, I haven't seen anything like 53, especially since some date from well before the blanket coverage of the game on TV. Also, like some of my readers perhaps, the dominance of Liverpool in the 1970s and Manchester United in the 1990s makes it difficult for an old man like me to distinguish between the seasons. Writing this book has been somewhat cathartic then. I hope you will not feel I have over-simplified the identification of key events and players in each season; in any case, the statistics are included to allow you to draw your own conclusions.

There is just enough detail about each season to fix it in my mind, and hopefully in yours too. It is not intended to take the place of detailed accounts in club histories, to which you may need to refer for other facts and stories. I've presented the seasons in club order in the first section of the book, though the results and line-ups grids are in date order.

Today's concept of a team manager is something that was quite slow to develop. Everton and West Bromwich Albion managed perfectly well without one until after the Second World War. They had a club secretary of course, who would deal with players' contracts and sometimes team selection, though often both these issues were in the hands of the club directors. Tom Watson, manager of championship teams at Sunderland and Liverpool, is sometimes recognized as the first manager, but I suspect he would have expected to be called club secretary rather than team manager. I have followed the example set by Messrs White and Turner, authors of 'The Breedon Book of Football Managers' and included a (sec) for secretary after some of the managers' names when their tasks are thought to have been mainly administrative.

The "first at top" and "last at top" entries work as follows. I disregard the first three games of the season, so the first League table is calculated at the fourth game. The "first at top" date is when the eventual champions first get to the top of the table. This might be after the fourth game of course, and you will find a couple of examples where clubs waited until the last day of the season! The "last at top" date needs a little more definition. This is the date after which the eventual champions did not lose their place at the top.

The "date won" entry is the date at which the eventual champions could not be caught. Some clubs could be assumed to have won the title at an earlier date, given a massively superior goal average or difference. However, given the unpredictability of football, I think it better only to take the points totals into account when identifying the date won.

There are a number of references to a 'Scots Count'. Most clubs in the first few seasons of the Football League were as dependent on 'imports' as the leading Premiership teams are today. The Scots Count is a rough average of the number of players, out of 11, that were regular members of the team and born north of the border. We can play the same game with today's champions, although we will have to rename it as a "Non-UK Count". I have resisted the urge to classify the Premier League champions in this way, but since it is recent history you are welcome to have a go yourself!

Tony Brown
October 2007

ROLL OF HONOUR

In 108 years of competition, 23 clubs have been champions of the Football League or the Premier League. They are as follows.

Liverpool	18
Manchester United	16
Arsenal	13
Everton	9
Aston Villa	7
Sunderland	6
Newcastle United	4
Sheffield Wednesday	4
Blackburn Rovers	3
Chelsea	3
Huddersfield Town	3
Leeds United	3
Wolverhampton Wanderers	3
Burnley	2
Derby County	2
Manchester City	2
Portsmouth	2
Preston North End	2
Tottenham Hotspur	2

and with one title:

Ipswich Town, Nottingham Forest, Sheffield United, West Bromwich Albion

Four clubs led the table at the halfway point at the end of December, but never went on to win the title. They are Oldham Athletic (1914/15), Cardiff City (1923/24), Brentford (1937/38) and Norwich City (1992/93).

The 15 Premier League winners (included in the table above) are Manchester United (nine times), Arsenal (three), Chelsea (two) and Blackburn Rovers (once).

DOUBLE WINNERS

The 'double' of League championship and FA Cup has now been achieved 10 times as follows:

1888/89	Preston North End
1896/97	Aston Villa
1960/61	Tottenham Hotspur
1970/71	Arsenal
1985/86	Liverpool
1993/94	Manchester United
1995/96	Manchester United
1997/98	Arsenal
1998/99	Manchester United
2001/02	Arsenal

CHAMPIONS ALL!

Arsenal 1931

Manager:	Herbert Chapman
Leading scorer:	Jack Lambert, 38 (7 hat-tricks)
Ever-present:	Cliff Bastin
First at top:	At start
Latest at top:	Feb 5
Date won:	Apr 18
Players used:	22

It took Herbert Chapman six years at Arsenal to mould his first championship team, with only one top-six finish before 1931. One wonders if today's managers would be granted as much time! Five straight wins at the start of the season took Arsenal to the head of the table. Aston Villa and Sheffield Wednesday (bidding for a third consecutive title) both had spells at the top, but just one defeat in their last 19 games saw Arsenal home. They scored a new club record of 127 goals and their 66 points was also a record until Leeds United's 67, 38 years later.

127 remains the highest number of goals scored by a championship-winning club. It is second in the all-clubs list, only being bettered by Aston Villa, who scored 128, also in 1930/31. There was just one game in which Arsenal did not score – against Huddersfield Town, Chapman's former club.

Jack Lambert scored 98 League goals in 143 games for Arsenal, having joined them from Doncaster Rovers in 1926. He was a strong player with a powerful shot but won no England caps. David Jack (with 31) and Cliff Bastin (28) also made major contributions to the goal total.

This was the first time a southern club had won the championship. Of the 108 titles to date, only 20 have been won by clubs south of the Midlands and East Anglia.

Arsenal 1933

Manager:	Herbert Chapman
Leading scorer:	Cliff Bastin, 33
Ever-present:	Cliff Bastin
First at top:	Oct 29
Latest at top:	Nov 19
Date won:	Apr 22
Players used:	22

After finishing second in both League and Cup in 1931/32, Arsenal returned to the top this season. Their two wingers, Hulme and Bastin, scored 53 of Arsenal's 118 goals. Lambert was not so productive this season, but scored five in one game in a 9-2 win over Sheffield United. Arsenal set the pace all season, winning the title with a comfortable four point margin over Aston Villa.

Cliff Bastin enjoyed a long career at Arsenal, from 1929 to 1947, having joined them from Exeter, aged just 17. He was just 21 years of age in this championship season. 5ft 8in tall, Bastin had a powerful left foot shot and won 21 England caps. His overall career figures for Arsenal were 151 goals in 353 League appearances.

The season was notable for Arsenal's FA Cup defeat at Third Division Walsall, although admittedly they were without five first-team regulars.

Arsenal 1934

Managers:	Herbert Chapman, Joe Shaw
Leading scorers:	Cliff Bastin, Ray Bowden, 13
Ever-present:	No-one
First at top:	Nov 25
Latest at top:	Apr 2
Date won:	Apr 28
Players used:	24

Tragedy struck on January 6, 1934 when manager Herbert Chapman died of pneumonia, aged 55. Trainer Joe Shaw took over team management for the remainder of the season, with George Allison as general manager.

Perhaps as a consequence, a run of three defeats in January followed, dropping Arsenal to second place. However, just two defeats in their last 15 games ensured Arsenal of their second successive championship.

Inside-right Ray Bowden joined from Plymouth Argyle in March 1933. He won six England caps whilst with Arsenal and moved to Newcastle United in 1937 after scoring 42 goals in 123 League games.

Ted Drake made his debut in March and made an immediate impact, scoring seven goals in the 10 games he played.

Arsenal 1935

Manager:	George Allison
Leading scorers:	Ted Drake, 42 (7 hat-tricks)
Ever-present:	No-one
First at top:	Oct 13
Latest at top:	Jan 19
Date won:	Apr 22
Players used:	25

Arsenal won their third consecutive championship by a four point margin over a Sunderland team that went on to win the 1936 championship. At halfway, Arsenal were two points behind Sunderland and Manchester City, but as these clubs lost form in January Arsenal won four on the trot and retained their lead to the end of the season.

This was Ted Drake's season. He had joined from Southampton in March 1934 and was 23 years-old in 1935. He was a brave and powerful centre-forward who won five England caps, despite the competition from Dean and Lawton. His seven hat-tricks in 1934/35 included four 4-goal hauls. Later, he managed the Chelsea championship team of 1955. He also played first-class cricket for Hampshire. His career totals for Arsenal were 128 goals in 169 League games.

Allison's important signings this season were Jack Crayston, a 6ft centre-half from Bradford Park Avenue, and Leeds United's English international Wilf Copping, an ex-miner and one of the real 'hard men' of the game.

The England team that played Italy at Highbury in November 1934 included seven Arsenal players.

Arsenal 1938

Manager:	George Allison
Leading scorer:	Ted Drake, 17
Ever-present:	No-one
First at top:	Feb 19
Latest at top:	Mar 5
Date won:	May 7 (last day)
Players used:	29

Many of the triple-championship players had retired or left the club, so there were new faces in the Arsenal teams of 1937/38. They included cricketer Denis Compton, who joined brother Les in the team. Alex James had retired in 1937 and finding a successor proved difficult. The team featured George Swindin in goal, amateur Bernard Joy at centre-half and centre-forward Eddie Carr, who scored important goals as the season reached its climax.

Brentford were the surprise club of the season. They built up a three-point lead over their rivals by the end of December, but fell away in the second half of the season to finish 6th. With three games to play, Preston North End had the same points total as Arsenal, and their first championship since 1890/91 looked possible. However, Arsenal beat them 3-1 in Preston, leaving the Gunners in a straight fight with Wolves for the title. Wolves had a difficult last game at Sunderland and lost 0-1, so Arsenal's 5-0 win at home to Bolton gave them the championship by a single point. Arsenal equalled Sheffield Wednesday's record championship low total (for a 42-game season) of 52 points.

Arsenal used 29 players in League games this season, a total not exceeded until Chelsea's 30 in 2004/05.

Arsenal 1948

Manager:	Tom Whittaker
Leading scorer:	Ronnie Rooke, 33
Ever-present:	Ronnie Rooke
First at top:	At start
Latest at top:	Never headed
Date won:	Apr 10
Players used:	19

Unbeaten in their first 17 games, Arsenal never looked like being caught. They were three points ahead of Burnley at the turn of the year, and finished a comfortable seven points clear of Manchester United. A 1-1 draw with Huddersfield Town in April gave them the title with four games still to play. Five of the 1938 championship team made regular appearances this season and wing-half Joe Mercer had played for the 1939 Everton team.

5ft 9in Ronnie Rooke joined from Fulham in December 1946. He was a 37-year-old veteran in this championship season. Never capped, but he was blessed with a thunderball shot that brought him 68 goals in his 88 career appearances for Arsenal.

Arsenal 1953

Manager:	Tom Whittaker
Leading scorer:	Doug Lishman, 22
Ever-present:	No-one
First at top:	Apr 15
Latest at top:	Same
Date won:	May 1 (last game)
Players used:	21

Five consecutive wins in April took the Gunners' supporters minds off climbers on Everest and invitations to the coronation of HM QE2. A defeat at challengers Preston in the penultimate game meant that the title race boiled down to a last game 'must win' against Burnley. Preston had finished their programme with a two-point lead, so Arsenal knew a win was good enough for them to take the title on goal average. Late goals from Burnley made for an exciting finish, but Arsenal held out to win 3-2. This was only the third time that goal average was needed to settle the title.

Doug Lishman was a 5ft 11in inside-left with a knack of scoring goals, 125 in 226 League games for Arsenal. He joined from Walsall in May 1948. He was not capped by England, but is well thought of by your author, thanks to his hat-trick for Forest in a vital end-of-season promotion decider at Bramall Lane in 1957!

Arsenal 1971

Manager:	Bertie Mee
Leading scorer:	Ray Kennedy, 19
Ever-present:	George Armstrong, Frank McLintock, Bob Wilson
First at top:	Apr 17
Latest at top:	May 3
Date won:	May 3 (last game)
Players used:	16

Leeds United and Arsenal were well clear of the pack at the halfway point of the season, with Leeds three points clear. However, an excellent second half saw Arsenal to the championship; all their last nine home games were won. Leeds finished their programme with 64 points; good enough to win the title in most seasons. Arsenal had a game in hand, played two days later at White Hart Lane. A goal from Ray Kennedy gave Arsenal a 1-0 win and the championship.

With the title won, attention switched to the FA Cup final. An unforgettable Charlie George goal in extra time won Arsenal the Cup and the League and Cup double.

Ray Kennedy, just 19 at the time, had an outstanding season. He was a tall powerful inside forward who was later to win more championship honours after his move to Liverpool.

In addition to the three ever-presents, Kennedy, McNab, Radford, Rice and Storey also made 40 or more appearances this season. George Graham, later to manage the club to two championships, played in 38 games and scored 11 goals.

Arsenal 1989

Manager:	George Graham
Leading scorer:	Alan Smith, 23
Ever-present:	John Lukic, Nigel Winterburn, David Rocastle
First at top:	Dec 26
Latest at top:	The same
Date won:	May 26 (last game)
Players used:	17

This season saw the closest-ever finish. The last day of the season found Liverpool top after winning games in hand, needing only a draw from their home game with Arsenal. Even a 0-1 defeat would have left them top. In a moment that is etched into folk memory, Michael Thomas skipped away in the last minute of the game to score Arsenal's second in their 2-0 win. It left the clubs level on points and level on goal difference; Arsenal took the title because they had scored more goals. If goal average was still the rule, it would have been Liverpool's championship.

Alan Smith was a tall (6ft 3in) striker who joined Arsenal from Leicester City. He was Arsenal Player of the Year in 1989. His career totals for the club were 87 goals in 242+22 League games.

Only Paul Merson also scored ten goals or more this season.

Arsenal 1991

Manager:	George Graham
Leading scorer:	Alan Smith, 22
Ever-present:	David Seaman, Lee Dixon, Nigel Winterburn, Steve Bould
First at top:	Dec 8
Latest at top:	Dec 31
Date won:	May 6
Players used:	19

This is the only occasion that a championship winning team has had points deducted during the season. Arsenal were docked two points (on November 12) and Manchester United one point after being found guilty of bringing the game into disrepute following a 21-man brawl during the game at Old Trafford in October. Arsenal still finished 7 points clear of second placed Liverpool, losing only one League game. Just 8 goals were conceded in the 19 away games, equalling Preston's record from 1889 (when only 11 away games were played).

The line-up was remarkably similar to that of 1989, except that Anders Limpar had replaced Brian Marwood on the wing. Tony Adams was the kingpin of a defence that only conceded 18 goals.

Arsenal 1998

Manager:	Arsène Wenger
Leading scorer:	Dennis Bergkamp, 16
Ever-present:	No-one
First at top:	Sep 24
Latest at top:	Apr 7
Date won:	May 3
Players used:	26

Arsène Wenger's championship-winning career started on a high note as Arsenal produced a League and Cup double. There were little signs of this at the end of December, with Arsenal in sixth place, 12 points behind Manchester United. A run of 10 consecutive victories (five of them "1-0 to the Arsenal") in March and April gave them the title with two games to spare – both of which they lost. However, the FA Cup was won 2-0 against Newcastle United.

Dennis Bergkamp was one of the first 'stellar' players to join the Premier League. He was a £7.5m signing from Internationale in July 1995. This was his greatest season for Arsenal, culminating in two Player of the Year awards. He went on to make 245+46 League appearances for the Gunners, scoring 85 goals.

Seaman, Adams, Bould and Winterburn were still most effective in defence. Ian Wright and Marc Overmars followed Bergkamp in the scorers' list this season.

Arsenal 2002

Manager:	Arsène Wenger
Leading scorer:	Thierry Henry, 24
Ever-present:	No-one
First at top:	Sep 15
Latest at top:	Apr 1
Date won:	May 8
Players used:	25

Another double season, and the first occasion since the very first season when a championship club was unbeaten away from home. Arsenal scored in every game, the only time in all 108 seasons that the champions have done this.

At the end of March, Arsenal were in third place behind Liverpool and Manchester United but with games in hand. They were in the middle of a run of 13 consecutive wins to the end of the season. The title was won with a vital 1-0 win over Manchester United at Old Trafford in the penultimate game, thanks to a goal from Wiltord. This game came four days after the FA Cup was won at the Millennium Stadium, by 2-0 against Chelsea.

Thierry Henry signed for Arsenal from Juventus in July 1999 and made an immediate impact with his lightning pace and excellent ball skills. His goals to games ratio stands comparison with some of the great strikers of old. To watch him in full flight as he cut in towards the goal must have had Arsenal supporters counting on another goal before he even shot.

The 2001/02 Arsenal team was much changed from the previous championship year. Sol Campbell was now at the heart of the defence, with Ljungberg and Wiltord contributing goals.

Arsenal 2004

Manager:	Arsène Wenger
Leading scorer:	Thierry Henry, 30
Ever-present:	Jans Lehmann
First at top:	Aug 31
Latest at top:	Jan 18
Date won:	Apr 25
Players used:	22

When I was a lad, they used to say the double of League and Cup would never be done again. Well, since 1961, several clubs proved the experts wrong. There was one record that seemed on safer ground; repeating Preston's achievement in the first season of being unbeaten in the League. In what I think is Arsenal's greatest-ever season, 2003/04 is when they remained unbeaten to equal Preston's record. I doubt if I will see it happen again in my lifetime.

Manchester United seemed to be the main threat, and headed the table at the end of December. However, United fell away badly in the second half as Chelsea put in a challenge. A 2-2 draw at White Hart Lane in April gave Arsenal the title, with four games left to play.

Henry's 30 goals came in 20 separate games. You would have done nicely at the bookmakers if you had bet on him to score in each game Arsenal played!

Although Arsenal won none of the cups this season, they had good runs in all of them, losing in the semi-finals of the FA Cup and the League Cup.

Aston Villa 1894

Manager:	George Ramsey (sec)
Leading scorer:	Jack Devey, 20
Ever-present:	Jimmy Cowan
First at top:	Sep 16
Latest at top:	Oct 28
Date won:	Apr 7
Players used:	23

Villa were very much the club of the decade, with five championships and two FA Cup wins from 1894 to 1900. For the first two of these championship seasons, they were based at Wellington Road. Though reporters claimed gates of 20,000, it is not clear how many of these would have been able to see the game!

Villa built up a six-point lead by the end of December and maintained that margin to the end of the season, with only Sunderland providing a serious challenge.

Jack Devey was an all-round sportsman who enjoyed a long cricket career with Warwickshire. He played football for local clubs in Birmingham before joining Villa in 1891. He was capped twice by England.

Jimmy Cowan was an attacking centre-half in the days when this was a common tactic. He was well-known as a sprinter and won the famous Powderhall Handicap in 1896. He was just 5ft 6½in tall, but his quoted weight of 12st 3lbs indicates a sprinter's powerful build.

For the first time in the League's history, the 'Scots Count' fell below five. Maybe the lessons learned from the Scottish players had finally permeated the English game. The preponderance of Scots in championship teams was henceforth not so great – with the odd exception of course.

Aston Villa 1896

Manager:	George Ramsey (sec)
Leading scorer:	John Campbell, 26
Ever-present:	Jack Devey
First at top:	Sep 30
Latest at top:	Jan 11
Date won:	Apr 4
Players used:	18

Derby County won all 10 home games and led the table at the end of December, with Villa in third. Six consecutive wins took Villa to the top in January and they finished with a four-point margin over Derby, taking the title when Derby dropped a point on April 4.

Villa paid Burnley £250 for international back James Crabtree in the summer of 1895. Crabtree, Reynolds and Jimmy Cowan formed an outstanding line of half-backs.

John Campbell was a Scot from Celtic where he had won the Scottish championship twice, and later returned to the club. He had developed an outstanding reputation in Scotland, and emphasized his skill by scoring his 26 goals in just 26 games. 5ft 9in tall but nearly 12st in weight, he was said to be difficult to stop when running at the opposition's defence.

This was the season Villa lost the FA Cup – literally. Following their FA Cup win in 1894/95, it was on display in a shop window in Birmingham. Sometime during the night of September 11-12 1895 it was stolen and never seen again. A replica had to be made to the same design. Villa were fined £25.

Aston Villa 1897

Manager:	George Ramsey (sec)
Leading scorer:	Fred Wheldon, 18
Ever-present:	Charlie Athersmith, Jimmy Cowan, Fred Wheldon
First at top:	Nov 28
Latest at top:	The same
Date won:	Apr 10
Players used:	17

If 1895/96 was good, this season was outstanding. It got off to a slow start, with Villa recording only two wins in the first six games. An unbeaten run of 12 games took them to the top, where they finished with a lead of 11 points. The title was won when Derby County failed to win on April 10; Villa had three games left to play, all of which were won. For good measure, the FA Cup was also won, to make Villa the second team to complete "the double".

John Campbell was not quite as productive as in the previous season, and the leading scorer honours went to Fred Wheldon. Fred had been signed in 1896 from local rivals Small Heath (today's Birmingham City). He was a good dribbler with the ball and won four caps for England. He played first class cricket for Worcestershire.

Aston Villa 1899

Manager:	George Ramsey (sec)
Leading scorer:	Jack Devey, 21
Ever-present:	Tom Bowman
First at top:	Oct 29
Latest at top:	Apr 24
Date won:	Apr 29 (last game)
Players used:	23

Three of Villa's 1897 championship team joined Celtic in the summer of 1897, so 1897/98 proved to be a rebuilding period for the club. By the mid-point of 1898/99, Villa had a narrow lead over Everton and Burnley but a late season run by Liverpool dropped them to second place. It came down to 'last-game decider', with Villa at home to Liverpool. 41,000 spectators shoe-horned themselves into Villa Park to see an emphatic win by the home team, 5-0.

The season was notable for one of those one-off, never repeated events that enliven League history. The referee was late arriving for the match at Sheffield Wednesday. After some deliberation, it was decided to start without him. Though he took over at half-time, the delay meant that darkness fell with 10 minutes left to play. Wednesday were the better team on the day and led 3-1 at the time. The League, in their infinite wisdom, consulted the rule-book and decided that the last 10 minutes would have to be played at a later date. The first suggestion was that perhaps the 10 minutes could be played before the return game at Villa Park. In the end, Villa agreed to play Wednesday in a benefit match for one of their players, and the missing minutes were duly played out before the friendly game. Villa made one change for the second game, Garraty replacing Bedingfield: I've chosen to give Garraty a 'substitute' appearance in the records, even though he wasn't.

At the time, the League instructed that the game should count as a loss for Villa when calculating the League table. I've chosen not to do this when calculating Villa's position throughout the season; you never know, they might have knocked in three goals in those closing minutes!

Aston Villa 1900

Manager:	George Ramsey (sec)
Leading scorer:	Billy Garraty, 27
Ever-present:	Billy George, Fred Wheldon
First at top:	Feb 17
Latest at top:	The same
Date won:	Apr 23
Players used:	21

Sheffield United set the pace this season and built up a six point lead by the end of December. Villa grew stronger towards the end of the season, losing just one game in their last 13, to leave United in second place by two points. Villa finished their programme first, leaving a mathematical chance for the Blades if they scored plenty of goals in the last two games. Their last game at Burnley was lost, leaving Villa champions by two points.

Billy Garraty was a local man, signed from Aston Shakespeare, and just 21 years of age this season. He was an industrious player able to play in almost any position – one of the first great "utility" players. He was capped once by England. He scored 96 goals in 224 League games during his career at Villa.

Aston Villa 1910

Manager:	George Ramsey (sec)
Leading scorer:	Harry Hampton, 26
Ever-present:	Charlie Wallace
First at top:	Jan 29
Latest at top:	The same
Date won:	Apr 16
Players used:	18

This season saw a straight fight between Villa and Liverpool and they finished well clear of the rest. Villa's record included a 15-match run without defeat. They built on this to finish five points ahead of Liverpool.

The Villa team included centre-forward Harry Hampton and inside-forward Joe Bache. In their Villa careers, Hampton scored 213 goals in 338 appearances and Bache 167 in 431. Hampton was just 5ft 8in tall and was a fearless, fast moving player on the field.

The ever-present outside-right Charlie Wallace also enjoyed a long career at the club, scoring 54 goals in 314 League games.

Aston Villa 1981

Manager:	Ron Saunders
Leading scorer:	Peter Withe, 20
Ever-present:	Des Bremner, Gordon Cowans, Ken McNaught, Tony Morley, Dennis Mortimer, Jimmy Rimmer, Kenny Swain
First at top:	Oct 22
Latest at top:	Apr 4
Date won:	May 2
Players used:	14

This season was something of a throwback to the 19th Century. Not only were Villa champions again, but they did it with just 14 players, of whom no less than seven were ever-present.

Liverpool and Villa were top at the end of December, but Ipswich were just a point behind with games in hand. Villa finally edged in front of Ipswich on April 4 and remained in top spot to the end of the season. Ipswich were still in with a shout, but both clubs lost their games on May 2, leaving Villa as champions.

Peter Withe won 11 caps for England and championship honours with Nottingham Forest in 1978. He had also played for Southport, Barrow, Wolves, Birmingham and Newcastle before joining Villa and later played for Sheffield United and Huddersfield Town. His longest time at one club was at Villa, where he scored 74 goals in 182 League games.

Blackburn Rovers 1912

Manager:	RB Middleton (sec)
Leading scorer:	Watty Aitkenhead, 15
Ever-present:	None
First at top:	Nov 11
Latest at top:	Jan 20
Date won:	Apr 25
Players used:	21

One of the original 12 Football League clubs, and five times FA Cup winners, Rovers supporters had to wait until 1912 for their first championship. The strength of this team was the half-back line of Walmsley, Smith and Bradshaw. At right-back was English international Bob Crompton, who joined the club in 1896, made 530 League appearances and was later club manager. With 42 caps, Crompton was a regular in the England team for many years.

With only one win in their first four games, Rovers got off to a slow start. Briefly top in November, they dropped to sixth before a run of 11 games unbeaten took them to the top. A heavy 1-5 defeat at Woolwich Arsenal may have blunted confidence, but they bounced back three days later to beat West Bromwich 4-1 and win the championship.

Watty Aitkenhead was signed from Partick Thistle in 1907. He won one cap for Scotland. He was an effective utility player, noted for his ability to make goals for others as well as score them himself.

Blackburn Rovers 1914

Manager:	RB Middleton (sec)
Leading scorer:	Danny Shea, 27
Ever-present:	Arthur Cowell
First at top:	Sep 13
Latest at top:	Nov 8
Date won:	Apr 10
Players used:	21

Rovers set the pace from day one, with a ten-game unbeaten run at the start of the season. Manchester United kept up with the pace and took the lead briefly in November. Rovers returned to the top to build a three-point lead in December and finished seven clear of Aston Villa, winning the title with three games left to play.

Danny Shea set a new transfer record (£2,000) with his transfer from Southern League West Ham United and his 27 goals were an important part of Rovers' second championship success in three seasons. It is said he once headed his own centre into the net, though I'm not sure I believe that story! He scored 61 goals in 97 games for Blackburn before returning to West Ham in 1920.

Blackburn Rovers 1995

Manager:	Kenny Dalglish
Leading scorer:	Alan Shearer, 34 (four hat-tricks)
Ever-present:	Alan Shearer
First at top:	Nov 26
Latest at top:	The same
Date won:	May 14 (last game)
Players used:	21

There were signs that a good team was being built at Blackburn; fourth in 1992/93 and second in 1993/94. By the end of December 1994 Rovers had a three-point lead over Manchester United. United pressed them all the way, but Rovers did enough for the championship and finished one point clear. They needed to win their last game at Liverpool to be certain of the title; they lost, but Manchester United could only draw.

The twin-strike force of Alan Shearer and Chris Sutton scored 49 goals between them. Shearer's total included four hat-tricks.

Somewhat freakishly, Blackburn used the same number of players this season, 21, as they did in their two other championship seasons.

Burnley 1921

Manager:	John Haworth
Leading scorer:	Joe Anderson, 25
Ever-present:	Bill Watson
First at top:	Nov 20
Latest at top:	The same
Date won:	Apr 23
Players used:	23

Having finished second to West Bromwich in 1920, Burnley were certainly one of the favourites this season. In a topsy-turvy year, they lost their first three games but then went on to set a new League record of 30 games without defeat. By the time of their next defeat, at Manchester City in March, they were seven points clear. Although their season finished out of character with what had gone before, with no wins in their last six games, the title was won with three games left to play.

Joe Anderson was a Scot from Clydebank, renowned for powerful shots from distance. He scored 64 goals in 121 appearances for Burnley before returning to Clydebank. Burnley's half-back line of Halley, Boyle and Watson was said to be the best of the time.

Burnley 1960

Manager:	Harry Potts
Leading scorer:	John Connelly, 20
Ever-present:	Jimmy Adamson, Brian Miller, Ray Pointer
First at top:	May 2
Latest at top:	The same
Date won:	May 2 (last game)
Players used:	18

Though they only led the table after the final game of the season, Burnley were a good footballing team with successful cup runs to their credit and a publicity-aware chairman, Bob Lord. With Wolves having played their 42 games, Burnley needed a win against Manchester City at Maine Road to win the title. Leading scorer Connelly was injured, but a goal from his reserve, Trevor Meredith, gave Burnley the win.

John Connelly was a winger who won 20 England caps. He was just 22 this season, and later moved to Manchester United where he was part of their championship team of 1965. Connelly was a two-footed winger at home on either side of the field.

Chelsea 1955

Manager:	Ted Drake
Leading scorer:	Roy Bentley, 22
Ever-present:	Eric Parsons, Derek Saunders
First at top:	Mar 23
Latest at top:	The same
Date won:	Apr 18
Players used:	20

With no trophies to show for their first 50 years of history, it was somehow appropriate that Chelsea should be champions in their jubilee year. It was a very close-fought season, with many clubs in contention for the title. Sunderland were top at the end of December, but only two points separated the first six clubs. Chelsea's form was better than the rest in the second half of the season. They took the title with just 52 points, but still managed to finish four points clear of the pack bunched behind them. The championship was won on April 18 when Wolves lost.

Roy Bentley was a fast-moving centre-forward able to play in all parts of the forward line. Indeed, later in his career he could be found playing at centre-half and right-back. He signed for the club from Newcastle United in 1948 and scored 129 goals in 324 appearances for Chelsea. He won 12 England caps.

Chelsea 2005

Manager:	José Mourinho
Leading scorer:	Frank Lampard, 13
Ever-present:	Frank Lampard
First at top:	Nov 6
Latest at top:	The same
Date won:	Apr 30
Players used:	30

They use to say money was not a guarantee of success in football. Maybe the same is true today – but money certainly helps. Claudio Ranieri had started to spend the chairman's billions in 2003/04, but Mourinho was able to take things to a higher level in 2004/05. Once they had risen to the top in November they never looked like being caught. A 2-0 win at Bolton in April gave them the title with three games left to play.

Chelsea set a new record of 95 points from a 38-game season and finished 12 clear of second place Arsenal. Their 29 wins was also a record for a 38-game season, a feat they repeated in 2006. Just 15 goals were conceded all season, equalling Preston's count in the very first season when only 22 games were played. Another record, perhaps less welcome but symptomatic of the modern age, is that they used the most players ever in a single championship season.

Chelsea 2006

Manager:	José Mourinho
Leading scorer:	Frank Lampard, 16
Ever-present:	None
First at top:	Aug 27
Latest at top:	The same
Date won:	Apr 17
Players used:	25

Chelsea continued where they left off, and were never headed during the season. Nine consecutive victories at the start of the season had statisticians reaching for the record books. A defeat at Old Trafford was the only reverse in the first half of the season, by which point they had a 9-point lead. The title was won by a 3-0 victory over Everton with three games left to play.

Frank Lampard again led the scorers' list, a remarkable feat when you consider the world-class strikers in the Chelsea squad. Attacking mid-field players have been important to many of the championship teams.

Derby County 1972

Manager:	Brian Clough (with Peter Taylor)
Leading scorer:	Alan Hinton, 15
Ever-present:	Colin Boulton, Kevin Hector
First at top:	Apr 1
Latest at top:	May 1
Date won:	May 8
Players used:	16

Clough's first miracle (see also Nottingham Forest) took Derby to the Second Division championship in 1969 and the Championship itself three years later. Clough and Taylor had the ability to get the best out of every player and to mould them into footballing teams that never knew when they were beaten.

Dave Mackay had been a key player in the 1969 promotion team but left the club in the summer of 1971. Colin Todd was signed from Sunderland in February 1971 and proved to be the last piece in the jigsaw. Derby were there or thereabouts in the opening weeks of the season, which were also occupied with Texaco Cup games, a competition that included clubs from Northern Ireland and Scotland. The low point in the League came when they lost 0-3 to Leeds United in December, but Cloughie's tongue-lashings produced the usual results and Derby started their climb to the top. With one game left to play, they were in third place, with both Leeds and Liverpool looking the more likely champions. Famously, Clough was on holiday and Taylor and the squad were in Majorca when the last games were played on May 8; the results left Derby as champions.

Alan Hinton's runs down the wing and his explosive shots had thrilled at least this spectator at the City Ground, but it seemed to me that his form was never quite the same after he got married! He proved me wrong after his move to Derby, where (as Gerald Mortimer describes him) he was creator in chief in the championship sides of 1969 and 1972. His 15 goals included seven penalties and many "assists". He won three England caps whilst at Wolves and Forest.

Goalkeeper Colin Boulton was a safe, unspectacular but consistent goalkeeper who provided a firm basis for the defence. Kevin Hector had four seasons with Bradford Park Avenue, where he is fondly remembered, before making headlines in the local paper when he joined Derby in 1966. He was a natural footballer who would easily hold his own in today's game. He holds the appearance record for Derby and scored 201 goals in all games, second in the list behind Steve Bloomer.

Derby County 1975

Manager:	Dave Mackay
Leading scorer:	Bruce Rioch, 15
Ever-present:	Colin Boulton, Bruce Rioch
First at top:	Apr 9
Latest at top:	Same
Date won:	Apr 26
Players used:	16

Clough and Taylor had left the club under controversial circumstances in 1973. Dave Mackay found management difficult at first, but his management style (not dissimilar to his never-say-die attitude as a player) soon pulled things round. Derby finished in third place in his first season. A few key signings, notably Bruce Rioch and Francis Lee, produced a winning team for 1974/75.

By September 1974 Derby were in 14th place and there was little sign of what was to follow. Even at the turn of the year they were still mid-table. However, a string of victories and a lack of consistency from the other challengers saw them reach the top in April and stay there. At the end of the season, Ipswich had a game in hand and a chance to catch Derby, but a point from Derby's last game was enough to take the title.

Bruch Rioch was signed from Aston Villa in February 1974. He was that rare and valuable beast – a player who scored a hatful of goals from midfield. Three other players reached double figures of goals; this firepower undoubtedly made the difference in the Championship race. He was capped twice by Scotland.

Colin Boulton, ever-present in 1971/72, repeated the feat this time.

Everton 1891

Manager:	Dick Molyneux (sec)
Leading scorer:	Fred Geary, 20
Ever-present:	Edgar Chadwick, Fred Geary, Alf Milward
First at top:	Sep 27
Latest at top:	Dec 26
Date won:	Mar 14 (last game)
Players used:	20

Everton's League games were complete by January 10th, except for one. They then had a two-month wait while the other clubs played their games in hand. By March 14, when Everton and Preston had their last matches, North End had narrowed the gap sufficiently for them to take the title if they won with a clean sheet and Everton lost. Both clubs lost, leaving Everton as champions.

Everton were still playing at Anfield this season, with competition on Merseyside coming from Alliance club Bootle rather than the yet-to-be-formed Liverpool club. Attendances in Liverpool were a cut above those elsewhere, meaning there was more money about to attract good players. The 'Scots Count' (see Preston North End for an explanation) was 6 out of 11, with some outstanding English players in the team.

Fred Geary was a Nottingham man who had played for Notts Rangers and Notts County. He may well have been the first player to 'put the ball in the net', when Mr Brodie's patent nets were tried out in a trial match in Nottingham. He was a fast and tricky centre-forward who could run rings around some of the larger defenders of the time.

Everton 1915

Manager:	Will Cuff (sec)
Leading scorer:	Bobby Parker, 36
Ever-present:	None
First at top:	Apr 17
Latest at top:	The same
Date won:	Apr 26 (last game)
Players used:	24

The outbreak of war in 1914 caused a number of difficulties this season. Many players volunteered for active service in the armed forces. The Football Association and the Football League were criticized for continuing with their competitions, but to be fair, there was a view in 1914 that matters would be settled by Christmas. Certainly the authorities learned their lesson, and there was an abrupt cancellation of the 1939/40 season when a second war broke out later in the century.

It looked for most of the time as if this was going to be Oldham Athletic's season. They led by three points at the end of December. In the last week, with a home game in hand over Everton, and level on points, one win would probably have been enough for them. However, both games were lost, leaving Everton champions with just 46 points from 38 games. Only six points separated the first 11 clubs.

46 points is three fewer than the next lowest (Blackburn Rovers in 1912). If 3-points-for-win applied then, Everton would have reached 65, whereas totals in the high 80s and low 90s have become the norm these days.

Everton's success was largely due to the goalscoring abilities of the Scottish centre-forward Bobby Parker, who scored 36 of Everton's 76 goals. Just 24 this season, Parker's footballing career was interrupted by the Great War, but he scored 68 goals in 88 League appearances for Everton before moving to Nottingham Forest in 1921.

Everton 1928

Manager:	Tom McIntosh (sec)
Leading scorer:	Dixie Dean, 60 (7 hat-tricks)
Ever-present:	Jack O'Donnell, Alec Troup
First at top:	Oct 29
Latest at top:	Apr 18
Date won:	May 2
Players used:	24

Dean's 60 goals this season still stands as the record haul in a season and looks safe to do so for all time. He joined from Tranmere Rovers aged 18 in March 1925, so was just 21 this season. Arguably England's finest centre-forward, despite the claims of Tommy Lawton. Both players were great headers of the ball and prolific goalscorers, but Dean probably has the edge given that Lawton's most productive years were lost to the Second War. At 5ft 10in and 12½ stone Dean was powerfully built and athletic. His career total for Everton was 349 goals in 399 League games.

The title was won with a new record low of just 53 points from a 42-game season (two points for a win). The record was only to last for one year, when Sheffield Wednesday managed one fewer! On January 7, Everton were four points clear of Huddersfield. They then had a spell of nine games without a win and seemed to have lost their chance. However, other clubs failed to take advantage and by early April Everton were back on top. They were unbeaten in the last nine games.

Everton 1932

Manager:	Tom McIntosh (sec)
Leading scorer:	Dixie Dean, 45 (9 hat-tricks)
Ever-present:	None
First at top:	Oct 24
Latest at top:	The same
Date won:	Apr 30
Players used:	20

Everton dropped to the Second Division after their 1928 championship success. In 1930/31 they won the Second Division title by seven points and more-or-less the same squad outfought Arsenal to win the championship a year later. Everton scored 84 goals in their 21 home games, ten more than the second-best (Arsenal with 74 in 1935) and a record unlikely to be beaten.

West Bromwich made the early running until Everton went to the top in October and then were never headed, although Sheffield United were close behind. A 1-0 win over Bolton at the end of April gave Everton the title with two games left to play.

Everton 1939

Manager:	Theo Kelly (sec)
Leading scorer:	Tommy Lawton, 34
Ever-present:	Norman Greenhalgh
First at top:	Sep 5
Latest at top:	Feb 4
Date won:	Apr 22
Players used:	22

Everton repeated their trick of 1914/15 and won the championship in the last peacetime season before a World War. Luckily no such misfortune struck the world when next they won in 1963.

Six straight victories at the start of the season set them off at a good pace. A strong Derby County side led the way in December, but apart from a 0-7 reverse against Wolves in February Everton were the most consistent team in the second half of the season.

This was Lawton's year. Lawton was a great footballer whose misfortune was to realise that he was worth far more in marketing terms than the maximum wage allowed him to be paid. The circumstances of the time left him with no option to 'do anything about it' other than to look for other ways of adding to his income. Consequently, post-war years found him playing third division football; great times for the spectators at Notts County, but it meant an early end to Lawton's international career. At 5ft 11in and 12st, his build was very similar to that of Dixie Dean. He won 23 caps for England.

Aged just 20 in 1939, Lawton was probably not yet at his peak. His prolific goal scoring continued during the 1939-46 war, but these records are usually ignored because of the nature of wartime football.

Also in the team was wing-half Joe Mercer, later to play in Arsenal's team of 1952/53 and manage Manchester City when these clubs won the championship.

Everton 1963

Manager:	Harry Catterick
Leading scorer:	Roy Vernon, 24
Ever-present:	Dennis Stevens, Alex Young
First at top:	Aug 29
Latest at top:	Apr 20
Date won:	May 11 (last game)
Players used:	20

We were lucky to finish this season at all. A deep freeze set in across most of the country at the end of December and didn't lift until March. Those were the days! Actually, I missed it all, being safely ensconced in Bangor in North Wales. Warmed by the Gulf Stream, sheltered by the mountains, I think Bangor only had one day of snow all winter!

Harry Catterick had been active in the transfer market for Everton, and spent more money during the season for Tony Kay of Sheffield Wednesday. The players knitted together well and gave Everton an unbeaten home record. The decisive win came with a 1-0 victory over Spurs on April 20th. With games in hand towards the end of the season, Spurs were still a threat, but a 4-1 win over Fulham in the final game meant that Everton could not be caught.

Roy Vernon was team captain with a good return of 100 goals from 176 League appearances. He made 32 appearances for Wales. The ever-presents were Dennis Stevens, an inside-right signed from Bolton, and centre-forward Alex Young, who had a championship-winning career with Hearts in Scotland before signing for Everton in 1960.

Everton 1970

Manager:	Harry Catterick
Leading scorer:	Joe Royle, 23
Ever-present:	John Hurst, Joe Royle, Gordon West, Tommy Wright
First at top:	Aug 19
Latest at top:	Mar 11
Date won:	Apr 1
Players used:	17

This was the team of Harvey, Kendall and Ball, fondly recalled by many Evertonians and perhaps the best of the club's championship teams. They finished with 66 points, only one behind the record set by Leeds the previous season. Their defence only conceded 15 goals away from home.

A seven-game unbeaten run at the start of the season saw them top, though they were then overtaken briefly by Derby and Liverpool. Leeds United edged in front in the New Year, but an unbeaten run in their last 14 games saw Everton take the title with two games to spare.

Joe Royle was just 21 this season. He was Everton's youngest player on his debut in 1966. At 6ft 1in and 12st, Joe was good in the air and a consistent goal scorer. He won 23 England caps and later enjoyed managerial success at Oldham.

Howard Kendall returned as manager in 1981 and led the club to two championships.

Everton 1985

Manager:	Howard Kendall
Leading scorer:	Graeme Sharp 21
Ever-present:	Neville Southall
First at top:	Nov 3
Latest at top:	Jan 12
Date won:	May 6
Players used:	25

Everton gave notice of what was to come with a victory in the 1984 FA Cup final. 1984/85 was an excellent season for the club, winning the European Cup-Winners' Cup and reaching the final for the FA Cup for the second successive year. They set a new record, winning the League with a 13-point margin (3 points for a win), a feat that has only been beaten once since.

Only one win in the first four games found them in 15th place, but a string of victories took them top in November. A brief challenge from Spurs in December soon faded and a run of 18 games without defeat made the championship secure. A 2-0 win over Queen's Park Rangers won the title with five games left to play.

Graeme Sharp was signed from Dumbarton by Gordon Lee in April 1980. He was a regular scorer with some spectacular ones to his credit. He was capped by Scotland.

Goalkeeper Neville Southall was named as the Football Writers' Association Player of the Year. He played in non-League football before joining Bury in 1980, then signed for Everton a year later. Sometimes compared to Peter Shilton; he had excellent reflexes and made many outstanding saves. He won 92 Welsh caps during his career. Other honours went to midfielder Peter Reid, who was the PFA's Player of the Year, and Howard Kendall was Manager of the Year.

Everton 1987

Manager:	Howard Kendall
Leading scorer:	Trevor Steven, 14
Ever-present:	Kevin Ratcliffe
First at top:	Feb 7
Latest at top:	Apr 4
Date won:	May 4
Players used:	23

After a third successive FA Cup final appearance in 1986, Everton retained their momentum with another championship in 1987. Arsenal had built a 4-point lead over Everton by the end of December but dropped away as Liverpool mounted a challenge. Everton's goal difference took them back to the top in April, from which point they finished strongly to establish a 9-point margin.

A Howard Kendall signing from Burnley, Trevor Steven was a goal-scoring midfield player with excellent ball control. Capped by England. Joined Rangers.

Manager Howard Kendall resigned in June 1987 and joined Athletico Bilbao.

Kevin Ratcliffe was club captain for the two championships in the 1980s. He joined straight from school in 1977 and by 1980 was a regular member of the team. Good in the air and fast on his feet, he moved on to Cardiff City in 1992.

Huddersfield Town 1924

Manager:	Herbert Chapman
Leading scorer:	Charlie Wilson, 18
Ever-present:	Billy Watson
First at top:	Oct 27
Latest at top:	May 3
Date won:	May 3 (last day)
Players used:	22

The top club of the 1920s. Three successive championships, twice runners-up, three FA Cup finals. The key signings for the club were manager Herbert Chapman in 1920 and Clem Stephenson from Aston Villa. Chapman's playing record was not outstanding, but his management skills led Huddersfield to two of their championships before he moved on to even greater things at Arsenal.

Huddersfield were there or thereabouts throughout the whole of the season. With three games to go, they seemed to be in the driving seat, holding a narrow lead and having a game in hand. However, they could only draw at Forest and lost at Villa, leaving Cardiff City one point ahead and with a better goal average. A 3-0 win at home to Nottingham Forest and a draw for Cardiff meant Town were champions on goal average, 1.818 against 1.794; this was the first time that the title was decided this way. If today's goal difference rule had been in force, both clubs were level, but Cardiff would have taken the title having scored one more goal.

The club's results owed much to Billy Smith on the left wing. His long and accurate cross-field passes must have been a bit like watching Beckham's crosses today. He played 521 League games for Town, scoring 114 goals, in 20 years with the club.

Charlie Wilson was a consistent goal scorer with a powerful shot. He joined Huddersfield from Spurs in 1922. Billy Watson played for the club for 16 years; he was the father of Willie Watson, who won England caps at football and cricket.

Huddersfield Town 1925

Manager:	Herbert Chapman
Leading scorer:	Charlie Wilson, 24
Ever-present:	No-one
First at top:	At start
Latest at top:	Apr 10
Date won:	May 2 (last game)
Players used:	22

One win in nine games left Huddersfield down in ninth position in November, despite an opening 10 games without defeat. With West Bromwich Albion at the top of the table, there was a key meeting with them at Leeds Road in March. A draw left the door open for both clubs, but Town remained unbeaten until the end of the season to take their second title. They had it more or less won on April 29th with a far superior goal average to West Bromwich, and made certain when they drew their last game with Liverpool.

Charlie Wilson was again the leading scorer. George Brown got 20, giving the pair 44 of Town's 69 goals.

Huddersfield Town 1926

Manager:	Cecil Potter
Leading scorer:	George Brown, 35
Ever-present:	None
First at top:	Feb 6
Latest at top:	Feb 13
Date won:	Apr 12
Players used:	24

Herbert Chapman left for Arsenal in the summer of 1925. The other event of note this season was the change in the off-side law, which reduced to two (from three) the number of defenders between the attacker and the goal. 1925/26 saw a huge surge in goals as a consequence, until managers were able to devise new tactics to stem the flow.

An indifferent start found Huddersfield in 7th place in November, five points behind Sunderland. A 5-1 win at Manchester City took them top in February, and later there followed an eight game unbeaten run to open a seven-point gap on Arsenal. Although three end-of-season games were lost, Town finished five points clear of their former manager's new club.

Town signed Alex Jackson from Aberdeen in 1925. Jackson would be lauded today as an attacking mid-field player. His skills were an important contribution to the famous Scotland win over England at Wembley in 1928.

George Brown was a 23-year-old skilful forward who won nine England caps and scored 142 goals in 213 games for Huddersfield before moving to Aston Villa in 1929.

Ipswich Town 1962

Manager:	Alf Ramsey
Leading scorer:	Ray Crawford, 33
Ever-present:	Larry Carberry, Doug Moran, Andy Nelson
First at top:	Mar 31
Latest at top:	Apr 21
Date won:	Apr 28 (last game)
Players used:	16

Perhaps the biggest surprise winners in League history. Ipswich were promoted as Second Division champions in 1961 but were not expected to compete with the then-superpowers of Spurs and Burnley.

Like some wizard of old, Alf Ramsey waved a wand over a group of journeyman players and turned them into champions. Deserved champions as well, with Crawford and Ted Phillips scoring 61 goals between them. Ever-present Larry Carberry was one of four Ipswich players in the 1962 team than had won promotion from Division Three (South) four years before. Moran had signed from Falkirk in 1961 at a cost of £12,000 – this was more than the rest of the team cost, in total! Eight players made 40 or more appearances.

Burnley were secure at the top at the end of December, with games in hand over Spurs, who were fancied to repeat their title win of the season before. Ipswich put together a ten-game unbeaten run to reach the top in March, only to suffer a 0-5 reverse at Old Trafford. This proved to be a one-off, and they finished the season three points clear of Burnley.

Leading scorer Ray Crawford was signed from Portsmouth in 1958 and won two caps for England. He later played for Wolves and West Bromwich before returning to Ipswich in 1966.

Leeds United 1969

Manager:	Don Revie
Leading scorer:	Mick Jones, 14
Ever-present:	Billy Bremner, Norman Hunter, Reaney, Gary Sprake
First at top:	At start
Latest at top:	Feb 12
Date won:	Apr 28
Players used:	17

Time has not been kind to Don Revie's achievements, but we should put aside his England role and the subsequent odd career choice and look again at his remarkable record with Leeds. In eight years, he took Leeds from an average Second Division club to champions of England, and kept them at the top with a team of outstanding individual players. Leeds finished second in 1965 and 1966, fourth in 1967 and 1968. After the championship win in 1969 they had three successive second places in 1970, 1971 and 1972.

There was never much doubt about a 'goal of the week' when Peter Lorimer scored – they usually burst the back of the net! Billy Bremner, Jack Charlton and Norman Hunter were arguably the best half-back line of all time.

This was an outstanding season for Leeds that set a number of records; a new high number of points (67), just 26 goals conceded in the 42 games, and only two defeats. After a 1-5 drubbing at Burnley in October, Leeds remained unbeaten for the rest of the season, taking the title with a 0-0 draw at Liverpool in the penultimate game.

Mick Jones was a £100,000 purchase from Sheffield United in September 1967. He was a brave and strong centre-forward not afraid to get into the thick of things. He won three caps for England.

Leeds United 1974

Manager:	Don Revie
Leading scorer:	Mick Jones, 14
Ever-present:	Billy Bremner, Norman Hunter
First at top:	At start
Latest at top:	Never headed
Date won:	Apr 24
Players used:	20

It seems strange with hindsight that Leeds had to wait five years for the next championship team. Many of the 1969 team were still regulars, though Gordon McQueen had taken over Jack Charlton's role at centre-half and Joe Jordan was providing aggression and action up front.

Seven successive victories at the start of the season was part of an unbeaten run that looked as if it might continue all season. A 2-3 defeat at Stoke in February put paid to that idea and a run of three defeats in March gave the chasing clubs some excitement, but Leeds were never headed and ended worthy champions. A Liverpool loss on April 24th made Leeds' last game a formality.

Mick Jones was again the leading scorer, although only playing in 31 of the 42 games. His playing style seemed to attract injuries and he was forced to give up the game in August 1975 due to a knee problem,

Leeds United 1992

Manager:	Howard Wilkinson
Leading scorer:	Lee Chapman, 16
Ever-present:	John Lukic, Gary McAllister (1 as sub)
First at top:	Oct 26
Latest at top:	Apr 20
Date won:	Apr 26
Players used:	23

The present-day emphasis on the Premiership may lead some youngsters to write off all that happened before 1992/93 as 'pre-historic'. That would be a shame, especially for the team that Howard Wilkinson build at Leeds. Though perhaps not touching the heights of the Revie teams, this was a good squad with David Batty, Gary McAllister, Gordon Strachan, Gary Speed … and a certain Mr Cantona! Leading scorer Lee Chapman was a tall, slim and unspectacular centre-forward with the handy ability to score goals.

At the end of 1991, Manchester United were giving a slight foretaste of what was to follow in the 1990s; they were two points clear with games in hand. Inconsistent home form by the Reds let Leeds through to take the title by four points. A 3-2 win at Sheffield United gave Leeds the title with a game to spare.

Liverpool 1901

Manager:	Tom Watson
Leading scorer:	Sam Raybould, 16
Ever-present:	Bill Goldie, Bill Perkins, Tommy Robertson
First at top:	Apr 29
Latest at top:	Apr 29
Date won:	Apr 29 (last game)
Players used:	18

This was the first occasion in League history when the champions only got to the top as a result of the last game. Nottingham Forest led the way in December, with Liverpool down in seventh place. However, Liverpool were unbeaten in their last 12 games. Sunderland's better goal average kept them top, but Liverpool were left needing to win their last game to take the championship. A 1-0 victory at West Bromwich did the trick.

Manager Tom Watson had been persuaded to leave Sunderland in 1896; maybe the £7 a week that Liverpool offered was a strong incentive, at time when 10 shillings a week was a good income.

Sam Raybould was a Chesterfield man who had played a lot of non-League football in the East Midlands. He joined Liverpool from New Brighton Tower in 1899 and scored 119 goals in 211 appearances for the club.

Liverpool 1906

Manager:	Tom Watson
Leading scorer:	Joe Hewitt, 23
Ever-present:	Arthur Goddard
First at top:	Dec 16
Latest at top:	The same
Date won:	Apr 16
Players used:	21

Results were again up and down after the championship of 1901, culminating in relegation to Division Two. However, that title was won in 1904/05, so Liverpool became the first club to win the Second and First Division titles in consecutive seasons. A double looked possible, but Liverpool lost to Everton in the semi-final of the FA Cup.

The season did not get off to the best of starts, with Liverpool losing their first three games. Indeed, in mid-October, Liverpool were in 16th place. A run of 11 games unbeaten took them to the top in December, where they remained for the rest of the season. Preston's defeat on April 16th meant Liverpool were champions for the second time.

Joe Hewitt had played a few games for Sunderland in their 1902 team. He joined Liverpool in 1903 and later moved to Bolton Wanderers.

Liverpool 1922

Manager:	David Ashworth
Leading scorer:	Harry Chambers, 19
Ever-present:	Dick Forshaw, Fred Hopkin
First at top:	Nov 19
Latest at top:	Dec 17
Date won:	Apr 17
Players used:	22

Liverpool and Burnley led the way in the first half of the season. A 15-game unbeaten run from December to March established a four point lead and the championship was won in style with a 2-1 home win over Burnley.

This championship team was built on a strong defence that conceded only 36 goals. Irish international goalkeeper Elisha Scott joined Liverpool in 1912 and went on to make 429 League appearances. Bow-legged centre-forward Harry Chambers was a consistent goalscorer for Liverpool with a reported ability to bend it like Beckham. Well, it would have been reported that way 80 years in the future! He won eight caps for England and scored 135 goals in 310 League games for Liverpool.

Inside-right Dick Forshaw was an ever-present this season and next, and later was a member of Everton's 1928 championship team.

Liverpool 1923

Manager:	Matt McQueen
Leading scorer:	Harry Chambers, 22
Ever-present:	Dick Forshaw, Donald McKinlay, Elisha Scott
First at top:	Sep 16
Latest at top:	The same
Date won:	Apr 21
Players used:	19

Liverpool's defence went one better (well, five actually) and just 31 goals were conceded this season, a new record low for a 42-game season. They were never headed in the table this season, so remained at the top from December 1921 until the end of 1922/23.

I think we might recognize this team if we saw it playing today. It is reported that the players moved quickly into open spaces and passed the ball speedily between them; push-and-run 28 years before Spurs, and total-football 50 years before the Dutch!

Liverpool 1947

Manager:	George Kay
Leading scorers:	Jack Balmer, Albert Stubbins, 24
Ever-present:	None
First at top:	Nov 16
Latest at top:	May 24
Date won:	Jun 14 (after last game)
Players used:	26

This was the first season after a seven-year break due to the Second World War. Every club had it hard this season. Players rusty from service in the armed forces joined inexperienced young players, and problems were compounded by a severe winter. Transport difficulties were severe as Britain struggled to get back to peacetime normality.

Wolves built up a five-point lead by the end of December and stayed at the top through to April. At the end of the month, Liverpool were four points behind Wolves with only five games left to play. However, Wolves mustered only one win in these five games whist Liverpool won four of their five. With one game to play, any one of four clubs could have won the title. Liverpool's final game on May 31 left Stoke City two points behind with a game to play and a better goal average. The bad weather had caused many games to be postponed, so Stoke's final game at Sheffield United did not take place until June 14. Stoke lost 1-2, giving Liverpool the title. Just two points separated the top four clubs at the end of the season.

Jack Balmer scored hat-tricks in three successive matches, the first time this had been done at any club in a championship-winning season. He had made his debut for Liverpool in 1935 and scored 98 goals in 289 appearances for the club. Albert Stubbins had been a prolific scorer for Newcastle United during the wartime seasons and signed for Liverpool in September 1946.

A young Bob Paisley was one of the half-backs. He was later to manage the club to six championships.

Liverpool 1964

Manager:	Bill Shankly
Leading scorer:	Roger Hunt, 31
Ever-present:	Ian Callaghan, Gordon Milne, Peter Thompson
First at top:	Nov 23
Latest at top:	Mar 30
Date won:	Apr 18
Players used:	17

Strange as it seems now, Liverpool spent much of the 1950s in the Second Division. This despite the brilliance of Billy Liddell on the wing and other fine players such as Alan A'Court and Tommy Younger. A turning point came in December 1959 when Bill Shankly became manager, though there was to be no 'instant' recovery. Promotion came in 1962 with a fine side that included Ron Yeats and Ian St John.

There were mixed results for Liverpool at the start of the season; indeed the first three home games were lost. By the end of December 1963, Liverpool were in third place with a much better away record than at Anfield, where they had won 8 and lost 5. All their remaining home games were won, and although taking just one point from their last three games, they ended with a four-point margin over Manchester United.

Roger Hunt was small by today's standards, just 5ft 9in. He was a determined attacker with a good career record for Liverpool and England. Among his 34 caps was one for a certain game against Germany at Wembley in 1966. He scored 245 goals in 401+3 League games for Liverpool and spent four seasons at Bolton at the end of his career.

Peter Thompson signed from Preston for a club record fee of £40,000 at the start of the season and was one of the ever-present players.

Liverpool 1966

Manager:	Bill Shankly
Leading scorer:	Roger Hunt, 30
Ever-present:	Gerry Byrne, Ian Callaghan, Tommy Lawrence, Tommy Smith, Ron Yeats
First at top:	Nov 17
Latest at top:	The same
Date won:	Apr 30
Players used:	14

Liverpool set a new championship record by using just 14 players during the season, a record later equalled by Aston Villa in 1981.

An uncertain start to the season found them in seventh place in late October. A run of 18 games with only one defeat saw them sitting comfortably at the top of the table and they ended the season six points clear of Leeds United and Burnley.

Roger Hunt again headed the goalscorers list, with Ian St John the only other player in double figures. In addition to the five ever-presents, four other men had 40 or 41 games; Lawler, St John, Stevenson and Thompson.

Liverpool reached the final of the European Cup-Winners' Cup, where they lost 1-2 to Borussia Dortmund at Hampden Park, after extra time.

Liverpool 1973

Manager:	Bill Shankly
Leading scorer:	Kevin Keegan, John Toshack, 13
Ever-present:	Ian Callaghan, Chris Lawler, Larry Lloyd
First at top:	At start
Latest at top:	Feb 24
Date won:	Apr 28 (last game)
Players used:	16

There was not a lot in the way of trophies to show from the Shankly years 1966 to 1972, but the foundations had been laid for the unprecedented success in the years that followed. Liverpool were transformed from 'just another contender' into 'the team to beat'. Success in domestic and European cups just added to the glory.

By the end of December, Liverpool had built up a 3-point lead over Arsenal, thanks in part to 12 straight wins at Anfield. A home defeat by Arsenal in February saw them drop to second place, but a string of good results in the final weeks saw them restore the 3-point lead over Arsenal – and win the UEFA Cup for good measure.

The sorcerer in the 1973 team was Kevin Keegan. He always reminded me of those Weebles – "you can knock them but they don't fall down". (Apologies to younger readers, especially if Weebles are no more; they were egg-shaped things with a weight in the bottom, so they really didn't fall down). I'm not saying Keegan never fell over; the 70s were the days when defenders still had full licence to jump in feet first, but somehow he was always in the thick of things and always in the right place at the right time. When he was knocked over, he seemed to bounce up again pretty quickly. He won 63 caps for England, some of them as skipper and was later manager of the national team.

A decent bloke. My colleague once wrote to ask him to write a foreword to a book on Scunthorpe United I'd produced. One day the phone rang: "Hi, Kevin Keegan here". At first my colleague assumed it was a wind-up; but no, Keegan had rung to dictate the foreword. Good for him.

Ever-present Larry Lloyd was later to feature in Nottingham Forest's 1978 championship team.

Liverpool 1976

Manager:	Bob Paisley
Leading scorer:	John Toshack, 16
Ever-present:	Ray Clemence, Phil Neal
First at top:	Dec 20
Latest at top:	Apr 17
Date won:	May 4 (last game)
Players used:	19

Shankly retired in 1974 and the mantle passed to Bob Paisley. Though not blessed with the most charismatic media presence, Paisley ended up with more trophies than any other manager before him.

Liverpool had mixed results until March this season, with Ipswich, Queen's Park Rangers and Manchester United leading the way. However, only one point was dropped in the last nine games, with the original 'supersub', David Fairclough, scoring some important goals. Liverpool needed to win their last match at Wolves to take the title and knock QPR off the top. Goals from Keegan, Toshack and Kennedy game them a 3-1 victory. The UEFA cup was won later in May.

Liverpool 1977

Manager:	Bob Paisley
Leading scorer:	Kevin Keegan, 12
Ever-present:	Ray Clemence, Emlyn Hughes, Phil Neal
First at top:	Sep 18
Latest at top:	Apr 16
Date won:	May 14
Players used:	17

Despite the achievements of the 1980s Liverpool, many people would rate the 1970s team as the more attractive to watch. They led the way for much of the season, though suffered a strange reverse in December when they lost 1-5 at Villa Park, all the goals coming in the first half. Liverpool needed to beat challengers Ipswich in April, which they did by 2-1. A late challenge from Manchester City meant it was the penultimate game when a 0-0 draw with West Ham won the title.

Goals were hard to come by this season; just 62 in total. Keegan and Toshack (on 10) were the only players to reach double figures.

The European Cup was won for the first time with a 3-1 victory over Borussia Mönchengladbach.

Liverpool 1979

Manager:	Bob Paisley
Leading scorer:	Kenny Dalglish, 21
Ever-present:	Ray Clemence, Kenny Dalglish, Ray Kennedy, Phil Neal
First at top:	At start
Latest at top:	Never headed
Date won:	May 8
Players used:	15

Liverpool's most dominant season, setting a number of new records; most points, best goal average or difference, and only 4 goals conceded in 20 home games. Ray Clemence kept a clean sheet in 28 games this season.

Kenny Dalglish had signed from Celtic in 1977 to replace Kevin Keegan. Dalglish had an excellent record at Celtic but moved to even greater heights with Liverpool. His career total for the Reds was 342+13 League appearances and 118 goals, some of which were arguably among the best ever scored for the club.

The season opened in spectacular style for Liverpool, with 10 wins and one draw in the first 11 games. West Bromwich and Nottingham Forest tried to keep in touch, but never seriously threatened to thwart Liverpool's title challenge.

Liverpool 1980

Manager:	Bob Paisley
Leading scorer:	David Johnson, 21
Ever-present:	Phil Neal, Phil Thompson
First at top:	Nov 17
Latest at top:	Dec 8
Date won:	May 3
Players used:	17

Liverpool made a slow start to the season, a 0-1 defeat at Nottingham Forest leaving them in 9th place at the end of September. However, that set Liverpool off on a 16-game unbeaten run and a two-point lead over Manchester United in January. Though away results were mixed, a good home record gave them a final margin of two points ahead of United.

David Johnson is perhaps the 'forgotten man' of the great Liverpool line-ups. A local man, he played for Everton before heading for Ipswich in 1972. Liverpool signed him in 1976 and he returned to Everton in 1982 after losing his place to Ian Rush. Johnson won eight caps for England.

Liverpool 1982

Manager:	Bob Paisley
Leading scorer:	Ian Rush, 17
Ever-present:	Kenny Dalglish, Bruce Grobbelaar, Phil Neal
First at top:	Apr 2
Latest at top:	The same
Date won:	May 15
Players used:	16

Too many drawn games had spoiled Liverpool's chance of a hat-trick of championships in 1980/81, but it was only a temporary problem as they marched on to six more titles from 1981/82 to 1989/90.

One win in the first five games found Liverpool in the unaccustomed position of 17th. A Boxing Day defeat at home to Manchester City found them in 11th place, with only the real diehards thinking this would be a championship season. However, Liverpool turned on the magic after Christmas, with 11 consecutive victories, so that they were back on top by April. Ipswich were the only challengers, closing to within three points at one stage, but Liverpool remained unbeaten in their last 16 games.

Ian Rush scored 245 goals in English League football, in 536+34 appearances. He is the leading post-war scorer in FA Cup games and joint top (with Geoff Hurst) in League Cup goals. There were another 19 goals in 36+2 European cups appearances. To my mind, he was the best striker in recent memory and I'd have him in my fantasy forward line, even at the expense of Alan Shearer. There was more to Rush than his goal scoring ability; he was not afraid to tackle back and was effective at bringing other players into the game. He won 73 Welsh caps and it was unfortunate that his country could not win a place on the world stage.

Liverpool 1983

Manager:	Bob Paisley
Leading scorer:	Ian Rush, 24
Ever-present:	Kenny Dalglish, Bruce Grobbelaar, Alan Kennedy, Phil Neal
First at top:	At start
Latest at top:	Oct 30
Date won:	Apr 30
Players used:	16

Apart from some small blips in October, Liverpool spent most of the season at the top of the table. They were six points clear of Forest at the half-way point. On April 9th, they were 16 points ahead of Watford in second place and must have taken their foot off the pedal, with no wins in their last seven matches. They still took the title with three games to spare and an 11-point margin.

This was Bob Paisley's final season before he retired. The team picked itself I think; 10 of the squad made 30 or more appearances.

Phil Neal was again an ever-present player, the sixth time he had done this for Liverpool. Indeed, in a ten-year spell he missed only one League game. He had already played 182+2 games for Northampton Town when he signed in 1974. His Liverpool totals were 453+2 games and 41 goals, many of the goals coming from the penalty spot. Including cup and international appearances (50 caps for England) he played more than 900 games in his career.

Liverpool 1984

Manager:	Joe Fagan
Leading scorer:	Ian Rush, 32
Ever-present:	Bruce Grobbelaar, Alan Hansen, Alan Kennedy, Mark Lawrenson, Sammy Lee
First at top:	Nov 6
Latest at top:	The same
Date won:	May 12
Players used:	15

Liverpool became the third club to win a hat-trick of championships, after Huddersfield Town and Arsenal. Moreover, they added the League Cup and the European Cup this season. Was this the club's greatest season? I describe 1978/79 as their most dominant, yet 1987/88 may have been even better! You will have to form your own conclusion, but I think I would pick this season's team as the best. Whatever we decide, Joe Fagan won more trophies in his first year as manager than many achieve in a lifetime.

It took a little time to reach the top, but once there they were seldom threatened. Southampton enjoyed a fine season and came closest in the end.

This was Graeme Souness's last season for the club. Souness was a strong, determined and sometimes controversial character with a great influence on the team.

Liverpool 1986

Manager:	Kenny Dalglish
Leading scorer:	Ian Rush, 22
Ever-present:	Bruce Grobbelaar
First at top:	Mar 31
Latest at top:	The same
Date won:	May 3 (last game)
Players used:	18

Kenny Dalglish became Liverpool's first player-manager in the summer of 1985. A number of the established players were dropped and it looked as if it would take some time for the new men to become established. Far from it; Dalglish and his men marched to the League and Cup double.

For once, this was a season where Liverpool followed others in the table, and it was not until March 31 that they took first place. Even then, Everton had a game in hand and looked set to repeat their championship success of 1985. However, Liverpool won all their final seven games to finish two points clear of Everton.

This is Liverpool's only 'double' year; they beat Everton in the FA Cup final.

Ian Rush headed the scorers' list for the champions for a record fourth time, beating Sunderland's John Campbell's record of three in the early years of the League.

Bruce Grobbelaar was again ever-present. Always entertaining and unpredictable, I think he may have caused his managers to grow the odd grey hair during his career.

Liverpool 1988

Manager:	Kenny Dalglish
Leading scorer:	John Aldridge, 26
Ever-present:	Steve McMahon, Steve Nicol
First at top:	Oct 17
Latest at top:	Nov 24
Date won:	Apr 23
Players used:	22

Liverpool in their pomp. Ten points clear at the end of December and unbeaten in the League. Just two defeats came in the second half of the season and they finished nine points clear (in a 40-game season).

Liverpool firepower was impressive this season. Anfield spectators enjoyed three successive 4-0 wins, over Derby, Portsmouth and QPR. Later, Watford, Newcastle and Coventry lost by the same score, before Liverpool went one better to beat Forest 5-0. A 1-0 win at home to Spurs secured the title with four games left to play.

Ian Rush had left for Juventus in the summer of 1987. Dalglish signed Peter Beardsley and John Barnes, and later Roy Houghton was added to the mix.

John Aldridge seemed determined to prove Rush would not be missed by scoring in each of the first nine games of the season. He was 30 years old this season, having already scored 141 League goals for Newport County and Oxford United. His total for the Reds was 50 in 69+14 appearances.

Steve Nicol was a versatile player who made more than 300 League appearances for Liverpool over a 14-year period, after joining as a 20-year-old from Ayr United.

Liverpool 1990

Manager:	Kenny Dalglish
Leading scorer:	John Barnes, 22
Ever-present:	Bruce Grobbelaar, Steve McMahon (including 1 as sub)
First at top:	Sep 12
Latest at top:	Mar 31
Date won:	Apr 28
Players used:	22

Liverpool's most recent championship, at the time of writing. It is surprising how the momentum was lost. Cup successes since 1990 have helped the club's profile, but the big prize (discounting European Cup success of course) still awaits.

Ian Rush was back and John Aldridge left for Real Sociedad after two substitute appearances. Ronnie Rosenthal took over the supersub role and scored seven goals in eight appearances at the end of the season.

Though four points clear of Aston Villa in December, Villa kept on Liverpool's tail so well that they were level on points at the end of March. Liverpool's customary unbeaten end of season run, nine games this time, saw then home with some comfort.

John Barnes had cost £900,000 when he signed from Watford in 1987. Barnes was blessed with skill and power and was an exciting player to watch.

Manchester City 1937

Manager:	Wilf Wild
Leading scorer:	Peter Doherty, 30
Ever-present:	Eric Brook, Jack Percival, Frank Swift, Ernie Toseland
First at top:	Apr 10
Latest at top:	The same
Date won:	Apr 24
Players used:	22

It was a long wait for City fans, but two FA Cup final visits in 1933 and 1934 led to their first championship in 1937. Their success was largely owed to inside-forward Peter Doherty, only signed from Blackpool in February 1936. Doherty was probably the outstanding player of the period, a playmaker in today's jargon, but with the ability to score goals as well.

City did it the hard way, working their way up from 16th place at the end of October. By end December they were 9th, 5 points behind Arsenal, who were one of four clubs bunched on 28 points. City's unbeaten run of 22 games started on Boxing Day and carried them to the title with a 3-point margin over Charlton Athletic.

Ever-present Frank Swift was an excellent goalkeeper who made 23 appearances for England. Sadly, he was to die in the 1958 Munich disaster, when working as a journalist.

Manchester City 1968

Manager:	Joe Mercer (and Malcolm Allison)
Leading scorer:	Neil Young, 19
Ever-present:	Tony Book
First at top:	Mar 16
Latest at top:	Apr 29
Date won:	May 11 (last game)
Players used:	21

One of those great management partnerships was at the helm. Perhaps Mercer and Allison did not enjoy the same consistent success as Clough and Taylor, but nevertheless they pulled City out of the Second Division and followed this two years later with the Championship. The FA, League and European Cup-Winners' cups were to follow.

There were some big-money signings in the team, but as is often the case, the best was the perhaps the cheapest. Tony Book was well past 30 when he signed, but became an essential part of the team.

Manchester United were top for most of the season, with a five-point advantage at the end of December, so it was March 16 before City edged in front on goal average, thanks largely to an excellent home record and a vital win at Old Trafford. A last-day win at Newcastle was needed to give City the title; they and Manchester United were level on points with one game left to play, though City had the better goal average. City won 4-3.

Neil Young was a local-born player who turned professional in 1961. He scored more than 100 goals in his City career.

Manchester United 1908

Manager:	Ernest Mangnall
Leading scorer:	Sandy Turnbull, 25
Ever-present:	None
First at top:	At start
Latest at top:	Never headed
Date won:	Apr 11
Players used:	25

United's first championship came just six years after they arose from the wreckage of Newton Heath. Still playing on the mud heaps of Bank Street, they owed their consistency to a solid yet creative half-back line of Duckworth, Roberts and Bell. The club's good fortune was to snap up Manchester City players when that club listed 17 men for sale following allegations of illegal payments. The players signed included Sandy Turnbull (leading scorer in 1907/08) and the immortal Billy Meredith.

The season opened with three straight wins and United were never caught. They finished nine points clear of second place Aston Villa. They won the title after losing at home to Notts County, thanks to results elsewhere. They had five games still to play.

Manchester United 1911

Manager:	Ernest Mangnall
Leading scorer:	Enoch 'Knocker' West, 19
Ever-present:	No-one
First at top:	Oct 15
Latest at top:	Apr 29
Date won:	Apr 29 (last game)
Players used:	26

United moved to Old Trafford in 1910. With a capacity of 60,000 or so, United now had a revenue stream to attract the better players, even with the players' maximum wage in force.

Though consistently in first place after the turn of the year, United would have found themselves in second place if Aston Villa won their last game. They didn't. Only 7,000 spectators saw United beat Sunderland at Old Trafford to take the title when Villa lost at Liverpool.

Enoch West had already scored 100 goals for Nottingham Forest when United signed him in June 1910. He and Sandy Turnbull provided an effective strike force – the Yorke and Cole of their day. West was later banned for life by the F.A. for his alleged role in fixing the result of a game with Liverpool in 1915. Sandy Turnbull was killed in the First World War; in his playing career 1902 – 1914 he made 110 League appearances for Manchester City, scoring 53 goals, and 220 for United, with 90 goals.

Manchester United 1952

Manager:	Matt Busby
Leading scorer:	Jack Rowley, 30
Ever-present:	Allenby Chilton
First at top:	Sep 12
Latest at top:	Jan 26
Date won:	Apr 26 (last game)
Players used:	24

After their championship of 1911, United found the going tough, even spending time in the Second Division. Their change in fortune started with the offer of the manager's job to Matt Busby. An FA Cup win in 1948 started the ball rolling, even if he had to wait another four years for the championship.

Busby's first championship team was a mixture of youngsters and veterans, with signings such as Johnny Berry from Birmingham City.

Arsenal and Portsmouth were in with a chance of the title, particularly as United had five games to play in 10 days in April. However 3 of the 5 were won and two drawn. It came down to the last game, at home to Arsenal, though United's goal average was so superior that Arsenal would have needed a 6-0 win. As it happens, United won 6-1 with a Rowley hat-trick.

Jack Rowley was a 5ft 9in 12st forward at home anywhere in the forward line. He 'put himself about a bit' as they say today, to good effect. His aggression and hard shooting ability won him 6 caps for England.

Allenby Chilton was a no-nonsense 6ft tall centre-half who made over 350 appearances for United in his career.

Manchester United 1956

Manager:	Matt Busby
Leading scorer:	Tommy Taylor, 25
Ever-present:	Mark Jones
First at top:	Oct 29
Latest at top:	Dec 17
Date won:	Apr 7
Players used:	24

Another team with a well-known nickname. It's difficult to compare the Busby Babes of 50 years ago with the current crop of players. My perspective now is that they were the same 'breath of fresh air' that the Hungarians brought with them for their famous wins over England in 1953 and 1954. I don't mean to compare the playing styles of the two teams. The mixture of youth with experienced players produced an attractive side that got better as time went by. Just two players remained from the 1952 team and the average age was around 22.

Early season results left them in seventh place, but a fine end-of-season run of 14 games unbeaten left them 11 points clear. The title was won with a 2-1 victory over nearest challengers Blackpool.

It was said that Tommy Taylor was the 'new Tommy Lawton'. Taylor was 6ft tall and weighed in at nearly 13st, so was of heavier build than Lawton, but equally powerful in the air. He won 19 caps for England but was one of those lost at Munich.

Mark Jones was a 6ft 1in centre-half who took over from Allenby Chilton at the heart of the defence. He was just 22 years old this season.

Manchester United 1957

Manager:	Matt Busby
Leading scorer:	Liam (Billy) Whelan, 26
Ever-present:	No-one
First at top:	Sep 1
Latest at top:	Nov 17
Date won:	Apr 20
Players used:	24

If 1955/56 was good, 1956/57 was superlative. For the first time, a European Cup run was added to United's fixture list, giving them a chance of a treble. More youngsters were added to the team, including a certain Bobby Charlton, who scored two goals on his debut.

Tottenham were the only challengers as United built up two-point lead at halfway and finished eight points clear, scoring 103 goals in the process.

Billy Whelan was an inside-forward with good ball skills and an eye for goal. He won four caps for the Republic of Ireland.

Manchester United 1965

Manager:	Matt Busby
Leading scorer:	Denis Law, 28
Ever-present:	Shay Brennan, John Connelly, Tony Dunne, Bill Foulkes
First at top:	Oct 31
Latest at top:	Apr 26
Date won:	Apr 28 (last game)
Players used:	18

Thoughts of the Munich air crash of 1958 still trouble your author. Yes, the team would have grown old, and results would not always be as good, but what a shame that such talented players were lost to their families and the game.

It seems a long time ago now. I knew nothing about the accident until the paperboy delivered the Daily Mirror. There was a television in the house, but perhaps we didn't have it on that night, or perhaps I was out with the Boy Scouts. I could hardly believe my eyes when I opened the paper. I still have the battered remains somewhere in the attic.

In took some time for Matt Busby to recover the momentum that had been lost. Holding true to his principles, it was another squad of exciting young players, mixed with older heads. Now we had Charlton, Best and Law to admire. With TV recording in its infancy, we can relive the pleasure of watching these players any time we like – how fortunate we are, and what a pity only grainy newsreel film lets us catch a glimpse of Lawton and Dean in their prime.

With only one win in the first six games, United dropped as low as 16th in the table and there was little indication at this point as to what was to come. Having got to the top, some indifferent form in January and February dropped them to third, but seven consecutive wins saw them home. A huge defeat in their last game could conceivably have given Leeds the title, but a 1-2 reverse at Villa did little to dent their excellent goal average. It was bad luck for Leeds; 61 points would have won them the title in many years.

Manchester United 1967

Manager:	Matt Busby
Leading scorer:	Denis Law, 23
Ever-present:	George Best, Bobby Charlton
First at top:	Nov 30
Latest at top:	Feb 25
Date won:	May 6
Players used:	20

It was again an untidy start, but after losing 1-2 to Sheffield United in December they were unbeaten in their remaining games and ended with a four-point margin over Nottingham Forest in second place.

Though George Best might win most popularity pools, for sheer unbridled excitement and entertainment there was no one in my view to match Dennis Law. In an 11-year spell at Old Trafford, Law scored 171 goals in 305+4 appearances. OK, so they weren't all aerobatic bicycle kicks or diving headers; we just remember them that way.

George Best was ever-present this season; a noteworthy statistic given his reputation later in his career.

Manchester United 1993

Manager:	Alex Ferguson
Leading scorer:	Mark Hughes, 15
Ever-present:	Peter Schmeichel, Steve Bruce, Gary Pallister, Brian McClair
First at top:	Jan 9
Latest at top:	Apr 10
Date won:	May 3
Players used:	20

The first season of the Premiership, so here's a good trivia question – who was top at the end of December? The answer is Norwich City, three points clear of the rest.

On November 7, United were in 10th place, eight points behind the leaders Arsenal. There was little sign of the dominance that was to follow. Ten games without defeat took United to the top, but as late as April 5 they were in second place behind Aston Villa. Seven consecutive wins at the end of the season left them five points clear of Arsenal.

A succession of managers had all failed to live up to the expectations aroused during the Busby years. As with the non-championship years from 1911 to 1952, United had even dropped to the Second Division.

Alex Ferguson had had managerial success in Scotland and looked a good candidate for the job. I've not heard Ferguson speak about Busby, but you can see the same approach to management; they have the ability to throw young players in with the old, stir a bit, and throw out excellent teams that can win matches. However, not for the first time in this account, it took time to build a championship team. Ferguson arrived in 1986, and I well remember the publicity surrounding him when he brought the team to Forest for a cup-tie in January 1990: "lose this one and you're out!" He didn't, of course, and he wasn't.

Even so, there was still little sign in the summer of 1992 as to what the next decade or two would bring. Gates at Old Trafford were around the 30,000 mark, and there was no difficulty getting in to see a game. No doubt the whingers were still whinging when United lost to Villa in November, leaving themselves in 10th place. A certain Mr Cantona arrived in December, and although views are mixed as to his contribution that season, there's no doubt that something galvanized United. Apart from a couple of blips, they got to the top in January and stayed there to the end of the season.

Given the sustained success of United teams since 1992/93, it is difficult to pick out the key points of each one. I would put this one down to consistency of selection; in addition to four ever-presents, Messrs Giggs, Hughes, and Ince also made 40 or 41 appearances in the 42-game season.

Manchester United 1994

Manager:	Alex Ferguson
Leading scorer:	Eric Cantona, 18
Ever-present:	Denis Irwin
First at top:	At start
Latest at top:	Never headed
Date won:	May 4
Players used:	23

United started 1993/94 as they had ended the previous one. Having got to the top they stayed there throughout the season. Moreover, they added the FA Cup to the trophy cabinet and nearly won the League Cup also.

There was a particularly strong start to the season, so much so that at the end of December they held a record 14-point lead over Blackburn Rovers.

Roy Keane was added to the mix this season. I saw him make his debut for Forest. He looked the complete footballer from his first moment on the pitch, rare in someone so young. However great Keane's contribution, I have to label the 1994 championship as the year of Cantona. Though memories of the man largely involve his presence on the field, off-field petulance and kung-fu attacks, this rather obscures the fact that he was a regular scorer whose goals were vital to the club's success.

Manchester United 1996

Manager:	Alex Ferguson
Leading scorer:	Eric Cantona, 14
Ever-present:	None
First at top:	Sep 23
Latest at top:	Mar 24
Date won:	May 5 (last game)
Players used:	23

Another double season. What had once seemed impossible now seemed to be the norm. Cantona again headed the scorers' list.

This looked to be Newcastle United's season. Their four-point lead at the end of December had grown to nine by the end of January. But by the end of February it was back to four points and Manchester United smelled blood. The clubs met at St James' Park on March 4th, when a Cantona goal gave Manchester a 1-0 win; the gap was now just one point. Newcastle still had a game in hand, so the result was not necessarily decisive. However the tide had turned and the Reds took over at the top. With three games left; a recovery by the Geordies was still looked possible; they were six points adrift but with two games in hand. They won the first to close the gap to three points; the second was drawn, so the title chase went to the last day. Manchester United won 3-0 at Middlesbrough and the title was theirs.

Manchester United 1997

Manager:	Alex Ferguson
Leading scorer:	Ole Gunnar Solksjaer, 18
Ever-present:	None
First at top:	Sep 14
Latest at top:	Jan 29
Date won:	May 8
Players used:	23

The title was won with just 75 points, the lowest total in a 38-game season in the modern era. Liverpool made the best start and had a five-point lead at halfway. United did not find form until mid-November, when, after losing three games on the trot, they went into a 16-game unbeaten run. Only two defeats followed this run, and they finished seven points clear of the pack, winning the title with a 0-0 draw at Old Trafford against second-place Newcastle United..

Solksjaer signed from Norwegian club Molde in 1996 for £1.5M. Injuries plagued the latter stages of his career and he was forced to retire in 2007. He scored many excellent goals for United, often coming on as a substitute to great effect. He scored 91 goals in 151+85 Premier League appearances for the club.

Manchester United 1999

Manager:	Alex Ferguson
Leading scorer:	Dwight Yorke, 18
Ever-present:	None
First at top:	Dec 12
Latest at top:	May 9
Date won:	May 16 (last game)
Players used:	23

This was the first season of the great double act, Andy Cole and Dwight Yorke. Yorke won the goalscoring race, with Cole just one behind on 17. It was also United's treble season; League, FA Cup and European Cup.

Though briefly top in December, it was the end of January before United settled there. There was competition from Arsenal by late April who took the lead, though United had a game in hand. With two games to play the clubs were level on points and goal difference. A draw for United and a defeat for Arsenal gave United the advantage on the last day of the season; a 2-1 win at Old Trafford over Spurs won the title. Ten days later the FA Cup and the European Cup had been added to the trophy cabinet.

At the time of writing (2007) this was the last occasion that the title was won by a single point. There has been nothing less than a five-point gap since then.

Manchester United 2000

Manager:	Alex Ferguson
Leading scorer:	Dwight Yorke, Andy Cole, 19
Ever-present:	None
First at top:	At start
Latest at top:	Jan 29
Date won:	Apr 22
Players used:	29

United ran away with this one, finishing a record 18 points clear of Arsenal in second place. Interestingly, they trailed Leeds by one point at the end of December. The New Year found them almost invincible and they finished the League season with 11 consecutive wins. The title was won with a 3-1 win over Southampton, with four games remaining.

Schmeichel had gone, but the great double act continued to knock in the goals. The big controversy concerned United's trip to Brazil in January for the Club World Championship (not to be confused with the annual World Club Championship, one-off games played each year in Tokyo, which United had won this season). As a consequence, they did not play in the FA Cup.

Manchester United 2001

Manager:	Alex Ferguson
Leading scorer:	Teddy Sheringham, 15
Ever-present:	None
First at top:	At start
Latest at top:	Oct 14
Date won:	Apr 14
Players used:	29

The ease with which a third consecutive championship was achieved took some gloss off the event. It was just too predicable. Having said that, this was an immense achievement. One does not wish to belittle the fact by pointing out that Huddersfield Town and Arsenal had done it before; United performed the feat under the glare of the spotlight and with all the commercial pressures of the modern game. When the time comes to write Sir Alex's epitaph, perhaps this is the achievement that deserves pride of place. He is the only manager to win three titles in a row.

United were top all season, except for a defeat at Arsenal in October which let Leicester City in for a week or so. United put them in their place with a 3-0 win at Filbert Street on October 14. This was the first in a run of eight consecutive victories that more or less sealed the championship for United. The title was won on April 14th with five games still to play.

Alex Ferguson became the first manager to lead a club to a hat-trick of championships. Huddersfield Town, Arsenal and Liverpool each had a change of manager during their three-in-a-row seasons.

Manchester United 2003

Manager:	Alex Ferguson
Leading scorer:	Ruud van Nistelrooy, 25
Ever-present:	None
First at top:	Mar 22
Latest at top:	Apr 12
Date won:	May 4
Players used:	26

After another double, this time from Arsenal in 2001/02, United returned to the top. Beckham was still banging his crosses in from the wing, Giggs was still making incisive runs. On the end of their crosses now was van Nistelrooy, who crowned an excellent season by scoring in each of the last eight League games.

For much of the season, it looked as though Arsenal were going to make it two titles on the trot. By April 5, United and Arsenal were level on points, both with six games left to play. United won five of their six, to finish with a five-point margin. Arsenal lost their match on May 4th to seal United's win.

Manchester United 2007

Manager:	Sir Alex Ferguson
Leading scorer:	Cristiano Ronaldo, 17
Ever-present:	No-one
First at top:	Sep 9
Latest at top:	Oct 1
Date won:	May 6
Players used:	25

Just when you wondered if Sir Alex's time at the top was numbered, back came the red devils for another decisive championship win. Ryan Giggs was still there; now we had the exciting Wayne Rooney and Cristiano Ronaldo to admire. At the top consistently from October, they were never able to relax whilst Chelsea sat on their shoulders. A run of seven consecutive wins in February and March gave United some breathing space and they finished six points clear.

At 6ft 2in, it is no wonder defenders find Ronaldo rather a handful. His remarkable ball control skills and his pace of movement are a delight to watch. A Chelsea draw on May 6 gave United the title, which rather spoiled the build up to their meeting on May 9 (which in the event was a 0-0 draw).

Newcastle United 1905

Manager:	Frank Watt (sec)
Leading scorer:	Jim Howie, 14
Ever-present:	None
First at top:	Dec 3
Latest at top:	Apr 29
Date won:	Apr 29 (last day)
Players used:	21

The team of the decade. With a 'Scots Count' of seven, Frank Watt and the committee assembled a team with many internationals for Newcastle's first championship. They were beaten FA Cup finalists, so came close to 'the double'.

United were top around the turn of the year, but three consecutive defeats in January seemed to have handed the initiative to Everton. Everton completed their fixtures on April 26; Newcastle and Manchester City were a point behind, both with one game left to play. United won 3-0 at Middlesbrough and City lost.

Jim Howie won three Scottish caps. He was said to be the outstanding inside-forward of the 1900s. He joined Huddersfield in 1910 and later managed QPR and Middlesbrough.

Also in the team was local man Colin Veitch, an Englishman, although his middle names of Cambpell McKechnie betray Scottish roots. Veitch was a utility player who excelled wherever he was picked to play, and won six England caps.

Newcastle United 1907

Manager:	Frank Watt (sec)
Leading scorer:	Bill Appleyard, 17
Ever-present:	None
First at top:	Feb 2
Latest at top:	The same
Date won:	Apr 13
Players used:	27

Most of the team that won the 1905 championship were still regulars in the 1907 team. As in 1904/05, Everton set the pace and it was February before Newcastle hit the top. 18 home wins out of 18 gave United the advantage. A draw in their last home game with Sheffield United spoiled the perfect record but won the title for Newcastle.

Bill Appleyard was a strong, powerful centre-forward, 6ft tall and over 14st. He was well known for his ability to put both goalkeeper and ball into the net. He signed from Grimsby Town in 1902 and scored 71 goals in 128 League games for Newcastle.

Newcastle United 1909

Manager:	Frank Watt (sec)
Leading scorer:	Albert Shepherd, 11
Ever-present:	Jimmy Lawrence
First at top:	At start
Latest at top:	Jan 23
Date won:	Apr 12
Players used:	25

This was a season notable for one reverse for the champions; Newcastle were beaten 1-9 at home by Sunderland! Eight of Sunderland's goals came in the second half. Newcastle were four points behind Everton at this point, but won 1-0 at Goodison on January 1, the first of seven consecutive wins. When this run ended they were five points clear and extended this to seven by the season's end. A 3-0 win over Everton on April 12 gave them the title with four games left to play.

Albert Shepherd was a record signing in December 1908 when he joined from Bolton Wanderers for £850. At 5ft 8in and 12½ stone, he was a stocky centre-forward with an aggressive attitude and a powerful shot.

Goalie Jimmy Lawrence made 495 appearances for Newcastle from 1904 onwards. He was a member of the team in all three of the championship seasons and played in five FA Cup finals. He won one cap for Scotland.

Newcastle United 1927

Manager:	Frank Watt (sec)
Leading scorer:	Hughie Gallacher, 36
Ever-present:	Frank Hudspeth, Stan Seymour, Willie Wilson
First at top:	Dec 4
Latest at top:	Jan 1
Date won:	Apr 30
Players used:	21

A season enshrined in every Geordie's mind as they wait for the next championship. There have been great Newcastle teams since then, but the championship has always seemed a step too far.

With 36 goals in 38 games, the key player in this United team was Hughie Gallacher. Often described as the best centre-forward of all time, a memory of Gallacher remains strong on Tyneside, even at a distance of 80 years. He scored 132 goals in 160 League games for Newcastle before a surprise move to Chelsea in 1930. Only 5ft 6in tall, he was very quick off the mark and difficult for defenders to tackle.

United hit the top on January 1 and were never headed thereafter. Two defeats in February left Huddersfield just a point adrift, but four consecutive wins, including a 7-3 thrashing of Everton, restored a three-point advantage. The clubs met on April 15th, when a Gallacher goal gave United a 1-0 win. Though they lost at Huddersfield four days later, they still had a four-point lead and they wrapped up the title with a win against Sheffield Wednesday and with a game to spare.

Of the ever-presents, Frank Hudspeth was a veteran at 37 this season. He made 474 appearances for the club and won one England cap, at the age of 35. Stan Seymour became 'Mr Newcastle', serving the club as player, manager and director.

Wing-half Tom Curry played in five of the games this season. He was later the trainer at Manchester United and lost his life in the 1958 Munich air crash.

Nottingham Forest 1978

Manager:	Brian Clough (with Peter Taylor)
Leading scorer:	John Robertson, Peter Withe, 12
Ever-present:	John Robertson
First at top:	Oct 4
Latest at top:	The same
Date won:	Apr 22
Players used:	16

One of our oldest clubs, but still amateur when the League was created in 1888. In any case, it is said the rule was 'one club per town', so Notts County would have got the nod anyway. Apart from two FA Cup wins, all Forest had to show for their labours before this season was second place in 1966.

Brian Clough and Peter Taylor arrived with the club in the doldrums in Division Two. Promotion was sneaked by a whisker in 1976/77, and a place back in the top tier was good enough for most Forest fans. What actually unrolled during 1977/78 will never be forgotten by the good folk of Nottingham.

Having started with three wins, Arsenal scored three against Forest without reply in game four. "Well, it was good while it lasted", said the fans. Oh they of little faith. In fact there were only three more losses all season, in League and Cup, as they steamed on to the Championship and won the League Cup. The title was won with a 0-0 draw at Coventry with four games left to play.

Some of the team had 'been there before' with Clough, and knew what he wanted. Gemmill, O'Hare and McGovern were in the Derby championship side of 1972. John Robertson 'came good' on the wing and Martin O'Neill and Viv Anderson added young blood to the mix. Opinion is still divided as to whether the man of the season was a superb Peter Shilton in goal, or an inspired Kenny Burns at the back, once Cloughie had moved him from the forward line. The League Cup was won without Shilton, a young Chris Woods deputising, so I think we have to give the accolades to Burns.

I have seen John Robertson described as 'perky', which I mis-read as 'porky'! His build was just camouflage really; he was adept at avoiding his markers and his centres were almost guaranteed to find a Forest striker's head or foot.

They say clubs like Forest and Ipswich will never be able to win the championship again. "Rot" I say; it just needs another Clough to mould a team together!

Portsmouth 1949

Manager:	Bob Jackson
Leading scorer:	Peter Harris, Doug Reid, 17
Ever-present:	Ernie Butler, Jimmy Scoular
First at top:	At start
Latest at top:	Dec 25
Date won:	Apr 23
Players used:	18

This was a real surprise. An unsung club from the south coast, with no international players. The key, as with later 'surprise' winners, was outstanding teamwork. A settled side helped I'm sure; seven players making making 40 or more appearances in the 42 games. Portsmouth also reached the FA Cup semi-finals this season.

A unbeaten run of 13 games from the start of the season saw Portsmouth in first place. Derby were also unbeaten and edged in front at the end of October. After Newcastle had a spell at the top, Portsmouth took over again on Christmas Day and were never again headed. A 2-1 win at Bolton gave them the title with three games remaining.

Peter Harris was a goal-scoring winger who won two caps for England. Doug Reid was a Scotsman who scored 129 goals for Pompey in 309 appearances. Ever-present Jimmy Scoular is more usually associated with Newcastle United, but he made 247 appearances for Portsmouth before moving north.

Portsmouth 1950

Manager:	Bob Jackson
Leading scorer:	Ike Clarke, 17
Ever-present:	Ernie Butler, Harry Ferrier
First at top:	Apr 15
Latest at top:	The same
Date won:	May 6 (last game)
Players used:	25

If the 1949 win was a surprise, the fact that Pompey were able to retain the title was perhaps an even greater one. It was a close-run thing in the end, with Wolves and Sunderland close behind. A 5-1 win in their last game left them level on points with Wolves but Pompey's superior goal average gave them the title.

Centre-forward Ike Clarke had spent ten years at West Bromwich before joining Portsmouth in 1947. He scored 49 goals in 116 games for Pompey.

Preston North End 1889

Manager:	Major William Sudell (sec)
Leading scorer:	John Goodall, 20
Ever-present:	John Graham
First at top:	At start
Latest at top:	Never headed
Date won:	Jan 5
Players used:	18

The Invincibles. Who doesn't know their nickname? Preston had been an outstanding team before the League was created, though they lost the 1888 Cup Final to West Bromwich Albion. However, had bookmakers' odds been available in 1888, I'm sure they would have been favourites for the title. So it proved; unbeaten in the League and the FA Cup won without conceding a goal. The title was won as early as January 5th, with three games of the 22 remaining.

Just as Premiership teams raid Europe and Africa these days for outstanding talent, English clubs went north of the border for players in the late 1880s. Preston were one of the first; some of the original 12 (Notts County for example) came to realise they could not compete with their home-grown players and were late heading to Scotland. It was said that the place was swarming with English scouts in the summer of 1889, not all of whom were received hospitably by the locals!

Though team changes make a 'Scots Count' difficult, I think we can assess this season's Preston team as 8 out of 11.

John Goodall was a prolific goalscorer for Preston, netting 16 of the goals Preston scored in their famous 26-0 FA Cup win over Hyde. Except he didn't of course. Goal nets weren't used until 1891.

Preston North End 1890

Manager:	Major William Sudell (sec)
Leading scorer:	Nick Ross, 22
Ever-present:	Jack Gordon, Jimmy Trainer
First at top:	Nov 16
Latest at top:	The same
Date won:	Mar 27 (last game)
Players used:	19

Despite a 10-0 thrashing of Stoke in the opening fixture, Preston's second season got off to a stuttering start, with three defeats in their first seven games. However, a run of six consecutive victories took them back to the top. Everton were hot on their heels, with both clubs level on points and one game left to play. Everton lost their last game, leaving Preston needing a point, though their goal average was so superior that it would have taken a record defeat for them not to win the title. They won 1-0 at Notts County.

John Goodall had moved to Derby in 1889. Two new Scots, Nick Ross and Bob Kelso, joined the mix, making the 'Scots Count' nearer 9 out of 11. Nick was Jimmy's brother and had played for Everton in 1888/89.

Sheffield United 1898

Manager:	Joseph Wolstinholm (sec)
Leading scorer:	Walter Bennett, 12
Ever-present:	None
First at top:	Sep 25
Latest at top:	Jan 1
Date won:	Apr 8
Players used:	23

Just one championship out of 108 seems a poor return for Blades' supporters. United started the 1897/98 season with a run of 14 games undefeated and maintained their lead throughout the season. A 1-3 defeat at Sunderland followed by a 0-2 reverse at West Bromwich left Sunderland just a point behind United with a game in hand. United won a vital game at home to Sunderland on April 2 by 1-0 and a win at Bolton on April 8 gave them the title.

The star player of the 1898 team was left-half Ernest Needham, a cross between Nobby Stiles, David Batty and Norman Hunter. Needham was just 5ft 6in and weighed 10st 8lbs. He won 16 caps for England and was a good cricketer, scoring over 6,000 runs for Derbyshire. He made 464 League appearances for United, his only professional club.

Walter Bennett was a 5ft 7in outside-right who was said to have the hardest shot ever seen. He won two caps for England. Indeed, the "Scots Count" for the United team in 1897/98 was only one or two, the lowest at this point in the League's history.

Sheffield Wednesday 1903

Manager:	Arthur Dickinson (sec)
Leading scorer:	Harry Davis, 13
Ever-present:	Ambrose Langley, Harold Ruddlesdin, Andrew Wilson
First at top:	Oct 3
Latest at top:	Feb 28
Date won:	Apr 25
Players used:	23

What had Wednesday's committee and supporters made of Sheffield United's 1898 championship? United were the newcomers, Wednesday the established senior club. Wednesday put matters right this season, then went on to take a second championship next season.

Wednesday first reached the top on February 28th, though West Bromwich and Sunderland had games in hand. Two defeats for Wednesday in April left Sunderland a point behind with two games in hand, and seemingly destined to take the title. When Wednesday completed their programme on April 18 they were just a point ahead of Sunderland, but a better goal average meant Sunderland really needed to win their last game at Newcastle. They lost, leaving Wednesday as champions.

Harry Davis was a goalscoring winger who won three England caps. He signed from Barnsley in 1899. At just 5ft 4in but nearly 12st you can imagine he would have been rather a handful. His career was ended by a broken leg in 1907 and later he was assistant trainer for the club.

Of the ever-presents, Ambrose Langley was a veteran full-back with a good turn of speed. Andrew Wilson at centre-forward made 502 League appearances for Wednesday and scored 200 goals. He won 6 caps for Scotland.

Sheffield Wednesday 1904

Manager:	Arthur Dickinson (sec)
Leading scorer:	Harry Chapman, 16
Ever-present:	Harry Chapman, Billy Layton
First at top:	Oct 3
Latest at top:	Apr 23
Date won:	Apr 30 (last game)
Players used:	22

Wednesday's good form continued with a second consecutive championship. Their success this season was based on a solid defence that only conceded 28 goals in the 34 matches. At the halfway point they were six points behind local rivals Sheffield United, having won just once in six games. The New Year brought better form but three defeats in four games again put their title challenge under threat, with Newcastle United and Manchester City poised to take over. Wednesday needed a win in their last game at Derby, which they did by 2-0.

Inside-right Harry Chapman was the brother of Herbert Chapman, later the manager of Huddersfield and Arsenal. Harry was the better player of the two, with 94 goals in 269 games for Wednesday. Herbert made just 38 League appearances, with Grimsby Town, Sheffield United and Notts County.

Sheffield Wednesday 1929

Manager:	Bob Brown
Leading scorer:	Jack Allen, 33
Ever-present:	Jack Brown, Mark Hooper, Billy Marsden, Alf Strange
First at top:	Nov 24
Latest at top:	The same
Date won:	Apr 27
Players used:	22

The title was won with just 52 points, a new record "low". It remains the record for a two-points-for-a-win era, though it was later equalled by Arsenal (1938) and Chelsea (1955).

Indifferent away form meant it was the end of November before they displaced Derby County at the top. Subsequently they were never headed, with only Sunderland providing a challenge for most of the time.

Jack Allen was a powerful centre-forward with a strong shot. He signed from Brentford in 1926 and scored 76 goals in 104 games before moving to Newcastle United. Goalkeeper Jack Brown won six England caps and made 465 League appearances for Wednesday. Billy Marsden's career came to an end when he suffered a broken neck playing for England against Germany in 1930.

Sheffield Wednesday 1930

Manager:	Rob Brown
Leading scorer:	Jack Allen, 33
Ever-present:	Mark Hooper
First at top:	Dec 28
Latest at top:	Mar 15
Date won:	Apr 22
Players used:	22

Wednesday repeated the feat of the 1904 team and retained the championship for a second successive season. If Wednesday ever make it to the top again, it's a sure-fire bet they will win it the season after as well. A new signing, Harry Burgess from Stockport County, helped Wednesday towards 105 goals for the season.

The season unwound in a similar fashion to the previous one. This time, it was the end of December before they reached the top, with Leeds United and Manchester City making the early running. Once at the top they stayed there, except for a week in March when two defeats let in Derby County. Wednesday won the title in emphatic and pleasing style when they beat Derby 6-3 at Hillsborough, thanks to a Jack Allen hat-trick. They had four games to spare.

Jack Allen was again the leading scorer. Mark Hooper, also ever-present in 1929, was a fast and skilful winger and an accurate kicker of the dead ball.

Sunderland 1892

Manager:	Tom Watson
Leading scorer:	John Campbell, 32
Ever-present:	Ned Doig
First at top:	Mar 26
Latest at top:	The same
Date won:	Apr 16
Players used:	15

A club with another well-known nickname, "the team of all the talents." A strong home record and a run of 13 successive wins from the middle of November took the club to their first championship. Preston provided the only real challenge, and the title was won in style with a 6-1 victory over Blackburn Rovers, John Campbell scoring four of them.

Under astute management, and being much nearer the Scots border than most, the Sunderland team was a bit like the Chelsea of the 21st century: "all foreign". As it happens, full-back Porteous was English, but played for a Scots club before signing for Sunderland. So, we had better set the 'Scots Count' at 10 out of 11.

Tom Watson was the first great club manager. I have to admit to knowing little about him, and suspect I am not alone. His achievements put him alongside Chapman and Busby and we could do with someone writing a full-scale biography of the man. He won three championships for Sunderland before moving to Liverpool (I guess he was 'poached' in today's parlance) where he added more.

John Campbell was not related to Aston Villa's forward of the same name. Labelled as the best centre-forward of the time, Campbell's scoring record for Sunderland was outstanding. He signed from Renton in 1889 but was never capped by Scotland, presumably because of the anti-Anglo-Scots attitudes of the time.

Sunderland 1893

Manager:	Tom Watson
Leading scorer:	John Campbell, 30
Ever-present:	Ned Doig, William Gibson, Tom Porteous
First at top:	Dec 24
Latest at top:	Jan 3
Date won:	Apr 4
Players used:	15

A largely unchanged team retained the championship in 1893. In both 1892 and 1893 only 15 players were used for League games, a record that lasted until 1966. Sunderland were the first club to score 100 goals in a season, this in a campaign of only 30 games.

Once again, it was Preston that set the early season pace. Sunderland won both games against them; the second, a 2-1 win at Deepdale in January, secured Sunderland's place at the top. By the end of March they were ten points clear and the title was confirmed with a 6-0 thrashing of Newton Heath.

Goalkeeper Ned Doig is reckoned by many that knew him as the best goalkeeper of all time. He was ever-present for Sunderland for most of the 1890s, and that at a time when goalkeepers were 'fair game' for charging into the goal by the opposing forwards. He played 421 games for Sunderland before Tom Watson, then at Liverpool, persuaded him to join him there in 1904.

Sunderland 1895

Manager:	Tom Watson
Leading scorer:	John Campbell, 19
Ever-present:	John Campbell, Ned Doig
First at top:	Jan 1
Latest at top:	Jan 12
Date won:	Apr 15
Players used:	18

Sunderland were runners-up behind Aston Villa in 1894 and returned to the top this season. Everton were their closest challengers but Sunderland finished a comfortable five points clear with an unbeaten home record. A defeat for Everton on April 15 confirmed Sunderland as champions, but they beat Everton 2-1 in the final game of the season for good measure. John Campbell was again the leading scorer.

The season opened on an interesting note when Sunderland scored 11 against Derby County, only 8 of which counted. Referee Kirkham of Darwen missed his connection at York and sent a telegram to say he would not arrive until 5pm. With 9,000 spectators expecting a 3.30pm start the clubs decided to start with another referee. Two goals for Campbell, one a lucky deflection off Hannah, and one for Hyslop gave Sunderland a 3-0 lead at half-time. At this point Kirkham arrived and insisted that the full 90 minutes should be played with him in charge for the game to count as a League fixture. For the second time, Sunderland were 3-0 up at half-time. Derby tired in the third 45 minutes, but Sunderland seemed to thrive on the situation and added five more.

Sunderland 1902

Manager:	Alex Mackie
Leading scorers:	Jimmy Gemmell, Billy Hogg, 10
Ever-present:	Alex 'Sandy' McAllister
First at top:	Oct 12
Latest at top:	Jan 1
Date won:	Apr 16
Players used:	19

A seven-year gap from their last championship meant that only two players, Doig and Miller, were left from the 1895 squad. With a "Scots count" of 9, the team still relied heavily on the skills of the Scottish players.

A number of clubs were in contention in the first half of the season, with Everton having a slight advantage. An unbeaten spell of ten games saw Sunderland at the top in January and they were never overtaken. Four games without a win towards the end of the season saw Everton get within one point, but Sunderland had games in hand and won the title with two games to spare.

The two inside-forwards, Jimmy Gemmell and Billy Hogg, shared the goalscoring honours. Gemmell was a versatile forward who had two spells at the club. Hogg spent 10 years at Sunderland, scoring 83 goals in 281 appearances, before joining Glasgow Rangers.

Sunderland 1913

Manager:	Bob Kyle
Leading scorer:	Charles Buchan, 27
Ever-present:	Harry Martin
First at top:	Feb 15
Latest at top:	Apr 9
Date won:	Apr 26
Players used:	22

Just two points from the first seven games left the club in 19th place on October 5th. 10 wins out of the next 12 games took them to 7th place on Christmas Day but now only two points separated the top eight. Clubs continued to swap places, so that early in March there were still just five points separating the top nine, with Sheffield Wednesday a point ahead of Sunderland. From March 18, Sunderland won seven on the trot to establish a two-point lead over Wednesday and eventually finished four points clear of Aston Villa.

Sunderland were beaten finalists in the FA Cup this season, losing to Villa on the 19th, just four days before a vital League meeting between the clubs that drew a full house to Villa Park.

Charles Buchan was described as the greatest centre-forward of his day. At 6ft 1in and 12st, he was a powerfully built but nevertheless graceful player, whose fine play sometimes confused his own players as well as the opposition. He went into journalism when his playing days were over, and is remembered today (by people of a certain age) for his "Football Monthly" magazine in the 1960s. Buchan scored 209 goals in 380 games for Sunderland before a move to Arsenal, where he scored 49 goals in 102 games.

Harry Martin was a tall, long-legged outside-left who could skip past the defenders and provide accurate centres for his forwards. He won one cap for England. In a later spell at Nottingham Forest, he was sitting injured in the dressing room when his team won a penalty. He was summoned back to take the kick, scored, and limped off back to the dressing room.

Sunderland 1936

Manager:	Johnny Cochrane
Leading scorers:	Raich Carter, Bob Gurney, 31
Ever-present:	Jimmy Connor, Charlie Thompson
First at top:	Oct 26
Latest at top:	Nov 9
Date won:	Apr 13
Players used:	23

Sunderland were back at the top after 23 years with another team of Scots, though this time the count was a mere seven. Huddersfield Town had the best start, but Sunderland took over in November and were then never headed. By early March, they were eight points clear of Derby County, but five games without a win gave the chasing clubs some hope. A 7-2 victory at Birmingham sealed the title in some style, with Bob Gurney scoring four.

Two Englishmen, Raich Carter and Bob Gurney, were the leading goalscorers. Carter was just 23 years old this season, and had a long career with Sunderland, Derby County and Hull City before managing Leeds, Mansfield and Middlesbrough. He won 13 caps for England. At 5ft 8in and 10½st, he was a skilful ball player with a powerful shot. He also played cricket for Derbyshire.

Bob Gurney won one England cap. He broke both legs during his career (at different times), but you get the impression he could have played on in that condition and knocked in a goal or two.

Tottenham Hotspur 1951

Manager:	Arthur Rowe
Leading scorer:	Sonny Walters, 15
Ever-present:	Harry Clarke, Ted Ditchburn
First at top:	Dec 30
Latest at top:	The same
Date won:	Apr 28
Players used:	19

Always known as the 'push and run' team, this was perhaps the first taste for English football of today's passing game. The First Division was taken by surprise, with Spurs only promoted from Division Two the previous season. Push and run was attack orientated and actively encouraged team members to run into space to receive a pass. Bill Nicholson (later the club manager), Leslie Bennett and Eddie Baily were the hubs around which the wheel revolved to great effect.

After nine games, Spurs were in 13th place, six points behind Newcastle United. Eight consecutive wins moved them rapidly up the table, included in which was a 7-0 demolition job on the Geordies at White Hart Lane. A 1-0 win over Middlesbrough in December took Spurs top and they were then never headed. A 1-0 win against Sheffield Wednesday secured the title with a game to spare.

William 'Sonny' Walters came through Spurs' junior ranks. He was a speedy winger with an eye for goal. He won no England caps but did play one game for the England 'B' team.

Tottenham Hotspur 1961

Manager:	Bill Nicholson
Leading scorer:	Bobby Smith, 28
Ever-present:	Les Allen, Danny Blanchflower, Ron Henry, John White
First at top:	At start
Latest at top:	Never headed
Date won:	Apr 17
Players used:	17

The first double winners of modern times. The big surprise to me is that they failed to follow this season with more championships. There were 31 wins in the 42-game season, a record that still stands.

The first 11 games of the season were all won and the unbeaten run went to 16 games before losing 1-2 to second place Sheffield Wednesday at Hillsborough. An eight-game unbeaten run followed; by then there was a 10-point gap over Wolves. Three defeats in February and March allowed Wednesday to close the gap to four points, but Spurs put in a strong finish and won the title by beating Wednesday 2-1 at White Hart Lane.

They had three games in hand, only one of which was won, perhaps because of keeping one eye on the FA Cup. Leicester City were beaten 2-0 in the final.

Bobby Smith was a bustling busybody of a player, powerful and aggressive. He was only 5ft 9in in height, but 13st in weight. He had signed from Chelsea in 1955, where he had played in four games of their championship season.

West Bromwich Albion 1920

Manager:	Fred Everiss (sec)
Leading scorer:	Fred Morris, 37
Ever-present:	Bob McNeal
First at top:	Sep 8
Latest at top:	Dec 6
Date won:	Apr 10
Players used:	18

This was the first season after the First World War, a time of social unrest as the ex-service personnel readjusted to civilian life. West Bromwich were able to field an experienced team with half of them active before the war. With a strong defence, including Jesse Pennington at left-back, and an attack that scored more than 100 goals in a season for the first time since Sunderland in 1892/93, they were not seriously challenged for the title after reaching the top in December. They finished nine points clear of Burnley. A 3-1 win at the Hawthorns against Bradford Park Avenue gave them the title with four games left to play.

Manager Fred Everiss joined West Bromwich as a 14-year-old office boy in 1896, became secretary-manager in 1902 and stayed in the job until 1948; a remarkable 46 years in charge.

Inside-left Fred Morris had a powerful shot and scored 112 goals in 263 League games for the club. He won two England caps.

Wolverhampton Wanderers 1954

Manager:	Stan Cullis
Leading scorers:	Johnny Hancocks, Dennis Wilshaw, 25
Ever-present:	Johnny Hancocks
First at top:	Dec 5
Latest at top:	Apr 10
Date won:	Apr 24 (last game)
Players used:	22

The club of the 1950s. Though none of us had television coverage at the time, we could all imagine smoky nights in the Black Country when the Wolves hosted exotic foreign opposition in floodlit friendlies.

This was a good season for the region, with West Bromwich also going well and looking capable of beating Wolves to the title. The crunch meeting came on April 3, when Wolves won 1-0 at the Hawthorns. This left the two clubs level on 50 points with five games each left to play. Wolves took seven points from their five; the Baggies could only muster three. Even so, it needed a last-day win at home to Spurs to clinch the title.

Johnny Hancocks and Dennis Wilshaw shared the goalscoring honours. Hancocks was a small winger, just 5ft 4in, with a powerful shot that belied his size. One of his colleagues said "you should see his calf muscles". In pictures of the time he may be wearing shin pads….or he may not – it just might be those calf muscles. He won three England caps at a time when Matthews and Finney were in their pomp.

Inside-left Dennis Wilshaw won 12 England caps and is the only player to score in four in a game against Scotland. He was a versatile forward with a good scoring record, which included a hat-trick on his debut for Wolves in 1949. He was one of those once-common-but-now-vanished players for whom professional football was a part-time activity; in his case working as a teacher.

Wolverhampton Wanderers 1958

Manager:	Stan Cullis
Leading scorer:	Jimmy Murray, 29
Ever-present:	None
First at top:	Oct 2
Latest at top:	The same
Date won:	Apr 19
Players used:	21

The ultimate 'long-ball' team I think, but a cracking team to watch: 103 goals this season, 110 the next. Billy Wright was a rock in the centre of defence, allowing wing-halves Eddie Clamp and Ron Flowers to spray the ball out to the speedy forwards.

It took Wolves a little time to get started; after six games they were down in tenth place. An 18-game unbeaten run took them six points clear of West Bromwich at the end of December. Preston were the main challengers in the New Year, and, as fortune sometimes has it in these pages, the title was confirmed when the clubs met in April. Wolves won 2-0 and were champions with two games to spare.

Jimmy Murray was a skilful centre-forward with an excellent goalscoring record, 155 in 273 games for Wolves. He moved to Manchester City in 1963.

Wolverhampton Wanderers 1959

Manager:	Stan Cullis
Leading scorer:	Jimmy Murray, 21
Ever-present:	None
First at top:	Dec 26
Latest at top:	Mar 2
Date won:	Apr 22
Players used:	22

Wolves continued where they left off in 1958 and retained the championship after seeing off challenges from Arsenal and Manchester United.

Only one win in the first four games left them in 13th place. Further indifferent results meant it was Boxing Day before they reached the top. Wolves were then unbeaten in their last 13 games and won the title with a game to spare.

Jimmy Murray was again the leading scorer, closely followed by inside-forward Peter Broadbent on 20. Both players came from the same village in Kent, Elvington. In their time at Wolves, Murray scored 155 goals in 273 League appearances, Broadbent 127 in 452.

Manager Stan Cullis won his third title in six seasons. As a player, he was a commanding centre-half who won 12 England caps and was captain of the team that played the last international before the war, aged just 23. He played regularly between 1939 and 1945 while serving in the Army as a PT instructor and won a further 20 caps during that time. Injuries caused him to retire at the end of the 1946/47 season and he was assistant to Ted Vizard for a year before becoming manager of Wolves in 1948.

STATISTICS SECTION

PLAYERS

Played in most championship seasons:

On 9; Ryan Giggs

On 8; Nicky Butt, Kenny Dalglish, Alan Hansen, Phil Neal, Gary Neville

On 7; Denis Irwin, Roy Keane, Paul Scholes, Phil Thompson

Played in most games in championship seasons:

	Apps	Subs	Goals
Phil Neal	304	2	31
Alan Hansen	294		7
Ryan Giggs	258	31	62
Bruce Grobbelaar	244		
Kenny Dalglish	218	7	78
Phil Thompson	218	2	2
Denis Irwin	213	6	14
Ray Clemence	208		

Scored most goals in championship seasons:

	Apps	Goals
Ian Rush	183	113
Cliff Bastin	196	109
Dixie Dean	77	105
Jack Devey	143	87
John Campbell	81	83

Played for more than one championship club:
36 players have appeared in the teams of two championship clubs. Their names will be found in the player section of the book. They include Andy Cole (one sub appearance for Arsenal, followed by 5 seasons at Manchester United), Dick Forshaw, Kevin Sheedy and Frank Mitchell (each of whom played for Everton and Liverpool) and Reg Pickett, whose appearances for Portsmouth and Ipswich Town were 12 years apart.

The number of players (to end 2006/07) to have played for a championship club:
1464

MANAGERS

Won most championships:

Alex Ferguson	9
Bob Paisley	6
Matt Busby	5
Herbert Chapman	4 (plus part of a 5th)
Kenny Dalglish	4

Of the secretary-managers, George Ramsey won 6, Tom Watson 5 and Frank Watt 4.

CLUBS

Fewest players used:

14	Liverpool	1965/66
	Aston Villa	1980/81
15	Sunderland	1891/92
	Sunderland	1892/93
	Liverpool	1978/79
	Liverpool	1983/84

Most players used:

30	Chelsea	2004/05
29	Manchester United	1999/2000
	Manchester United	2000/01
	Arsenal	1937/38

Comparisons over the years are complicated by the changes from 2 points to 3 for a win (from 1981/82 onwards) and by the use of goal average (goals for divided by goals against), and goal difference, the latter in use from 1976/77 onwards. In the next four tables, to give the best perspective, points gained and goal average/difference have been calculated across all seasons, whatever the actual rules were at the time:

Most points – assuming always 3 points for a win

			Games
98	Liverpool	1978/79	42
97	Tottenham Hotspur	1960/61	42
95	Everton	1969/70	42
	Chelsea	2004/05	38

Most points – assuming always 2 points for a win

			Games
68	Liverpool	1978/79	42
67	Leeds United	1968/69	42
66	Tottenham Hotspur	1960/61	42
	Everton	1969/70	42
	Chelsea	2004/05	38
	Arsenal	1930/31	42

Best Goal Average:

			Games
5.31	Liverpool	1978/79	42
4.93	Preston NE	1888/89	22
4.80	Chelsea	2004/05	38

Best Goal Difference:

			Games
69	Liverpool	1978/79	42
	Arsenal	1934/35	42
68	Arsenal	1930/31	42

Most wins:

			Games
31	Tottenham Hotspur	1960/61	42
30	Liverpool	1978/79	42
29	Chelsea	2004/05	38
	Chelsea	2005/06	38
	Everton	1969/70	42
	Arsenal	1970/71	42

Fewest losses:

			Games
0	Preston NE	1888/89	22
	Arsenal	2003/04	38
1	Arsenal	1990/91	38
	Chelsea	2004/05	38
2	Leeds United	1968/69	42
	Liverpool	1987/88	40

29 clubs have remained unbeaten at home during a championship season. In addition to 2003/04, Arsenal were also unbeaten away from home in 2001/02

Most goals in total

			Games
137	Arsenal	1930/31	42
118	Arsenal	1932/33	42
116	Everton	1931/32	42

Fewest goals conceded in total (38 games or more)

			Games
15	Chelsea	2004/05	38
16	Liverpool	1978/79	42
18	Arsenal	1990/91	38

Fewest goals scored in total (38 games or more)

			Games
60	Blackburn Rovers	1911/12	38
	Huddersfield Town	1923/24	42
62	Liverpool	1976/77	42
63	Liverpool	1921/22	42

Most home goals:

			Games
84	Everton	1931/32	21
74	Arsenal	1934/35	21
71	Sunderland	1935/36	21
70	Arsenal	1932/33	21

Fewest home goals conceded:

			Games
4	Liverpool	1978/79	21

Most away goals:

			Games
60	Arsenal	1930/31	21
51	Manchester City	1936/37	21
50	Tottenham Hotspur	1960/61	21

Fewest away goals conceded:

			Games
8	Preston NE	1888/89	11
	Arsenal	1990/91	19
9	Chelsea	2004/05	19

Never headed (from game 4)

		Games
Preston NE	1888/89	22
Manchester United	1907/08	38
Arsenal	1947/48	42
Tottenham Hotspur	1960/61	42
Leeds United	1973/74	42
Liverpool	1978/79	42
Manchester United	1993/94	42
Chelsea	2005/06	38

Never top until last game

		Games
Liverpool	1900/01	34
Burnley	1959/60	42

Doubles (other than FA Cup)

League Cup

Nottingham Forest	1977/78
Liverpool	1981/82
Liverpool	1982/83
Liverpool	1983/84
Chelsea	2004/05

European Cup

Liverpool	1976/77
Liverpool[1]	1983/84
Manchester United[2]	1998/99

European Cup-Winners' Cup

| Everton | 1984/85 |

UEFA Cup

| Liverpool | 1972/73 |
| Liverpool | 1975/76 |

Inter-Cities Fairs Cup

| Leeds United[3] | 1968/69 |

Texaco Cup

| Derby County | 1971/72 |

[1] also League Cup winners
[2] also FA Cup winners
[3] strictly, this was the held-over final of 1967/68 season

Earliest Champions

The number of games remaining when the championship was won, not allowing for goal average or goal difference.

5	Manchester United	1907/08
	Everton	1984/85
	Manchester United	2000/01

Eight clubs achieved it with four games remaining.

ALL TIME TABLE 1888/89 TO 2006/07

The complete playing records of clubs in the top tier:

	p	w	d	l	f	a
Everton	4062	1652	998	1412	6373	5720
Aston Villa	3728	1541	868	1319	6202	5564
Arsenal	3678	1629	954	1095	5994	4693
Liverpool	3678	1692	913	1073	6019	4535
Manchester United	3322	1529	835	958	5663	4391
Manchester City	3164	1175	787	1202	4759	4768
Newcastle United	3084	1220	748	1116	4754	4427
Sunderland	2960	1165	676	1119	4745	4552
Chelsea	2942	1113	777	1052	4351	4334
Tottenham Hotspur	2938	1176	715	1047	4585	4227
West Bromwich Alb.	2766	1007	670	1089	4230	4408
Bolton Wanderers	2612	965	598	1049	3939	4160
Sheffield Wed.	2582	980	612	990	3976	4020
Blackburn Rovers	2530	960	599	971	4081	4048
Derby County	2430	905	577	948	3744	3821
Sheffield United	2356	871	560	925	3531	3762
Middlesbrough	2324	796	578	950	3328	3603
Wolverhampton Wan.	2308	918	518	872	3913	3748
Birmingham City	2192	695	546	951	2928	3489
Nottingham Forest	2178	800	549	829	3069	3171
Leeds United	2060	846	523	691	3079	2784
West Ham United	2054	709	504	841	2976	3263
Stoke City	1992	662	474	856	2657	3134
Burnley	1982	784	447	751	3163	3157
Leicester City	1900	603	500	797	2796	3247
Preston North End	1720	671	390	659	2701	2569
Southampton	1416	464	391	561	1868	2080
Coventry City	1390	430	396	564	1604	1954
Huddersfield Town	1260	480	317	463	1874	1854
Portsmouth	1242	451	295	496	1901	2045
Blackpool	1134	405	273	456	1733	1863
Ipswich Town	1084	402	265	417	1442	1500
Notts County	1068	341	253	474	1403	1712
Charlton Athletic	1050	355	253	442	1424	1651
Norwich City	864	264	263	337	1012	1254
Queen's Park Rgs.	822	277	223	322	1028	1111
Bury	804	279	180	345	1176	1340
Fulham	732	219	184	329	991	1246
Luton Town	658	213	168	277	863	1011
Cardiff City	630	224	154	252	865	993
Wimbledon	554	186	171	197	702	754
Crystal Palace	530	137	156	237	546	792
Grimsby Town	488	167	97	224	756	940
Oldham Athletic	484	159	129	196	604	713
Bradford City	468	152	126	190	584	671
Bristol City	358	114	94	150	428	510
Watford	326	104	77	145	450	508
Brentford	210	76	46	88	330	359
Brighton & Hove A.	168	47	48	73	182	244
Oxford United	124	27	38	59	150	229
Accrington	122	35	33	54	226	313
Bradford Park Ave.	122	40	27	55	172	204
Swansea City	84	31	17	36	109	120
Millwall	76	19	22	35	86	117
Wigan Athletic	76	25	14	37	82	111
Darwen	56	11	8	37	75	195
Carlisle United	42	12	5	25	43	59
Leyton Orient	42	6	9	27	37	81
Northampton Town	42	10	13	19	55	92
Swindon Town	42	5	15	22	47	100
Barnsley	38	10	5	23	37	82
Reading	38	16	7	15	52	47
Glossop	34	4	10	20	31	74

FOOTBALL LEAGUE CHAMPIONS 1993-2007

After the top clubs broke away to form the Premier League, the remaining three divisions of the Football League were re-numbered 1, 2 and 3. The champions of Division 1 continue to receive the old championship trophy and are entitled to call themselves "Football League Champions". In recognition of this fact, the Football League re-labelled Division One as "The Championship" for the 2004/05 season.

Though I have chosen not to include the results and line-up grids for these clubs, this is the list of champions:

1992/93	Newcastle United
1993/94	Crystal Palace
1994/95	Middlesbrough
1995/96	Sunderland
1996/97	Bolton Wanderers
1997/98	Nottingham Forest
1998/99	Sunderland
1999/2000	Charlton Athletic
2000/01	Fulham
2001/02	Manchester City
2002/03	Portsmouth
2003/04	Norwich City
2004/05	Sunderland
2005/06	Reading
2006/07	Sunderland

Sunderland have won four times, the other 11 clubs in the list once each.

FOUNDER MEMBERS

Of the twelve founder members of the Football League, four clubs have never won the championship. Derby County were the last of the twelve to break their duck. The four are:

Accrington. resigned in 1893.

Bolton Wanderers. Their best finish was third place in 1891/92, 1920/21 and 1924/25.

Notts County. Third in 1890/91 and 1900/01.

Stoke. Fourth in 1935/36 and 1946/47. A win in their last game would have given Stoke the championship in 1947.

THE GRIDS

Many of the results and line-up grids are taken from my 'Match by Match' series. Details of the volumes currently available will be found on the soccerdata.com web site. The books will provide authoritative match statistics for every Football League game from the first season (1888/89) to the start of the Rothmans Yearbooks in 1970. Matches played by the clubs in other major tournaments are included, including the FA Cup, the League Cup and the European cups.

In the pages that follow, the first column of each grid is the position held by the club in the League table on the day the game was played, taking that day's result into account. Strictly, there should be no entries before November in 1888/89 since the "two points for a win" system was not used until that date.

When compiling the grids, the results and dates of games are taken from a number of sources. A full account of the differences between those used in my books and elsewhere (including some publications of the Football League) will be found in 'Football League and Premiership Results and Dates' published in 2006. Home games are printed in upper case, away games in lower case.

Attendances are taken, with permission, from the records of Brian Tabner. Those to 1924/25 are from Brian's transcription of newspaper accounts. It was quite common in the early days for newspapers to use words such as 'small' or 'good'; if no other detail can be found I have left the number blank. From 1925/26 onwards, club secretaries were obliged to report attendance figures to the Football League. Brian transcribed the attendances from the League's ledgers, with their permission. It should be noted that official figures are invariably not the ones reported in the press at the time. I do not wish to enter into any arguments over which figure is right but merely re-state that, for better or worse, I have used the official figures.

Scorers' names were not recorded by the Football League and therefore I have to use press accounts. Before players wore numbered shirts (1939/40 season) it is understandable that reporters may sometimes have credited a goal to the wrong man. Also, goals in 19th century games are often described as 'rushed through' or scored 'in a scrimmage'. I have used 'unknown' where necessary, and followed club statisticians' selections in the majority of cases where doubt exists. A dubious goals panel has been used by the Premier League since 1992/93 to decide on goalscorers if any doubt exists.

Players' names include full initials as recorded by Michael Joyce in his 'Football League Players' Records 1888-1939' and also in Barry Hugman's post-war volume. You can refer to these books in order to trace players' careers at other clubs.

Line-ups. The bulk of the work in compiling the Match by Match books is to establish the line-ups used in each game. I am indebted to the late Morley Farror for his pioneering work at the British Newspaper Library at Colindale. Morley's work was used by the Association of Football Statisticians for the initial volumes of their 'AFS Annuals' series. In parallel with the publication of the Annuals, Breedon Books produced a pioneering series of 'complete records', which eventually covered more than 50 League clubs. Later, Dave Twydell (Yore Publications) and myself (with the 'Definitive' series) carried on the task of featuring every League club. Together with the valiant efforts of other club statisticians and publishers, the task of compiling complete records for every club is almost complete.

Newspaper accounts in local and national press are a prime source for line-ups, though in a (very) few cases we are fortunate to find records maintained by officials of the clubs themselves. The Football League has always required the clubs to notify them of the players used in a game. On receipt of the details, clerical staff at the League's offices transcribed them into ledgers. Fortunately most of these ledgers have survived and are now stored at the National Football Museum in Preston. Though I have used them to check many details, they cannot be regarded as authoritative because of clerical errors made in their compilation.

The best sources of line-up and goalscorer details are local newspaper accounts written by the regular reporters. We can rely on these men to recognize the players and give a true account of the game. Sometimes their best efforts were hampered by enthusiastic sub-editors, who would save a bit of typesetting time by setting 'the line-up announced before the game' at the beginning of the report, rather than the team that actually played. In almost every case, dedicated club statisticians have compiled their complete records by a painstaking review of every match report. Consequently, if any details are contradicted by other sources, I tend to side with the club statistician. This has the consequence that it may appear that I am simply copying details from complete record books. This is not the case; many other sources are consulted and the computer is then used to validate the line-ups and goalscorer details. I am indebted to many people who spend time on my behalf at Colindale, particularly Kit Bartlett. I am naturally indebted to all the club statisticians, who if paid by the hour for the time spent on their work, would all be rich men.

Shirt numbers reflect traditional positions as follows: 1, goalkeeper; 2 and 3, full-backs; 4, 5 and 6, half-backs, 7 and 11, outside-right and left; 8 and 10, inside-right and left; 9, centre-forward. It is almost impossible to follow such strict numbering in recent seasons; the numbers chosen hopefully give an indication of the player's position on the field.

Substitutes, from season 1965/66 onwards, have the numbers 12, 13 and 14. Number 12 is used if only one substitute was used (no matter what number was on the player's shirt). The players replaced are underlined. Unused substitutes are not included.

A full player list is provided for every player who has played in a championship winning team. This does not mean that they won a medal. It is impossible to establish which players were given medals; for many years, the Football League rule was "11 for the players", leaving the clubs to decide which 11 of their squad would get one. The clubs were able to have additional ones made, but we do not always know if this was done or not. Even today, the Football League award just 16 medals for the players.

Date and place of birth are shown, where known, and the year of death. The next three columns show the number of separate championship seasons played for each club, the year of the first championship, and the year of the last (if more than one). The years shown are the "last year" of the season; for example, 1972 is season 1971/72. Appearance and goals are totalled for each club a player represented. Please note these are appearances during championship seasons only, and not complete career records.

Full international caps are as follows: ar (Argentina), as (Austria), au (Australia), br (Brazil), ch (China), cm (Cameroon), cz (Czech Republic), de (Denmark), e (England), fr (France), ge (Germany), gh (Ghana), ho (Holland), i (Ireland), ic (Iceland), is (Israel), iv (Ivory Coast), la (Latvia), li (Liberia), n (Northern Ireland), ng (Nigeria), no (Norway), po (Poland), pt (Portugal), r (Republic of Ireland), ro (Romania), ru (Russia), s (Scotland), sa (South Africa), sm (Serbia), sp (Spain), sr (South Korea), sw (Sweden), tt (Trinidad & Tobago), un (Ukraine), uy (Uruguay), w (Wales) and zm (Zimbabwe).

I am indebted to Michael Joyce for the use of his player database in compiling this section of the book.

FURTHER READING

A good general account of the champions to 1972 will be found in Maurice Golesworthy's book "We Are The Champions", published by Pelham Books. Though long out of print, copies can sometimes be found on eBay or the Abebooks web sites.

Players' records can be found in two volumes of "Football League Players' Records". The volume for 1888-1939, by Michael Joyce, is a Soccerdata publication. That for 1946-2005, by Barry Hugman and Michael Joyce, is published by Queen Anne Press. The data is also on the internet at allfootballers.com.

A list of the complete record books for every League club can be found on soccerdata.com. Though some are long out of print, Breedon Books, Desert Island Books, Yore Publications and my Soccerdata imprint continue to produce new and updated volumes.

Preston North End 1888/89

Deepdale

					Dewhurst F	Drummond G	Edwards J	Goodall AL	Goodall J	Gordon JB	Graham J	Graham W	Holmes R	Howarth RH	Inglis J	Mills-Roberts RH	Robertson T	Ross JD	Russell D	Thomson S	Trainer J	Whittle R
Sep	8	BURNLEY	5-2	Gordon, Ross 2, Dewhurst 2	5000	10	11			9	7	6	5	3	2				4	8			1	
	15	Wolverhampton Wan.	4-0	Gordon, Ross, J Goodall, A Goodall	5000		2		10	9	7	6	5	3					4	8		11	1	
	22	BOLTON WANDERERS	3-1	Gordon 2, Drummond	5000	10	11				7	6		3	2				4	8	5	9	1	
1	29	Derby County	3-2	Robertson, Ross 2	6000		11		10	9	7	6	5	3	2				4	8			1	
1	Oct 6	STOKE	7-0	Ross 4, Whittle, J Goodall, Dewhurst	3000	10	11			9	7	6		3					4	8	5		1	2
1	13	WEST BROMWICH ALB.	3-0	Dewhurst, Edwards, Ross	10000	10	2	11		9	7	6		3					4	8	5		1	
1	20	Accrington	0-0		6000	10	11			9	7	6		3	2				4	8	5		1	
	27	WOLVERHAMPTON W.	5-2	Gordon, Ross, J Goodall 3	5000			11		9	7	6		3	2				4	8	5	10	1	
1	Nov 3	Notts County	7-0	J Goodall 3, Gordon 3, Ross	7000		11			9	7	6		3	2				4	8	5	10	1	
	10	ASTON VILLA	1-1	J Goodall	10000	10		7		9		6		3	2				4	8	5	11	1	
	12	Stoke	3-0	Ross, Thomson, Robertson	4500	10	11			9		6	4	3					2	8	5	7	1	
1	17	ACCRINGTON	2-0	Gordon, Dewhurst	7000	10				9	7	6		3	2				4	8	5	11	1	
	24	Bolton Wanderers	5-2	Ross 2, Robertson, Dewhurst, J Goodall	10000	10				9	7	6	5	3	2				4	8		11	1	
1	Dec 8	DERBY COUNTY	5-0	Inglis, J Goodall 2, Dewhurst 2	4000	10				9	7	6		3	2	8			4		5	11	1	
1	15	Burnley	2-2	Thomson, Ross	8000	10				9	7	6		3	2		1		4	8	5	11		
1	22	EVERTON	3-0	J Goodall 2, Dewhurst	8000	10	11			9	7	6		3	2				4	8	5		1	
1	26	West Bromwich Albion	5-0	J Goodall 2, Ross 2, Gordon	5150	10				9	7	6		3	2				4	8	5	11	1	
1	29	BLACKBURN ROVERS	1-0	J Goodall	8000	10				9	7	6		3	2				4	8	5	11	1	
1	Jan 5	NOTTS COUNTY	4-1	J Goodall 2, Edwards 2	4000			10		9	7	6		3	2				4	8	5	11	1	
1	12	Blackburn Rovers	2-2	Thomson, Dewhurst	10000	11				9	7	6		3	2				4	8	5	10	1	
1	19	Everton	2-0	Ross, J Goodall	15000		8			9	7	6		3	2				4	10	5	10	1	
1	Feb 9	Aston Villa	2-0	Dewhurst 2	10000	10	4			9	7	6		3	2		1			8	5	11		
				Apps		16	12	4	2	21	20	22	5	22	18	1	2	21	21	18	16	20	1
				Goals		12	1	3	1	20	10					1			3	19		3		1

F.A. Cup

R1	Feb 2	Bootle	3-0	J Goodall, Gordon, Thomson			10			9	7	6		3	2			1	4	8	5	11		
R2	16	Grimsby Town	2-0	J Goodall, Ross	8000	10	4			9	7	6		3	2			1		8	5	11		
R3	Mar 2	BIRM'HAM ST GEORGES	2-0	Holmes, Thomson	8000	10	4			9	7	6		3	2			1		8	5	11		
SF	16	West Bromwich Albion	1-0	Russell	22688	10	4			9	7	6		3	2			1		8	5	11		
F	30	Wolverhampton Wan.	3-0	Dewhurst, Ross, Thomson	25000	10	4			9	7			3	2			1		8	5	11		

SF at Bramall Lane, Sheffield. Final at The Oval.

Back (non-players): , Rt Hon. RW Hanbury MP, Sir WEM Tomlinson MP, W Sudell (secretary/manager), Back (players): Drummond, Howarth, Russell, Holmes, Graham, Dr Mills-Roberts. Front: Gordon, Jimmy Ross, Goodall, Dewhurst, Thomson

Preston North End 1889/90

Deepdale

						Dewhurst F	Drummond G	Gordon JB	Graham J	Gray FJS	Heaton C	Hendry WH	Holmes R	Howarth RH	Inglis J	Johnstone W	Kelso R	Pauls CA	Robertson T	Ross JD (Jimmy)	Ross NJ (Jack)	Russell D	Thomson S	Trainer J
	Sep	14	STOKE	10-0	J Ross 2, N Ross 3, Thomson 2, Drummond 2, Russell	9000		11	7	6				3	2			4			8	9	5	10	1
		21	Aston Villa	3-5	N Ross, J Ross 2	8000		11	7	6				3	2			4			8	9	5	10	1
		28	Burnley	3-0	N Ross 3			11	7	6				3	2	8		5		4		9		10	1
3	Oct	5	WEST BROMWICH ALB.	5-0	J Ross 3, N Ross, Inglis	10000		11	7	6				3	2	10		4			8	9	5		1
2		12	Bolton Wanderers	6-2	Drummond, J Ross 3, N Ross, Thomson	10000		11	7	6				3	2			4			8	9	5	10	1
3		19	Derby County	1-2	J Ross	5000		11	7	4				3				2		6	8	9	5	10	1
7		26	WOLVERHAMPTON W.	0-2		8000	9	11	7	6				3	2			4			8		5	10	1
4	Nov	2	Blackburn Rovers	4-3	J Ross, Drummond 2, N Ross	15000	10	11	7	6				3	2			4			8	9	5		1
4		9	ACCRINGTON	3-1	Drummond, N Ross, Gordon	8000		11	7	6				3	2			4			8	9	5	10	1
2		11	Stoke	2-1	Thomson, Gordon	5500		11	7					3	2			4		5	8	9	6	10	1
1		16	Everton	5-1	Thomson, J Ross, Russell 2, Gordon	18000	9	11	7	6					2			4			8	3	5	10	1
1		23	BOLTON WANDERERS	3-1	Drummond, J Ross, Russell	8000		11	7	6				3	2					4	8	9	5	10	1
1		30	BURNLEY	6-0	N Ross 2, J Ross 2, Gordon, Gray	4000			7	6	11			3	2					4	8	9	5	10	1
1	Dec	7	BLACKBURN ROVERS	1-1	J Ross	12000	10		7	6		11			2			4			8	3	5	9	1
1		21	EVERTON	1-2	Drummond	7000	10	11	7	6					2			4			8	3	5	9	1
1		25	ASTON VILLA	3-2	N Ross 3	9000		11	7	6				3	2		10	4			8	9	5		1
1		26	West Bromwich Albion	2-2	J Ross 2	10065		11	7	6				3	2		10	4			8	9	5		1
1	Jan	4	Wolverhampton Wan.	1-0	Heaton	10000		10	7			11		3	2			4		6	8		5	9	1
1		11	DERBY COUNTY	5-0	N Ross 4, Drummond	5000		11	7					3	2			4		6	8	9	5	10	1
1	Mar	1	NOTTS COUNTY	4-3	Thomson 2, J Ross, Drummond	3000		11	7					4	2			6	10		8	3	5	9	1
1		15	Accrington	2-2	J Ross, Haworth (og)	5000	10		7					4	2			6	11		8	3	5	9	1
1		27	Notts County	1-0	Thomson	3000			7	6			9		2			4	11		8	3	5	10	1

	Apps	6	18	22	17	1	2	1	18	21	2	2	20	3	7	21	20	21	18	22
	Goals		10	5		1	1				1					19	22	4	7	

One own goal

F.A. Cup

R1	Jan	18	NEWTON HEATH	6-1	Drummond 3, J Ross, N Ross, Gordon	7000		11	7	6				3	2			4			8	9	5	10	1
R2	Feb	1	LINCOLN CITY	4-0	Gillespie 2, J Ross, N Ross			6	7		11			3	2			4			8	5		9	1
R3		15	BOLTON WANDERERS	2-3	Pauls, Thomson			6	7					3	2			4	11		8	9	5	10	1

Played in R2: Gillespie (at 10)

Back: J Woods, Robertson, Howarth, Drummond, W Sudell (secretary-manager), Trainer, Holmes, Graham, MP Betts. Front: Gordon, Jimmy Ross, Goodall, Dewhurst, Thompson. Goodall had gone to Derby County this season.

Bob Holmes

Jimmy Ross

James Trainer

39

Everton 1890/91

Anfield

						Angus JA	Brady A	Campbell WC	Chadwick EW	Doyle D	Elliott J	Geary F	Gordon P	Hannah AB	Holt J	Jardine D	Kirkwood D	Latta A	Lochhead A	McLean D	Milward A	Parry CF	Robertson H	Smalley RE	Wylie TC
	Sep	6	West Bromwich Albion	4-1	Geary 2, Campbell, Brady	3000	1	8	6	10	3		9		2	5		4	7			11				
		13	WOLVERHAMPTON W.	5-0	Milward 2, Geary 2, Chadwick	10000	1	8	6	10	3		9		2	5		4	7			11				
		20	Bolton Wanderers	5-0	Geary 2, Milward 2, Latta	12000	1	8	6	10	3		9		2	5		4	7			11				
1		27	Accrington	2-1	Geary, Milward	5000	1	8	6	10	3		9		2	5		4	7			11				
1	Oct	4	DERBY COUNTY	7-0	Milward 2, Geary 2, Kirkwood, Chadwick, Brady	5000	1	8	6	10	3		9		2	5		7				11	4			
1		11	Aston Villa	2-2	Geary 2	12000	1	8	6	10	3		9		2	5		7				11	4			
1		18	BOLTON WANDERERS	2-0	Brady 2	12000	1	8		10	3		9	7	2	5		6				11	4			
1		25	WEST BROMWICH ALB.	2-3	Latta, Holt	8000	1	8	2	10	3		9			5		6	7			11	4			
1	Nov	1	Notts County	1-3	Geary	13000	1	8	5	10	3	7	9		2						4	11	6			
2		8	Blackburn Rovers	1-2	Chadwick	10000		8		10	3		9		2	5					6	11	4	7	1	
1		15	SUNDERLAND	1-0	Robertson	15000	1	8	6	10	3		7		2	5		4				11		9		
2		22	Preston North End	0-2		12000	1	8	4	10	3		9	7	2	5		6				11				
2		29	BLACKBURN ROVERS	3-1	Geary 2, Brady	11000		8	6	10	3		9	7	2	5	1	4				11				
1	Dec	6	Wolverhampton Wan.	1-0	Geary	8000		8		10			9		2	5	1	4		3		11	6			7
1		13	Derby County	6-2	Wylie 4, Geary, Brady	3000		8	6	10			9		2	5	1	4		3		11				7
2		20	Sunderland	0-1		6500		8	6	10	3		9		2	5	1	4				11				7
1		26	ACCRINGTON	3-2	Chadwick, Milward 2	16000		8		10	3		9		2	5	1	4				11	6			7
1		27	BURNLEY	7-3	Latta 2, Chadwick 3, Brady, Milward	8000		8		10	3		9		2	5	1	4	7			11	6			
1	Jan	1	ASTON VILLA	5-0	Chadwick, Geary, Brady 2, one og	10000		8		10	3		9		2	5	1	4	7			11	6			
1		3	NOTTS COUNTY	4-2	Chadwick 2, Milward, Geary	13000				10	3		9		2	5	1	4	7			11	6	8		
1		10	PRESTON NORTH END	0-1		16000		8		10	3		9		2	5	1	4	7			11	6			
1	Mar	14	Burnley	2-3	Geary 2	10000		8		10	3		9			5	1		7	4	2	11	6			

	Apps	11	21	13	22	20	1	22	3	20	21	10	19	10	1	5	22	13	3	1	4
	Goals		9	1	10			20			1		1	4			11		1		4

One own goal

F.A. Cup

| R1 | Jan | 17 | Sunderland | 0-1 | | 21000 | 1 | | | 10 | 2 | | 9 | | | 5 | | 6 | 7 | | 3 | 11 | 4 | 8 | | |

Players only. Back row: Hannah, Smalley, Doyle. Centre: Brady, Kirkwood, Holt, Parry, Chadwick. Front: Latta, Geary, Milward

Sunderland 1891/92

Newcastle Road

							Auld JR	Campbell JM	Doig JE	Gibson W	Gow DR	Hannah D	Hannah J	Logan J	Millar J	Murray JW	Oliver JS	Porteous TS	Scott J	Smith J	Wilson H
	Sep	5	WOLVERHAMPTON W.	5-2	Campbell 2, Millar 3	4000	5	9	1	4		10			8	6	2	3	11	7	
		12	Preston North End	1-3	Millar	7000	5	9	1	4		10		7	8	6	2	3	11		
		19	Bolton Wanderers	3-4	Campbell, Millar, Wilson (p)	8000	5	9	1		3	10			8	6		2	11	7	4
14		28	Aston Villa	3-5	Campbell 2, Wilson	6000	5	9	1		3	10			8	6		2	11	7	4
12	Oct	3	EVERTON	2-1	Campbell, Scott	10000	5	9	1	4	3	10	8			6		2	11	7	
10		17	West Bromwich Albion	5-2	Millar, Campbell 2, Scott 2	3000	5	9	1	6			7	10	8	3		2	11		4
6		24	WEST BROMWICH ALB.	4-0	Campbell 2, Wilson (p), J Hannah	7000	5	9	1	6	3		8		10			2	11	7	4
6		31	ACCRINGTON	4-1	J Hannah 2, Campbell, Scott	10000	5	9	1	6			8		10	3		2	11	7	4
5	Nov	7	Blackburn Rovers	1-3	Arthur (og)	8000	5	9	1	6			8		10	3		2	11	7	4
4		14	DERBY COUNTY	7-1	J Hannah, Scott, Campbell 4, Millar	5000	5	9	1	6			8		10	3		2	11	7	4
4		21	BURNLEY	2-1	Wilson (p), Smith	4000	5	9	1	6			8		10	3		2	11	7	4
4		28	Stoke	3-1	Campbell, Scott 2	1500	5	9	1		3		8		10	4		2	11	7	6
4	Dec	5	NOTTS COUNTY	4-0	J Hannah 2, Campbell (p), Wilson	5000	5	9	1	6	3	8	7		10	4		2			11
3		12	DARWEN	7-0	Millar 3, D Hannah, Campbell 2, Wilson	4000	5	9	1			8	7		10	6	3	2	11		
3		25	Everton	4-0	Campbell, D Hannah, J Hannah, Auld	16000	5	9	1		3	8	7		10	6		2	11		4
3		26	Wolverhampton Wan.	3-1	Campbell, Wilson, J Hannah	20000	5	9	1		3	8	10			6		2	11	7	4
3	Mar	1	BOLTON WANDERERS	4-1	Millar, J Hannah 2, Scott	5000	5		1	6	3	8	7		10			2	11	9	4
3		5	Accrington	5-3	Scott, Millar 2, J Hannah, McLellan (og)	2000			1	6	3	8	7		10	2			11	9	4
2		12	PRESTON NORTH END	4-1	Campbell, Auld 2, D Hannah	12000	5	9	1	6	3	8	7		10			2	11		4
2		19	Derby County	1-0	Auld	6000	5	9	1	6	3	8	7		10	4		2	11		
1		26	ASTON VILLA	2-1	Wilson, J Hannah	18000	5	9	1	6			7		10	4		2	11		8
1	Apr	2	STOKE	4-1	Campbell 2, J Hannah 2	3000	5	9	1	6	3	8	7		10			2	11		4
1		9	Notts County	0-1		10000		9	1	5	3	8	7		10	4		2	11		6
1		16	BLACKBURN ROVERS	6-1	Campbell 4, J Hannah, Millar	10000		9	1	5	3	11	7		10	4		2		8	6
1		23	Darwen	7-1	Campbell 3, J Hannah 2, Scott, Wilson	4000	5	9	1	6		8	7		10	3		2	11		4
1		30	Burnley	2-1	Millar, Campbell	10000	5	9	1	6		8	7		10	3		2	11		4

						Apps	24	24	26	20	16	18	22	2	24	22	3	25	24	14	22
						Goals	4	32				3	17		15				10	1	9

Two own goals

F.A. Cup

R1	Jan	23	NOTTS COUNTY	4-0	J Hannah, Smith, Campbell 2	12000	5	9	1	6	3	8	7			4		2	11	10	
R2	Feb	6	Accrington	3-1	Campbell 3	8000	5	9	1	6	3	8	7		10	4		2	11		
R3		13	Stoke	2-2	Millar, Campbell	9000	5	9	1		3	8			10	6		2	11	7	4
rep		20	STOKE	4-0	Campbell, D Hannah, J Hannah, Millar	9000	5	9	1		3	8	7		10	6		2	11		4
SF		27	Aston Villa	1-4	Scott	28000	5	9	1		3	8	7		10	6		2	11		4

R3 a.e.t. SF at Bramall Lane.

Void FA Cup Games:

R1	Jan	16	NOTTS COUNTY	3-0	Millar, Campbell, J Hannah	16000	5	9	1		3	8	7		10	6		2	11		4
R2		30	Accrington	0-1			5	9	1	6	3	8	7			4		2	11	10	

Games replayed after protests

Back: Porteous, Dunlop, Doig, Auld, Smellie. Centre: Gillespie, D Hannah, J Hannah, Scott. Front: Wilson, Harvie, Campbell, Millar, Gibson.

41

Sunderland 1892/93

Newcastle Road

	Date	Opponent	Score	Scorers	Att	Auld JR	Campbell JM	Doig JE	Dunlop W	Gibson W	Gillespie, Jas	Gillespie, John	Hannah D	Hannah J	Harvie J	Millar J	Porteus TS	Scott J	Smellie RI	Wilson H
	Sep 3	Accrington	6-0	Campbell 3, Scott, Millar, D Hannah	3000	5	9	1		6			8	7		11	2	10	3	4
	10	NOTTS COUNTY	2-2	Campbell, Wilson	10000	5	9	1		6	11		8	7		10	2		3	4
	17	Aston Villa	6-1	Wilson, Campbell 2, J Hannah 2, Harvie	12000	5	9	1		6	7		10	11	8		2		3	4
2	24	BLACKBURN ROVERS	5-0	Campbell 2, J Hannah, Millar, Harvie	8000	5	9	1		6	7			11	8	10	2		3	4
2	Oct 1	STOKE	3-1	Campbell, J Hannah 2	10000	5	9	1		6	7			11	8	10	2		3	4
2	8	Everton	4-1	Wilson, Gillespie 2, Millar	18000	5	9	1		6	7			11	8	10	2		3	4
2	15	ACCRINGTON	4-2	Campbell 2 (1p), Millar, Gibson	6000	5	9	1		6			7	11	8	10	2		3	4
2	22	WEST BROMWICH ALB.	8-1	Wilson, Campbell 2, Millar 3, Gibson, Scott	7000	5	9	1		6				7	8	10	2	11	3	4
2	29	Sheffield Wednesday	2-3	Campbell, Scott	20000	5	9	1		6				7	8	10	2	11	3	4
2	Nov 5	BURNLEY	2-0	Campbell, Scott	6000	5	9	1		6	7				10	8	2	11	3	4
2	19	NOTTM. FOREST	1-0	Campbell	5000	5	9	1		6			10	7	8		2	11	3	4
2	26	Notts County	1-3	J Hannah	8000	5		1		6	9		10	7	8		2	11	3	4
2	Dec 3	Nottingham Forest	3-2	Gillespie, Wilson, Campbell 3	8000	5	9	1		6	7		10	11	8		2		3	4
2	17	PRESTON NORTH END	2-0	Campbell, J Hannah	20000	5	9	1		6	7		10	11	8		2		3	4
1	24	West Bromwich Albion	3-1	J Hannah, D Hannah, Campbell	8000	5	9	1		6	7		10	11	8		2		3	4
2	26	Wolverhampton Wan.	0-2		14000	5	9	1		6	7		10	11	8		2		3	4
2	Jan 2	WOLVERHAMPTON W.	5-2	J Hannah 4, Millar	7000	5		1		6	7		10	11	8	9	2		3	4
1	3	EVERTON	4-3	Millar 2, Gillespie, Jardine (og)		5		1		6	7		11	10	8	9	2		3	4
1	7	Preston North End	2-1	Gillespie 2	16000	5	9	1		6	7		11	10		8	2		3	4
1	14	ASTON VILLA	6-0	D Hannah, J Hannah, Gillespie 2, Campbell 2	7000	5	9	1		6	7		11	10		8	2		3	4
1	28	SHEFFIELD WEDNESDAY	4-2	Gillespie, J Hannah 2, Millar	10000		9	1	5	6	7		11	10		8	2		3	4
1	Feb 14	BOLTON WANDERERS	3-3	D Hannah, J Hannah, Gibson	6000	5	9	1		6	7		11	10		8	2		3	4
1	Mar 4	Newton Heath	5-0	Campbell 2, Harvie, Scott, Gillespie	13000	5	9	1	4	6	7	3			8	10	2	11		
1	11	DERBY COUNTY	3-1	Campbell 2, Gillespie	6000	5	9	1		6	7	3			8	10	2	11		4
1	18	Stoke	1-0	Wilson	10000	5	9	1		6	7	3	8	11		10	2			4
1	31	Blackburn Rovers	2-2	J Hannah, Gillespie	12000	5	9	1		6	7		8	11		10	2		3	4
1	Apr 1	Bolton Wanderers	1-2	Campbell	13000		9	1		6	7	3	8	11	5	10	2			4
1	4	NEWTON HEATH	6-0	J Hannah, Campbell 2, Millar 2, Wilson	5000	5	9	1	6	3				8	7	10	2	11		4
1	8	Derby County	1-1	J Hannah	7000		9	1		6	7	3	8	11		10	2			4
1	15	Burnley	3-2	Harvie 2, Wilson	9000	5	9	1		6	3			8	7	10	2	11		4

All Gillespie goals are James Gillespie

	Auld JR	Campbell JM	Doig JE	Dunlop W	Gibson W	Gillespie, Jas	Gillespie, John	Hannah D	Hannah J	Harvie J	Millar J	Porteus TS	Scott J	Smellie RI	Wilson H
Apps	27	27	30	5	30	23	5	20	28	21	22	30	10	23	29
Goals		30			3	12		4	19	5	13		5		8

One own goal

F.A. Cup

	Date	Opponent	Score	Scorers	Att	Auld JR	Campbell JM	Doig JE	Dunlop W	Gibson W	Gillespie, Jas	Gillespie, John	Hannah D	Hannah J	Harvie J	Millar J	Porteus TS	Scott J	Smellie RI	Wilson H
R1	Jan 21	ROYAL ARSENAL	6-0	Millar 3, Campbell 2, D Hannah	3000	5	9	1		6	7		10	11		8	2		3	4
R2	Feb 4	Sheffield United	3-1	Campbell, Millar 2	14769	5	9	1		6	7		10	11		8	2		3	4
R3	18	Blackburn Rovers	0-3		20000	5	9	1		6	7	2	10	8			3	11		4

John Campbell

Donald Gow

Hugh Wilson

Ned Doig

Jimmy Millar

Aston Villa 1893/94

Wellington Road

		Date	Opponent	Score	Scorers	Att	Athersmith WC	Baird J	Benwell LA	Brown AA	Burton GF	Chatt RS	Coulton F	Cowan J	Devey JHG	Devey W	Dunning JW	Elliott JAE	Gillan JS	Groves W	Hare CB	Hodgetts D	Logan J	Randle WW	Reynolds J	Russell G	Smith S	Welford JW	Woolley A
	Sep	2	WEST BROMWICH ALB.	3-2	Reynolds(p), J Devey, Woolley	15000	7	3				6		5	9		1	2				10	8		4				11
		9	Sunderland	1-1	Hodgetts	10000	7	3				6		5	9		1	2				10	8		4				11
		11	STOKE	5-1	Hodgetts 2, Woolley 2, Logan	8000	7	3				6		5	8		1	2				10	9		4				11
1		16	Everton	2-4	Woolley, Athersmith	20000	7	3				6		5	8		1	2				10	9		4				11
1		23	EVERTON	3-1	Woolley 2, Athersmith	10000	7	2						5	9	8	1		6			10			4			3	11
2		30	DERBY COUNTY	1-1	Reynolds	10000		2				6		5	8	7	1			9		10			4			3	11
3	Oct	2	Sheffield United	0-3		10000		2				6		5	8	7	1			9		10			4			3	11
3		7	Nottingham Forest	2-1	J Devey, Groves	12000		2						5	8		1		6	9	7	10			4			3	11
3		14	Darwen	1-1	J Devey	3000	7	2						5	8		1		6	9					4			3	11
2		16	Stoke	3-3	Athersmith, J Devey, Clare (og)	4000	7					6		5	9		1	2			8	10			4			3	11
2		21	West Bromwich Albion	6-3	J Devey 2, Athersmith, Hare, Woolley, Cowan	15000	7	2						5	9		1			6	8	10			4			3	11
1		28	BURNLEY	4-0	Smith, Hare, Athersmith, J Devey	10000	7	2						5	9		1			6	8	10			4		11	3	
1		30	SHEFFIELD UNITED	4-0	Hare 3, Reynolds	9500	7	2						5	9		1			6	8	10			4		11	3	
1	Nov	4	Blackburn Rovers	0-2		8000	7	2						5	9		1			6	8	10			4		11	3	
1		11	SUNDERLAND	2-1	J Devey, Reynolds(p)	15000		2						5	9		1			6	8	10		7	4		11	3	
1		18	Bolton Wanderers	1-0	Hare	4500		2	1	7	4			5	9					6	8	10					11	3	
1		25	PRESTON NORTH END	2-0	J Devey, Hare	10300	7	2			4			5	9		1			6	8	10					11	3	
1	Dec	2	Derby County	3-0	Hodgetts 2, Athersmith	7000	7	2						5	9		1			6	8	10			4		11	3	
1		9	SHEFFIELD WEDNESDAY	3-0	Hodgetts, Athersmith, RN Brown (og)	8000	7	2	8					5	9		1			6		10			4		11	3	
1		16	Newton Heath	3-1	J Devey, Mitchell 2 (2 og)	8000	7	2	8					5	9		1			10		11			4	6		3	
1		23	Wolverhampton Wan.	0-0		14000	7	2	8					5	9		1			6		10			4		11	3	
1		26	DARWEN	9-0	J Devey 2, Brown 2,Hodgetts 2, Athersmith, Reynolds	12500	7	2	8					5	9		1			6		10			4		11	3	
1	Jan	6	Sheffield Wednesday	2-2	Reynolds, Woolley	3000	7	2	8					5	9		1					10			4	6		3	11
1		18	Preston North End	5-2	J Devey 2, Cowan 2,Hodgetts	4000	7	2						5	9		1					10			4	6			11
1	Feb	3	NEWTON HEATH	5-1	J Devey 3, Hodgetts, Reynolds	4000	7	2						5	9		1	3		6		10			4				11
1	Mar	3	BOLTON WANDERERS	2-3	Chatt	8000	7	2			6	8	1	5		9		3		10						4	11		
1		24	BLACKBURN ROVERS	2-1	Chatt 2	20000	7	2				8		5	9		1	3		6		10			4		11		
1		26	WOLVERHAMPTON W.	1-1	Athersmith	15000	7	2				8		5	9		1	3		6		10			4		11		
1	Apr	7	Burnley	6-3	Hodgetts 2, Groves 2, J Devey 2	7000	7	2			4			5	9		1	3		6		10				6	11		
1		14	NOTTM. FOREST	3-1	Athersmith, Chatt, J Devey	4700	7	2				8		5	9		1	3		6		10			4		11		

	Apps	Goals
Athersmith WC	25	10
Baird J	29	
Benwell LA	1	
Brown AA	6	2
Burton GF	4	
Chatt RS	13	5
Coulton F	1	
Cowan J	30	3
Devey JHG	29	20
Devey W	4	
Dunning JW	28	
Elliott JAE	12	3
Gillan JS	3	
Groves W	22	3
Hare CB	10	7
Hodgetts D	29	12
Logan J	4	1
Randle WW	1	
Reynolds J	26	7
Russell G	5	
Smith S	15	2
Welford JW	19	
Woolley A	14	8

Four own goals

F.A. Cup

		Date	Opponent	Score	Scorers	Att																						
R1	Jan	27	WOLVERHAMPTON W.	4-2	J Devey 2, Chatt, Cowan	22981	7	3				8		5	9		1	2		6		10			4				11
R2	Feb	10	Sunderland	2-2	Cowan, Hodgetts	15956	7	3				8		5	9		1	2		6		10			4				11
rep		21	SUNDERLAND	3-1	Athersmith, Hodgetts, Chatt	25000	7	3				8		5	9		1	2		6		10			4				11
R3		24	Sheffield Wednesday	2-3	Chatt 2	20000	7	3				8		5	9		1	2		6		10			4				11

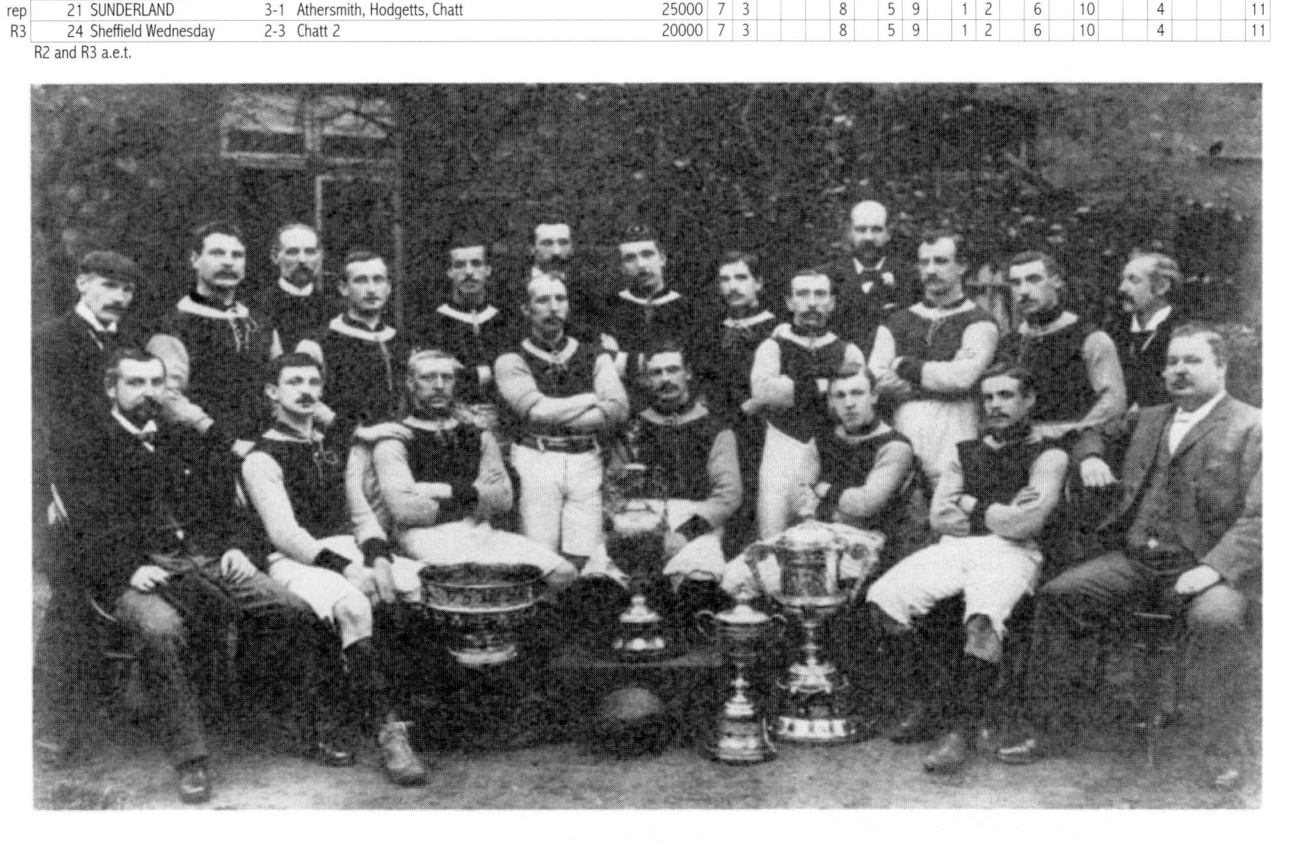

R2 and R3 a.e.t.

Players only. Back: Hodgetts, Bird, Hare, Reynolds, Johnson, Dunning, Groves, Welford, Moon. Front: Athersmith, Chatt, Devey, Woolley, Smith

Sunderland 1894/95

Newcastle Road

				Score	Scorers	Att	Auld JR	Campbell JM	Doig JE	Dunlop W	Gillespie J	Goodchild G	Gow DR	Hannah D	Hannah J	Harvie J	Hyslop T	Johnston H	McCreadie A	McNeill R	Meehan P	Millar J	Scott J	Wilson H
	Sep	1	DERBY COUNTY	8-0	J Hannah, Campbell, Millar 2, Hyslop 2, Gillespie 2	9000		9	1		7		3		11		10	6	5		2	8		4
		8	BURNLEY	3-0	Hyslop 3	7000	5	9	1						7	8	10	6	4	3	2		11	
		15	Aston Villa	2-1	Campbell, J Hannah	15000		9	1		7				11		10	6	5	3	2	8		4
2		22	WEST BROMWICH ALB.	3-0	Campbell, Gillespie 2	8000		9	1		7				11		10	6	5	3	2	8		4
3		29	Bolton Wanderers	1-4	Campbell	13000		9	1		7			10	11			6	5	3	2	8		4
2	Oct	6	STOKE	3-1	Hyslop, Millar, Clare (og)	6000		9	1		7				11		10	6	5	3	2	8		4
2		13	Derby County	2-1	Hyslop, Campbell (p)	7000		9	1		7				11		10	6	5	3	2	8		4
4		27	Everton	2-2	Millar 2	35000		9	1		7				11		10	6	5	3	2	8		4
3	Nov	3	WOLVERHAMPTON W.	2-0	Campbell, Millar	6000		9	1		7					8		6	5		2	10	11	4
2		10	Blackburn Rovers	1-1	McCreadie	15000		9	1		7				11		10	6	5	3	2	8		4
2		17	BOLTON WANDERERS	4-0	J Hannah 2, Campbell, Gillespie	8500		9	1	3	7				11		10	6	5		2	8		4
2		24	LIVERPOOL	3-2	J Hannah, Campbell, Gillespie	8000		9	1	4	7				11		10	3	5		2	8		6
3	Dec	8	SMALL HEATH	7-1	Gillespie 2, Wilson 2, Campbell, Millar, McCreadie	6000		9	1	4	7				10			3	5		2	8	11	6
2		15	BLACKBURN ROVERS	3-2	Campbell, Gillespie 2	8000		9	1	4	7				10			3	5		2	8	11	6
3		26	West Bromwich Albion	2-0	Meechan, Wilson	15086		9	1	4	7				10			3	5		2	8	11	6
3		27	Nottingham Forest	1-2	Campbell	7000		9	1	4	7					8		3	5	2		10	11	6
3		29	Preston North End	0-1		7000		9	1	4	7				10			3		5	2	8	11	6
1	Jan	1	PRESTON NORTH END	2-0	Campbell, J Hannah	10000	5	9	1	6	7				10			3	4	2		8	11	
1		2	ASTON VILLA	4-4	Gillespie 2, J Hannah, Millar	12000		9	1	4	7				10			6	5	3	2	8	11	
2		5	NOTTM. FOREST	2-2	Millar, Campbell	6000	5	9	1	4	7				10			3	6	2		8	11	
1		12	Wolverhampton Wan.	4-1	J Hannah, Millar, Campbell 2	4000		9	1	4	7				10				11	3	2	8		6
1		26	Stoke	5-2	J Hannah, McCreadie, Millar, Campbell 2	1000		9	1	4	7				11			3	5	2		8	10	6
1	Feb	9	Small Heath	1-1	J Hannah	15000	5	9	1	4	7				11			3		2		8	10	6
1		23	SHEFFIELD UNITED	2-0	McCreadie, Campbell	7000		9	1		7				10			6	5	3	2	8	11	4
1		26	SHEFFIELD WEDNESDAY	3-1	McCreadie, Campbell, Johnston	7000		9	1	6	7		3		10			11	5		2	8		4
1	Mar	9	Sheffield United	0-4		10000		9	1	4		7	3		11			6	5		2	8		10
1		23	Sheffield Wednesday	2-1	Dunlop, Campbell	6000		9	1	5			3		10	7		6		2		8	11	4
1		25	Liverpool	3-2	Campbell, Wilson, Millar	20000		9	1	5			3		10	7		6		2		8	11	4
1	Apr	13	Burnley	3-0	McCreadie, Gillespie 2	8000		9	1		7		3		10			6	5	2		8	11	4
1		20	EVERTON	2-1	McCreadie, J Hannah	16000		9	1	4	7		3		11	8		6	5	2		10		

Game 1 was a game of three halves. 0-3 down at half-time, the late-arriving referee decided to replay the first half. Sunderland's three goal scorers are therefore not included in the official records

	Apps	4	30	30	18	26	1	7	1	28	6	12	29	27	22	19	29	16	25
	Goals		19		1	12				12		7	2	8		1	12	1	4

One own goal

F.A. Cup

				Score	Scorers	Att																		
R1	Feb	2	FAIRFIELD	11-1	Millar 5, J Hannah 3, Gillespie, McCreadie, Scott	1500		9	1	4	7				11			3	5	2		8	10	6
R2		16	PRESTON NORTH END	2-0	Campbell 2	15000		9	1	5	7					8		6		3	2	10	11	4
R3	Mar	2	BOLTON WANDERERS	2-1	Wilson 2	14000		9	1	4	7				10			11	5	3	2	8		6
SF		16	Aston Villa	1-2	Millar	15000		9	1				3		7	8		6	5	2		10	11	4

SF at Ewood Park, Blackburn

Back: Wallace (financial secretary), Dodds (trainer), McNeil, Doig, Wilson, Gow, McCreadie, James Henderson (director), Reynolds (groundsman). Centre: Potts (director), Watson (secretary/manager), Dunlop, Millar, Hannah, Harvie, JP Henderson (President), Marshall (diirector), Wilson (director). Front: Auld, Gillespie, Campbell, Scott, Johnston

Aston Villa 1895/96

Wellington Road

							Athersmith WC	Burton GF	Campbell JJ	Chatt RS	Cowan, James	Cowan, John	Crabtree JW	Devey JHG	Dorrell W	Elliott JAE	Griffiths JA	Harris EI	Hodgetts D	Reynolds J	Smith S	Spencer H	Welford JW	Wilkes TH
	Sep	2	WEST BROMWICH ALB.	1-0	Devey	18150	7		9		5		6	8					10	4	11	2	3	1
		7	SMALL HEATH	7-3	Campbell 4, Devey 2, Jas Cowan	14000	7		9		5		6	8					10	4	11	2	3	1
		14	Sheffield United	1-2	Hodgetts	10000	7		9		5		6	8					10	4	11	2	3	1
3		21	DERBY COUNTY	4-1	John Cowan, Jas Cowan, Campbell, Devey	12000	7	6	9		5	11	2	8					10	4			3	1
3		28	Blackburn Rovers	1-1	Campbell	15000	7		9		5	11	6	8					10	4		2	3	1
1		30	EVERTON	4-3	Campbell 2, Devey, Athersmith	15000	7		9		5	11	6	8					10	4		2	3	1
1	Oct	5	SUNDERLAND	2-1	Campbell, John Cowan	15000	7		9		5	11	6	8					10	4		2	3	1
1		12	West Bromwich Albion	1-1	Campbell	15000	7		9		5	11	6	8					10	4		2	3	1
1		19	BLACKBURN ROVERS	3-1	Crabtree, Dorrell, Hodgetts	18000	7			5		8	6	9	11				10	4		2	3	1
1		26	Small Heath	4-1	Devey 2, Reynolds, Campbell	10000	7		9		5		6	8		3			10	4	11	2		1
1	Nov	2	BURNLEY	5-1	Athersmith 3, Smith, Devey	6000	7	6			5	11	3	9					10	4	8	2		1
1		9	Sunderland	1-2	Hodgetts	15000	7	6	8		5	11	3	9					10	4		2		1
1		16	SHEFFIELD UNITED	2-2	Chatt, John Cowan	4000		4		8	5	7	6	9	11			1	10			2	3	
1		23	Burnley	4-3	Athersmith 2, Devey, Reynolds	6000	7			8	5	10	6	9						4	11	2	3	1
3	Dec	7	Preston North End	3-4	Campbell 2, Devey	5000	7		10	5		8	6	9						4	11	2	3	1
3		14	BOLTON WANDERERS	2-0	Welford, Campbell	8000	7		10	5		8	6	9						4	11	2	3	1
3		21	Everton	0-2		30000	7		10	5		8	6	9						4	11	2	3	1
3		26	Wolverhampton Wan.	2-1	Smith, Spencer	22200	7		10	5		8	6	9						4	11	2	3	1
3		28	BURY	2-0	Campbell 2	5000	7		10	5			6	9			4		8		11	2	3	1
3	Jan	4	Stoke	2-1	Campbell 2	12000	7	4	9	5		11	6	9					10			2	3	1
1		11	PRESTON NORTH END	1-0	John Cowan	10000	7	4	9	6	5	11	3	8					10			2		1
1		18	Sheffield Wednesday	3-1	John Cowan, Devey, Crabtree	15000	7	4	9	6	5	11	3	8					10			2		1
1		25	NOTTM. FOREST	3-1	Chatt, Devey, John Cowan	5000	7	4	9	6	5	11	3	8					10			2		1
1	Feb	8	Derby County	2-2	Devey, Athersmith	20000	7	6	10	8	5	11		9						4		2	3	1
1		22	STOKE	5-2	Campbell 3, Chatt, one og	15000	7	4	10	8	5	11	6	9								2	3	1
1	Mar	7	Bolton Wanderers	2-2	Devey 2	14364	7	6	10	8	5	11		9						4		2	3	1
1		14	SHEFFIELD WEDNESDAY	2-1	John Cowan, Campbell	10000	7		10	8	5	11	6	9						4		2	3	1
1		21	Bury	3-5	Devey, Campbell, John Cowan	13000	7	6	10	8	5	11	4	9								2	3	1
1	Apr	3	Nottingham Forest	2-0	Athersmith, Campbell	10000	7	6	10		5	11	9	8						4		2	3	1
1		6	WOLVERHAMPTON W.	4-1	Campbell 2, Crabtree, John Cowan	15000	7	6	10		5	11	9	8						4		2	3	1
						Apps	29	14	26	17	23	25	28	30	2	1	1	1	18	22	11	29	24	29
						Goals	8		26	3	2	9	3	16	1				3	2	2	1	1	

One own goal

F.A. Cup

| R1 | Feb | 1 | Derby County | 2-4 | Burton, Hodgetts | 25000 | 7 | 4 | 9 | 6 | 5 | 11 | 3 | 8 | | | | | 10 | | | 2 | | 1 |

Players only: Back: Spencer, Wilkes, Hodgetts, Welford. Centre: Chatt, Crabtree, Reynolds, James Cowan, Devey, Burton, Athersmith, Campbell. Front: Smith, John Cowan

45

Aston Villa 1896/97

Wellington Road/Villa Park

							Athersmith WC	Burton GF	Campbell JJ	Chatt RS	Cowan J (James)	Cowan J (John)	Crabtree JW	Devey JHG	Evans AJ	Griffiths JA	Reynolds J	Smith S	Spencer H	Welford JW	Wheldon GF	Whitehouse J	Wilkes TH
	Sep	2	STOKE	2-1	John Cowan, Devey	6000	7		10		5	11	6	9			4		2	3	8		1
		5	West Bromwich Albion	1-3	Devey	12000	7		10		5	11	6	9			4		2	3	8	1	
		12	SHEFFIELD UNITED	2-2	Wheldon, Burton	10000	7	6	10		5	11	3	9			4		2		8		1
6		19	Everton	3-2	Campbell 2, Devey	25000	7	6	10		5	11	3	9			4		2		8	1	
10		26	EVERTON	1-2	Devey	15000	7	6	9		5	11	2	8			4			3	10	1	
8	Oct	3	Sheffield United	0-0		12000	7	6	10		5	11	3	9			4		2		8	1	
7		10	WEST BROMWICH ALB.	2-0	Wheldon, Campbell	15000	7		9		5	11	6	8			4		2	3	10	1	
4		17	Derby County	3-1	John Cowan, Campbell, Wheldon	10000	7		9		5	11	6	8			4		2	3	10	1	
4		24	DERBY COUNTY	2-1	Wheldon, John Cowan	10000	7		9		5	11	6	8			4		2	3	10	1	
3		31	Stoke	2-0	Wheldon, Smith	8000	7	6	9		5			8			4	11	2	3	10	1	
4	Nov	7	BURY	1-1	Athersmith	4000	7		9				6	8	2		4	11		3	10	1	
3		14	Sheffield Wednesday	3-1	Wheldon, Athersmith, Campbell	10000	7		9	4	5		6	8				11	2	3	10	1	
2		21	SHEFFIELD WEDNESDAY	4-0	Smith, Devey, Wheldon, Athersmith	12000	7		9	4	5		6	8				11	2	3	10	1	
1		28	Blackburn Rovers	5-1	Wheldon 3, Devey, Smith	5000	7		9	4	5		6	8	3			11	2		10	1	
1	Dec	19	NOTTM. FOREST	3-2	Devey, Athersmith, Reynolds	5000	7			6	5			9	8	3	4	11	2		10	1	
1		25	Liverpool	3-3	Wheldon, Athersmith, James Cowan	15000	7		9	6	5			3	8		4	11	2		10	1	
1		26	Wolverhampton Wan.	2-1	Chatt, Athersmith	15000	7		9	6	5			3	8		4	11	2		10	1	
1	Jan	2	BURNLEY	0-3		12000	7		9	6	5			8	3		4	11	2		10	1	
1		9	Sunderland	2-4	Campbell, Ferguson (og)	10000	7	6	9	4	5		8			3		11	2		10	1	
1		16	SUNDERLAND	2-1	Devey, Wheldon	15000	7		9	6	5			3	8		4	11	2		10		1
1	Feb	6	Bury	2-0	Campbell 2	10000	7		9	4	5		6	8	3			11	2		10		1
1		8	Burnley	4-3	Devey 3, Campbell	4000	7		9	4	5		6	8	3			11	2		10		1
1		22	PRESTON NORTH END	3-1	Devey 2, Athersmith	14000	7		9		5		6	8	3		4	11	2		10		1
1	Mar	6	Nottingham Forest	4-2	Devey 2, Wheldon, John Cowan	10000	7		9		5	11	6	8	3		4		2		10		1
1		13	LIVERPOOL	0-0		18000	7		9		5	11	6	8	3		4		2		10	1	
1		22	BOLTON WANDERERS	6-2	Wheldon 2, Athersmith, Reynolds, Devey, Campbell	8000	7		9		5			8	3	6	4	11	2		10		1
1		27	Bolton Wanderers	2-1	Wheldon 2	8000	7	6	9		5	11		8	3		4		2		10	1	
1	Apr	17	BLACKBURN ROVERS	3-0	Campbell, John Cowan, Kelean (og)	15000	7		9		5	11	6	8	3		4		2		10	1	
1		19	WOLVERHAMPTON W.	5-0	John Cowan 2, Campbell 2, Devey	35000	7	6	9		5	11		8	3		4		2		10	1	
1		26	Preston North End	1-0	Wheldon	3000	7		9		5	11	6	8	3		4		2		10	1	

April 17 and April 19 games at Villa Park

	Apps	30	8	29	11	30	15	25	29	15	1	24	15	28	10	30	22	8
	Goals	8	1	13	1	1	7		17				2	3		18		

Two own goals

F.A. Cup

R1	Jan	30	NEWCASTLE UNITED	5-0	Wheldon 2, Athersmith, Smith, White (og)	6000	7		9	4	5		6	8	3			11	2		10		1
R2	Feb	13	NOTTS COUNTY	2-1	Wheldon, Campbell	4000	7		9		5		6	8	3		4	11	2		10		1
R3		27	Preston North End	1-1	Campbell	14000	7		9		5		6	8	3		4	11	2		10		1
rep	Mar	3	PRESTON NORTH END	0-0		12000	7		9		5		6	8	3		4	11	2		10		1
rep2		10	Preston North End	3-2	Athersmith 2, Campbell	22000	7		9		5	11	6	8	3		4		2		10		1
SF		20	Liverpool	3-0	John Cowan 2, Athersmith	30000	7		9		5	11		8	3	6	4		2		10	1	
F	Apr	4	Everton	3-2	Campbell, Wheldon, Crabtree	65891	7		9		5	11	6	8	3		4		2		10	1	

R3 replay 2 and semi-final at Bramall Lane; Final at the Crystal Palace
R3 replay a.e.t.

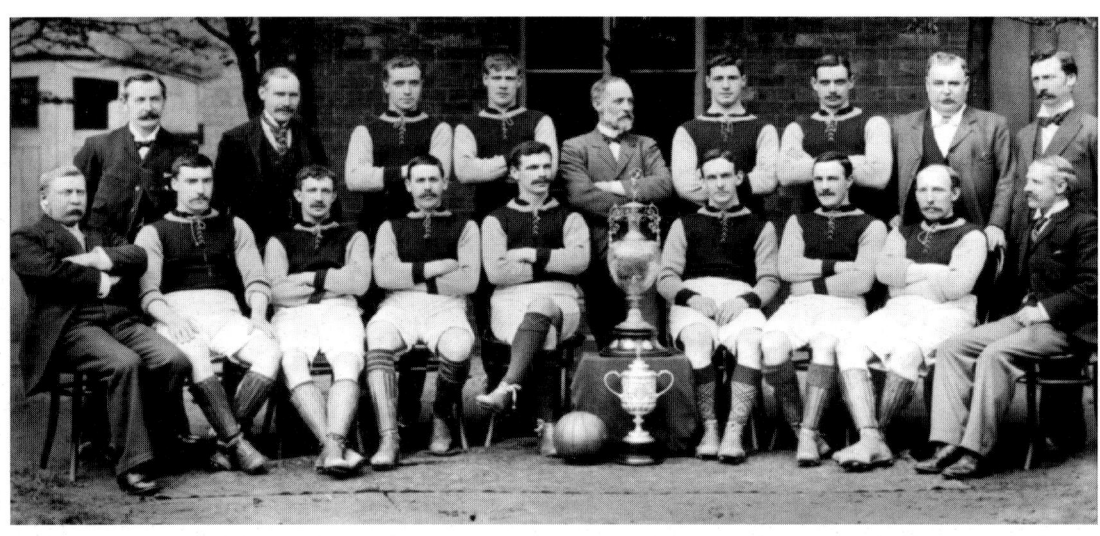

Back: George Ramsey (secretary), Jack Grierson (trainer), Spencer, Whitehouse, Margoschis (chairman), Evans, Crabtree, Lees and Johnstone (directors). Seated: Jones (director), James Cowan, Athersmith, Campbell, Devey, Wheldon, John Cowan, Reynolds, Rinder (vice-chairman)

Sheffield United 1897/98

Bramall Lane

							Almond J	Bennett W	Blair J	Bradshaw AE	Cain R	Cunningham J	Foulke WH	French A	Gaudie R	Hedley GA	Howard H	Howell R	Jenkinson TJ	Johnson WH	Logan N	McKay K	Morren T	Morton D	Needham E	Priest AE	Thickett H	White H	Whitham M
	Sep	1	DERBY COUNTY	2-1	Bennett, Needham	2500	10	7	5		3		1					4						8	6	11	2		9
		4	Preston North End	3-1	Bennett, Priest 2	4500	10	7			3		1					4				8	5		6	11	2		9
		11	STOKE	4-3	Morren, McKay 2, Bennett	11000	10	7			3		1					4				8	5		6	11	2		9
2		18	Nottingham Forest	1-1	Almond	8500	10	7			3		1					4				8	5		6	11	2		9
1		25	BURY	1-1	Priest	11000	10	7			3		1					4				8	5		6	11	2		9
2	Oct	2	Wolverhampton Wan.	1-1	Almond	8500	10	7			3		1					4				8	5	9	6	11	2		
1		4	BLACKBURN ROVERS	5-2	Bennett, Almond, Needham 3 (1p)	8000	9	7			3	10	1					4				8	5		6	11			2
1		9	Bury	5-2	Needham, Bennett, Almond, Morren, Cunningham	5531	9	7			3	10	1					4				8	5		6	11	2		
1		16	Wednesday	1-0	Bennett	24000	9	7			3	10	1					4				8	5		6	11	2		
		23	PRESTON NORTH END	2-1	McKay, Needham	10500		7			3	10	1					4		6		8	5		11		2	9	
1		30	Everton	4-1	Cunningham, Almond 2, Bennett	33000	9	7			3	10	1					4				8	5		6	11	2		
1	Nov	13	Derby County	1-1	McKay	10000	9	7			3	10	1					4				8	5		6	11	2		
		20	Blackburn Rovers	1-1	Cunningham	7000	9				3	10	1					4	7			8	5		6	11	2		
1	Dec	4	NOTTM. FOREST	1-1	Almond	9700	9				3	10	1					4		6		8	5		7	11	2		
1		11	Stoke	1-2	Needham	6000	9				3	10	1					4	7			8	5		6	11	2		
2		27	WEDNESDAY	1-1	Earp (og)	37389	9	7			3	10	1					4				8	5		6	11	2		
2		29	LIVERPOOL	1-2	unknown	4000	9	7			3	10	1					4		5		8			6	11	2		
1	Jan	1	Notts County	3-1	Gaudie 2, Bennett	11000		7			3	10	1	8	9						4		5		6	11	2		
1		8	ASTON VILLA	1-0	Bennett	23887		7			3	10	1		9			4				8	5		6	11	2		
1		15	Aston Villa	2-1	Cunningham 2	43000		7			3	10	1		9			4				8	5		6	11	2		
1		22	WOLVERHAMPTON W.	2-1	Almond, McKay	11500	9	7			3	10	1					4				8	5		6	11	2		
1	Feb	5	Liverpool	4-0	Cunningham, Logan 2, Johnson	17500		7			3	10	1								4	9	8	5		6	11	2		
1		7	BOLTON WANDERERS	4-0	Priest, Logan 2, Bennett	5000		7			3	10	1								4	9	8	5		6	11	2		
1		19	NOTTS COUNTY	0-1		8500		7			3	10	1					4				9	8	5		6	11	2		
1		22	EVERTON	0-0		9500					3	10	1	7				4				9	8	5		6	11	2		
1	Mar	5	Sunderland	1-3	Cunningham	23500		7			2	10	1		9			4		5		8			6	11	3		
		26	West Bromwich Albion	0-2		4200		7			3	10	1			9		4				5	8		6	11	2		
1	Apr	2	SUNDERLAND	1-0	Johnson	23000	10				3	8	1		9		6			4			5			11	2		
1		8	Bolton Wanderers	1-0	Needham	19395	9	7			3	10	1				6			4			5		8	11	2		
1		11	WEST BROMWICH ALB.	2-0	Bennett 2	9000	8	7		1	3	10			9		6			4			5		11		2		

Apps: 20 26 1 1 30 24 29 1 6 2 3 24 2 10 5 25 26 2 29 28 29 6 1
Goals: 8 12 7 2 2 4 5 2 8 4

One own goal, one unknown

F.A. Cup

R1	Jan	29	BURSLEM PORT VALE	1-1	Needham (p)	13250	9	7				10	1					4				8	5		6	11	2		
R2	Feb	2	Burslem Port Vale	1-2	Thickett	13000		7				10	1					4			9	8	5		6	11	2		

R2 a.e.t. GP Simpson played at 3 in both games

Sheriff of London's Charity Shield

	Mar	19	Corinthians	0-0		19707		7			3	10	1		9			4				8	5		6	11	2		
rep	Apr	4	Corinthians	1-1	Almond	7500	10	7			3	8	1		9			4					5		6	11	2		

Both games at the Crystal Palace. United declined to play extra time in the replay. Shield held jointly.

Players only: Back: Hedley, Johnson, Boyle, Foulkes, Almond, Morren. Front: Bennett, Beers, Needham, Thickett, Priest

Aston Villa 1898/99

Villa Park

		Date	Opponent	Score	Scorers	Att	Aston CL	Athersmith WC	Bedingfield F	Bowman T	Cowan, James	Cowan, John	Crabtree JW	Devey JHG	Evans AJ	Garraty W	Gaudie R	George W	Haggart W	Johnson G	Leigh WH	Sharp A	Sharp J	Smith S	Spencer H	Templeton RB	Wheldon GF	Wilkes A	Wilkes TH
	Sep	3	STOKE	3-1	Athersmith, Devey, Gaudie	19002		7		2	5		6	8	3		10			9				11				4	1
		10	Bury	1-2	Devey	7000		7		2	5		3	8			6			9				11			10	4	1
		17	Burnley	4-2	Smith, Athersmith, Johnson, Wheldon	9000		7		2	5		3	8			6			9				11			10	4	1
8		24	SHEFFIELD UNITED	1-1	Devey	25421		7		2	5		3	8			6			9				11			10	4	1
7	Oct	1	Newcastle United	1-1	Devey	27500		7		2	5		4	8	3		6	1		9				11			10		
4		8	PRESTON NORTH END	4-2	Devey 2, Jas Cowan, Johnson	18899	2	7		4	5		6	8	3			1		9				11			10		
3		15	Liverpool	3-0	Johnson, Devey, Wheldon	20000	2	7		4	5		6	8	3			1		9				11			10		
2		22	NOTTM. FOREST	3-0	J Sharp 2, Devey	16889	3			4	5		6	8				1	2	9			7	11			10		
1		29	BOLTON WANDERERS	2-1	Devey, Wheldon	17402	2			4	5	11	6	8	3			1		9			7				10		
1	Nov	5	DERBY COUNTY	7-1	Devey 2, Johnson 2, Wheldon 2, John Cowan	16786	2			4	5	11		8	3			1		9			7				10	6	
1		12	West Bromwich Albion	1-0	Johnson	18000	2			4	5	11	6	8	3			1		9			7				10		
1		19	BLACKBURN ROVERS	3-1	Wheldon 2, Devey	21220	2	7		4	5	11	6	9	3			1					8				10		
1		26	Sheffield Wednesday		* see note below	17000	2	7	9	4	5		6	8	3			1						11			10		
1	Dec	3	SUNDERLAND	2-0	J Sharp 2	24983	2	7		4	5		6	9	3			1					8	11			10		
1		10	WOLVERHAMPTON W.	1-1	Crabtree	17357	2	7		4	5		6	9	3			1		8				11			10		
1		17	EVERTON	3-0	Wheldon, Devey, Johnson	21335		7		4			6	8	3			1		9			2	11			10	5	
1		24	Notts County	0-1		16000		7		4	5		6	8	3			1		9			2	11			10		
1		26	NEWCASTLE UNITED	1-0	Athersmith	30000		7		4	5		6	8	3			1		9			2	11			10		
1		31	Stoke	0-3		10000		7		4	5		6		3			1		9			2	10	11		8		
1	Jan	7	BURY	3-2	Devey 2, Wheldon	15400		7		4	5		6	2	8	3		1		9				11			10	6	
1		14	BURNLEY	4-0	Wheldon, Bowman, Athersmith, Taylor (og)	21000		7		4	5	11	2	8	3			1		9							10	6	
1		21	Sheffield United	3-1	John Cowan 2, Wilkes	12000		7		4	5	11	2	8	3			1		9							10	6	
1	Feb	4	Preston North End	0-2		10000		7		4	5	11	2	8	3			1		9							10	6	
1		18	Nottingham Forest	0-1		16000				4	5			8	3			1		9			7	11	2		10	6	
1	Mar	4	Derby County	1-1	Johnson	10000		7		4	5		6	8	3			1		9				11	2		10		
2		13	Sheffield Wednesday	1-4	Bedingfield	3000										9													
1		18	Blackburn Rovers	0-0		14000	3	7		4	5		6			8		1		9				11	2		10		
1		25	SHEFFIELD WEDNESDAY	3-1	Wheldon, Garraty, Johnson	14000		7		4	5		6		3	8		1		9				11	2		10		
1	Apr	1	Sunderland	2-4	Devey, John Cowan	18000	6			4	5			8	3	9		1						11	2	7	10		
1		3	Wolverhampton Wan.	0-4		18000	2	7		4	5		6	8	3	9		1						11			10		
2		15	Everton	1-1	Smith	15000		7		4	5		6		3	8		1			9			11	2		10		
2		17	Bolton Wanderers	0-0		7000		7		4	5		6	8	3	9		1						11	2		10		
2		22	NOTTS COUNTY	6-1	Devey 3, Garraty 2, Wheldon	18900		7		4	5		6	8	3	9		1						11	2		10		
1		24	WEST BROMWICH ALB.	7-1	Garraty 3, Wheldon 2, Bowman, Jas Cowan	12500		7		4	5		6	8	3	9		1						11	2		10		
1		29	LIVERPOOL	5-0	Devey 2, Wheldon 2, Crabtree	41000		7		4	5		6	8	3	9		1						11	2		10		
			Apps				13	28	1	34	33	7	31	30	29	10	5	30	1	24	1	4	8	27	10	1	33	11	4
			Goals					4	1	2	2	4	2	21		6	1			9			4	2			16	1	

Mar 13th was last ten mins of game started Nov 26th but abandoned because of bad light. Wednesday led 3-1 on Nov 26th.
The only change to the Villa team was that Garraty replaced Bedingfield

One own goal

F.A. Cup

R1	Jan	28	Nottingham Forest	1-2	Johnson	32000		7		4	5		2	8	3			1		9				11			10	6	

Sheriff of London's Charity Shield

	Mar	11	Queen's Park	0-0		14000	2	7		4	5		6		3	8		1		9				11			10		

After extra time. Played at the Crystal Palace. Shield held jointly.

Players only: Back: Bowman, Crabtree, Garraty, Spencer, George, Evans. Front: Johnson, Athersmith, Devey, Wheldon, James Cowan, Smith

Aston Villa 1899/1900

Villa Park

						Aston CL	Athersmith WC	Bowman T	Cowan, James	Crabtree JW	Devey JHG	Evans AJ	Garfield JH	Garraty W	George W	Haggart W	Johnson G	Mann CJ	McEleny CR	Noon MT	Smith S	Spencer H	Templeton RB	Watkins AE	Wheldon GF	Wilkes A
	Sep	2	Sunderland	1-0	Garraty	18000		7	4	5	6	8	3		9	1						11	2			10	
		4	GLOSSOP	9-0	Garraty 4, Wheldon 2, Athersmith, Devey, Smith	15000		7	4	5	6	8	3		9	1						11	2			10	
		9	WEST BROMWICH ALB.	0-2		25000	3	7	4	5	6	8			9	1						11	2			10	
2		16	Everton	2-1	Wheldon, Garraty	30000		7	4	5	6	8	3		9	1						11	2			10	
2		23	BLACKBURN ROVERS	3-1	Devey 2, Wheldon	15000		7	4	5	6	8	3		9	1						11	2			10	
3		30	Derby County	0-2		9000		7	4	5	6		3		8	1		9				11	2			10	
3	Oct	7	BURY	2-1	Johnson, Wheldon	18000		7	4	5					8	1	3	9				11	2			10	6
3		14	Notts County	4-1	Johnson 3, Devey	10000		7	4			8	3			1		9				11	2			10	6
2		21	MANCHESTER CITY	2-1	Devey, Wheldon (p)	25000			4	5		8	3		9	1						11	2	7		10	6
2		28	Sheffield United	1-2	Smith	30000		7	4	5	6	8	3		9	1						11	2			10	
2	Nov	4	NEWCASTLE UNITED	2-1	Devey, Wheldon	12000			4	5	6	8	3		9	1						11	2	7		10	
3		11	WOLVERHAMPTON W.	0-0		12000	2		4			8	3		9	1			5			11		7		10	6
2		13	Stoke	2-0	Garfield, Devey	15000			4			8	3	7	9	1			5			11	2			10	6
2		18	Liverpool	3-3	Devey, Wilkes, Storer (og)	15000			4			8	3		9	1			5			11	2	7		10	6
2		25	BURNLEY	2-0	Templeton, Wheldon	20000			4			8	3		9	1			5		2	11		7		10	6
2	Dec	2	Preston North End	5-0	Smith 3, Garraty, Dunn (og)	6000						8	3		9	1			5	4	2	11		7		10	6
2		9	NOTTM. FOREST	2-2	Garraty, Devey	15000			4			8	3		9	1			5		2	11		7		10	6
2		16	Glossop	0-1		6000		7	4			8			9	1			5		3	11	2			10	6
2		23	STOKE	4-1	Wheldon 2, Smith, Garraty	5000		7		5	3				8	1		9			4	11	2			10	6
2		30	SUNDERLAND	4-2	Garraty 3, Johnson	60000		7		5	3				8	1		9			4	11	2			10	6
2	Jan	1	Bury	0-2		14266		7		5	3				8	1		9			4	11	2			10	6
2		6	West Bromwich Albion	2-0	Garraty 2	5000		7		5	3				8	1		9			4	11	2			10	6
2		13	EVERTON	1-1	Athersmith	12000		7		5	3				8	1		9			4	11	2			10	6
2		20	Blackburn Rovers	4-0	Garraty 2, Athersmith, Smith	8000		7		5	8		3		9	1					4	11	2			10	6
2	Feb	3	DERBY COUNTY	3-2	Garraty 2, Wheldon	7000		7	4	5	6	8	3		9	1						11	2			10	
1		17	NOTTS COUNTY	6-2	Garraty 3, Devey, Athersmith, Cowan	16000		7	4	5	6	8	3		9	1						11	2			10	
1	Mar	3	SHEFFIELD UNITED	1-1	Garraty	50000		7	4	5		8	3		9	1					6	11	2			10	
1		10	Newcastle United	2-3	Devey, Garraty	25000		7	4	5		8	3		9	1					6	11	2			10	
1		19	Manchester City	2-0	Garraty 2	15000		7	4	5		8	3		9	1						11	2			10	6
1		24	LIVERPOOL	1-0	Devey	12000		7	4	5	6	8	3		9	1						11	2			10	
1		31	Burnley	2-1	Devey, Woolfall (og)	7000	3		4			9	2		7	1					5			11	8	10	6
1	Apr	7	PRESTON NORTH END	3-1	Garraty 2, Templeton	18000			4	5		10	3		8	1					2	7		11		9	6
1		14	Nottingham Forest	1-1	Templeton	10000		7	4	5		8	3		10	1							2	11		9	6
1		16	Wolverhampton Wan.	1-0	Templeton	18000		7	4				3		9	1		8			6		2	11		10	5

Apps	3	24	27	25	17	25	26	1	33	34	1	9	7	1	15	31	28	11	1	34	21
Goals		4		1		13		1	27			5				7		4		11	1

Three own goals

F.A. Cup

R1	Jan	27	Manchester City	1-1	Devey	30000		7		5		8	3		9	1					4	11	2			10	6
rep		31	MANCHESTER CITY	3-0	Garraty 2, Wheldon	20000		7	4	5	6	8	3		9	1						11	2			10	
R2	Feb	10	Bristol City	5-1	Devey 4, Garraty	12000		7	4	5	6	8	3		9	1						11	2			10	
R3		24	Millwall Athletic	1-1	Wheldon	25000		7	4	5	6	8	3		9	1						11	2			10	
rep		28	MILLWALL ATHLETIC	0-0		15000		7	4	5	6	8	3		9	1						11	2			10	
rep2	Mar	5	Millwall Athletic	1-2	Johnson	15000		7	4			8	3		9	1		10			6		2	11			5

R3 replay a.e.t. R3 replay 2 at Elm Park, Reading

Sheriff of London's Charity Shield

| Nov | 8 | Corinthians | 1-2 | Garraty | 8000 | | 7 | 4 | | | 8 | 3 | | 9 | 1 | | | 6 | | | 11 | 2 | | | 10 | 5 |

At the Crystal Palace

Players only. Back: Moon, Bowman, Crabtree, George, Spencer, Evans. Front: Wilkes, James Cowan, Wheldon, Devey, Athersmith, Garraty, Smith, Templeton

Liverpool 1900/01

Anfield

							Cox J	Davies JO	Dunlop WTP	Glover JW	Goldie WG	Howell R	Hunter JB	Hunter TJ	McGuigan A	Parry MP	Perkins WH	Raisbeck AG	Raybould SF	Robertson JT	Robertson T	Satterthwaite CO	Walker J	Wilson C
	Sep	1	BLACKBURN ROVERS	3-0	T Robertson, Satterthwaite, Raybould	20000	7		3		6						1	5	9	2	11	10	8	4
		8	Stoke	2-1	T Robertson, Raybould	15000	7		3		6						1	5	9	2	11	10	8	4
		15	WEST BROMWICH ALB.	5-0	Raybould 2, Goldie, Walker, T Robertson	15000	7		3		6						1	5	9	2	11	10	8	4
2		22	Everton	1-1	Raybould	50000	7		3		6						1	5	9	2	11	10	8	4
4		29	SUNDERLAND	1-2	Wilson	15000	7		3		6						1	5	9	2	11	10	8	4
4	Oct	6	Derby County	3-2	T Robertson 2, Walker	8000	7		3		6				9		1	5		2	11	10	8	4
2		13	BOLTON WANDERERS	2-1	Cox, Satterthwaite	10000	7		3		6				9	5	1			2	11	10	8	4
5		20	Notts County	0-3		18000	7			3	6						1	5	9	2	11	10	8	4
4		27	PRESTON NORTH END	3-2	Cox, Raybould, McGuigan	8000	7			3	6						1	5	9	2	11	10	8	4
4	Nov	3	Wolverhampton Wan.	1-2	Walker	6000	7		3		6				10		1	5	9	2	11		8	4
3		10	ASTON VILLA	5-1	Raybould 2, Walker 2, McGuigan	18000			3		6				10		1	5	9	2	11	7	8	4
5		17	Sheffield Wednesday	2-3	Raybould, Raisbeck	10000	7		3		6						1	5	9	2	11	10	8	4
5		24	Newcastle United	1-1	Cox	12000	7		3		6						1	5	9	2	11	10	8	4
6	Dec	1	SHEFFIELD UNITED	1-2	Satterthwaite	15000	7		3		6						1	5	9	2	11	10	8	4
6		8	Manchester City	4-3	Raybould, Cox, T Robertson, McGuigan	15000	7		3		6				10		1	5	9	2	11		8	4
4		15	BURY	1-0	Cox	15000	7		3		6				10		1	5	9	2	11		8	4
5		22	Nottingham Forest	0-0		10000	7		3		6	8			10		1	5	9	2	11			4
2		25	DERBY COUNTY	0-0		18000	7		3		6	8			10		1	5	9	2	11			4
7		29	Blackburn Rovers	1-3	Raybould	6000	7		3		6	4			10		1	5	9	2	11	8		
6	Jan	1	STOKE	3-1	T Robertson, Cox, McGuigan	15000	7		3		6	4			10		1	5	9	2	11	8		
8		19	EVERTON	1-2	Cox	20000	7		3		6				10		1	5	9	2	11		8	4
8	Feb	16	Bolton Wanderers	0-1		9461	7		3		6				10		1	5	9	2	11	8		4
7		23	Sunderland	1-0	Cox	10000	7		3	2	6						1	5	9		11	10	8	4
7	Mar	2	Preston North End	2-2	Satterthwaite, Raybould	5000	7		3	2	6						1	5	9		11	10	8	4
6		9	WOLVERHAMPTON W.	1-0	Raybould	15000		7	3	2	6						1	5	9		11	10	8	4
6		16	Aston Villa	2-0	McGuigan, J Hunter	15000	7		3	2	6		9		10		1	5			11		8	4
4		23	SHEFFIELD WEDNESDAY	1-1	Raybould	15000	7		3	2	6		10				1	5	9		11		8	4
3		30	NEWCASTLE UNITED	3-0	J Hunter 2, Raybould	10000	7		3	2	6		10	5		4	1		9		11		8	
4	Apr	8	NOTTS COUNTY	1-0	Raybould	20000	7		3	2	6		10			4	1	5	9		11		8	
3		13	MANCHESTER CITY	3-1	T Robertson 2, Cox	10000	7		3	2	6		10			4	1	5	9		11		8	
4		20	Bury	0-0		6000	7		3	2	6		10			4	1	5	9		11		8	
2		22	Sheffield United	2-0	Raybould, Satterthwaite	7000	7		3		6			5		4	1		9	2	11	10	8	
2		27	NOTTM. FOREST	2-0	Cox, Goldie	16000	7		3		6					4	1	5	9	2	11	10	8	
1		29	West Bromwich Albion	1-0	Walker	8974	7		3		6					4	1	5	9	2	11	10	8	

	Apps	32	1	32	11	34	2	8	2	13	8	34	31	31	25	34	22	29	25
	Goals	10				2		3		5			1	16		9	5	7	1

F.A. Cup

IR	Jan	5	West Ham United	1-0	Raybould	6000	7		3		6	8			10		1	5	9	2	11			4
R1	Feb	9	Notts County	0-2		15000	7		3		6				10		1	5	9	2	11		8	4

Back: Ottey, Glover, McGuigan, Foster, S Hunter, J Hunter, Howell. Centre: Soulsby, Wilson, Raybould, Robertson, Perkins, Goldie, Parry, ano. Front: Walker, Dunlop, Raisbeck, Cox, Robertson

Sunderland 1901/02

Roker Park

							Common A	Craggs J	Doig JE	Farquhar JW	Ferguson M	Gemmell J	Gibson WK	Hewitt J	Hogg R	Hogg W	Jackson RW	McAllister A	McCombie A	McLatchie CC	Mearns FC	Millar J	Murray WB	Prior G	Watson J
	Sep	2	SHEFFIELD UNITED	3-1	Common 2, R Hogg	10000	7	1			4	9			8		6	5	2	11		10			3
		7	MANCHESTER CITY	1-0	W Hogg	13000	7	1			4				8	9	6	5	2	11		10			3
		14	Wolverhampton Wan.	2-4	Millar, R Hogg	7000	8	1	1	4					10	7	6	5	2	11		9			3
5		21	LIVERPOOL	1-1	Jackson	15000	7		1	4		9			8		6	5	2	11		10			3
2		28	Newcastle United	1-0	Gemmell	30000		1			4	10			8	7	6	5	2	11		9			3
2	Oct	5	ASTON VILLA	1-0	R Hogg	8000					4	10			8	7	6	5	2	11	1	9			3
1		12	Sheffield United	1-0	Gemmell	12000		1			4	10			8	7	6	5	2	11		9			3
1		19	NOTTM. FOREST	4-0	Millar 3, Jackson	14000		1			4	10			8	7	6	5	2	11		9			3
1		26	Bury	0-1		14000		1			4	10			8	7	6	5	2	11		9			3
1	Nov	2	BLACKBURN ROVERS	3-2	W Hogg, McCombie, Millar	10000		1			4	10			8	7	6	5	2	11		9			3
1		9	Stoke	0-3		10000		1			4	10			8	7	6	5	2	11				9	3
2		16	EVERTON	2-4	Gemmell, McLatchie	15000	7	1			4	10			8		6	5	2	11		9			3
2		23	Grimsby Town	3-3	Gemmell 2, W Hogg	5000		1			4	10			8	7	6	5	2	11				9	3
2		30	Small Heath	3-2	W Hogg, McLatchie, Millar	18000		1			4	10			8	7	6	5	2	11		9			3
2	Dec	14	Sheffield Wednesday	1-1	R Hogg	3000		1			4	10			8	7	6	5	2	11		9			3
2		21	NOTTS COUNTY	2-1	Gemmell, W Hogg	5000		1			4	10			8	7	6	5	2	11		9			3
2		26	Liverpool	1-0	McLatchie	20000		1	6	4	10				8	7		5	2	11		9			3
3		28	Bolton Wanderers	0-0		5848		1			4	10			8	7	6	5	2	11		9			3
1	Jan	1	DERBY COUNTY	1-0	Jackson	20000		1			4	10			8	7	6	5	2	11		9			3
1		4	Manchester City	3-0	W Hogg 2, Gemmell	6000		1				10				7	6	5	2	11		9		8	3
1		11	WOLVERHAMPTON W.	2-0	W Hogg 2	10000		1	1	4		10				7	6	5	2	11		9		8	3
1	Feb	1	Aston Villa	1-0	McLatchie	25000		1	6	4	10				8	7	3	5	2	11		9			
1		15	Nottingham Forest	1-2	R Hogg	10000		1	6	4	10				8	7		5	2	11		9			3
1	Mar	1	Blackburn Rovers	1-0	Gemmell	25000		1			4	10		8			7	6	5	2	11		9			3
1		8	STOKE	2-0	Craggs, Gemmell	10000	7	1			4	10			8		6	5	2	11		9			3
1		15	Everton	0-2		25000	11	1			4	10			8	7	6	5	2			9			3
1		22	GRIMSBY TOWN	3-1	Craggs, McAllister, Murray	8000	7	1		4	2	10			8			6	5				9	11		3
1		29	SMALL HEATH	1-1	Hewitt	8000		1	6	4	10			8			7	2	5				9	11		3
1		31	NEWCASTLE UNITED	0-0		35000	11	1	6	4			10	8	7			2	5			9			3
1	Apr	5	Derby County	0-1		2000	7		6	4	10				8			2	5		1	9	11		3
1		12	SHEFFIELD WEDNESDAY	1-2	Murray	8000		1	6	4	10				8	7		2	5			9	11		3
1		16	BURY	3-0	Millar 3	10000		1		4	10	2		8	7	6		2	5			9	11		3
1		19	Notts County	0-2		10000		1	4		10		6			7		2	5			9	11	8	3
1		26	BOLTON WANDERERS	2-1	Gemmell, W Hogg	6000		1	4		10		6	8	7			2	5			9	11		3

Apps	4	6	32	13	29	31	1	5	29	28	32	34	26	25	2	32	7	5	33
Goals	2	2				10		1	5	10	3	1	1	4		9	2		

F.A. Cup

R1	Jan	25	Sheffield Wednesday	1-0	Millar	30096		1			4	10			8	7	6	5	2	11		9			3
R2	Feb	12	Newcastle United	0-1		19700		1			4	10			8	7	6	5	2	11		9			3

Players only. Back: McCombie, Doig, Watson, Prior. Centre: Craggs, Ferguson, McAllister, Jackson, Farquahar, Hewitt, Murray. Front: W Hogg, R Hogg, Millar, Gemmell, McLatchie

Sheffield Wednesday 1902/03

Hillsborough

							Barron GW	Beech GC	Chapman H	Crawshaw P	Crawshaw TH	Davis H	Ferrier R	Hounsfield RE	Langley A	Layton W	Lyall J	Malloch JM	Marrison T	Moralee MW	Ruddlesdin H	Ryalls J	Simpson G	Simpson VS	Spiksley F	Stewart J	Stubbs FL	Thackeray F	Wilson AMcC
	Sep	1	Sheffield United	3-2	Davis, Spiksley, Wilson	20113			8		5	7	4		3	2	1	10			6				11				9
		6	Bolton Wanderers	2-0	Davis, Wilson	15000			8		5	7	4		3	2	1	10			6				11				9
		13	MIDDLESBROUGH	2-0	Davis, Wilson	20000			8		5	7	4		3	2	1	10			6				11				9
2		20	Newcastle United	0-3		23000			8		5	7	4		3	2	1	10			6				11				9
4		27	WOLVERHAMPTON W.	1-1	Chapman (p)	15000			8		5	7	4		3	2	1	10			6				11				9
1	Oct	3	Notts County	3-0	Spiksley 3	6000			8		5		4	7	3	2	1	10			6				11				9
3		4	Liverpool	2-4	Chapman, Spiksley	16000			8		5		4	7	3	2	1	10			6				11				9
6		11	SHEFFIELD UNITED	0-1		20000			8			7	4		3	2	1	10		5	6				11				9
4		18	Grimsby Town	1-0	Chapman	6000	8	7		4	5				3	2	1	10			6				11				9
3	Nov	1	Nottingham Forest	4-1	Wilson 2, Chapman, Davis	10000			8		5	7	4		3	2	1	10			6				11				9
3		8	BURY	2-0	Chapman, Wilson	4000			8		5	7	4		3	2	1	10			6				11				9
4		15	Blackburn Rovers	1-2	Langley (p)	7000					5	7	4		3	2	1	10			6			8	11				9
4		22	SUNDERLAND	1-0	Chapman	12000			8		5	7	4		3	2	1	10			6				11				9
6		29	Stoke	0-4		10000			8		5	7	4		3	2	1	10			6				11				9
5	Dec	6	EVERTON	4-1	Wilson 3, Spiksley	12000			8		5	7	4		3		1	10			6				11			2	9
5		13	DERBY COUNTY	0-1		14000	10		8		5	7	4		3	2	1	11			6								9
4		20	West Bromwich Albion	3-2	Davis 2, Chapman	12000			8		5	7	4		3	2		10			6				11	1			9
6		26	Aston Villa	0-1		30000			8		5	7	4		3	2	1	10			6				11				9
5		27	NOTTS COUNTY	2-0	Chapman, Davis	25000			8		5	7	4		3	2	1	10			6				11				9
2	Jan	1	ASTON VILLA	4-0	Ruddlesdin 2, Malloch, Wilson	28000			8		5	7	4		3	2	1	10			6				11				9
2		3	BOLTON WANDERERS	3-0	Davis 3	13000			8		5	7	4		3	2	1	10			6				11				9
2		10	Middlesbrough	1-2	Davis	7000			8		5	7	4		3	2	1	10			6				11				9
2		17	NEWCASTLE UNITED	3-0	Chapman 2, Spiksley	10000			8		5	7	4		3	2	1	10			6				11				9
2		24	Wolverhampton Wan.	1-2	Davis	7000			8		5	7	4		3	2	1	10			6				11				9
2		31	LIVERPOOL	3-1	Chapman 2, Davis	12000			8		5	7	4		3	2	1	10			6				11				9
2	Feb	14	GRIMSBY TOWN	1-1	Langley (p)	8000	8	7			5		4		3		1				6				11	10		2	9
1		28	NOTTM. FOREST	1-0	Langley (p)	12000			8		5	7	4		3	2	1	10			6				11				9
1	Mar	14	BLACKBURN ROVERS	0-0		8000			8		5		4		3	2	1	10			6	7	11						9
1		21	Sunderland	1-0	Wilson	20000			8		5	7	4		3		1	10			6				11			2	9
1		28	STOKE	1-0	Marrison	7000					5	7	4		3		1	10	8		6				11			2	9
1	Apr	4	Everton	1-1	Langley (p)	14000			8		5		4		3		1	10			6			7	11			2	9
1		6	Bury	0-4		2200	7		8		5		4		3	2	1	10			6				11				9
1		11	Derby County	0-1		10000			8		5	7	4		3	2	1	10			6				11				9
1		18	WEST BROMWICH ALB.	3-1	Spiksley, Wilson, Langley (p)	16000			8		5		4		3	2	1	10			6			7	11				9
						Apps	1	3	32	1	33	26	33	2	34	29	33	33	1	1	34	1	1	3	32	1	1	5	34
						Goals			12			13			5			1	1		2				8				12

F.A. Cup

| R1 | Feb | 7 | Blackburn Rovers | 0-0 | | 12000 | | | 8 | | 5 | 7 | 4 | | 3 | 2 | 1 | 10 | | | 6 | | | | 11 | | | | 9 |
| rep | | 12 | BLACKBURN ROVERS | 0-1 | | 25410 | | | 8 | | 5 | 7 | 4 | | 3 | | 1 | 10 | | | 6 | | | | 11 | | | 2 | 9 |

Players only: Back: Ferrier, Hemingfield, Thackery. Centre: Layton, Langley, Lyall, Crawshaw, Ruddlesdin. Front: V Simpson, Davies, Chapman, Wilson, Mallock, Spiksley, G Simpson

52

Sheffield Wednesday 1903/04

Hillsborough

							Bartlett WJ	Beech GC	Burton HA	Chapman H	Crawshaw TH	Davis H	Eyre IJ	Ferrier R	Hemmingfield WE	Hoyland GA	Jarvis TR	Langley A	Layton W	Lyall J	Malloch JV	Moralee MW	Ruddlesdin H	Ryalls J	Simpson G	Simpson VS	Stewart J	Wilson AMcC
	Sep	2	West Bromwich Albion	1-0	Chapman	7000				8	5	7		4				3	2	1	10		6		11			9
		5	MIDDLESBROUGH	4-1	Chapman, Malloch, G Simpson, Wilson	20000				8	5	7		4				3	2	1	10		6		11			9
		12	Liverpool	3-1	Wilson 2, Davis	20000				8	5	7		4				3	2	1	10		6		11			9
2		19	BURY	1-1	Wilson	16000				8	5	7		4				3	2	1	10		6		11			9
2		26	Blackburn Rovers	0-0		10000				8	5	7		4				3	2	1	10		6		11			9
1	Oct	3	NOTTM. FOREST	2-1	Wilson, og (Henderson)	15000				8	5	7		4				3	2	1			6		11		10	9
3		10	Wolverhampton Wan.	1-2	Davis	12000			3	8		7		4					2	1		5	6		11		10	9
2		17	Sunderland	1-0	Wilson	15000				8	5	7		4				3	2	1			6		11		10	9
2		24	WEST BROMWICH ALB.	1-0	Chapman	12000			3	8	5	7		4					2	1	10		6		11			9
2		31	Small Heath	0-0		12000			3	8	5	7		4					2	1	10		6		11			9
1	Nov	7	EVERTON	1-0	Chapman	12000			3	8	5	7		4					2	1	10		6		11			9
2		14	Stoke	1-3	Wilson	10000			3	8	5	7		4					2	1	10		6		11			9
2		21	DERBY COUNTY	1-0	G Simpson	5000			3	8	5	7		4					2	1	10		6		11			9
2		28	Manchester City	1-1	Chapman	6000			3	8	5	7		4					2	1	10		6		11			9
3	Dec	12	Sheffield United	1-1	Wilson	30000			3	8	5	7		4					2	1	10		6		11			9
3		19	NEWCASTLE UNITED	1-1	Langley (p)	8000				8	5	7		4				3	2	1	11		6			10		9
4		26	Aston Villa	1-2		40000			3	8	5	7		4					2	1	11		6			10		9
3	Jan	1	WOLVERHAMPTON W.	4-0	V Simpson 2, Malloch, Chapman (p)	15000			3	8	5	7		4					2	1	11		6			10		9
2		2	Middlesbrough	1-0	Chapman (p)	15000			3	8	5	7		4					2	1	11		6				10	9
2		9	LIVERPOOL	2-1	Crawshaw, Stewart	14000			3	8	5	7		4					2	1	11		6				10	9
3		16	Bury	0-1		7000			3	8	5	7		4					2	1	11		6			10		9
2		23	BLACKBURN ROVERS	3-1	Chapman 2, Crawshaw	14000			3	8	5	7			4				2	1	11		6			10		9
1		30	Nottingham Forest	1-0	Wilson	15000			3	8	5	7		4					2	1	11		6			10		9
1	Feb	13	SUNDERLAND	0-0		8000		9	3	8	5	7		4					2	1	11		6			10		
1		22	NOTTS COUNTY	2-0	G Simpson 2	7000	6		3	8	5	7		4					2	1					11	10	9	
1		27	SMALL HEATH	3-2	Chapman, Davis, Hemmingfield	7000			3	8	5	7		4	9				2	1			6		11	10		
1	Mar	12	STOKE	1-0	Chapman	12000	6		3	8		7	9	4	5				2	1	10				11			
1		26	MANCHESTER CITY	1-0	Chapman	18000		10	3	8	5	7		4		9			2	1			6		11			
1	Apr	2	Notts County	0-1		13000		10	3	8	5	7		4			1		2				6		11			9
1		4	Everton	0-2		30000		10	3	8	5			4	7				2	1			6		11			9
		9	SHEFFIELD UNITED	3-0	Chapman 2, G Simpson	16000			3	8	5			4					2	1			6	7	11		10	9
2		16	Newcastle United	0-4		30000			3	8	5	7		4					2	1			6		11		10	9
1		23	ASTON VILLA	4-2	G Simpson 2, Chapman, Davis	14000	6		3	8	5	7		4					2	1	10				11			9
1		30	Derby County	2-0	Chapman, Davis	6000	6		3	8	5	7			4				2	1	10				11			9

	Apps	4	4	26	34	32	32	1	31	6	1	1	8	34	33	24	1	30	1	25	7	10	29
	Goals				16	2	5			1					1		2				7	2	1	10

One own goal

F.A. Cup

R1	Feb	6	Plymouth Argyle	2-2	Wilson 2	20103			3	8	5	7		4					2	1	11		6			10		9
rep		10	PLYMOUTH ARGYLE	2-0	Davis, Chapman (p)	18845			3	8	5	7		4					2	1	11		6			10		9
R2		20	MANCHESTER UNITED	6-0	Simpson 3, Davis 2, G Simpson	22051	9		3	8	5	7		4					2	1			6		11	10		
R3	Mar	5	Tottenham Hotspur	1-1	Davis	15500	9		3	8	5	7		4					2	1			6		11	10		
rep		9	TOTTENHAM HOTSPUR	2-0	Chapman, Davis	30011			3	8	5	7		4	9				2	1			6		11	10		
SF		19	Manchester City	0-3		53000			3	8	5	7		4					2	1	10		6		11			9

SF at Goodison Park

Back:- Hemmingfield, Stewart, Jarvis, Bartlett. Centre: Davis (assistant trainer), Ferrier, Langley, Lyall, Crawshaw, Layton, Burton, Ruddlesdin, Frith (trainer). Front: Davis, Chapman, Wilson, Malloch, Simpson

Newcastle United 1904/05

St James' Park

						Aitken A	Appleyard W	Carr J	Crumley RJ	Gardner A	Gosnell AA	Graham S	Howie J	Innerd W	Lawrence J	McClarence JP	McCombie A	McCracken WR	McIntyre EP	McWilliam P	Orr R	Rutherford J	Templeton RB	Veitch CCMcK	Watts C	Wills T
	Sep	3	WOOLWICH ARSENAL	3-0	Orr 2, Rutherford	18000	5	9	6		4		8					3	2				10	7	11		1	
		10	Derby County	1-1	Appleyard	10000	5	9	6		4		8					3	2				10	7	11		1	
		17	EVERTON	3-2	Veitch 2, Rutherford	20000	5		6		4		8					3	2	10				7	11	9	1	
7		24	Small Heath	1-2	Veitch	13000	5	9	6		4		8					3	2					7	11	10	1	
4	Oct	1	MANCHESTER CITY	2-0	Veitch, Appleyard	22000	5	9			4		8	1				2	3		6			7	11	10		
3		8	Notts County	3-0	Rutherford 2, Howie	12000	5	9			4		8	1				3	2		6			7	11	10		
3		15	SHEFFIELD UNITED	1-1	Howie	23000	5	9			4		8	1				3	2		6			7	11	10		
5		22	Stoke	0-1		12000	5	9			4		8	1				3	2				10	7	11	6		
7		29	Preston North End	0-1		10000	5			6	4		8	1				3	2				10	7	11	9		
7	Nov	5	MIDDLESBROUGH	3-0	Orr, Howie, Rutherford	25000	5		3		4	11	8	1				2					6	10	7			
5		12	Wolverhampton Wan.	3-1	Howie 3	7000	5	9	3		4	11	8	1				2					6	10	7			
3		19	BURY	3-1	Gosnell, Appleyard, Veitch	12000	5	9	3		4	11		1				2					6	10	7	8		
3		26	Aston Villa	1-0	Appleyard	12000	5	9	3		4	11		1				2					6	10	7	8		
1	Dec	3	BLACKBURN ROVERS	1-0	McClarence	14000		9	3		4	11	7	8			1	10	2				6			5		
1		10	Nottingham Forest	3-1	Gosnell, Appleyard, Veitch	5000		9	3		4	11	8	1				2					6	10	7	5		
1		17	SHEFFIELD WEDNESDAY	6-2	Rutherford 2, Orr, Appleyard, Howie, McWilliam	18000		9	3		4	11	8	1				2					6	10	7	5		
1		24	Sunderland	1-3	McWilliam	30000		9	3		4	11	8	1				2					6	10	7	5		
3		31	Woolwich Arsenal	2-0	Rutherford, Veitch	20000		9	3		4	11	8	1				2					6	10	7	5		
1	Jan	2	NOTTS COUNTY	1-0	Orr	20000	5	9			4	11	8	1				2	3				6	10	7			
1		7	DERBY COUNTY	2-0	Veitch, Gardner	25000	5	9	3		4	11	8	1				2					6		7	10		
1		14	Everton	1-2	Howie	30000	5	9	3		4	11	10	8	1			2					6		7			
1		21	SMALL HEATH	0-1		24000	5	9	3		4	11	8	1				2					6	10	7			
4		28	Manchester City	2-3	Howie 2	30000	5	9	3		4	11	8	1				2					6	10	7			
3	Feb	11	Sheffield United	3-1	Gosnell, McClarence, og	18000	5		3		4	11	8		1	9	2					6	10		7			
2		25	PRESTON NORTH END	1-0	Appleyard	20000	5	9			4	11	8	1				2					6	10	7			3
3	Mar	11	WOLVERHAMPTON W.	3-0	Appleyard, Rutherford, McWilliam	20000	5	9	3		4	11	8	1			10	2					6		7			
2		18	Bury	4-2	Appleyard 3, Aitken	15000	5	9	3		4	11	8	1				2					6		7	10		
3	Apr	1	Blackburn Rovers	0-2		8000		9	3		5	11	8		4	1	10			2	6			7				
2		5	ASTON VILLA	2-0	Veitch, Appleyard	25000	5	9	3		4	11	8	1				2					6		7	10		
2		8	NOTTM. FOREST	5-1	Howie 2, Gosnell, McClarence, Aitken	20000	5		3		4	11	8	1		9		2					6		7	10		
2		21	STOKE	4-1	Orr 2, McClarence, Howie	24000	5		3		4	11	8	1		9		2						10	7	6		
2		22	SUNDERLAND	1-3	Veitch	30000	5	9	3		4	11	8	1				2					6		7	10		
2		26	Sheffield Wednesday	3-1	Howie, McWilliam, Orr (p)	12000	5	9		1		11	8					2					4	10	7	6		3
1		29	Middlesbrough	3-0	Orr, Appleyard, Rutherford	12000	5	9	3			11	8		1						2	4		10	7	6		

Apps	28	28	27	1	32	25	3	31	1	29	6	31	13	2	26	20	31	10	24	4	2
Goals	2	13			1	4		14			4					4	9	10		10		

One own goal

F.A. Cup

R1	Feb	4	PLYMOUTH ARGYLE	1-1	Gosnell	28385	5	9	3		4	11	7	8			1		2				6	10				
rep		8	Plymouth Argyle	1-1	Gosnell	20000	5		3		4	11	8		1	9	2					6	10					
rep2		13	Plymouth Argyle	2-0	Orr 2 (1p)	11570	5		3		4	11	8		1	9	2					6	10	7				
R2		18	Tottenham Hotspur	1-1	Howie	19013	5		3		4	11	8	1				2					6	10	7	9		
rep		22	TOTTENHAM HOTSPUR	4-0	Orr 2, Appleyard, Howie	26735	5	9	3		4	11	8	1				2					6	10	7			
R3	Mar	4	Bolton Wanderers	2-0	Appleyard, Howie	35574	5	9	3		4	11	8	1				2					6	10	7			
SF		25	Sheffield Wednesday	1-0	Howie	40000	5	9	3		4	11	8	1				2					6		7	10		
F	Apr	15	Aston Villa	0-2		101117	5	9	3		4	11	8	1				2					6		7	10		

R1 replay 2 at the Manor Ground, Plumstead
SF at Hyde Road, Manchester
Final at the Crystal Palace

G Thompson played at 7 in R1 replay

Back: McCombie, Milne, JW Bell and Archibald (directors), Lawrence. Next to back: R and JP Oliver (directors), Carr, McCracken, Cameron (chairman), J Bell (vice-chairman), McWilliam, McClarence. Graham (director), F Watt jnr (assistant secretary). Seated: F Watt (secretary), Aitken, Rutherford, Howie, Appleyard, Orr, Gosnell, McPherson (trainer). Front: Veitch, Gardner

Liverpool 1905/06

Anfield

						Bradley JE	Carlin J	Chorlton T	Cox J	Doig JE	Dunlop WTP	Fleming G	Garside JA	Goddard AM	Gorman J	Griffiths H	Hardy S	Hewitt J	Latham G	Murray DB	Parkinson J	Parry MP	Raisbeck AG	Raybould SF	Robinson RS	West A
	Sep	2 Woolwich Arsenal	1-3	Robinson	25000				11	1	3	6		7								10	4	5	9	8	2
		9 BLACKBURN ROVERS	1-3	Cox	20000				11	1		6		7						9			3	4	5	10	8	2
		11 Aston Villa	0-5		15000				11	1		6		7						9			3	4	5	10	8	2
18		16 Sunderland	2-1	Raybould 2	20000				11	1				7						9	6			4	5	10	8	2
14		23 BIRMINGHAM	2-0	Robinson, Hewitt	24000	6			11	1	3			7						9				4	5	10	8	2
16		30 Everton	2-4	Hewitt, Goddard	45000	6			11	1				7						9			3	4	5	10	8	2
13	Oct	7 DERBY COUNTY	4-1	Cox 2, Robinson, Goddard	22000	6			11	1	3			7						9				4	5	10	8	2
16		14 Sheffield Wednesday	2-3	Robinson, Hewitt	12000	6	10				1	3			11	7		2		9				4	5		8	
14		21 NOTTM. FOREST	4-1	Hewitt, Cox, Raybould, Robinson	20000				11		3			7						9		1		4	5	10	8	2
10		28 Manchester City	1-0	Hewitt	25000	6	10		11		3			7						9		1		4	5		8	2
9	Nov	4 BURY	3-1	Robinson 2, Carlin	12000	6	10		11		3			7						9		1		4	5		8	2
8		11 Middlesbrough	5-1	Hewitt 3, Carlin 2	8000	6	10		11		3			7						9		1		4	5		8	2
7		18 PRESTON NORTH END	1-1	Hewitt	15000	6	10		11		3			7						9		1		4	5		8	2
6		25 Newcastle United	3-2	West 2 (2p), Raybould	20000	6					3			7						9	5	1		4		10	8	2
3	Dec	2 ASTON VILLA	3-0	Cox, Hewitt, Spence (og)	28000	6			11		3			7						9		1		4	5	10	8	2
2		9 WOLVERHAMPTON W.	4-0	Hewitt 2, Raybould, Goddard	10000				11		3	6		7						9		1		4	5	10	8	2
1		16 Sheffield United	2-1	Parry, Robinson	16000	6			11		3			7						9		1		4	5	10	8	2
1		23 NOTTS COUNTY	2-0	Robinson, Hewitt	15000	6			11		3			7						9		1		4	5	10	8	2
1		25 BOLTON WANDERERS	2-2	Hewitt, Goddard	22000	6			11		3			7						9		1		4	5	10	8	2
1		26 Stoke	1-2	Hewitt	12000	6			11		3			7						9		1		4	5	10	8	2
1		30 WOOLWICH ARSENAL	3-0	Raisbeck, Goddard, Raybould	12000	6			11		3			7						9		1		4	5	10	8	2
1	Jan	1 STOKE	3-1	Raybould 2, Hewitt	25000	6			11		3			7						9		1		4	5	10	8	2
1		6 Blackburn Rovers	0-0		12000	6	10		11		3			7						9		1		4	5		8	2
1		20 SUNDERLAND	2-0	Hewitt, Carlin	18000	6	10				3			7			11			9		1		4	5		8	2
1		27 Birmingham	0-1		8000	6	10				3			7			11			9		1		4	5		8	2
1	Feb	10 Derby County	3-0	Hewitt, Raybould, Robinson	3000	6			11		3			7						9		1		4	5	10	8	2
1		17 SHEFFIELD WEDNESDAY	2-1	Cox 2	20000				11		3			7						9	6	1		4	5	10	8	2
1	Mar	3 MANCHESTER CITY	0-1		30000	6			11		3			7						9		1		4	5	10	8	2
1		14 Nottingham Forest	2-1	Hewitt 2	6000	6			11		3			7						9	4	1			5	10	8	2
1		17 MIDDLESBROUGH	6-1	Carlin 2, Parkinson, Hewitt, Cox, Goddard	25000	6	8		11		3			7						10		1	9	4	5			2
1		21 Notts County	0-3		6000	6	8				3			7						10		1	11	4	5	9		2
1		24 Preston North End	2-1	Chorlton, Hewitt	15000		4	6	11		3			7						9		1	10		5		8	2
1	Apr	2 Bury	0-0		7000	6					3		11	7						9		1		4	5	10	8	2
1		9 NEWCASTLE UNITED	3-0	Parkinson 2, Raybould	15000	6	8	3						7						9		1	11	4	5	10		2
1		13 EVERTON	1-1	West (p)	30000	6	8	3						7						9		1	11	4	5	10		2
1		14 Wolverhampton Wan.	2-0	Hewitt, Goddard	8000	6	10	3						7						9		1	11	4	5		8	2
1		16 Bolton Wanderers	2-3	Parkinson 2	23000	6					3			7						9		1	11	4			8	2
1		21 SHEFFIELD UNITED	3-1	Parkinson 2, Robinson	6000	6			3					7	10					9	5	1	11	4			8	2

| | Apps | 31 | 14 | 6 | 28 | 8 | 31 | 4 | 4 | 38 | 1 | 1 | 30 | 37 | 5 | 3 | 9 | 36 | 36 | 25 | 34 | 37 |
| | Goals | | 6 | 1 | 8 | | | | | 7 | | | | 23 | | | 7 | 1 | 1 | 10 | 11 | 3 |

One own goal

F.A. Cup

R1	Jan	13 LEICESTER FOSSE	2-1	Raybould, Goddard	12000	6	10		11		3			7						9		1		4	5	8		2
R2	Feb	3 BARNSLEY	1-0	West	10000	6			11		3			7						9		1		4	5	10	8	2
R3		24 BRENTFORD	2-0	Hewitt, Goddard	20000	6			11		3			7						9	5	1		4		10	8	2
R4	Mar	10 SOUTHAMPTON	3-0	Raybould 3	20000	6			11		3			7						9		1		4	5	10	8	2
SF		31 Everton	0-2		37000	6	10				3			7						9		1	11	4	5		8	2

SF at Villa Park

Sheriff of London's Charity Shield

| Apr | 28 Corinthians | 5-1 | Hewitt 2, Raybould, Goddard, og (Hunt) | 25000 | 6 | | | 11 | | 3 | | | 7 | | | | | | 9 | | | 8 | 4 | 5 | 10 | | 2 |

At Craven Cottage

Back: Carlin, West, Wilson, Hardy, Doig, Dunlop, Murray, Hewitt. Seated, at back: Connell (trainer), James Hughes, Latham, John Hughes, Parry, Raisbeck, Fleming, Chorlton, Watson (secretary/manager). Seated in front centre: R Robinson, Parkinson, Raybould. On ground: G Robinson, Gorman, Goddard, Cox, Garside

Newcastle United 1906/07

St James' Park

	Sep	1	SUNDERLAND	4-2	Rutherford 2, Appleyard, Howie	55000
		3	Sheffield Wednesday	2-2	Appleyard 2	8000
		8	Birmingham	4-2	Brown 3, Veitch (p)	20000
2		15	EVERTON	1-0	McWilliam	40000
5		22	Woolwich Arsenal	0-2		27000
3		29	SHEFFIELD WEDNESDAY	5-1	Speedie 2, Appleyard, Gosnell, Kirkcaldy	30000
6	Oct	6	Bury	2-3	Appleyard, Veitch (p)	15000
6		13	MANCHESTER CITY	2-0	Appleyard 2	20000
4		20	Middlesbrough	3-0	Appleyard 3	18000
2		27	PRESTON NORTH END	2-1	Brown, Howie	30000
2	Nov	3	Derby County	0-0		9000
2		10	Aston Villa	0-0		30000
2		17	LIVERPOOL	2-0	Gardner, Speedie	35000
4		24	Bristol City	1-2	Brown	20000
3	Dec	1	NOTTS COUNTY	4-3	Appleyard 2, Speedie, Veitch	28000
3		8	Sheffield United	0-0		12000
2		15	BOLTON WANDERERS	4-0	Speedie 2, McClarence, Orr	25000
2		22	Manchester United	3-1	Speedie, McClarence, Veitch (p)	4000
2		25	Blackburn Rovers	0-4		30000
2		26	Stoke	2-1	Howie, Speedie	7000
2	Jan	1	DERBY COUNTY	2-0	Orr, Speedie	25000
2		5	BIRMINGHAM	2-0	Rutherford 2	28000
2		19	Everton	0-3		30000
2		26	WOOLWICH ARSENAL	1-0	Howie	36000
1	Feb	2	MANCHESTER UNITED	5-0	Veitch 2, Gosnell, Orr, Rutherford	35000
1		9	BURY	3-2	Brown, Howie, Rutherford	25000
1		16	Manchester City	1-1	Brown	40000
1		23	MIDDLESBROUGH	4-0	Appleyard 2, McWilliam, McCracken (p)	50000
1	Mar	2	Preston North End	2-2	Gosnell, Howie	10000
1		16	ASTON VILLA	3-2	Appleyard 2, Rutherford	50000
1		20	Sunderland	0-2		30000
1		23	Liverpool	1-4	Brown	20000
1		29	STOKE	1-0	Rutherford	35000
1		30	BRISTOL CITY	3-0	Rutherford 2, Howie	35000
1	Apr	1	BLACKBURN ROVERS	3-1	Duffy, Appleyard, Speedie (p)	30000
1		6	Notts County	0-1		12000
1		13	SHEFFIELD UNITED	0-0		26000
1		20	Bolton Wanderers	2-4	Orr, Veitch	4000

F.A. Cup

R1	Jan	12	CRYSTAL PALACE	0-1		28000

Sheriff of London's Charity Shield

	Mar	9	Corinthians	5-2	Brown 2, Appleyard, Rutherford, Timmis(og)	34000

At Craven Cottage

Back: Howie, McCracken, Speedie, McWilliam, McClarence, Orr. Next to back: Rutherford, Veitch, Carr, Gosnell. Seated: Appleyard, Gardner. Front: Duffy, Lawrence, Sinclair, Brown. The Sheriff of London's Shield takes centre stage!

Manchester United 1907/08

Bank Street

	Date	Opponent	Score	Scorers	Att	Bannister J	Bell A	Berry WA	Broomfield HC	Burgess H	Dalton E	Downie ALB	Duckworth R	Halse HJ	Holden RH	Hulme A	McGillivray J	Menzies AW	Meredith WH	Moger HH	Picken JB	Roberts C	Stacey GW	Thomson E	Turnbull A	Turnbull J McL	Wall G	Whiteside KD	Williams H	Wilson TC
	Sep 2	Aston Villa	4-1	Meredith 2, Bannister, Wall	20000	8	6			3			4		2				9	7	1		5			10		11			
	7	LIVERPOOL	4-0	A Turnbull 3, Wall	8000	8	6			3			4		2				9	7	1		5			10		11			
	9	MIDDLESBROUGH	2-1	A Turnbull 2	15000	8	6			3			4		2				9	7	1		5			10		11			
1	14	Middlesbrough	1-2	Bannister	18000	8				3			4		2				9	7	1		5		6	10		11			
1	21	SHEFFIELD UNITED	2-1	A Turnbull 2	22000	8	6			3			4		2				9	7	1		5			10		11			
	28	Chelsea	4-1	Meredith 2, Bannister, A Turnbull	14000	8	6			3			4		2					7	1		5			10	9	11			
1	Oct 5	NOTTM. FOREST	4-0	Bannister, J Turnbull, Wall, og (Maltby)	25000	8	6			3			4		2					7	1		5			10	9	11			
1	12	Newcastle United	6-1	Wall 2, Meredith, Roberts, A Turnbull, J Turnbull	25000	8	6						4		2					7	1		5	3		10	9	11			
	19	Blackburn Rovers	5-1	A Turnbull 3, J Turnbull 2	35000	8	6			3			4		2					7	1		5			10	9	11			
	26	BOLTON WANDERERS	2-1	A Turnbull, J Turnbull	40000	8	6			3			4		2					7	1		5			10	9	11			
1	Nov 2	Birmingham	4-3	Meredith 2, J Turnbull, Wall	20000	8	6			3			4		2					7	1	10	5			9		11			
1	9	EVERTON	4-3	Wall 2, Meredith, Roberts	30000	8	6			3			4		2					7	1		5			10	9	11			
	16	Sunderland	2-1	A Turnbull 2	30000	8	6			3			4		2					7	1		5			10	9	11			
	23	WOOLWICH ARSENAL	4-2	A Turnbull 4	8000	8	6			3			4		2					7	1		5			10	9		11		
	30	Sheffield Wednesday	0-2		30000	8	6			3			4		2					7	1		5			10	9	11			
1	Dec 7	BRISTOL CITY	2-1	Wall 2	10000	8	6						4		2					7	1		5	3		10	9	11			
1	14	Notts County	1-1	Meredith	7000	8	6						4		2					7	1		5			10	9	11			
1	21	MANCHESTER CITY	3-1	A Turnbull 2, Wall	35000	8	6			3			4		2					7	1		5			10	9	11			
	25	BURY	2-1	Meredith, J Turnbull	44000	8	6						4		2					7	1		5	3		10	9	11			
1	28	Preston North End	0-0		12000	8	6						4		2					7	1		5	3		10	9	11			
1	Jan 1	Bury	1-0	Wall	31000	8	6						4		2					7	1		5	3		10	9	11			
	18	Sheffield United	0-2		15000	8	6			3					2		5			7	1	10					9	11	4		
1	25	CHELSEA	1-0	J Turnbull	18000		6			3	4				2			10	7	1		8	5			9	11			
1	Feb 8	NEWCASTLE UNITED	1-1	J Turnbull	45000	8	6			3	5	4			2					7	1					10	9	11			
	15	BLACKBURN ROVERS	1-2	A Turnbull	9000	8	6			3			4		2					7	1		5			10	9				11
	29	BIRMINGHAM	1-0	A Turnbull	10000	8	6						4		2					7	1		5	3		10	9	11			
1	Mar 14	SUNDERLAND	3-0	Bell, Berry, Wall	10000	8	6	9		3			4							7	1		5	2		10		11			
1	21	Woolwich Arsenal	0-1		17000	8	6	9	1	3			4							7		10	5	2				11			
	25	Liverpool	4-7	Wall 2, Bannister, J Turnbull	12000	8					3	6	4							7	1	10	5	2			9	11			
1	28	SHEFFIELD WEDNESDAY	4-1	Wall 2, Halse, A Turnbull	20000	8	6		1	3		5	4	9						7				2		10		11			
1	Apr 4	Bristol City	1-1	Wall	12000	8	6		1	3			4	9						7			5	2		10		11			
	8	Everton	3-1	Halse, Wall, A Turnbull	20000	8			1	3		6	4	9						7			5	2		10		11			
1	11	NOTTS COUNTY	0-1		14000	8	6	7	1	3		5	4											2		10	9	11			
1	17	Nottingham Forest	0-2		20000		6		1	3			4	8						7			5	2		10	9	11			
1	18	Manchester City	0-0		40000	8	6		1				4	2						7			5	3		10	9	11			
1	20	ASTON VILLA	1-2	Picken	10000	8	6		1				4	2						7		9	5	3			10	11			
1	22	Bolton Wanderers	2-2	Halse, Stacey	18000	8	6		1				4	2	9					7		10		3	5			11			
1	25	PRESTON NORTH END	2-1	Halse, og (Rodway)	8000	8	6						4		9	3				7	1	10		2	5			11			

	Apps	36	35	3	9	27	1	10	35	6	26	1	1	6	37	29	8	32	18	3	30	26	36	1	1	1
	Goals	5	1	1					4						10		1	2	1		25	10	19			

Two own goals

F.A. Cup

	Date	Opponent	Score	Scorers	Att																									
R1	Jan 11	BLACKPOOL	3-1	Wall 2, Bannister	11747	8	6						4		2		5			7	1			3		10	9	11			
R2	Feb 1	CHELSEA	1-0	A Turnbull	25184	8	6			3			4		2					7	1		5			10	9	11			
R3	22	Aston Villa	2-0	A Turnbull, Wall	12777	8	6	9		4					3					7	1		5	2		10		11			
R4	Mar 7	Fulham	1-2	J Turnbull	41000	8	6			3			4							7	1		5	2		10	9	11			

FA Charity Shield

	Date	Opponent	Score	Scorers	Att																									
	Apr 27	Queen's Park Rangers	1-1	Meredith	12000	8	6			3			4							7	1		5	2		10	9	11			

At Stamford Bridge
Manchester United won a replay 4-0 in August 1908

Players only. Back row: Downie, Burgess. Next to back: Broomfield, Stacey, Duckworth, Holden, Bell, Moger. Seated: Picken, A (Sandy) Turnbull, J Turnbull, Roberts, Halse, Whiteside. At front: Meredith, Wall. The trophies are the FA Charity Shield, the League Championship trophy and the Manchester Cup. On the extreme right is Ernest Mangnall.

Newcastle United 1908/09

St James' Park

						Allan SJE	Anderson AL	Blanthorne R	Carr J	Duncan ASM	Gardner A	Gosnell AA	Higgins A	Howie J	Jobey G	Lawrence J	Liddell R	McCombie A	McCracken WR	McWilliam P	Pudan AE	Randall CE	Ridley J	Rutherford J	Shepherd A	Stewart J	Veitch CCMcK	Whitson TT	Willis DL	Wilson GW
	Sep	2	BRADFORD CITY	1-0	Veitch	26000			9	3		4		8			1			2	6				7		10	5			11
		5	LEICESTER FOSSE	2-0	Howie, Veitch	20000	9					4		8			1			2	6				7		10	5	3		11
		9	BRISTOL CITY	2-1	Howie 2	12000	9					4		8			1			2	6				7		10	5	3		11
1		12	Woolwich Arsenal	2-1	Rutherford, Stewart	18000		11				4		8			1			2	6				7		9	5	3		10
1		19	NOTTS COUNTY	1-0	Wilson	35000		11				4		8			1			2	6				7		9	5	3		10
2		26	Sheffield Wednesday	0-2		25000		11				4		8			1	6		2					7		9	5	3		10
2	Oct	3	Bristol City	3-3	Veitch 2, Higgins	16000						4	9	8			1			2					7		10	5	3	6	11
2		10	PRESTON NORTH END	2-0	Higgins, Stewart	30000					7		9	8			1			2	6						10	5	3	4	11
2		17	Middlesbrough	0-0		20000							9	8			1			2	6				7		10	5	3	4	11
2		24	MANCHESTER CITY	2-0	Howie 2	30000							9	8	4	1			2	6				7		10	5	3		11
2		31	Liverpool	1-2	Wilson	25000							9	8	4		1			2	6				7		10	5	3		11
2	Nov	7	BURY	3-1	Ridley, Rutherford, Veitch	20000					2		9	8	4	1					6			11	7		5	3			10
2		14	Sheffield United	1-1	Veitch (p)	15000							9	8	4	1			2	6				11	7		10	5	3		
3		21	ASTON VILLA	0-2		30000							9	8	4	1			2	6					7		10	5	3		11
2		28	Nottingham Forest	4-0	Wilson, Shepherd, Higgins, Liddell	12000				7			11	8			1	4				3				9		5	2	6	10
2	Dec	5	SUNDERLAND	1-9	Shepherd (p)	50000				7			11	8			1	4				3				9		5	2	6	10
2		12	Chelsea	2-1	Allan, Veitch (p)	30000	9			3	7		11	8		4	1			2								10	5		6	
2		19	BLACKBURN ROVERS	2-0	Anderson, Duncan	20000		11			7			8			1			2	6					9		5	3	4	10
2		25	MANCHESTER UNITED	2-1	Shepherd, Wilson	43000		11			7			8			1			2	6					9		5	3	4	10
2		26	Manchester United	0-1		40000		11			7			8			1			2	6					9		5	3	4	10
2	Jan	1	Everton	1-0	Howie	40000		11				4		8			1		2		6				7	9		5	3		10
2		2	Leicester Fosse	4-0	Higgins 2, Shepherd, Stewart	12000		11			7	4		8			1				6					9	10	2	3	5	
2		9	WOOLWICH ARSENAL	3-1	Anderson, Shepherd, Veitch (p)	30000		11				4	10	8			1			2	6				7	9		5	3		
1		23	Notts County	4-0	Shepherd 4	12000		11			2	4		8			1				6				7	9		5	3		10
1		30	SHEFFIELD WEDNESDAY	1-0	Veitch	35000		11				4		8			1			2	6				7	9	10	5	3		
1	Feb	13	Preston North End	1-0	Anderson	10000		11						8	5		1			2	6				7	9			3	4	10
1		27	Manchester City	2-0	Jobey, Stewart	25000		11		3	7			9	8	6	1			2							10	5		4	
1	Mar	13	Bury	1-1	og	20000					7		11	8	5	6	1			2						9	10			3	4	10
1		20	SHEFFIELD UNITED	4-0	Duncan, Shepherd, Stewart, Willis	30000				3	7						1			2	6			11		9	8	5		4	10
1		23	Bradford City	2-1	Allan, Stewart	10000	9			2						6	1						10	11	7		8	5	3	4	
1		31	MIDDLESBROUGH	1-0	Allan	12000	9				7			8	4		1			2		3		11			5			6	10
1	Apr	3	NOTTM. FOREST	1-1	Allan	16000	9	11		3	7			8	4		1			2							10	5		6	
1		10	Sunderland	1-3	Shepherd	30000		11						4			1			2	6				7	9	8	5	3		10
1		12	EVERTON	3-0	Stewart 2, McCracken (p)	40000		11		3				9	4		1			2	6				7		8	5			10
1		17	CHELSEA	1-3	Wilson	20000		11						9	4		1			2	6				7		8	5	3		10
1		24	Blackburn Rovers	4-2	Rutherford 3, Allan	7000	9	11		3					8		1			2	6				7			10	5		4	
1		26	Aston Villa	0-3		9000	9					7		11	8	6	1	5		2								3	4	10	
1		30	LIVERPOOL	0-1		8000	9	11		2				8			1	5			6				7			3	4	10	

	Apps	9	19	1	11	14	12	5	26	26	10	38	5	1	30	27	3	1	5	24	14	25	34	30	20	28
	Goals	5	3			2			5	6	1		1		1					1	5	11	8	9		1	5

One own goal

FA Charity Shield

| | Apr | 28 | Northampton Town | 2-0 | Allan, Rutherford | 7500 | 9 | 11 | | | | | | 8 | | | 1 | | | 2 | 6 | | | | 7 | | | 5 | 3 | 4 | 10 |

Played at Stamford Bridge

F.A. Cup

R1	Jan	16	CLAPTON ORIENT	5-0	Wilson 3, Anderson, Shepherd	23670		11				4		8			1		2		6				7	9		5	3		10
R2	Feb	6	BLACKPOOL	2-1	Howie, Rutherford	32137		11				4		8			1			2	6				7	9		5	3		10
R3		20	West Ham United	0-0		17000		11						8			1			2	6				7	9		5	3	4	10
rep		24	WEST HAM UNITED	2-1	Anderson, Shepherd (p)	36526		11						8	4		1			2	6				7	9		5	3		10
R4	Mar	6	SUNDERLAND	2-2	Rutherford, Wilson	53353		11						8	4		1			2	6				7	9		5	3		10
rep		10	Sunderland	3-0	Shepherd 2, Wilson	27512					7			8	4		1			2	6					9	10	5	3		11
SF		27	Manchester United	0-1		40118					7			8	4		1			2	6					9	10	5	3		11

SF at Bramall Lane

Back: G Hardy (assistant trainer), Soye, FG Watt (assistant secretary), Allan, Anderson, Liddell, GT Milne (director), Higgins, GG Archibald (director). Next to back: W Bramwell (director), Willis, Whitson, Crawford (director), McCracken, Stewart, JP Oliver (director), Pudan, Gosnell, R Oliver (director). Seated: J Graham (director), Wilson, McWilliam, Veitch, J Lunn (vice chairman), Gardner, Jos. Bell (chairman), Howie, Rutherford, Carr, J Cameron (director). Front: Duncan, Frank G Watt (secretary), Lawrence, JO McPherson (trainer), Sinclair. Inset, top right: Blanthorne.

Aston Villa 1909/10

Villa Park

							Bache JW	Buckley CS	Cartlidge A	Eyre E	George W	Gerrish WWN	Hall AE	Hampton JH	Hunter GC	Kearns JH	Layton AEC	Logan JL	Lyons AT	Miles A	Moss AJ	Tranter GH	Wallace CW	Walters J
	Sep	1	WOOLWICH ARSENAL	5-1	Bache 2, Gerrish, Hall, Walters	14000	10	5	1			9	11		6				4	2	3		7	8
		4	Bolton Wanderers	2-1	Wallace, Hall (p)	20000	10	5	1			9	11		6				4	2	3		7	8
		11	CHELSEA	4-1	Gerrish 3, Bache	20000	10	5	1			9	11		6				4	2	3		7	8
4		18	Blackburn Rovers	2-3	Gerrish, Wallace	20000	10	5	1			9	11		6				4	2	3		7	8
5		25	NOTTM. FOREST	0-0		30000	10	5	1			9	11		6				4	2	3		7	8
6	Oct	2	Sunderland	1-1	Hall	20000	10	5	1			9	11		6				4	2	3		7	8
4		9	EVERTON	3-1	Hampton 2, Hunter	30000		5	1			9	11	10	6				4	2	3		7	8
8		16	Manchester United	0-2		15000		5	1			9	11	10	6				4	2	3		7	8
7		23	BRADFORD CITY	3-1	Hampton, Hall, Gerrish	20000	8	5	1			9	11	10	6				4	2	3		7	
9		30	Sheffield Wednesday	2-3	Hampton 2	10000	8	5	1			9	11	10	6				4	2	3		7	
7	Nov	6	BRISTOL CITY	1-0	Gerrish	25000	8	5	1			9	11	10					4	2	3	6	7	
6		13	Bury	2-0	Bache 2	12000	8	5	1			9	11	10					4	2	3	6	7	
5		20	TOTTENHAM HOTSPUR	3-2	Gerrish, Bache, Hampton	15000	10	5	1				8	11	9				4	2	3	6	7	
8		27	Preston North End	0-1		8000	10	5	1				8	11	9		3		4	2		6	7	
6	Dec	4	NOTTS COUNTY	1-1	Hampton	6000	10	5	1				8	11	9	6	3	2				4	7	
7		11	Newcastle United	0-1		15000	10	5	1				8	11	9	6	3				2	4	7	
6		18	LIVERPOOL	3-1	Bache 2, Hampton	18000	10	5	1				8	11	9	6	3				2	4	7	
6		25	Sheffield United	1-0	Gerrish	25000	10	5	1	11		8			9	6				2	3	4	7	
4		27	SHEFFIELD UNITED	2-1	Hampton, Bache	25000	10	5	1	11		8			9	6				2	3	4	7	
5	Jan	1	Nottingham Forest	4-1	Hampton 3, Bache	7000	10	5		11	1	8			9	6		2		3		4	7	
3		8	BOLTON WANDERERS	3-1	Bache 2, Gerrish	17000	10	5			1	8	11	9	6			2		3		4	7	
4		22	Chelsea	0-0		30000	10	5			1	8	11	9	6					2	3	4	7	
1		29	BLACKBURN ROVERS	4-3	Hampton 3, Bache	12000	10		1			8	11	9	6					2	3	5	4	7	
1	Feb	12	SUNDERLAND	3-2	Walters, Buckley, Gerrish	20000		5	1	11		8			9	6				2	3		4	7	10
1		26	MANCHESTER UNITED	7-1	Walters 3, Gerrish 2, Hampton 2	20000		5	1	11		8			9	6				2	3		4	7	10
1	Mar	5	Bradford City	2-1	Bache, Robinson (og)	22000	10	5	1	11		8			9	6				2	3		4	7	
1		12	SHEFFIELD WEDNESDAY	5-0	Hall 2, Bache 2, Wallace (p)	12000	10	5	1				11	9	6					2	3		4	7	8
1		14	Everton	0-0		15000	10	5	1			8	11	9	6					2	3		4	7	
1		19	Bristol City	0-0		15000	10	5	1	11		8		9	6			2	3				4	7	
1		25	MIDDLESBROUGH	4-2	Hampton 3, Bache	30000	10	5	1			8	11	9	6					2	3		4	7	
1		26	BURY	4-1	Hampton 3, Walters	30000		5	1	11		8			9	6	3		2			4	7	10
1		28	Middlesbrough	2-3	Wallace 2 (2p)	25000	10	5	1			8	11	9	6				2	3		4	7	
1	Apr	2	Tottenham Hotspur	1-1	Bache	35000	10	5	1				11	9	6	3		2				4	7	8
1		9	PRESTON NORTH END	3-0	Hampton, Gerrish, Bache	20000	10	5	1	11		8		9	6				2	3		4	7	
1		11	Woolwich Arsenal	0-1		8000		5	1	11		8		9	6	3		2				4	7	10
1		16	Notts County	3-2	Wallace, Eyre, Hampton	11000	10	5	1	11		8		9	6	3		2				4	7	
1		27	NEWCASTLE UNITED	4-0	Bache, Wallace (p), Eyre, Hampton	15000	10	5	1	11		8		9		3	6	2				4	7	
1		30	Liverpool	0-2		25000	10	5	1	11		8		9		3	6	2				4	7	

Apps	32	37	35	13	3	36	25	32	32	10	4	16	35	27	1	28	38	14
Goals	20	1		2		14	6	26	1								7	6

One own goal

F.A. Cup

R1	Jan	15	Oldham Athletic	2-1	Bache, Hall	17000	10	5			1	8	11	9	6					2	3		4	7	
R2	Feb	5	DERBY COUNTY	6-1	Hampton 3, Wallace, Bache, Scattergood (og)	45000	10	5	1			8	11	9	6					2	3		4	7	
R3		19	MANCHESTER CITY	1-2	Gerrish	45000	10	5	1			8	11	9	6					2	3		4	7	

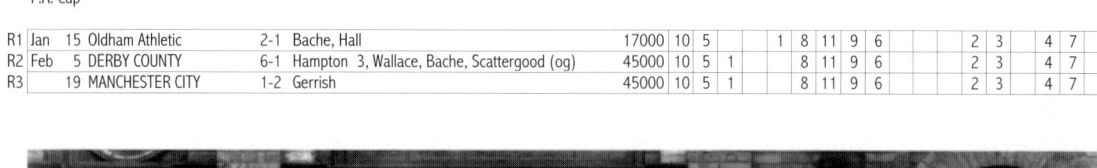

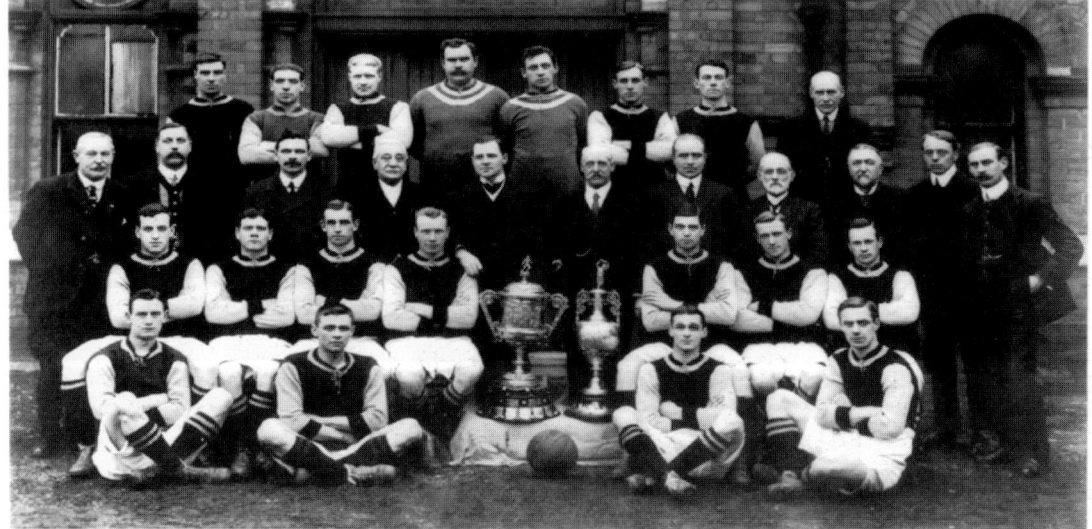

Back: Lyons, Layton, Logan, George, Cartlidge, Miles, Kearns. Next to back: Ramsey, Bate, Devey, Cooper, Jones, Rinder, Spencer, Margoschis, Whitehouse, Jessop, Strange. Seated: Gerrish, Hunter, Eyre, Bache, Tranter, Buckley, Hall. Front: Walters, Moss, Hampton, Wallace

Manchester United 1910/11

Old Trafford

						Bell A	Blott SP	Connor JE	Curry JJ	Donnelly A	Duckworth R	Edmonds H	Halse HJ	Hayes IV	Hodge J	Hofton LB	Holden RH	Homer TP	Hooper AH	Linkson OHS	Livingstone GT	Meredith WH	Moger HH	Picken JB	Roberts C	Sheldon J	Stacey GW	Turnbull A	Wall G	West EJ	Whalley A
	Sep	1	Woolwich Arsenal	2-1	Halse, West	15000	6					4		8				2						7	1		5		3	10	11	9	
		3	BLACKBURN ROVERS	3-2	Meredith, Turnbull, West	30000	6					4		8				2						7	1		5		3	10	11	9	
		10	Nottingham Forest	1-2	Turnbull	14000	6					4		8	3									7	1		5		2	10	11	9	
3		17	MANCHESTER CITY	2-1	Turnbull, West	50000	6					4		8								2		7	1		5		3	10	11	9	
2		24	Everton	1-0	Turnbull	25000	6					4		8				2						7	1		5		3	10	11	9	
2	Oct	1	SHEFFIELD WEDNESDAY	3-2	Wall 2, West	12000	6					4		8				2						7	1		5		3	10	11	9	
2		8	Bristol City	1-0	Halse	20000	6							8				2					4	7	1	10	5		3		11	9	
1		15	NEWCASTLE UNITED	2-0	Halse, Turnbull	50000						4		8				2					6	7	1		5		3	10	11	9	
1		22	Tottenham Hotspur	2-2	West 2	30000			11			4		8				2					6	7	1		5		3	10		9	
2		29	MIDDLESBROUGH	1-2	Turnbull	12000			11			4		8								2	6	7	1		5		3	10		9	
2	Nov	5	Preston North End	2-0	Turnbull, West	14000			11	6		4		8								2		7	1		5		3	10		9	
2		12	NOTTS COUNTY	0-0		7000				6		4		8								2		7	1		5		3	10	11	9	
2		19	Oldham Athletic	3-1	Turnbull 2, Wall	30000				6				8								2	4	7	1		5		3	10	11	9	
3		26	Liverpool	2-3	Roberts, Turnbull	10000				6				8							9	2	4	7	1		5		3	10	11		
3	Dec	3	BURY	3-2	Homer 2, Turnbull	6000				6								9			2	4	7	1	8	5		3	10	11		
3		10	Sheffield United	0-2		10000												2	9			4	7	1	8	5		3	10	11		6
3		17	ASTON VILLA	2-0	Turnbull, West	15000	6				2													7	1	8	5		3	10	11	9	4
1		24	Sunderland	2-1	Meredith, Turnbull	30000	6				2													7	1	8	5		3	10	11	9	4
1		26	WOOLWICH ARSENAL	5-0	Picken 2, West 2, Meredith	40000	6				2													7	1	8	5		3	10	11	9	4
1		27	Bradford City	0-1		35000					2												6		1	8	5	7	3	10	11	9	4
2		31	Blackburn Rovers	0-1		18000					2														1	8	5	7	3	10	11	9	4
1	Jan	2	BRADFORD CITY	1-0	Meredith	40000	6				2												4	7	1	8			3	10	11	9	5
1		7	NOTTM. FOREST	4-2	Homer, Picken, Wall, og (Needham)	8000	6				2							9						7	1	8	5		3		11	10	4
1		21	Manchester City	1-1	Turnbull	42000	6				2	4		8										7	1		5		3	10	11	9	
1		28	EVERTON	2-2	Duckworth, Wall	15000	6				2	4		8											1		5	7	3	10	11	9	
1	Feb	11	BRISTOL CITY	3-1	Homer, Picken, West	15000	6				2	4	1					8						7		10	5		3		11	9	
1		18	Newcastle United	1-0	Halse	40000	6				3	4	1	8			2							7			5			10	11	9	
1	Mar	4	Middlesbrough	2-2	Turnbull, West	8000	6				2	4	1					8						7					3	10	11	9	5
1		11	PRESTON NORTH END	5-0	West 2, Connor, Duckworth, Turnbull	12000	6		11			4	1			2								7		8	5		3	10		9	
1		15	TOTTENHAM HOTSPUR	3-2	Meredith, Turnbull, West	13000	6		11			4	1			2								7		8	5		3	10		9	
1		18	Notts County	0-1		8000	6		11		2	4	1											7		8	5		3	10		9	
1		25	OLDHAM ATHLETIC	0-0		18000	6					4	1			2								7		5	8	3	10	11	9	
1	Apr	1	LIVERPOOL	2-0	West 2	12000	6						1	8			2							7		5	11	3	10		9	4
1		8	Bury	3-0	Homer 2, Halse	16000	6						1	8			2	9						7			5		3	10		11	4
1		15	SHEFFIELD UNITED	1-1	West	20000	6						1	8			2	9						7			5		3	10		11	4
1		17	Sheffield Wednesday	0-0		25000	6			3			1	8	4	2					9			7						10		11	5
2		22	Aston Villa	2-4	Halse 2	50000	6		11			4	1	8			2							7					3	10		9	5
1		29	SUNDERLAND	5-1	Halse 2, Turnbull, West, og (Milton)	7000			11		2	4	1	8	6									7					3	10		9	5
					Apps		27	1	7	5	15	22	13	23	1	2	9	8	7	2	7	10	35	25	14	33	5	36	35	26	35	15
					Goals			1				2		9				6					5		4	1			18	5	19	

Two own goals

F.A. Cup

R1	Jan	14	BLACKPOOL	2-1	Picken, West	12000	6					2	4										7	1	8	5		3	10	11	9	
R2	Feb	4	ASTON VILLA	2-1	Halse, Wall	65101	6					2	4	8										7	1		5		3	10	11	9	
R3		25	West Ham United	1-2	Turnbull	26000	6					2	4	1	8									7			5		3	10	11	9	

Back: JE Mangall (secretary/manager), Bacon, Picken, Edmonds, Mr Murray (director), Moger, Mr Davies (chairman), Homer, Mr Lawton (director), Bell, Mr Deakin (director). Centre: Meredith, Duckworth, Roberts, A (Sandy) Turnbull, West, Stacey. Front: Whalley, Hofton, Halse, Wall

Blackburn Rovers 1911/12

Ewood Park

						Aitkenhead WCA	Anthony W	Ashcroft J	Bradshaw W	Cameron WS	Chapman GR	Clennell J	Cowell A	Crompton R	Davies W	Dennison H	Garbutt WT	Johnston J	Latheron EG	Orr J	Proctor BJ	Robinson A	Simpson J	Smith PJ	Suttie T	Walmsley A
	Sep	2	BURY	2-0	Aitkenhead 2	20000	9	11		6				10	3	2					8			1	7	5		4
		6	Sunderland	0-3		20000	9	11		6				10	3	2					8			1	7	5		4
		9	Middlesbrough	1-2	Aitkenhead	18000	9			6	11			10	3	2					8			1	7	5		4
14		16	NOTTS COUNTY	0-0		15000	10	11		6			8	3	2	9		7						1		5		4
10		23	Tottenham Hotspur	2-0	Aitkenhead, Davies	40000	10	11		6					3	2	9					8		1	7	5		4
8		30	MANCHESTER UNITED	2-2	Orr 2	30000	10	11		6					3	2	9					8		1	7	5		4
6	Oct	7	Liverpool	2-1	Aitkenhead, Orr	40000	10	11		6		5			3	2	9					8		1	7			4
3		14	ASTON VILLA	3-1	Aitkenhead, Chapman, Latheron	25000	10	11		6		5			3	2	9				8			1	7	4		
8		21	Newcastle United	2-4	Davies, Latheron	25000	10	11		6		5			3	2	9				8			1	7			4
5		28	SHEFFIELD UNITED	1-0	Aitkenhead	15000	10	11		6		5			3	2	9				8			1	7			4
3	Nov	4	Oldham Athletic	1-0	Smith	20000	10	11			6	5			3	2					8			1	7	9		4
1		11	BOLTON WANDERERS	2-0	Anthony, Latheron	20000	10	11		6		5			3	2					8			1	7	9		4
3		18	Bradford City	0-1		35000	10	11		6		5			3	2	9				8			1	7			4
2		25	WOOLWICH ARSENAL	4-0	Aitkenhead, Chapman, Latheron, Bradshaw (p)	10000	10	11		6		9			3	2					8			1	7	5		4
4	Dec	2	Manchester City	0-3		36000	10	11		6	9	5			3	2					8			1	7			4
2		9	EVERTON	2-1	Chapman, Bradshaw (p)	13724	10	11		6		9			3	2					8			1	7	5		4
4		16	West Bromwich Albion	0-2		13176	10	11	1	6		5				2	9				8				7		3	4
6		23	SUNDERLAND	2-2	Aitkenhead, Orr	12000	9	11	1	6		5	10			2						8			7		3	4
5		25	SHEFFIELD WEDNESDAY	0-0		25000		11	1	6	9		10			2						8			7	5	3	4
4		26	Preston North End	2-2	Clennell, Simpson	25000	9		1	6	11		10			2						8			7	5	3	4
2		30	Bury	2-1	Clennell, Orr	10000			1	6	11		10			2	9					8			7	5	3	4
2	Jan	1	PRESTON NORTH END	3-0	Aitkenhead, Chapman, Simpson	40000	10		1	6	11	9							2			8			7	5	3	4
2		6	MIDDLESBROUGH	2-1	Aitkenhead, Chapman	5000	10			6	11	9							2			8		1	7	5	3	4
1		20	Notts County	3-1	Aitkenhead, Cameron, Orr	3000	10			6	11				3	2					9	8		1	7	5		4
1		27	TOTTENHAM HOTSPUR	0-0		15000	10			6	11				3	2					9	8		1	7	5		4
1	Feb	10	LIVERPOOL	1-0	Chapman	15000	10				6	9	11	3						2	7	8		1		5		4
1		17	Aston Villa	3-0	Chapman 2, Orr	28000	10	11		6		9			3					2		8		1	7	5		4
1	Mar	2	Sheffield United	1-1	Orr	25000	10	11		6		9			3	2						8			7	5		4
1		16	Bolton Wanderers	0-2		30175		11	1	6		9	10	3	2							8			7	5		4
1		23	BRADFORD CITY	3-1	Aitkenhead, Orr, Bradshaw (p)	10000	10	11		6		9			3					2		8	7	1		5		4
1	Apr	6	MANCHESTER CITY	2-0	Chapman, Clennell	20000		11		6		9	10	3	2							8		1	7	5		4
1		8	Sheffield Wednesday	1-1	Clennell	15000				6	11		10	3	2					9	8			1	7	5		4
1		13	Everton	3-1	Clennell 2, Latheron	40000				6	11	9	10	3	2						8			1	7	5		4
1		15	OLDHAM ATHLETIC	1-0	Latheron	10000		11		6		9	10	3	2						8			1	7	5		4
1		22	Woolwich Arsenal	1-5	Ducat (og)	7000		11		6		9	10	3	2						8			1	7	5		4
1		25	WEST BROMWICH ALB.	4-1	Aitkenhead 2, Clennell 2	12000	9	11		6			10	3	2							8		1	7	5		4
1		27	NEWCASTLE UNITED	1-1	Latheron	10000				6			10	3	2	9	11			8				1	7	5		4
1		29	Manchester United	1-3	Clennell	6000	9	11		6			10	3	2						8			1	7	5		4

Apps	29	27	8	36	13	23	18	31	33	11	1	1	5	22	19	1	30	35	31	7	37
Goals	15	1		3	1	9	9			2				7	9			2	1			

One own goal

FA Cup

R1	Jan	13	NORWICH CITY	4-1	Chapman 2, Simpson 2	22947	10			6	11	9			3	2						8		1	7	5		4
R2	Feb	3	Derby County	2-1	Chapman, Orr	22023	10			6		9	11	3	2						8		1	7	5		4
R3		24	WOLVERHAMPTON W.	3-2	Aitkenhead 2, Chapman	45711	10	11	1	6		9			3	2						8			7	5		4
R4	Mar	9	Manchester United	1-1	Aitkenhead	59296	10			6	11	9			3	2						8			7	5		4
rep		14	MANCHESTER UNITED	4-2	Chapman 2, Aitkenhead, Simpson	39286	10	11		6		9			3	2						8			7	5		4
SF		30	West Bromwich Albion	0-0		30063	10	11		6		9			3	2						8		1	7	5		4
rep	Apr	3	West Bromwich Albion	0-1		20050	10	11		6		9			3	2						8		1	7	5		4

R4 replay and SF replay a.e.t.
SF at Anfield, Liverpool. SF replay at Hillsborough, Sheffield

Charity Shield

| May | 4 | QUEEN'S PARK RANGERS | 2-1 | Aitkenhead 2 | 10000 | 9 | 11 | | 6 | | | | 10 | 3 | 2 | | | | | 8 | | | 1 | 7 | 5 | | 4 |

At White Hart Lane

Players only: Back: Brooksbank, McEvoy, Porteus, Robinson, Dennison, Proctor. Next to back: Orr, Garbutt, Bradshaw, Walmsley, Johnston, Jones, Ashcroft, Suttie, Davies. Seated: Cameron, Latheron, Smith, Crompton, Cowell, Anthony, Stevenson. Front: Chapman, Clennell, Byrom, Simpson

Sunderland 1912/13

Roker Park

						Anderson GA	Best RB	Buchan CM	Butler JH	Connor JC	Cringan WC	Cuggy FC	Gladwin CE	Hall TH	Hobson AH	Holley GH	Low HF	Martin HM	Milton AM	Mordue JM	Ness HM	Richardson JR	Scott WS	Small JS	Thomson CB	Tinsley WT	Troughear WB
	Sep	7 Newcastle United	1-1	Mordue	56000			8				4				10	6	11		7	3	9	1		5		2
		9 Blackburn Rovers	0-4		15000			8				4				10	6	11		7	3	9	1		5		2
		14 DERBY COUNTY	0-2		18000			8				4				10	6	11		7	3	9	1		5		2
16		18 BLACKBURN ROVERS	2-4	Buchan, Mordue	18000			8		9		4				10	6	11		7	3		1		5		2
19		21 Oldham Athletic	0-3		16000	1		8		9	6	4					10	11	3	7	7	2			5		
17		28 TOTTENHAM HOTSPUR	2-2	Hall, Mordue	10000	1		8				4		9		10	6	11	3	7	7	2			5		
19	Oct	5 Chelsea	0-2		25000			8	1		6			9		10	4	11	3	7					5		2
17		12 MIDDLESBROUGH	4-0	Hall, Holley, Low, Mordue	20000			8	1			4	2	9		10	6	11	3	7					5		
17		19 Woolwich Arsenal	3-1	Mordue 2 (1p), Holley	12000			8	1			4	2	9		10	6	11	3	7					5		
14		26 NOTTS COUNTY	4-0	Hall, Martin, Buchan 2	8000			8	1			4	2	9		10	6	11	3	7					5		
12	Nov	2 Bradford City	5-1	Holley 3, Buchan, Low	20000			8	1			4	2	9		10	6	11	3	7					5		
11		9 MANCHESTER UNITED	3-1	Hall, Mordue (p), Tinsley	20000			8	1			4	2	9			6	11	3	7					5	10	
12		16 Manchester City	0-1		12000			8	1			4	2	9		10	6	11	3	7					5		
10		23 ASTON VILLA	3-1	Buchan, Holley, Mordue (p)	30000			8	1		4		2	9		10	6	11	3	7					5		
12		30 West Bromwich Albion	1-3	Holley	13529			8	1		4		2	9		10	6	11	3	7					5		
10	Dec	7 LIVERPOOL	7-0	Buchan 5, Martin, Mordue	8000			8	1			4		9		10	6	11	3	7					5		2
10		14 Everton	4-0	Richardson 2, Buchan, Mordue	6000			8	1			4	2			10	6	11	3	7		9			5		
9		21 BOLTON WANDERERS	2-1	Buchan, Mordue (p)	20000			8	1			4	2	9		10	6	11	3	7					5		
7		25 Sheffield Wednesday	2-1	Holley, Mordue (p)	30000			8	1			4	2	9		10	6	11	3	7					5		
9		26 SHEFFIELD WEDNESDAY	0-2		10000			8	1			4	2	9		10	6	11	3	7					5		
7		28 NEWCASTLE UNITED	2-0	Holley 2	30000			8	1			4	2			10	6	11	3	7		9			5		
5	Jan	1 WOOLWICH ARSENAL	4-1	Buchan, Cuggy, Mordue, Richardson	20000			8	1			4	2				6	11		7	3	9			5	10	
7		18 OLDHAM ATHLETIC	1-1	Buchan	12000			8	1			4	2			10	6	11	3	7		9			5		
4		25 Tottenham Hotspur	2-1	Low, Martin	40000			8	1			4	2	9		10	6	11	3	7					5		
3	Feb	8 CHELSEA	4-0	Buchan 2, Low, Richardson	20000			8	1			4	2	10			6	11	3	7		9			5		
1		15 Middlesbrough	2-0	Martin, Richardson	14000		7		1		4		2	10		8	6	11	3			9			5		
1		26 Derby County	3-0	Hall 2 (1p), Mordue	6000			8	1		6	4	2	9		10	5	11	3	7							
2	Mar	1 Notts County	1-2	Hall	10000		7		1			4	2	9		10	8	6	11	3					5	10	
2		15 Manchester United	3-1	Buchan 2, Richardson	20000		7	8	1		6	5	2			10		11	3			9		4			
2		21 SHEFFIELD UNITED	1-0	Thomson	25500			8	1			4	2			10	6	11	3	7		9			5		
1		22 MANCHESTER CITY	1-0	Buchan	20000			8	1			4	2			10	6	11	3	7		9			5		
1		24 Sheffield United	3-1	Buchan 2, Holley	32500			8	1			4	2		9	2	10	6	11	7	3					5		
2	Apr	5 WEST BROMWICH ALB.	3-1	Buchan, Mordue (p), Tinsley	17000			8	1		6	4	2				5	11		7	3	9				10	
1		9 EVERTON	3-1	Buchan, Holley, Richardson	15000			8	1			4			2	10	6	11	3	7		9			5		
1		12 Liverpool	5-2	Buchan 3, Richardson 2	30000			8	1		4				2		6	11		7	3	9			5	10	
1		23 Aston Villa	1-1	Tinsley	60000			8	1			4	2				6	11		7	3	9			5	10	
1		26 Bolton Wanderers	3-1	Richardson 2, Mordue (p)	11857			8	1			4	2				6	11		7	3	9			5	10	
1		30 BRADFORD CITY	1-0	Buchan	15000			8	1			4	2			10	6	11		7	3	9			5		
					Apps	2	3	36	32	2	10	32	27	20	3	30	37	38	27	35	13	18	4	1	35	7	6
					Goals			27				1		7		12	4	5		15		11				1	3

F.A. Cup

R1	Jan	11 CLAPTON ORIENT	6-0	Richardson 4, Holley, Mordue	12895			8	1			4	2			10	6	11	3	7		9			5		
R2	Feb	5 MANCHESTER CITY	2-0	Holley, Mordue	27974			8	1			4	2			10	6	11	3	7		9			5		
R3		22 SWINDON TOWN	4-2	Richardson 2, Buchan, Gladwin	24865			8	1			4	2			10	6	11	3	7		9			5		
R4	Mar	8 NEWCASTLE UNITED	0-0		29111			8	1			4	2			10	6	11	3	7		9			5		
rep		12 Newcastle United	2-2	Buchan, Holley	56717			8	1			4	2			10	6	11	3	7		9			5		
rep2		17 Newcastle United	3-0	Mordue 2 (1p), Holley	49354			8	1			4	2			10	6	11	3	7		9			5		
SF		29 Burnley	0-0		33656			8	1			4	2			10	6	11	3	7		9			5		
rep	Apr	2 Burnley	3-2	Buchan, Holley, Mordue (p)	30000			8	1			4	2			10	6	11		7	3	9			5		
F		19 Aston Villa	0-1		120081			8	1			4	2			10	6	11		7	3	9			5		

SF at Bramall Lane, replay at St Andrews, Birmingham. Final at Crystal Palace
R4 replay a.e.t

Back: Butler, Cuggy, Ness, Richardson, Martin, Tinsley, Mordue. Front: Cringan, Gladwin, Buchan, Thompson, Low, Holley

Blackburn Rovers 1913/14

Ewood Park

	Date		Opponent	Score	Scorers	Att	Aitkenhead WCA	Anthony W	Bell A	Bradshaw W	Chapman GR	Clennell J	Cowell A	Crabtree JI	Crompton R	Dawson PH	Hodkinson IC	Johnston J	Latheron EG	McGhie A	Orr J	Porteous G	Robinson A	Shea DH	Simpson J	Smith PJ	Walmsley A
	Sep	1	NEWCASTLE UNITED	3-0	Latheron 2, Chapman	20000				6	9		3		2		11		10				1	8	7	5	4
		6	LIVERPOOL	6-2	Shea 4, Latheron, Bradshaw (p)	30000				6	9		3		2		11		10				1	8	7	5	4
		8	Burnley	2-1	Chapman, Smith	40000				6	9		3		2		11		10				1	8	7	5	4
1		13	Aston Villa	3-1	Chapman, Shea, Bradshaw (p)	40000				6	9		3		2		11		10				1	8	7	5	4
1		20	MIDDLESBROUGH	6-0	Chapman 3, Shea 3	25000				6	9		3		2		11		10				1	8	7	5	4
1		27	Sheffield United	1-1	Chapman	30000				6	9	10	3		2		11						1	8	7	5	4
1	Oct	4	DERBY COUNTY	3-1	Clennell, Latheron, McGhie	30000		6				9	3		2		11		10	7			1	8		5	4
1		11	Manchester City	2-1	Smith, Hughes (og)	40000		6				9	3		2		11		10				1	8	7	5	4
1		18	BRADFORD CITY	0-0		25000		6				9	3		2		11		10				1	8	7	5	4
1		25	Tottenham Hotspur	3-3	Hodkinson, Latheron, Shea	48000				6	9		3		2		11		10				1	8	7	5	4
2	Nov	1	Sunderland	1-2	Orr	50000				6	9		3		2		11		10	7	8		1			5	4
1		8	EVERTON	6-0	Latheron 3, Chapman, McGhie, Bradshaw (p)	20000			5	6	9		3		2		11		10	7			1	8			4
1		15	West Bromwich Albion	0-2		30000				6	9		3		2		11		10	7			1			5	4
1		22	SHEFFIELD WEDNESDAY	3-2	Chapman, Latheron, Shea	20000		6			9		3		2		11		10				1	8	7	5	4
1		29	Bolton Wanderers	0-1		53747				6	9		3		2		11		10				1	8	7	5	4
1	Dec	6	CHELSEA	3-1	Shea 2, Hodkinson	20000					4		3		2		11		10		9	6	1	8	7	5	
1		13	Oldham Athletic	1-1	Shea	20000	6						3		2		11		10		9		1	8	7	5	4
1		20	MANCHESTER UNITED	0-1		35000	6				9		3		2		11		10				1	8	7	5	4
1		25	PRESTON NORTH END	5-0	Aitkenhead 3, Shea 2	25000	9			6			3		2		11		10				1	8	7	5	4
1		26	Preston North End	5-1	Shea 3, Aitkenhead, Simpson	28000	9		5	6			3		2		11		10				1	8	7		4
1		27	Liverpool	3-3	Shea 2, Aitkenhead	30000	9			6			3		2		11		10				1	8	7	5	4
1	Jan	1	BURNLEY	0-0		40000	9			6	2		3				11		10				1	8	7	5	4
		3	ASTON VILLA	0-0		15000	9			6	2		3				11		10				1	8	7	5	4
1		17	Middlesbrough	0-3		15000	9		6				3		2		11		10				1	8	7	5	4
1		24	SHEFFIELD UNITED	3-2	Shea 2, Latheron	15000	9		6				3		2		11		10				1	8	7	5	4
1	Feb	7	Derby County	3-2	Aitkenhead, Latheron, Shea	10000	9			6			3		2		11		10				1	8	7	5	4
		14	MANCHESTER CITY	2-1	Aitkenhead, Smith	18000	9			6			3				11	2			10	8	1		7	5	4
		25	Bradford City	2-0	Shea 2	17000	9						3	1	2		11		10					8	7	5	4
		28	TOTTENHAM HOTSPUR	1-1	Simpson	25000	10	11		6	5		3	1	2	9								8	7		
1	Mar	14	Everton	0-0		36080				6			3	1	2	9	11		10					8	7	5	4
1		21	WEST BROMWICH ALB.	2-0	Dawson, McGhie	20000	6						3	1		9		2	10	11				8	7	5	4
1		23	SUNDERLAND	3-1	Orr, Walmsley, Ness (og)	8000	5			6			3	1	2				10	11	9			8	7		4
1		28	Sheffield Wednesday	1-3	Shea	12000	6						3	1	2	9			10	11				8	7	5	4
1	Apr	4	BOLTON WANDERERS	3-2	Dawson, Latheron, Shea	25000				6	2		3			9			10	11		1		8	7	5	4
1		10	Newcastle United	0-0		40000				6			3	1	2	9	11		10					8	7	5	4
1		11	Chelsea	0-2		40000				6			3	1	2	9	11		10					8	7	5	4
1		18	OLDHAM ATHLETIC	2-1	Dawson, Latheron	20000	5			6			3	1	2	9	11		10					8	7		4
1		25	Manchester United	0-0		15000				6	9		3	1	2		11		10					8	7	5	4

	Apps	17	1	8	27	19	4	38	10	33	8	33	2	35	9	5	1	28	36	34	33	37
	Goals	7			3	9	1				3	2		13	3	2			27	2	3	1

Two own goals

FA Cup

	Date		Opponent	Score	Scorers	Att																					
R1	Jan	10	MIDDLESBROUGH	3-0	Aitkenhead 3	25395	9		6				3		2		11		10				1	8	7	5	4
R2		31	BURY	2-0	Shea 2	29098	9			6			3		2		11		10				1	8	7	5	4
R3	Feb	21	MANCHESTER CITY	1-2	Aitkenhead	41250	9			6			3		2		11		10				1	8	7	5	4

Players only: Back: Shea, Simpson, Chapman, Robinson, Smith, Walmsley. Front: Latheron, Cowell, Crompton, Bradshaw, Hodkinson

63

Everton 1914/15

Goodison Park

							Brown W	Chedgzoy S	Clennell J	Fern TE	Fleetwood T	Galt JH	Grenyer A	Harrison G	Houston J	Howarth HR	Jefferis F	Kirsopp WHJ	Maconnachie JSJ	Makepeace JWH	Mitchell FWG	Nuttall TAB	Palmer W	Parker RN	Roberts J	Simpson RH	Thompson R	Wareing W	Weller LC	Wright WP
	Sep	2	Tottenham Hotspur	3-1	Clennell 3	8000		7	10	1	4	5	6	11			8		3					9			2			
		5	Newcastle United	1-0	Jefferis	12000		7	10	1	4	5	6	11			8		3					9			2			
		7	Burnley	0-1		20000		7	10	1	4	5	6	11			8		3					9			2			
6		12	MIDDLESBROUGH	2-3	Parker 2	12000		7	10	1	4	5	6						3			8	11	9			2			
12		19	Sheffield United	0-1		20000		7	10	1	4	5	6						3			8	11	9			2			
11		26	ASTON VILLA	0-0		25000		7	10	1	4	5					8		3	6			11	9			2			
5	Oct	3	Liverpool	5-0	Parker 3, Clennell 2	25000		7	10	1	4	5					8		3	6			11	9			2			
4		10	BRADFORD PARK AVE.	4-1	Parker 2, Chedgzoy, Galt	20000		7	10	1	4	5					8		3	6			11	9			2			
4		17	Oldham Athletic	1-1	Jefferis	10000		7	10	1	4	5					8		3	6			11	9	2					
4		24	MANCHESTER UNITED	4-2	Parker 2, Makepeace, Palmer	18000		7	10	1	4	5					8		3	6			11	9	2					
4		31	Bolton Wanderers	0-0		10000		7	10	1	4	5					8		3	6			11	9	2					
7	Nov	7	BLACKBURN ROVERS	1-3	Parker	25000		7	10	1	4	5					8		3	6			11	9	2					
8		14	Notts County	0-0		10000		7	10	1	4	5		11			8		3	6				9			2			
5		21	SUNDERLAND	7-1	Parker 3, Clennell 2, Harrison, Jefferis	13000		7	10	1	4	5		11			8		3	6				9			2			
5		28	Sheffield Wednesday	4-1	Parker 4	14000		7	10	1	4	5		11			8		3	6				9			2			
4	Dec	5	WEST BROMWICH ALB.	2-1	Clennell, Parker	20000		7	10	1	4	5		11			8		3	6				9			2			
3		12	MANCHESTER CITY	4-1	Parker 3, Clennell	18000	4	7	10	1		5		11			8		3					9			2	6		
5		19	Chelsea	0-2		4000		7	10	1	4	5		11			8		3	6				9			2			
4		25	BRADFORD CITY	1-1	Jefferis	20000		7	10	1	4	5		11			8		3	6				9			2			
3		26	Bradford City	1-0	Chedgzoy	30000		7	10	1	4	5		11			8		3	6				9			2			
4	Jan	1	TOTTENHAM HOTSPUR	1-1	Kirsopp	10000		7	10	1	4	5		11				8	3	6				9			2			
2		2	NEWCASTLE UNITED	3-0	Harrison, Kirsopp, Parker	20000	4		10	1		5		11	7			8	3	6				9			2			
3		16	Middlesbrough	1-5	Parker	7500		7	10	1	4	5		11				8	3	6				9			2			
4		23	SHEFFIELD UNITED	0-0		18000		7	10	1	4	5								6		8	11			3	2			9
4	Feb	6	LIVERPOOL	1-3	Clennell	35000		7	10	1	4	5					8		3	6			11	9			2			
4		10	Aston Villa	5-1	Parker 3, Galt, Kirsopp	7000		7	10	1	4	5					8		3	6				9	11		2			
2		27	Manchester United	2-1	Harrison, Parker	18000		7	10	1	4	5		11			8		3	6				9			2			
5	Mar	13	Blackburn Rovers	1-2	Kirsopp	15000		7	10	1	4						8		3	6				9			2	5		
5		17	OLDHAM ATHLETIC	3-4	Parker 2, Kirsopp	11000				1	4		6	11			8	3					7	9			2	5		10
5		20	NOTTS COUNTY	4-0	Kirsopp 2, Clennell, Parker	16000	4		10					11				8		6	1		7	9			2	5	3	
2		22	BOLTON WANDERERS	5-3	Parker 3, Clennell 2	5000			10		4		6	11		8					1		7	9		3	2	5		
5	Apr	2	BURNLEY	0-2				7	10	1	4	5	6				8							9		3	2			
5		3	SHEFFIELD WEDNESDAY	0-1		12000			10	1	4	5	6	11			8							7	9		3	2			
4		6	Sunderland	3-0	Parker 2, Kirsopp	10000			10	1	4		6	11			8							7	9			2	5	3	
4		10	West Bromwich Albion	2-1	Fleetwood, Harrison	8748	4		10	1	9		6	11			8							7			2		5	3	
2		14	Bradford Park Avenue	2-1	Grenyer, Kirsopp	6000		7		1	4	5	10	11			8					9						2	6	3	
1		17	Manchester City	1-0	Clennell	30000			10	1	4	5	6	11			8						7		9			2		3	
1		26	CHELSEA	2-2	Fleetwood, Parker	30000		7	10	1	4	5	6	11			8								9			2		3	
						Apps	4	30	36	36	35	32	14	26	1	1	18	16	28	23	2	5	17	35	1	9	33	8	6	2
						Goals		2	14		2	2	1	4			4	9		1			1	36				1			

F.A. Cup

R1	Jan	9	BARNSLEY	3-0	Galt 2, Parker			7	10	1	4	5		11			8		3	6				9			2			
R2		30	BRISTOL CITY	4-0	Clennell, Kirsopp, Parker, Wareing	24500		7	10	1	4						8			6			11	9		3	2	5		
R3	Feb	20	Queen's Park Rangers	2-1	Clennell, og	33000		7	10	1	4	5		11			8		3	6				9			2			
R4	Mar	6	Bradford City	2-0	Chedgzoy, Clennell	26100		7	10	1	4	5		11			8		3	6				9			2			
SF		27	Chelsea	0-2		22000		7	10		4	5		11			8			6	1			9		3	2			

SF at Villa Park

Back: Fleetwood, Granger, Thompson, Galt, Fern, McConnochie, Makepeace.
Front: Chedgzoy, Kirksopp, Parker, Clennell, Roberts

64

West Bromwich Albion 1919/20

The Hawthorns

							Bentley A	Bowser S	Cook AF	Crisp J	Gregory J	Hatton SEO	Jephcott AC	Magee TP	McNeal R	Moorwood L	Morris F	Pearson HP	Pennington J	Reed FWM	Richardson S	Smith AW	Smith J	Waterhouse F
	Aug	30	OLDHAM ATHLETIC	3-1	Morris 2, Gregory	18000		5		7	11			8	6		10	1	3		4	9	2	
	Sep	3	Newcastle United	2-0	Magee, Gregory	40000		5		7	11			8	6		10	1	3		4	9	2	
		6	Oldham Athletic	1-2	Bowser (p)	10000		5		7	11			8	6		10	1	3		4	9	2	
1		8	NEWCASTLE UNITED	3-0	A Smith, Bowser (p), Morris	20000		5		7	11			8	6		10	1	3		4	9	2	
2		13	EVERTON	4-3	Magee, Morris, Gregory, Crisp	35000		5		7	11			8	6		10	1	3		4	9	2	
1		20	Everton	5-2	Jephcott, Crisp 2, A Smith 2	35000		5			11		7	8	6		10	1	3		4	9	2	
1		27	BRADFORD CITY	4-1	Bowser 3 (2p), Morris	30000		5			11		7	8	6		10	1	3		4	9	2	
1	Oct	4	Bradford City	0-3		20000		5			11		7	8	6		10	1	3		4	9	2	
1		11	BOLTON WANDERERS	4-1	Magee, Bowser (p), Crisp, A Smith	30000		5			11		7	8	6		10	1	3		4	9	2	
1		18	Bolton Wanderers	2-1	Morris, Gregory	24000		5	2	11	10		7	8	6	1	9		3		4			
1		25	NOTTS COUNTY	8-0	Morris 5, Foster(og), Gregory, Magee	30000			2	7	11			8	6	1	10		3	5	4	9		
2	Nov	1	Notts County	0-2		14000		5		7	11			8	6	1	10		3		4	9	2	
3		10	ASTON VILLA	1-2	Gregory	20000		5		7	11			8	6		10	1	3		4	9	2	
3		15	Aston Villa	4-2	Gregory 2, Morris 2	60000		5		8	11		7		6		10	1	3		4	9	2	
3		22	SHEFFIELD WEDNESDAY	1-3	A Smith	20000		5		8	11		7		6		10	1	3		4	9	2	
2		29	Sheffield Wednesday	3-0	Bowser (p), Bentley, Morris	30000	9	5			11		7	8	6		10	1	3		4		2	
1	Dec	6	Manchester City	3-2	Bowser (p), Morris 2	25000	9	5			11		7	8	6		10	1	3		4		2	
1		13	MANCHESTER CITY	2-0	Morris 2, Gregory	25000	9	5		7	11			8	6		10	1	3		4		2	
1		20	Derby County	4-0	Bentley, Morris 2, Gregory	14000	9	5		7	11			8	6		10	1	3		4		2	
1		26	SUNDERLAND	4-0	Magee, Morris 2, Bentley	40000	9	5		7	11			8	6		10	1	3		4		2	
1		27	DERBY COUNTY	3-0	Morris 2, Magee	35000	9	5		7	11			8	6		10	1	3		4		2	
1	Jan	1	Sunderland	1-4	Morris	40000	9	5		7	11			8	6		10	1	3		4		2	
1		3	Blackburn Rovers	5-1	Bentley 3, Morris, Gregory	20000	9	5		7	11			8	6		10	1	3		4		2	
1		17	BLACKBURN ROVERS	5-2	Magee, Bentley, Morris, Crisp, Gregory	30000	9	5		7	11			8	6		10	1	3		4		2	
1		24	MANCHESTER UNITED	2-1	Bowser, Morris	30000		5		7	11			8	6		10	1	3		4	9	2	
1	Feb	7	SHEFFIELD UNITED	0-2		25000		5		7	11	9		8	6		10	1	3		4		2	
1		14	Sheffield United	0-1		45000	9				11		7		6		10	1	3		4	8	2	
1		21	MIDDLESBROUGH	4-1	Bentley 2, Morris 2	25000	9	5			11		7		6		10	1	3		4	8	2	
1		25	Manchester United	2-1	Bentley 2	20000	9	5	3	11	10		7		6			1			4	8	2	
1		28	Middlesbrough	0-0		30000	9	5			11		7		6		10	1	3			8	2	4
1	Mar	6	Burnley	2-2	Jephcott, Crisp	25000	9	5		8	11		7		6		10	1	3			2		4
1		13	BURNLEY	4-1	Bentley, Morris 2, Crisp	25000	9	5		8	11		7		6		10	1	3		4		2	
1		20	Preston North End	1-0	Crisp	20000	9	5	3	11	10		7		6			1			4	8	2	
1		27	PRESTON NORTH END	4-1	Jephcott 2, Morris 2	25000	9	5			11		7		6		10	1	3		4	8	2	
1	Apr	3	Bradford Park Avenue	4-0	Bentley, Morris, McNeal (p), A Smith	15000	9	5			11		7		6		10	1	3		4	8	2	
1		5	Arsenal	0-1		40000	9	5			11		7		6		10	1	3		4	8	2	
1		6	ARSENAL	1-0	Morris	20000		5	3	8	11		7		6		10	1			4	9	2	
1		10	BRADFORD PARK AVE.	3-1	Jephcott, Bentley, Bowser (p)	10000	9	5	3	11	10		7		6			1			4	8	2	
1		17	Liverpool	0-0		45000	9	5		7	11				6		10	1	3		4	8	2	
1		24	LIVERPOOL	1-1	Morris	35000	9	5	3	7	11				6		10	1			4	8	2	
1		26	Chelsea	0-2		25000	9	5		7	11				6		10	1	3		4	8	2	
1	May	1	CHELSEA	4-0	McNeal, Gregory, A Smith, Bentley	35000	9	5		7	11				6		10	1	3		4	8	2	
					Apps		24	41	7	38	34	1	21	24	42	3	39	39	37	1	40	29	40	2
					Goals		15	10		8	12		5	7	2		37					7		

One own goal

F.A. Cup

| R1 | Jan | 10 | BARNSLEY | 0-1 | | 32327 | | 9 | 5 | | 7 | 11 | | | 8 | 6 | | 10 | 1 | 3 | | 4 | | 2 | |

FA Charity Shield

| | May | 16 | Tottenham Hotspur | 2-0 | AW Smith 2 | 38168 | 9 | 5 | | 7 | 11 | | | | 6 | | 10 | 1 | 3 | | 4 | 8 | 2 | |

Back row: Barber (trainer), Pearson, Gopsill (masseur), Smith (assistant secretary). Next to back: Unknown, D Nurse (director), Cook, Bassett (chairman), Keys (director), Jephcott, Seymour and Lt. Col. Ely (directors). Seated: Crisp, A Smith, McNeal, Pennington, Bowser, Morris, Gregory. Front: J Smith, Magee, Bentley, Richardson

Burnley 1920/21

Turf Moor

							Anderson J	Basnett A	Birchenough F	Boyle TW	Brophy TJ	Cross B	Dawson J	Douglas GH	Freeman BC	Halley G	Jones C	Kelly RF	Lane JW	Lindsay JJ	McGrory R	Moorwood L	Mosscrop E	Nesbitt W	Smelt L	Taylor D	Taylor W	Watson W	Weaver W
	Aug	28	BRADFORD CITY	1-4	Anderson	20000	9			5			1		7	4		8		10				11		2	3	6	
		30	Huddersfield Town	0-1		25000	9	1							7	4		8		10						2	3	5	6	11
	Sep	4	Bradford City	0-2		35000	9	1							8	4				10					7	2	3	5	6	11
19		6	HUDDERSFIELD TOWN	3-0	Kelly, Boyce, Nesbit	40000	9			5		10	1			4		8							7	2	3		6	11
16		11	MIDDLESBROUGH	2-1	Cross, Anderson	30000	9			5		10	1			4		8							7	2	3		6	11
15		18	Middlesbrough	0-0		20000	9			5		10	1			4		8							7	2	3		6	11
10		25	CHELSEA	4-0	Boyce. Cross, Kelly, Nesbit	30000	9			5		10	1			4		8							7	2	3		6	11
11	Oct	2	Chelsea	1-1	Anderson	40000	9			5		10	1			4		8			2			7		3		6	11
10		9	Bradford Park Avenue	3-1	Kelly 2, Dickinson (og)	12000	9			5		10	1			4		8			2			7		3		6	11
7		16	BRADFORD PARK AVE.	1-0	Anderson	30000	9			5		10	1			4	3	8			2			7				6	11
6		23	Tottenham Hotspur	2-1	Anderson 2	40000	9			5		8	1			4				10				7		2	3	6	11
4		30	TOTTENHAM HOTSPUR	2-0	Kelly, Cross	35000	9			5		10	1			4	3	8						7		2		6	11
4	Nov	6	Newcastle United	2-1	Boyce, Kelly	50000	9			5		10	1			4	3	8						7		2		6	11
2		13	NEWCASTLE UNITED	3-1	Kelly, Cross, Boyce	40000	9			5		10	1			4	3	8						7		2		6	11
1		20	Oldham Athletic	2-2	Anderson, Weaver	15000	9			5		10	1			4	3	8						7		2		6	11
1		27	OLDHAM ATHLETIC	7-1	Kelly 4, Cross 2, Boyce	20000	9			5		10	1			4	3	8						7		2		6	11
1	Dec	4	Liverpool	0-0		40000	9			5		10	1			4	3	8						7		2		6	11
1		11	LIVERPOOL	1-0	Weaver	30000	9			5		10	1			4	3	8						7		2		6	11
1		18	PRESTON NORTH END	2-0	Anderson 2	30000	9			5		10	1			4	3	8						7		2		6	11
1		25	SHEFFIELD UNITED	6-0	Anderson 4, Cross, Kelly	40000	9			5		10	1			4	3	8						7		2		6	11
1		27	Sheffield United	1-1	Kelly	50000	9			5		10	1			4	3	8						7		2		6	11
1	Jan	1	Preston North End	3-0	Cross, Kelly, Anderson	32000	9			5		10	1			4	3	8						7		2		6	11
1		15	BLACKBURN ROVERS	4-1	Cross 2, Kelly, Boyce	35000	9			5		10	1			4	3	8						7		2		6	11
1		22	Blackburn Rovers	3-1	Kelly, Mosscrop. Anderson	45000	9			5		10	1			4	3	8						11	7	2		6	
1	Feb	5	ASTON VILLA	7-1	Anderson 5, Watson, Lindsay	40000	9				5		1			4	3	8		10				11	7	2		6	
1		9	Aston Villa	0-0		40000	9			5			1			4	3	8		10				11	7	2		6	
1		12	DERBY COUNTY	2-1	Anderson, Lindsay	35000	9				5	4	10	1			3				8			11	7	2		6	
1		23	Derby County	0-0		16000		4		5		10	1	9			3	8							7	2		6	11
1		26	BOLTON WANDERERS	3-1	Kelly, Cross, Nesbitt	40000	9	4		5		10	1				3	8							7	2		6	11
1	Mar	5	Bolton Wanderers	1-1	Anderson	54809	9	4		5		10	1				3	8							7	2		6	11
1		12	ARSENAL	1-0	Watson	30000	9	4		5		10	1				3				8				7	2		6	11
1		19	Arsenal	1-1	Anderson	40000	9	4			5	10	1				3	8						11	7	2		6	
1		25	MANCHESTER UNITED	1-0	Cross	40000	9	4		5		10	1				3	8						11	7	2		6	
1		26	Manchester City	0-3		47500	9	4		5		10	1				3	8						11	7	2		6	
1		28	Manchester United	3-0	Boyce, Kelly, Anderson	30000	9	4		5		10	1				3	8						11	7	2		6	
1	Apr	2	MANCHESTER CITY	2-1	Nesbitt, Anderson	40000	9	4		5		10	1				3	8						11	7	2		6	
1		9	West Bromwich Albion	0-2		25000	9	4		5		10	1	11			3		8						7	2		6	
1		16	WEST BROMWICH ALB.	1-1	Kelly	30000	9	4		5		10	1				3	8						11	7	2		6	
1		23	Everton	1-1	Cross	55000	9	4		5		10	1				3	8						11	7	2		6	
1		30	EVERTON	1-1	Cross	22066	9	4		5		10	1				3	8						11	7	2		6	
1	May	2	Sunderland	0-1		20000	9	4		5		10	1				3	8							7	2		6	11
1		7	SUNDERLAND	2-2	Nesbitt, Kelly	25000	9	4		5		10						8					1	11	7	2	3	6	
					Apps		41	15	2	38	3	37	39	2	3	26	31	37	1	8	3	1	14	40	39	11	2	42	27
					Goals		25			7		14						20		2			1	5				2	2

One own goal

F.A. Cup

R1	Jan	8	Leicester City	7-3	Anderson 5, Cross, Kelly	29149	9			5		8	1			6	2	10						11	3			4	7
R2		29	QUEEN'S PARK RANGERS	4-2	Kelly 2, Anderson 2	41007	9			5		10	1			4	3	8						11	7	2		6	
R3	Feb	19	Hull City	0-3		26000				5		10	1	9			3	8						7	4	2		6	11

FA Charity Shield

	May	16	Tottenham Hotspur	0-2		18000	9	4		5		10	1					8						11	7	2	3	6	

At White Hart Lane

Players only: Back: Halley, Boyle, Dawson, Jones, Watson. Front: Nesbitt, Kelly, Anderson, Lindsay, Mosscrop, Smelt

Liverpool 1921/22

Anfield

			Opponent	Score	Scorers	Att	Bamber J	Beadles GH	Bromilow TG	Chambers H	Checkland FJ	Cunningham W	Forshaw R	Gilhespy TWC	Hopkin F	Lacey W	Lewis H	Longworth E	Lucas T	Matthews RW	McKinlay D	McNab JS	Mitchell FWG	Parry E	Scott E	Shone D	Wadsworth H	Wadsworth W
	Aug	27	Sunderland	0-3		24000	4		6	10			8		11	7		2			3				1	9		5
		31	MANCHESTER CITY	3-2	Matthews 2, Forshaw	27000	4		6	10			8		11	7			2	9	3				1			5
	Sep	3	SUNDERLAND	2-1	Matthews, Forshaw	40000	4		6	10			8		11	7			2	9	3				1			5
8		7	Manchester City	1-1	Chambers	25000	4		6	10			8		11	7			2	9	3				1			5
4		10	Sheffield United	1-0	Bromilow	25000			6	10	4		8		11	7			2	9	3				1			5
5		17	SHEFFIELD UNITED	1-1	Chambers	35000			6	10	4		8		11	7			2	9	3				1			5
2		24	Chelsea	1-0	Matthews	35000	10		6		4		8		11	7			2	9	3				1			5
4	Oct	1	CHELSEA	1-1	Forshaw	40000	10		6		4		8		11	7		2		9				3	1			5
5		8	Preston North End	1-1	Beadles	20000	10		6		4		8		11	7	9		2		3				1			5
2		15	PRESTON NORTH END	4-0	Chambers, Forshaw, Beadles, Lucas (p)	45000	9		6	10			8		11	7			2	3		4			1			5
2		22	Tottenham Hotspur	1-0	Beadles	35000	9		6	10			8		11						3	4	1				7	5
2		29	TOTTENHAM HOTSPUR	1-1	Lewis	40000			6				8		11	7	10		2		3	4			1	9		5
3	Nov	5	Everton	1-1	Shone	35000			6				8		11	7	10	2			3	4			1	9		5
2		12	EVERTON	1-1	Forshaw	50000			6				8		11	7	10	2			3	4			1	9		5
1		19	MIDDLESBROUGH	4-0	Shone 3, Lucas (p)	35000			6				8		11	7			2		3	4			1	9		5
2		26	Middlesbrough	1-3	Shone	25000			6				8		11	7	10		2		3	4			1	9		5
3	Dec	3	Aston Villa	1-1	Chambers	25000			6	10			8		11	7			2		3	4	1			9		5
2		10	ASTON VILLA	2-0	Shone, Forshaw	40000			6	10			8		11	7		2	3		5	4	1			9		
1		17	MANCHESTER UNITED	2-1	Lacey, Chambers	30000			6	10			8		11	7		2	3		5	4			1	9		
1		24	Manchester United	0-0		20000			6	10			8		11	7		2	3		5	4			1	9		
1		26	NEWCASTLE UNITED	1-0	Chambers	40000			6	10			8		11	7		2	3		5	4			1	9		
1		27	HUDDERSFIELD T	2-0	Chambers 2	35000			6	10			8		11	7			2		3	4			1	9		5
1		31	Bradford City	0-0		25000		9	6	10			8		11	7			2		3	4			1			5
1	Jan	2	Newcastle United	1-1	Forshaw	45000			6	10			8		11	7			2	3		4			1	9		5
1		14	BRADFORD CITY	2-1	Chambers, Forshaw	23000	4		6	10			8		11	7	9		2		3				1			5
1		21	Huddersfield Town	1-0	Chambers	10000			6	10			8		11	7	9		2		3	4			1			5
1	Feb	4	Birmingham	2-0	Chambers 2	10000			6	10			8		11	7	9	2	3						1			5
1		11	BIRMINGHAM	1-0	Forshaw	30000			6				8		11	7	10		2		3	4			1	9		5
1		25	ARSENAL	4-0	Forshaw 3, Turnbull (og)	35000			6	10			8		11	7	9		2		3	4			1			5
1	Mar	4	Blackburn Rovers	0-0		20000	4	9	6				8	7	11				2	3					1			5
1		11	BLACKBURN ROVERS	2-0	McKinlay, Forshaw	30000			6				8		11	7	9		2		3	4			1			5
1		18	BOLTON WANDERERS	0-2		30000	9					6	8		11	7	10	2			3	4			1			5
1		22	Arsenal	0-1		12000			6	10			8		11	7			2	3		4			1	9		5
1		25	Bolton Wanderers	3-1	Forshaw 2, Chambers	30000			6	10			8		11	7	9	2				4		3	1			5
1	Apr	1	OLDHAM ATHLETIC	2-0	Chambers, Gilhespy	25000	4		6	10			8	7	11		9	2						3	1			5
1		8	Oldham Athletic	0-4		10000	4			10			8		11	7	9	2			3			6	1			5
1		14	Burnley	1-1	Chambers	30000			6	10			8		11	7	9	2				4		3	1			5
1		15	CARDIFF CITY	5-1	Chambers 3, Bromilow, McNab	45000			6	10			8		11	7	9	2				4		3	1			5
1		17	BURNLEY	2-1	Chambers, Forshaw	60000			6	10			8		11	7	9	2				4		3	1			5
1		22	Cardiff City	0-2		37000	9		6	10			8		11	7			2	3		4			1			5
1		29	WEST BROMWICH ALB.	1-2	Beadles	25000	9	6	10				8		11	7			2	3		4			1			5
1	May	6	West Bromwich Albion	4-1	Beadles 2, Forshaw, McNab	15000	9	6	10				8		11	7			2		3	4			1			5

	Apps	8	11	40	32	5	1	42	2	42	39	19	26	27	7	29	29	3	7	39	15	1	38
	Goals		6	2	19			17	1		1	1		2	4	1	2				6			

One own goal

F.A. Cup

			Opponent	Score	Scorers	Att																						
R1	Jan	7	Sunderland	1-1	Forshaw	30000			6	10			8		11	7	9		2		3	4			1			5
rep		11	SUNDERLAND	5-0	Forshaw 2, Chambers 2, W Wadsworth	46000			6	10			8		11	7	9		2		3	4			1			5
R2		28	WEST BROMWICH ALB.	0-1		50000			6	10			8		11	7	9		2		3	4			1			5

FA Charity Shield

			Opponent	Score	Scorers	Att																						
	May	10	Huddersfield Town	0-1		20000		9	6	10			8		11	7			2		3	4			1			5

At Old Trafford

Players only: Back: Wadsworth, McNabb, Scott, Walsh, Bromilow. Front: Longworth, Gilhespy, Forshaw, Chambers, Hopkin

Liverpool 1922/23

Anfield

						Bamber J	Beadles GH	Bromilow TG	Chambers H	Forshaw R	Gilhespy TWC	Hopkin F	Johnson RK	Lacey W	Longworth E	Lucas T	McKinlay D	McNab JS	Pratt D	Sambrook JH	Scott E	Shone D	Wadsworth H	Wadsworth W
	Aug	26	ARSENAL	5-2	Johnson 3, Bromilow, Chambers	35000			6	10	8		11	9	7	2		3	4			1			5
		30	Sunderland	0-1		30000			6	10	8		11	9	7	2		3	4			1			5
	Sep	2	Arsenal	0-1		25000		11	6	10	8			9	7	2		3	4			1			5
9		6	SUNDERLAND	5-1	* see below	30000			6	10	8			9	7	2		3	4			1		11	5
6		9	Preston North End	3-1	Johnson, W Wadsworth, Chambers	37000			6	10	8		11	9	7	2		3	4			1			5
1		16	PRESTON NORTH END	5-2	Forshaw 3, Chambers, Bromilow	40000			6	10	8		11	9	7	2		3	4			1			5
1		23	BURNLEY	3-0	Forshaw 2, Chambers	45000			6	10	8		11	9	7	2		3	4			1			5
1		30	Burnley	0-2		25000			6	10	8		11		7	2		3	4			1	9		5
1	Oct	7	EVERTON	5-1	Chambers 3, McNab, Bromilow	54368			6	10	8		11	9	7	2		3	4			1			5
1		14	Everton	1-0	Johnson	58000			6	10	8		11	9	7	2		3	4			1			5
1		21	CARDIFF CITY	3-1	Gilhespy, Forshaw, W Wadsworth	35000		10	6		8	7	11	9		2		3	4			1			5
1		28	Cardiff City	0-3		40000			6	10	8	7	11	9		2		3	4			1			5
1	Nov	4	Tottenham Hotspur	4-2	Chambers 2, Forshaw, Gilhespy	40000			6	10	8	7	11	9		2		3	4			1			5
1		11	TOTTENHAM HOTSPUR	0-0		35000			6	10	8	7	11	9		2		3	4			1			5
1		18	ASTON VILLA	3-0	McKinlay, Chambers, Johnson	30000			6	10	8	7	11	9		2		3	4			1			5
1		25	Aston Villa	1-0	Chambers	40000			6	10	8		11	9		2		3	4			1		7	5
1	Dec	2	NEWCASTLE UNITED	0-2		35000			6	10	8		11	9		2		3	4			1		7	5
1		9	Newcastle United	1-0	Chambers	35000			6	10	8	7	11	9		2		3	4			1			5
1		16	NOTTM. FOREST	2-1	Johnson, McKinlay	20000			6	10	8	7	11	9		2		3	4			1			5
1		23	Nottingham Forest	3-1	Forshaw 2, Johnson	20000			6	10	8	7	11	9		2		3	4			1			5
1		25	Oldham Athletic	2-0	McKinlay, Johnson	20776	4		6	10	8	7	11	9		2		3				1			5
1		26	OLDHAM ATHLETIC	2-1	McKinlay, Forshaw	30000	9		6	10	8	7	11			2		3	4			1			5
1		30	Chelsea	0-0		40000	4		6		8		11		7	2		3	4		9	1			5
1	Jan	6	CHELSEA	1-0	Lacey	28000			6	10	8		11		7	2		3	4		9	1			5
1		20	Middlesbrough	2-0	Chambers, Johnson	25000			6	10	8		11	9	7	2		3	4			1			5
1		27	MIDDLESBROUGH	2-0	Chambers, Johnson	40000			6	10	8		11	9	7	2		3	4			1			5
1	Feb	7	WEST BROMWICH ALB.	2-0	Forshaw, Johnson	30000			6	10	8		11	9	7	2		3	4			1			5
1		10	West Bromwich Albion	0-0		15000			6	10	8		11	9	7	2		3	4			1			5
1		17	BLACKBURN ROVERS	3-0	Forshaw 3	30000		10			8		11	9	7	2		3	4	6		1			5
1	Mar	3	BOLTON WANDERERS	3-0	Forshaw, Johnson, Hopkin	20000			6	10	8		11	9	7	2		3	4			1			5
1		12	Blackburn Rovers	0-1		8000			6	10	8		11	9	7	2		3	4			1			5
1		17	Manchester City	0-1		32000	4		6	10	8		11	9	7	2		3		5		1			
1		24	MANCHESTER CITY	2-0	Chambers, Forshaw	25000			6	10	8		11	9	7	2		3	4	5		1			
1		30	SHEFFIELD UNITED	2-1	Chambers 2	45000			6	10	8		11	9	7	2		3	4	5		1			
1		31	Birmingham	1-0	Chambers	35000			6	10	8		11	9	7	2		3	4			1			5
1	Apr	2	Sheffield United	1-4	Forshaw	35000			6	10	8		11	9	7	2		3	4	5		1			
1		7	BIRMINGHAM	0-0		28000			6	10	8		11	9	7	2		3	4			1			5
1		14	Huddersfield Town	0-0		15000		10	6		8		11	9	7		2	3	4			1			5
1		18	Bolton Wanderers	1-1	Forshaw	15000			6	10	8		11	9	7	2		3	4			1			5
1		21	HUDDERSFIELD T	1-1	Chambers	35000			6	9	8		11		7	2		10	4	3		1			5
1		28	Stoke	0-0		18000			6	10	8		11	9	7	2		3	4			1			5
1	May	5	STOKE	1-0	Chambers	20000			6	10	8		11	9	7	2		3	4			1			5

Scorers in game 4: Chambers 2, Forshaw, Johnson, McKinlay

					Apps	4	4	41	39	42	10	40	37	30	41	1	42	39	7	2	42	1	3	37
					Goals			3	22	19	2	1	14	1			5	1						2

F.A. Cup

R1	Jan	13	ARSENAL	0-0		37000			6	10	8		11	9	7	2		3	4			1			5
rep		17	Arsenal	4-1	Chambers 2, Johnson, McKinlay (p)	40000			6	10	8		11	9	7	2		3	4			1			5
R2	Feb	3	Wolverhampton Wan.	2-0	Johnson, Forshaw	40079			6	10	8		11	9	7	2		3	4			1			5
R3		24	SHEFFIELD UNITED	1-2	Chambers	51859			6	10	8		11	9	7	2		3	4			1			5

Back: Connell (trainer), Chambers, McNab, Scott, Waddsworth, Bromilow, Forshaw. Seated: Ashworth (manager), Lacey, Longworth, McKinlay, Lucas, Hopkin, Patterson (secretary). Front: Shone, Lewis

Huddersfield Town 1923/24

Leeds Road

						Barkas E	Boot LGW	Brown G	Cawthorne H	Cook GW	Cowell W	Goodall FR	Islip E	Johnstone WG	Richardson E	Richardson GEH	Shaw GE	Smith Aw	Smith WH	Steele DM	Stephenson C	Taylor EH	Wadsworth SJ	Walter JD	Watson W	Wilson C	Wilson T
	Aug	25	MIDDLESBROUGH	1-0	C Wilson	25000	2							8			7		4	11		10		3		6	9	5
		27	Preston North End	3-1	WH Smith, C Wilson, Stephenson	18500	2				8								4	11		10	1	3	7	6	9	5
	Sep	1	Middlesbrough	0-2		20000	2				8		3				7		4	11		10	1			6	9	5
2		4	PRESTON NORTH END	4-0	C Wilson 2, WH Smith, Stephenson	20000	2				7	1			8				4	11		10		3		6	9	5
6		8	Notts County	0-1		20000	2				7	1		8					4	11		10		3		6	9	5
8		15	NOTTS COUNTY	0-0		15000	2							8					4	11		10	1	3	7	6	9	5
9		22	Everton	1-1	Brown	40000	2		9		8								4	11		10	1	3	7	6		5
4		29	EVERTON	2-0	Brown, Stephenson	15000	2		9	4	8									11		10	1	3	7	6		5
4	Oct	6	West Bromwich Albion	4-2	WH Smith 2, Cook 2	25000	2		9	4	8									11		10	1	3	7	6		5
5		13	WEST BROMWICH ALB.	0-0		15000	2		9		8									11	4	10	1	3	7	6		5
3		20	Birmingham	1-0	WH Smith	20000	2	1			8		3							11	4	10			7	6	9	5
1		27	BIRMINGHAM	1-0	Stephenson	10000	2				8								5	11	4	10	1	3	7	6	9	
2	Nov	3	Liverpool	1-1	Stephenson	40000	2				8									11	4	10	1	3	7	6	9	5
2		10	LIVERPOOL	3-1	Cook 2, H Wadsworth (og)	12000	2				8									11	4	10	1	3	7	6	9	5
2		17	Bolton Wanderers	1-3	C Wilson	17630	2				8									11	4	10	1	3	7	6	9	5
2		24	BOLTON WANDERERS	1-0	Cook	15000					8	2								11	4	10	1	3	7	6	9	5
3	Dec	1	Sunderland	1-2	C Wilson	25000					8	2								11	4	10	1	3	7	6	9	5
3		8	SUNDERLAND	3-2	C Wilson 2, WH Smith	17000					8	2								11	4	10	1	3	7	6	9	5
2		15	Arsenal	3-1	C Wilson 3	30000					8	2								11	4	10	1	3	7	6	9	5
2		22	ARSENAL	6-1	Cook, C Wilson 3, Stephenson 2	15000					8	2								11	4	10	1	3	7	6	9	5
3		25	Tottenham Hotspur	0-1		40000					8	2								11	4	10	1	3	7	6	9	5
3		26	TOTTENHAM HOTSPUR	2-1	WH Smith 2	30000					8	2								11	4	10	1	3	7	6	9	5
3		29	Blackburn Rovers	0-1		20000			9		8	2		10						11	4		1	3	7	6		5
4	Jan	5	BLACKBURN ROVERS	1-0	Stephenson	12000			9			2		8	11						4	10	1	3	7	6		5
4		19	CHELSEA	0-1		10000			9	7		2		8						11	4	10	1	3		6		5
4		26	Chelsea	1-0	Stephenson	30000	2		9	4				8						11		10	1	3	7	6		5
4	Feb	9	Newcastle United	1-0	Stephenson	30000				4			2	8						11		10	1	3	7	6	9	5
4		16	WEST HAM UNITED	1-1	WH Smith	10000	2							8						11	4	10	1	3	7	6	9	5
4		27	NEWCASTLE UNITED	1-1	Stephenson	6000			8									2		11	4	10	1	3	7	6	9	5
3	Mar	1	CARDIFF CITY	2-0	Brown 2	25000	2		8	4								3		11	7	10	1			6	9	5
4		15	Sheffield United	1-0	Brown	24000	2	1	8	4								3		11	7	10				6	9	5
3		22	SHEFFIELD UNITED	1-0	C Wilson	18000		1	8	4								2		11	7	10		3		6	9	5
1		27	West Ham United	3-2	Smith W, C Wilson 2	15000		1	8	4								2		11	7	10		3		6	9	5
3	Apr	5	ASTON VILLA	1-0	WH Smith (p)	25000			8	4								2		11	7	10	1	3		6	9	5
2		12	MANCHESTER CITY	1-1	Brown	10000	2	1	8	4			3							11	7	10				6	9	5
1		14	Cardiff City	0-0		30000			8	2	10									11	4		1	3	7	6	9	5
2		18	Burnley	1-1	Brown	25000			8	4								2		11	7	10	1	3		6	9	5
2		19	Manchester City	1-1	C Wilson	40000			8	4						11		2			7	10	1	3		6	9	5
1		22	BURNLEY	1-0	WH Smith	33000			8	2							7			11	4	10	1	3		6	9	5
2		26	Nottingham Forest	1-1	Cook	10000			9	2	8					11					4	10	1	3	7	6		5
2		30	Aston Villa	1-3	WH Smith	14000			9	4				8				2		11	7	10	1	3		6		5
1	May	3	NOTTM. FOREST	3-0	Cook 2, Brown	20000	2		8		9					7				11	4	10	1	3		6		5
						Apps	21	5	22	16	25	2	14	3	8	5	2	9	8	39	31	40	35	37	26	42	31	41
						Goals			8		9									13		11					18	

One own goal

F.A. Cup

R1	Jan	12	BIRMINGHAM	1-0	Johnstone	30924			9		7		2	8						11	4	10	1	3		6		5
R2	Feb	2	Manchester United	3-0	C Wilson 2, Stephenson	66678	2							8						11	4	10	1	3	7	6	9	5
R3		23	Burnley	0-1		54775	2							8						11	4	10	1	3	7	6	9	5

Back: Cawthorne, T Wilson, Taylor, Barkas, Wadsworth. Front: Walter, Cook, Brown, Stephenson, WH Smith, Watson

Huddersfield Town 1924/25

Leeds Road

						Barkas E	Binks S	Boot LGW	Brown G	Cawthorne H	Cook GW	Goodall FR	Mercer W	Richardson E	Shaw GE	Smith N	Smith WH	Spence MB	Steele DM	Stephenson C	Taylor EH	Wadsworth SJ	Walter JD	Watson W	Williams JJ	Wilson C	Wilson T
	Aug	30	Newcastle United	3-1	Brown, C Wilson, Stephenson	45000				8		2					11	4		10	1	3		6	7	9	5
	Sep	2	NOTTM. FOREST	3-0	C Wilson 3	13500				8		10	2				11	4			1	3		6	7	9	5
		6	SHEFFIELD UNITED	2-1	C Wilson, Brown	15000				8			2				11	4		10	1	3		6	7	9	5
1		8	Nottingham Forest	1-0	Cook	10000				8		10	2				11	4			1	3		6	7	9	5
1		13	West Ham United	0-0		30000				8		10	2	11				4			1	3		6	7	9	5
1		20	BLACKBURN ROVERS	0-0		18000				8		10	2				11	4			1	3		6	7	9	5
1		27	Leeds United	1-1	WH Smith	42000				8		10	2				11	4			1	3		6	7	9	5
1	Oct	4	Aston Villa	1-1	Cook	30000				8		10	2				11	4			1	3		6	7	9	5
1		11	ARSENAL	4-0	WH Smith, Cook, C Wilson, Brown	15000				8	3	10	2				11	5	4		1			6	7	9	
1		18	Manchester City	1-1	Brown	58000				8		10	2				11	4			1	3		6	7	9	5
2		25	BIRMINGHAM	0-1		18000			1	8		9	2				11		4	10		3		6	7		5
5	Nov	1	West Bromwich Albion	0-1		10000			1	8		9	2				11		4	10		3		6	7		5
9		8	TOTTENHAM HOTSPUR	1-2	C Wilson	18000			1			8	2			6	11		4	10		3			7	9	5
3		12	Liverpool	3-2	WH Smith, Cook, C Wilson	30000	2		1	8							11	4		10		3		6	7	9	5
5		15	Bolton Wanderers	0-1		32291			1	8			2				11	4		10		3		6	7	9	5
7		22	NOTTS COUNTY	0-0		10000				8		2	1				11		4	10		3		6	7	9	5
5		29	Everton	2-0	Cook, C Wilson	30000				8		2	1				11		4	10		3		6	7	9	5
2	Dec	6	SUNDERLAND	4-0	C Wilson 2, Stephenson, WH Smith	15000				8		2	1				11		4	10		3		6	7	9	5
4		13	Cardiff City	2-2	Cook 2	25000				8		2	1				11		4	10		3		6	7	9	5
2		20	PRESTON NORTH END	1-0	C Wilson	15000			10	8		2	1				11		4			3		6	7	9	5
2		25	Burnley	5-1	C Wilson 4, Brown	23000			10	8		2	1				11		4			3		6	7	9	5
2		26	BURNLEY	2-0	WH Smith, Cook	25000				8		2	1				11		4	10		3		6	7	9	5
2		27	NEWCASTLE UNITED	0-0		10000				8			2	1		3	11		4	10				6	7	9	5
2	Jan	3	Sheffield United	1-1	WH Smith	25000						8	2	1		3	11		4	10				6	7	9	5
3		17	WEST HAM UNITED	1-2	Cook	14000		9				8	2	1			11		4	10		3	7	6			5
3		24	Blackburn Rovers	3-2	Brown 2, Walter	12000		9		8			2	1		3	11		4	10			7	6			5
2		31	LEEDS UNITED	2-0	WH Smith, Brown	8000				8			2	1		3	11		4	10			7	6		9	5
1	Feb	7	ASTON VILLA	4-1	Brown 3, Stephenson	15000				8			2	1		3	11		4	10			7	6		9	5
2		14	Arsenal	5-0	Brown, Stephenson, C Wilson 3	20000				8			2	1		3	11		4	10			7	6		9	5
1		21	MANCHESTER CITY	1-1	WH Smith	18000				8			2	1		3	11		4	10			7	6		9	5
1		28	Birmingham	1-0	Brown	12000				8			2	1			11		4	10		3		6	7	9	5
1	Mar	11	WEST BROMWICH ALB.	1-1	Brown	15000				8			2	1			11		4	10		3		6	7	9	5
1		14	Tottenham Hotspur	2-1	Stephenson, Brown	35000				8			2	1			11	5	4	10		3		6	7	9	
1		21	BOLTON WANDERERS	0-0		30000				8			2	1			11		4	10		3		6	7	9	5
2	Apr	4	EVERTON	2-0	C Wilson 2 (1p)	15000				8			2	1		3	11		4	10				6	7	9	5
1		10	Bury	1-0	WH Smith	30000				8			2	1			11		4	10		3		6	7	9	5
1		11	Sunderland	1-1	Brown	30000				8			2	1			11		4	10		3		6	7	9	5
1		14	BURY	2-0	Brown, C Wilson	30000				8		10	2	1			11		4			3	7	6		9	5
1		18	CARDIFF CITY	0-0		16000				8		10		1		2	11		4			3		6	7	9	5
1		25	Preston North End	4-1	C Wilson, Brown 3	10000			10	8				1		2	11		4			3		6	7	9	5
1		29	Notts County	1-1	C Wilson	8000				8			2	1			11		4	10		3		6	7	9	5
1	May	2	LIVERPOOL	1-1	Cawthorne	20000				8	4			1		2	11			10		3		6	7	9	5
					Apps		1	2	5	32	2	25	38	27	1	11	1	41	4	39	29	10	33	7	41	35	38	40
					Goals					20	1	9					9			5			1			24	

F.A. Cup

| R1 | Jan | 10 | Bolton Wanderers | 0-3 | | 50512 | | | | 8 | 2 | 1 | | | | | 11 | | 4 | 10 | | 3 | | 6 | 7 | 9 | 5 |

A 1923/24 group: Wilson, A Smith, Shaw, Taylor, Wadsworth, Cook, ano, Watson. Front: Steele, Johnston, Stevenson, Brown, WH Smith, Cawthorne

70

Huddersfield Town 1925/26

Leeds Road

						Barkas E	Binks S	Brown G	Cawthorne H	Cook GW	Dennis H	Devlin WA	Goodall FR	Hobson RGE	Jackson AS	Mercer W	Raw H	Shaw GE	Smith AWT	Smith WH	Spence MB	Steele DM	Stephenson C	Taylor EH	Wadsworth SJ	Watson W	Williams J	Wilson C	Wilson T
	Aug	29	WEST BROMWICH ALB.	1-1	Williams	21975			8					2		7							4	10	1	3	6	11	9	5
	Sep	5	Sheffield United	3-2	C Wilson, Jackson, Brown	23013	2		8							7							4	10	1	3	6	11	9	5
		8	BURY	2-1	Binks, Brown	11933	2	9	8							7							4	10	1	3	6	11		5
4		12	CARDIFF CITY	1-1	Stephenson	19033	2	9	8							7							4	10	1	3	6	11		5
4		16	Birmingham	3-1	Cook 2, Brown	16320	2		9		8					7							4	10	1	3	6	11		5
4		19	Tottenham Hotspur	5-5	Jackson 3, Cook, Brown	20880	2		9		8					7							4	10	1	3	6	11		5
5		26	MANCHESTER CITY	2-2	Cook, Williams	19541	2		9		8					7							4	10	1	3	6	11		5
3	Oct	3	Everton	3-2	Brown 3	35665	2		9		8					7	1						4	10		3	6	11		5
3		10	BURNLEY	2-1	Brown 2	18963	2		9		8					7	1						4	10		3	6	11		5
2		17	Leeds United	4-0	Cook 2, Williams, Brown	33008	2		9		8					7	1		3				4	10			6	11		5
4		24	NEWCASTLE UNITED	0-1		18285	2		9		8					7	1		3				4	10			6	11		5
3		31	Manchester United	1-1	Cook	37213	2		9		8							1	3		11		4	10			6	7		5
7	Nov	14	Aston Villa	0-3		33401			9		8			2		7	1		3		11		4	10			6			5
6		21	LEICESTER CITY	3-0	Brown 2, Williams	14386			8					2		9	1				11		4	10		3	6	7		5
5		25	LIVERPOOL	0-0		7285			8					2		9	1				11		4	10		3	6	7		5
5		28	West Ham United	3-2	Jackson 2, Brown	13914			8					2		9	1				11		4	10		3	6	7		5
4	Dec	5	ARSENAL	2-2	Jackson 2	22115			8	6				2		9	1				11		4	10		3		7		5
4		12	Bolton Wanderers	1-6	Brown	25823			9	6	8			2		7	1						4	10		3		11		5
3		19	NOTTS COUNTY	2-0	C Wilson (p), Brown	7972			8	4				2		7								10	1	3	6	11	9	5
3		26	SUNDERLAND	1-1	Brown	27136			8	4				2		7								10	1	3	6	11	9	5
3		28	BIRMINGHAM	4-1	WH Smith,Stephenson,Brown,Jackson	16565			8	4	9			2		7					11			10	1	3	6			5
2	Jan	2	West Bromwich Albion	2-2	Williams, Brown	22435			8	4	10			2		9					11				1	3	6	7		5
2		16	SHEFFIELD UNITED	4-1	Goodall (p), Cook, Brown, WH Smith	16181			9	4	8			2		7					11			10	1	3	6			5
3		20	Sunderland	1-4	Brown	27833			9	4	8			2		7					11			10	1	3	6			5
3		23	Cardiff City	2-1	Cook, Jackson	13049			9	4	10			2		8					11				1	3	6	7		5
1	Feb	6	Manchester City	5-1	Brown 3, Goodall (p), WH Smith	34645			9		10			2	4	7		8			11				1	3	6			5
2		11	Blackburn Rovers	1-2	Brown	21437			9		10			2	4	7		8			11	5			1	3	6			
1		13	EVERTON	3-0	Brown 2, Raitt (og)	17278			9	4	8			2		7					11			10	1	3	6			5
1		20	Burnley	1-1	WH Smith	21482			9	4	8			2		7					11			10	1	3	6			5
1		27	LEEDS UNITED	3-1	Cook, Brown, Williams	26248			9	4	8			2							11			10	1	3	6	7		5
1	Mar	3	TOTTENHAM HOTSPUR	2-1	Brown 2	13005			9	4	10			2		8					11				1	3	6	7		5
1		6	Newcastle United	2-0	Brown 2	56496			8	4			9	2		7					11			10	1	3	6			5
1		13	MANCHESTER UNITED	5-0	Cook 2, Devlin 2, WH Smith	27842	2			4	8		9			7					11			10	1	3	6			5
1		20	Liverpool	2-1	Devlin, Stephenson	35255			8	4			9	2		7					11			10	1	3	6			5
1		27	ASTON VILLA	5-1	Jackson 2, Brown 2, Cook	28442			9	4	8			2		7					11			10	1	3	6			5
1	Apr	3	Leicester City	0-2		29903			9	4	8			2		7					11			10	1	3	6			5
1		5	Bury	0-0		27144			9	4	8			2		7					11			10	1	3	6			5
1		6	BLACKBURN ROVERS	3-1	Brown 2, AW Smith	34821			8	4	10			2		7				9	11				1	3	6			5
1		10	WEST HAM UNITED	2-1	Jackson 2	21116			9	4	8			2		7					11			10	1	3	6			5
1		12	BOLTON WANDERERS	3-0	WH Smith, Jackson, Stephenson	20829			8	4	9			2		7					11			10	1	3	6			5
1		17	Arsenal	1-3	Devlin	34110	2		8	4		7	9			1					11			10		3	6			5
1	May	1	Notts County	2-4	Cook, Jackson	4715			8	4	9			2		7	1				11			10		3	6			5
					Apps		13	2	41	24	29	1	4	29	2	39	13	2	4	1	28	1	18	36	29	38	40	23	4	41
					Goals			1	35		14		4	2		16				1	6			4				6	2	

One own goal

F.A. Cup

R3	Jan	9	Charlton Athletic	1-0	Goodall (p)	21184			8	4	9			2		7					11			10	1	3	6			5
R4		30	Manchester City	0-4		74799	2		9	4				8							11			10	1	3	6	7		5

Back: Steele, Barkas, Taylor, Wadsworth, Watson. Front: Jackson, Cook, Brown, Stephenson, Williams, T Wilson

Newcastle United 1926/27

St James' Park

							Boyd JM	Chandler A	Clark JR	Curry T	Gallacher HR	Gibson WM	Hampson W	Harris J	Hudspeth FC	Loughlin J	Low J	Maitland AE	McDonald TH	McKay R	MacKenzie RR	Mooney EP	Park O	Seymour GS	Spencer CW	Urwin T	Wilson W
	Aug	28	ASTON VILLA	4-0	Gallacher 4	36057		2	8		9	6			3				10		4	5		11		7	1
	Sep	1	BURNLEY	1-5	Hudspeth (p)	33069		2	8		9	6			3				10		4	5		11		7	1
		4	Bolton Wanderers	1-2	Seymour	25049		2	8	6					3	9			10		4	5		11		7	1
14		6	Burnley	3-3	Gallacher, McDonald, Seymour	25374			8		9	6			2			3	10		4			11	5	7	1
11		11	MANCHESTER UNITED	4-2	McDonald 2, Seymour, Gallacher	28050			8		9	6			2			3	10		4			11	5	7	1
12		18	Derby County	1-1	Crilly (og)	26306		2	8		9	6			3				10		4			11	5	7	1
13		20	Cardiff City	1-1	Urwin	14048	7				9	6			3			2	10		4			11	5	8	1
7		25	SHEFFIELD UNITED	2-0	Gallacher 2	27611					9	6			3	8		2	10		4			11	5	7	1
8	Oct	2	Arsenal	2-2	Clark, Seymour	38842			8		9	6			3			2	10		4			11	5	7	1
9		9	LIVERPOOL	1-0	Gallacher	21515			8		9			6	3			2	10		4		5	11		7	1
6		16	Everton	3-1	Clark, Gallacher, McDonald	41746			8		9			6	3			2	10		4			11	5	7	1
2		23	BLACKBURN ROVERS	6-1	Seymour 3, Clark, McDonald, MacKenzie	27145			8		9	6			3			2	10		4			11	5	7	1
5		30	Sunderland	0-2		31152			8			6			3	9		2	10		4			11	5	7	1
2	Nov	6	WEST BROMWICH ALB.	5-2	McKay 3, Gallacher 2	28864					9	6			3			2	10	8	4			11	5	7	1
5		13	Bury	2-3	Gallacher, Hudspeth (p)	19973					9	6			3			2	10	8	4			11	5	7	1
3		20	BIRMINGHAM	5-1	Gallacher,Hudspeth,McDonald,McKay,Seymour	30056					9	6			3			2	10	8	4			11	5	7	1
2		27	Tottenham Hotspur	3-1	Gallacher 3	33325					9	6		4	3			2	10	8				11	5	7	1
1	Dec	4	WEST HAM UNITED	2-0	Gallacher, Seymour	35079					9	6		4	3			2	10	8				11	5	7	1
4		11	Sheffield Wednesday	2-3	Gallacher, McKay	38422					9	6		4	3			2	10	8				11	5	7	1
3		18	LEICESTER CITY	1-1	Seymour	35702	7				9	6			3			2	10	8	4			11	5		1
2		25	CARDIFF CITY	5-0	McDonald 3, Gallacher 2	36250					9	6			3			2	10	8	4			11	5	7	1
2		27	Leeds United	2-1	Seymour, Urwin	48590					9	6		4	3			2	10	8			5	11		7	1
1	Jan	1	LEEDS UNITED	1-0	Gallacher	51343				6	9				3			2	10	8	4		5	11		7	1
1		15	Aston Villa	2-1	Gallacher , McDonald	46723					9	6			3			2	10	8	4			11	5	7	1
1		22	BOLTON WANDERERS	1-0	McKay	57431					9	6			3			2	10	8	4			11	5	7	1
1	Feb	5	DERBY COUNTY	3-0	Gallacher, McDonald, Urwin	30849					9	6			3			2	10	8	4			11	5	7	1
1		9	Manchester United	1-3	McDonald	25402					9	6			3			2	10	8	4			11	5	7	1
1		12	Sheffield United	1-2	Seymour	31633					9	6			3	10		2		8	4			11	5	7	1
1		26	Liverpool	2-1	Seymour 2	34493		9				6			3			2	10	8	4			11	5	7	1
1	Mar	5	EVERTON	7-3	Gallacher 3,McDonald,McKay,MacKenzie,Seymour	40202					9	6			3			2	10	8	4			11	5	7	1
1		12	Blackburn Rovers	2-1	Gallacher 2	35334					9	6			3			2	10	8	4			11	5	7	1
1		19	SUNDERLAND	1-0	Gallacher	67067					9	6			3		7	2	10	8	4			11	5	7	1
1		26	West Bromwich Albion	2-4	Gallacher, McDonald	21046					9	6			3			2	10	8	4		5	11		7	1
1	Apr	2	BURY	3-1	Clark, McDonald, McKay	26057		9				6			3			2	10	8	4			11	5	7	1
1		6	ARSENAL	6-1	Gallacher 3, McKay 2, McDonald	33635					9	6	2		3				10	8	4			11	5	7	1
1		9	Birmingham	0-2		27918				6	9		2		3				10	8	4			11	5	7	1
1		15	HUDDERSFIELD T	1-0	Gallacher	60149					9	6			3			2	10	8	4			11	5	7	1
1		16	TOTTENHAM HOTSPUR	3-2	Seymour 2, Urwin	32151			8		9			6	3			2	10		4			11	5	7	1
1		19	Huddersfield Town	0-1		44636			8		9			6	3			2	10		4			11	5	7	1
1		23	West Ham United	1-1	Seymour	29722			8		9			6	3			2	10		4			11	5	7	1
1		30	SHEFFIELD WEDNESDAY	2-1	Gallacher 2	28421			8	6	9				3			2	10		4			11	5	7	1
1	May	7	Leicester City	1-2	Low	26621				6	9				3		7	2	10	8	4		5	11			1
						Apps	2	4	17	5	38	32	2	9	42	4	2	36	41	25	38	3	5	42	34	39	42
						Goals			4		36				3		1		17	10	2			18		4	

One own goal

F.A. Cup

R3	Jan	8	NOTTS COUNTY	8-1	Gallacher 3, McDonald 3, Seymour, Urwin	32564					9	6			3			2	10	8	4			11	5	7	1
R4		29	Corinthians	3-1	McDonald 2, McKay	56338					9	6			3			2	10	8	4			11	5	7	1
R5	Feb	19	Southampton	1-2	McDonald (p)	21406					9	6			3			2	10	8	4			11	5	7	1

Players only: Back: Lee, Burns, Davis, Mathison, Curry. Next to back: Patten, Boyd, Bradley, Carlton, Wilkinson, Park, Lang. Next to front: Barber, Little, Clarke, Spencer, Wilson, Harris, T Curry, Gillespie. Front: Urwin, McKay, MacKenzie, Hudspeth, Gallacher, McDonald, Maitland, Low

Everton 1927/28

Goodison Park

						Bain D	Brown W	Cresswell W	Critchley E	Davies AL	Dean WR	Dominy AA	Easton WC	Forshaw R	Hardy HJ	Hart H	Houghton H	Irvine RW	Kelly J	Martin GS	Meston SW	O'Donnell J	Raitt D	Rooney WF	Taylor EH	Troup A	Virr AE	Weldon A	White TA
	Aug	27	SHEFFIELD WEDNESDAY	4-0	Dean, Forshaw, Troup, Welson	39485			2			9			8		5		7	4			3			1	11	6	10	
	Sep	3	Middlesbrough	2-4	Critchley, Dean	30229			2	7		9			8		5			4			3			1	11	6	10	
		5	Bolton Wanderers	1-1	Dean	18734				7		9			8		5			4			3	2		1	11	6	10	
8		10	BIRMINGHAM	5-2	Dean 2, Troup 2, Forshaw	37386				7		9			8		5			4			3	2		1	11	6	10	
5		14	BOLTON WANDERERS	2-2	Dean, Forshaw	22726			2	7		9			8		5			4			3			1	11	6	10	
7		17	Newcastle United	2-2	Dean 2	50359			2	7		9			8		5			4			3			1	11	6	10	
7		24	HUDDERSFIELD T	2-2	Dean 2	37269			2	7		9			8		5			4			3			1	11	6	10	
5	Oct	1	Tottenham Hotspur	3-1	Dean 2, Troup	7718			2	7		9			8		5			4			3			1	11	6	10	
3		8	MANCHESTER UNITED	5-2	Dean 5	40080			2	7		9			8		5			4			3			1	11	6	10	
3		15	LIVERPOOL	1-1	Troup	65729			2	7		9			8		5			4			3			1	11	6	10	
2		22	WEST HAM UNITED	7-0	* See below	20151			2	7					8		5			4			3			1	11	6	10	9
1		29	Portsmouth	3-1	Dean 3	23326			2	7		9			8		5			4			3			1	11	6	10	
1	Nov	5	LEICESTER CITY	7-1	Dean 3, Weldon 2, Critchley, Troup	30392	4		2	7		9			8		5						3			1	11	6	10	
1		12	Derby County	3-0	Dean 2, Weldon	21590			2	7	1	9			8		5			4			3				11	6	10	
1		19	SUNDERLAND	0-1		35993			2	7	1	9			8		5			4			3				11	6	10	
1		26	Bury	3-2	Dean 2, Critchley	24727			2	7		9			8		5			10	4		3			1	11	6	10	
1	Dec	3	SHEFFIELD UNITED	0-0		36141			2	7		9			8		5			4			3			1	11	6	10	
1		10	Aston Villa	3-2	Dean 3	40353			2	7		9			8		5			4			3		6	1	11		10	
1		17	BURNLEY	4-1	Critchley, Forshaw, Kelly, Troup	30180			2	7		9			8		5			4			3			1	11	6	10	
1		24	Arsenal	2-3	Dean, Troup	27995			2	7		9			8		5			4			3			1	11	6	10	
1		26	CARDIFF CITY	2-1	Dean 2	56305				7		9			8		5			4			3	2		1	11	6	10	
1		27	Cardiff City	0-2		25387				7		9					5		8	4			3	2	6	1	11	5	10	
1		31	Sheffield Wednesday	2-1	Dean 2	18354				7		9					5		8	4			3	2		1	11	6	10	
1	Jan	2	Blackburn Rovers	2-4	Dean 2	39300				7		9					5		8	4			3	2		1	11	6	10	
1		7	MIDDLESBROUGH	3-1	Dean 2, Irvine	46432			2	7		9					5		8	4			3		6	1	11		10	
1		21	Birmingham	2-2	Irvine 2	33675			2	7		9	10				5		8	4			3		6	1	11			
1	Feb	4	Huddersfield Town	1-4	Dean	50012			2	7		9					5		8	4			3			1	11	6	10	
1		11	TOTTENHAM HOTSPUR	2-5	Troup 2	27149		4	2	7		9					5		8				3			1	11	6	10	
1		25	Liverpool	3-3	Dean 3	55361			2	7		9			8	1	5			4			3				11	6	10	
1	Mar	3	West Ham United	0-0		31997			2	7		9			8	1	5			4			3				11	6	10	
2		10	PORTSMOUTH	0-0		29803			2	7			8			1	5	10		4			3				11	6	9	
2		14	Manchester United	0-1		25667			2	7			8			1	5			4			3				11	6	10	
2		17	Leicester City	0-1		26625			2	7		9				1	5			4	8		3				11	6	10	
2		24	DERBY COUNTY	2-2	Dean 2	28541	8		2	7	1	9					5			4	10		3				11	6		
2		31	Sunderland	2-0	Easton, Virr	15407	9		2	7	1		8				5			4	10		3				11	6		
2	Apr	6	BLACKBURN ROVERS	4-1	Dean 2, Hart, Martin	48521			2	7	1	9					5			4	8		3				11	6	10	
1		7	BURY	1-1	Dean	37597			2	7		9				1	5			4	8		3				11	6	10	
2		14	Sheffield United	3-1	Dean 2, Martin	26252			2		1	9					5			4	8	7	3				11	6	10	
1		18	NEWCASTLE UNITED	3-0	Critchley, Dean, Weldon	28266			2	7	1	9					5			4	8		3				11	6	10	
1		21	ASTON VILLA	3-2	Dean 2, Weldon	39825			2	7	1	9					5			4	8		3				11	6	10	
1		28	Burnley	5-3	Dean 4, Martin	24485			2	7	1	9					5			4	8		3				11	6	10	
1	May	5	ARSENAL	3-3	Dean 3	48715			2	7	1	9					5			4	8		3				11	6	10	

Scorers in game 11: White 2, Critchley, Forshaw, O'Donnell, Weldon, Henderson (og)

Apps	2	2	36	40	10	39	1	3	23	6	41	1	9	40	10	1	42	4	4	26	42	39	38	1
Goals				6		60		1	5		1		3	1	3		1				10	1	7	2

One own goal

F.A. Cup

| R3 | Jan | 14 | Preston North End | 3-0 | Dean, Irvine, Ward (og) | 37788 | | | 2 | 7 | | 9 | | | | | 5 | | 8 | 4 | | | 3 | | 6 | 1 | 11 | | 10 | |
| R4 | | 28 | Arsenal | 3-4 | Dean 2, Troup | 44328 | | | 2 | 7 | | 9 | | | | | 5 | | 8 | 4 | | | 3 | | | 1 | 11 | 6 | 10 | |

Players only: Back: Kelly, Hart, Davies, O'Donnell, Virr. Front: Critchley, Martin, Dean, Cresswell, Weldon, Troup

Sheffield Wednesday 1928/29

Hillsborough

						Allen.JDW	Blenkinsop.E	Brown.JH	Burridge.H	Felton.W	Gregg.R	Hargraves.L	Harper.E	Hatfield.E	Hill.H	Hooper.M	Kean.F	Leach.T	Marsden.W	Rimmer.EJ	Seed.J	Strange.AH	Trotter.J	Walker.T	Whitehouse.J	Wilkinson.J	Wilson.C
	Aug	25	ARSENAL	3-2	Hooper 2, Marsden	23684	10	3	1								7		5	6	11	8	4	9	2			
		29	Everton	0-0		39011	10	3	1								7	5		6	11	8	4	9	2			
	Sep	1	Blackburn Rovers	1-4	Seed	18647		3	1							10	7	5		6	11	8	4	9	2			
5		3	EVERTON	1-0	Seed	24322	10	3	1								7	5		6		8	4	9	2		11	
5		8	SUNDERLAND	2-1	Trotter, Strange	25716		3	1			10					7	5		6		8	4	9	2		11	
7		15	Derby County	0-6		22762	10	3	1					9			7		5	6		8	4		2		11	
3		22	SHEFFIELD UNITED	5-2	Hooper 2, Allen 2, Rimmer	44699	10		1			3		9			7		5	6	11	8	4		2			
7		29	BOLTON WANDERERS	0-0		25098	10	3	1					9			7		5	6	11	8	4		2			
10	Oct	6	Portsmouth	2-3	Hooper, Allen	22732	9	3	1			10					7		5	6	11	8	4		2			
7		13	BIRMINGHAM	3-0	Allen 3	21677	9	3	1			10					7		5	6	11	8	4		2			
4		20	Bury	4-0	Allen 4	12273	9	3	1	5		10					7			6	11	8	4		2			
4		27	CARDIFF CITY	1-0	Hooper	20116	9	3	1	5		10					7			6	11	8	4		2			
4	Nov	3	Leicester City	1-1	Allen	29522	9	3	1			10					7		5	6		8	4		2		11	
3		10	MANCHESTER UNITED	2-1	Hooper, Gregg	18113	9	3	1			10					7		5	6		8	4		2		11	
2		17	Leeds United	2-0	Seed, Gregg	25579	9		1		3	10					7		5	6	11	8	4		2			
1		24	LIVERPOOL	3-2	Allen 2, Rimmer	14624	9	3	1			10					7		5	6	11	8	4		2			
1	Dec	1	West Ham United	2-3	Allen 2	18536	9	3	1			8					7		5	6	11		4		2			10
1		8	NEWCASTLE UNITED	3-1	Allen 2, Hooper	25835	9	3	1			8					7		5	6	11		4		2			10
1		15	Burnley	2-0	Allen 2	16173	9	3	1			10					7		5	6	11	8	4		2			
1		22	ASTON VILLA	4-1	Seed 2, Allen, Hooper	24822	9	3	1			10					7		5	6	11	8	4		2			
1		25	MANCHESTER CITY	4-0	Allen 2, Hooper, Gregg	45093	9	3	1			10					7		5	6	11	8	4		2			
1		26	Manchester City	2-2	Allen 2	42826	9	3	1			10					7		5	6	11	8	4		2			
1		29	Arsenal	2-2	Hooper, Gregg	39255	9	3	1			10					7		5	6	11	8	4		2			
1	Jan	1	HUDDERSFIELD T	1-1	Gregg	57143	9	3	1			10					7		5	6	11	8	4		2			
1		5	BLACKBURN ROVERS	1-0	Allen	28136	9	3	1			10					7		5	6	11	8	4		2			
1		19	Sunderland	3-4	Allen 2, Gregg	36475	9	3	1			10					7		5	6	11	8	4		2			
1	Feb	2	Sheffield United	1-1	Hooper	44576		3	1			10					7		5	6	11	8	4	9	2			
1		9	Bolton Wanderers	2-2	Allen, Blenkinsop	18802	9	3	1			10					7		5	6	11	8	4		2			
1		18	DERBY COUNTY	5-0	Harper 3, Gregg, Strange	16026		3	1			10		9			7		5	6	11	8	4		2			
1		23	Birmingham	1-4	Harper	28599		3	1	2		10		9			7		5	6	11	8						
1	Mar	2	BURY	3-1	Harper, Seed, Whitehouse	23826		3	1					9			7		5	6	11	8	4		2	10		
1		4	PORTSMOUTH	2-1	Hooper, Wilson	13705		3	1								7		5	6	11	8	4		2	10		9
1		9	Cardiff City	1-3	Seed	18636	9	3	1								7		5	6		8	4		2	10	11	
1		16	LEICESTER CITY	1-0	Allen	30176	9	3	1				11				7		5	6		8	4		2	10		
1		23	Manchester United	1-2	Hargreaves	27095	9	3	1				11				7		5	6		10	4		2	8		
1		30	LEEDS UNITED	4-2	Rimmer 3, Seed	30655	9	3	1			10					7		5	6	11	8	4		2			
1	Apr	2	Huddersfield Town	0-0		32555	9	3	1			10					7		5	6	11	8	4		2			
1		6	Liverpool	2-3	Rimmer, Allen	29878	9	3	1			10					7		5	6	11	8	4		2			
1		13	WEST HAM UNITED	6-0	Strange 2 (1p), Hooper 2, Rimmer, Allen	22596	9		1			10			3		7		5	6	11	8	4		2			
1		20	Newcastle United	1-2	Allen	26401	9	3	1			10					7		5	6	11	8	4		2			
1		27	BURNLEY	1-1	Allen	33314	9	3	1			10					7		5	6	11	8	4		2			
1	May	4	Aston Villa	1-4	Strange	25075	9	3	1			10					7		5	6	11		4		2	8		
						Apps	35	39	42	2	3	30	2	6	1	1	42	4	36	42	34	39	42	6	41	6	6	3
						Goals	33	1				7	1	5			15			1	7	8	5	1		1	1	1

F.A. Cup

R3	Jan	12	Wigan Borough	3-1	Allen 2, Hooper	30651	9	3	1			10					7		5	6	11	8	4		2			
R4		26	Reading	0-1		29248	9	3	1			10					7		5	6	11	8	4		2			

Back: Strange, Felton, Brown, Blenkinsop, Marsden. Front: Hooper, Seed, Harper, Gregg, Rimmer, Leach

Sheffield Wednesday 1929/30

Hillsborough

							Allen IDA	Beeson GW	Blenkinsop E	Brown JH	Burgess H	Burridge BJH	Gregg RE	Hooper M	Jones TJ	Leach TJ	Mackey TS	Marsden W	Mellors RD	Millership W	Rimmer EJ	Seed JM	Smith WS	Strange AH	Walker T	Whitehouse JC	Wilkinson J	Wilson C
	Aug	31	Portsmouth	4-0	Rimmer 2, Allen 2	27537	9		3	1			10	7		5		6			11			4	2	8		
	Sep	2	BOLTON WANDERERS	1-0	Allen	26480	9		3	1			10	7		5		6			11			4	2	8		
		7	ARSENAL	0-2		31735	9		3	1			10	7		5		6			11			4	2	8		
3		14	Aston Villa	3-1	Burgess, Allen 2	36209	9		3	1	10			7		5		6			11	8		4	2			
9		21	LEEDS UNITED	1-2	Seed	21353	9		3	1	10			7		5		6			11	8		4	2			
5		25	Bolton Wanderers	3-1	Seed, Allen, Hooper	11136	9		3	1	10			7		5		6			11	8		4	2			
3		28	Sheffield United	2-2	Seed, Allen	47039	9		3	1	10			7		5		6			11	8		4	2			
2	Oct	5	Burnley	4-2	Marsden, Burgess 2, Hooper	17294	9		3	1	10			7		5		6			11	8		4	2			
2		12	SUNDERLAND	1-1	Burgess	23158	9		3	1	10			7		5		6			11	8		4	2			
2		19	HUDDERSFIELD T	3-1	Burgess, Allen, Rimmer	25998	9				10			7		5		6	1		11	8		4	2			3
4		26	Birmingham	0-1		27221	9		3	1	10			7		5		6			11	8		4				2
4	Nov	2	LEICESTER CITY	4-0	Burgess, Allen 3	19159	9	2		1	10	6		7		5					11	8		4				3
3		9	Newcastle United	3-1	Rimmer, Allen 2	29505	9		3	1	10			7		5		6			11	8		4				2
2		16	MANCHESTER UNITED	7-2	Rimmer 2, Allen 4, Hooper	14264	9		3	1	10			7		5		6			11	8		4				2
2		23	West Ham United	1-1	Burgess	18753	9		3	1	10			7		5		6			11	8		4				2
2		30	LIVERPOOL	2-1	Strange, Hooper	19701	9		3	1	10			7		5		6			11	8		4				2
2	Dec	7	Middlesbrough	1-4	Allen	21265	9		3	1	10			7		5		6			11			4		8		2
2		14	BLACKBURN ROVERS	4-0	Seed, Allen 2, Burgess	19278	9		3	1	10			7		5		6			11	8		4	2			
2		25	Everton	4-1	Allen, Hooper 3	30835	9		3	1	10			7		5		6			11	8		4	2			
2		26	EVERTON	4-0	Burgess, Leach 2, Allen	45559	9		3	1	10			7		5		6			11	8		4	2			
1		28	PORTSMOUTH	1-1	Strange	23548			3	1	9	5	10	7				6			11	8		4	2			
1	Jan	1	Manchester City	3-3	Burgess, Allen, Seed	55930	9		3	1	10			7		5					11	8		4	2			
1		4	Arsenal	3-2	Burgess 2, Seed	40766	9		3	1	10			7		5		6			11	8		4	2			
1		18	ASTON VILLA	3-0	Rimmer, Marsden, Hooper	34911	9		3	1	10			7		5		6			11	8		4	2			
1	Feb	1	SHEFFIELD UNITED	1-1	Burgess	54459	9		3	1	10			7		5					11	8	6	4	2			
1		5	Grimsby Town	5-0	Burgess 2, Allen, Rimmer, Seed	12514	9		3	1	10			7		5		6			11	8		4	2			
1		8	BURNLEY	4-1	McCluggage (og), Seed, Rimmer 2	23864	9		3	1	10			7		5		6			11	8		4	2			
1		22	Huddersfield Town	1-4	Burgess	26705	9		3	1	10			7		5		6			11	8		4	2			
2	Mar	8	Leicester City	1-2	Marsden	29644	9		3	1	10			7		5		6				8		4	2		11	
1		15	NEWCASTLE UNITED	4-2	Rimmer 2, Allen, Burgess	9350	9		3	1	10			7		5		6			11	8		4	2			
1		29	WEST HAM UNITED	2-1	Hooper, Burgess	25092	9		3	1	10			7		5		6			11	8		4	2			
1	Apr	5	Liverpool	3-1	Allen, Hooper, Burgess	35563	9			1	10			7	11	5				8			4	6			3
1		9	Leeds United	0-3		3590	9		3	1	10			7		5		6		8	11			4	2			
1		12	MIDDLESBROUGH	1-0	Rimmer	23087	9		3	1	10			7		5		6		8	11			4	2			
1		14	Manchester United	2-2	Allen 2	12806	9		3	1	10			7		5		6		8	11			4	2			
1		19	Blackburn Rovers	1-0	Hooper	17768	9		3	1	10		8	7		5		6			11			4	2			
1		21	Derby County	1-4	Hooper	25442	9		3	1	10			7		5		6		8	11			4	2			
1		22	DERBY COUNTY	6-3	Allen 3, Rimmer, Millership, Hooper	41218	9		3	1	10			7		5				8	11		6	4	2			
1		26	GRIMSBY TOWN	1-0	Jacobson (og)	22524	9		3	1	10			7		5					11	8	6	4	2			
1		28	BIRMINGHAM	1-1	Strange	9310	9		3	1	10			7				5	6		11	8		4	2			
1		30	Sunderland	4-2	Hooper 2, Burgess, Allen	26351	9		3	1	10			7		5		6			11	8		4	2			
1	May	3	MANCHESTER CITY	5-1	Allen, Hooper 3, Seed	23293	9	2	3	1	10			7		5		6			11	8		4				

	Apps	41	2	39	41	39	2	5	42	1	40	1	37	1	6	40	32	4	41	34	4	1	9
	Goals	33				19			18		2		3		1	15	9		3				

Two own goals

F.A. Cup

R3	Jan	11	BURNLEY	1-0	Allen	31794	9		3	1	10			7		5		6			11	8		4	2			
R4		25	Oldham Athletic	4-3	Allen 2, Hooper, Seed	46471	9		3	1	10			7		5		6			11	8		4	2			
R5	Feb	15	BRADFORD PARK AVE.	5-1	Seed, Rimmer, Allen, Hooper, Bentley (og)	53268	9		3	1	10			7		5		6			11	8		4	2			
R6	Mar	1	Nottingham Forest	2-2	Allen, Rimmer	44166	9		3	1	10			7		5		6			11	8		4	2			
rep		5	NOTTM FOREST	3-1	Seed, Allen, Burgess	59205	9		3	1	10			7		5		6			11	8		4	2			
SF		22	Huddersfield Town	1-2	Hooper	69292	9		3	1	10			7		5		6			11	8		4	2			

SF at Old Trafford

Back:- Hopkins, Francis, E.Flint, S.Nixon, Dickinson (directors). Next to back: Turner, Hodgkiss, Webster, Johnson, Neale, Brown, Dodds, Hargreaves, Mellors, Mills, Feanehough, Rhind (directors). Front standing row: Wardley (director), Jones, Hooper, Harston, Whitehouse, Leach, Blenkinsop, Burgess, Amith, Barton, Trotman, Gunstone, Blanchard (directors). Seated on chairs: Brown (manager), Hooper, Stange, Walker, William Clegg, Charles Clegg, Allen, Rimmer, Gregg, Wilson, Smith, Dean, Stephen. Front of seats: Craig (trainer), Beeson, Seed, Marsden, Hatfield, Goddard, Burridge. Front, with pennants: Wilkinson, Trotter

Arsenal 1930/31

Highbury

						Baker A	Bastin CS	Brain J	Cope HW	Hapgood EA	Harper W	Haynes AE	Hulme JHA	Jack DBN	James AW	John RF	Johnstone W	Jones C	Keizer GP	Lambert J	Male CG	Parker TR	Preedy CJF	Roberts H	Seddon WC	Thompson L	Williams JJ
	Aug	30	Blackpool	4-1	Bastin 2 (1p), Jack 2	28723		11		3			7	8	10	6			4	1	9		2		5			
	Sep	1	Bolton Wanderers	4-1	Lambert 3, Hulme	20684		11		3			7	8	10	6			4	1	9		2		5			
		6	LEEDS UNITED	3-1	Lambert 2, Jack	40828		11		3			7	8	10	6			4	1	9		2		5			
1		10	BLACKBURN ROVERS	3-2	Bastin, Johnstone	20863		11		3			7	8		6	10	4	1	9		2		5			
1		13	Sunderland	4-1	Lambert 3, Hulme	26525		11		3			7	8		6	10		1	9		2		5	4		
2		15	Blackburn Rovers	2-2	Hulme, Lambert	25572		11	8	3			7		10	6			1	9		2		5	4		
1		20	LEICESTER CITY	4-1	Hulme, Lambert 2, Bastin	37851		11	8	3			7		10	6			1	9		2		5	4		
1		27	Birmingham	4-2	Bastin, Lambert 3	31693		11	8	3			7		10	6			1	9		2		5	4		
1	Oct	4	SHEFFIELD UNITED	1-1	Lambert	47113		11	8	3			7		10	6			1	9		2		5	4		
2		11	Derby County	2-4	Bastin, Roberts	29783		11		3			7	8	10	6			1	9		2		5	4		
1		18	Manchester United	2-1	Williams, Lambert	23406		11	8	3					10	6			1	9		2		5	4		7
1		25	WEST HAM UNITED	1-1	Bastin	51918		11	8	3					10	6			1	9		2		5	4		7
1	Nov	1	Huddersfield Town	1-1	Jack	25772		11		3	1			8	10	6				9		2		5	4		7
1		8	ASTON VILLA	5-2	Bastin 2, Lambert, Jack 2	56417		11		3				8	10	6				9		2	1	5	4		7
1		15	Sheffield Wednesday	2-1	Lambert 2	43671		11		3	1			8	10	6				9		2		5	4		7
1		22	MIDDLESBROUGH	5-3	Lambert 3, Bastin 2 (1p)	32517		11		3	1			8	10	6				9		2		5	4		7
1		29	Chelsea	5-1	Jack 3, Williams, Lambert	74667		11		3	1			8	10	6				9		2		5	4		7
2	Dec	13	Liverpool	1-1	Jack	44342		11		3	1			8	10	6				9		2		5	4		7
2		20	NEWCASTLE UNITED	1-2	Jack	32212		11		3	1			8	10	6				9		2		5	4		7
1		25	Manchester City	4-1	Bastin (p), Jack, Lambert, Hulme	56750		11		3	1		7	8	10	6				9		2		5	4		
1		26	MANCHESTER CITY	3-1	Bastin, John, Hulme	17624		11		3	1		7	8	10	6	4			9		2		5			
1		27	BLACKPOOL	7-1	Brain 3, Jack 3, Bastin	35113		11	8		1		7	9	10	3		4			6	2		5			
2	Jan	17	SUNDERLAND	1-3	James	35975		11	8	3	1		7	9	10	6						2		5	4		
1		28	GRIMSBY TOWN	9-1	Jack 4, Lambert 3, Bastin, Hulme	15751		11		3			7	8	10	6	4			9		2	1	5			
2		31	BIRMINGHAM	1-1	Lambert	30913		11		3			7	8	10	6	4			9		2	1	5			
1	Feb	5	Leicester City	7-2	Lambert 3, Bastin 2, Hulme, Jack	17416		11		3			7	8	10	6				9		2	1	5	4		
1		7	Sheffield United	1-1	Hulme	49602		11	8	3			7	9	10	6	4					2	1	5			
1		14	DERBY COUNTY	6-3	Bastin 3 (1p), Hulme, James, Jack	34785		11	8	2	3		7	9	10	6	4						1	5			
1		21	MANCHESTER UNITED	4-1	Hulme, Jack, Brain, Bastin	41510		11	8	3			7	9	10	6	4					2	1	5			
1		28	West Ham United	4-2	Bastin, Jack 2, John	30361		11		3			7	8	10	6	4					2	1	5			
1	Mar	7	HUDDERSFIELD T	0-0		31058	3	11	8				7	9	10		4				6	2	1	5			
1		11	Leeds United	2-1	Bastin, James	12212		11	8				7		10	6	4		9	3	2	1	5		6	
1		14	Aston Villa	1-5	Jack	60997		11	8				7	9	10	3	4					2	1	5		6	
1		21	SHEFFIELD WEDNESDAY	2-0	Jack, Bastin	47872		11	8	3	1			7	10	6	4			9		2		5			
1		28	Middlesbrough	5-2	Lambert 3, Jack 2	23476		11		3	1	5	7	8	10	6	4			9		2					
1	Apr	3	Portsmouth	1-1	Bastin	31398		11		3	1		7	8	10	6	4			9		2		5			
1		4	CHELSEA	2-1	Hulme, Bastin	53867		11		3	1		7	8	10	6	4			9		2		5			
1		6	PORTSMOUTH	1-1	James	40490		11		3	1		7	8	10	6	4			9		2		5			
1		11	Grimsby Town	1-0	Lambert	22394		11		3	1	5	7	8	10	6	4			9		2					
1		18	LIVERPOOL	3-1	Jack, Bastin, Lambert	39143		11		3	1		7	8	10	6	4			9		2		5			
1		25	Newcastle United	3-1	Jones, Hulme 2	21747		11		3	1		7	8	10	6	4		9			2		5			
1	May	2	BOLTON WANDERERS	5-0	Jack 2, Lambert 2, James	35406		11		3	1		7	8	10	6	4			9		2		5			
						Apps	1	42	16	1	38	19	2	32	35	40	40	2	24	12	34	3	41	11	40	18	2	9
						Goals		28	4					14	31	5	2	1	1		38				1			2

F.A. Cup

R3	Jan	10	ASTON VILLA	2-2	Lambert, Jack	40864		11		3	1		7	8	10	6				9		2		5	4		
rep		14	Aston Villa	3-1	Hulme 2, Jack	73632		11	8	3	1		7	9	10	6						2		5	4		
R4		24	Chelsea	1-2	Bastin	62475		11		3	1		7	8	10	6				9		2		5	4		

F.A. Charity Shield

Oct	8	Sheffield Wednesday	2-1	Hulme, Jack	18000		11	8		3			7	10		6			1	9		2		5	4		

At Stamford Bridge

Sheriff of London Shield

Apr	22	CORINTHIANS	5-3	Hulme 2, Lambert 2, John	12000		11		3	1	5	7	8	10	6	4			9		2					

Players only: Back: Thompson, Roberts, Preedy, Seddon, Lambert. Front: Hulme, Jack, Parker, James, Williams, Hapgood

Everton 1931/32

Goodison Park

						Bocking W	Clark A	Coggins WH	Cresswell W	Critchley E	Dean WR	Dunn J	Gee GW	Griffiths PH	Johnson TCF	Lowe H	Martin GS	McClure JH	McPherson L	Rigby A	Sagar E	Stein J	Thompson JR	White TA	Williams BD
	Aug	29	BIRMINGHAM	3-2	Dunn 3	39146	2	4		3		9	8	5	7	10						1	11	6		
	Sep	2	Portsmouth	3-0	White 3	23075	2	4		3			8	5	7	10						1	11	6	9	
		5	Sunderland	3-2	Johnson, Griffiths, Stein	28474	2	4		3		9	8	5	7	10						1	11	6		
7		12	MANCHESTER CITY	0-1		32510	2	4		3		9	8	5	7	10						1	11	6		
10		16	Derby County	0-3		12491	2	4		3		9	8	5	7	10						1	11	6		
5		19	Liverpool	3-1	Dean 3	53220	2			3	7	9	8	5		10			4	6		1	11			
4		23	DERBY COUNTY	2-1	Johnson 2	19130	2			3	7	9	8	5		10			4	6		1	11			
6		26	Arsenal	2-3	Critchley, Dean	47637	2			3	7	9	8	5		10			4	6		1	11			
4	Oct	3	BLACKPOOL	3-2	Johnson 2, White	31651		4		3	7	9		5		10						1	11	6	8	2
2		10	Sheffield United	5-1	Johnson, Dean 3, Stein	26651		4		3	7	9		5		10						1	11	6	8	2
2		17	SHEFFIELD WEDNESDAY	9-3	Stein, Dean 5, White, Critchley, Johnson	38186		4		3	7	9		5		10						1	11	6	8	2
1		24	Aston Villa	3-2	Critchley 2, White	61663		4		3	7	9		5		10						1	11	6	8	2
1		31	NEWCASTLE UNITED	8-1	Johnson 2, White 2, Stein, Critchley, Dean 2	30765		4		3	7	9		5		10						1	11	6	8	2
1	Nov	7	Huddersfield Town	0-0		17605		4		3	7			5		10			9			1	11	6	8	2
1		14	CHELSEA	7-2	Dean 5, Johnson, Stein	32758		4		3	7	9		5		10						1	11	6	8	2
1		21	Grimsby Town	2-1	White, Stein	16508		4		3	7	9		5		10						1	11	6	8	2
1		28	LEICESTER CITY	9-2	Dean 4, White 2, Johnson 2, Clark	33513		4		3	7	9		5		10						1	11	6	8	2
1	Dec	5	West Ham United	2-4	Johnson, Stein	34109		4		3	7	9		5		10						1	11	6	8	2
1		12	MIDDLESBROUGH	5-1	White 2, Critchley, Johnson, Dean	33182		4		3	7	9		5		10						1	11	6	8	2
1		19	Bolton Wanderers	1-2	Dean	33619		4		3	7	9		5		10						1	11	6	8	2
1		25	Blackburn Rovers	3-5	White 2, Dean	40059		4		3	7	9		5		10						1	11	6	8	2
1		26	BLACKBURN ROVERS	5-0	Dean 3, Johnson, White	52991		4		3	7	9		5		10						1	11	6	8	2
1	Jan	2	Birmingham	0-4		26256		4		3	7			5		10						1	11	6	8	2
		16	SUNDERLAND	4-2	Griffiths 2, White, Dean	29491		4	1		7	9		5	11	10	3							6	8	2
		27	Manchester City	0-1		26363		4		3	7	9		5	11	10						1		6	8	2
1		30	LIVERPOOL	2-1	White, Critchley	46537	3	4			7	9				10		5			11	1		6	8	2
1	Feb	6	ARSENAL	1-3	Johnson	56698		4		3	7	9		5		10					11	1		6	8	2
1		13	Blackpool	0-2		16346		4		3	7	9				10		5			11	1		6	8	2
1		20	SHEFFIELD UNITED	5-1	Dunn 2, Dean, Critchley, Johnson	38190		4		3	7	9	8	5		10						1	11	6		2
1		27	Sheffield Wednesday	3-1	Dunn, Dean 2	24279		4		3	7	9	8	5		10						1	11	6		2
1	Mar	5	ASTON VILLA	4-2	Dean 2, Dunn, Johnson	39190		4		3	7	9	8	5		10						1	11	6		2
1		19	HUDDERSFIELD T	4-1	Johnson, Dean 3	30748		4		3	7	9	8	5		10						1	11	6		2
1		25	WEST BROMWICH ALB.	2-1	Dean, Dunn	51783		4		3	7	9	8	5		10						1	11	6		2
1		26	Chelsea	0-0		56298		4		3	7	9	8	5		10						1	11	6		2
1		28	West Bromwich Albion	1-1	Stein	32428		4		3	7	9	8	5		10						1	11	6		2
1	Apr	2	GRIMSBY TOWN	4-2	Dunn 2, Dean, Johnson	28456		4		3	7	9	8	5		10						1	11	6		2
		9	Leicester City	1-0	Dean	23229	2	4		3	7	9	8	5								1	11	6	10	
1		16	WEST HAM UNITED	6-1	Dean 3, Stein, Johnson 2	26997		4		3	7	9	8	5		10						1	11	6		2
1		23	Middlesbrough	0-1		10728		4		3	7	9	8	5		10						1	11	6		2
1		30	BOLTON WANDERERS	1-0	Dean	28546		4		3	7	9	8	5		10						1	11	6		2
1	May	4	Newcastle United	0-0		30898		4		3	7		8			10		5				1	11	6	9	2
1		7	PORTSMOUTH	0-1		24011		4		3	7	9	8			10		5				1	11	6		2

	Apps	Goals
Bocking W	10	
Clark A	39	1
Coggins WH	1	
Cresswell W	40	
Critchley E	37	8
Dean WR	38	45
Dunn J	22	10
Gee GW	38	
Griffiths PH	7	3
Johnson TCF	41	22
Lowe H	1	
Martin GS	2	
McClure JH	7	
McPherson L	3	
Rigby A	3	
Sagar E	41	
Stein J	37	9
Thompson JR	39	
White TA	23	18
Williams BD	33	

F.A. Cup

R3	Jan	9	LIVERPOOL	1-2	Dean	57090	3	4			7	9		5		10						1	11	6	8	2

Back: Thomson, Clark, Gee, Sagar, Williams, Cresswell, Bocking. Front: Critchely, Dunn, Dean, Johnson, Stein, White

Arsenal 1932/33

Highbury

						Bastin CS	Bowden ER	Coleman E	Compton LH	Cope HW	Hapgood EA	Haynes AE	Hill FR	Hulme JHA	Jack DBN	James AW	John RF	Jones C	Lambert J	Male CG	Moss F	Parker TR	Parkin R	Preedy CJF	Roberts H	Sidey NW	Stockill RR
Aug	27	Birmingham	1-0	Stockhill	31592	11			2		3			7	8	10	6			4	1				5		9
	31	WEST BROMWICH ALB.	1-2	Stockhill	37748	11			2		3			7	8	10	6			4	1				5		9
Sep	3	SUNDERLAND	6-1	Hulme 3, Coleman, Jack, Bastin	28896	11		9	2		3	5		7	8	10	6	4			1						
5	10	Manchester City	3-2	Jack, Coleman 2	36542	11		9	2		3	5		7	8	10	6	4			1						
5	14	West Bromwich Albion	1-1	Jack	45038	11		9			3	5		7	8	10	6	4			1	2					
4	17	BOLTON WANDERERS	3-2	Hulme, Coleman, Bastin	42395	11		9			3	5		7	8	10	6	4			1	2					
2	24	EVERTON	2-1	Coleman, Jack	51182	11		9			3			7	8	10	6	4			1	2			5		
2	Oct 1	Blackpool	2-1	Coleman, Bastin	30218	11		9			3			7	8	10	6	4				2		1	5		
2	8	DERBY COUNTY	3-3	Coleman 2, Hulme	32055	11		9			3			7	8	10	6	4		1		2			5		
2	15	Blackburn Rovers	3-2	Bastin, Jack, Coleman	28799	11		9			3			7	8	10	6				2	1			5		
2	22	Liverpool	3-2	Bastin 2, Coleman	38548	11		9			3	5	4	7	8	10	6				2	1					
1	29	LEICESTER CITY	8-2	Coleman 2, Jack, Hulme 3, Bastin 2	36714	11		9			3		4	7	8	10	6				2	1			5		
1	Nov 5	Wolverhampton Wan.	7-1	Lambert 2, Bastin 2, Jack 3	43570	11					3		4	7	8	10	6		9		2	1			5		
1	12	NEWCASTLE UNITED	1-0	Hulme	56498	11		9			3		4	7	8	10	6				2	1			5		
2	19	Aston Villa	3-5	Jack, Lambert, Bastin	58066	11					3		4	7	8	10	6		9		2	1			5		
1	26	MIDDLESBROUGH	4-2	Coleman 2, Hulme, Jack	34640	11		9			3		4	7	8		6				2	1		10	5		
1	Dec 3	Portsmouth	3-1	Bastin 2, Jack	31401	11		9			3		4	7	8	10	6				2	1			5		
1	10	CHELSEA	4-1	Bastin 2, Hulme, Coleman	53206	11		9			3		4	7	8	10	6				2	1			5		
1	17	Huddersfield Town	1-0	Coleman	23198	11		9			3		4	7	8	10	6				2	1			5		
1	24	SHEFFIELD UNITED	9-2	Bastin 3, Jack, Lambert 5	41520	11					3		4	7	8	10	6		9		2	1			5		
1	26	LEEDS UNITED	1-2	Hulme	55876	11					3		4	7	8	10	6		9		2	1			5		
1	27	Leeds United	0-0		56776	11					3	5		7	9	10	6				2	1				4	8
1	31	BIRMINGHAM	3-0	James, Jack, Bastin	37800	11		9			3		4	7	8	10	6				2	1			5		
1	Jan 2	Sheffield Wednesday	2-3	Jack, Bastin (p)	64492	11		9			3		4	7	8	10	6				2	1			5		
1	7	Sunderland	2-3	Lambert 2	36707	11					3		4	7	8	10	6		9		2	1			5		
1	21	MANCHESTER CITY	2-1	Bastin 2	32456	11				3			4	7	8	10					2	1			5	6	
1	Feb 1	Bolton Wanderers	4-0	Coleman 3, Bastin	13401	11		9		3			4	7		10	6				2	1	8		5		
1	4	Everton	1-1	Coleman	55463	11		9		3			4	7	8	10	6				2	1			5		
1	11	BLACKPOOL	1-1	Coleman	35180	11		9		3				7	8	10	6				2	1		4	5		
1	22	Derby County	2-2	Jack, Bastin	23148	11		9			3			7	8	10	6				2	1		4	5		
1	25	BLACKBURN ROVERS	8-0	Stockhill, Coleman 3, Bastin 2, Hulme 2	27576	11		9			3			7		10	6	4			2	1			5		8
1	Mar 4	LIVERPOOL	0-1		42868	11		9			3			7	8	10	6	4			2	1			5		
1	11	Leicester City	1-1	James	32228	11		9			3			7	8	10	6	4			2	1			5		
1	18	WOLVERHAMPTON W.	1-2	Bowden	44711	11	8	9			3			7		10	6	4			2	1			5		
1	25	Newcastle United	1-2	Hulme	51215	11		9			3		6	7	8	10		4			2	1			5		
1	Apr 1	ASTON VILLA	5-0	Jack, Lambert 2, Bowden, James	54265	11	8				3		4	7		10	6		9		2	1			5		
1	8	Middlesbrough	4-3	Hulme 3, Bastin	22137	11					3		4	7		10	6		9		2	1	8		5		
1	14	SHEFFIELD WEDNESDAY	4-2	Lambert, Hulme 2, Bastin	61945	11	8				3		4	7		10	6		9		2	1			5		
1	15	PORTSMOUTH	2-0	Lambert, Bastin	42809	11	8				3		4	7		10		6	9		2	1			5		
1	22	Chelsea	3-1	Jack, Bstin 2	72260	11	8				3		4		7	10		6	9		2	1			5		
1	29	HUDDERSFIELD T	2-2	Bastin 2	30779	11	8				3		4	7		10		6	9		2	1			5		
1	May 6	Sheffield United	1-3	Hill	18620	11	8				3		4	7			10	6	9		2	1			5		
				Apps		42	7	27	4	4	38	6	26	40	34	40	37	16	12	35	41	5	5	1	36	2	4
				Goals		33	2	24				1	20	18	3		14										3

F.A. Cup

| R3 | Jan 14 | Walsall | 0-2 | | 11149 | 11 | | | | | | 4 | | 8 | 10 | | | 2 | 1 | | | | | | 5 | 6 | |

Also played: T Black (at 3), WH Warnes (7), CH Walsh (9)

Sheriff of London Shield

| | Oct 26 | CORINTHIANS | 9-2 | Coleman 5, Jack, Hulme, Bastin, John (p) | 9493 | 11 | | 9 | | | 3 | 5 | 10 | 7 | 8 | | 6 | | | | 2 | 1 | | 4 | | | |

Back: Male, Compton, Moss, Roberts, Hapgood, Front: Hulme, Jack, Stockhill, James, Bastin, John

78

Arsenal 1933/34

Highbury

						Bastin CS	Beasley AE	Birkett RJE	Bowden ER	Coleman E	Cox G	Dougal PG	Drake EJ	Dunne J	Hapgood EA	Haynes AE	Hill FR	Hulme JHA	Jack DBN	James AW	John RF	Jones C	Lambert J	Male CG	Moss F	Parkin R	Roberts H	Sidey NW	Wilson AA
	Aug	26	BIRMINGHAM	1-1	Jack	44662	11				9					3		4	7	8	10	6			2	1		5		
	Sep	2	Sheffield Wednesday	2-1	Bastin, Jack	23186	11		7	10	9					3		4		8		6			2	1		5		
		6	WEST BROMWICH ALB.	3-1	Bastin 2 (1p), Lambert	34688	11			10	7					3		4		8		6		9	2	1		5		
3		9	MANCHESTER CITY	1-1	Coleman	43412	11			10	7					3		4		8		6		9	2	1		5		
4		13	West Bromwich Albion	0-1		29429	11			8	7					3		6			10		4	9	2	1		5		
6		16	Tottenham Hotspur	1-1	Bowden	56612	11			9						3		4		8	10	6			2	1	7	5		
12		23	Everton	1-3	Bowden	53792	11			9						3		4		8	10	6			2	1	7	5		
6		30	MIDDLESBROUGH	6-0	Birkett 2, Jack 2, Bastin, Bowden	28293	11		7	8					9	3				10		6	4		2	1		5		
3	Oct	7	Blackburn Rovers	2-2	Bastin, Bowden	31636	11		7	8					9	3	5			10		6	4		2	1				
2		14	NEWCASTLE UNITED	3-0	Birkett, Bowden, og (Fairhurst)	32821			7	8					9			6		11	10	3	4		2	1		5		
2		21	LEICESTER CITY	2-0	Dunne 2	44014	11		7	8					9	3					10	6	4		2	1		5		
2		28	Aston Villa	3-2	Dunne 2, Bastin	54323	11			8					9	3		7			10	6	4		2	1		5		
2	Nov	4	PORTSMOUTH	1-1	Bastin	51765	11			8					9	3		7			10	6	4		2	1		5		
2		11	Wolverhampton Wan.	1-0	Bowden	37210	11			10	8				9	3		7				6	4		2	1		5		
2		18	STOKE CITY	3-0	Hulme, Dunne, John	32972	11			10	8				9	3			7			6	4		2	1		5		
1		25	Huddersfield Town	1-0	Dunne	29407	11			8	10				9	3			7			6	4		2	1		5		
1	Dec	2	LIVERPOOL	2-1	Hulme, Dunne	38362	11			8					9	3			7		10	6	4		2	1		5		
1		9	Sunderland	0-3		35166	11			8	9					3			7		10	6	4		2	1		5		
1		16	CHELSEA	2-1	Beasley 2	43897	8	11	7	9						3					10	6	4		2	1		5		
1		23	Sheffield United	3-1	Beasley 2, Bowden	31453	10	11	7	8					9	3						6	4		2	1		5		
1		25	Leeds United	1-0	Bastin	33193	10	11	7	8					9	3		6					4		2	1		5		
1		26	LEEDS UNITED	2-0	Bowden, Dunne	22817	10	11	7	8					9	3						6	4		2	1		5		
1		30	Birmingham	0-0		34771	10	11	7	8					9	3		6					4		2	1		5		
1	Jan	6	SHEFFIELD WEDNESDAY	1-1	Dunne	45156	10	11		8	7				9	3		6					4		2	1		5		
1		20	Manchester City	1-2	Beasley	60401	10	11	7	8					9	3						6	4		2	1		5		
2		31	TOTTENHAM HOTSPUR	1-3	Bastin	68674	10	11	7	8					9	3						6	4		2	1		5		
2	Feb	3	EVERTON	1-2	Birkett	24025	10	11	7	8					9	3		4				6			2	1		5		
2		10	Middlesbrough	2-0	Birkett, Bowden	15894		11	7	8			10		9	3							4		2	1		5	6	
1		21	BLACKBURN ROVERS	2-1	Bastin, Beasley	29886	11	7					10		9	3				8	6				2	1	4	5		
1		24	Newcastle United	1-0	Beasley	40065	11	7					10		9	3		6		8			4		2	1			5	
2	Mar	8	Leicester City	1-4	Bowden	23976	11	7		8		9	10			3		6					4		2	1		5		
2		10	ASTON VILLA	3-2	Jack, Roberts, Hulme	41169		11			9					3			7	8	10	6			2		4	5		1
2		24	WOLVERHAMPTON W.	3-2	Drake, James, Bastin	41143	11							9		3			7	8	10	6	4		2	1		5		
1		30	DERBY COUNTY	1-0	James	69007	11	7		8				9		3					10	6	4		2			5		1
2		31	Stoke City	1-1	Bastin	43163	11	7					10	9		3		6					4		2			5		1
1	Apr	2	Derby County	4-2	Drake 2, Bowden 2	32180	11	7		8				9		3		4			10	6			2			5		
1		7	HUDDERSFIELD T	3-1	Beasley, Bowden, Drake	55930	11	7		8				9		3		4			10	6			2	1		5		
1		14	Liverpool	3-2	Hulme 2, Beasley	43027		11		8				9				6	7		10	3	4		2			5		1
1		18	Portsmouth	0-1		28442	11	7		8				9		3		6			10		4		2	1		5		
1		21	SUNDERLAND	2-1	Drake, Beasley	37783	10	11	7					9		3		6		8					2	1	4	5		
1		28	Chelsea	2-2	James, Bastin	65344	11	7		8				9		3		6			10		4		2	1		5		
1	May	5	SHEFFIELD UNITED	2-0	Drake 2	25265	11	7						9		3		4		8	10	6			2	1		5		

	Apps	38	23	15	32	12	2	5	10	21	40	1	25	8	14	22	31	29	3	42	37	5	30	12	5
	Goals	13	10	5	13	1			7	9			5	5	3	1		1					1			

One own goal

F.A. Cup

R3	Jan	13	Luton Town	1-0	Dunne	18641	10	11		8	7				9	3						6	4		2	1		5		
R4		27	CRYSTAL PALACE	7-0	Dunne 2, Bastin 2, Beasley 2, Birkett	56177	10	11	7	8					9	3						6	4		2			5		1
R5	Feb	17	DERBY COUNTY	1-0	Jack	66905	11	7					10		9	3				8		6	4		2	1		5		
R6	Mar	3	Aston Villa	1-2	Dougall	67366	11	7					10		9	3				8		6	4		2	1		5		

F.A. Charity Shield

Oct	18	Everton	3-0	Birkett 2, Bowden	20000			7	9	8					3		11			10	6	4		2	1		5		

At Goodison Park

Back: Sidey, Dunne, Moss, Male, John. Front: Hill, Bowden, Jones, James, Bastin, Hapgood

Arsenal 1934/35

Highbury

							Bastin CS	Beasley AE	Birkett RJE	Bowden ER	Compton LH	Copping W	Crayston WJ	Davidson RT	Dougal PG	Drake EJ	Dunne J	Hapgood EA	Hill FR	Hulme JHA	James AW	John RF	Kirchen AJ	Male CG	Marshall J	Moss F	Roberts H	Rogers E	Sidey NW	Trim RF	Wilson AA
	Aug	25	Portsmouth	3-3	Bowden, Drake, Bastin	39710	11			8		6				9			4	7	10	3		2		1	5				
	Sep	1	LIVERPOOL	8-1	Drake 3, Bowden 3, Bastin, Crayston	54062	11	7		8		6	4			9		3			10			2		1	5				
		5	BLACKBURN ROVERS	4-0	Drake 2, Bowden, Bastin	39654	11	7		8		6	4			9		3			10			2		1	5				
5		8	Leeds United	1-1	Drake	29447	11	7		8		6	4			9		3			10			2		1	5				
4		15	WEST BROMWICH ALB.	4-3	Drake, James, Bastin, Bowden	40016	11	7		8		6	4			9		3			10			2		1	5				
4		17	Blackburn Rovers	0-2		25472	11	7		8			4			9		3					6	2	10	1			5			
5		22	Sheffield Wednesday	0-0		24751	11			8		6	4			9		3		7	10			2		1	5				
3		29	BIRMINGHAM	5-1	Drake 4, Bastin	47868	11					6	4			9				7	10	3		2	8	1	5				
3	Oct	6	Stoke City	2-2	Bastin 2	45340	11			8		6	4			9		3		7	10			2		1	5				
1		13	MANCHESTER CITY	3-0	Bowden 2, Bastin	68145	11	7		8		6	4			9		3			10			2		1	5				
1		20	TOTTENHAM HOTSPUR	5-1	Drake 3, Beasley, og (T Evans)	70544	11	7		8			4			9		3			10	6		2		1	5				
2		27	Sunderland	1-2	Drake	43744	11	7		8		6	4			9		3			10			2		1	5				
1	Nov	3	EVERTON	2-0	Bastin 2	50350	11	7				6	4		9			3			10			2		1	5				
2		10	Grimsby Town	2-2	Drake, Hulme	26288	11			8		6	4			9		3		7	10			2		1	5				
3		17	ASTON VILLA	1-2	Bastin (p)	54226	11					6	4			9		3		7	10			2	8	1	5				
2		24	Chelsea	5-2	Drake 4, Hulme	43419	11			8		6				9		3	4	7	10			2		1	5				
1	Dec	1	WOLVERHAMPTON W.	7-0	Drake 4, Birkett 2, Bowden	39532	11		7	8		6	4			9		3			10			2		1	5				
2		8	Huddersfield Town	1-1	og (Houghton)	36113	11		7	8		6	4			9		3			10			2		1	5				
2		15	LEICESTER CITY	8-0	Drake 3, Hulme 3, Bastin 2	23689	11			8		6	4			9		3		7	10			2		1	5				
2		22	Derby County	1-3	Bowden	26091	11		7	8		6	4			9		3			10			2		1	5				
1		25	PRESTON NORTH END	5-3	Hulme 2, Bowden, Bastin, og (Hough)	40201	11		8	2		6	4			9		3		7	10					1	5				
3		26	Preston North End	1-2	Hill	39411	10					6	4			9		3	11	7				2	8	1			5			
3		29	PORTSMOUTH	1-1	Drake	36054	11			8		6				9		3	4	7		10		2		1	5				
2	Jan	5	Liverpool	2-0	Drake, Hapgood	55794	11			8		6	4			9		3		7	10			2		1	5				
1		19	LEEDS UNITED	3-0	Bowden 2, Bastin	37026	11			8		6	4	10		9		3		7				2		1	5				
1		30	West Bromwich Albion	3-0	Drake, Bastin, Hulme	30713	8	11			2	6		10		9		3	4	7					1				5			
1	Feb	2	SHEFFIELD WEDNESDAY	4-1	James 3, Bastin	57922	8	11				6	4			9		3		7	10			2		1	5				
1		9	Birmingham	0-3		50188	8	11				6	4			9		3		7	10			2		1	5				
1		20	STOKE CITY	2-0	Davidson, Hill	27067			7			6	4	8	10	9		3	11					2		1			5			
1		23	Manchester City	1-1	Bowden	79491	11			7		6	4	8	10	9						3		2		1	5				
1	Mar	6	Tottenham Hotspur	6-0	Kirchen 2, Drake 2, Dougall, Bastin (p)	47714	11						3	6	4	8	10	9						7	2		1	5		5	
1		9	SUNDERLAND	0-0		73295	11					6	4	8		9		3			10			7	2	1	5				
1		16	Everton	2-0	Moss, Drake	50389	11					6	4	8	10	9		3						7	2	1	5				
1		23	GRIMSBY TOWN	1-1	Drake	33591	11						4	8	10	9		3	6					7	2		5				1
1		30	Aston Villa	3-1	Beasley, Drake, Bastin (p)	59572	10	11					4	8		9		3	6					7	2		5				1
1	Apr	6	CHELSEA	2-2	Drake, Compton (p)	54020		11			2		4	8		9			6		10	3	7				5				1
1		13	Wolverhampton Wan.	1-1	Hill	40888	8	11				3	4			9			6		10			7	2		5				1
1		19	MIDDLESBROUGH	8-0	Drake 4, Rogers 2, Bastin, Beasley	45719	8	11					4			9		3	6		10				2		5	7			1
1		20	HUDDERSFIELD T	1-0	Beasley	41892		11					4	8	10	9		3	6						2		5	7			1
1		22	Middlesbrough	1-0	Drake	29171		11		8			4			9			6		10	3			2			7	5		1
1		27	Leicester City	5-3	Beasley 2, Crayston 2, Davidson	26958		11					4	8		9		3	6		10				2		5	7			1
1	May	4	DERBY COUNTY	0-1		36421		11							8	9			4		10	6		2			5	7		3	1
						Apps	36	20	4	24	5	31	37	11	8	41	1	34	15	16	30	9	7	39	4	33	36	5	6	1	9
						Goals	20	6	2	14	1		3	2	1	42		1	3	8	4		2			1		2			

Three own goals

F.A. Cup

R3	Jan	12	Brighton & Hove Albion	2-0	Hulme, Drake	22343	11			8		6	4			9		3		7	10			2		1	5				
R4		26	Leicester City	1-0	Hulme	39494	11			8		6				9		3	4	7	10			2		1	5				
R5	Feb	16	Reading	1-0	Bastin	30621	8	11	7			6	4			9		3			10			2		1	5				
R6	Mar	2	Sheffield Wednesday	1-2	og (Catlin)	66945	11	7				6	4	8		9					10	3		2		1	5				

F.A. Charity Shield

	Nov	28	MANCHESTER CITY	4-0	Birkett, Marshall, Drake, Bastin	11000	11		7			6				9		3	4		10			2	8	1			5			

Players only: Back: Bowden, Hill, Compton, Moss, Sidey, Drake, Crayston. Front: Hulme, Beasley, Bastin, Hapgood, Dougal, Copping.

Sunderland 1935/36

Roker Park

	Aug	31	Arsenal	1-3	Gurney	66428	
	Sep	4	West Bromwich Albion	3-1	Carter, Gallacher 2	24396	
		7	MANCHESTER CITY	2-0	Bray (og), Gurney	38224	
4		11	WEST BROMWICH ALB.	6-1	Davis, Carter 4, Gallacher	35276	
2		14	Stoke City	2-0	Davis, Gallacher	34516	
2		16	Aston Villa	2-2	Carter, Gurney	24717	
2		21	BLACKBURN ROVERS	7-2	Davis, Carter, Gurney 2, Gallacher 3	29704	
4		28	Chelsea	1-3	Gallacher	61051	
2	Oct	5	LIVERPOOL	2-0	Carter, Goddard	30114	
3		12	Grimsby Town	0-4		11751	
3		19	Wolverhampton Wan.	4-3	Davis, Carter 2, Goddard	29006	
1		26	SHEFFIELD WEDNESDAY	5-1	Thomson, Davis, Carter 2, Gallacher	32890	
2	Nov	2	Portsmouth	2-2	Carter 2	22709	
1		9	PRESTON NORTH END	4-2	Duns 2, Carter, Gurney	16739	
1		16	Brentford	5-1	Duns, Carter, Gurney 2, Gallacher	24720	
1		23	MIDDLESBROUGH	2-1	Carter 2	58902	
1		30	Everton	3-0	Carter, Gurney, Connor	39366	
1	Dec	7	BOLTON WANDERERS	7-2	Carter, Gurney 5, Gallacher	27375	
1		14	Huddersfield Town	0-1		30690	
1		21	DERBY COUNTY	3-1	Carter 2, Gurney	33665	
1		26	LEEDS UNITED	2-1	Gurney 2	25296	
1		28	ARSENAL	5-4	Davis, Carter 2 (1p), Gallacher, Connor	58773	
1	Jan	1	ASTON VILLA	1-3	Gallacher	34476	
		4	Manchester City	1-0	Carter	48732	
		18	STOKE CITY	1-0	McNab	16946	
1	Feb	1	CHELSEA	3-3	Gurney 2, Gallacher	23755	
1		8	Liverpool	3-0	Gurney 2, Gallacher	33332	
1		15	Blackburn Rovers	1-1	Gurney	18628	
1		19	GRIMSBY TOWN	3-1	Davis 2, Gurney	12108	
1		22	WOLVERHAMPTON W.	3-1	Davis, Carter 2	26461	
1		29	Preston North End	2-3	Gurney, Gallacher	18718	
1	Mar	7	EVERTON	3-3	Duns, Carter, Gurney	23268	
		14	Sheffield Wednesday	0-0		31787	
1		21	BRENTFORD	1-3	Duns	26348	
1		28	Middlesbrough	0-6		29990	
1	Apr	4	PORTSMOUTH	5-0	Carter, Gurney, Gallacher, Connor 2	19101	
1		10	BIRMINGHAM	2-1	Gallacher 2	40660	
1		11	Bolton Wanderers	1-2	Carter	32306	
1		13	Birmingham	7-2	Hornby, Gurney 4, Carter, Connor	21693	
1		18	HUDDERSFIELD T	4-3	Davis, Hornby, Gurney, Connor	27859	
1		22	Leeds United	0-3		16682	
1		25	Derby County	0-4		15712	

Apps: 39 28 42 25 17 37 3 39 38 31 8 10 7 1 13 9 21 21 3 1 1 42 26
Goals: 31 7 10 5 19 1 31 2 1 1
One own goal

Players: Carter HS, Clarke MMcNC, Connor J, Davis H, Duns L, Gallacher P, Goddard G, Gurney R, Hall AW, Hastings AC, Hornby CF, Johnston R, Mapson JD, McDowell LJ, McNab A, Middleton MY, Morrison TK, Murray W, Rodgerson R, Russell JW, Shaw HV, Thomson CM, Thorpe JH

F.A. Cup

R3	Jan	11	PORT VALE	2-2	Gallacher, Connor	29270	
rep		13	Port Vale	0-2		16677	

Players only: Back: Carter, Thomson, Hall, Mapson, Hastings, Collin, Clark. Front: Davis, Gurney, Gallacher, Connor

Manchester City 1936/37

Maine Road

							Barkas S	Bray J	Brook EF	Cassidy JA	Clark GV	Dale W	Doherty PD	Donnelly R	Freeman RH	Heale JA	Herd A	Marshall RS	McCullough K	McLeod JS	Neilson R	Percival J	Regan RH	Rodger C	Rogers JH	Swift FV	Tilson SF	Toseland E
	Aug	29	Middlesbrough	0-2		23081	3	6	11			2	10			8					5	4				1	9	7
	Sep	2	LEEDS UNITED	4-0	Brook, Doherty, Herd, Tilson	24726		6	11		2	3	10			8		5				4				1	9	7
		5	WEST BROMWICH ALB.	6-2	Doherty 2, Herd 2, Brook, Heale	33063		6	11		2	3	9		10	8		5				4				1		7
4		9	Leeds United	1-1	Heale	13933		6	11		2	3	9	5		10	8					4				1		7
7		12	Manchester United	2-3	Bray, Heale	68796	3	6	11			2	10	5		9	8					4				1		7
5		16	BIRMINGHAM	1-1	Doherty	20280		6	11		2	3	10			9		5	8			4				1		7
12		19	Portsmouth	1-2	McLeod	24600		6	11		2	3	10					5	4	9		8				1		7
11		26	CHELSEA	0-0		30004		6	11	8	2	3	9			10		5				4				1		7
12	Oct	3	Stoke City	2-2	Doherty, Heale	36400		6	9		2	3	10			8		5				4	11			1		7
12		10	CHARLTON ATHLETIC	1-1	Heale	33664	3	6	9			2	10			8		5				4	11			1		7
8		17	DERBY COUNTY	3-2	Doherty, Heale, Toseland	21245	3	6	9			2	10			8		5				4	11			1		7
13		24	Wolverhampton Wan.	1-2	Doherty	20888	3	6	9			2	10			8		5				4	11			1		7
16		31	SUNDERLAND	2-4	Doherty, McLeod	39444	3	6	11			2	10			8		5		9		4				1		7
15	Nov	7	Huddersfield Town	1-1	Brook	18438	3	6	11			2	10					8	5		9	4				1		7
14		14	EVERTON	4-1	Rodger 2, Brook, Toseland	27818	3	6	11			2	10					8	5			4		9		1		7
12		21	Bolton Wanderers	2-0	Brook, Herd	32003	3	6	11			2	10					8	5			4		9		1		7
9	Dec	5	Arsenal	3-1	Rodger 2, Doherty	41783	3	6	11			2	10					8	5			4		9		1		7
8		12	PRESTON NORTH END	4-1	Toseland 2, Brook, Doherty	20093	3	6	11			2	10					8	5			4		9		1		7
9		19	Sheffield Wednesday	1-5	Doherty	18826	3	6	11			2	10					8	5			4		9		1		7
12		25	Grimsby Town	3-5	Brook, Doherty, Rodger	17921	3	6	11			2	10					8	5			4		9		1		7
11		26	MIDDLESBROUGH	2-1	Brook, Rodger	56227		6	11			2	10	3				8	5			4		9		1		7
9		28	GRIMSBY TOWN	1-1	Tilson	16146		6	11		2		10	3				8	5			4				1	9	7
10	Jan	2	West Bromwich Albion	2-2	Herd, Tilson	18137		6	11			2	10	3				8	5			4				1	9	7
10		9	MANCHESTER UNITED	1-0	Herd	64862	3	6	11			2	10					8	5			4				1	9	7
8		23	PORTSMOUTH	3-1	Brook, Herd, Toseland	19595	3	6	11			2			10			8	5			4				1	9	7
8	Feb	3	Chelsea	4-4	Doherty 2, Bray, Tilson	11620	3	6	11			2	10					8	5			4				1	9	7
6		6	STOKE CITY	2-1	Doherty, Tilson	34767	3	6	11			2	10					8	5			4				1	9	7
8		13	Charlton Athletic	1-1	Herd	35509	3	6	11			2	10					8	5			4				1	9	7
6		24	Derby County	5-0	Tilson 3, Brook, Rodger	12572	3	6	11			2	8						5			4		10		1	9	7
3		27	WOLVERHAMPTON W.	4-1	Tilson 3, Herd	42133	3	6	11		2		10					8	5			4				1	9	7
4	Mar	13	HUDDERSFIELD T	3-0	Doherty 2, Brook	28240	3	6	11			2	10					8	5			4				1	9	7
7		20	Everton	1-1	Percival	31921	3	6	11			2	10					8	5			4				1	9	7
4		26	Liverpool	5-0	Brook 3, Doherty, Herd	34088	3	6	11			2	10					8	5			4				1	9	7
4		27	BOLTON WANDERERS	2-2	Doherty, Herd	51714	3	6	11			2	10					8	5			4				1	9	7
3		29	LIVERPOOL	5-1	Herd 2, Brook, Neilson, Tilson	38763	3	6	11			2	10					8			5	4				1	9	7
3	Apr	3	Brentford	6-2	Doherty 2, Brook, Herd, Tilson, Toseland	29028	3	6	11			2	10					8	5			4				1	9	7
2		7	BRENTFORD	2-1	Brook, Doherty	24629	3	6	11			2	10					8	5			4				1	9	7
1		10	ARSENAL	2-0	Doherty, Toseland	74918	3	6	11			2	10					8	5			4				1	9	7
1		14	Sunderland	3-1	Doherty 2, Brook	14827			11		2		8	3					5			4		10	6	1	9	7
1		17	Preston North End	5-2	Doherty 3, Donnelly, Herd	21804			11		2		10	3				8	5			4			6	1	9	7
1		24	SHEFFIELD WEDNESDAY	4-1	Brook 2, Doherty, Tilson	50985	3	6	11		2		10					8	5			4				1	9	7
1	May	1	Birmingham	2-2	Doherty, Tilson	17325	3	6	11		2		10					8	5			4				1	9	7
						Apps	30	40	42	1	13	36	41	7	1	10	32	38	2	3	2	42	4	9	2	42	23	42
						Goals		2	20				30	1		6	15			2	1	1		7			15	7

FA Cup

R3	Jan	16	Wrexham	3-1	Brook, Herd, Tilson	20600	3	6	11		2		10					8	5			4				1	9	7
R4		30	Accrington Stanley	2-0	Doherty, Tilson	39135	3	6	11			2	10					8	5			4				1	9	7
R5	Feb	20	Bolton Wanderers	5-0	Herd 2, Brook, Doherty, Tilson	60979	3	6	11			2	10					8	5			4				1	9	7
R6	Mar	6	Millwall	0-2		42474	3	6	11			2	10					8	5			4			4	1	9	7

Back: McCullough, Dale, Corlton (trainer), Swift, Marshall, Bray. Centre: Toseland, Herd, Tilson, Wilf Wild (secretary/manager), Barkas, Doherty, Brook. Front: Heale, Rodger, Clarke, Percival

82

Arsenal 1937/38

Highbury

						Bastin CS	Biggs AG	Boulton FP	Bowden ER	Bremner GH	Carr EM	Cartwright S	Collett E	Compton DCS	Compton LH	Copping W	Crayston WJ	Davidson RT	Drake EJ	Drury GB	Griffiths WM	Hapgood EA	Hulme JHA	Hunt GS	Jones LJ	Joy B	Kirchen AJ	Lewis RJ	Male CG	Milne JV	Roberts H	Sidey NW	Swindin GH	Wilson AA
	Aug	28	Everton	4-1	Drake 3, Bastin	53856	10			8							6	4		9		3						7		2	11	5			1
	Sep	1	HUDDERSFIELD T	3-1	Drake, Crayston, Bastin	32758	10			8							6	4		9		3	7							2	11	5			1
		4	WOLVERHAMPTON W.	5-0	Drake 2,Crayston,Hulme,Bastin(p)	67311	10			8							6	4		9		3	7							2	11	5			1
2		8	Huddersfield Town	1-2	Bowden	28405	10			8							6	4		9		3	7							2	11	5			1
2		11	Leicester City	1-1	Drake	39106	10		1	8						11	6	4		9		3								2	7	5			
5		15	Bolton Wanderers	0-1		39750	10	11	1	8					2	6	4			9		3									7	5				
2		18	SUNDERLAND	4-1	Milne, Drake, Hulme, Davidson	65635	10		1								6	4	10	9		3	7							2	11	5			
7		25	Derby County	0-2		33101	8										6	4	10	9		3	7							2	11	5			1
6	Oct	2	MANCHESTER CITY	2-1	Milne, Kirchen	68353	8								2		6	4	10			3		9				7			11	5			1
6		9	Chelsea	2-2	Kirchen 2	75952	10								2		6	4				3		9				7			11	5			
6		16	PORTSMOUTH	1-1	Hunt	45150	10		1	8					2		6	4				3		9				7			11	5			
6		23	Stoke City	1-1	Davidson	35684	4			8				6	2				10			3		9				7			11	5			1
9		30	MIDDLESBROUGH	1-2	Milne	39066	8			9					2		6	4	10			3	7								11	5			1
11	Nov	6	Grimsby Town	1-2	Jones	20244	10							11	2		6	4				3				9	8	5		7					1
10		13	WEST BROMWICH ALB.	1-1	L Compton	34324		8						11	2	6						3					10	5	9	7						1
9		20	Charlton Athletic	3-0	Bastin, Drake, og (Ford)	55078	11		1								6	4		9		3					8	10	5	7		2				
6		27	LEEDS UNITED	4-1	Drake 2, Bastin (p), Kirchen	34350	11		1								6	4		9		3					8	10	5	7		2				
4	Dec	4	Birmingham	2-1	Kirchen, Cartwright	18440	11		1				4	6						9		3					8	10	5	7		2				
2		11	PRESTON NORTH END	2-0	Bastin, Milne	35679	11		1				4				6			9		3					8	10	5			2	7			
4		18	Liverpool	0-2		32093	11		1				4				6			9		3	7	8	10	5					2				
4		25	Blackpool	1-2	Bastin (p)	23229	11		1								6	4		9		3					8	10	5	7		2				
3		27	BLACKPOOL	2-1	Bastin, Cartwright	54163	11		1				4				6			9		3					8	10	5	7		2				
2	Jan	1	EVERTON	2-1	Lewis, Hunt	36953	11		1				4				6					3					8	10		7	9	2		5		
3		15	Wolverhampton Wan.	1-3	Drake	39383		1							11	6	4		9		3					8	10	5	7		2					
6		29	Sunderland	1-1	Hunt	42638	11		1								6	4				3					8	10	5	7	9	2				
3	Feb	2	LEICESTER CITY	3-1	Drake, Bastin, Jones	23839	11										6	4		9	7	3					8	10	5			2			1	
3		5	DERBY COUNTY	3-0	Crayston 2, Lewis	47263	11										6	4			7	3					8	10	5		9	2			1	
2		16	Manchester City	2-1	Drake, D Compton	34299					10				11		6	4		9		3						8	5	7		2			1	
1		19	CHELSEA	2-0	Griffiths, Drake	49573	11				10						6	4		9	7	3						8	5			2			1	
2		26	Portsmouth	0-0		43991	11										6	4		9	7	3			10		8	5			2			1	
1	Mar	5	STOKE CITY	4-0	Griffiths 2, Carr, Drake	35296	11				10	6						4		9	7	3					8	5			2			1	
1		12	Middlesbrough	1-2	Bastin	46747	11										6	4		9	10	7	3					8			2			5	1	
1		19	GRIMSBY TOWN	5-1	Griffiths 2,Bastin 2(1p),Jones	40701	11				9						6	4			10	7	3					8				2			5	1	
1		26	West Bromwich Albion	0-0		33954	11				8						6	4		9	10	7	3						5			2			1		
1	Apr	2	CHARLTON ATHLETIC	2-2	Drake, Carr	52858	11				10	4					6			9	7	3					8	5	7			2			1	
1		9	Leeds United	1-0	Bremner	29365					7	9		6	11	3		4							10		8	5				2			1	
1		15	BRENTFORD	0-2		51299	11					4					6				9	10	7	3				8	5				2			1	
1		16	BIRMINGHAM	0-0		35161	11					8					6					10		3				4	5	7	9		2			1	
1		18	Brentford	0-3		34601	10								11		6			9	8			3				4	5	7			2			1	
1		23	Preston North End	3-1	Carr 2, Bastin	42684	11					9					6	4			10		3					8	5	7			2			1	
1		30	LIVERPOOL	1-0	Carr	34703	11					9					6	4			7	10	3					8	5				2			1	
1	May	7	BOLTON WANDERERS	5-0	Bastin 2, Carr 2, Kirchen	40500	11				8	9					6					10		3				4	5	7		2			1		

Apps: 38 2 15 10 2 11 6 5 7 9 38 31 5 27 11 9 41 7 18 28 26 19 4 34 16 13 3 17 10
Goals: 15 1 1 7 2 1 1 4 2 17 5 2 3 3 6 2 4

One own goal

F.A. Cup

R3	Jan	8	BOLTON WANDERERS	3-1	Bastin 2, Kirchen	64016	11		1								6	4		9		3					8	10	5	7		2				
R4		22	Wolverhampton Wan.	2-1	Kirchen, Drake	61267	11		1								6	4		9		3					8	10	5	7		2				
R5	Feb	12	PRESTON NORTH END	0-1		72121	11										6	4		9		3					8	10	5	7		2			1	

Players only: Back: Pryde, Drake, Crayston, Swindon, Joy, Male, Kirchen. Front: Griffiths, Carr, Hapgood, Drury, Bastin, Copping

Everton 1938/39

Goodison Park

						Barber AW	Bell RC	Bentham SJ	Boyes WE	Britton CS	Caskie J	Cook W	Cunliffe JN	Gee CW	Gillick T	Greenhalgh N	Jackson G	Jones TG	Lawton T	Mercer J	Milligan GH	Morton H	Sagar E	Stevenson AE	Thomson JR	Trentham DH	Watson TG
	Aug	27	Blackpool	2-0	Lawton, Stevenson	29647			8	11			2			7	3		5	9	4			1	10	6		
		31	GRIMSBY TOWN	3-0	Lawton 2, Gillick	25017			8	11			2			7	3		5	9	4			1	10	6		
	Sep	3	BRENTFORD	2-1	Lawton 2	35989			8	11			2			7	3		5	9	4			1	10	6		
1		5	Aston Villa	3-0	Stevenson 2, Lawton	34105			8	11			2			7	3		5	9	4			1	10	6		
1		10	Arsenal	2-1	Lawton, Stevenson	64555			8	11			2			7	3		5	9	4			1	10	6		
1		17	PORTSMOUTH	5-1	Bentham, Boyes, Gillick, Lawton, Morgan (og)	43913			8	11			2			7	3		5	9	4			1	10	6		
1		24	Huddersfield Town	0-3		27710			8	11			2			7	3		5	9	4			1	10	6		
1	Oct	1	LIVERPOOL	2-1	Bentham, Boyes	64977			8	11			2			7	3		5	9	4			1	10	6		
1		8	WOLVERHAMPTON W.	1-0	Lawton	36681	7		8	11				10			3	2	5	9	4			1		6		
1		15	Bolton Wanderers	2-4	Lawton, Stevenson	57989			8	11			2			7	3		5	9	4			1	10			
1		22	LEEDS UNITED	4-0	Bell 3, Trentham	30747		9	8				2		5	7	3			4				1	10		11	6
2		29	Leicester City	0-3		23964			8	11			2			7	3		5	9	4			1	10			6
2	Nov	5	MIDDLESBROUGH	4-0	Lawton 3, Stevenson	35683			8	11			2			7	3		5	9	4			1	10	6		
2		12	Birmingham	0-1		27548			8	11			2		5	7	3			9	4			1	10	6		
2		19	MANCHESTER UNITED	3-0	Lawton 2, Gillick	31809			8	11			2			7	3		5	9	4			1	10	6		
2		26	Stoke City	0-0		26725			8	11			2			7	3		5	9	4			1	10	6		
2	Dec	3	CHELSEA	4-1	Lawton 2, Gillick, Stevenson	27959			8	11			2			7	3		5	9	4			1	10	6		
2		10	Preston North End	1-0	Lawton	26549			8	11			2			7	3		5	9	4			1	10	6		
2		17	CHARLTON ATHLETIC	1-4	Gillick	22053			8	11			2			7	3		5	9	4			1	10	6		
2		24	BLACKPOOL	4-0	Cunliffe 2, Cook, Gillick	24040			8	11			2	10		7	3		5	9	4			1				6
2		26	DERBY COUNTY	2-2	Cook, Gillick	55401		9	8	11			2	10		7	3		5		4			1		6		
2		27	Derby County	1-2	Cook	35683			8	11			2	10		7	3		5	9	4			1		6		
2		31	Brentford	0-2		27861			8	11			2	10		7	3		5	9	4			1		6		
2	Jan	14	ARSENAL	2-0	Boyes, Lawton	47178			8	11			2			7	3		5	9	4			1	10	6		
2		28	HUDDERSFIELD T	3-2	Cook, Lawton, Stevenson	37269			8	11			2			7	3		5	9	4			1	10	6		
2	Feb	1	Portsmouth	1-0	Lawton	17371			8	11			2			7	3		5	9	4			1	10	6		
1		4	Liverpool	3-0	Lawton 2, Bentham	55994			8	11			2			7	3		5	9	4			1	10	6		
1		18	BOLTON WANDERERS	2-1	Gillick, Hubbick (og)	38961		9	8	11			2			7	3		5		4			1	10	6		
1		22	Wolverhampton Wan.	0-7		39774		9		11			2			7	3		5	8	4		1		10	6		
1		25	Leeds United	2-1	Bentham, Cunliffe	21728	7		8	11				10			3	2	5	9	4			1				6
1	Mar	8	LEICESTER CITY	4-0	Boyes, Greenhalgh, Lawton, Stevenson	8199			8	11			2			7	3		5	9	4			1	10			6
1		11	Middlesbrough	4-4	Lawton 4	20014			8	11			2			7	3		5	9	4			1	10			6
1		18	BIRMINGHAM	4-2	Lawton 2, Bentham, Gillick	29687			8	11			2			7	3		5	9	4			1	10			6
1		29	Manchester United	2-0	Gillick, Lawton	18348			8	11			2			7	3		5	9	4			1	10			6
1	Apr	1	STOKE CITY	1-1	Lawton	38601			8	11			2			7	3		5	9	4			1	10			6
1		7	Sunderland	2-1	Gillick, Lawton	40521			8	11			2			7	3		5	9	4			1	10			6
1		8	Chelsea	2-0	Gillick, Stevenson	51481			8				11	2		7	3		5	9	4			1	10			6
1		10	SUNDERLAND	6-2	Bentham 3, Caskie, Lawton, Stevenson	46016			8				11	2		7	3			9	4			1	10	5		6
1		15	PRESTON NORTH END	0-0		31987			8		4	11	2	9		7	3		5					1	10			6
1		22	Charlton Athletic	1-2	Gillick	26338			8			11	2			7	3		5	9	4			1	10			6
1		29	ASTON VILLA	3-0	Bentham, Cook, Gillick	23667			8			11	2			7	3		5	9	4			1	10			6
1	May	6	Grimsby Town	0-3		11016			8	11			2			7	3		5	9	4			1	10			6

		Apps	2	4	41	36	1	5	40	7	2	40	42	2	39	38	41	1	1	41	36	26	1	16
		Goals		3	9	4		1	5	3		14	1			34					11	1		

Two own goals

F.A. Cup

R3	Jan	7	Derby County	1-0	Boyes	22237			8	11			2			7	3		5	9	4			1	10	6		
R4		21	DONCASTER ROVERS	8-0	Lawton 4, Boyes 2, Gillick, Stevenson	41115			8	11			2			7	3		5	9	4			1	10	6		
R5	Feb	11	Birmingham	2-2	Boyes, Stevenson	67341			8	11			2			7	3		5	9	4			1	10	6		
rep		15	BIRMINGHAM	2-1	Cook, Gillick	64796			8	11			2			7	3		5	9	4			1	10	6		
R6	Mar	4	Wolverhampton Wan.	0-2		59545			8	11			2			7	3		5	9	4			1	10			6

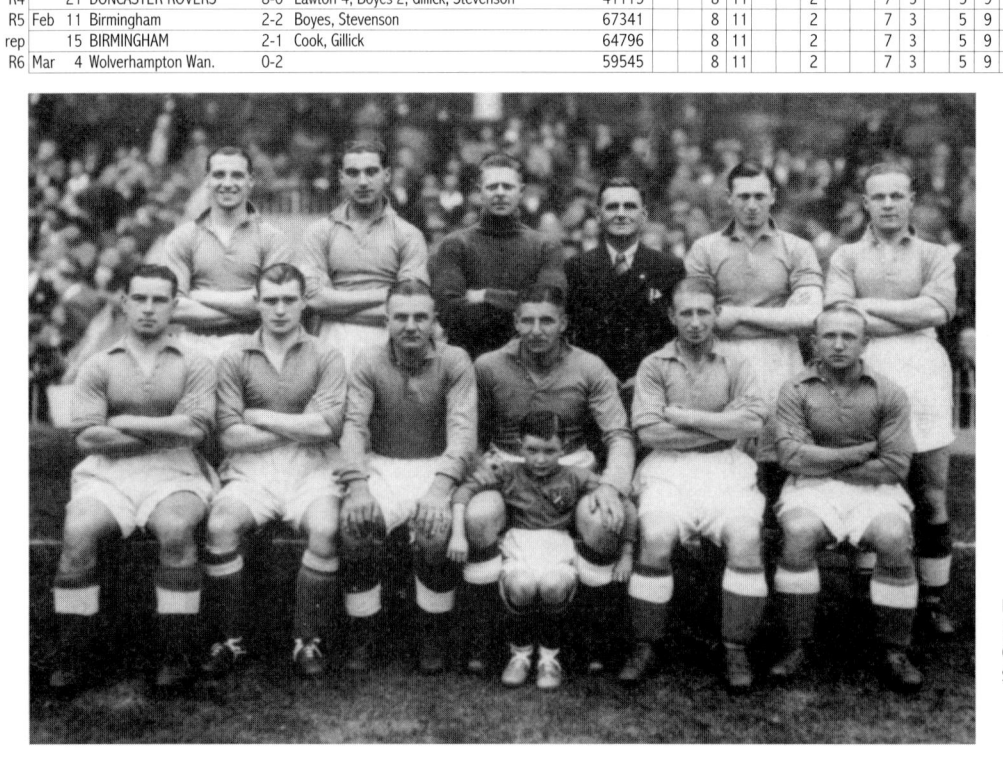

Back: Lawton, Jones, Sagar, H Cooke (trainer), Mercer, Greenhalgh. Front: Cook, Gillick, Bentham, Thomson, Stevenson, Boyes

Liverpool 1946/47

Anfield

							Ashcroft CT	Balmer J	Bush WT	Carney LF	Done CC	Easdale J	Eastham H	Fagan W	Harley J	Hughes L	Jones WH	Kaye GH	Lambert R	Liddell WB	McLeod T	Minshull R	Nieuwenhuys B	Paisley R	Polk S	Priday RH	Ramsden B	Sidlow C	Spicer EW	Stubbins A	Taylor PH	Watkinson WW
	Aug	31	Sheffield United	1-0	Carney	28296		8		10					2	5	9							7			11	3	1	6		4	
	Sep	4	MIDDLESBROUGH	0-1		34140		8		10					2	5	9							7			11	3	1	6		4	
		7	CHELSEA	7-4	Fagan 2, Jones 2, Liddell 2, Balmer	49995	1	8						10	2	5	9			11				7	6			3				4	
12		11	Manchester United	0-5		40874	1	8						10	2	5	9							7	6		11	3				4	
8		14	Bolton Wanderers	3-1	Nieuwenhuys, Stubbins, Balmer	35861		8								5	10		2	11				7	6			3	1		9	4	
9		21	EVERTON	0-0		49875		8								5	10		2	11				7	6			3	1		9	4	
7		28	LEEDS UNITED	2-0	Balmer, Nieuwenhuys	51042		8					6			5	10		2	11				7				3	1		9	4	
4	Oct	5	Grimsby Town	6-1	Stubbins 2,Liddell 2,Balmer,Fagan(p)	20189		8						7	10	5			2	11					6			3	1		9	4	
3		9	Middlesbrough	2-2	Liddell 2	37382		8						7	10	5			2	11					6			3	1		9	4	
6		12	CHARLTON ATHLETIC	1-1	Done	51127		8		10				7	9	5			2	11					6			3	1			4	
4		19	Huddersfield Town	4-1	Done 3, Balmer	17323		8		10				7		2	5					1			6		11	3			9	4	
3		26	BRENTFORD	1-0	Stubbins	43892		8		10				7		5			2	11					6			3	1		9	4	
2	Nov	2	Blackburn Rovers	0-0		29072		8		10				7		5			2	11					6			3	1		9	4	
2		9	PORTSMOUTH	3-0	Balmer 3 (1p)	43525		8		10				7		5			2	11					6			3	1		9	4	
1		16	Derby County	4-1	Balmer 4	28444		8		10				7		5			2	11					6			3	1		9	4	
1		23	ARSENAL	4-2	Balmer 3 (1p), Stubbins	51435		8		10				7		5			2	11					6			3	1		9	4	
1		30	Blackpool	2-3	Balmer, Done	23565		8		10				7		5	6		2	11								3	1		9	4	
2	Dec	7	WOLVERHAMPTON W.	1-5	Balmer (p)	52512		8		10				7		5			2	11					6			3	1		9	4	
2		14	Sunderland	4-1	Balmer,Liddell,Nieuwenhuys,Stubbins	33291		8						10		5	3		2	11				7	6			1			9	4	
2		21	ASTON VILLA	4-1	Balmer 2, Stubbins, Nieuwenhuys	35389		8						10		5	3		2	11				7	6			1			9	4	
2		25	Stoke City	1-2	Stubbins	30473		8				5	10				3		2	11	1			7	6						9	4	
2		26	STOKE CITY	2-0	Nieuwenhuys, Stubbins	49465		8	5				10				3		2	11	1			7	6						9	4	
2		28	SHEFFIELD UNITED	1-2	Stubbins	50961		8	5				10				3		2	11	1			7	6					4	9		
4	Jan	4	Chelsea	1-3	Balmer	59226		8						10		5	3		2	11				7	6			1			9	4	
5		18	BOLTON WANDERERS	0-3		49820		8						10		5	3		2	11	1			7	6						9	4	
6		29	Everton	0-1		30612		8		10			7		2	5			3	11					6			1			9	4	
6	Feb	1	Leeds United	2-1	Stubbins 2	25430		8						10	2	5			3	11				7	6			1			9	4	
2		12	GRIMSBY TOWN	5-0	Done 3, Fagan 2	20648				10				8		5			2	11					6	7		3	1		9	4	
4		22	HUDDERSFIELD T	1-0	Stubbins	42130		8		10				7		5			2	11					6			3	1		9	4	
2	Mar	8	BLACKBURN ROVERS	2-1	Done, Stubbins	49378		8		10				7	2	5			3	11					6				1		9	4	
2		15	Portsmouth	2-1	Stubbins 2	30296		8		10			7		2	5			4	11					6			3	1		9		
3		22	DERBY COUNTY	1-1	Taylor	50848		8		10	5			7	2				3	11					6				1			9	4	
3	Apr	4	Preston North End	0-0		32542		8		10				7		5			2		9						11	3	1	6		4	
5		5	BLACKPOOL	2-3	Fagan, Done	47320				10				7	2		5	4	3	11						8			1	6	9		
5		7	PRESTON NORTH END	3-0	Stubbins 2, Balmer	46477		8	5						2					11	10	1				7		3		6	9	4	
5		19	SUNDERLAND	1-0	Stubbins	41589		8							2	5			3	11	10				6	7			1		9	4	
5		26	Aston Villa	2-1	Watkinson, Fagan	35429								7	2	5			3						6	8			1		9	4	10
4	May	3	MANCHESTER UNITED	1-0	Stubbins	48800		8								5	4		2	11					6	7			1	3	9		10
4		10	Charlton Athletic	3-1	Stubbins 3	45608		8						7		5	3	2							6		11		1		9	4	10
4		17	Brentford	1-1	Priday	18228		8						7	2	5		3							6		11		1	4	9		10
1		24	Arsenal	2-1	Balmer, Priday	44265		8						7	2	5	4	3									11		1	6	9		10
1		31	Wolverhampton Wan.	2-1	Balmer, Stubbins	50765		8							2	5	4	3		7							11		1	6	9		10

| | | | | | Apps | 2 | 39 | 3 | 2 | 17 | 2 | 19 | 18 | 17 | 30 | 26 | 1 | 36 | 34 | 3 | 6 | 15 | 33 | 6 | 9 | 23 | 34 | 10 | 36 | 35 | 6 |
| | | | | | Goals | | 24 | | 1 | 10 | | | 7 | | | 2 | | | 7 | | | | 5 | | | 2 | | | | 24 | 1 | 1 |

F.A. Cup

R3	Jan	11	Walsall	5-2	Done, Liddell, Balmer 2, Foulkes (og)	18370		8			10			7		5	2		3	11					6				1		9	4	
R4		25	GRIMSBY TOWN	2-0	Stubbins, Done	45256		8			10			7			5		2	11					6			3	1		9	4	
R5	Feb	8	DERBY COUNTY	1-0	Balmer	44493		8			10			7	2	5			3	11					6				1		9	4	
R6	Mar	1	BIRMINGHAM CITY	4-1	Stubbins 3, Balmer	51911		8			10			7	2	5			3	11					6				1		9	4	
SF		29	Burnley	0-0	(aet)	53000		8			10			7	2	5			3	11					6				1		9	4	
rep	Apr	12	Burnley	0-1		72000		8			10			7	2	5			3	11					6				1		9	4	

SF at Ewood Park, SF replay at Maine Road

Arsenal 1947/48

Highbury

						Barnes W	Compton DCS	Compton LH	Fields AG	Forbes AR	Jones B	Lewis RJ	Logie JT	Macaulay AR	Male CG	McPherson IB	Mercer J	Rooke RL	Roper DGB	Scott L	Sloan JW	Smith L	Swindin GH	Wade SJ
Aug	23	SUNDERLAND	3-1	Logie, Rooke, McPherson	58184	3			5			9	8	4		11	6	10	7	2			1	
	27	Charlton Athletic	4-2	Roper, Logie, Lewis, McPherson	60323	3			5			9	8	4		11	6	10	7	2			1	
	30	Sheffield United	2-1	Roper, Rooke	39124	3			5			9	8	4		11	6	10	7	2			1	
Sep	3	CHARLTON ATHLETIC	6-0	Lewis 4, Rooke 2	54684	3			5			9	8	4		11	6	10	7	2			1	
	6	MANCHESTER UNITED	2-1	Lewis, Rooke	64905	3			5			9	8	4		11	6	10	7	2			1	
	10	BOLTON WANDERERS	2-0	Rooke (p), McPherson	46969	3			5			9	8	4		11	6	10	7	2			1	
	13	Preston North End	0-0		40040	3		5					8	4		11	6	10	7	2	9		1	
	20	STOKE CITY	3-0	McPherson 2, Logie	61579	3		5			10		8	4	2	11	6	9	7				1	
	27	Burnley	1-0	Lewis	46958	3		5				9	8	4		11		10	7	2	6		1	
Oct	4	PORTSMOUTH	0-0		62461	3		5				9	8		4	11		10	7	2	6		1	
	11	ASTON VILLA	1-0	Rooke	60427	3		5			10		8	4		11	6	9	7	2			1	
	18	Wolverhampton Wan.	1-1	Rooke (p)	55998			5				9	8	4	2	11	6	10	7				1	3
	25	EVERTON	1-1	Lewis	56645	3		5				9	8	4		11	6	10	7	2			1	
Nov	1	Chelsea	0-0		67277	3		5				9	8	4		11	6	10	7	2			1	
	8	BLACKPOOL	2-1	Rooke (p), Roper	67057	3		5				8	10	4		11	6	9	7	2			1	
	15	Blackburn Rovers	1-0	Rooke	37447	3		5				9	8	4		11	6	10	7	2			1	
	22	HUDDERSFIELD T	2-0	Rooke, Logie	47514	3		5				9	8	4		11	6	10	7	2			1	
	29	Derby County	0-1		35713	3		5				9	8	4		11	6	10	7	2			1	
Dec	6	MANCHESTER CITY	1-1	Rooke (p)	41274	3		5				9	8	4		11	6	10	7	2			1	
	13	Grimsby Town	4-0	Rooke 2, Roper, Logie	18700	3		5			10		8	4		11	6	9	7	2			1	
	20	Sunderland	1-1	Jones	58397	3		5			10		8	4		11	6	9	7	2			1	
	25	Liverpool	3-1	Rooke 2, Roper	53604			5				9	8	4		11	6	10	7	2			1	3
	27	LIVERPOOL	1-2	Lewis	56650			5				9	8	4		11	6	10	7	2			1	3
Jan	1	Bolton Wanderers	1-0	Lewis	30028			5				9	8	4	2	11	6	10	7	3			1	
	3	SHEFFIELD UNITED	3-2	Rooke 2, Lewis	48993			5				9	8	4	2	11	6	10	7	3			1	
	17	Manchester United	1-1	Lewis	83260	3		5				9	8	4		11	6	10	7	2			1	
	31	PRESTON NORTH END	3-0	Lewis 2, Rooke	63162	3		5				9	8	4		11	6	10	7	2			1	
Feb	7	Stoke City	0-0		44836	3		5				9	8	4		11	6	10	7	2			1	
	14	BURNLEY	3-0	Rooke 2, Roper	62125	3	11	5			10		8	4			6	9	7	2			1	
	28	Aston Villa	2-4	Rooke, Moss (og)	65690	3	11	5			10	8		4			6	9	7	2			1	
Mar	6	WOLVERHAMPTON W.	5-2	Rooke 2, Forbes, Roper, Logie	57711	3	11	5	10				8	4			6	9	7	2			1	
	13	Everton	2-0	D Compton 2	64059	3	11	5	10			7	8	4			6	9		2			1	
	20	CHELSEA	0-2		56596	3	11	5	10				8	4			6	9	7	2			1	
	26	MIDDLESBROUGH	7-0	Rooke 3, D Compton 2, Roper, Robinson (og)	57557	3	11	5	10				8	4			6	9	7	2			1	
	27	Blackpool	0-3		32678	3	11	5				10	8	4		7	6	9		2			1	
	29	Middlesbrough	1-1	Rooke	38249	3	11	5	10				8	4			6	9	7	2			1	
Apr	3	BLACKBURN ROVERS	2-0	Logie, Rooke	45801	3	11	5	10				8	4			6	9	7	2			1	
	10	Huddersfield Town	1-1	Roper	38110	3	11	5	4			10	8		2		6	9	7				1	
	17	DERBY COUNTY	1-2	Roper	49677	3	11	5	10				8	4			6	9	7	2			1	
	21	Portsmouth	0-0		42250	3	11	5	10	8				4			6	9	7	2			1	
	24	Manchester City	0-0		23391		11	5	10	8			8	4	2		6	9	7	3			1	
May	1	GRIMSBY TOWN	8-0	Rooke 4, D Compton 2, Logie (p), Forbes	34644		11		10				8	4	2		6	9	7	3		5	1	

Apps	35	14	35	6	11	7	28	39	40	8	29	40	42	40	39	3	1	42	3
Goals		6			2	1	14	8			5		33	10					

Two own goals

F.A. Cup

| R3 | Jan | 10 | BRADFORD PARK AVE. | 0-1 | | 47738 | | | 5 | | | | 9 | 8 | 4 | 2 | 11 | 6 | 10 | 7 | 3 | | | 1 | |

Portsmouth 1948/49

Fratton Park

						Barlow H	Bowler GC	Butler EA	Clarke I	Delapenha LL	Dickinson JW	Ferrier HR	Flewin R	Froggatt J	Harris PP	Hindmarsh JW	Parker CH	Phillips, Len	Reid JD	Rookes PW	Scoular J	Thompson WG	Youell JH
	Aug	21	Preston North End	2-2	Reid, Barlow	37062	11		1			6	3	5	9	7				10	8	2	4		
		25	EVERTON	4-0	Froggatt 2, Barlow 2	31433	8		1			6	3	5	11	7				10	9	2	4		
		28	BURNLEY	1-0	Froggatt	37846	8		1			6	3	5	11	7				10	9	2	4		
1	Sep	1	Everton	5-0	Harris, Reid, Froggatt 2, Barlow	41511	8	5	1			6	3		11	7				10	9	2	4		
1		4	Stoke City	1-0	Harris	31151	8	5	1			6	3		11	7				10	9	2	4		
1		8	MIDDLESBROUGH	1-0	Reid	33275	8		1			6	3	5	11	7				10	9	2	4		
1		11	CHARLTON ATHLETIC	3-1	Reid 3	39459	8		1			6	3	5	11	7				10	9	2	4		
1		15	Middlesbrough	1-1	Barlow	33247	8		1			6	3	5	11	7				10	9	2	4		
1		18	Manchester City	1-1	Reid	51490	8		1			6	3	5	11	7				10	9	2	4		
1		25	SHEFFIELD UNITED	3-0	Harris 2, Phillips	36240	8		1			6	3	5	11	7				10	9	2	4		
1	Oct	2	NEWCASTLE UNITED	1-0	Phillips	45827	8		1			6	3	5	11	7				10	9	2	4		
1		9	Aston Villa	1-1	Reid	57649	8		1			6	3	5	11	7				10	9	2	4		
1		16	SUNDERLAND	3-0	Harris, Reid, Froggatt	35205	8		1			6	3	5	11	7				10	9	2	4		
1		23	Wolverhampton Wan.	0-3		48604	8		1			6	3	5	11	7				10	9	2	4		
2		30	BOLTON WANDERERS	0-0		29760	10		1			6	3	5	11	7				8	9	2	4		
2	Nov	6	Liverpool	1-3	Harris	43665	10		1			6	3	5	11	7				8	9	2	4		
2		13	BLACKPOOL	1-1	Harris	44869		1	10	8		6	3	5	11	7					9	2	4		
3		20	Derby County	0-1		34087	10	1	9	8		6	3	5	11	7						2	4		
2		27	ARSENAL	4-1	Froggatt, Phillips, Barlow, Clarke	43000	8		1	9		6	3	5	11	7				10		2	4		
2	Dec	4	Huddersfield Town	0-0		21785	8		1	9		6	3	5	11	7				10		2	4		
3		11	MANCHESTER UNITED	2-2	Froggatt, Clarke	29966	8		1	9		6	3	5	11	7				10		2	4		
2		18	PRESTON NORTH END	3-1	Harris, Phillips, Barlow (p)	26545	8		1	9		6	3	5	11	7				10		2	4		
1		25	Chelsea	2-1	Harris 2	43422	8		1	9		6	3	5	11	7				10		2	4		
1		27	CHELSEA	5-2	Harris 2, Barlow(p), Clarke, Winter(og)	43624	8		1	9		6	3	5	11	7				10		2	4		
1	Jan	1	Burnley	1-2	Bray (og)	31045	8		1	9		6	3	5	11	7				10		2	4		
1		15	STOKE CITY	1-0	Froggatt	34538	8		1	9		6	3	5	11	7				10			4		2
1		22	Charlton Athletic	1-0	Clarke	61475	8		1	9		6	3	5	11	7				10			4		2
1	Feb	5	MANCHESTER CITY	3-1	Harris, Clarke 2	34949	8		1	9		6	3	5	11	7				10			4		2
1		19	Sheffield United	1-3	Froggatt	42876	8		1	9		6	3	5	7				11	10			4		2
1	Mar	5	ASTON VILLA	3-0	Froggatt, Phillips 2	34264	8		1	9		6	3	5	11	7				10			4		2
		12	Sunderland	4-1	Reid 2, Froggatt, Phillips	57229			1			6	3	5	9	7			11	10	8		4		2
1		19	DERBY COUNTY	1-0	Phillips	43188			1			6	3	5	9	7			11	10	8		4		2
1	Apr	2	LIVERPOOL	3-2	Harris, Phillips, Clarke	35013			1	9		6	3	5	11	7	2			10	8		4		
1		6	Newcastle United	5-0	Harris 2, Froggatt 3	60611			1	9		6	3	5	11	7	2			10	8		4		
1		9	Blackpool	0-1		18723			1	9		6	3	5	11	7	2			10	8		4		
1		15	BIRMINGHAM CITY	3-1	Reid 2, Clarke	38456			1	9		6	3	5	11	7	2			10	8		4		
1		16	WOLVERHAMPTON W.	5-0	Reid 2, Phillips, Clarke 2	44225			1	9		6	3	5	11	7	2			10	8		4		
1		18	Birmingham City	0-3		29983			1	9		6	3	5		7	2		11	10	8		4		
1		23	Bolton Wanderers	2-1	Harris, Clarke	31063			1	9		6	3	5	11	7	2			10	8		4		
1		30	HUDDERSFIELD T	2-0	Reid (p), Clarke	37042			1	9			3	5	11	7	2			10	8		4	6	
1	May	4	Arsenal	2-3	Clarke 2	56973			1	9		6		5	11		2	7		10	8		4	3	
1		7	Manchester United	2-3	Harris, Reid	52661			1	9		6			11	7	2			10	8		4	5	3

| | | Apps | 29 | 2 | 42 | 24 | 2 | 41 | 40 | 39 | 41 | 40 | 10 | 5 | 40 | 29 | 25 | 42 | 3 | 8 |
| | | Goals | 8 | | | 14 | | | | | 15 | 17 | | | 11 | 17 | | | | |

Two own goals

F.A. Cup

R3	Jan	8	STOCKPORT COUNTY	7-0	Harris 3, Phillips 2, Clarke 2	33590	8		1	9		6	3	5	11	7				10		2	4		
R4		29	SHEFFIELD WEDNESDAY	2-1	Harris, Phillips	47188	8		1	9		6	3	5	11	7				10			4		2
R5	Feb	12	NEWPORT COUNTY	3-2	Froggatt, Phillips 2	48581	8		1	9		6	3	5	11	7				10			4		2
R6		26	DERBY COUNTY	2-1	Clarke 2	51385	8		1	9		6	3	5	11	7				10			4		2
SF	Mar	26	Leicester City	1-3	Harris	62000	8		1	9		6	3	5	11	7				10			4		2

R5 a.e.t. SF at Highbury.

Portsmouth 1949/50

Fratton Park

						Barlow H	Bennett R	Butler EA	Clarke I	Dawson JEIB	Delapenha LL	Dickinson JW	Ekner DH	Elder J	Ferrier HR	Flewin R	Froggatt J	Harris PP	Higham P	Hindmarsh JW	Parker CH	Phillips, Len	Pickett RA	Reid ID	Rookes PW	Scoular J	Spence WJ	Stephen JF	Thompson WG	Youell JH
	Aug	20	Newcastle United	3-1	Harris, Clarke, Phillips	54258			1	9			6			3	5	11	7				10		8		4			2
		24	MANCHESTER CITY	1-1	Reid (p)	43965			1	9			6			3	5	11	7				10		8		4			2
		27	BLACKPOOL	2-3	Clarke, Phillips	46927			1	9			6			3	5	11	7				10		8		4			2
16		31	Manchester City	0-1		32732			1	9			6			3	5	11	7		2		10		8		4			
8	Sep	3	Middlesbrough	5-1	Harris 3, Clarke, Froggatt	41974			1	9		8	6			3	5	11	7		2		10				4			
11		5	Aston Villa	0-1		38360			1	9		8	6			3	5	11	7		2		10				4			
9		10	EVERTON	7-0	Harris,Reid 3,Clarke,Phillips,Froggatt	36012			1	9			6			3	5	11	7		2		10		8		4			
7		17	Huddersfield Town	1-0	Clarke	26222			1	9			6			3	5	11	7		2		10		8		4			
7		24	BOLTON WANDERERS	1-1	Clarke	35188			1	9			6			3	5	11	7				10		8		4			2
7	Oct	1	WOLVERHAMPTON W.	1-1	Reid	49831			1	9			6			3		11	7		2		10		8		4		5	
6		8	Birmingham City	3-0	Reid, Clarke 2	37944			1	9			6			3		11	7		2		10		8		4		5	
4		15	DERBY COUNTY	3-1	Reid, Clarke, Froggatt	36849			1	9						3		11	7		2		10	6	8		4		5	
5		22	West Bromwich Albion	0-3		40808	10		1		7		6			3		9			2	11			8		4		5	
5		29	MANCHESTER UNITED	0-0		40586			1	9			6			3		11	7		2		10	8			4	5		
5	Nov	5	Chelsea	4-1	Clarke 2, Froggatt 2	31650			1	9			6			3		11	7		2		10		8		4	5		
6		12	STOKE CITY	0-0		32809			1	9			6			3		11	7		2		10				4	5		
7		19	Burnley	1-2	Barlow	28541	10		1	9			6			3		11	7		2				8		4	5		
7		26	SUNDERLAND	2-2	Harris, Clarke	36035			1	10			6	9	4	3		11	7						8			5	2	
7	Dec	3	Liverpool	2-2	Harris, Clarke	44851			1	9			6	8		3		11	7		2		10				4	5		
7		10	ARSENAL	2-1	Clarke, Froggatt	39027			1	9			6	8		3	5	11	7		2		10				4			
7		17	NEWCASTLE UNITED	1-0	Clarke	30066			1	8			6	9		3	5	11	7		2		10				4			
7		24	Blackpool	1-2	Harris	25953			1	8			6			3	5	11	7		2		10		9		4			
6		26	Charlton Athletic	2-1	Phillips, Froggatt	37539			1	8			6	9		3	5	11	7		2		10				4			
4		27	CHARLTON ATHLETIC	1-0	Harris	43325			1	9		8	6			3	5	11	7		2		10				4			
5		31	MIDDLESBROUGH	1-1	Froggatt	32644			1	9		8	6			3	5	11	7		2		10				4			
4	Jan	14	Everton	2-1	Harris, Phillips	50428			1	9			6			3	5		7		2	11	10		8		4			
4		21	HUDDERSFIELD T	4-0	Reid, Froggatt 3	29327			1	9			6			3	5	11	7		2		10		8		4			
4	Feb	4	Bolton Wanderers			32441			1	9			6			3	5	11			2	7	10				4			
5		18	Wolverhampton Wan.	0-1		46679			1	9			6			3	5	11	7				10	8		2	4			
4		25	BIRMINGHAM CITY	2-0	Harris 2	28051		11	1				6			3			7	9			10	8		2	4		5	
7	Mar	8	Derby County	1-2	Pickett	17713			1				6			3		11	7				10	8	9	2	4		5	
5		11	BURNLEY	2-1	Clarke, Froggatt	26344			1	9			6			3	5	11	7		2		10	8			4			
5		18	Sunderland	1-1	Bennett	44591		11	1	10			6			3	5		7		2			8	9		4			
4		25	CHELSEA	4-0	Harris, Reid 3	29100			1	9			6			3	5	11	7		2			10	8		4			
5	Apr	1	Stoke City	1-0	Harris	26521			1	9			6			3	5	11	7		2			10	8		4			
4		7	FULHAM		Harris 2, Froggatt	38932			1	9			6			3	5	11	7		2			10	8		4	5		
5		8	WEST BROMWICH ALB.	0-1		33494			1	9			6			3		11	7		2		8	10			4	5		
3		10	Fulham	1-0	Clarke	24812			1	9		8	6			3		11	7		2			10			4	5		
1		15	Manchester United	2-0	Reid, Froggatt	46709			1	9						3		11	7		2		10		8		4	5	6	
1		22	LIVERPOOL	2-1	Reid, Froggatt	46927			1	9			6			3		11	7		2		10		8		4	5		
1	May	3	Arsenal	0-2		63124			1				6			3		11	7		2		10	9	8		5	4		
1		6	ASTON VILLA	5-1	D Reid 3, Thompson 2	41638			1				6			3	5	11	7		2		10		8		4		9	

	Apps	2	2	42	37	1	5	40	5	1	42	24	39	40	1	34	3	34	14	27	3	36	16	1	9	4
	Goals	1	1		17								15	16				5	1	16					2	

F.A. Cup

R3	Jan	7	NORWICH CITY	1-1	Delapenha	42059			1	9		8	6			3	5		7		2		10	11			4			
rep		12	Norwich City	2-0	Reid 2	43129			1	9			6			3	5	11	7		2		10		8		4			
R4		28	GRIMSBY TOWN	5-0	Clarke 2, Phillips, Froggatt 2	39364			1	9			6			3	5	11			2	7	10		8		4			
R5	Feb	11	Manchester United	3-3	Ferrier, Clarke, Parker	53688			1	8			6			3	5	9	7		2	11	10				4			
rep		15	MANCHESTER UNITED	1-3	Harris	49962			1	8			6			3	5	9	7		2	11	10				4			

F.A. Charity Shield

Oct	19	Wolverhampton Wan.	1-1	Reid	25000	10		1	9			6			3		11	7		2				8		4		5	

At Highbury

Tottenham Hotspur 1950/51

White Hart Lane

						Baily EF	Bennett LD	Brittan C	Burgess WAR	Clarke HA	Ditchburn EG	Duquemin LS	McClellan SB	Medley LD	Murphy P	Nicholson WE	Ramsey AE	Scarth JW	Tickridge S	Uphill EDH	Walters WE	Willis A	Withers CF	Wright AM
	Aug	19	BLACKPOOL	1-4	Baily	64978	10	8		6	5	1	9			11						7		3	
		23	Bolton Wanderers	4-1	Murphy, Duquemin, Walters, Medley	21745	10			6	5	1	9		11	8	4	2				7		3	
		26	Arsenal	2-2	Burgess, Walters	64638	10			6	5	1	9		11	8	4	2				7	3		
4		28	BOLTON WANDERERS	4-2	Duquemin 2, Baily, Howe (og)	44246	10	8		6	5	1	9		11		4	2				7	3		
9	Sep	2	Charlton Athletic	1-1	Ramsey (p)	61480	10	8		6	5	1	9		11		4	2				7	3		
12		6	Liverpool	1-2	Medley	39015	10			6	5	1	9		11	8	4	2				7	3		
9		9	MANCHESTER UNITED	1-0	Walters	60621	10	8		6	5	1	9			11	4	2				7	3		
12		16	Wolverhampton Wan.	1-2	Chatham (og)	55364	10	8		6	5	1	9		11		4	2				7	3		
13		23	SUNDERLAND	1-1	Baily	59190	10			6	5	1		9	11		4	2			8	7	3		
9		30	Aston Villa	3-2	Murphy, Duquemin, Medley	36538	10			6	5	1	9		11	8	4	2				7	3		
7	Oct	7	BURNLEY	1-0	Medley	46518		10	6		5	1	9		11	8	4			2		7	3		
5		14	Chelsea	2-0	Walters, Duquemin	65992	10	8		6	5	1	9		11		4	2				7	3		
4		21	STOKE CITY	6-1	Bennett 2, Duquemin 2, Walters, Medley	54124	10	8	6		5	1	9		11		4	2				7	3		
5		28	West Bromwich Albion	2-1	Walters, Medley	44543	10	8		6	5	1	9		11		4	2				7	3		
4	Nov	4	PORTSMOUTH	5-1	Baily 3, Walters, Duquemin	66402	10	8		6	5	1	9		11		4	2				7	3		
4		11	Everton	2-1	Baily, Medley	47125	10	8		6	5	1	9		11		4	2				7	3		
2		18	NEWCASTLE UNITED	7-0	* See below	70336	10	8	6		5	1	9		11		4	2				7	3		
4		25	Huddersfield Town	2-3	Nicholson, Walters	39519	10	8	6		5	1	9		11		4	2				7	3		
4	Dec	2	MIDDLESBROUGH	3-3	Ramsey (p), Walters, Duquemin	61148	10	8		6	5	1	9		11		4	2				7	3		
4		9	Sheffield Wednesday	1-1	Bennett	44367	10	8		6	5	1	9		11		4	2				7	3		
4		16	Blackpool	1-0	Duquemin	22203	10	8	6		5	1	9		11		4	2				7	3		
3		23	ARSENAL	1-0	Baily	54898	10	8		6	5	1	9		11		4	2				7	3		
2		25	Derby County	1-1	Murphy	32301		8	6		5	1	9		11	10	4	2				7	3		
2		26	DERBY COUNTY	2-1	McClellan 2	59885	10			6	5	1		9	11	8	4	2	7				3		
1		30	CHARLTON ATHLETIC	1-0	Walters	54667	10	8		6	5	1	9		11		4	2				7	3		
1	Jan	13	Manchester United	1-2	Baily	45104	10		4		5	1		9	11	8	6	2				7	3		
1		20	WOLVERHAMPTON W.	2-1	Walters, McClellan	66796	10			6	5	1		9	11	8	4	2				7	3		
1	Feb	3	Sunderland	0-0		56817	10			6	5	1	9		11	8	4	2				7	3		
1		17	ASTON VILLA	3-2	Ramsey (p), Baily, Medley	47842	10		4	6	5	1		9	11	8		2				7	3		
1		24	Burnley	0-2		33047	10			6	5	1		9	11	8	4	2				7	3		
1	Mar	3	CHELSEA	2-1	Wright, Burgess	59449	10			6	5	1			11	8	4	2				7	3		9
1		10	Stoke City	0-0		24236	10			6	5	1			11	8	4	2				7	3		9
1		17	WEST BROMWICH ALB.	5-0	Duquemin 3, Baily, Bennett	45353	10	8		6	5	1	9			11	4	2				7	3		
1		23	Fulham	1-0	Murphy	47391	10	8		6	5	1	9			11	4	2				7	3		
1		24	Portsmouth	1-1	Uphill	49716	10			6	5	1	9			11	4	2			8	7	3		
1		26	FULHAM	2-1	Bennett, Murphy	51862	10	8		6	5	1	9		7	11	4	2					3		
1		31	EVERTON	3-0	Murphy, Walters, Bennett	46651	10	8		6	5	1	9			11	4	2				7	3		
1	Apr	7	Newcastle United	1-0	Walters	41241	10	8		6	5	1	9			11	4	2				7	3		
1		14	HUDDERSFIELD T	0-2		55014	10	8		6	5	1	9			11	4					7	2	3	
1		21	Middlesbrough	1-1	Murphy	36689	10			6	5	1	9		11	8	4	2				7	3		
1		28	SHEFFIELD WEDNESDAY	1-0	Duquemin	46645	10			6	5	1	9		11	8	4	2				7	3		
1	May	5	LIVERPOOL	3-1	Murphy 2, Walters	49072	10			6	5	1	9		11	8	4	2				7	3		

Scorers in game 17: Medley 3, Baily, Bennett, Walters, Ramsey (p)

	Apps	40	25	8	35	42	42	33	7	35	25	41	40	1	1	2	40	39	4	2
	Goals	12	7		2			14	3	11	9	1	4			1	15			1

Two own goals

F.A. Cup

| R3 | Jan | 6 | Huddersfield Town | 0-2 | | 25390 | 10 | 8 | | 6 | 5 | 1 | 9 | | 11 | | 4 | 2 | | | | 7 | 3 | | |

Manchester United 1951/52

Old Trafford

							Allen AR	Aston J	Berry RJ	Birch B	Blanchflower J	Bond JE	Byrne RW	Carey JJ	Cassidy L	Chilton AC	Clempson F	Cockburn H	Crompton J	Downie JD	Gibson TRD	Jones M	McGlen W	McNulty T	McShane H	Pearson SC	Redman W	Rowley JF	Walton JA	Whitefoot J
	Aug	18	West Bromwich Albion	3-3	Rowley 3	29769	1					11		2		5		4		10				6		7	8	3	9	
		22	MIDDLESBROUGH	4-2	Pearson, Rowley 3	39176	1					11		2		5		6		10	4					7	8	3	9	
		25	NEWCASTLE UNITED	2-1	Rowley, Downie	53673	1					11		2		5		6		10	4					7	8	3	9	
2		29	Middlesbrough	4-1	Pearson 2, Rowley 2	44434	1					11		2		5		6		10	4					7	8	3	9	
5	Sep	1	Bolton Wanderers	0-1		55477	1		7			11		2		5		6		10	4						8	3	9	
3		5	CHARLTON ATHLETIC	3-2	Rowley 2, Downie	28627	1		7			11		2		5		6		10	4						8	3	9	
3		8	STOKE CITY	4-0	Pearson, Rowley 3	45494	1		7					2		5		6		10	4					11	8	3	9	
1		12	Charlton Athletic	2-2	Downie 2	27048	1		7					2		5		6		10	4					11	8	3	9	
1		15	Manchester City	2-1	Berry, McShane	52520	1		7					2	9	5		6		10	4					11	8	3		
3		22	Tottenham Hotspur	0-2		70882	1		7					2		5		6		10	4					11	8	3	9	
6		29	PRESTON NORTH END	1-2	Aston	55267	1	9	7					2		5		6			4						10	3	11	8
3	Oct	6	DERBY COUNTY	2-1	Berry, Pearson	41563	1		7					2		5		6								11	10	3	9	8
1		13	Aston Villa	5-2	Pearson 2, Rowley 2, Bond	47765	1		7			11				5		6		10	4		2				8	3	9	
3		20	SUNDERLAND	0-1		42707	1		7					2		5				8	4		6			11	10	3	9	
3		27	Wolverhampton Wan.	2-0	Pearson, Rowley	46167	1			10		11		2		5		6			4					7	8	3	9	
2	Nov	3	HUDDERSFIELD T	1-1	Pearson	27420	1			10		11		2		5		6			4					7	8	3	9	
5		10	Chelsea	2-4	Pearson, Rowley	48960	1	9	7					2		5		6		10	4						8	3	11	
7		17	PORTSMOUTH	1-3	Downie	37703	1	9	7					2		5		6		10	4						8	3	11	
7		24	Liverpool	0-0		42378			7		4	11	3	2		5		6	1	10							8		9	
6	Dec	1	BLACKPOOL	3-1	Rowley, Downie 2	35977			7			11	3	4		5		6	1	10				2			8		9	
3		8	Arsenal	3-1	Daniel (og), Pearson, Rowley	53451			7			11	3	4		5		6	1	10				2			8		9	
2		15	WEST BROMWICH ALB.	5-1	Berry, Pearson 2, Downie 2	29402	1		7			11	3	4		5		6		10				2			8		9	
2		22	Newcastle United	2-2	Cockburn, Bond	45414	1		7			11	3	4		5		6		10				2			8		9	
2		25	FULHAM	3-2	Berry, Rowley, Bond	35697	1		7			11	3			4		6		10		5		2			8		9	
2		26	Fulham	3-3	Pearson, Rowley, Bond	32671	1		7			11	3			4		6		10		5		2			8		9	
1		29	BOLTON WANDERERS	1-0	Pearson	55073	1		7			11	3			4		6		10		5		2			8		9	
2	Jan	5	Stoke City	0-0		36389	1		7			11	3	4		5		6		10				2			8		9	
2		19	MANCHESTER CITY	1-1	Carey	56122	1	9	7				3	4		5		6		10				2			8		11	
1		26	TOTTENHAM HOTSPUR	2-0	Ramsay (og), Pearson	42668	1	9	7				3	4		5	8	6						2			10		11	
1	Feb	9	Preston North End	2-1	Berry, Aston	38792	1	9	7				3	4		5	8	6						2			10		11	
1		16	Derby County	3-0	Aston, Pearson, Rowley	27693		9	7				3	4		5	8	6	1					2			10		11	
1	Mar	1	ASTON VILLA	1-1	Berry	41717		9	7				3	4		5	8	6	1					2			10		11	
1		8	Sunderland	2-1	Cockburn, Rowley	48078		9	7				3	4		5	8	6	1					2			10		11	
1		15	WOLVERHAMPTON W.	2-0	Clempson, Aston	46933		9	7				3	4		5	8	6	1					2			10		11	
1		22	Huddersfield Town	2-3	Clempson, Pearson	30316		9	7				3	4		5	8	6	1					2			10		11	
1	Apr	5	Portsmouth	0-1		25522		9	7			11	3	4		5	8		1	10				2						6
1		11	Burnley	1-1	Byrne	38907	1	3	7					11	4	5		6		8				2			10		9	
1		12	LIVERPOOL	4-0	Downie, Rowley, Byrne 2	44899	1	3	7					11	4	5				8				2			10		9	6
1		14	BURNLEY	6-1	Carey, Downie, Rowley, Pearson, Byrne 2	46339	1	3	7					11	4	5				8				2			10		9	6
1		19	Blackpool	2-2	Byrne, Rowley	29118	1	3	7					11	4	5		6		8				2			10		9	
1		21	CHELSEA	3-0	Carey, Pearson, McKnight (og)	39272	1	3	7					11	4	5		6		8				2			10		9	
1		26	ARSENAL	6-1	Rowley 3, Pearson 2, Byrne	55516	1	3	7					11	4	5		6		8				2			10		9	

| | Apps | 33 | 18 | 36 | 2 | 1 | 19 | 24 | 38 | 1 | 42 | 8 | 38 | 9 | 31 | 17 | 3 | 2 | 24 | 12 | 41 | 18 | 40 | 2 | 3 |
| | Goals | | | 4 | 6 | | | 4 | 7 | 3 | | | 2 | 2 | | 11 | | | | 1 | | 22 | | 30 | | |

Three own goals

F.A. Cup

| R3 | Jan | 12 | HULL CITY | 0-2 | | 43517 | 1 | | 7 | | | 11 | 3 | 4 | | 5 | | 6 | | 10 | | | | 2 | | | 8 | | 9 | | |

Arsenal 1952/53

Highbury

						Bowen DL	Chenhall JC	Cox FJA	Daniel WR	Dodgin W	Forbes AR	Goring H	Holton CC	Kelsey AJ	Lishman DJ	Logie JT	Marden RJ	Mercer J	Milton CA	Oakes DJ	Platt EH	Roper DGB	Shaw A	Smith L	Swindin GH	Wade SJ
	Aug	23	Aston Villa	2-1	Oakes, Lishman	50930				5		7	9		10			6		8		11	4	3	1	2
		27	MANCHESTER UNITED	2-1	Cox, Goring	57831			7	5			9		10			6		8		11	4	3	1	2
		30	SUNDERLAND	1-2	Lishman	56873		2	7	5			8	9	10			6				11	4		1	3
6	Sep	3	Manchester United	0-0		39193	6	2	7	5			8	9	10							11	4		1	3
6		6	Wolverhampton Wan.	1-1	Roper	43371			7	5			8	9	10			6				11	4	3	1	2
3		10	PORTSMOUTH	3-1	Milton, Goring, Roper	39743				5		4	9				8	6	7			11	10	3	1	2
9		13	CHARLTON ATHLETIC	3-4	Daniel, Milton, Goring	60102				5		4	9				8	6	7			11	10	3	1	2
7		17	Portsmouth	2-2	Holton 2	37356	6	2		5		8	10	9					7		1	11	4	3		
7		20	Tottenham Hotspur	3-1	Milton, Logie, Goring	69247		2		5		6	9			10	8		7		1	11	4	3		
7		27	Derby County	0-2		24582		2		5		6	9			10	8		7		1	11	4			3
5	Oct	4	BLACKPOOL	3-1	Roper 2, Logie	66642		2		5		6	9		1	10	8		7			11	4			3
6		11	SHEFFIELD WEDNESDAY	2-2	Logie, Roper	54678		2		5		6	9		1	10	8		7			11	4			3
5		25	NEWCASTLE UNITED	3-0	Roper 2, Lishman	63744				5		4	9		1	10	8	6	7			11		3		2
7	Nov	1	West Bromwich Albion	0-2		42911				5		4	9		1	10	8	6	7			11		3		2
7		8	MIDDLESBROUGH	2-1	Milton, Holton	48564				5		6		9	1	10	8		7			11	4	3		2
4		15	Liverpool	5-1	Holton 3, Marden 2	45010		2		5		4		9	1	10	8	11	6	7						3
3		22	MANCHESTER CITY	3-1	Logie 2, Lishman	38161				5		4		9	1	10	8		6	7			11		3		2
3		29	Stoke City	1-1	Holton	24057		2		5		4		9	1	10	8		6	7			11				3
4	Dec	13	Burnley	1-1	Milton	32753				5		4		9	1	10	8		6	7			11		3		2
3		20	ASTON VILLA	3-1	Holton, Lishman, Roper	30064				5				9	1	10	8		6	7			11	4	3		2
2		25	Bolton Wanderers	6-4	Holton 2, Daniel, Milton, Logie, Roper	45432				5				9	1	10	8		6	7			11	4	3		2
6	Jan	3	Sunderland	1-3	Lishman	54912				5		4		9	1	10	8		6	7			11		3		2
4		17	WOLVERHAMPTON W.	5-3	Lishman 2, Milton, Daniel, Logie	57983				5		4		9	1	10	8			7			11	6	3		2
5		24	Charlton Athletic	2-2	Lishman, Roper	66555				5		4		9	1	10	8		6	7			11		3		2
4	Feb	7	TOTTENHAM HOTSPUR	4-0	Holton 2, Logie, Lishman	69051				5		4		9	1	10	8		6	7			11		3		2
2		18	DERBY COUNTY	6-2	Holton 2, Lishman 2, Daniel 2	32681				5		4	8	9	1	10				7			11	6	3		2
5		21	Blackpool	2-3	Mercer, Goring	30034		3		5		4	8	9	1	10			6	7			11				2
5	Mar	2	Sheffield Wednesday	4-1	Holton 4	32814		3	7	5			8	9	1	10			6				11	4			2
5		7	CARDIFF CITY	0-1		59780			7	5				9	1	10	8		6				11	4	3		2
5		14	Newcastle United	2-2	Lishman 2	51618				5			9		1	10	8		6	7			11	4	3		2
5		19	PRESTON NORTH END	1-1	Mercer	33597				5		4	9		1	10	8		6	7			11		3		2
6		21	WEST BROMWICH ALB.	2-2	Holton, Roper	49078			7	5			6		9	1	10	8					11	4	3		2
6		28	Middlesbrough	0-2		25911			7	5		4	8	9	1	10			6				11		3		2
6	Apr	3	Chelsea	1-1	Goring	72614			7	5			6	9	1	10	8						11	4	3		2
4		4	LIVERPOOL	5-3	Roper 2, Goring, Lishman, Hughes (og)	39564				5			6	9	1	10	8			7			11	4	3		2
3		6	CHELSEA	2-0	Marden, Lishman	40536				5		4		9		10	8	11	6				7		3	1	2
3		11	Manchester City	4-2	Goring 2, Logie, Roper	50018				5		4		9		10	8	11	6				7		3	1	2
1		15	BOLTON WANDERERS	4-1	Lishman 2, Marden, Goring	35381		3			5	4		9		10	8	11	6				7			1	2
1		18	STOKE CITY	3-1	Lishman 3	47376		3		5		4		9		10	8	11	6				7			1	2
1		22	Cardiff City	0-0		57893				5		4		9		10	8	11					7	6	3	1	2
1		25	Preston North End	0-2		39537				5		4		9		10	8	11					7	6	3	1	2
1	May	1	BURNLEY	3-2	Forbes, Logie, Lishman	51586				5		4		9		10	8	11	6				7		3	1	2
						Apps	2	13	9	41	1	33	29	21	25	39	32	8	28	25	2	3	41	25	31	14	40
						Goals			1	5		1	10	19		22	10	4	2	7		1	14				

One own goal

F.A. Cup

R3	Jan	10	DONCASTER ROVERS	4-0	Logie, Holton, Lishman, Roper	57443				5		6		9	1	10	8			7			11	4	3		2
R4		31	BURY	6-2	Milton, Logie, Holton, Lishman, Roper, Daniel(og)	45701				5		4		9	1	10	8		6	7			11		3		2
R5	Feb	14	Burnley	2-0	Holton, Lishman	51025				5		4		9	1	10	8		6	7			11		3		2
R6		28	BLACKPOOL	1-2	Logie	69158				5		4		9	1	10	8		6	7			11		3		2

Wolverhampton Wanderers 1953/54

Molineux

							Baxter W	Broadbent PF	Chatham RH	Clamp HE	Deeley NV	Flowers R	Gibbons L	Guttridge WH	Hancocks J	Mullen J	Pritchard RT	Short J	Shorthouse WH	Sims DN	Slater WJ	Smith JL	Stockin R	Stuart EA	Swinbourne RH	Williams BF	Wilshaw DJ	Wright WA
	Aug	19	Burnley	1-4	Swinbourne	32822									7	11	3	2	5	1	4				8	9		10	6
		22	Manchester City	4-0	Swinbourne 2, Slater, Wilshaw	22729									7	11	3	2	5	1	4				8	9		10	6
		26	Sunderland	2-3	Hancocks (p), Wilshaw	57135									7	11	3	2	5	1	4				8	9		10	6
9		29	CARDIFF CITY	3-1	Hancocks (p), Mullen, Wilshaw	33221		8							7	11	3	2	5	1	4					9		10	6
5		31	SUNDERLAND	3-1	Mullen, Swinbourne, Wilshaw	41442		8							7	11	3	2	5	1	4					9		10	6
4	Sep	5	Arsenal	3-2	Broadbent, Hancocks, Wilshaw	60460		8							7	11	3	2	5		4					9	1	10	6
3		7	LIVERPOOL	2-1	Broadbent, Swinbourne	35701		8							7	11	3	2	5		4					9	1	10	6
2		12	PORTSMOUTH	4-3	Wilshaw 3, Swinbourne	36524		8			4		2		7	11	3		5							9	1	10	6
2		16	Liverpool	1-1	Wilshaw	29848		8			4				7	11	3		5		6					9	1	10	2
3		19	Blackpool	0-0		35074	6	8	4						7	11	3		5							9	1	10	2
3		26	CHELSEA	8-1	* see below	36134		8							7	11	3	2	5		4					9	1	10	6
3	Oct	3	Sheffield United	3-3	Hancocks, Swinbourne, Wilshaw	35961		8							7	11	3	2	5		4					9	1	10	6
2		10	Newcastle United	2-1	Smith, Swinbourne	39913		8			6				7		3	2	5		4	11	10		9	1			
2		17	MANCHESTER UNITED	3-1	Broadbent, Hancocks (p), Swinbourne	40084		8					3		7	11		2	5		4					9	1	10	6
3		24	Bolton Wanderers	1-1	Hancocks	40027	4	8					3		7	11		2	5		6					9	1	10	
2		31	PRESTON NORTH END	1-0	Wilshaw	34211	4	8							7	11		2	5		6		10			1		9	3
2	Nov	7	Middlesbrough	3-3	Hancocks, Swinbourne, Wilshaw	24284	4	8							7	11		2	5		6					9	1	10	3
2		14	WEST BROMWICH ALB.	1-0	Mullen	56590	4								7	11	3	2	5					8		9	1	10	6
2		21	Charlton Athletic	2-0	Broadbent, Hancocks	35595		8							7	11	3	2	5		4					9	1	10	6
2		28	SHEFFIELD WEDNESDAY	4-1	Hancocks 2 (1p), Swinbourne 2	35154		8							7	11	3	2	5		4					9	1	10	6
1	Dec	5	Tottenham Hotspur	3-2	Broadbent, Hancocks, Wilshaw	48164		8							7	11	3	2	5		4					9	1	10	6
2		12	BURNLEY	1-2	Hancocks	35043		8							7	11	3	2	5		4					9	1	10	6
1		19	MANCHESTER CITY	3-1	Hancocks 2 (1p), Wilshaw	27606		8							7	11	3	2	5		4					9	1	10	6
1		24	ASTON VILLA	1-2	Wilshaw	40536		8							7	11	3	2	5	1	4					9		10	6
1		26	Aston Villa	2-1	Hancocks, Wilshaw	49123		8							7	11	3	2	5	1	4					9		10	6
1	Jan	2	Cardiff City	3-1	Hancocks, Swinbourne, Wilshaw	42521		8				6			7	11	3		5	1	4					9		10	2
2		16	ARSENAL	0-2		45974		8				6			7	11	3	2			4					9	1	10	5
2		23	Portsmouth	0-2		35312		10				8	6		7	11		2	5		4					9	1		3
2	Feb	6	BLACKPOOL	4-1	Swinbourne 3, Hancocks	27795		8				8			7	11	3	2	5		4					9	1	10	6
2		13	Chelsea	2-4	Swinbourne, Wilshaw	60289						8			7	11	3	2	5		4					9	1	10	6
2		20	SHEFFIELD UNITED	6-1	Hancocks 2, Swinbourne 2, Broadbent, Wilshaw	27823		8				6			7	11	3				4			2		9	1	10	5
2		27	NEWCASTLE UNITED	3-2	Broadbent, Slater, Wilshaw	38592		8				6			7	11		3			4			2		9	1	10	5
2	Mar	6	Manchester United	0-1		40774		8		6		9			7	11		3			4			2		1	1	10	5
2		20	Preston North End	1-0	Wilshaw	24376		8			6				7			3			4	11		2		9	1	10	5
2		24	BOLTON WANDERERS	1-1	Broadbent	19617		8		10	6				7			3			4	11		2		9	1		5
2		27	MIDDLESBROUGH	2-4	Broadbent 2	29145		8			6				7	11		3			4			2		9	1	10	5
2	Apr	3	West Bromwich Albion	1-0	Swinbourne	49669		8				6			11		3		5		4	7		2		9	1		
1		10	CHARLTON ATHLETIC	5-0	Hancocks 2, Mullen 2, Wilshaw	35028		8				6			7	11			5		4			2		9	1	10	3
1		17	Sheffield Wednesday	0-0		40707		8				6			7	11			5		4			2		9	1	10	3
1		19	HUDDERSFIELD T	4-0	Broadbent, Hancocks, Mullen, Wilshaw	42862		8				6			7	11			5		4			2		9	1	10	3
1		20	Huddersfield Town	1-2	Wilshaw	35814		8				6			7	11			5		4			2		9	1	10	3
1		24	TOTTENHAM HOTSPUR	2-0	Swinbourne 2	44055		8				6			7	11			5		4			2		9	1	10	3

Sep 26 scorers: Hancocks 3 (1p), Swinbourne 2, Broadbent, Mullen, Wilshaw

Apps	5	36	1	2	6	15	1	2	42	38	27	26	40	8	39	4	6	12	40	34	39	39
Goals		12							25	7					2	1			24		25	

F.A. Cup

R3	Jan	9	BIRMINGHAM CITY	1-2	Wilshaw	36784		8							7	11	3	2	5	1	4					9		10	6

Chelsea 1954/55

Stamford Bridge

		Date	Opponent	Score	Scorers	Att	Armstrong K	Bentley TRF	Blunstone F	Brabrook P	Dicks AV	Edwards RH	Greenwood R	Harris J	Lewis IL	McNichol J	O'Connell SCP	Parsons EG	Robertson WG	Saunders DW	Sillett RPT	Smith RA	Stubbs LL	Thomson CR	Wicks SM	Willemse SB
	Aug	21	Leicester City	1-1	Bentley	38941		9	11				5	4		8		7	1	6	2		10			3
		23	BURNLEY	1-0	Parsons	30239							5	4	11	8		7	1	6	2	9	10			3
		28	BOLTON WANDERERS	3-2	Bentley, Lewis, Ball (og)	52756	4	9					5	2	11	8		7	1	6			10			3
2		31	Burnley	1-1	Bentley	28472	4	9					5	2	11	8		7	1	6			10			3
6	Sep	4	CARDIFF CITY	1-1	Lewis	42688	4	9					5	2	11	8		7	1	6			10			3
8		6	PRESTON NORTH END	0-1		35947	4	9				10	5	2	11	8		7	1	6						3
10		11	Manchester City	1-1	Bentley	36230	4	9					5	2	11	8		7	1	6			10			3
8		15	Preston North End	2-1	Parsons, McNichol	27549	4	9					5	2	11	8		7	1	6			10			3
10		18	EVERTON	0-2		59199	4	9					5	2	11	8		7	1	6			10			3
6		20	Sheffield United	2-1	Stubbs, Lewis	14137	4	9					5	2	11	8		7	1	6			10			3
4		25	Newcastle United	3-1	Bentley 2, McNichol	45659	4	9					5	2	11	8		7	1	6		10				3
4	Oct	2	WEST BROMWICH ALB.	3-3	Parsons, Bentley, Lewis	67440	4	9					5	2	11	8		7	1	6		10				3
9		9	Huddersfield Town	0-1		29556	4	9					5	2	11	8		7	1	6			10			3
11		16	MANCHESTER UNITED	5-6	O'Connell 3, Armstrong, Lewis	55966	4	9					5	2	11	8	10	7	1	6						3
12		23	Blackpool	0-1		19694	4	9					5	2	11	8	10	7	1	6						3
12		30	CHARLTON ATHLETIC	1-2	Parsons	54113	4	9					5	2	11		10	7	1	6		8				3
12	Nov	6	Sunderland	3-3	McNichol 2, Stubbs	42416	4	9	11					2		8		7	1	6			10		5	3
12		13	TOTTENHAM HOTSPUR	2-1	Bentley, Lewis	52961	4	9						2	11	8		7	1	6			10		5	3
12		20	Sheffield Wednesday	1-1	McNichol	25913	4	9	11					2		8		7	1	6			10		5	3
11		27	PORTSMOUTH	4-3	McNichol, Bentley, Stubbs, Blunstone	40358	4	9	11				5	2		8		7	1	6			10			3
8	Dec	4	Wolverhampton Wan.	4-3	Bentley 2, McNichol, Stubbs	32095	4	9	11				5	2		8		7	1	6			10			3
4		11	ASTON VILLA	4-0	McNichol 2, Parsons, Bentley	36162	4	9	11				5	2		8		7	1	6			10			3
4		18	LEICESTER CITY	3-1	Parsons, McNichol, Milburn/Froggatt(og)	33215	4	9	11				5	2		8		7	1	6	3		10			
5		25	Arsenal	0-1		47178	4	9	11				5	2		8		7	1	6			10			3
5		27	ARSENAL	1-1	O'Connell	65922	4	9	11							8	10	7	1	6	2				5	3
4	Jan	1	Bolton Wanderers	5-2	Bentley 2, Sillett, O'Connell, Higgins (og)	30998	4	9	11								8	7	1	6	2		10		5	3
6		22	MANCHESTER CITY	0-2		34160	4	9	11							8		7		6	2		10	1	5	3
6	Feb	5	Everton	1-1	Bentley	50658	4	9	11							8		7		6	2		10	1	5	3
5		12	NEWCASTLE UNITED	4-3	Bentley 3, McNichol	50667	4	9	11							8		7		6	2		10	1	5	3
3		26	HUDDERSFIELD T	4-1	Parsons, Bentley, Stubbs, Blunstone	35786	4	9	11							8		7		6	2		10	1	5	3
5	Mar	5	Aston Villa	2-3	Parsons, McNichol	24467	4	9							11	8		7		6	2		10	1	5	3
3		9	West Bromwich Albion	4-2	Sillett 2, Saunders, Bentley	7651	4	9	11					2		8		7		6	3		10	1	5	
2		12	BLACKPOOL	0-0		55227	4	9	11					2		8		7		6	3		10	1	5	
2		19	Charlton Athletic	2-0	O'Connell, Blunstone	41553	4	9	11					2		8	10	7		6	3			1	5	
1		23	Cardiff City	1-0	O'Connell	16649	4	9	11					2		8	10	7		6	3			1	5	
1		29	SUNDERLAND	2-1	Willemse, Bentley	33203	4	9	11		10			2		8		7		6	3			1	5	11
1	Apr	2	Tottenham Hotspur	4-2	McNichol 2, Sillett, Wicks	53159		9			10	4		2		8		7		6	3			1	5	11
1		8	SHEFFIELD UNITED	1-1	Parsons	50978	4	9	11	10				2		8		7		6	3			1	5	
1		9	WOLVERHAMPTON W.	1-0	Sillett (p)	75043	4	9	11							8	10	7		6	2			1	5	3
1		16	Portsmouth	0-0		40230	4	9	11							8		7		6	2		10	1	5	3
1		23	SHEFFIELD WEDNESDAY	3-0	Parsons 2, Sillett (p)	51421	4	9	11							8	10	7		6	2			1	5	3
1		30	Manchester United	1-2	Bentley	34933	4	9	11							8	10	7		6	2			1	5	3

	Apps	39	41	23	3	1	1	21	31	17	40	10	42	26	42	21	4	27	16	21	36
	Goals	1	22	3						6	14	7	11		1	6		5		1	1

Three own goals

F.A. Cup

		Date	Opponent	Score	Scorers	Att	Armstrong	Bentley	Blunstone							McNichol	O'Connell	Parsons	Robertson	Saunders	Sillett		Stubbs	Thomson	Wicks	Willemse
R3	Jan	8	WALSALL	2-0	O'Connell, Stubbs	40020	4	9	11								8	7	1	6	2		10		5	3
R4		29	Bristol Rovers	3-1	Parsons, McNichol, Blunstone	35972	4	9	11							8		7		6	2		10	1	5	3
R5	Feb	19	Notts County	0-1		41930	4	9	11							8		7		6	2		10	1	5	3

93

Manchester United 1955/56

Old Trafford

							Bent G	Berry RJ	Blanchflower J	Byrne RW	Colman E	Crompton J	Doherty JH	Edwards D	Foulkes WA	Goodwin F	Greaves ID	Jones M	Lewis E	McGuinness W	Pegg D	Scanlon AJ	Scott J	Taylor T	Viollet DS	Webster C	Whelan WA	Whitefoot J	Whitehurst W	Wood RE
	Aug	20	Birmingham City	2-2	Viollet 2	37612			8	3				6	2			5						11	9	10	7		4		1
		24	TOTTENHAM HOTSPUR	2-2	Berry, Webster	28713		7	8	3				6	2			5						11		10	9		4		1
		27	WEST BROMWICH ALB.	3-1	Lewis, Scanlon, Viollet	32267			8	3				6	2			5	9					11		10	7		4		1
5		31	Tottenham Hotspur	2-1	Edwards 2	27453			8	3				6	2			5	9					11		10	7		4		1
7	Sep	3	Manchester City	0-1		59192			8	3			10	2	6			5	9					11			7		4		1
4		7	EVERTON	2-1	Blanchflower, Edwards	28062			8	3			10	2	6			5	9					11			7		4		1
7		10	Sheffield United	0-1		28027		7	10	3					2	6		5			11						9	8	4		1
7		14	Everton	2-4	Blanchflower, Webster	35238		11	9	3		10			2	6		5									7	8		4	1
6		17	PRESTON NORTH END	3-2	Pegg, Taylor, Viollet	33362			8	3					2	6		5			11			9	10	7		4		1
6		24	Burnley	0-0		26723			8	3					2	6		5			11			9	10	7		4		1
4	Oct	1	LUTON TOWN	3-1	Taylor 2, Webster	34661	3	7	8						2	6		5			11			9		10		4		1
3		8	WOLVERHAMPTON W.	4-3	Taylor 2, Doherty, Pegg	48890	3	7		2			8					5		6	11			9		10		4		1
3		15	Aston Villa	4-4	Pegg 2, Blanchflower, Webster	29478		7	8	3					2			5		6	11			9		10		4		1
2		22	HUDDERSFIELD T	3-0	Berry, Pegg, Taylor	34201	3	7	8			1		6	2			5			11			9	10			4		
1		29	Cardiff City	1-0	Taylor	27795		7	8	3				6	2			5			11			9	10			4		1
1	Nov	5	ARSENAL	1-1	Taylor	41836		7	8	3				6	2			5			11			9	10			4		1
3		12	Bolton Wanderers	1-3	Taylor	41829		7	8	3	4			6	2			5			11			9		10				1
2		19	CHELSEA	3-0	Taylor 2, Byrne (p)	22365		7		3	4		8	6	2			5			11			9	10					1
2		26	Blackpool	0-0		26240		7		3	4		8	6			2	5			11			9	10					1
1	Dec	3	SUNDERLAND	2-1	Doherty, Viollet	40150		7		3	4		8	6	2			5			11			9	10					1
2		10	Portsmouth	2-3	Pegg, Taylor	24186		7		3	4		8	6	2			5			11			9	10					1
1		17	BIRMINGHAM CITY	2-1	Jones, Viollet	27936		7		3	4		8	6	2			5			11			9	10					1
1		24	West Bromwich Albion	4-1	Viollet 3, Taylor	25168		7		3	4		8	6	2			5			11			9	10					1
1		26	CHARLTON ATHLETIC	5-1	Viollet 2, Byrne, Doherty, Taylor	44838		7		3	4		8	6	2			5			11			9	10					1
1		27	Charlton Athletic	0-3		41340		7		3	4		8	6	2			5			11			9	10					1
1		31	MANCHESTER CITY	2-1	Taylor, Viollet	61194		7		3	4		8	6	2			5			11			9	10					1
1	Jan	14	SHEFFIELD UNITED	3-1	Berry, Pegg, Taylor	30388		7		3	4			6	2			5			11			9	10		8			1
1		21	Preston North End	1-3	Whelan	28047				3	4			6	2			5			11		7		10	9	8			1
1	Feb	4	BURNLEY	2-0	Taylor, Viollet	27542		7		3	4			6			2	5			11			9	10		8			1
1		11	Luton Town	2-0	Viollet, Whelan	16368		7	6	3						4	2	5			11			9	10		8			1
1		18	Wolverhampton Wan.	2-0	Taylor 2	40014		7		3	4			6			2	5			11			9	10		8			1
1		25	ASTON VILLA	1-0	Whelan	36476		7		3	4			6			2	5			11			9	10		8			1
1	Mar	3	Chelsea	4-2	Viollet 2, Pegg, Taylor	32050		7		3	4			6			2	5			11			9	10		8			1
1		10	CARDIFF CITY	1-1	Byrne (p)	44914		7		3	4			6			2	5			11			9	10		8			1
1		17	Arsenal	1-1	Viollet	50758		7		3	4			6			2	5			11			9	10		8			1
1		24	BOLTON WANDERERS	1-0	Taylor	46346		7		3	4			6			2	5			11			9	10		8			1
1		30	NEWCASTLE UNITED	5-2	Viollet 2, Doherty, Pegg, Taylor	58994		7		3	4		8	6			2	5			11			9	10					1
1		31	Huddersfield Town	2-0	Taylor 2	37780		7		3	4			6			2	5			11			9	10					1
1	Apr	2	Newcastle United	0-0		37395		7		3	4		8	6			2	5			11			9	10					1
1		7	BLACKPOOL	2-1	Berry, Taylor	62522		7		3	4		8	6			2	5			11			9	10					1
1		14	Sunderland	2-2	McGuinness, Whelan	19855	3	7	9		4						2	5		6	11				10		8			1
1		21	PORTSMOUTH	1-0	Viollet	38672		7		3	4		8	6			2	5			11			9	10					1
					Apps		4	34	18	39	25	1	16	33	26	8	15	42	4	3	35	6	1	33	34	15	13	15	1	41
					Goals			4	3	3			4	3				1	1	1	9	1		25	20	4	4			

FA Cup

R3	Jan	7	Bristol Rovers	0-4		35872		7		3	4		8		2			5			11			9	10			6		1

94

Manchester United 1956/57

Old Trafford

	Date	Opponent	Score	Scorers	Att	Bent G	Berry RJ	Blanchflower J	Byrne RW	Charlton R	Clayton G	Colman E	Cope R	Dawson AD	Doherty JH	Edwards D	Foulkes WA	Goodwin F	Greaves ID	Hawksworth A	Jones M	McGuinness W	Pegg D	Scanlon AJ	Taylor T	Viollet DS	Webster C	Whelan WA	Wood RE
	Aug 18	BIRMINGHAM CITY	2-2	Viollett 2	32958		7		3			4				6	2				5		11		9	10		8	1
	20	Preston North End	3-1	Whelan, Taylor 2	32569		7		3			4				6	2				5		11		9	10		8	1
	25	West Bromwich Albion	3-2	Whelan, Taylor, Violett	26387		7		3			4				6	2				5		11		9	10		8	1
3	29	PRESTON NORTH END	3-2	Violett 3	32515		7		3			4				6	2				5		11		9	10		8	1
1	Sep 1	PORTSMOUTH	3-0	Violett, Pegg, Berry	40595		7		3			4				6	2				5		11		9	10		8	1
1	5	Chelsea	2-1	Whelan, Taylor	29082		7		3			4				6	2				5		11		9	10		8	1
1	8	Newcastle United	1-1	Whelan	50133		7		3			4				6	2				5		11		9	10		8	1
1	15	SHEFFIELD WEDNESDAY	4-1	Whelan, Taylor, Berry, Violett	48306		7		3			4				6	2				5		11		9	10		8	1
1	22	MANCHESTER CITY	2-0	Whelan, Violett	53751		7		3			4				6	2				5		11		9	10		8	1
1	29	Arsenal	2-1	Whelan, Berry	62479		7		3			4	5			6	2						11		9	10		8	1
1	Oct 6	CHARLTON ATHLETIC	4-2	Berry, Charlton 2, Whelan	41698	3	7			9		4					2				5	6	11			10		8	1
1	13	Sunderland	3-1	Whelan, Violett, Morrison (og)	49487		7		3			4				6	2				5		11		9	10		8	1
1	20	EVERTON	2-5	Whelan, Charlton	43677		7		3	10		4				6	2				5		11		9			8	1
1	27	Blackpool	2-2	Taylor 2	32632		7		3			4				6	2			1	5		11		9	10		8	
1	Nov 3	WOLVERHAMPTON W.	3-0	Whelan, Taylor, Pegg	55071		7		3	10		4				6	2				5		11		9			8	1
2	10	Bolton Wanderers	0-2		39922		7		3	10		4				6	2				5		11		9			8	1
1	17	LEEDS UNITED	3-2	Whelan 2, Charlton	52402		7		3	10		4					2				5	6	11		9			8	1
1	24	Tottenham Hotspur	2-2	Colman, Berry	57724		7	5	3			4				10	2					6	11		9			8	1
1	Dec 1	LUTON TOWN	3-1	Taylor, Edwards, Pegg	34954		7		3			4				10	2				5	6	11		9			8	1
1	8	Aston Villa	3-1	Taylor 2, Violett,	42530	3	7					4				6	2				5		11		9	10		8	1
1	15	Birmingham City	1-3	Whelan	36146	3	7					4				6	2				5		11		9	10		8	1
1	26	CARDIFF CITY	3-1	Whelan, Taylor, Violett	28810		7		3			4				6	2				5		11		9	10		8	1
1	29	Portsmouth	3-1	Edwards, Violett, Pegg	32052		7		3			4				9	2				5	6	11			10		8	1
1	Jan 1	CHELSEA	3-0	Whelan, Taylor 2	42282		7		3			4				6	2				5		11		9	10		8	1
1	12	NEWCASTLE UNITED	6-1	Whelan 2, Violett 2, Pegg 2	45132		7		3			4				6	2				5		11		9	10		8	1
1	19	Sheffield Wednesday	1-2	Taylor	49398		7		3			4				6	2				5		11		9	10		8	1
1	Feb 2	Manchester City	4-2	Edwards, Whelan, Taylor, Violett	63872		7		3			4				6	2				5		11		9	10		8	1
1	9	ARSENAL	6-2	Edwards, Berry 2, Whelan 2, Taylor	61628		7		3			4				6	2				5		11		9	10		8	1
1	18	Charlton Athletic	5-1	Taylor 2, Charlton 3	16408	3	7			2	10	4					2				5	6	11		9			8	1
1	23	BLACKPOOL	0-2		42707		7		3	10		4				6	2				5		11		9			8	1
1	Mar 6	Everton	2-1	Webster 2	34029	3	7	5	2						10		4					6	11				9	8	1
1	9	ASTON VILLA	1-1	Charlton	55686		7	5	3	10						9	2	4				6	11					8	1
1	16	Wolverhampton Wan.	1-1	Charlton	53238		7	5	3	10	1	4				6	2						11				9	8	1
1	25	BOLTON WANDERERS	0-2		61101		7	5	3	10		4				9	2					6	11					8	1
1	30	Leeds United	2-1	Berry, Charlton	47216		7	5	3	10		4				6	2						11				9	8	1
1	Apr 6	TOTTENHAM HOTSPUR	0-0		60583	3	7	5				4					2					6		11	9	10		8	1
1	13	Luton Town	2-0	Taylor 2	21244		7	5	3	10						6	2	4					11	9	8				1
1	19	Burnley	3-1	Whelan 3	37823		7	5	3	10						6	2	4					11		9			8	1
1	20	SUNDERLAND	4-0	Whelan 2, Edwards, Taylor	58725		7	5	3	10		4				6	2						11		9			8	1
1	22	BURNLEY	2-0	Webster, Dawson	41540									5	9	8	2	4	3			6	11			10	7		1
1	27	Cardiff City	3-2	Dawson, Scanlon 2	17708			5				4		9			2		3			6	11			10	7	8	1
1	29	WEST BROMWICH ALB.	1-1	Dawson	20976		7		3		1			9	8			4	2		5	6	11			10			1

	Apps	6	40	11	36	14	2	36	2	3	3	34	39	6	3	1	29	13	37	5	32	27	5	39	39
	Goals		8			10		1		3		5							6	2	22	16	3	26	

One own goal

FA Cup

Rd	Date	Opponent	Score	Scorers	Att																								
R3	Jan 5	Hartlepools United	4-3	Whelan 2, Berry, Taylor	17264		7		3			4				6	2				5		11		9	10		8	1
R4	26	Wrexham	5-0	Whelan 2, Byrne (p), Taylor 2	34445				3			4				6	2				5		11		9	10	7	8	1
R5	Feb 16	EVERTON	1-0	Edwards	61803		7		3			4				6	2				5		11		9	10		8	1
R6	Mar 2	Bournemouth	2-1	Berry 2	28799		7		3			4				9	2				5	6	11			10		8	1
SF	23	Birmingham City	2-0	Berry, Charlton	65107		7	5	3	9		4				6	2						11			10		8	1
F	May 14	Aston Villa	1-2	Taylor	100000		7	5	3	10		4				6	2						11					8	1

SF at Hillsborough, Final at Wembley

European Cup

Rd	Date	Opponent	Score	Scorers	Att																								
PR1	Sep 12	Anderlecht	2-0	Viollet, Taylor	35000		7	6	3			4					2				5		11		9	10		8	1
PR2	26	Anderlecht	10-0	Viollet 4, Taylor 3, Whelan 2, Berry	43635		7		3			4				6	2				5		11		9	10		8	1
R1/1	Oct 17	Borussia Dortmund	3-2	Viollet 2, Pegg	75598		7		3			4				6	2				5		11		9	10		8	1
R1/2	Nov 21	Borussia Dortmund	0-0		44570		7		3			4				10	2				5	6	11		9			8	1
QF1	Jan 16	Atletico Bilbao	3-5	Taylor, Viollet, Whelan	30000		7		3			4				6	2				5		11		9	10		8	1
QF2	Feb 6	Atletico Bilbao	3-0	Viollet, Taylor, Berry	70000		7		3			4				6	2				5		11		9	10		8	1
SF1	Apr 11	Real Madrid	1-3	Taylor	120000		7	5	3			4				6	2						11		9	10		8	1
SF2	25	REAL MADRID	2-2	Taylor, Charlton	65000		7	5	3	10		4				6	2						11		9			8	1

Home leg matches on Sep 26, Oct 17 and Feb 6 played at Maine Road, Manchester since there were no floodlights at Old Trafford

FA Charity Shield

Date	Opponent	Score	Scorers	Att																								
Oct 24	Manchester City	1-0	Viollet	30495		7		3			4				6	2				5		11		9	10		8	1

At Maine Road

J Gaskell replaced Wood in goal at half-time

Wolverhampton Wanderers 1957/58

Molineux

	Date		Opponent	Score	Scorers	Att	Booth C	Broadbent PF	Clamp HE	Deeley NV	Dwyer NM	Finlayson MJ	Flowers R	Harris GW	Henderson JG	Howells R	Jackson A	Jones G	Lill MJ	Mason RH	Mullen J	Murray JR	Showell GW	Slater WJ	Stuart EA	Wilshaw DJ	Wright WA
	Aug	24	Everton	0-1		58229	8	10	4	7		1	6	3							11	9			2		5
		28	BOLTON WANDERERS	6-1	Deeley 2, Murray 2, Booth, Broadbent	30790	8	10	4	7		1	6	3							11	9			2		5
		31	SUNDERLAND	5-0	Murray 2, Booth, Deeley, Mullen	38645	10	8	4	7		1	6	3							11	9			2		5
5	Sep	4	Bolton Wanderers	1-1	Deeley	25845	10	8	4	7		1	6	3							11	9			2		5
8		7	Luton Town	1-3	Wilshaw	22030	10	8	4	7		1	6	3								9			2	11	5
10		14	BLACKPOOL	3-1	Broadbent, Mullen, Murray	38496		10	4	7		1	6	3						8	11	9			2		5
5		16	ASTON VILLA	2-1	Deeley, Murray	26033		10	4	7		1	6	3						8	11	9			2		5
5		21	Leicester City	3-2	Murray 2, Clamp	35498	7	8	4			1	6	3							11	9			2	10	5
3		23	Aston Villa	3-2	Broadbent, Deeley, Murray	20904		8	4	7	1		6								11	9	3		2	10	5
2		28	MANCHESTER UNITED	3-1	Deeley 2, Wilshaw	48825		8	4	7		1	6	3							11	9	2			10	5
1	Oct	2	TOTTENHAM HOTSPUR	4-0	Broadbent 2, Flowers, Murray	36024		8	4	7		1	6	3							11	9			2	10	5
1		5	Leeds United	1-1	Deeley	28635	10	8	4	7		1	6	3							11				2	9	5
1		12	Birmingham City	5-1	Clamp 2, Deeley, Murray, Wilshaw	43005		8	4	7		1	6	3							11	9			2	10	5
1		19	CHELSEA	2-1	Deeley, Wilshaw	37524		8	4	7		1	6	3			2				11	9	5			10	
1		26	Newcastle United	1-1	Deeley	44361		8	4	7		1	6	3							11	9			2	10	5
1	Nov	2	NOTTM. FOREST	2-0	Broadbent, Deeley	47858		8	4	7		1	6	3							11	9			2	10	5
		9	Portsmouth	1-1	Clamp	38430		8	4	7	1		6	3							11	9			2	10	5
1		16	WEST BROMWICH ALB.	1-1	Clamp	55618		8	4	7	1		6	3							11	9			2	10	5
1		23	Manchester City	4-3	Murray 2, Broadbent, Mason	45121		8	4	7	1		6	3						10	11	9			2		5
1		30	BURNLEY	2-1	Broadbent, Murray	32888		8	4	7		1	6	3						10	11	9			2		5
1	Dec	7	Preston North End	2-1	Lill, Murray	22771	10	8	4	7		1	6	3					11			9			2		5
1		14	SHEFFIELD WEDNESDAY	4-3	Broadbent, Clamp (p), Mason, Murray	28082		8	4	7		1	6	3						10	11	9			2		5
1		21	EVERTON	2-0	Clamp, Mullen	29447			4	7		1	6	3						10	11	9		8	2		5
1		26	Tottenham Hotspur	0-1		58393		8	4	7		1		3						10	11	9			2		5
		28	Sunderland	2-0	Broadbent, Murray	46479		8	4	7		1		3						10	11	9	5	6	2		
1	Jan	11	LUTON TOWN	1-1	Mason	30805		8	4	7		1		3						10	11	9		6	2		5
1		18	Blackpool	2-3	Deeley, Murray	17953		8	4	7		1		3						10	11	9		6	2		5
1	Feb	1	LEICESTER CITY	5-1	Murray 2, Broadbent, Deeley, Mason	36400		8	4	7		1		3						10	11	9		6	2		5
1		19	LEEDS UNITED	3-2	Broadbent, Deeley, Mason	35527		8	4	7		1		3						10	11	9		6	2		5
1		22	BIRMINGHAM CITY	5-1	Murray 3, Deeley 2	36941	10	8	4	7		1		3							11	9		6	2		5
1	Mar	8	NEWCASTLE UNITED	3-1	Broadbent, Deeley, Mason	34058		8	4	7		1		3	6					10	11	9			2		5
1		11	Chelsea	2-1	Deeley, Showell	46835		8	4	7		1			6					10	11	9	3	6	2		5
1		15	Nottingham Forest	4-1	Murray 3, Broadbent	40197		8	4	7		1		3						10	11	9		6	2		5
1		22	MANCHESTER CITY	3-3	Deeley, Mullen, Ewing (og)	34932		8	4	7		1		3						10	11	9		6	2		5
1		29	West Bromwich Albion	3-0	Murray 2, Mason	56904		8	4	7		1		3						10	11	9		6	2		5
1	Apr	5	PORTSMOUTH	1-0	Clamp (p)	31259		8	4	7		1		3						10	11	9		6	2		5
		7	Arsenal	2-0	Broadbent, Murray	51340		8	4	7		1	6	3		11				10		9			2		5
1		8	ARSENAL	1-2	Broadbent	47501		8	4	7		1		3		11				10		9		6	2		5
1		12	Burnley	1-1	Clamp (p)	28539	10	8	4	7		1	6	3							11	9	5		2		
1		19	PRESTON NORTH END	2-0	Deeley, Milne (og)	46001	10	8	4	7		1	6	3							11	9	5		2		
1		21	Manchester United	4-0	Broadbent, Clamp, Deeley, Flowers	35467	10	8	4	7	1		6					3			11	9			2		5
1		26	Sheffield Wednesday	1-2	Flowers	23523	10			7		1	6	3	8						11	9		4	2		5
			Apps				13	40	41	41	5	37	28	39	1	2	2	2	1	20	38	41	7	14	40	12	38
			Goals				2	17	10	23			3						1	7	4	29	1		4		

Two own goals

F.A. Cup

	Date		Opponent	Score	Scorers	Att	Broadbent PF	Clamp HE	Deeley NV	Finlayson MJ	Flowers R	Harris GW	Mason RH	Mullen J	Murray JR	Slater WJ	Stuart EA	Wright WA
R3	Jan	4	Lincoln City	1-0	Mullen	21741	8	4	7	1		3	10	11	9	6	2	5
R4		25	PORTSMOUTH	5-1	Broadbent, 2, Mason, Mullen, Rutter (og)	43522	8	4	7	1		3	10	11	9	6	2	5
R5	Feb	15	DARLINGTON	6-1	Murray, 3, Broadbent, 2, Mason	55778	8	4	7	1		3	10	11	9	6	2	5
R6	Mar	1	Bolton Wanderers	1-2	Mason	56306	8	4	7	1	6	3	10	11	9		2	5

Wolverhampton Wanderers 1958/59

Molineux

							Booth C	Broadbent PF	Clamp HE	Deeley NV	Durandt CM	Finlayson MJ	Flowers R	Harris GW	Henderson JG	Horne DT	Jackson A	Jones G	Kelly JPV	Lill MJ	Mason RH	Mullen J	Murray JR	Showell GW	Sidebottom G	Slater WJ	Stuart EA	Wright WA
	Aug	23	NOTTM. FOREST	5-1	Mason 3, Broadbent, Deeley	52656		8		7		1	6	3	9	11					10					4	2	5
		25	West Ham United	0-2		37487		8		7		1	6	3	9	11					10					4	2	5
		30	Chelsea	2-6	Mason, Slater	62118		8		7		1	6	3	9						10	11				4	2	5
13	Sep	3	WEST HAM UNITED	1-1	Broadbent	52317	10	8		7		1	6	3	9							11				4	2	5
11		6	BLACKPOOL	2-0	Broadbent, Henderson	46219		8	6	7		1		3	11						10		9			4	2	5
9		8	Aston Villa	3-1	Booth, Broadbent, Murray	43138	10	8	6	7		1		3								11	9			4	2	5
4		13	Blackburn Rovers	2-1	Home, Woods (og)	43192	10	8	6	7		1	4	3		11							9				2	5
2		17	ASTON VILLA	4-0	Henderson 2, Murray 2	41845	10	8	4	7		1		3	11								9			6	2	5
7		20	NEWCASTLE UNITED	1-3	Broadbent,	39130	10	8	4			1		3	11			7					9			6	2	5
9		27	Tottenham Hotspur	1-2	Clamp	48563		8	6			1		3	7						10	11	9			4	2	5
5	Oct	4	MANCHESTER UNITED	4-0	Murray 2, Mason, Mullen	36840			6	7	8	1		3							10	11	9	5		4	2	
4		11	MANCHESTER CITY	2-0	Broadbent, Deeley	33769		8	6	7		1		3							10	11	9			4	2	5
3		18	Arsenal	1-1	Showell	49199		8	6	7		1		3							10	11		9		4	2	5
2		25	BIRMINGHAM CITY	3-1	Mullen 2, Showell	36156		8		7		1	6	3							10	11		9		4	2	5
5	Nov	1	West Bromwich Albion	1-2	Deeley	48771		8		7			6	3							10	11		9	1	4	2	5
3		8	PRESTON NORTH END	1-2	Mason 2	35593		8		7			6	3							10	11		9	1	4	2	5
2		15	Burnley	2-0	Deeley, Jackson	23067		8	4	7			6	3		11	9				10				1		2	5
3		22	BOLTON WANDERERS	1-2	Deeley	33489		8	6	7		1		3			9				10	11				4	2	5
3		29	Luton Town	1-0	Mullen	20648		8		7		1	6	3							10	11	9			4	2	5
2	Dec	6	EVERTON	1-0	Broadbent	27074		8		7		1	6	3							10	11	9			4	2	5
4		13	Leicester City	0-1		25964		8		7		1	6	3							10	11	9			4	2	5
2		20	Nottingham Forest	3-1	Broadbent, Horne, Mason	28079	10	9		7		1	6	3		11					8					4	2	5
1		26	Portsmouth	5-3	Broadbent 3, Booth, Deeley	28022	10	9		7		1	6	3		11					8					4	2	5
1		27	PORTSMOUTH	7-0	Booth 3, Deeley 3, Horne	41347	10	9		7		1	6	3		11					8					4	2	5
1	Jan	3	CHELSEA	1-2	Deeley	36093	10	9		7		1	6	3		11					8					4	2	5
2		31	BLACKBURN ROVERS	5-0	Mason 2, Deeley, Lill, Murray	30743		10		11		1	6					3		7	8		9			4	2	5
1	Feb	7	Newcastle United	4-3	Lill 2, Mason, Murray	42377		10	6	11		1						3		7	8		9			4	2	5
1		14	LEEDS UNITED	6-2	Broadbent 2, Deeley 2, Murray 2	26790		10	4	11		1	6	3						7	8		9				2	5
1		21	Manchester United	1-2	Mason	62794		10	4	11		1	6	3						7	8		9				2	5
2		28	Manchester City	4-1	Murray 2, Lill, Brannagan (og)	42776		10	4			1	6	3						7	8	11	9				2	5
1	Mar	2	TOTTENHAM HOTSPUR	1-1	Lill	30437		10	4			1	6	3						7	8	11	9				2	5
1		7	ARSENAL	6-1	Broadbent 2, Deeley 2, Lill, Murray	40480		10	4	11		1	6	3						7	8		9				2	5
1		14	Birmingham City	3-0	Murray 2, Broadbent,	37725		10	4	11		1	6	3						7	8		9				2	5
1		21	WEST BROMWICH ALB.	5-2	Lill 3, Deeley, Mason	44240		10	4	11		1	6	3						7	8		9				2	5
1		28	Preston North End	2-1	Lill 2	22465		10	4	11		1	6	3			2			7	8		9					5
1		31	Leeds United	3-1	Broadbent, Clamp, Murray	35819		10	4	11		1	6	3						7	8		9	2				5
1	Apr	4	BURNLEY	3-3	Broadbent, Harris, Murray	39810		10	4	11		1	6	3			2			7	8		9					5
1		11	Bolton Wanderers	2-2	Booth, Murray	26019	10		4	11		1		3					2	7	8		9	5		6		
1		13	Blackpool	1-0	Murray	22328		10	4	11		1	6	3						7	8		9				2	5
1		18	LUTON TOWN	5-0	Broadbent 2, Booth, Clamp, Murray	40981	8	10	4	11		1	6	3						7			9				2	5
1		22	LEICESTER CITY	3-0	Deeley, Lill, Murray	41220	8	10	4	11		1	6	3						7			9				2	5
1		25	Everton	1-0	Murray	29414	8	10		11		1	6	3						7			9	5		4	2	

Apps	13	40	26	38	1	39	31	40	8	8	2	4	1	18	34	16	28	8	3	27	38	39
Goals	7	20	3	17			1	3	3	1				12	13	4	21	2		1		

Two own goals

F.A. Cup

| R3 | Jan | 10 | Barrow | 4-2 | Deeley 2, Booth, Lill | 16340 | 10 | 9 | | 11 | | 1 | 6 | 3 | | | | | | 7 | 8 | | | | | 4 | 2 | 5 |
| R4 | | 24 | BOLTON WANDERERS | 1-2 | Hennin (og) | 55621 | 10 | 9 | | 7 | | 1 | 6 | 3 | | 11 | | | | | 8 | | | | | 4 | 2 | 5 |

European Cup

| R1.1 | Nov | 12 | FC SCHALKE | 2-2 | Broadbent 2 | 45767 | | 8 | | 7 | | | 6 | 3 | | | 9 | | | | 10 | 11 | | | 1 | 4 | 2 | 5 |
| R1.2 | | 18 | FC Schalke | 1-2 | Jackson | 25000 | | 8 | 4 | 7 | | 1 | 6 | 3 | | | 9 | | | | 10 | 11 | | | | | 2 | 5 |

FA Charity Shield

| Oct | 6 | Bolton Wanderers | 1-4 | Durandt | 15596 | | | 4 | | 8 | 1 | 6 | 3 | | 11 | | | | | 10 | | 9 | | | | 2 | 5 |

At Burnden Park

GP Mannion played at 7

Burnley 1959/60

Turf Moor

							Adamson J	Angus J	Blacklaw AS	Connelly JM	Cummings TS	Elder AR	Furnell J	Harris G	Lawson FIA	Marshall W	McIlroy J	Meredith TG	Miller BG	Pilkington B	Pointer R	Robson J	Seith R	White WH
	Aug	22	Leeds United	3-2	Connelly, Pointer, Pilkington	20233	6	2	1	7	3						8		5	11	9	10	4	
		25	EVERTON	5-2	Connelly 2, Robson, Pointer, Pilkington	29165	6	2	1	7	3						8		5	11	9	10	4	
		29	WEST HAM UNITED	1-3	Connelly	26756	6	2	1	7	3						8		5	11	9	10	4	
5	Sep	2	Everton	2-1	Pointer 2	39416	6	2	1	7	3						8		5	11	9	10	4	
6		5	Chelsea	1-4	Connelly	36023	6	2	1	7	3						8		5	11	9	10	4	
3		8	PRESTON NORTH END	2-1	Pointer, Robson	29195	6	2	1	7	3						8		5	11	9	10	4	
3		12	WEST BROMWICH ALB.	2-1	Robson, Pilkington	23907	6	2	1	7	3						8		5	11	9	10	4	
4		15	Preston North End	0-1		27299	4	2	1	7	5	3							6	11	9	10		8
4		19	Newcastle United	3-1	Connelly 2, McIlroy	38576	4	2	1	7	5	3					8		6	11	9	10		
4		26	BIRMINGHAM CITY	3-1	Connelly, McIlroy, Pointer	23848	4	2	1	7	5	3					8		6	11	9	10		
3	Oct	3	Tottenham Hotspur	1-1	Miller	42717	4	2	1	7	5	3							6	11	9	10		8
4		10	BLACKPOOL	1-4	Robson	28104	4	2	1	7	5	3					8		6	11	9	10		
7		17	Blackburn Rovers	2-3	Pilkington, Douglas (og)	33316	5	2	1			3		11			8		6	7	9		4	10
6		24	MANCHESTER CITY	4-3	White 2, Pointer, Pilkington	28653	6	2	1	7		3					8		5	11	9		4	10
7		31	Luton Town	1-1	Pointer	15638	6	2	1	7		3					8		5	11	9		4	10
5	Nov	7	WOLVERHAMPTON W.	4-1	Pointer 2, Connelly, Robson	27793	6	2	1	7		3					8		5	11	9	10	4	
6		14	Sheffield Wednesday	1-1	Robson	18420	6	2	1	7		3					8		5	11	9	10	4	
4		21	NOTTM. FOREST	8-0	Robson 5, Pointer 2, Pilkington	24349	6	2	1	7		3					8		5	11	9	10	4	
6		28	Fulham	0-1		29582	6	2	1	7		3					8		5	11	9	10	4	
6	Dec	5	BOLTON WANDERERS	4-0	McIlroy 2 (1p), Connelly, Pointer	26510	6	2	1	7		3					8		5	11	9	10	4	
3		12	Arsenal	4-2	Connelly 3, Adamson (p)	26056	6	2	1	7		3					8		5	11	9	10	4	
4		19	LEEDS UNITED	0-1		17398	6	2	1	7		3							5	11	9	10	4	8
3		26	Manchester United	2-1	Lawson, Robson	62673	6	2	1	7		3			8				5	11	9	10	4	
3		28	MANCHESTER UNITED	1-4	Robson	47696	6	2	1	7		3					8		5	11	9	10	4	
2	Jan	2	West Ham United	5-2	Connelly 2, Lawson 2, Pilkington	25752	6	2	1	7		3			8				5	11	9	10	4	
2		16	CHELSEA	2-1	Robson 2	21916	6	2	1	7		3			8				5	11	9	10	4	
2		23	West Bromwich Albion	0-0		23512	6	2	1	7		3		11	8				5		9	10	4	
2	Feb	6	NEWCASTLE UNITED	2-1	Pointer, Robson	26998	6	2	1	7		3			8				5	11	9	10	4	
4		27	Bolton Wanderers	1-2	Connelly	28772	4	2	1	7	5	3			10		8		6	11	9			
3	Mar	1	TOTTENHAM HOTSPUR	2-0	Connelly, Pointer	32992	4	2	1	7	5	3					8		6	11	9	10		
3		5	BLACKBURN ROVERS	1-0	Robson	32331	6	2	1	7		3					8		5	11	9	10	4	
3		19	ARSENAL	3-2	Miller, Connelly, Pointer	20327	5	2	1	7		3			8				6	11	9	10	4	
3		30	Wolverhampton Wan.	1-6	Pointer	33953	6		1	7	2	3					8		5	11	9	10	4	
3	Apr	2	SHEFFIELD WEDNESDAY	3-3	Miller, Connelly, McIlroy (p)	23123	5	2	1	7		3					8		6	11	9	10	4	
4		9	Nottingham Forest	1-0	Pointer	24640	4	2	1		5					3	8	7	6	11	9	10		
3		15	LEICESTER CITY	1-0	Connelly	23777	4	2	1	7	5	3					8		6	11	9	10		
3		16	LUTON TOWN	3-0	McIlroy (p), Pointer, Robson	20893	4	2	1		5	3					8	7	6	11	9	10		
3		18	Leicester City	1-2	Meredith	24429	4	2	1		5	3					8	7	6	11	9	10		
3		23	Blackpool	1-1	Meredith	23753	4	2			5	3	1				8	7	6	11	9	10		
2		27	Birmingham City	1-0	Pilkington	37032	4	2	1		5	3					8	7	6	11	9	10		
3		30	FULHAM	0-0		30807	4	2	1		5	3			8			7	6	11	9	10		
1	May	2	Manchester City	2-1	Meredith, Pilkington	65981	4	2	1		5	3					8	7	6	11	9	10		
					Apps		42	41	41	34	23	34	1	2	8	1	32	7	42	41	42	38	27	6
					Goals		1			20					3		6	3	3	9	19	18		2

One own goal

F.A. Cup

R3	Jan	9	Lincoln City	1-1	Pointer	21693	6	2	1	7		3			8				5	11	9	10	4	
rep		12	LINCOLN CITY	2-0	McIlroy (p), Pilkington	35416	6	2	1	7		3					8		5	11	9	10	4	
R4		30	Swansea Town	0-0		30060	6	2	1	7		3					8		5	11	9	10	4	
rep	Feb	2	SWANSEA TOWN	2-1	Robson 2	37038	6	2	1	7		3							5	11	9	10	4	8
R5		20	Bradford City	2-2	Connelly 2	26227	6	2	1	7		3					8		5	11	9	10	4	
rep		23	BRADFORD CITY	5-0	Pointer 2, Robson 2, Connelly	52850	6	2	1	7		3					8		5	11	9	10	4	
R6	Mar	12	BLACKBURN ROVERS	3-3	Pointer, Pilkington, Connelly	51501	6	2	1	7		3					8		5	11	9	10	4	
rep		16	Blackburn Rovers	0-2		53839	6	2	1	7		3					8		5	11	9	10	4	

R6 replay a.e.t.

Tottenham Hotspur 1960/61

White Hart Lane

						Allen LW	Baker PRB	Barton KR	Blanchflower RD	Brown WDF	Dyson TK	Henry RP	Hollowbread JF	Jones CW	Mackay DC	Marchi AV	Medwin TC	Norman M	Saul FL	Smith J	Smith RA	White JA
	Aug	20	EVERTON	2-0	Smith, Allen	50393	10	2		4	1	11	3		7	6			5			9	8
		22	Blackpool	3-1	Dyson 2, Medwin	27656	10	2		4	1	11	3			6		7	5			9	8
		27	Blackburn Rovers	4-1	Smith 2, Allen, Dyson	26819	10	2		4	1	11	3			6		7	5			9	8
1		31	BLACKPOOL	3-1	Smith 3	45684	10	2		4	1	11	3			6		7	5			9	8
1	Sep	3	MANCHESTER UNITED	4-1	Smith 2, Allen 2	55442	10	2		4	1	11	3			6		7	5			9	8
1		7	Bolton Wanderers	2-1	White, Allen	41565	10	2		4	1	11	3			6		7	5	9			8
1		10	Arsenal	3-2	Saul, Allen, Dyson	59868	10	2		4	1	11	3			6		7	5	9			8
1		14	BOLTON WANDERERS	3-1	Smith 2, Blanchflower (p)	43559	10	2		4	1	11	3		7	6			5			9	8
1		17	Leicester City	2-1	Smith 2	30129	10	2		4	1	11	3		7	6			5			9	8
1		24	ASTON VILLA	6-2	White 2, Smith, Allen, Dyson, Mackay	61356	10	2		4	1	11	3		7	6			5			9	8
1	Oct	1	Wolverhampton Wan.	4-0	Blanchflower, Jones, Allen, Dyson	52829	10	2		4	1	11	3		7		6		5			9	8
1		10	MANCHESTER CITY	1-1	Smith	58916	10	2		4	1	11	3		7	6			5			9	8
1		15	Nottingham Forest	4-0	Jones 2, Mackay, White	37248	10	2		4	1	11	3		7	6			5			9	8
1		29	Newcastle United	4-3	Norman, Jones, White, Smith	51369	10	2		4	1	11	3		7	6			5			9	8
1	Nov	2	CARDIFF CITY	3-2	Blanchflower (p), Dyson, Medwin	47605	10	2		4	1	11	3			6		7	5			9	8
1		5	FULHAM	5-1	Jones 2, Allen 2, White	56270	10	2		4	1	11	3		7	6			5			9	8
1		12	Sheffield Wednesday	1-2	Norman	53988	10	2		4	1	11	3		7	6			5			9	8
1		19	BIRMINGHAM CITY	6-0	Jones 2, Dyson 2, White, Smith (p)	46010	10	2		4	1	11	3		7	6			5			9	8
1		26	West Bromwich Albion	3-1	Smith 2, Allen	39017	10	2		4	1	11	3		7	6			5			9	8
1	Dec	3	BURNLEY	4-4	Jones 2, Mackay, Norman	58737	10	2		4	1	11	3		7	6			5			9	8
1		10	Preston North End	1-0	White	21657	10	2		4	1	11	3		7	6			5	9			8
1		17	Everton	3-1	Mackay, White, Allen	61052	10	2		4	1	11	3		7	6			5			9	8
1		24	WEST HAM UNITED	2-0	White, Dyson	54930	10	2		4	1	11	3		7	6			5			9	8
		26	West Ham United	3-0	White, Allen, Brown (og)	34351	10	2		4		11	3	1		6		7	5			9	8
1		31	BLACKBURN ROVERS	5-2	Smith 2, Allen 2, Blanchflower	48742	10	2		4	1	11	3				6	7	5			9	8
	Jan	16	Manchester United	0-2		65535	10		2	4	1	11	3			6			5		7	9	8
		21	ARSENAL	4-2	Allen 2, Blanchflower (p), Smith	65251	10	2		4	1	11	3		7	6			5			9	8
1	Feb	4	LEICESTER CITY	2-3	Allen, Blanchflower (p)	53627	10	2		4	1	11	3		7	6			5			9	8
		11	Aston Villa	2-1	Smith, Dyson	50786	10	2		4	1	11	3		7	6			5			9	8
		22	WOLVERHAMPTON W.	1-1	Smith	62261	10	2		4	1	11	3		7	6			5			9	8
		25	Manchester City	1-0	Medwin	40278	10	2		4	1	11	3			6	5	7				9	8
1	Mar	11	Cardiff City	2-3	Allen, Dyson	45463	10	2		4	1	11	3		7	6			5			9	8
		22	NEWCASTLE UNITED	1-2	Allen	46470	10	2		4	1	11	3		7	6			5			9	8
		25	Fulham	0-0		38536	10	2		4	1	11	3		7		6		5	9			8
		31	CHELSEA	4-2	Jones 2, Saul, Allen	65032	10	2		4	1	11	3		7		6		5	9			8
1	Apr	1	PRESTON NORTH END	5-0	Jones 3, White, Saul	46325	10	2		4	1		3		7		6	11	5	9			8
		3	Chelsea	3-2	Norman, Smith, Medwin	57103	10	2		4	1		3		7	6		11	5			9	8
		8	Birmingham City	3-2	White, Smith, Allen	40961	10	2		4	1	11	3		7	6			5			9	8
		17	SHEFFIELD WEDNESDAY	2-1	Smith, Allen	61205	10	2		4	1	11	3		7	6			5			9	8
		22	Burnley	2-4	Baker, Smith	28991	10	2		4	1	11	3			6		7	5			9	8
1		26	NOTTM. FOREST	1-0	Medwin	35743	10	2		4	1	11	3			6		7	5			9	8
1		29	WEST BROMWICH ALB.	1-2	Smith	52054	10	2		4	1	11	3		7	6			5			9	8

All Smith goals are R Smith

	Apps	42	41	1	42	41	40	42	1	29	37	6	14	41	6	1	36	42
	Goals	23	1		6		12				15	4		5	4	3		28	13

One own goal

F.A. Cup

R3	Jan	7	CHARLTON ATHLETIC	3-2	Allen 2, Dyson	54969	10	2		4	1	11	3			6		7	5			9	8
R4		28	CREWE ALEXANDRA	5-1	Mackay, Jones, Smith, Allen, Dyson	53721	10	2		4	1	11	3		7	6			5			9	8
R5	Feb	18	Aston Villa	2-0	Jones, Neal (og)	69672	10	2		4	1	11	3		7	6			5			9	8
R6	Mar	4	Sunderland	1-1	Jones	61236	10	2		4	1	11	3		7	6			5			9	8
rep		8	SUNDERLAND	5-0	Dyson 2, Smith, Allen, Mackay	64797	10	2		4	1	11	3		7	6			5			9	8
SF		18	Burnley	3-0	Smith 2, Jones	69968	10	2		4	1	11	3		7	6			5			9	8
F	May	6	Leicester City	2-0	Smith, Dyson	100000	10	2		4	1	11	3		7	6			5			9	8

SF at Villa Park, Final at Wembley Stadium

Ipswich Town 1961/62

Portman Road

						Bailey RN	Baxter WA	Carberry LJ	Compton JF	Crawford R	Curtis DP	Elsworthy JT	Hall W	Leadbetter JH	Malcolm KC	Moran DW	Nelson AN	Owen AW	Phillips EJ	Pickett RA	Stephenson RA
	Aug	19	Bolton Wanderers	0-0		16708	1	4	2		9		6		11	3	8	5		10		7
		22	Burnley	3-4	Phillips 2, Crawford	24577	1	4	2		9		6		11	3	8	5		10		7
		26	MANCHESTER CITY	2-4	Brett (og), Ewing (og)	21473	1	4	2		9		6		11	3	8	5		10		7
11		29	BURNLEY	6-2	Crawford 2, Miller (og), Moran, Phillips, Leadbetter	23835	1	4	2	3	9		6		11		8	5		10		7
9	Sep	2	West Bromwich Albion	3-1	Moran 2, Crawford	19016	1	4	2	3	9		6		11		8	5		10		7
6		5	BLACKBURN ROVERS	2-1	Stephenson, Phillips	24928	1	4	2	3	9		6		11		8	5		10		7
5		9	BIRMINGHAM CITY	4-1	Crawford, Phillips 2, Moran	20017	1	4	2	3	9		6		11		8	5		10		7
7		16	Everton	2-5	Phillips, Moran	35259		4	2	3	9		6	1	11		8	5		10		7
5		18	Blackburn Rovers	2-2	Phillips 2 (1p)	19904		4	2	3	9		6	1	11		8	5		10		7
8		23	FULHAM	2-4	Crawford 2	23050		4	2	3	9		6	1	11		8	5		10		7
6		30	Sheffield Wednesday	4-1	Phillips 2, Crawford, Leadbetter	26565		4	2	3	9		6	1	11		8	5		10		7
4	Oct	7	WEST HAM UNITED	4-2	Crawford 2, Phillips 2	28059	1	4	2	3	9		6		11		8	5		10		7
6		14	Sheffield United	1-2	Leadbetter	22194	1	4	2	3	9		6		11		8	5		10		7
4		21	TOTTENHAM HOTSPUR	3-2	Phillips, Crawford 2	28778	1	4	2	3	9		6		11		8	5		10		7
4		28	Blackpool	1-1	Phillips	19773	1	4	2	3	9		6		11		8	5		10		7
3	Nov	4	NOTTM. FOREST	1-0	Phillips	19068	1	4	2	3	9		6		11		8	5		10		7
5		11	Wolverhampton Wan.	0-2		21711	1	4	2	3	9		6		11		8	5		10		7
3		18	MANCHESTER UNITED	4-1	Phillips 2, Crawford, Elworthy	25755	1	4	2	3	9	7	6		11		8	5		10		
2		25	Cardiff City	3-0	Phillips 2, Rankmore (og)	22823	1	4	2	3	9		6		11		8	5		10		7
2	Dec	2	CHELSEA	5-2	Crawford 3, Moran, Stephenson	22726	1	4	2	3	9		6		11		8	5		10		7
3		9	Aston Villa	0-3		31924	1	4	2	3	9		6		11		8	5		10		7
2		16	BOLTON WANDERERS	2-1	Crawford 2	16587	1	4	2	3	9		6		11		8	5		10		7
5		23	Manchester City	0-3		18376	1	4	2	3	9		6		11		8	5		10		7
4		26	LEICESTER CITY	1-0	Crawford	18146	1	4	2	3	9		6				8	5	11	10		7
3	Jan	13	WEST BROMWICH ALB.	3-0	Stephenson, Moran, Leadbetter	18378	1	4	2	3	9		6		11		8	5		10		7
4		20	Birmingham City	1-3	Crawford	26968		4	2	3	9		6	1	11		8	5		10		7
2	Feb	3	EVERTON	4-2	Phillips, Moran, Elsworthy, Crawford	22572	1	4	2	3	9		6		11		8	5		10		7
3		10	Fulham	2-1	Stephenson, Crawford	25209	1	4	2	3	9		6		11		8	5		10		7
3		24	West Ham United	2-2	Leadbetter, Phillips (p)	27763	1	4	2	3	9		6		11		8	5		10		7
2	Mar	3	SHEFFIELD UNITED	4-0	Moran, Leadbetter, Crawford 2	20158	1	4	2	3	9		6		11		8	5		10		7
2		9	SHEFFIELD WEDNESDAY	2-1	Crawford, Stephenson	23713	1	4	2	3	9		6		11		8	5		10		7
2		14	Tottenham Hotspur	3-1	Crawford, Phillips 2	51098	1	4	2	3	9		6		11		8	5		10		7
2		17	BLACKPOOL	1-1	Moran	22450	1	4	2	3	9		6		11		8	5		10		7
2		24	Nottingham Forest	1-1	Moran	26053	1	4	2	3	9	10	6		11		8	5				7
2		28	Leicester City	2-0	Crawford, Stephenson	19068	1		2	3	9	10	6		11		8	5			4	7
1		31	WOLVERHAMPTON W.	3-2	Phillips (p), Crawford, Moran	23153	1		2	3	9		6		11		8	5		10	4	7
2	Apr	7	Manchester United	0-5		24976	1	4	2	3		9	6		11		8	5		10		7
1		14	CARDIFF CITY	1-0	Moran	17693	1	4	2	3	9				11		8	5		10	6	7
2		20	ARSENAL	2-2	Phillips (p), Leadbetter	30649	1	4	2	3	9		6		11		8	5		10		7
1		21	Chelsea	2-2	Crawford, Phillips (p)	28462	1	4	2	3	9		6		11		8	5		10		7
1		23	Arsenal	3-0	Phillips, Crawford 2	44694	1	4	2	3	9		6		11		8	5		10		7
1		28	ASTON VILLA	2-0	Crawford 2	28932	1	4	2	3	9		6		11		8	5		10		7
					Apps		37	40	42	39	41	4	41	5	41	3	42	42	1	40	3	41
					Goals						33	2			7		13			28		6

Four own goals

F.A. Cup

							Bailey RN	Baxter WA	Carberry LJ	Compton JF	Crawford R	Curtis DP	Elsworthy JT	Hall W	Leadbetter JH	Malcolm KC	Moran DW	Nelson AN	Owen AW	Phillips EJ	Pickett RA	Stephenson RA
R3	Jan	6	LUTON TOWN	1-1	Phillips	18450	1	4	2	3	9		6				8	5	11	10		7
rep		10	Luton Town	1-1	Elsworthy	23818	1	4	2	3	9		6				8	5	11	10		7
rep2		15	Luton Town	5-1	Phillips 2 (1p), Stephenson 2, Moran	29438		4	2	3	9		6	1	11		8	5				7
R4		27	Norwich City	1-1	Leadbetter	39890	1	4	2	3	9		6		11		8	5		10		7
rep		30	NORWICH CITY	1-2	Crawford	29796	1	4	2	3	9		6		11		8	5		10		7

R3 replay a.e.t.   R3 replay 2 at Highbury

F.L. Cup

							Bailey RN	Baxter WA	Carberry LJ	Compton JF	Crawford R	Curtis DP	Elsworthy JT	Hall W	Leadbetter JH	Malcolm KC	Moran DW	Nelson AN	Owen AW	Phillips EJ	Pickett RA	Stephenson RA
R1	Sep	11	MANCHESTER CITY	4-2	Crawford 2, Moran 2	14919		4	2	3	9		6	1	11		8	5		10		7
R2	Oct	3	Swansea Town	3-3	Stephenson, Crawford, Phillips (p)	13541		4		3	9		6	1	11		8	5		10		7
rep		24	SWANSEA TOWN	3-2	Stephenson, Phillips, Moran	11010	1	4	2	3	9		6		11		8	5		10		7
R3	Nov	21	Aston Villa	3-2	Phillips 2 (1p), Leadbetter	22541	1	4	2	3		9	6		11		8	5	7	10		
R4	Dec	11	Blackburn Rovers	1-4	Phillips (p)	11071	1	4	2	3	9		6		11		8	5		10		7

Played at 2 in R2: D Millward

Everton 1962/63

Goodison Park

						Bingham WL	Dunlop A	Gabriel J	Harris B	Heslop GW	Kay AH	Labone BL	Meagan MK	Morrissey JJ	Parker AH	Scott AS	Sharples GFV	Stevens D	Temple DW	Thomson GM	Veall RJ	Vernon TR	West G	Wignall F	Young A
	Aug	18	Burnley	3-1	Bingham, Vernon, Young	37100	7		4	6			5	2					8		3	11	10	1		9
		22	MANCHESTER UNITED	3-1	Young 2, Parker	69500	7		4	6			5			2			8		3	11	10	1		9
		25	SHEFFIELD WEDNESDAY	4-1	Vernon 2 (1p), Stevens, Young	51504	7			6			5		11	2		4	8		3		10	1		9
1		29	Manchester United	1-0	Vernon	63675	7		4	6			5		11	2			8		3		10	1		9
2	Sep	1	Fulham	0-1		30582	7		4	6			5		11	2			8		3		10	1		9
1		5	LEYTON ORIENT	3-0	Bingham, Gabriel, Vernon (p)	51542	7		4	6			5	2	11				8		3		10	1		9
1		8	LEICESTER CITY	3-2	Stevens, Vernon (p), Young	48738	7		4	6			5	2	11				8		3		10	1		9
2		12	Leyton Orient	0-3		21847				6			5	2	11		4		8		3		10	1		9
2		15	Bolton Wanderers	2-0	Bingham, Gabriel	27404	7		4	6			5	2	11				8		3		10	1		9
2		22	LIVERPOOL	2-2	Morrissey, Vernon (p)	72488	7		4	6			5	2	11				8		3		10	1		9
2		29	WEST BROMWICH ALB.	4-2	Morrissey 3, Young	45471	7		4	6			5	2	11				8		3		10	1		9
1	Oct	6	Wolverhampton Wan.	2-0	Bingham, Young	44506	7		4	6			5	2	11				8		3		10	1		9
1		13	ASTON VILLA	1-1	Vernon (p)	53035	7		4	6			5	2	11				8		3		10	1		9
2		27	IPSWICH TOWN	3-1	Morrissey 2, Vernon (p)	39695	7		4	6			5	3	11	2			8				10	1		9
2	Nov	3	Manchester City	1-1	Wignall	40336			4	6			5	3	7	2			8			11			1	10	9
2		10	BLACKPOOL	5-0	Young 2, Bingham, Gabriel, Stevens	39517	7		4	6			5	3		2			8			11	10	1		9
1		13	Nottingham Forest	4-3	Vernon 2, Gabriel, Veall	31610	7		4	6			5	3		2			8			11	10	1		9
2		17	Blackburn Rovers	2-3	Harris, Stevens	30243	7		4	6			5	3		2			8			11	10	1		9
1		24	SHEFFIELD UNITED	3-0	Vernon 2, Stevens	42017	7		4	6			5	3		2			8			11	10	1		9
1	Dec	1	Tottenham Hotspur	0-0		60626	7		4	6			5	3		2			8			11	10	1		9
1		8	WEST HAM UNITED	1-1	Stevens	38701	7		4	6			5	3		2			8			11	10	1		9
1		15	BURNLEY	3-1	Stevens, Vernon, Young	48443	7		4	6			5	3		2			8			11	10	1		9
1		22	Sheffield Wednesday	2-2	Bingham, Young	26280	7		4	6			5	3		2			8			11	10	1		9
2	Feb	12	Leicester City	1-3	Vernon	35743			4			6	5	3	11	2		7	8				10	1		9
3		23	WOLVERHAMPTON W.	0-0		65616			4			6	5	3	11	2			8	7			10	1		9
3	Mar	9	NOTTM. FOREST	2-0	Parker, Young	45068			4			6	5	3	11	2		7	8				10	1		9
3		19	Ipswich Town	3-0	Young 2, og (Elsworthy)	19712			4			6	5		11	2		7	8		3		10	1		9
3		23	MANCHESTER CITY	2-1	Morrissey, Young	46101			4			6	5		11	2		7	8		3		10	1		9
3		26	Arsenal	3-4	Kay, Vernon, Young	38061	7		4			6	5		11	2			8		3		10	1		9
3		30	Sheffield United	1-2	Scott	21839			4			6	5		11	2		7	8		3		10	1		9
3	Apr	1	Aston Villa	2-0	Gabriel, Young	31377			4			6	5		11	2		7	8		3		10	1		9
3		6	BLACKBURN ROVERS	0-0		39790			4			6	5		11	2		7	8		3		10	1		9
3		8	Liverpool	0-0		56060			4			6	5	3	11	2		7	8				10	1		9
3		13	Blackpool	2-1	Scott, Young	27842			4			6	5	3	11	2		7	8				10	1		9
3		15	BIRMINGHAM CITY	2-2	Scott, Young	50122			5	4		6		3	11	2		7	8				10	1		9
3		16	Birmingham City	1-0	Vernon	29719			4		5	6		3	11	2		7	8				10	1		9
1		20	TOTTENHAM HOTSPUR	1-0	Young	67650			4			6	5	3	11	2		7	8				10	1		9
1		24	ARSENAL	1-1	Vernon	56034			4			6	5	3	11	2		7	8				10	1		9
1		27	West Ham United	2-1	Temple, Vernon	28391		1	4			6	5	3		2		7	8	11			10			9
1	May	4	BOLTON WANDERERS	1-0	Vernon	52047		1	4			6	5	3		2		7	8	11			10			9
1		7	West Bromwich Albion	4-0	Young 2, Vernon (p), og (Williams)	25280		1	4			6	5	3		2		7	8	11			10			9
1		11	FULHAM	4-1	Vernon 3, Scott	60578		1	4			6	5	3		2		7	8	11			10			9

	Apps	23	4	40	24	1	19	40	32	28	33	17	2	42	5	19	11	41	38	1	42
	Goals	6		5	1		1			7	2	4		7	1		1	24		1	22

Two own goals

F.A. Cup

R3	Jan	15	Barnsley	3-0	Harris, Stevens, Vernon	30011	7		4	6			5	3	11	2			8				10	1		9
R4		29	Swindon Town	5-1	Vernon 2, Bingham, Gabriel, Morrissey	25239	7		4			6	5	3	11	2			8				10	1		9
R5	Mar	16	West Ham United	0-1		31770	7		4			6	5	3	11	2			8				10	1		9

Inter-Cities Fairs Cup

R1.1	Oct	24	DUNFERMLINE ATH.	1-0	Stevens	40244	7		4	6			5		11	2			8		3		10	1		9
R1.2		31	Dunfermline Athletic	0-2		21813	7		4	6			5	3	11	2			8				10	1		9

101

Liverpool 1963/64

Anfield

						Arrowsmith AW	Byrne G	Callaghan IR	Ferns P	Furnell J	Hunt R	Lawler C	Lawrence TJ	Melia JJ	Milne G	Moran R	St John I	Stevenson W	Thompson P	Thomson R	Wallace GH	Yeats R
	Aug	24	Blackburn Rovers	2-1	Moran, Callaghan	34390		2	7			8		1	10	4	3	9	6	11			5
		28	NOTTM. FOREST	1-2	og (McKinlay)	49829		2	7			8		1	10	4	3	9	6	11			5
		31	BLACKPOOL	1-2	Melia	42767		2	7			8		1	10	4	3	9	6	11			5
12	Sep	3	Nottingham Forest	0-0		21979		2	7	6		8		1	10	4	3	9		11			5
9		7	Chelsea	3-1	St John 2, Hunt	38202		2	7	6		8		1	10	4	3	9		11			5
4		9	Wolverhampton Wan.	3-1	Hunt 2, Melia	23962		2	7	6		8		1	10	4	3	9		11			5
11		14	WEST HAM UNITED	1-2	Hunt	45497		2	7	6	1	8			10	4	3	9		11			5
6		16	WOLVERHAMPTON W.	6-0	Hunt 2, Arrowsmith, Thompson, Callaghan, Milne	44050	9	2	7		1	8			10	4	3		6	11			5
10		21	Sheffield United	0-3		24932	9	2	7			8		1	10	4	3		6	11			5
8		28	EVERTON	2-1	Callaghan 2	51976		2	7	3		8		1	10	4		9	6	11			5
8	Oct	5	ASTON VILLA	5-2	Hunt 2, St John, Callaghan, Thompson	39106		2	7	3		8		1	10	4		9	6	11			5
8		9	SHEFFIELD WEDNESDAY	3-1	St John 2, Melia	46107		2	7	3		8		1	10	4		9	6	11			5
5		19	WEST BROMWICH ALB.	1-0	Milne	43099		2	7	3		8		1	10	4		9	6	11			5
3		26	Ipswich Town	2-1	Melia, Hunt	16322		2	7	3		8		1	10	4		9	6	11			5
6	Nov	2	LEICESTER CITY	0-1		47438		2	7	3		8		1	10	4		9	6	11			5
4		9	Bolton Wanderers	2-1	Hunt, Callaghan	24049			7	2		8		1	10	4	3	9	6	11			5
2		16	FULHAM	2-0	St John, Hunt	38478			7	2		8		1	10	4	3	9	6	11			5
1		23	Manchester United	1-0	Yeats	54884			7	2		8		1	10	4	3	9	6	11			5
1		30	BURNLEY	2-0	St John, Hunt (p)	42968			7	2		8		1	10	4	3	9	6	11			5
1	Dec	7	Arsenal	1-1	Callaghan	40551			7	2		8		1	10	4	3	9	6	11			5
4		14	BLACKBURN ROVERS	1-2	Hunt	45182			7	2		8		1	10	4	3	9	6	11			5
3		21	Blackpool	1-0	St John	13254			7	2		8		1	10	4	3	9	6	11			5
3		26	STOKE CITY	6-1	Hunt 4, Arrowsmith, St John	49942	10		7	2		8		1		4	3	9	6	11			5
2	Jan	11	CHELSEA	2-1	Hunt, Arrowsmith	45848	10					8	5	1		4	3	9	6	11	2		
3		18	West Ham United	0-1		25546	10	2	7			8	5	1		4		9	6	11	3		
2	Feb	1	SHEFFIELD UNITED	6-1	St John 3, Hunt 2, Thompson	43309		2	7			8		1	10	4	3	9	6	11			5
3		8	Everton	1-3	St John	66515		2	7			8		1	10	4	3	9	6	11			5
3		19	Aston Villa	2-2	Hunt, Arrowsmith	13793	10	2	7			8		1		4	3	9	6	11			5
2		22	BIRMINGHAM CITY	2-1	Milne, St John	41823	10	2	7			8		1		4	3	9	6	11			5
2	Mar	4	Sheffield Wednesday	2-2	St John, Stevenson	22946	10	2	7			8		1		4	3	9	6	11			5
2		7	IPSWICH TOWN	6-0	Hunt 2, Arrowsmith 2, St John, Thompson	35575	10	2	7			8		1		4	3	9	6	11			5
4		14	Fulham	0-1		14022	10	2	7			8		1		4	3	9	6	11			5
1		20	BOLTON WANDERERS	2-0	Arrowsmith, St John	38583	10	2	7			8	5	1		4	3	9	6	11			
2		27	Tottenham Hotspur	3-1	Hunt 3	57022	10	2	7			8	5	1		4	3	9	6	11			
2		28	Leicester City	2-0	Hunt, Arrowsmith	31209	10	2	7			8	5	1		4	3	9	6	11			
1		30	TOTTENHAM HOTSPUR	3-1	St John 2, Arrowsmith	52904	10	2	7			8		1		4	3	9	6	11			5
1	Apr	4	MANCHESTER UNITED	3-0	Arrowsmith 2, Callaghan	52559	10	2	7			8		1		4	3	9	6	11			5
1		14	Burnley	3-0	Arrowsmith 2, St John	34804	10	2	7					1		4	3	9	6	11		8	5
1		18	ARSENAL	5-0	Thompson 2, Arrowsmith, St John, Hunt	48623	10	2	7			8		1		4	3	9	6	11			5
1		22	Birmingham City	1-3	Hunt	22630	10	2	7			8		1		4	3	9	6	11			5
1		25	West Bromwich Albion	2-2	Hunt 2	17833	10	2	7			8		1		4	3	9	6	11			5
1		29	Stoke City	1-3	Arrowsmith	32170	10	2	7			8	5	1		4	3	9	6	11			

	Apps	20	33	42	18	2	41	6	40	24	42	35	40	38	42	2	1	36
	Goals	15		8			31			4	3	1	21	1	6			1

One own goal

F.A. Cup

R3	Jan	4	DERBY COUNTY	5-0	Arrowsmith 4, Hunt	46460	10		7	2		8		1		4	3	9	6	11			5
R4		25	PORT VALE	0-0		52327	10	3	7			8		1		4		9	6	11	2		5
rep		27	Port Vale	2-1	Hunt, Thompson	42179		2	7			8		1	10	4	3	9	6	11			5
R5	Feb	15	Arsenal	1-0	St John	61295	10	2	7			8		1		4	3	9	6	11			5
R6		29	SWANSEA TOWN	1-2	Thompson	52608	10	2	7			8		1		4	3	9	6	11			5

R4 replay a.e.t.

102

Manchester United 1964/65

Old Trafford

						Aston J	Best G	Brennan JSA	Cantwell NEC	Charlton R	Connelly JM	Crerand PT	Dunne AP	Dunne PAJ	Fitzpatrick JHN	Foulkes WA	Gaskell JD	Herd DG	Law D	Moir I	Sadler D	Setters ME	Stiles NP
	Aug	22	WEST BROMWICH ALB.	2-2	Charlton, Law	52268		11	2		8	7		3			5	1	9	10			4	6
		24	West Ham United	1-3	Law	37298		11	2		8	7		3			5	1	9	10			4	6
		29	Leicester City	2-2	Law, Sadler	32373		11	2		8	7	4	3			5	1		10		9		6
13	Sep	2	WEST HAM UNITED	3-1	Best, Connelly, Law	45415		11	2		8	7	4	3			5	1		10		9		6
16		5	Fulham	1-2	Connelly	36291		11	2		8	7	4	3			5	1		10		9		6
15		8	Everton	3-3	Connelly, Herd, Law	63465		11	2		8	7	4	3	1		5		9	10				6
14		12	NOTTM. FOREST	3-0	Herd 2, Connelly	46437		11	2		8	7	4	3	1		5		9				6	10
11		16	EVERTON	2-1	Best, Law	50286		11	2		8	7	4	3	1		5		9	10				6
7		19	Stoke City	2-1	Connelly, Herd	40064		11	2		8	7	4	3	1		5		9				6	10
4		26	TOTTENHAM HOTSPUR	4-1	Crerand 2, Law 2	53362		11	2		8	7	4	3	1		5		9	10				6
2		30	Chelsea	2-0	Best, Law	60769		11	2		8	7	4	3	1		5		9	10				6
3	Oct	6	Burnley	0-0		31056		11	2		8	7	4	3	1		5		9	10				6
2		10	SUNDERLAND	1-0	Herd	48862		11	2		8	7	4	3	1		5		9	10				6
2		17	Wolverhampton Wan.	4-2	Law 2, Herd, og (Harris)	26763		11	2		8	7	4	3	1		5		9	10				6
2		24	ASTON VILLA	7-0	Law 4, Herd 2, Connelly	37233		11	2			7	4	3	1		5		9	10			6	8
1		31	Liverpool	2-0	Crerand, Herd	52402		11	2		8	7	4	3	1		5		9	10				6
1	Nov	7	SHEFFIELD WEDNESDAY	1-0	Herd	50446		11	2		8	7	4	3	1		5		9	10				6
1		14	Blackpool	2-1	Connelly, Herd	31129			2		8	7	4	3	1		5		9	10	11			6
1		21	BLACKBURN ROVERS	3-0	Best, Connelly, Herd	49928		11	2		8	7	4	3	1		5		9	10				6
1		28	Arsenal	3-2	Law 2, Connelly	59637		11	2		8	7	4	3	1		5		9	10				6
1	Dec	5	LEEDS UNITED	0-1		53651		11	2		8	7	4	3	1		5		9	10				6
2		12	West Bromwich Albion	1-1	Law	28126		11	2		8	7	4	3	1		5		9	10				6
1		16	BIRMINGHAM CITY	1-1	Charlton	25938		11	2		8	7	4	3	1		5		10			9		6
1		26	Sheffield United	1-0	Best	37295		11	2		8	7	4	3	1		5		10			9		6
1		28	SHEFFIELD UNITED	1-1	Herd	42219		11	2		8	7	4	3	1		5		10			9		6
3	Jan	16	Nottingham Forest	2-2	Law 2	43009		11	2		8	7	4	3	1		5		9	10				6
3		23	STOKE CITY	1-1	Law	51978		11	2		8	7	4	3	1		5		9	10				6
3	Feb	6	Tottenham Hotspur	0-1		58639		11	2		8	7	4	3	1		5		9	10				6
3		13	BURNLEY	3-2	Best, Charlton, Herd	39135		11	2		8	7	4	3	1		5		9	10				6
3		24	Sunderland	0-1		51336		11	2		8	7	4	3	1	6	5		9	10				
3		27	WOLVERHAMPTON W.	3-0	Charlton 2, Connelly	38587		11	2		8	7	4	3	1		5		9	10				6
3	Mar	13	CHELSEA	4-0	Herd 2, Best, Law	57662		11	2		8	7	4	3	1		5		9	10				6
3		15	FULHAM	4-1	Connelly 2, Herd 2	45631		11	2		8	7	4	3	1		5		9	10				6
3		20	Sheffield Wednesday	0-1		32782		11	2		8	7	4	3	1		5		9	10				6
3		22	BLACKPOOL	2-0	Law 2	42586		11	2		8	7	4	3	1		5		9	10				6
3	Apr	3	Blackburn Rovers	5-0	Charlton 3, Connelly, Herd	29363		11	2		8	7	4	3	1		5		9	10				6
2		12	LEICESTER CITY	1-0	Herd	35906	11	10	2		8	7	4	3	1		5		9					6
3		17	Leeds United	1-0	Connelly	52368		11	2		8	7	4	3	1		5		9	10				6
1		19	Birmingham City	4-2	Best 2, Cantwell, Charlton	28914		11	2	9	8	7	4	3	1		5			10				6
2		24	LIVERPOOL	3-0	Law 2, Connelly	56058		11	2	9	8	7	4	3	1		5			10				6
1		26	ARSENAL	3-1	Law 2, Best	53350		11	2		8	7	4	3	1		5		9	10				6
1		28	Aston Villa	1-2	Charlton	36005		11	2		8	7		3	1	4	5		9	10				6

Apps	1	41	42	2	41	42	39	42	37	2	42	5	37	36	1	6	5	41
Goals		10			1	10	15	3					20	28		1		

One own goal

F.A. Cup

R3	Jan	9	CHESTER	2-1	Kinsey, Best	40000		11	2		8	7	4	3	1		5		9					6
R4		30	Stoke City	0-0		53009		11	2		8	7	4	3	1		5		9	10				6
rep	Feb	3	STOKE CITY	1-0	Herd	50814		11	2		8	7	4	3	1		5		9	10				6
R5		20	BURNLEY	2-1	Crerand, Law	54000		11	2		8	7	4	3	1		5		9	10				6
R6	Mar	10	Wolverhampton Wan.	5-3	Law 2, Crerand, Herd, Best	53581		11	2		8	7	4	3	1		5		9	10				6
SF		27	Leeds United	0-0		65000		11	2		8	7	4	3	1		5		9	10				6
rep		31	Leeds United	0-1		46300		11	2		8	7	4	3	1		5		9	10				6

SF at Hillsborough, SF replay at the City Ground, Nottingham   AJ Kinsey played at 10 in R3

Inter-Cities Fairs Cup

R1.1	Sep	23	Djurgaardens	1-1	Herd	6537		11	2		8	7	4	3	1		5		9				10	6
R1.2	Oct	27	DJURGAARDENS	6-1	Law 3, Charlton 2, Best	38437		11	2		8	7	4	3	1		5		9	10				6
R2.1	Nov	11	Borussia Dortmund	6-1	Charlton 3, Herd, Law, Best	25000		11	2		8	7	4	3	1		5		9	10				6
R2.2	Dec	2	BORUSSIA DORTMUND	4-0	Charlton 2, Connelly, Law	31896		11	2		8	7	4	3	1		5		9	10				6
R3.1	Jan	20	EVERTON	1-1	Connelly	50000		11	2		8	7	4	3	1		5		9	10				6
R3.2	Feb	9	Everton	2-1	Connelly, Herd	54397		11	2		8	7	4	3	1		5		9	10				6
QF1	May	12	RC Strasbourg	5-0	Law 2, Connelly, Charlton, Herd	30000		11	2		8	7	4	3	1		5		9	10				6
QF		19	RC STRASBOURG	0-0		34188		11	2		8	7	4	3	1		5		9	10				6
SF1		31	FERENCVAROS	3-2	Herd 2, Law	39902		11	2		8	7	4	3	1		5		9	10				6
SF2	Jun	6	Ferencvaros	0-1		50000		11	2		8	7	4	3	1		5		9	10				6
rep		16	Ferencvaros	1-2	Connelly	60000		11	2		8	7	4	3	1		5		9	10				6

SF replay at Ferencvaros

Liverpool 1965/66

Anfield

						Arrowsmith AW	Byrne G	Callaghan IR	Graham R	Hunt R	Lawler C	Lawrence TJ	Milne G	Smith T	St John I	Stevenson W	Strong GH	Thompson P	Yeats R
	Aug	21	Leicester City	3-1	Hunt 2, Strong	29696		3	7		8	2	1	4	10	9	6	11		5
		25	SHEFFIELD UNITED	0-1		47295		3	7		8	2	1	4	10	9	6	11		5
	Sep	1	Sheffield United	0-0		20798		3	7		8	2	1	4	10	9	6		11	5
9		4	Blackpool	3-2	Hunt 2, Callaghan	25616		3	7		8	2	1	4	10	9		6	11	5
3		6	West Ham United	5-1	Hunt 3, Milne, Callaghan	32144		3	7		8	2	1	4	10	9	6		11	5
4		11	FULHAM	2-1	Lawler, Hunt	46382		3	7		8	2	1	4	10	9	6		11	5
6		15	WEST HAM UNITED	1-1	Strong	44553		3	7		8	2	1	4	10	9	6	12	11	5
8		18	Tottenham Hotspur	1-2	Strong	46925		3	7		8		1	4	10	9	6	2	11	5
6		25	EVERTON	5-0	Hunt 2, Smith, Stevenson, St John	53557	12	3	7		8		1	4	10	9	6	2	11	5
2	Oct	2	ASTON VILLA	3-1	Thompson 2, St John	43859		3	7		8	2	1		10	9	6	4	11	5
6		9	Manchester United	0-2		58461		3	7		8	2	1		10	9	6	4	11	5
3		16	NEWCASTLE UNITED	2-0	Hunt, Callaghan	47984		3	7		8	2	1		10	9	6	4	11	5
7		23	West Bromwich Albion	0-3		29905		3	7		8	2	1		10	9	6	4	11	5
5		30	NOTTM. FOREST	4-0	Hunt 2, Stevenson (p), St John	38418		3	7		8	2	1		10	9	6	4	11	5
2	Nov	6	Sheffield Wednesday	2-0	Hunt, Thompson	23889		3	7		8	2	1		10	9	6	4	11	5
2		13	NORTHAMPTON T	5-0	St John, Thompson, Stevenson (p), Callaghan, Hunt	41904		3	7		8	2	1		10	9	6	4	11	5
1		17	BLACKBURN ROVERS	5-2	St John 2, Hunt, Smith, Stevenson (p)	36450		3	7		8	2	1		10	9	6	4	11	5
1		20	Stoke City	0-0		28435		3	7		8	2	1	4	10	9	6		11	5
1		27	BURNLEY	2-1	Hunt, Milne	50282		3	7		8	2	1	4	10	9	6		11	5
1	Dec	4	Chelsea	1-0	Hunt	36839		3	7		8	2	1		10	9	6	4	11	5
1		11	ARSENAL	4-2	Thompson, St John, Strong, Hunt	43727		3	7		8	2	1		10	9	6	4	11	5
1		18	Newcastle United	0-0		34153		3	7		8	2	1		10	9	6	4	11	5
1		27	LEEDS UNITED	0-1		53430		3	7		8	2	1	4	10	9	6		11	5
1		28	Leeds United	1-0	Milne	49192		3	7		8	2	1	4	10	9	6		11	5
1	Jan	1	MANCHESTER UNITED	2-1	Smith, Milne	53970		3	7		8	2	1	4	10	9	6		11	5
1		8	Arsenal	1-0	Yeats	43931		3	7		8	2	1	4	10	9	6		11	5
1		15	WEST BROMWICH ALB.	2-2	Milne, Byrne	46687		3	7		8	2	1	4	10	9	6		11	5
1		29	LEICESTER CITY	1-0	Lawler	45409		3	7		8	2	1	4	10	9	6		11	5
1	Feb	5	Blackburn Rovers	4-1	St John 2, Lawler, Hunt	30414		3	7		8	2	1	4	10	9	6		11	5
1		12	SUNDERLAND	4-0	Hunt 3, Yeats	43859	12	3	7		8	2	1	4	10	9	6		11	5
1		19	BLACKPOOL	4-1	Hunt 2, Arrowsmith, Milne	45046	9	3	7		8	2	1	4	10		6		11	5
1		26	Fulham	0-2		31616		3	7		8	2	1	4	10	9	6		11	5
1	Mar	12	TOTTENHAM HOTSPUR	1-0	Hunt	50760		3	7		8	2	1	4	10	9	6		11	5
1		19	Everton	0-0		62337		3	7		8	2	1		4	9	6	10	11	5
1		26	Aston Villa	3-0	Hunt 2, Callaghan	23298	10	3	7		8	2	1		4	9	6		11	5
1	Apr	6	SHEFFIELD WEDNESDAY	1-0	Stevenson	44792		3	7		8	2	1		4	9	6	10	11	5
1		9	Northampton Town	0-0		20029		3	7			2	1	4	10	9	6	8	11	5
1		11	Sunderland	2-2	Lawler 2	38355		3	7			2	1	4	10	9	6	8	11	5
1		16	STOKE CITY	2-0	Strong, St John	41106		3	7			2	1	4	10	9	6	8	11	5
1		23	Burnley	0-2		36530	8	3	7			2	1	4	10	9	6		11	5
1		30	CHELSEA	2-1	Hunt 2	53754		3	7		8	2	1	4	10	9	6		11	5
1	May	10	Nottingham Forest	1-1	Milne	22105		3	7	8		2	1	4	10	9	6		11	5

						Apps	3	42	42	1	37	40	42	28	42	41	41	21	40	42
						Subs	2											1		
						Goals	1	1	5		30	5		7	3	10	5	5	5	2

F.A. Cup

| R3 | Jan | 22 | CHELSEA | 1-2 | Hunt | 54097 | | 3 | 7 | | 8 | 2 | 1 | 4 | 10 | 9 | 6 | | 11 | 5 |

European Cup-Winners Cup

R1.1	Sep	29	Juventus	0-1		23000	4	3	7		8		1		10	9	6	2	11	5
R1.2	Oct	13	JUVENTUS	2-0	Lawler, Strong	51055		3	7		8	2	1		10	9	6	4	11	5
R2.1	Dec	1	STANDARD LIEGE	3-1	Lawler 2, Thompson	46112		3	7		8	2	1	4	10	9	6		11	5
R2.1		15	Standard Liege	2-1	Hunt, St John	30000		3	7		8	2	1		10	9	6	4	11	5
QF1	Mar	1	Honved	0-0		25000		3	7		8	2	1	4	10	9	6		11	5
QF2		8	HONVED	2-0	Lawler, St John	54631		3	7		8	2	1	4	10	9	6		11	5
SF1	Apr	14	Celtic	0-1		80000		3	7		8	2	1	4	10	9	6		11	5
SF2		19	CELTIC	2-0	Smith, Strong	54208		3	7			2	1	4	10	9	6	8	11	5
F	May	5	Borussia Dortmund	1-2	Hunt	41657		3	7		8	2	1	4	10	9	6		11	5

Final at Hampden Park, a.e.t
P Chisnall played at 8 in SF1

F.A. Charity Shield

| Aug | 14 | Manchester United | 2-2 | Stevenson, Yates | 48502 | | 3 | 7 | | 8 | 2 | 1 | 4 | 10 | 9 | 6 | | 11 | | 5 |

At Old Trafford

Manchester United 1966/67

Old Trafford

						Anderson WJ	Aston J	Best G	Brennan JSA	Cantwell NEC	Charlton R	Connelly JM	Crerand PT	Dunne AP	Fitzpatrick JHN	Foulkes WA	Gaskell JD	Gregg H	Herd DG	Law D	Noble R	Ryan J	Sadler D	Stepney AC	Stiles NP
	Aug	20	WEST BROMWICH ALB.	5-3	Law 2, Best, Stiles, Herd	41543			7	2		9	11	3	4		5	1		10	8					6
		23	Everton	2-1	Law 2	60657			7	2		9	11	3	4		5	1		10	8					6
		27	Leeds United	1-3	Best	45092			7	2		9	11	3	4		5	1		10	8					6
6		31	EVERTON	3-0	Connelly, Foulkes, Law	61114			11	2		9	11	4	3		5			10	8					6
5	Sep	3	NEWCASTLE UNITED	3-2	Connelly, Herd, Law	44438			11	2		9	7	4	3		5		1	10	8					6
7		7	Stoke City	0-3		44420			11	2		9	7	4	3		5		1	10	8					6
9		10	Tottenham Hotspur	1-2	Law	56295		12	7	2		11		4	3		5	1		10	8			9		6
9		17	MANCHESTER CITY	1-0	Law	62085		11	7	2		10		4	3		5							9	1	6
5		24	BURNLEY	4-1	Crerand, Herd, Law, Sadler	52717		12	11	2		10		4	3		5			7	8			9	1	6
8	Oct	1	Nottingham Forest	1-4	Charlton	41854		11	7	2		8		4	3		5			10				9	1	6
6		8	Blackpool	2-1	Law 2	33555			11		5	10		4	2					7	8	3		9	1	6
6		15	CHELSEA	1-1	Law	56789			11		5	10		4	2					7	8	3		9	1	6
5		29	ARSENAL	1-0	Sadler	45417			11		5	10		4	2					7	8	3		9	1	6
4	Nov	5	Chelsea	3-1	Aston 2, Best	56452		8	11	2		10		4			5			7		3		9	1	6
2		12	SHEFFIELD WEDNESDAY	2-0	Charlton, Herd	46946		12	11			10		4	2		5			7	8	3		9	1	6
3		19	Southampton	2-1	Charlton 2	29458		12	11		5	10		4	2					7	8	3		9	1	6
2		26	SUNDERLAND	5-0	Herd 4, Law	44687		11	7			9		4	2					10	8	3		5	1	6
1		30	Leicester City	2-1	Best, Law	39014		11	7			9		4	2					10	8	3		5	1	6
1	Dec	3	Aston Villa	1-2	Herd	40016		11	7			9		4	2					10	8	3		5	1	6
1		10	LIVERPOOL	2-2	Best 2	61768	12	11	7	2		9		4	6					10		3	8	5	1	
1		17	West Bromwich Albion	4-3	Herd 3, Law	32080		11	7	2		9		4						10	8	3		5	1	6
2		26	Sheffield United	1-2	Herd	42752		11	7			9		4	2		5			10	8	3		6	1	
1		27	SHEFFIELD UNITED	2-0	Crerand, Herd	59392		11	7			9		4	2		5			10	8	3		6	1	
1		31	LEEDS UNITED			51578		11	7			9		4	2		5			10	8	3		6	1	
2	Jan	14	TOTTENHAM HOTSPUR	1-0	Herd	57365		11	7			9		4	2		5			10		3	8	6	1	
2		21	Manchester City	1-1	Foulkes	62983			11			8		4	2		5			10		3	7	9	1	6
2	Feb	4	Burnley	1-1	Sadler	40265			7			11		4	2		5			10	8	3		9	1	6
2		11	NOTTM. FOREST	1-0	Law	62727			7			11		4	2		5			10	8	3	12	9	1	6
1		25	BLACKPOOL	4-0	Charlton 2, Law, og (Hughes)	47157		11	7			10		4	2		5				8	3		9	1	6
1	Mar	3	Arsenal	1-1	Aston	63563		11	7			10		4	2		5				8	3		9	1	6
1		11	Newcastle United	0-0		38202		11	7			10		4	2		5				8	3		9	1	6
1		18	LEICESTER CITY	5-2	Aston, Charlton, Herd, Law, Sadler	50281		11	7			9		4	2		5			10	8	3		12	1	6
1		25	Liverpool	0-0		53813		11	7			10		4	2		5				8	3		9	1	6
1		27	Fulham	2-2	Best, Stiles	47290		11	7			10		4	2		5				8	3		9	1	6
1		28	FULHAM	2-1	Foulkes, Stiles	51673		11	7			10		4	2		5				8	3		9	1	6
1	Apr	1	WEST HAM UNITED	3-0	Best, Charlton, Law	61308		11	7			10		4	2		5				8	3		9	1	6
1		10	Sheffield Wednesday	2-2	Charlton 2	50315		11	7			10		4	2		5				8	3		9	1	6
1		18	SOUTHAMPTON	3-0	Charlton, Law, Sadler	55121		11	7			10		4	2		5				8	3		9	1	6
1		22	Sunderland	0-0		43570		11	7			10		4	2		5				8	3		9	1	6
1		29	ASTON VILLA	3-1	Aston, Best, Law	55763		11	7	2		10		4	3		5				8			9	1	6
1	May	6	West Ham United	6-1	Law 2, Best, Charlton, Crerand, Foulkes	38424		11	7	2		10		4	3		5				8			9	1	6
1		13	STOKE CITY	0-0		61071		11	7	2		10		4	3		5						8	9	1	6

						Apps	0	26	42	16	4	42	6	39	40	3	33	5	2	28	36	29	4	35	35	37
						Subs	1	4															1	1		
						Goals			5	10		12	2	3			4			16	23			5		3

One own goal

F.A. Cup

| R3 | Jan | 28 | STOKE CITY | 2-0 | Law, Herd | 63500 | | | 7 | | | 11 | | 4 | 2 | | 5 | | | 10 | 8 | 3 | | 9 | 1 | 6 |
| R4 | Feb | 18 | NORWICH CITY | 1-2 | Law | 63409 | | | 11 | | | 9 | | 4 | 2 | | | | | 10 | 8 | 3 | 7 | 5 | 1 | 6 |

F.L. Cup

| R2 | Sep | 14 | Blackpool | 1-5 | Herd | 15570 | | 11 | 8 | 2 | | | 7 | 4 | 3 | | 5 | | | 10 | | | | 9 | | 6 |

P Dunne played in goal

105

Manchester City 1967/68

Maine Road

						Bell C	Book AK	Bowles S	Cheetham RAJ	Clay JH	Coleman AG	Connor DR	Dowd HW	Doyle M	Heslop GW	Hince PF	Horne SF	Jones CMN	Kennedy R	Lee FH	Mulhearn KJ	Oakes AA	Ogley A	Pardoe G	Summerbee MG	Young NJ
	Aug	19	LIVERPOOL	0-0		49531	8	2				11	4			5			10				6	1	3	7	9
		23	Southampton	2-3	Bell, Coleman	23675	8	2				11	4		10	5							6	1	3	7	9
		26	Stoke City	0-3		22426	8	2		4			9	1	10	5							6		3	7	11
18		30	SOUTHAMPTON	4-2	Bell 2, Young 2	22002	8	2		4		11		1	12	5	7						6		3	9	10
11	Sep	2	NOTTM. FOREST	2-0	Coleman, Summerbee	29547	8	2				11		1	4	5	7						6		3	9	10
8		6	NEWCASTLE UNITED	2-0	Hince, Young	29978	8	2				11		1	4	5	7						6		3	9	10
5		9	Coventry City	3-0	Bell, Hince, Summerbee	34578	8	2				11		1	4	5	7						6		3	9	10
3		16	SHEFFIELD UNITED	5-2	Bowles 2, Bell, Summerbee, Young	31922	8	2	11					1	4	5	7						6		3	9	10
5		23	Arsenal	0-1		41567	8	2				11	12	1	4	5	7						6		3	9	10
7		30	MANCHESTER UNITED	1-2	Bell	62942	8	2	7			11			4	5		12				1	6		3	9	10
10	Oct	7	Sunderland	0-1		27885	8	2	7			11				5		4				1	6		3	9	10
8		14	WOLVERHAMPTON W.	2-0	Doyle, Young	36476	8	2			12	11			4	5					7	1	6		3	9	10
6		21	Fulham	4-2	Summerbee 2, Lee, Young	22108	8	2				11	3		4	5					7	1	6			9	10
4		28	LEEDS UNITED	1-0	Bell	39713	8	2				11			4	5					7	1	6		3	9	10
4	Nov	4	Everton	1-1	Connor	47144	8	2				11	10		4	5					7	1	6		3	9	
3		11	LEICESTER CITY	6-0	Lee 2, Young 2, Doyle, Oakes	29039	8	2				11			4				5		7	1	6		3	9	10
3		18	West Ham United	3-2	Lee 2, Summerbee	25495	8	2				11			4	5					7	1	6		3	9	10
3		25	BURNLEY	4-2	Coleman 2 (1p), Summerbee, Young	37098	8	2				11			4	5					7	1	6		3	9	10
3	Dec	2	Sheffield Wednesday	1-1	Oakes	38207	8	2				11			4	5					7	1	6		3	9	10
3		9	TOTTENHAM HOTSPUR	4-1	Bell, Coleman, Summerbee, Young	35792	8	2				11			4	5					7	1	6		3	9	10
3		16	Liverpool	1-1	Lee	53268	8	2				11			4	5				12	7	1	6		3	9	10
2		23	STOKE CITY	4-2	Lee 2, Coleman, Young	40121	8	2				11			4	5					7	1	6		3	9	10
3		26	West Bromwich Albion	2-3	Lee, Summerbee	44897		2	8	12		11				5		4			7	1	6		3	9	10
4		30	WEST BROMWICH ALB.	0-2		45754		2			8	11				5		4			7	1	6		3	9	10
4	Jan	6	Nottingham Forest	3-0	Coleman (p), Summerbee, Young	39581		2				11	8		4	5					7	1	6		3	9	10
4		20	Sheffield United	3-0	Bell, Doyle, Lee (p)	32142	8	2				11	12		4	5					7	1	6		3	9	10
4	Feb	3	ARSENAL	1-1	Lee	42392	8	2				11			4	5					7	1	6		3	9	10
4		24	SUNDERLAND	1-0	Lee	28624	8	2				11	10		4	5			9		7	1	6		3		
3	Mar	2	Burnley	1-0	Lee (p)	23486	8	2				11			4	5					7	1	6		3	9	10
2		9	COVENTRY CITY	3-1	Bell, Summerbee, Young	33310	8	2				11			4	5				12	7	1	6		3	9	10
1		16	FULHAM	5-1	Young 2, Bell, Lee, Summerbee	30773	8	2				11			4	5				6	7	1			3	9	10
3		23	Leeds United	0-2		51818	8	2				11			4	5					7	1	6		3	9	10
2		27	Manchester United	3-1	Bell, Heslop, Lee (p)	62243	8	2				11	12		4	5					7	1	6		3	9	10
3	Apr	6	Leicester City	0-1		24925		2				11	8		4	5					7	1	6		3	9	10
3		12	CHELSEA	1-0	Doyle	47132		2				11			8	5				4	7	1	6		3	9	10
3		13	WEST HAM UNITED	3-0	Young 2, Doyle	38755		2				11			8	5				4	7	1	6		3	9	10
3		16	Chelsea	0-1		36466		2					11		8	5				4	7	1	6		3	9	10
3		20	Wolverhampton Wan.	0-0		39632	8	2					11		4	5					7	1	6		3	9	10
3		25	SHEFFIELD WEDNESDAY	1-0	og (Usher)	32999	8	2				11			4	5					7	1	6		3	9	10
1		29	EVERTON	2-0	Book, Coleman	37786	8	2				11			4	5					7	1	6		3	9	10
1	May	4	Tottenham Hotspur	3-1	Bell 2, Summerbee	51242	8	2				11			4	5					7	1	6		3	9	10
1		11	Newcastle United	4-3	Young 2, Lee, Summerbee	46492	8	2				11			4	5					7	1	6		3	9	10

	Bell C	Book AK	Bowles S	Cheetham RAJ	Clay JH	Coleman AG	Connor DR	Dowd HW	Doyle M	Heslop GW	Hince PF	Horne SF	Jones CMN	Kennedy R	Lee FH	Mulhearn KJ	Oakes AA	Ogley A	Pardoe G	Summerbee MG	Young NJ
Apps	35	42	4	2	1	38	10	7	37	41	6	4	2	4	31	33	41	2	41	41	40
Subs					1		1		3		1			2							
Goals	14	1	2			8	1		5	1	2				16		2			14	19

One own goal

F.A. Cup

							Bell C	Book AK	Coleman AG	Connor DR	Doyle M	Heslop GW	Lee FH	Mulhearn KJ	Oakes AA	Pardoe G	Summerbee MG	Young NJ
R3	Jan	27	READING	0-0		40343	8	2	11		4	5	7	1	6	3	9	10
rep		31	Reading	7-0	Summerbee 3, Bell, Coleman, Heslop, Young	25659	8	2	11	12	4	5	7	1	6	3	9	10
R4	Feb	17	LEICESTER CITY	0-0		51009	8	2	11		4	5	7	1	6	3	9	10
rep		19	Leicester City	3-4	Bell, Lee, Summerbee	39112	8	2	11		4	5	7	1	6	3	9	10

F.L. Cup

							Bell C	Book AK	Bowles S	Coleman AG	Connor DR	Doyle M	Heslop GW	Hince PF	Jones CMN	Kennedy R	Oakes AA	Pardoe G	Summerbee MG	Young NJ
R2	Sep	13	LEICESTER CITY	4-0	Bowles 2, Book (p), Young	25653	8	2	12	11		1	4	5	7			6	3	9	10
R3	Oct	11	BLACKPOOL	1-1	Summerbee	27633	8	2		11			5	7	4		6	3	9	10
rep		18	Blackpool	2-0	Summerbee, og (Craven)	23405	8	2		11	12		4	5	7		6	3	9	10
R4	Nov	1	Fulham	2-3	Bell, Oakes	11732	8	2		11		1	4	5	7	12	6	3	9	10

TJ Corrigan played in R3 and R3 replay in goal

Leeds United 1968/69

Elland Road

							Bates MJ	Belfitt RM	Bremner WJ	Charlton J	Cooper T	Giles MJ	Gray E	Greenhoff J	Hibbitt TA	Hunter N	Johanneson AL	Jones MD	Lorimer PP	Madeley PE	O'Grady M	Reaney P	Sprake G
	Aug	10	Southampton	3-1	Hibbitt, Jones, Lorimer	25479			4	5			10	11	8	12	6		9	7	3		2	1
		14	QUEEN'S PARK RANGERS	4-1	Giles, Hibbitt, Jones, Reaney	31612			4	5	3	10			8	11	6		9	7			2	1
		17	STOKE CITY	2-0	Johannesson, Jones	30383		7	4	5	3		10	8		11	6	12	9				2	1
1		20	Ipswich Town	3-2	Belfitt, Hibbitt, O'Grady	30388		8	4	5	3		10			11	6		9			7	2	1
2		28	SUNDERLAND	1-1	Belfitt	37797		8	4	5	3		10			11	6		9			7	2	1
2		31	LIVERPOOL	1-0	Jones	38930	12	10	4	5	3					11	6		9	8		7	2	1
2	Sep	7	WOLVERHAMPTON W.	2-1	Cooper, Charlton	31277			4	5	3					11	6		9	8	10	7	2	1
2		14	Leicester City	1-1	Madeley	28654			4	5	3					11	6		9	8	10	7	2	1
1		21	ARSENAL	2-0	Charlton, O'Grady	39946			4	5	3					11	6		9	8	10	7	2	1
3		28	Manchester City	1-3	O'Grady	46431			4	5	3			12		11	6		9	8	10	7	2	1
3	Oct	5	Newcastle United	1-0	Charlton	41999			4	5	3	10	11				6			8	9	7	2	1
1		9	Sunderland	1-0	Jones	33535			4	5	3	8	11				6		9		10	7	2	1
1		12	WEST HAM UNITED	2-0	Lorimer, Giles (p)	40686			4	5	3	8					6		9	11	10	7	2	1
1		19	Burnley	1-5	Bremner	26434			4	5	3	8	11				6		9	12	10	7	2	1
3		26	WEST BROMWICH ALB.	0-0		33926	10		4	5				8			6		9	7	3	11	2	1
3	Nov	2	Manchester United	0-0		53839	8		4	5		10					6		9	7	3	11	2	1
3		9	TOTTENHAM HOTSPUR	0-0		38995			4	5	3	10	11				6		9		8	7	2	1
3		16	Coventry City	1-0	Madeley	33224			4	5	3	10	11				6		9		8	7	2	1
2		23	EVERTON	2-1	Gray, Giles (p)	41716			4	5	3	10	11				6		9		8	7	2	1
3		30	Chelsea	1-1	O'Grady	43286			4	5	3	10					6		9	7	8	11	2	1
2	Dec	7	SHEFFIELD WEDNESDAY	2-0	Lorimer 2	32718			4	5		10	11				6		9	8	3	7	2	1
2		14	West Ham United	1-1	Gray	27418			4	5		10	11				6		9	8	3	7	2	1
2		21	BURNLEY	6-1	Lorimer 2, Bremner, Gray, Giles, Jones	31409			4	5		10	11				6		9	8	3	7	2	1
2		26	NEWCASTLE UNITED	2-1	Madeley, Lorimer (p)	44995			4	5			10				12	6	9	8	3	7	2	1
2	Jan	11	MANCHESTER UNITED	2-1	Jones, O'Grady	48145			4	5	12	10	11				6		9	8	3	7	2	1
2		18	Tottenham Hotspur	0-0		42396			4	5	3	10	11				6		9		8	7	2	1
2		24	Queen's Park Rangers	1-0	Jones	26163		12	4	5	3	10	11				6		9	7	8		2	1
2	Feb	1	COVENTRY CITY	3-0	Bremner 2, O'Grady	32314			4	5	3		10				12	6	9	7	8	11	2	1
1		12	IPSWICH TOWN	2-0	Belfitt, Jones	24494		8	4	5	3	10	11				6		9			7	2	1
1		15	CHELSEA	1-0	Lorimer	35789		12	4	5	3	10	11				6		9	8		7	2	1
1		25	Nottingham Forest	2-0	Jones, Lorimer	36249		8	4	5	3	10	11				6		9	12		7	2	1
1	Mar	1	SOUTHAMPTON	3-2	Jones, Giles (p), og (Kirkup)	33205			4	5	3	10	11				6		9	8		7	2	1
1		8	Stoke City	5-1	Bremner 2, O'Grady 2, Jones	24345			4	5	3	10	11				6		9		8	7	2	1
1		29	Wolverhampton Wan.	0-0		27986			4	5	3	10	11				6		9	12	8	7	2	1
1	Apr	1	Sheffield Wednesday	0-0		35062			4	5	3	10	11				6		9	8		7	2	1
1		5	MANCHESTER CITY	1-0	Giles	43176			4	5	3	10	11				6		9	8		7	2	1
1		9	West Bromwich Albion	1-1	Gray	28286			4	5	3	10	11				6		9		8	7	2	1
1		12	Arsenal	2-1	Giles, Jones	44715	8		4		3	10	11				6		9	12	5	7	2	1
1		19	LEICESTER CITY	2-0	Gray, Jones	38931			4	5	3	10	11				6		9		8	7	2	1
1		22	Everton	0-0		59022			4	5	3	10	11				6			9	8	7	2	1
1		28	Liverpool	0-0		53570			4	5	3	10	11				6		9	8		7	2	1
1		30	NOTTM. FOREST	1-0	Giles	46508			4	5	3	10					6		9	7	8	11	2	1

Apps	3	6	42	41	34	32	32	3	9	42	0	40	25	31	38	42	42
Subs	1	2			1		1		3		1	4					
Goals		3	6	3	1	8	5		3			1	14	9	3	8	1	

One own goal

F.A. Cup

| R3 | Jan | 4 | Sheffield Wednesday | 1-1 | Lorimer (p) | 52111 | 10 | | 4 | 5 | | | 11 | | | | 6 | | 9 | 8 | 3 | 7 | 2 | 1 |
| rep | | 8 | SHEFFIELD WEDNESDAY | 1-3 | Johanneson | 48234 | 10 | 12 | 4 | 5 | | | 7 | | | | 6 | 11 | 9 | 8 | 3 | | 2 | 1 |

F.L. Cup

R2	Sep	4	CHARLTON ATHLETIC	1-0	Jones	18860	12	8	4	5	3				10	6			9	7		11	2	1
R3		25	BRISTOL CITY	2-1	Johanneson, Jones	16359			4			3	10	6				11	9	8	5	7	2	1
R4	Oct	16	Crystal Palace	1-2	Madeley	26217				5	3	8	4			6			9	11	10	7	2	1

Inter-Cities Fairs Cup (Final of 1967/68 season)

| F1 | Aug | 7 | FERENCVAROS | 1-0 | Jones | 25268 | | 12 | 4 | 5 | 3 | | 10 | 11 | 13 | | 6 | | 9 | 7 | 8 | | 2 | 1 |
| F2 | Sep | 11 | Ferencvaros | 0-0 | | 76000 | 12 | | 4 | 5 | 3 | | | | | 11 | 6 | | 9 | 8 | 10 | 7 | 2 | 1 |

Won 1-0 on aggregate

Inter-Cities Fairs Cup

R1.1	Sep	18	Standard Liege	0-0		35000			4	5	3					11	6		9	8	10	7	2	1
R1.2	Oct	23	STANDARD LIEGE	3-2	Bremner, Charlton, Lorimer	24178	12		4	5	3			13		11	6		9	8	10	7	2	1
R2.1	Nov	13	NAPOLI	2-0	Charlton 2	26967		9	4	5		10					6		8	11	3	7	2	1
R2.2		27	Napoli	0-2		15000			4	5	3	10	11				6			8	7		2	1
R3.1	Dec	18	HANNOVER 96	5-1	Lorimer 2, Charlton, Hunter, O'Grady	25162			4	5		10	11			12	6		9	8	3	7	2	1
R3.2	Feb	4	Hannover 96	2-1	Belfitt, Jones	15000		10	4	5	3		11				6		9	8		7	2	1
R4.1	Mar	5	UJPESTI DOZSA	0-1		30906			4	5		10	11				6		9	12	3	7	2	1
R4.2		19	Ujpesti Dozsa	0-2		40000	2	8	4		3	10	11			13	6		9	7	5		2	1

R2 won on the toss of a coin   T Yorath played at 12 in final game

Everton 1969/70

Goodison Park

								Ball AJ	Brown AD	D'Arcy FA	Harvey JC	Humphreys G	Hurst JW	Husband J	Jackson TA	Kendall H	Kenyon RN	Labone BL	Morrissey JJ	Newton KR	Royle J	West G	Whittle A	Wright TI
	Aug	9	Arsenal	1-0	Hurst		44364		3		6		10	7	8	4	12	5	11		9	1		2
		13	Manchester United	2-0	Ball, Hurst		57752	8	3		6		10	7	4			5	11		9	1		2
		16	CRYSTAL PALACE	2-1	Morrissey, Royle		51241	8	3		6		10	7	4			5	11		9	1		2
1		19	MANCHESTER UNITED	3-0	Ball, Morrissey, Royle		53185	8	3	12	6		10	7	4			5	11		9	1		2
		23	Manchester City	1-1	Morrissey		43366	8	3		6		10	7	4			5	11		9	1		2
1		26	SHEFFIELD WEDNESDAY	2-1	Ball, Royle		46480	8	3		6		10	7	4			5	11		9	1		2
1		30	LEEDS UNITED	3-2	Royle 2, Husband		53253	8	3		6		10	7	4			5	11		9	1		2
2	Sep	6	Derby County	1-2	Kendall		37708	8	3		6		10	7		4		5	11		9	1		2
3		13	WEST HAM UNITED	2-0	Ball, Husband		49052	8	3		6		10	7		4		5	11		9	1		2
1		17	Newcastle United	2-1	Husband 2		37094	8	3		6		10	7		4		5	11		9	1		2
1		20	Ipswich Town	3-0	Ball, Harvey, Royle		23258	8	3		6		10	7		4		5	11		9	1		2
		27	SOUTHAMPTON	4-2	Royle 3, Hurst		46942	8	3		6		10	7		4		5	11		9	1		2
1	Oct	4	Wolverhampton Wan.	3-2	Harvey, Morrissey, Royle		40838	8	3		6		10	7		4		5	11		9	1		2
		8	Crystal Palace	0-0			33967	8	3		6		10	7		4		5	11		9	1		2
1		11	SUNDERLAND	3-1	Kendall, Morrissey, Royle		47271	8	3		6		10	7		4		5	11		9	1		2
1		18	STOKE CITY	6-2	Morrissey 2, Royle 2, Ball, Husband		48663	8	3		6		10	7		4		5	11		9	1		2
1		25	Coventry City	1-0	Royle		37816	8	3		6		10	7		4		5	11		9	1		2
1	Nov	1	NOTTM. FOREST	1-0	Wright		49610	8	3		6		10	7		4		5	11		9	1		2
1		8	West Bromwich Albion	0-2			34298	8	3		6		10	7		4		5	11		9	1		2
		15	Chelsea	1-1	Husband		49895	8	3		6		10	7		4		5	11		9	1		2
1		22	BURNLEY	2-1	Hurst, Royle		46380	8	3	12			10	7	6	4		5	11		9	1		2
1	Dec	6	LIVERPOOL	0-3			57370	8	3				10		6	4		5	11		9	1	7	2
		13	West Ham United	1-0	Whittle		26689	8	3	12			10		6	4		5	11		9	1	7	2
1		20	DERBY COUNTY	1-0	Ball		44914	8	12				10	7	6	4		5	11	3	9	1		2
1		23	MANCHESTER CITY	1-0	Whittle		51864	8	12			11	10		6	4		5		3	9	1	7	2
1		27	Leeds United	1-2	Whittle		46770	8					10		6	4		5	11	3	9	1	7	2
1	Jan	10	IPSWICH TOWN	3-0	Royle 2, Kendall		42510	8					10	7	6	4		5	11	3	9	1		2
2		17	Southampton	1-2	Morrissey		27156		10		6		8	7	12	4		5	11	3	9	1		
2		24	NEWCASTLE UNITED	0-0			42845		12		6		10	7		4		5	11	3	9	1	8	2
2		31	WOLVERHAMPTON W.	1-0	Royle		45681		12		6		10	7		4		5	11	3	9	1	8	2
2	Feb	14	ARSENAL	2-2	Whittle 2		48564				6		10	7		4		5	11	3	9	1	8	2
2		21	COVENTRY CITY	0-0			45934	8			6		10	7		4		5	11	3	9	1		2
2		28	Nottingham Forest	1-1	Royle		29174	8			6		10	7		4		5	11	3	9	1		2
2	Mar	7	Burnley	2-1	Ball, Hurst		21114	8			6		10			4		5	11	3	9	1	7	2
1		11	Tottenham Hotspur	1-0	Whittle		27764	8	12		6		10			4	5		11	3	9	1	7	2
1		14	TOTTENHAM HOTSPUR	3-2	Ball, Royle, Whittle		51533	8	3		6		10			4	5		11		9	1	7	2
1		21	Liverpool	2-0	Royle, Whittle		54496	8	3		6		10			4	5		11		9	1	7	2
1		28	CHELSEA	5-2	Royle 2, Ball, Kendall, Whittle		58337	8	3		6		10			4	5		11		9	1	7	2
1		30	Stoke City	1-0	Whittle		33111	8	3		6		10			4	5		11		9	1	7	2
1	Apr	1	WEST BROMWICH ALB.	2-0	Harvey, Whittle		58523	8	3		6		10			4	5		11		9	1	7	2
1		4	Sheffield Wednesday	1-0	Morrissey		30696	8	3	12	6		10			4	5		11		9	1	7	2
1		8	Sunderland	0-0			28774	8	3	12	6		10	7		4	5		11		9	1		2

	Apps	Subs	Goals
Ball AJ	37		10
Brown AD	31	5	
D'Arcy FA	0	5	
Harvey JC	35		3
Humphreys G	1		
Hurst JW	42		5
Husband J	30		6
Jackson TA	14	1	4
Kendall H	36	1	
Kenyon RN	8		
Labone BL	34		
Morrissey JJ	41		9
Newton KR	12		
Royle J	42		23
West G	42		
Whittle A	15		11
Wright TI	42		1

F.A. Cup

R3	Jan	3	Sheffield United	1-2	Ball		29116	8	12				10		6	4		5	11	3	9	1	7	2

F.L. Cup

R2	Sep	3	Darlington	1-0	Ball		18000	8	3		6		10	7		4		5	11		9	1		2
R3		24	Arsenal	0-0			36119	8	3		6		10			4	12	5	11		9	1	7	2
rep		30	ARSENAL	1-0	Kendall		41140	8	3		6		10	7		4		5	11		9	1		2
R4	Oct	14	Manchester City	0-2			45463		3			11			6	4		5			9	1	7	2

Brindle (at 8) and Bennett (at 10) played in R4

108

Arsenal 1970/71

Highbury

		Date	Opponent	Score	Scorers	Att	Armstrong G	George FC	Graham G	Kelly EP	Kennedy R	Marinello P	McLintock F	McNab R	Nelson S	Radford J	Rice PJ	Roberts JG	Sammels JC	Simpson PF	Storey PE	Wilson RP
	Aug	15	Everton	2-2	George, Graham	50248	7	10	11	4		12	6	3		9	2	5			8	1
		17	West Ham United	0-0		39004	7		11	4	9	10	5	3		8		6			2	1
		22	MANCHESTER UNITED	4-0	Radford 3, Graham	54137	7		11	4	10	12	5	3		9	2	6			8	1
2		25	HUDDERSFIELD T	1-0	Kennedy	34848	7		11	4	10		5	3	12	9	2	6			8	1
7		29	Chelsea	1-2	Kelly	53722	7		11	4	10		5	3	9		2	6			8	1
7	Sep	1	LEEDS UNITED	0-0		47769	7		11	4	10		5	3		9	2	6			8	1
3		5	TOTTENHAM HOTSPUR	2-0	Armstrong 2	48931	7		11	4	10		5	3	12	9	2	6			8	1
4		12	Burnley	2-1	Radford, Kennedy	12710	7		11	4	10		5	3		9	2	6			8	1
3		19	WEST BROMWICH ALB.	6-2	Kennedy 2, Graham 2, Armstrong, og (Cantello)	33303	7		11	4	10		5	3		9	2	6			8	1
4		26	Stoke City	0-5		18196	7		11	4	10		5	3		9	2	6			8	1
3	Oct	3	NOTTM. FOREST	4-0	Kennedy 3, Armstrong	32073	7		11	4	10		5	3		9	2	6			8	1
4		10	Newcastle United	1-1	Graham	38024	7		11	4	10		5	3		9	2	6			8	1
2		17	EVERTON	4-0	Kennedy 2, Storey (p), Kelly	50053	7		11	4	10		5	3		9	2	6			8	1
2		24	Coventry City	3-1	Radford, Kennedy, Graham	29975	7		11	4	10		5	3		9	2	6			8	1
2		31	DERBY COUNTY	2-0	Kelly, Radford	43013	7		11	4	10		5	3		9	2	6			8	1
2	Nov	7	Blackpool	1-0	Radford	17115	7		11	4	10		5	3		9	2	6			8	1
3		14	CRYSTAL PALACE	1-1	Radford	34503	7		11	4	10		5	3		9	2	6			8	1
2		21	Ipswich Town	1-0	Armstrong	22867	7			4	10		5	3		9	2		11	6	8	1
2		28	LIVERPOOL	2-0	Radford, Graham	45097	7		12	4	10		5	3		9	2		11	6	8	1
2	Dec	5	Manchester City	2-0	Armstrong, Radford	33036	7		4		10		5	3		9	2		11	6	8	1
2		12	WOLVERHAMPTON W.	2-1	Radford, Graham	38816	7		11		10		5	3		9	2		8	6	4	1
2		19	Manchester United	3-1	McLintock, Kennedy, Graham	31381	7		11		10		5	3		9	2		8	6	4	1
2		26	SOUTHAMPTON	0-0		34431	7		11		10		5	3		9	2		8	6	4	1
2	Jan	9	WEST HAM UNITED	2-0	Kennedy, Graham	49057	7		11		10		5		3	9	2		8	6	4	1
2		16	Huddersfield Town	1-2	Kennedy	30455	7		11		10		5	3		9	2		8	6	4	1
2		30	Liverpool	0-2		43847	7		11		10		5	3		9	2		8	6	4	1
2	Feb	6	MANCHESTER CITY	1-0	Radford	46162	7	11			10		5	3		9	2		8	6	4	1
2		20	IPSWICH TOWN	3-2	McLintock, George, Radford	39872	7	11			10		5	3		9	2		8	6	4	1
2		27	Derby County	0-2		35771	7	11	12		10		5	3		9	2		8	6	4	1
2	Mar	2	Wolverhampton Wan.	3-0	Armstrong, Radford, Kennedy	33644	7	11			10		5	3		9	2		8	6	4	1
2		13	Crystal Palace	2-0	Graham, Sammels	35002	7	11	8		10		5	3		9	2		12	6	4	1
2		20	BLACKPOOL	1-0	Storey	37412	7	11	8		10		5	3		9	2			6	4	1
2	Apr	3	CHELSEA	2-0	Kennedy 2	62056	7	11	8	12	10		5	3		9	2			6	4	1
2		6	COVENTRY CITY	1-0	Kennedy	37141	7	11	8		10		5	3		9	2			6	4	1
2		10	Southampton	2-1	McLintock, Radford	30231	7	11	8		10		5	3		9	2			6	4	1
2		13	Nottingham Forest	3-0	McLintock, Kennedy, George	40692	7	11	8		10		5	3		9	2			6	4	1
1		17	NEWCASTLE UNITED	1-0	George	48131	7	11	8		10		5	3		9	2			6	4	1
1		20	BURNLEY	1-0	George (p)	47591	7	11	8	4	10		5			9	2	3		6		1
1		24	West Bromwich Albion	2-2	McLintock, og (Hartford)	36621	7	11	8		10		5	3		9	2		12	6	4	1
2		26	Leeds United	0-1		48350	7	11	8		10		5	3		9	2			6	4	1
2	May	1	STOKE CITY	1-0	Kelly	54896	7	11	8	12	10		5	3		9	2			6	4	1
1		3	Tottenham Hotspur	1-0	Kennedy	51992	7	11	8	4	10		5	3		9	2			6		1

	Armstrong G	George FC	Graham G	Kelly EP	Kennedy R	Marinello P	McLintock F	McNab R	Nelson S	Radford J	Rice PJ	Roberts JG	Sammels JC	Simpson PF	Storey PE	Wilson RP
Apps	42	17	36	21	41	1	42	40	2	41	41	18	13	25	40	42
Subs			2	2		2			2				2			
Goals	7	5	11	4	19		5			15		1		2		

Two own goals

F.A. Cup

		Date	Opponent	Score	Scorers	Att																
R3	Jan	6	Yeovil Town	3-0	Radford 2, Kennedy	4374	7		11	12	10		5	3		9	2		8	6	4	1
R4		23	Portsmouth	1-1	Storey (p)	39659	7	12	11		10		5	3		9	2		8	6	4	1
rep	Feb	1	PORTSMOUTH	3-2	Storey (p), Simpson, George	47865	7	11			10		5	3		9	2		8	6	4	1
R5		17	Manchester City	2-1	George 2	45105	7	11			10		5	3		9	2		8	6	4	1
R6	Mar	6	Leicester City	0-0		42000	7	11			10		5	3		9	2		8	6	4	1
rep		15	LEICESTER CITY	1-0	George	57443	7	11	8		10		5	3		9	2			6	4	1
SF		27	Stoke City	2-2	Storey 2 (1p)	53436	7	11	8		10		5	3		9	2		12	6	4	1
SF		31	Stoke City	2-0	Kennedy, Graham	62500	7	11	8		10		5	3		9	2			6	4	1
F	May	8	Liverpool	2-1	Kelly, George	100000	7	11	8	12	10		5	3		9	2			6	4	1

SF at Hillsborough, SF replay at Villa Park. Final at Wembley Stadium, a.e.t.

F.L. Cup

		Date	Opponent	Score	Scorers	Att																
R2	Sep	8	Ipswich Town	0-0		21564	7		11	4	10		5	3	9		2	6			8	1
rep		28	IPSWICH TOWN	4-0	Kennedy 2, Radford, Roberts	26542	7		11	4	10		5	3		9	2	6			8	1
R3	Oct	6	Luton Town	1-0	Graham	27023	7		11	4	10		5	3		9	2	6			8	1
R4		28	Crystal Palace	0-0		40451	7		11	4	10		5	3		9	2	6			8	1
rep	Nov	9	CRYSTAL PALACE	0-2		45026	7		11	4	10		5	3		9	2	6			8	1

Inter-City Fairs Cup

		Date	Opponent	Score	Scorers	Att																
R1.1	Sep	16	Lazio	2-2	Radford 2	60000	7		11	4	10		5	3		9	2	6			8	1
R1.2		23	LAZIO	2-0	Armstrong, Radford	53013	7		11	4	10		5	3	12	9	2	6			8	1
R2.1	Oct	21	Sturm Graz	0-1		13000	7		11	4	10		5	3		9	2	6			8	1
R2.2	Nov	4	STURM GRAZ	2-0	Storey (p), Kennedy	37667	7		11	4	10		5	3		9	2	6			8	1
R3.1	Dec	2	SK BEVEREN	4-0	Kennedy 2, Graham, Sammels	33444	7		11		10		5	3		9	2		4	6	8	1
R3.2		16	SK Beveren	0-0		16000	7	13	11		10	12		3		9	2	5	8	6	4	1
QF1	Mar	9	COLOGNE	2-1	Storey, McLintock	40007	7	11	12		10		5	3		9	2		8	6	4	1
QF2		23	Cologne	0-1		50000	7	11	8		10		5	3		9	2			6	4	1

QF lost on away goals

Derby County 1971/72

Baseball Ground

							Bailey AD	Boulton CD	Durban WA	Gemmill A	Hector KJ	Hennessey WT	Hinton AT	McFarland RL	McGovern JP	O'Hare J	Powell S	Robson JD	Todd C	Walker JMcI	Webster R	Wignall F
	Aug	14	MANCHESTER UNITED	2-2	Wignall, Hector	35386	1			7	10	5	11		4	9		3	6		2	8
		18	WEST HAM UNITED	2-0	Wignall, O'Hare	30783	1			7	10	5	11		4	9		3	6		2	8
		21	Leicester City	2-0	Hector, Hinton (p)	35460	1			7	10	5	11		4	9		3	6		2	8
3		24	Coventry City	2-2	Wignall, O'Hare	27759	1			7	10		11	5	4	9		3	6		2	8
4		28	SOUTHAMPTON	2-2	McGovern, Hector	28498	1		8		10	4	11	5	6	9		3	2			
2		31	Ipswich Town	0-0		18687	1		8	7	10	4	11	5	6			3	2			9
3	Sep	4	Everton	2-0	Wignall, Hector	41024	1		8	7	10		11	5	6			3	4		2	9
2		11	STOKE CITY	4-0	Todd, Gemmill, O'Hare, Hinton	32545	1		7	6	10		11	5		9		3	4		2	8
3		18	Chelsea	1-1	McFarland	42872	1			7	10		11	5	6	9		3	4		2	8
3		25	WEST BROMWICH ALB.	0-0		30628	1		7	6	10		11	5	12	9		3	4		2	8
3	Oct	2	Newcastle United	1-0	Hinton	32077	1		8		10	4	11	5	7	9		3	6		2	
4		9	TOTTENHAM HOTSPUR	2-2	Todd, McFarland	35744	1		8	7	10		11	5	6	9		3	4		2	12
4		16	Manchester United	0-1		53247	1		8	7	10	4	11	5	6	9		3	2			
3		23	ARSENAL	2-1	O'Hare, Hinton (p)	36480	1		8	7	10		11	5	6	9	12	3	4		2	
2		30	Nottingham Forest	2-0	Robson, Hinton (p)	37170	1			8	10		11	5	7	9	4	3	6		2	
2	Nov	6	CRYSTAL PALACE	3-0	Wignall, Hector, Bell (og)	30388	1		7		10	5	11		6	9		3	4		2	8
2		13	Wolverhampton Wan.	1-2	O'Hare	32957	1			8	10	6	11	5	7	9		3	4		2	
2		20	SHEFFIELD UNITED	3-0	Hinton 2 (2p), Hector	35326	1			8	10	6	11	5	7	9		3	4		2	
3		27	Huddersfield Town	1-2	McGovern	15329	1			8	10	6	11	5	7	9		3	4		2	
2	Dec	4	MANCHESTER CITY	3-1	Webster, Durban, Hinton (p)	35384	1		7	8	10		11	5	6	9		3	4		2	
4		11	Liverpool	2-3	O'Hare 2	44601	1		7	8	10	4	11	5	6	9			2	12	3	
3		18	EVERTON	2-0	Hinton 2	27895	1		7	8	10	4	11	5	6	9		3			2	
5		27	Leeds United	0-3		44214	4	1		8	10	6	11	5	7	9		3			2	
4	Jan	1	CHELSEA	1-0	Gemmill	33063	1		7	8	10		11	5	6	9		3	4		2	
4		8	Southampton	2-1	O'Hare, Durban	19321	1		4	8	10		11	5	7	9		3	6		2	
4		22	West Ham United	3-3	Hector, Hinton, Durban	31045	1		4	8	10		11	5	7	9		3	6		2	
3		29	COVENTRY CITY	1-0	Robson	29385	1		4	8	10		11	5	7	9		3	6		2	
3	Feb	12	Arsenal	0-2		52102	1		4	8	10		11	5	7	9		3	6		2	
3		19	NOTTM. FOREST	4-0	Hinton 2, Hector, O'Hare	31801	1		4	8	10		11	5	7	9		3	6		2	
3	Mar	4	WOLVERHAMPTON W.	2-1	McFarland, Hinton (p)	33456	1		4	8	10		11	5	7	9		3	6		2	
3		11	Tottenham Hotspur	1-0	Hinton	36310	1			8	10	4	11	5	7	9		3	6		2	
2		18	LEICESTER CITY	3-0	O'Hare, Hector, Durban	34019	1		4	11	10	8		5	7	9		3	6	12	2	
2		22	IPSWICH TOWN	1-0	Hector	26738	1		4	8	10		11	5	7	9		3	6	12	2	
2		25	Stoke City	1-1	Durban	33771	1		4	8	10			5	7	9		3	6	11	2	
2		28	Crystal Palace	1-0	Walker	21158	1		4	8	10	7		5		9		3	6	11	2	
1	Apr	1	LEEDS UNITED	2-0	O'Hare, Hunter (og)	38611	1		4	8	10			5	7	9		3	6	11	2	
1		3	NEWCASTLE UNITED	0-1		38119	1		4	8	10			5	7	9		3	6		2	
1		5	West Bromwich Albion	0-0		32439	1		4	8	10		11	5	7	9		3	6		2	
1		8	Sheffield United	4-0	Gemmill, O'Hare, Hector, Durban	38238	1		4	8	10		11	5	7	9		3	6		2	
1		15	HUDDERSFIELD T	3-0	McFarland, O'Hare, Hector	31414	1		4	8	10		11	5	7	9		3	6		2	
3		22	Manchester City	0-2		55023	1		4	8	10	12	11	5	7	9		3	6		2	
1	May	1	LIVERPOOL	1-0	McGovern	39159	1		4	8	10		11	5	7	9	2	3	6			

	Apps	Subs	Goals
Bailey	1		
Boulton	42		
Durban	31		6
Gemmill	40	1	3
Hector	42		12
Hennessey	17	1	
Hinton	38		15
McFarland	38		4
McGovern	39	1	3
O'Hare	40		13
Powell	2	1	
Robson	41		2
Todd	40		2
Walker	3	3	1
Webster	38	1	1
Wignall	10	1	5

Two own goals

F.A. Cup

R3	Jan	15	SHREWSBURY TOWN	2-0	Hector 2	33463	1		4	8	10		11	5	7	9		3	6		2	
R4	Feb	5	NOTTS COUNTY	6-0	Durban 3, Robson, Hector, Hinton	39450	1		4	8	10		11	5	7	9	12	3	6		2	
R5		26	ARSENAL	2-2	Durban, Hinton	39622	1		4	8	10		11	5	7	9		3	6		2	
rep		29	Arsenal	0-0		63077	1		4	8	10		11	5	7	9		3	6		2	
rep2	Mar	13	Arsenal	0-1		40000	1		4	8	10	12	11	5	7	9		3	6		2	

R5 replay a.e.t. Replay 2 at Filbert Street, Leicester

F.L. Cup

R2	Sep	8	LEEDS UNITED	0-0		34023	1			7	6	10		11	5		9		3	4		2	8
rep		27	Leeds United	0-2		29132	1				6	10		11	5	7	9		3	4		2	8

Texaco Cup

R1.1	Sep	15	DUNDEE UNITED	6-2	Durban, Hector, Walker, O'Hare, Hinton, Robson	20059		1	8		10	5	11		6	9		3	4	12	2	
R1.2		29	Dundee United	2-3	Hinton, Butlin	6000	5	1		6		4	11		7			3		10		8
R2.1	Oct	20	STOKE CITY	3-2	O'Hare 2, Hector	21487	12	1			10	4	11	5		9	8		6			7
R2.2	Nov	3	Stoke City	1-1	Wignall	23461		1	7		10	5	11		6	9		3	4		2	8
SF1		24	NEWCASTLE UNITED	1-0	O'Hare 2, Hector	20201		1		8	10	6	11	5	7	9		3	4		2	
SF2	Dec	8	Newcastle United	3-2	McGovern, Todd, Walker	37000	5	1	7		10	4	11		8	9			2	12	3	
F1	Jan	26	Airdrieonians	0-0		16000		1		8		6	11					3	4	10	2	
F2	Apr	26	AIRDRIEONIANS	2-1	Hinton (p), Davies	25102		1	4		10	6	11		7		2	3				

SF2 a.e.t. Final won 2-1 on aggregate

Daniel played in 5 games: R1.2 and R2.1 at 2, SF2 at 6, F1 and F2 at 5
Butlin played in 3 games: R1.2 and F1 at 9, F2 at 8
Bourne played at 7 in R1.1
Lewis played at 3 in R2.1
Parry played in F1 at 7
Davies played in F2 at 9

110

Liverpool 1972/73

Anfield

	Date		Opponent	Score	Scorers	Att	Boersma P	Callaghan IR	Clemence RN	Cormack PB	Hall BW	Heighway SD	Hughes EW	Keegan JK	Lane F	Lawler C	Lindsay A	Lloyd LV	Smith T	Storton TG	Thompson PB	Toshack JB
	Aug	12	MANCHESTER CITY	2-0	Hall, Callaghan	55383		11	1		8	9	6	7		2	3	5	4			10
		15	MANCHESTER UNITED	2-0	Toshack, Heighway	54779		11	1		8	9	6	7		2	3	5	4			10
		19	Crystal Palace	1-1	Hughes	30054		11	1		8	9	6	7		2	3	5	4			10
1		23	Chelsea	2-1	Toshack, Callaghan	35375		11	1		8	9	6	7		2	3	5	4			10
1		26	WEST HAM UNITED	3-2	Toshack, Hughes, og (Ferguson)	50491		11	1		8	9	6	7		2	3	5	4			10
4		30	Leicester City	2-3	Toshack 2	26706		11	1		8	9	6	7		2	3	5	4			10
6	Sep	2	Derby County	1-2	Toshack	32524		11		8	6	9	3	7	1	2		5	4			10
4		9	WOLVERHAMPTON W.	4-2	Hughes, Cormack, Smith (p), Keegan	43886		11	1	8		9	6	7		2	3	5	4			10
5		16	Arsenal	0-0		47367		11	1	8		9	6	7		2	3	5	4			10
1		23	SHEFFIELD UNITED	5-0	Boersma, Lindsay, Heighway, Cormack, Keegan (p)	42940	10	11	1	8		9	6	7		2	3	5	4			
1		30	Leeds United	2-1	Lloyd, Boersma	46468	10	11	1	8		9	6	7		2	3	5		4		
1	Oct	7	EVERTON	1-0	Cormack	55975	10	11	1	8		9	6	7		2	3	5		4		
1		14	Southampton	1-1	Lawler	24100	10	11	1	8		9	6	7		2	3	5		4		
1		21	STOKE CITY	2-1	Hughes, Callaghan	45604	10	11	1	8		9	6	7		2	3	5	4			
1		28	Norwich City	1-1	Cormack	36500	10	11	1	8		9		7		2	3	5	4	6		
1	Nov	4	CHELSEA	3-1	Toshack 2, Keegan	48932		11	1	8		9	6	7		2	3	5	4			10
1		11	Manchester United	0-2		53944		11	1	8		9	6	7		2	3	5	4		12	10
1		18	NEWCASTLE UNITED	3-2	Cormack, Lindsay, Toshack	46153		11	1	8		9	6	7		2	3	5	4			10
1		25	Tottenham Hotspur	2-1	Heighway, Keegan	45497		11	1	8		9	6	7		2	3	5	4			10
1	Dec	2	BIRMINGHAM CITY	4-3	Lindsay 2, Cormack, Toshack	45407		11	1	8		9	6	7		2	3	5	4			10
1		9	West Bromwich Albion	1-1	Boersma	27171	7	11	1	8		9	6			2	3	5			4	10
1		16	Ipswich Town	1-1	Heighway	25990	10	11	1	8	12	9	6	7		2	3	5		4		
1		23	COVENTRY CITY	2-0	Toshack 2	41550		11	1	8		9	6	7		2	3	5		4		10
1		26	Sheffield United	3-0	Boersma, Lawler, Heighway	34040	10	11	1	8		9	6	7		2	3	5		4		
1		30	CRYSTAL PALACE	1-0	Cormack	50862		11	1	8		9	6	7		2	3	5		4		10
1	Jan	6	West Ham United	1-0	Keegan	34480	10	11	1	8		9	6	7		2		5	4	3		
1		20	DERBY COUNTY	1-1	Toshack	45996		11	1	8		9	6	7		2	3	5	4			10
1		27	Wolverhampton Wan.	1-2	Keegan	32957		11	1	8		9	6	7		2	3	5	4			10
2	Feb	10	ARSENAL	0-2		49898	9	11	1		8		6	7		2	3	5	4			10
2		17	Manchester City	1-1	Boersma	41709	9	11	1			12	10	6	7		2	3	5	4	8	
1		24	IPSWICH TOWN	2-1	Heighway, Keegan	43875	8	11	1			9	6	7		2	3	5	4		12	10
1	Mar	3	Everton	2-0	Hughes 2	54856	9	11	1		8	10	6	7		2	3	5	4			
1		10	SOUTHAMPTON	3-2	Keegan 2, Lloyd	41674	9	11	1		8		6	7		2	3	5	4			10
1		17	Stoke City	1-0	og (Mahoney)	33658	9	11	1	8	12	9	6	7		2	3	5	4			
1		24	NORWICH CITY	3-1	Lawler, Hughes, Hall	42995		11	1	8	9		6	7		2	3	5	4			
1		31	TOTTENHAM HOTSPUR	1-1	Keegan	48477		11	1	10	8	9	6	7		2	3	5	4			
1	Apr	7	Birmingham City	1-2	Smith	48114		11	1	8	10	9	6	7		2	3	5	4			
1		14	WEST BROMWICH ALB.	1-0	Keegan (p)	43853		11	1	8	9	10	6	7		2	3	5	4			
1		17	Coventry City	2-1	Boersma 2	27324	10	11	1	8	9		6	7		2		5	4	3		
1		21	Newcastle United	1-2	Keegan	36810	10	11	1	8	9		6	7		2		5	4	3		
1		23	LEEDS UNITED	2-0	Cormack, Keegan	55738		11	1	8	9	10	6	7		2		5	4	3		
1		28	LEICESTER CITY	0-0		56202	8	11	1		12	10	6	7		2	3	5	4	9		

	Apps	19	42	41	30	17	38	41	41	1	42	37	42	33	4	12	22
	Subs					4										2	
	Goals	7	3		8	2	6	7	13		3	4	2	2			13

Two own goals

F.A. Cup

	Date		Opponent	Score	Scorers	Att																
R3	Jan	13	Burnley	0-0		35730		11	1	8		9	6	7		2	3	5	4			10
rep		16	BURNLEY	3-0	Toshack 2, Cormack	56124		11	1	8		9	6	7		2	3	5	4			10
R4	Feb	3	MANCHESTER CITY	0-0		56296		11	1	8		9	6	7		2	3	5		4		10
rep		7	Manchester City	0-2		49572	12	11	1	8		9	6	7		2	3	5		4		10

F.L. Cup

	Date		Opponent	Score	Scorers	Att																
R2	Sep	5	Carlisle United	1-1	Keegan	16257		11		6	8	9	3	7	1	2		5	4			10
rep		19	CARLISLE UNITED	5-1	Boersma 2, Keegan (p), Lawler, Heighway	11182	12	11	1	8		9	6	7		2	3	5	4			10
R3	Oct	3	West Bromwich Albion	1-1	Heighway	17756	10	11	1	8		9	6	7		2	3	5		4		
rep		10	WEST BROMWICH ALB.	2-1	Hughes, Keegan	26461	10	11	1	8	12	9	6	7		2	3	5		4		
R4		31	LEEDS UNITED	2-2	Keegan, Toshack	44609		11	1	8		9	6	7		2	3	5	4			10
rep	Nov	22	Leeds United	1-0	Keegan	34856		11	1	8		9	6	7		2	3	5	4			10
R5	Dec	4	TOTTENHAM HOTSPUR	1-1	Hughes	48677		11	1	8		9	6	7		2	3	5		4		10
rep		6	Tottenham Hotspur	1-3	Callaghan	34565		11	1	8		9	6	7		2	3	5		4	12	10

R3 replay a.e.t.

UEFA Cup

	Date		Opponent	Score	Scorers	Att																
R1.1	Sep	12	EINTRACHT FRANKFURT	2-0	Keegan, Hughes	33380		11	1	8		9	6	7		2	3	5	4			10
R1.2		26	Eintracht Frankfurt	0-0		20000	10	11	1	8	12	9	6	7		2	3	5	4	14		
R2.1	Oct	24	AEK (ATHENS)	3-0	Boersma, Cormack, Smith (p)	31906	10	11	1		8	14	9	6	7		2	3	5		12	
R2.2	Nov	7	AEK (Athens)	3-1	Hughes 2, Boersma	25000	12	11	1			9	6	7		2	3	5	4			10
R3.1		29	Dynamo Berlin	0-0		20000		11	1	8	12	9	6	7		2	3	5		4		10
R3.2	Dec	13	DYNAMO BERLIN	3-1	Boersma, Heighway, Toshack	34140	7	11	1	8		9	6			2	3	5			4	10
QF1	Mar	7	DYNAMO DRESDEN	2-0	Hall, Boersma	33270	9	11	1		8		6	7		2	3	5	4			12
QF2		21	Dynamo Dresden	1-0	Keegan	35000		11	1	10	8	9	6	7		2	3	5	4			12
SF1	Apr	10	TOTTENHAM HOTSPUR	1-0	Lindsay	42174	12	11	1	8	9		10	6	7		2	3	5	4		
SF2		25	Tottenham Hotspur	1-2	Heighway	46919	8	11	1			9	10	6	7		2		5	4	3	
F1	May	10	BORUSSIA MO'GLADBACH	3-0	Keegan 2, Lloyd	41169		11	1	8	12	9	6	7		2	3	5	4			10
F2		23	Borussia Monch'gladbach	0-2		35000	12	11	1	8		9	6	7		2	3	5	4			10

SF won on away goals. Final won 3-2 on aggregate.   J Whitham played at 12 in R3.2

Leeds United 1973/74

Elland Road

						Bates MJ	Bremner WJ	Cherry TJ	Clarke AJ	Cooper T	Ellam R	Giles MJ	Gray E	Gray FT	Harvey D	Hunter N	Jones MD	Jordan J	Liddell G	Lorimer PP	Madeley PE	McQueen G	Reaney P	Stewart DS	Yorath TC
Aug	25	EVERTON	3-1	Bremner, Giles, Jones	39425		4		8			10	11		1	6	9			7	3	5	2		
	28	Arsenal	2-1	Lorimer, Madeley	47273		4		8			10	11		1	6	9			7	3	5	2		
Sep	1	Tottenham Hotspur	3-0	Bremner 2, Clarke	42091		4	12	8			10	11		1	6	9			7	3	5	2		
	5	WOLVERHAMPTON W.	4-1	Lorimer 2 (1p), Jones, Bremner	39946		4		8			10	11		1	6	9	12		7	3	5	2		
	8	BIRMINGHAM CITY	3-0	Lorimer 3 (1p)	39746		4		8			10	11		1	6	9	12		7	3	5	2		
	11	Wolverhampton Wan.	2-0	Clarke, Jones	36980	12	4	2	8			10			1	6	9	11			3	5			7
	15	Southampton	2-1	Clarke 2	27770		4	3	8				11		1	6	9	7			10	5	2		
	22	MANCHESTER UNITED	0-0		47058		4	2	8			10	11		1	6	9	7			3	5			
	29	Norwich City	1-0	Giles	31798		4	3	8			10			1	6	9	7			11	5	2		
Oct	6	STOKE CITY	1-1	Jones	36553	11	4	3	8			10			1	6	9			7	5		2		12
	13	Leicester City	2-2	Bremner, Jones	36978	11	4	2	8			10			1	6	9	12		7	3	5			
	20	LIVERPOOL	1-0	Jones	44901	10	4	3	8						1	6	9			7	2	5			11
	27	Manchester City	1-0	Bates	45363	11	4	2	8			10			1	6	9	12		7	3	5			
Nov	3	WEST HAM UNITED	4-1	Jones 2, Bates, Clarke	35869	10	4	3	8						1	6	9			7	11	5	2		
	10	Burnley	0-0		40087	10	4	3	8						1	6	9	12		7	11	5	2		
	17	COVENTRY CITY	3-0	Bremner, Clarke, Jordan	35522	10	4	3	8						1	6		9		7	11	5	2		12
	24	Derby County	0-0		36003	10	4	3	8						1	6		9		7		5	2		11
Dec	1	QUEEN'S PARK RANGERS	2-2	Bremner, Jones	32194	10	4	3	8						1	6	9	12		7		5	2		11
	8	Ipswich Town	3-0	Clarke, Jones, Yorath	27313		4	3	8						1	6	9	12		7	11	5	2		10
	15	Chelsea	2-1	Jones, Jordan	40768		4	3							1	6	9	8		7	11	5	2		10
	22	NORWICH CITY	1-0	Yorath	34747		4	3							1	6	9	8		7	11	5	2		10
	26	Newcastle United	1-0	Madeley	55638		4	3							1	6	9	8		7	11	5	2		10
	29	Birmingham City	1-1	Jordan	50451		4	3							1	6	9	8		7	11	5	2		10
Jan	1	TOTTENHAM HOTSPUR	1-1	Jones	46545		4	3	8						1	6	9	10		7	11	5	2		12
	12	SOUTHAMPTON	2-1	Jones, Jordan	35000		4	3						11	1	6	9	8		7	5		2		10
	19	Everton	0-0		55740		4	3		12				11	1	6	9	8		7	5		2		10
Feb	2	CHELSEA	1-1	Cherry	41520		4	3	8	10					1	6		9		7	11	5	2		12
	5	ARSENAL	3-1	Jordan 2, og (Simpson)	26778		4	3	8	5					1	6		9		7	11		2		10
	9	Manchester United	2-0	Jones, Jordan	60025		4	3	8						1	6	9	12		7	11	5	2		10
	23	Stoke City	2-3	Bremner, Clarke	39687		4	3	8	12	5	10			1	6		9		7	11				2
	26	LEICESTER CITY	1-1	Lorimer (p)	30543		4	3	8	5				12		6		9		7	11		2	1	10
Mar	2	NEWCASTLE UNITED	1-1	Clarke	46611		4	3	8					11		6		9	12	7		5	2	1	10
	9	MANCHESTER CITY	1-0	Lorimer (p)	36578		4	3	8							6		9		7	11	5	2	1	10
	16	Liverpool	0-1		56003		4	3	8						1	6	12	9		7	11	5	2		10
	23	BURNLEY	1-4	Clarke	39453		4	3	8						1	6	12	9		7	11	5	2		10
	30	West Ham United	1-3	Clarke	38416		4	3	8			7			1	6	12	9			11	5	2		10
Apr	6	DERBY COUNTY	2-0	Bremner, Lorimer	37838		4	3				8			1	6		9		7	11	5	2		10
	13	Coventry City	0-0		35206		4	3				10			1	6		9		7	11	5	2		8
	15	SHEFFIELD UNITED	0-0		41140		4	3	8			10		12	1	6	9			7	11	5	2		
	16	Sheffield United	2-0	Lorimer 2 (1p)	39972		4	3	8					12	1	6	9	8		7	11	5	2		10
	20	IPSWICH TOWN	3-2	Bremner, Clarke, Lorimer	44015		4	3	8				11		1	6	9			7	10	5	2		
	27	Queen's Park Rangers	1-0	Clarke	35353		4	3	8			10			1	6		9		7	11	5	2		12

	Apps	9	42	37	34	1	3	17	8	3	39	42	28	25	0	37	39	36	36	3	23
	Subs	1		1		1		1		3			3	8	1							5
	Goals	2	10	1	13			2					14	7		12	2					2

One own goal

FA Cup

R3	Jan	5	Wolverhampron Wan.	1-1	Lorimer (p)	38132		4	3					12	1	6	9	8		7	11	5	2		10
rep		9	WOLVERHAMPTON W.	1-0	Jones	42747		4	3	8							6	9	10		7	11	5	2	1	12
R4		26	Peterborough United	4-1	Jordan 2, Lorimer, Yorath	28000		4	10		3	5				1	6		9		7	11		2		8
R5	Feb	16	Bristol City	1-1	Bremner	37000		4	3	12			10			1	6	9	8		7	11	5			2
rep		19	BRISTOL CITY	0-1		47128		4	2	8	3	5	10			1	6	9	12		7	11				

FL Cup

R2	Oct	8	Ipswich Town	0-2		26385		4	3			5			11	1	6	9			7		10		2	8

O'Neill played at 12

UEFA Cup

R1.1	Sep	19	Stromgodset IF	1-1	Clarke	16276	10		3	8				11	6			9		7		2	5			4
R1.2	Oct	3	STROMGODSET IF	6-1	Clarke 2, Jones 2, Bates, F Gray	18711	10	4	3	8		5			11	1		9			7			2		6
R2.1		24	HIBERNIAN	0-0		27157	10	4	2	8		5			11	1		9	12		7	3				6
R2.2	Nov	7	Hibernian	0-0		36051	10	4	3	8		5			11			9			7			2		6
R3.1		28	VITORIA SETUBAL	1-0	Cherry	14196	10	4	3	8					13	1	6	9			7		5	2		11
R3.2	Dec	12	Vitoria Setubal	1-3	Liddell	25000			3				6		11	1			9	12	7		5	2		4

R2 won 5-4 on penalties, a.e.t. in R2.2

Davey played in R3.1 at 12
Hampton played in R3.2 at 10
Letheran played in R2.2 at 12
Mann played in R3.2 at 8
McGinley played in R1.2 at 13
O'Neill played at 12 in R1.2 and 13 in R2.1
Sprake played in R1.1 in goal
Shaw played in R2.2 in goal

Derby County 1974/75

Baseball Ground

							Boulton CD	Bourne JA	Daniel PA	Davies R	Gemmill A	Hector KJ	Hinton AT	Lee FH	McFarland RL	Newton HA	Nish DJ	Powell S	Rioch BD	Thomas RJ	Todd C	Webster R
	Aug	17	Everton	0-0		42293	1	12	5	9	8	10		11				3	7	4	6	2
		21	COVENTRY CITY	1-1	Lee	25717	1	12	5	9	8	10		11				3	7	4	6	2
		24	SHEFFIELD UNITED	2-0	Davies, Hector	23088	1	12		9	8	10		11		5	3	7	4		6	2
4		27	Coventry City	1-1	Davies	18659	1			9	8	10		11				3	7	4	5	6	2
12		31	Tottenham Hotspur	0-2		20670	1	12	5	9	8	10		11			7	3		4		6	2
11	Sep	7	NEWCASTLE UNITED	2-2	Lee, Davies	21197	1	12	5	9	8	10		11			7	3		4		6	2
14		14	Birmingham City	2-3	Rioch, Davies	27345	1		5	9	8	10		11		12	3		7	4		6	2
10		21	BURNLEY	3-2	Hector, Lee, Rioch (p)	21377	1		5	9	8	10		11			7	3		4		6	2
7		25	CHELSEA	4-1	Webster, Rioch, Daniel, Hector	22036	1		5	9	8	10		11			7	3		4		6	2
8		28	Stoke City	1-1	Lee	23590	1		5	9	8	10		11			7	3	12	4		6	2
9	Oct	5	West Ham United	2-2	Hector, Lee	32938	1		5	9	8	10		11			7	3		4		6	2
5		12	LEICESTER CITY	1-0	Rioch	24753	1		5	9	8	10		11			7	3		4		6	2
3		15	Sheffield United	2-1	Lee 2	21882	1		5	9	8	10		11			7	3		4		6	2
7		19	Carlisle United	0-3		13353	1		5	9	8	10		11			7	3		4		6	2
7		26	MIDDLESBROUGH	2-3	Hector, Hinton	24036	1		5	9	8	10	12	11			7	3	6	4			2
7	Nov	2	Leeds United	1-0	Lee	33551	1		5	9	8	10		11			7	3	6	4			2
5		9	QUEEN'S PARK RANGERS	5-2	Hector 3, Lee, Rioch	23339	1	12	5	9	8	10		11			7	3	6	4			2
10		16	Arsenal	1-3	Rioch (p)	32286	1		5	9	8	10		11			7	3		4		6	2
5		23	IPSWICH TOWN	2-0	Rioch, Hector	24341	1		5	9	8	10		11			7	3		4		6	2
8	Dec	7	Liverpool	2-2	Davies, Bourne	41058	1	9	5	12	8	10		11			7			4	3	6	2
9		14	EVERTON	0-1		24891	1	10	5	9	8		12	11			7			4	3	6	2
10		21	Luton Town	0-1		12862	1	10	5	9	8		12	11			7			4	3	6	2
10		26	BIRMINGHAM CITY	2-1	Rioch, Bourne	26121	1	10	5	9	8			11			7	3		4		6	2
9		28	Manchester City	2-1	Lee, Newton	40188	1	10	5	9	8			11			7	3		4		6	2
7	Jan	11	LIVERPOOL	2-0	Lee, Newton	33463	1		5	9	8	10		11			7	3		4	2	6	
5		18	Wolverhampton Wan.	1-0	Newton	24515	1		5	9	8	10		11			7	3		4	2	6	
8	Feb	1	Queen's Park Rangers	1-4	Rioch	20686	1	12	5	9	8	10		11			7	3		4	2	6	
9		8	LEEDS UNITED	0-0		33641	1	12	5	9	8	10		11			7	3		4	2	6	
7		22	ARSENAL	2-1	Powell 2	24002	1	9	5			10		11			7	3	8	4	2	6	
8		25	Ipswich Town	0-3		23132	1	9	5		8	10		11			7	3	12	4	2	6	
7	Mar	1	TOTTENHAM HOTSPUR	3-1	Rioch, Daniel, Davies	22995	1		5	9	8	10	11				7	3	12	4	2	6	
3		8	Chelsea	2-1	Daniel, Hinton	22644	1		5	9	8	10	11				7	3		4	2	6	
6		15	STOKE CITY	1-2	Hector	29985	1		5	9	8	10	11				7	3		4	2	6	
7		22	Newcastle United	2-0	Nish, Rioch	32201	1	12	5	9	8	10	11				7	3		4	2	6	
6		29	LUTON TOWN	5-0	Davies 5	24619	1		5	9	8	10	11					3	7	4	2	6	
5		31	Burnley	5-2	Hector 2, Davies, Nish, Rioch	24317	1		5	9	8	10	11					3	7	4	2	6	
3	Apr	1	MANCHESTER CITY	2-1	Rioch 2	32966	1		5	9	8	10	11					3	7	4	2	6	
4		5	Middlesbrough	1-1	Hector	30066	1	12	5	9	8	10	11				7	3		4	2	6	
1		9	WOLVERHAMPTON W.	1-0	Lee	30109	1		5	9	8	10		11		3	7			4	2	6	
1		12	WEST HAM UNITED	1-0	Rioch	31536	1			9	8	10	12	11		5	7	3		4	2	6	
1		19	Leicester City	0-0		38143	1			9	8	10		11		5	7	3		4	2	6	
1		26	CARLISLE UNITED	0-0		36882	1			9	8	10	12	11		5	7	3		4	2	6	

	Boulton	Bourne	Daniel	Davies	Gemmill	Hector	Hinton	Lee	McFarland	Newton	Nish	Powell	Rioch	Thomas	Todd	Webster
Apps	42	7	37	39	41	38	8	34	4	35	38	12	42	22	39	24
Subs		10		1			5			1		3				
Goals		2	3	12		13	2	12		3	2	2	15			1

F.A. Cup

R3	Jan	3	Orient	2-2	Todd 2	12490	1	10	5	9	8		12	11			7	3		4		6	2
rep		8	ORIENT	2-1	Lee, Rioch	26501	1	10	5	9	8		12	11			7	3		4		6	2
R4		27	BRISTOL ROVERS	2-0	Hector, Rioch (p)	27980	1	12	5	9	8	10		11			7	3		4	2	6	
R5	Feb	18	LEEDS UNITED	0-1		35298	1	9	5	12		10		11			7	3	8	4	2	6	

F.L. Cup

R2	Sep	11	Portsmouth	5-1	Hector 2, Lee, Rioch, og (Roberts)	13582	1		5	9	8	10		11		12	3	7		4		6	2
R3	Oct	8	Southampton	0-5		14911	1	12	5	9	8	10		11			7	3		4		6	2

UEFA Cup

R1.1	Sep	18	SERVETTE	4-1	Hector 2, Daniel, Lee	17716	1	9	5		8	10	12	11			7	3		4		6	2
R1.2	Oct	2	Servette	2-1	Lee, Hector	9600	1	9	5		8	10		11			7	3		4		6	2
R2.1		23	ATLETICO MADRID	2-2	Nish, Rioch (p)	29347	1	9	5		8	10	12	11			7	3		4		6	2
R2.2	Nov	6	Atletico Madrid	2-2	Rioch, Hector	35000	1		5	9	8	10		11			7	3	6	4			2
R3.1		27	VELEZ MOSTAR	3-1	Bourne 2, Hinton	26131	1	12	5	9	8	10	13	11			7	3		4		6	2
R3.2	Dec	11	Velez Mostar	1-4	Hector	15000	1	9	5	12	8	10	13	11		7				4	3	6	2

R2 won 7-6 on penalties a.e.t. in the second leg

Liverpool 1975/76

Anfield

							Boersma P	Callaghan IR	Case JR	Clemence RN	Cormack PB	Fairclough D	Hall BW	Heighway SD	Hughes EW	Jones JP	Keegan JK	Kennedy R	Kettle B	Lindsay A	McDermott T	Neal PG	Smith T	Thompson PB	Toshack JB
	Aug	16	Queen's Park Rangers	0-2		27113		11		1	5			9	6	3	7				8	2		4	10
		19	WEST HAM UNITED	2-2	Callaghan, Toshack	40564		11		1	5			9	6	3	7				8	2		4	10
		23	TOTTENHAM HOTSPUR	3-2	Keegan (p), Case, Heighway	42729			11	1	5			9	6	3	7				8	2		4	10
8		26	Leeds United	3-0	Callaghan 2, Kennedy	36186	9	11		1	5		12		6	3	7	10			8	2		4	
8		30	Leicester City	1-1	Keegan	25008	12	11		1	5			9	6	3	7	10			8	2		4	
5	Sep	6	SHEFFIELD UNITED	1-0	Kennedy	37340		11		1	5			9	6		7	10		3	8	2		4	
7		13	Ipswich Town	0-2		28154		11		1	5			9	6	3	7	10			8	2	4		
4		20	Aston Villa	3-0	Toshack, Keegan, Case	42779			11	1	5		8	9	6		7			3		2		4	10
8		27	Everton	0-0		55769		11		1	5		8	9	6		7			3		2		4	10
6	Oct	4	WOLVERHAMPTON W.	2-0	Hall, Case	36391		11	9	1	5		8		6		7			3		2		4	10
4		11	BIRMINGHAM CITY	3-1	Toshack 3	36532		11	5	1	12		8	9	6		7			3		2		4	10
5		18	Coventry City	0-0		20919		11		1	5		8	9	6		7			3		2		4	10
5		25	DERBY COUNTY	1-1	Toshack	46324	12	11		1	5		8	9	6	3	7					2		4	10
5	Nov	1	Middlesbrough	1-0	McDermott	30952		11		1		9	8			3	7	6			12	2	5	4	10
4		8	MANCHESTER UNITED	3-1	Heighway, Toshack, Keegan	49136		11		1			5	9	6	3	7	8				2		4	10
2		15	Newcastle United	2-1	Hall, Kennedy	41181		11		1			5	9	6	3	7	8				2		4	10
3		22	COVENTRY CITY	1-1	Toshack	36929		11	7	1			8	9	6	3		5				2		4	10
6		29	NORWICH CITY	1-3	Hughes	34780		11		1			8	9	6		7	5				3	2	4	10
5	Dec	2	ARSENAL	2-2	Neal 2 (2p)	27447		11		1			8	9	6		7	5	3			2		4	10
5		6	Burnley	0-0		18524		11	8	1				9	6	3	7	5				2		4	10
2		13	Tottenham Hotspur	4-0	Keegan, Case, Neal, Heighway	29891		11	8	1	5	12		9	6		7					3	2	4	10
1		20	QUEEN'S PARK RANGERS	2-0	Toshack, Neal (p)	39182		11	8	1	5			9	6		7					3	2	4	10
1		26	Stoke City	1-1	Toshack	32176		11	8	1	5			9	6		7	12				3	2	4	10
1		27	MANCHESTER CITY	1-0	Cormack	53386		11	8	1	5			9	6		7					3	2	4	10
3	Jan	10	IPSWICH TOWN	3-3	Keegan 2, Case	40547		11	8	1				9	6		7	5				3	2	4	10
3		17	Sheffield United	0-0		31255		11	8	1		12		9	6		7	5				3	2	4	10
2		31	West Ham United	4-0	Toshack 3, Keegan	26741		11	8	1				9	6		7	5				3	2	4	10
1	Feb	7	LEEDS UNITED	2-0	Keegan, Toshack	54525		11	8	1				9	6		7	5			12	3	2	4	10
1		18	Manchester United	0-0		59709		11	8	1				9	6		7	5				3	2	4	10
1		21	NEWCASTLE UNITED	2-0	Keegan, Case	43404		11	8	1		12		9	6		7	5				3	2	4	10
1		24	Arsenal	0-1		36141		11	8	1				9	6	2	7	5				3		4	10
1		28	Derby County	1-1	Kennedy	32800		11	8	1		10		9	6		7	5				3	2	4	
2	Mar	6	MIDDLESBROUGH	0-2		41391		11	8	1		10		9	6		7	5				3	2	4	
2		13	Birmingham City	1-0	Neal (p)	31797		11	8	1				9	6		7	5				3	2	4	10
3		20	Norwich City	1-0	Fairclough	28728		11	8	1		10		9	6		7	5				3	2	4	
4		27	BURNLEY	2-0	Fairclough 2	36708		11	8	1		12		9	6		7	5				3	2	4	10
2	Apr	3	EVERTON	1-0	Fairclough	54632		11	8	1		12		9	6		7	5				3	2	4	10
2		6	LEICESTER CITY	1-0	Keegan	35290		11	8	1		12		9	6		7	5				3	2	4	10
2		10	Aston Villa	0-0		44250		11	8	1		12		9	6		7	5				3	2	4	10
1		17	STOKE CITY	5-3	Neal (p), Toshack, Kennedy, Hughes, Fairclough	44069		11	8	1		12		9	6		7	5				3	2	4	10
1		19	Manchester City	3-0	Fairclough 2, Heighway	50439		11		1			8	9	6		7	5				3	2	4	10
1	May	4	Wolverhampton Wan.	3-1	Keegan, Toshack, Kennedy	46097		11	8	1		12		9	6		7	5				3	2	4	10

	Apps	1	40	27	42	16	5	12	39	41	13	41	29	1	6	7	42	24	41	35
	Subs	2				1	9	1					1		2					
	Goals		3	6		1	7	2	4	2		12	6			1	6			16

F.A. Cup

R3	Jan	3	West Ham United	2-0	Keegan, Toshack	32363		11	8	1				9	6		7	5				3	2	4	10
R4		24	Derby County	0-1		38200		11	8	1				12	9	6		7	5				3	2	4	10

F.L. Cup

R2	Sep	10	York City	1-0	Lindsay	9421		11		1	5			9	6		7	10		3	8	2		4	
R3	Oct	7	BURNLEY	1-1	Case	24607		11	9	1	5		8		6		7			3		2		4	10
rep		14	Burnley	0-1		19857	12	11		1	5		8	9	6		7			3		2		4	10

UEFA Cup

R1.1	Sep	17	Hibernian	0-1		19219	12	11		1	5		8	9	6	3	7	10				2			14
R1.2		30	HIBERNIAN	3-1	Toshack 3	29963		11	12	1	5		8	9	6		7			3		2		4	10
R2.1	Oct	22	Real Sociedad	3-1	Heighway, Callaghan, Thompson	20000		11		1	5		8	9	6		7			3		2		4	10
R2.2	Nov	4	REAL SOCIEDAD	6-0	Kennedy 2, Toshack, Fairclough, Heighway, Neal	23796		11		1		14	8	9			7	6	3			2	5	4	10
R3.1		26	Slask Wroclaw	2-1	Kennedy, Toshack	40000		11	7	1			8	9	6			5				3	2	4	10
R3.2	Dec	10	SLASK WROCLAW	3-0	Case 3	17886		11	9	1	12		8		6		7	5				3	2	4	10
QF1	Mar	3	Dynamo Dresden	0-0		33000		11	8	1			10	12	9		7	5				3	2	4	
QF2		17	DYNAMO DRESDEN	2-1	Case, Keegan	39300		11	8	1		12		9			7	5				3	2	4	10
SF1		30	Barcelona	1-0	Toshack	70000		11	8	1				12	9	6		7	5				3	2	4	10
SF2	Apr	14	BARCELONA	1-1	Thompson	55104		11	8	1				12	9	6		7	5				3	2	4	10
F1		28	CLUB BRUGGE KV	3-2	Kennedy, Case, Keegan (p)	49981		11	12	1		8		9	6		7	5				3	2	4	10
F2	May	19	Club Brugge KV	1-1	Keegan	33000		11	8	1		12		9	6		7	5				3	2	4	10

Final won 4-3 on aggregate

C Lawler played at 4 in game R1.1
M Thompson played at 12 in R2.2

Liverpool 1976/77

Anfield

						Callaghan IR	Case JR	Clemence RN	Fairclough D	Heighway SD	Hughes EW	Johnson DE	Jones JP	Keegan JK	Kennedy R	Kettle B	Lindsay A	McDermott T	Neal PG	Smith T	Thompson PB	Toshack JB
	Aug 21	NORWICH CITY	1-0	Heighway	49753	11		1		9	6	8	3	7	5				2		4	10
	25	West Bromwich Albion	1-0	Toshack	29735	11		1		9	6	8	3	7	5				2		4	10
	28	Birmingham City	1-2	Johnson	33228	11		1	12	9	6	8	3	7	5				2		4	10
3	Sep 4	COVENTRY CITY	3-1	Keegan, Johnson, Toshack	40371	11		1		9	6	8	3	7	5				2		4	10
1	11	Derby County	3-2	Kennedy, Toshack, Keegan	26833	11		1		9	6	8	3	7	5				2	4		10
1	18	TOTTENHAM HOTSPUR	2-0	Johnson, Heighway	47421	11	10	1		9	6	8	3	7	5				2	4		
1	25	Newcastle United	0-1		34813	11	10	1	12	9	6	8	3	7	5				2	4		
3	Oct 2	MIDDLESBROUGH	0-0		45107	11	12	1		9	6	8	3	7	5			10	2		4	
1	16	EVERTON	3-1	Heighway, Neal (p), Toshack	55141	11		1	12	9	6		3	7	5			8	2		4	10
3	23	Leeds United	1-1	Kennedy	44696	11		1		9	6	12	3	7	5			8	2		4	10
1	27	Leicester City	1-0	Toshack	29384	11	12	1		9	6		3	7	5			8	2		4	10
1	30	ASTON VILLA	3-0	Callaghan, McDermott, Keegan	51751	11		1		9	6	12	3	7	5			8	2		4	10
1	Nov 6	Sunderland	1-0	Fairclough	39843	11	8	1	12	9	6	10	3	7	5				2		4	
1	9	LEICESTER CITY	5-1	Heighway, Toshack, Neal (p), Jones, Keegan (p)	39851	11	8	1		9	6		3	7	5				2		4	10
1	20	Arsenal	1-1	Kennedy	45016	11		1		9	6		3	7	5			8	2		4	10
1	27	BRISTOL CITY	2-1	Keegan, Jones	44323	11		1		9	6		3	7	5			8	2		4	10
1	Dec 4	Ipswich Town	0-1		35109	11		1	12	9	6		3	7	5			8	2		4	10
1	11	QUEEN'S PARK RANGERS	3-1	Toshack, Keegan, Kennedy	37154	11		1		9	6	12	3	7	5			8	2		4	10
1	15	Aston Villa	1-5	Kennedy	42851	11		1		9	6	10	3	7	5			8	2		4	10
2	18	West Ham United	0-2		24175	11	12	1		9	6		3	7	5			8	2		4	10
1	27	STOKE CITY	4-0	Thompson, Neal (p), Keegan, Johnson	50371	11		1		9	6	12	3	7	5			8	2		4	10
1	29	Manchester City	1-1	og (Watson)	50020	11	7	1	12	9	6	10	3		5			8	2		4	
1	Jan 1	SUNDERLAND	2-0	Kennedy, Thompson	44687	11		1		9	6	7	3		5			8	2		4	10
	15	WEST BROMWICH ALB.	1-1	Fairclough	39195	11	8	1	10	9	6	12		7	5	3			2	4		
1	22	Norwich City	1-2	Neal	25617	11	8	1	10	9	6			7	5	3			2	4		
1	Feb 5	BIRMINGHAM CITY	4-1	Toshack 2, Neal, Heighway	41072	11	8	1		9	6		3	7	5				2		4	10
2	16	Manchester United	0-0		57487	11	8	1		9	6		3	7	5				2		4	10
1	19	DERBY COUNTY	3-1	Toshack, Jones, Keegan	44202	11	5	1	8	9	6		3	7					2		4	10
1	Mar 5	NEWCASTLE UNITED	1-0	Heighway	45553	11	7	1	8	9	6		3		5			12	2		4	10
1	9	Tottenham Hotspur	0-1		32098	11	8	1		9	6		3	7	5				2	4		10
1	12	Middlesbrough	1-0	Hughes	29166	11	8	1	10	9	6	12	3	7	5				2	4		
2	22	Everton	0-0		56562		8	1	10	9	6		3	7	5			11	2	4		
1	Apr 2	LEEDS UNITED	3-1	Neal (p), Fairclough, Heighway	48791		8	1	10	9	6		3	7	5			11	2	4		
2	9	MANCHESTER CITY	2-1	Keegan, Heighway	55283		8	1		9	6		3	7	5			11	2	4		
2	11	Stoke City	0-0		29908		8	1	10	9	6	12	3	7	5			11	2	4		
1	16	ARSENAL	2-0	Neal, Keegan	48174		8	1		9	6	10	3	7	5			11	2	4		
1	30	IPSWICH TOWN	2-1	Kennedy, Keegan	56044		8	1	12	9	6	10	3	7	5			11	2	4		
1	May 3	MANCHESTER UNITED	1-0	Keegan	53046		8	1	10		6	9	3	7	5			11	2	4		
1	7	Queen's Park Rangers	1-1	Case	29382	12	8	1		9		6	10	3	7	5			11	2	4		
1	10	Coventry City	0-0		38160		8	1		9	6	10	3	7	5			11	2	4		
1	14	WEST HAM UNITED	0-0		54341		8	1	12	9	6	10	3	7	5			11	2	4		
1	16	Bristol City	1-2	Johnson	37265	7	8	1	9		6	10			5		3	11	2	4		

Apps	32	24	42	12	39	42	19	39	38	41	2	1	25	42	16	26	22
Subs	1	3		8			7						1				
Goals	1	1		3	8	1	5	3	12	7			1	7		2	10

One own goal

F.A. Cup

R3	Jan 8	CRYSTAL PALACE	0-0		44730	11		1	12	9	6	8	3	7	5			10	2		4	
rep	11	Crystal Palace	3-2	Heighway 2, Keegan	42664	11	8	1	10	9	6		3	7	5				2		4	
R4	29	CARLISLE UNITED	3-0	Keegan, Toshack, Heighway	45358	11	8	1		9	6		3	7	5				2		4	10
R5	Feb 26	OLDHAM ATHLETIC	3-1	Keegan, Case, Neal (p)	52455	11	8	1		9	6		3	7	5				2		4	10
R6	Mar 19	MIDDLESBROUGH	2-0	Fairclough, Keegan	55881		8	1	10	9	6		3	7	5			11	2	4		
SF	Apr 23	Everton	2-2	McDermott, Case	52637		8	1	10	9	6	12	3	7	5			11	2	4		
rep	27	Everton	3-0	Neal (p), Case, Kennedy	52579		8	1	10		6	9	3	7	5			11	2	4		
F	May 21	Manchester United	1-2	Case	100000	12	8	1		9	6	10	3	7	5			11	2	4		

SF and SF replay at Maine Road, Manchester. Final at Wembley Stadium

F.L. Cup

R2	Aug 31	WEST BROMWICH ALB.	1-1		23378	11		1		9	6	8	3	7	5				2		4	10
rep	Sep 6	West Bromwich Albion	0-1	Callaghan	22662	11	10	1	12	9	6	8	3	7	5				2		4	

European Cup

R1.1	Sep 14	CRUSADERS (BELFAST)	2-0	Neal (p), Toshack	22442	11		1		9	6	8	3	7	5				2	4		10
R1.2	28	Crusaders (Belfast)	5-0	Johnson 2, Keegan, McDermott, Heighway	10000	11	10	1		9	6	8	3	7	5			12	2	4		
R2.1	Oct 20	Trabzonspor	0-1		25000	11		1	12	9	6	14	3	7	5			8		2	4	10
R2.2	Nov 3	TRABZONSPOR	3-0	Heighway, Johnson, Keegan	42275	11		1		9	6	10	3	7	5			8	2		4	
QF1	Mar 2	Saint-Etienne	0-1		28000	11	8	1		9	6		3		5			7	2	12	4	10
QF2	16	SAINT-ETIENNE	3-1	Keegan, Kennedy, Fairclough	55043	11	8	1	12	9	6		3	7	5				2	4		10
SF1	Apr 6	FC Zurich	3-1	Neal 2 (1p), Heighway	30500		8	1	10	9	6		3	7	5			11	2	4		
SF2	20	FC ZURICH	3-0	Case 2, Keegan	50611		8	1		9	6	10	3	7	5			11	2	4		
F	May 25	B'sia Moenchengladbach	3-1	McDermott, Smith, Neal (p)	57000	11	8	1		9	6		3	7	5			10	2	4		

Final at the Olympic Stadium, Rome   Played at 12 in SF2: Waddle

F.A. Charity Shield

Aug 14	Southampton	1-0	Toshack	76500	11	8	1		9	6		3	7	5				2		4	10

At Wembley Stadium

Nottingham Forest 1977/78

						Anderson VA	Barrett C	Bowyer I	Burns K	Clark FA	Gemmill A	Lloyd LV	McGovern JP	Middleton J	Needham DW	O'Hare J	O'Neill MHM	Robertson JN	Shilton PL	Withe P	Woodcock AS
	Aug	20	Everton	3-1	O'Neill, Robertson, Withe	38001	2		8	6	3		5	4	1			7	11		9	10
		23	BRISTOL CITY	1-0	Withe	21743	2		8	6	3		5	4	1			7	11		9	10
		27	DERBY COUNTY	3-0	Withe 2, Robertson	28807	2		8	6	3		5	4	1			7	11		9	10
4	Sep	3	Arsenal	0-3		40810	2	12	8	6	3		5	4	1			7	11		9	10
3		10	Wolverhampton Wan.	3-2	Bowyer, Withe, Woodcock	24522	2	3	8	6			5	4	1			7	11		9	10
3		17	ASTON VILLA	2-0	Robertson, Woodcock	31016	2	3	8	6			5	4				7	11	1	9	10
2		24	Leicester City	3-0	O'Neill, Woodcock, Robertson (p)	21447	2	3	8	6			5	4			9	7	11	1		10
2	Oct	1	NORWICH CITY	1-1	Burns	23741	2	3	4	6		8	5					7	11	1	9	10
1		4	IPSWICH TOWN	4-0	Withe 4	26845	2	3	8	6			5	4				7	11	1	9	10
1		8	West Ham United	0-0		26128	2	3	8	6		12	5	4				7	11	1	9	10
1		15	MANCHESTER CITY	2-1	Withe, Woodcock	35572	2	3	8	6		12	5	4				7	11	1	9	10
1		22	Queen's Park Rangers	2-0	Bowyer, Burns	24449	2	3	8	6		4	5					7	11	1	9	10
1		29	MIDDLESBROUGH	4-0	Anderson 2, Bowyer, McGovern	27373	2	3	8	6		7	5	4				12	11	1	9	10
1	Nov	5	Chelsea	0-1		36116	2	3	8	6		7	5	4				12	11	1	9	10
1		12	MANCHESTER UNITED	2-1	Burns, Gemmill	30183	2	3	8	6		7	5	4					11	1	9	10
1		19	Leeds United	0-1		42925	2	3	8	6		7	5	4					11	1	9	10
1		26	WEST BROMWICH ALB.	0-0		31908	2	3		6		7	5	4				8	11	1	9	10
1	Dec	3	Birmingham City	2-0	O'Neill, Woodcock	29925	2	3		6		8	5	4				7	11	1	9	10
1		10	COVENTRY CITY	2-1	McGovern, O'Neill	29823	2	3		6		8	5	4				7	11	1	9	10
1		17	Manchester United	4-0	Woodcock 2, Robertson, og (B Greenhoff)	54374	2	3		6		8		4		5		7	11	1	9	10
1		26	LIVERPOOL	1-1	Gemmill	47218	2	3		6		8		4		5		7	11	1	9	10
1		28	Newcastle United	2-0	McGovern, Needham	41612	2	3	12	6		8		4		5		7	11	1	9	10
1		31	Bristol City	3-1	Needham, O'Neill, Woodcock	31506	2	3		6		8		4		5		7	11	1	9	10
1	Jan	2	EVERTON	1-1	Robertson (p)	44030	2	3		6		8		4		5		7	11	1	9	10
1		14	Derby County	0-0		33384	2	3		6		8		4		5		7	11	1	9	10
1		21	ARSENAL	2-0	Gemmill, Needham	35743	2	3		6		8		4		5		7	11	1	9	10
1	Feb	4	WOLVERHAMPTON W.	2-0	McGovern, Woodcock	28803	2	3		6		8		4		5		7	11	1	9	10
1		25	Norwich City	3-3	Barrett, O'Neill, Withe	25705	2	3		6		8		4		5		7	11	1	9	10
1	Mar	4	WEST HAM UNITED	2-0	Needham, Robertson (p)	33924			2	6	3	8				5	4	7	11	1	9	10
1		14	LEICESTER CITY	1-0	Robertson (p)	32355			2	9	6	3	8			5	4	7	11	1		10
1		25	NEWCASTLE UNITED	2-0	Anderson, Robertson (p)	35552	2		12	6	3	8				5	4	7	11	1	9	10
1		29	Middlesbrough	2-2	O'Neill, Woodcock	25445			2	6	3	8				5	4	7	11	1	9	10
1	Apr	1	CHELSEA	3-1	Burns, O'Neill, Robertson (p)	31262		12	2	6	3	8	5				4	7	11	1	9	10
1		5	Aston Villa	1-0	Woodcock	44215	2	3		6		8	5				4	7	11	1	9	10
1		11	Manchester City	0-0		43428	2	3		6		8	5				4	7	11	1	9	10
1		15	LEEDS UNITED	1-1	Withe	38662		2		10	6	3	8	5	4			7	11	1	9	
1		18	QUEEN'S PARK RANGERS	1-0	Robertson (p)	30339		2		10	6	3	8	5	4			7	11	1	9	
1		22	Coventry City	0-0		36894	2	3		8	6		10				5	4	7	11	1	9	
1		25	Ipswich Town	2-0	Clark, og (Mariner)	30092	2	3		8	6	12	10				5	4	7	11	1	9	
1		29	BIRMINGHAM CITY	0-0		37625	2	3	12	6		8				4	5	7	11	1	9	10
1	May	2	West Bromwich Albion	2-2	Bowyer, Robertson (p)	23523	2	3	10	6		8	5	4				7	11	1	9	
1		4	Liverpool	0-0		50021	2	3	10		6	8	5	4				7	11	1	9	

						Apps	37	33	26	41	12	32	26	31	5	16	10	38	42	37	40	36
						Subs		2	3		1	2						2				
						Goals	3	1	4	4	1	3		4			4	8	12		12	11

Two own goals

F.A. Cup

R3	Jan	7	SWINDON TOWN	4-1	Woodcock 2, Robertson, Withe	28593	2	3		6		8		4		5	12	7	11	1	9	10
R4		24	MANCHESTER CITY	2-1	Robertson, Withe	38509	2	3		6		8		4		5		7	11	1	9	10
R5	Feb	18	Queen's Park Rangers	1-1	O'Neill	26803	2	3		6		8		4		5		7	11	1	9	10
rep		27	QUEEN'S PARK RANGERS	1-1	Robertson (p)	40097	2		8	6	3		4			5		7	11	1	9	10
rep2	Mar	2	QUEEN'S PARK RANGERS	3-1	Woodcock 2, O'Neill	33950	2		8	6	3		4			5		7	11	1	9	10
R6		11	West Bromwich Albion	0-2		36506			2	6	3	8				4	5	7	11	1	9	10

R5 replay a.e.t.

F.L. Cup

R2	Aug	30	WEST HAM UNITED	5-0	Bowyer 2, O'Neill, Withe, Woodcock	18224	2		8	6	3		5	4	1			7	11		9	10
R3	Oct	25	NOTTS COUNTY	4-0	Bowyer 2, Woodcock, Robertson	26931	2	3	8	6			5	4				7	11		9	10
R4	Nov	29	ASTON VILLA	4-2	Anderson, Lloyd, Withe, Woodcock	29333	2	3	8	6			5	4				7	11		9	10
R5	Jan	17	Bury	3-0	Bowyer, O'Neill, Robertson	21500	2	5	8	6	3			4				7	11		9	10
SF1	Feb	8	Leeds United	3-1	Withe 2, O'Hare	43222	2	3	8	5				4			6	7	11		9	10
SF2		22	LEEDS UNITED	4-2	Bowyer, O'Neill, Withe, Woodcock	38131	2	3	8	6			5	4				7	11		9	10
F	Mar	18	Liverpool	0-0		100000	2		8	6	3		5	4				12	7	11		9	10
rep		22	Liverpool	1-0	Robertson (p)	54375	2		8	6	3		5					4	7	11		9	10

Final at Wembley Stadium, replay at Old Trafford
Final a.e.t.

C Woods in goal for all but first match

116

Liverpool 1978/79

Anfield

						Case JR	Clemence RN	Dalglish KM	Fairclough D	Hansen AD	Heighway SD	Hughes EW	Johnson DE	Kennedy AP	Kennedy R	Lee S	McDermott T	Neal PG	Souness GJ	Thompson PB
	Aug	19	QUEEN'S PARK RANGERS	2-1	Dalglish, Heighway	50793	8	1	7			9	6		3	5		10	2	11	4
		22	Ipswich Town	3-0	Dalglish 2, Souness	27806	8	1	7			9	6		3	5		10	2	11	4
		26	Manchester City	4-1	Souness 2, R Kennedy, Dalglish	46710	8	1	7			9	6		3	5		10	2	11	4
1	Sep	2	TOTTENHAM HOTSPUR	7-0	Dalglish 2, Johnson 2, R Kennedy, Neal (p), McDermott	50705	8	1	7			9	6	12	3	5		10	2	11	4
1		9	Birmingham City	3-0	Souness 2, A Kennedy	31740	8	1	7		6	9			3	5		10	2	11	4
1		16	COVENTRY CITY	1-0	Souness	51130	8	1	7			9	6		3	5		10	2	11	4
1		23	West Bromwich Albion	1-1	Dalglish	33772	8	1	7			9	6	12	3	5		10	2	11	4
1		30	BOLTON WANDERERS	3-0	Case 3	47099	8	1	7		6	9			3	5		10	2	11	4
1	Oct	7	Norwich City	4-1	Heighway 2, Johnson, Case	26661	8	1	7		6	9		10	3	5			2	11	4
1		14	DERBY COUNTY	5-0	R Kennedy 2, Dalglish 2, Johnson	47475	8	1	7		6	9		10	3	5			2	11	4
1		21	CHELSEA	2-0	Johnson, Dalglish	45775	8	1	7		6	9		10	3	5			2	11	4
1		28	Everton	0-1		53141	8	1	7		6	9		10	3	5		12	2	11	4
1	Nov	4	LEEDS UNITED	1-1	McDermott (p)	51697	8	1	7		6	9		10	3	5		12	2	11	4
1		11	Queen's Park Rangers	3-1	Heighway, R Kennedy, Johnson	26626	8	1	7		6	9		10	3	5			2	11	4
1		18	MANCHESTER CITY	1-0	Neal (p)	47765	8	1	7		6	9		10	3	5			2	11	4
1		22	Tottenham Hotspur	0-0		50393	8	1	7		6	9		10	3	5		12	2	11	4
1		25	MIDDLESBROUGH	2-0	McDermott, Souness	39812	8	1	7		6	9			3	5		10	2	11	4
1	Dec	2	Arsenal	0-1		51902	8	1	7		6	9		12	3	5		10	2	11	4
1		9	NOTTM. FOREST	2-0	McDermott 2 (1p)	51469	8	1	7		6	9			3	5		10	2	11	4
1		16	Bristol City	0-1		28347	8	1	7		6	9		12	3	5		10	2	11	4
1		26	Manchester United	3-0	R Kennedy, Case, Fairclough	54910	8	1	7	9	6		3			5		10	2	11	4
1	Feb	3	WEST BROMWICH ALB.	2-1	Dalglish, Fairclough	52211	8	1	7	9	4	12	6		3	5		10	2	11	
1		13	BIRMINGHAM CITY	1-0	Souness	35207		1	7	9	6	8	3		4	5		10	2	11	
1		21	NORWICH CITY	6-0	Dalglish 2, Johnson 2, A Kennedy, R Kennedy	33754		1	7		6	9	3	8	4	5		10	2	11	
1		24	Derby County	2-0	Dalglish, R Kennedy	27859		1	7			9	3	8	4	5		10	2	11	6
1	Mar	3	Chelsea	0-0		40686		1	7			9	3	8	4	5		10	2	11	6
1		6	Coventry City	0-0		26638	9	1	7		6		3	8		5		10	2	11	4
1		13	EVERTON	1-1	Dalglish	52352	9	1	7	12	6		3	8		5		10	2	11	4
1		20	WOLVERHAMPTON W.	2-0	McDermott, Johnson	39695	9	1	7		6		3	8		5		10	2	11	4
1		24	IPSWICH TOWN	2-0	Dalglish, Johnson	43243	9	1	7		6		3	8		5		10	2	11	4
1	Apr	7	ARSENAL	3-0	Case, Dalglish, McDermott	47297	8	1	7		6			9	3	5		10	2	11	4
1		10	Wolverhampton Wan.	1-0	Hansen	30857	9	1	7		6			8	3	5		10	2	11	4
1		14	MANCHESTER UNITED	2-0	Dalglish, Neal	46608	8	1	7		6			9	3	5		10	2	11	4
1		16	Aston Villa	1-3	Johnson	44029		1	7		6	8		9	3	5		10	2	11	4
1		21	BRISTOL CITY	1-0	Dalglish	43191	8	1	7		6	12		9	3	5		10	2	11	4
1		24	Southampton	1-1	Johnson	23182	8	1	7		6			9	3	5	11	10	2		4
1		28	Nottingham Forest	0-0		41898	8	1	7		6	9			3	5	12	10	2	11	4
1	May	1	Bolton Wanderers	4-1	R Kennedy 2, Johnson, Dalglish	35200	8	1	7		6			9	3	5		10	2	11	4
1		5	SOUTHAMPTON	2-0	Neal 2	46687	8	1	7		6			9	3	5		10	2	11	4
1		8	ASTON VILLA	3-0	A Kennedy, Dalglish, McDermott	50576	8	1	7		6			9	3	5		10	2	11	4
1		11	Middlesbrough	1-0	Johnson	32214	8	1	7		6			9	3	5		10	2	11	4
1		17	Leeds United	3-0	Johnson 2, Case	41324	8	1	7		6			9	3	5		10	2	11	4

	Apps	Subs	Goals
Case JR	37		7
Clemence RN	42		
Dalglish KM	42	1	21
Fairclough D	3	2	2
Hansen AD	34	4	1
Heighway SD	26		4
Hughes EW	16	1	
Johnson DE	26	3	16
Kennedy AP	37		3
Kennedy R	42		10
Lee S	1		
McDermott T	34		8
Neal PG	42		5
Souness GJ	41		8
Thompson PB	39		

F.A. Cup

R3	Jan	10	Southend United	0-0		31033	8	1	7	9	6	12	3			5		10	2	11	4
R3		17	SOUTHEND UNITED	3-0	Case, Dalglish, R Kennedy	37797	8	1	7	9	6		3			5		10	2	11	4
R4		30	BLACKBURN ROVERS	1-0	Dalglish	43432	8	1	7	9	6	12	3		4	5		10	2	11	
R5	Feb	28	BURNLEY	3-0	Johnson 2, Souness	47161		1	7			9	3	8	4	5		10	2	11	6
R6	Mar	10	Ipswich Town	1-0	Dalglish	31322	9	1	7		6		3	8		5		10	2	11	4
SF		31	Manchester United	2-2	Dalglish, Hansen	52584	9	1	7		6	12	3	8		5		10	2	11	4
rep	Apr	4	Manchester United	0-1		53069	12	1	7		6	9	3	8		5		10	2	11	4

SF at Maine Road, Manchester; SF replay at Goodison Park

F.L. Cup

R2	Aug	28	Sheffield United	0-1		35753	8	1	7	12		9	6		3	5		10	2	11	4

European Cup

R1.1	Sep	13	Nottingham Forest	0-2		38316	8	1	7			9	6	12	3	5		10	2	11	4
R1.2		27	NOTTM FOREST	0-0		51679	8	1	7	12		9	6	14	3	5		10	2	11	4

Liverpool 1979/80

Anfield

						Case JR	Clemence RN	Cohen A	Dalglish KM	Fairclough D	Hansen AD	Heighway SD	Irwin CT	Johnson DE	Kennedy AP	Kennedy R	Lee S	McDermott T	Neal PG	Ogrizovic S	Souness GJ	Thompson PB
	Aug	21	BOLTON WANDERERS	0-0		45900	8	1		7		6	12		9	3			10	2		11	4
		25	WEST BROMWICH ALB.	3-1	Johnson 2, McDermott	48021	8	1		7				6	9	3	5		10	2		11	4
	Sep	1	Southampton	2-3	Johnson, Irwin	21402	8	1		7				6	9	3	5		10	2		11	4
8		8	COVENTRY CITY	4-0	Johnson 2, Case, Dalglish	39926	8	1		7				6	9	3	5		10	2		11	4
8		15	Leeds United	1-1	McDermott	39779	8	1	5	7		6			9	3			10	2		11	4
7		22	NORWICH CITY	0-0		44120	8	1		7	5		12	6	9	3			10	2		11	4
9		29	Nottingham Forest	0-1		28262	8			7	9	6		12		3	5		10	2	1	11	4
8	Oct	6	BRISTOL CITY	4-0	Johnson, Dalglish, Kennedy, McDermott	38213	8	1		7		6			9	3	5		10	2		11	4
7		9	Bolton Wanderers	1-1	Dalglish	25571	8	1		7		6			9	3	5		10	2		11	4
6		13	Ipswich Town	2-1	Johnson, og (Hunter)	24969	8	1		7		6	10		9	3	5			2		11	4
5		20	EVERTON	2-2	Kennedy, og (Lyons)	52201	8	1		7		6			9	3	5		10	2		11	4
3		27	Manchester City	4-0	Dalglish 2, Johnson, Kennedy	48128	8	1		7		6	10		9	3	5			2		11	4
3	Nov	3	WOLVERHAMPTON W.	3-0	Dalglish 2, Kennedy	49541	8	1		7		6			9	3	5		10	2		11	4
2		10	Brighton & Hove Albion	4-1	Dalglish 2, Kennedy, Johnson	29690	8	1		7		6	12		9	3	5		10	2		11	4
1		17	TOTTENHAM HOTSPUR	2-1	McDermott 2	51092	8	1		7		6			9	3	5		10	2		11	4
2		24	Arsenal	0-0		55561	8	1		7		6			9	3	5		10	2		11	4
2	Dec	1	MIDDLESBROUGH	4-0	McDermott, Hansen, Johnson, Kennedy	39885	8	1		7		6			9	3	5		10	2		11	4
1		8	Aston Villa	3-1	Kennedy, Hansen, McDermott	41160	8	1		7		6			9	3	5		10	2		11	4
1		15	CRYSTAL PALACE	3-0	Case, Dalglish, McDermott	42898	8	1		7		6			9	3	5		10	2		11	4
1		22	Derby County	3-1	McDermott (p), Johnson, og (Davies)	24945	8	1		7		6			9	3	5		10	2		11	4
1		26	MANCHESTER UNITED	2-0	Hansen, Johnson	51073	8	1		7		6			9	3	5		10	2		11	4
1		29	West Bromwich Albion	2-0	Johnson 2	34993	8	1		7		6	12		9	3	5		10	2		11	4
1	Jan	12	SOUTHAMPTON	1-1	McDermott (p)	44655	8	1		7		6			9	3	5		10	2		11	4
1		19	Coventry City	0-1		31644	8	1		7		6	12		9	3	5		10	2		11	4
1	Feb	9	Norwich City	5-3	Fairclough 3, Dalglish, Case	25418	8	1		7	9	6				3	5	11	10	2			4
1		19	NOTTM. FOREST	2-0	McDermott, Kennedy	45163	8	1		7	9	6				3	5		10	2		11	4
1		23	IPSWICH TOWN	1-1	Fairclough	47566	8	1		7	9	6				3	5		10	2		11	4
1		26	Wolverhampton Wan.	0-1		36693	8	1		7	9	6	12			3	5		10	2		11	4
1	Mar	1	Everton	2-1	Johnson, Neal (p)	53018	8	1		7	12	6			9	3	5		10	2		11	4
1		11	MANCHESTER CITY	2-0	Souness, og (Caton)	40443	8	1		7		6			9	3	5		10	2		11	4
1		15	Bristol City	3-1	Dalglish 2, Kennedy	27523	8	1		7		6			9	3	5		10	2		11	4
1		19	LEEDS UNITED	3-0	Johnson 2, Kennedy	37088	8	1		7	12	6			9	3	5		10	2		11	4
1		22	BRIGHTON & HOVE ALB	1-0	Hansen	42738	8	1		7	12	6			9	3	5		10	2		11	4
1		29	Tottenham Hotspur	0-2		32114	8	1		7		6			9	3	5		10	2		11	4
1	Apr	1	STOKE CITY	1-0	Dalglish	36415	8	1		7		6			9	3	5		10	2		11	4
1		5	Manchester United	1-2	Dalglish	57342	8	1		7		6			9	3	5	12	10	2		11	4
1		8	DERBY COUNTY	3-0	Irwin, Johnson, og (Osgood)	40939	8	1		7	12	6		3	9		5		10	2		11	4
1		19	ARSENAL	1-1	Dalglish	46878		1		7	8	6	12	3	9		5	10		2		11	4
1		23	Stoke City	2-0	Johnson, Fairclough	32699		1	12	7	8	6			3	9	5	10		2		11	4
1		26	Crystal Palace	0-0		45746		1		7	8	6			9	3	5	10		2		11	4
1	May	3	ASTON VILLA	4-1	Johnson 2, Cohen, og (Blake)	51541		1	3	7		6			9		5	8	10	2		11	4
1		6	Middlesbrough	0-1		24458		1	3	7	12	6			9		5	8	10	2		11	4

					Apps	37	41	3	42	9	38	2	7	37	37	40	6	37	42	1	41	42
					Subs			1		5		7	1			1						
					Goals	3		1	16	5	4			2	21	1	9	11	1		1	

Six own goals

F.A. Cup

R3	Jan	5	GRIMSBY TOWN	5-0	Johnson 3, Souness, Case	49706	8	1		7		6			9	3	5		10	2		11	4
R4		26	Nottingham Forest	2-0	Dalglish, McDermott (p)	33277	8	1		7		6			9	3	5		10	2		11	4
R5	Feb	16	BURY	2-0	Fairclough 2	43769	8	1		7	12	6			9	3	5		10	2		11	4
R6	Mar	8	Tottenham Hotspur	1-0	McDermott	48033	8	1		7		6			9	3	5		10	2		11	4
SF	Apr	12	Arsenal	0-0		50174	8	1		7	12	6		3	9		5	10		2		11	4
rep		16	Arsenal	1-1	Fairclough	40679		1		7	8	6		3	9		5	10		2		11	4
rep2		28	Arsenal	1-1	Dalglish	42975		1		7	12	6			9	3	5	8	10	2		11	4
rep3	May	1	Arsenal	0-1		35335		1	3	7	12	6			9		5	8	10	2		11	4

SF replay and replay 2 a.e.t. SF at Hillsborough, SF replay and replay 2 at Villa Park, SF replay 3 at Highfield Road, Coventry

F.L. Cup

R2	Aug	29	Tranmere R	0-0		16759	8	1		7	12			6	9	3	5		10	2		11	4
R2	Sep	4	TRANMERE ROVERS	4-0	Dalglish 2, Fairclough, Thompson	24785	8	1		7	12	6			9	3	5		10	2		11	4
R3		25	CHESTERFIELD	3-1	Fairclough, Dalglish, McDermott	20960	8	1		7	5		9	6		3			10	2		11	4
R4	Oct	30	EXETER CITY	2-0	Fairclough 2	21019	8	1		7	12	6			9	3	5		10	2		11	4
R5	Dec	5	Norwich C	3-1	Johnson 2, Dalglish	23000	8	1		7		6			9	3	5		10	2		11	4
SF1	Jan	22	Nottm Forest	0-1		32234	8	1		7		6			9	3	5		10	2		11	4
SF2	Feb	12	NOTTM FOREST	1-1	Fairclough	50880	8	1		7	12	6			9	3	5		10	2		11	4

European Cup

R1.1	Sep	19	DINAMO TBILISI	2-1	Johnson, Case	35270	8	1		7	5		12	6	9	3			10	2		11	4
R1.2	Oct	3	Dinamo Tbilisi	0-3		80000	8	1		7	12	6		3	9		5		10	2		11	4

F.A. Charity Shield

	Aug	11	Arsenal	3-1	McDermott 2, Dalglish	92000	8	1		7		6			9	3	5		10	2		11	4

At Wembley Stadium

Aston Villa 1980/81

		Date	Opponent	Score	Scorers	Att.	Bremner DG	Cowans GS	Deacy ES	Evans AI	Geddis D	Gibson CJ	McNaught K	Morley WA	Mortimer DG	Rimmer JJ	Shaw GR	Swain KM	Williams G	Withe P
	Aug	16	Leeds United	2-1	Morley, Shaw	23401	7	10	3				5	11	6	1	8	2	4	9
		20	NORWICH CITY	1-0	Shaw	25970	7	10		4		3	5	11	6	1	8	2		9
		23	Manchester City	2-2	Withe 2	30017	7	10		4		3	5	11	6	1	8	2		9
3		30	COVENTRY CITY	1-0	Shaw	20050	7	10		4		3	5	11	6	1	8	2		9
4	Sep	6	Ipswich Town	0-1		23192	7	10		4		3	5	11	6	1	8	2		9
10		13	EVERTON	0-2		25673	7	10		4		3	5	11	6	1	8	2		9
6		20	WOLVERHAMPTON W.	2-1	Geddis, Hughes (og)	26881	7	10		4	8	3	5	11	6	1		2		9
4		27	Crystal Palace	1-0	Shaw	18398	7	10		4		3	5	11	6	1	8	2		9
4	Oct	4	SUNDERLAND	4-0	Evans 2, Morley, Shaw	26914	7	10	12	4		3	5	11	6	1	8	2		9
4		8	Manchester United	3-3	Withe, Shaw, Cowans (p)	38831	7	10	3	4			5	11	6	1	8	2		9
3		11	Birmingham City	2-1	Evans, Cowans (p)	33879	7	10	3	4			5	11	6	1	8	2		9
2		18	TOTTENHAM HOTSPUR	3-0	Morley 2, Withe	30940	7	10		4		3	5	11	6	1	8	2		9
1		22	BRIGHTON & HOVE ALB	4-1	Mortimer, Withe, Bremner, Shaw	27367	7	10		4		3	5	11	6	1	8	2		9
1		25	Southampton	2-1	Morley, Withe	21249	7	10	12	4		3	5	11	6	1	8	2		9
1	Nov	1	LEICESTER CITY	2-0	Shaw, Cowans	29953	7	10	3	4			5	11	6	1	8	2	12	9
1		8	West Bromwich Albion	0-0		34001	7	10		4			5	11	6	1	8	2	3	9
1		12	Norwich City	3-1	Shaw 2, Evans	17050	7	10		4			5	11	6	1	8	2	3	9
1		15	LEEDS UNITED	1-1	Shaw	29106	7	10		4			5	11	6	1	8	2	3	9
1		22	Liverpool	1-2	Evans	48114	7	10		4			5	11	6	1	8	2	3	9
1		29	ARSENAL	1-1	Morley	30140	7	10		4			5	11	6	1	8	2	3	9
2	Dec	6	Middlesbrough	1-2	Shaw	15597	7	10		4	9		5	11	6	1	8	2	3	
1		13	BIRMINGHAM CITY	3-0	Geddis 2, Shaw	41101	7	10		4	9		5	11	6	1	8	2	3	
2		20	Brighton & Hove Albion	0-1		16425	7	10	12	4	9		5	11	6	1	8	2	3	
2		26	STOKE CITY	1-0	Withe	34658	7	10		4			5	11	6	1	8	2	3	9
2		27	Nottingham Forest	2-2	Shaw, Lloyd (og)	33930	7	10		4	9		5	11	6	1	8	2	3	
1	Jan	10	LIVERPOOL	2-0	Withe, Mortimer	47960	7	10		4		3	5	11	6	1	8	2		9
2		17	Coventry City	2-1	Morley, Withe	27020	7	10		4		3	5	11	6	1	8	2		9
2		31	MANCHESTER CITY	1-0	Shaw	33682	7	10	3	4	12		5	11	6	1	8	2		9
2	Feb	7	Everton	3-1	Morley, Mortimer, Cowans (p)	31434	7	10		4			5	11	6	1	8	2	3	9
2		21	CRYSTAL PALACE	2-1	Withe 2	27203	7	10		4		12	5	11	6	1	8	2	3	9
2		28	Wolverhampton Wan.	1-0	Withe	34693	7	10		4			5	11	6	1	8	2	3	9
2	Mar	7	Sunderland	2-1	Evans, Mortimer	27278	7	10		4		12	5	11	6	1	8	2	3	9
2		14	MANCHESTER UNITED	3-3	Withe 2, Shaw	42182	7	10		4			5	11	6	1	8	2	3	9
2		21	Tottenham Hotspur	0-2		35091	7	10		4	9		5	11	6	1	8	2	3	
2		28	SOUTHAMPTON	2-1	Morley, Geddis	32467	7	10		4	9		5	11	6	1	8	2	3	
1	Apr	4	Leicester City	4-2	Withe 2, Bremner, Morley	26032	7	10		4			5	11	6	1	8	2	3	9
1		8	WEST BROMWICH ALB.	1-0	Withe	47998	7	10		4	8	3	5	11	6	1		2		9
1		14	IPSWICH TOWN	1-2	Shaw	47495	7	10				3	5	11	6	1	8	2	4	9
1		18	NOTTM. FOREST	2-0	Withe, Cowans (p)	34707	7	10				3	5	11	6	1	8	2	4	9
1		20	Stoke City	1-1	Withe	23500	7	10	12	4		3	5	11	6	1	8	2		9
1		25	MIDDLESBROUGH	3-0	Shaw, Withe, Evans	38018	7	10		4		3	5	11	6	1	8	2		9
1	May	2	Arsenal	0-2		57472	7	10		4		3	5	11	6	1	8	2		9

	Bremner	Cowans	Deacy	Evans	Geddis	Gibson	McNaught	Morley	Mortimer	Rimmer	Shaw	Swain	Williams	Withe
Apps	42	42	5	39	8	19	42	42	42	42	40	42	21	36
Subs			4		1	2							1	
Goals	2	5		7	4			10	4		18			20

Two own goals

F.A. Cup

		Date	Opponent	Score		Att.														
R3	Jan	3	Ipswich Town	0-1		27721	7	10		4			5	11	6	1	8	2	3	9

F.L. Cup

		Date	Opponent	Score	Scorers	Att.														
R2	Aug	27	LEEDS UNITED	1-0	Morley	24238	7	10		4		3	5	11	6	1	8	2		9
R2s	Sep	3	Leeds United	3-1	Shaw 2, Withe	12236	7	10	12	4		3	5	11	6	1	8	2		9
R3		23	Cambridge United	1-2	Morley	7628	7	10		4	8	3	5	11	6	1		2		9

Liverpool 1981/82

Anfield

	Date		Opponent	Score	Scorers	Att	Dalglish KM	Grobbelaar BD	Hansen AD	Johnson DE	Johnston CP	Kennedy AP	Kennedy R	Lawrenson MT	Lee S	McDermott T	Neal PG	Rush IJ	Sheedy KM	Souness GJ	Thompson PB	Whelan RA
	Aug	29	Wolverhampton Wan.	0-1		28001	7	1	6	9	12		5	3	8	10	2			11	4	
	Sep	1	MIDDLESBROUGH	1-1	Neal (p)	31963	7	1	6	9			5	3	8	10	2			11	4	
		5	ARSENAL	2-0	McDermott, Johnson	35269	7	1	6	9	12		5	3	8	10	2			11	4	
16		12	Ipswich Town	0-2		26682	7	1	6	9	12	3	5		8	10	2			11	4	
17		19	ASTON VILLA	0-0		37474	7	1	6	9			3	5	8	10	2			11	4	
10		22	Coventry City	2-1	Kennedy, McDermott (p)	16738	7	1	6	9			3	5	12	8	10	2			11	4	
12		26	West Ham United	1-1	Johnson	30802	7	1	6	9			3	5		8	10	2			11	4	
11	Oct	3	SWANSEA CITY	2-2	McDermott 2 (2p)	47845	7	1		9			3		5	8	10	2		12	11	4	6
8		10	LEEDS UNITED	3-0	Rush 2, og (Cherry)	35840	7	1					3	6	5	8	10	2	9		11	4	
8		17	Brighton & Hove Albion	3-3	Dalglish, Kennedy, McDermott	26328	7	1	6				3	5	12	8	10	2	9		11	4	
12		24	MANCHESTER UNITED	1-2	McDermott (p)	41438	7	1	6	9				5	3	8	10	2			11	4	12
8		31	Sunderland	2-0	Souness, McDermott	27854	7	1	6					5	3		10	2	9		11	4	8
7	Nov	7	EVERTON	3-1	Dalglish 2, Rush	48461	7	1	6	12				5	3		10	2	9		11	4	8
7		21	West Bromwich Albion	1-1	Dalglish	20706	7	1	6	9		12		5	3		10	2			11	4	8
10		28	SOUTHAMPTON	0-1		35189	7	1	6	12				5	3		10	2	9		11	4	8
10	Dec	5	Nottingham Forest	2-0	Lawrenson, Kennedy	24521	7	1	6					5	3		10	2	9		11	4	8
11		26	MANCHESTER CITY	1-3	Whelan	37929	7	1	6		10	12			3	8		2	9		11	4	5
9	Jan	5	WEST HAM UNITED	3-0	McDermott, Whelan, Dalglish	28427	7	1	6				8		3		10	2	9		11	4	5
8		16	WOLVERHAMPTON W.	2-1	Whelan, Dalglish	26438	7	1	6	12			8		3		10	2	9		11	4	5
5		26	Notts County	4-0	Rush 3, Whelan	14399	7	1	6				4		3	8	10	2	9		11		5
4		30	Aston Villa	3-0	McDermott 2, Rush	35947	7	1	6				4		3	8	10	2	9		11		5
3	Feb	6	IPSWICH TOWN	4-0	McDermott, Rush, Dalglish, Whelan	41316	7	1	6				4		3	8	10	2	9		11		5
6		16	Swansea City	0-2		22604	7	1	6				4		3	8	10	2	9		11		5
5		20	COVENTRY CITY	4-0	Souness, Lee, Rush, McDermott (p)	28275	7	1	6				4		3	8	10	2	9		11		5
4		27	Leeds United	2-0	Souness, Rush	33689	7	1	6	12			4		3	8	10	2	9		11		5
6	Mar	6	BRIGHTON & HOVE ALB	0-1		28574	7	1	6				4		3	8	10	2	9	12	11		5
4		9	Stoke City	5-1	McDermott, Dalglish, Souness, Lee, Whelan	16781	7	1	6				4		3	8	10	2	9		11		5
4		20	SUNDERLAND	1-0	Rush	30344	7	1		12	10	4			3	8		2	9		11	6	5
4		27	Everton	3-1	Souness, Whelan, Johnston	51806	7	1			10	4			3	8		2	9		11	6	5
2		30	BIRMINGHAM CITY	3-1	Rush 2, McDermott	24224	7	1			11	4			3	8	10	2	9			6	5
1	Apr	2	NOTTS COUNTY	1-0	Dalglish	30126	7	1			11	4			3	8	10	2	9			6	5
1		7	Manchester United	1-0	Johnston	48371	7	1			10	4			3	8	12	2	9		11	6	5
1		10	Manchester City	5-0	Lee, Neal (p), Johnston, Kennedy, Rush	40112	7	1	11		10	4			3	8		2	9			6	5
1		13	STOKE CITY	2-0	Kennedy, Johnston	30419	7	1	11		10	4			3	8		2	9			6	5
1		17	WEST BROMWICH ALB.	1-0	Dalglish	34286	7	1	11		10	4			3	8		2	9			6	5
1		24	Southampton	3-2	Whelan 2, Rush	24704	7	1	11		10	4			3	8		2	9			6	5
1	May	1	NOTTM. FOREST	2-0	Johnston 2	34321	7	1	11		10	4			3	8		2	9			6	5
1		3	Tottenham Hotspur	2-2	Dalglish 2	38091	7	1	11		10	4			3	8		2	9		12	6	5
1		8	Birmingham City	1-0	Rush	26381	7	1	10			12	4		3	8		2	9		11	6	5
1		11	Arsenal	1-1	Rush	30932	7	1	10			12	4		3	8		2	9		11	6	5
1		15	TOTTENHAM HOTSPUR	3-1	Lawrenson, Dalglish, Whelan	48122	7	1	10				4		3	8		2	9		11	6	5
1		18	Middlesbrough	0-0		17431	7	1	10		5	4			3	8		2	9		11	6	

	Dalglish	Grobbelaar	Hansen	Johnson	Johnston	Kennedy AP	Kennedy R	Lawrenson	Lee	McDermott	Neal	Rush	Sheedy	Souness	Thompson	Whelan
Apps	42	42	35	10	13	32	15	37	35	28	42	32	0	34	34	31
Subs				5	5	2		2		1			2	1		1
Goals	13			2	6	3	2	2	3	14	2	17		5		10

One own goal

F.A. Cup

	Date		Opponent	Score	Scorers	Att																
R3	Jan	2	Swansea City	4-0	Rush 2, Hansen, Lawrenson	24179	7	1	6				3		5		10	2	9		11	4	8
R4		23	Sunderland	3-0	Dalglish 2, Rush	28582	7	1	6	12			4		3	8	10	2	9		11		5
R5	Feb	13	Chelsea	0-2		41422	7	1	6			12	4		3	8	10	2	9		11		5

F.L. Cup

	Date		Opponent	Score	Scorers	Att																
R2	Oct	7	EXETER CITY	5-0	Rush 2, McDermott, Dalglish, Whelan	11478	7	1					3		5	8	10	2	9		11	4	6
R2s		28	Exeter City	6-0	Rush 2, Dalglish, Neal, Sheedy, og (Marker)	11740	7	1	6					5	3		10	2	9	11		4	8
R3	Nov	10	MIDDLESBROUGH	4-1	Johnson 2, Sheedy, Rush	16145	7	1	6	8	12				3		10	2	9	5	11	4	
R4	Dec	1	Arsenal	0-0		37917	7	1	6	12				5	3		10	2	9		11	4	8
rep		8	ARSENAL	3-0	Johnston, McDermott, Dalglish	21375	7	1	6			12	4	5	3	8		2	9		11		
R5	Jan	12	BARNSLEY	0-0		33707	7	1	6				3		8		10	2	9		11	4	5
rep		19	Barnsley	3-1	Souness, Johnson, Dalglish	29639	7	1	6	12					3	8	10	2	9		11	4	5
SF1	Feb	2	Ipswich Town	2-0	McDermott, Rush	26690	7	1	6				4		3	8	10	2	9		11		5
SF2		9	IPSWICH TOWN	2-2	Rush, Dalglish	34933	7	1	6				4		3	8	10	2	9		11		5
F	Mar	13	Tottenham Hotspur	3-1	Whelan 2, Rush	100000	7	1			12		4		3	8	10	2	9		11	6	5

R4 replay and Final a.e.t. Final at Wembley Stadium

European Cup

	Date		Opponent	Score	Scorers	Att																
R1.1	Sep	16	OPS (Oulu)	1-0	Dalglish	8400	7	1	6	9			3	5	8	10		2			11	4	
R1.2		30	OPS (OULU)	7-0	McDermott 2, Dalglish, R Kennedy, Johnson, Rush, Lawrenson	20789	7	1	6	9			3	5	12	8	10	2	14		11	4	
R2.1	Oct	21	AZ (Alkmaar)	2-2	Johnson, Lee	15000	7	1	6	9				5	3	8	10	2			11	4	12
R2.2	Nov	4	AZ (ALKMAAR)	3-2	McDermott, Rush, Hansen	29703	7	1	6					5	3		10	2	9		11	4	8
QF1	Mar	3	CSKA (SOFIA)	1-0	Whelan	27388	7	1	6				3		5	8	10	2	9		11		4
QF2		17	CSKA (Sofia)	0-2		60000	7	1		14	12	4			3	8	10	2	9		11	6	5

120

Liverpool 1982/83

Anfield

		Date	Opponent	Score	Scorers	Att	Dalglish KM	Fairclough D	Grobbelaar BD	Hansen AD	Hodgson DJ	Johnston CP	Kennedy AP	Lawrenson MT	Lee S	McDermott T	Neal PG	Nicol S	Rush II	Souness GI	Thompson PB	Whelan RA
	Aug	28	WEST BROMWICH ALB.	2-0	Lee, Neal (p)	35652	7		1		10	12	3	6	8		2		9	11	4	5
		31	Birmingham City	0-0		20976	7		1		10		3		8		6	2	9	11	4	5
	Sep	4	Arsenal	2-0	Hodgson, Neal	36429	7		1		10		3	5	8		2		9	11	4	6
1		7	NOTTM. FOREST	4-3	Hodgson 2, Souness, Rush	27145	7		1		10		3	5	8		2		9	11	4	6
4		11	LUTON TOWN	3-3	Souness, Rush, Johnston	33694	7		1		10	12	3	5	8		2		9	11	4	6
2		18	Swansea City	3-0	Rush 2, Johnston	20322	7		1			10	3	5	8	12	2		9	11	4	
1		25	SOUTHAMPTON	5-0	Whelan 2, Lawrenson 2, Souness	32996	7		1			10	3	6	8	12	2		9	11	4	5
1	Oct	2	Ipswich Town	0-1		23766	7	12	1	6		9	3	10	8		2			11	4	5
5		9	West Ham United	1-3	Souness	32500	7		1	6		12	3	10	8		2		9	11	4	5
3		16	MANCHESTER UNITED	0-0		40853	7		1	6			3	10	8		2		9	11	4	5
4		23	Stoke City	1-1	Lawrenson	29501	7		1	6			3	10	8		2		9	11	4	5
1		30	BRIGHTON & HOVE ALB	3-1	Dalglish 2, Lawrenson	27929	7		1	6			3	10	8		2		9	11	4	5
1	Nov	6	Everton	5-0	Rush 4, Lawrenson	51726	7		1	6	12	5	3	10	8		2		9	11	4	
1		13	COVENTRY CITY	4-0	Rush 3, Dalglish	27870	7		1	6		5	3	10	8		2		9	11	4	
1		20	Notts County	2-1	Johnston, Dalglish	16897	7		1	6		5	3	10	8		2		9	11	4	
1		27	TOTTENHAM HOTSPUR	3-0	Dalglish 2, Neal (p)	40691	7		1	6		5	3	10	8		2		9	11	4	
1	Dec	4	Norwich City	0-1		22826	7		1	6		5	3	10	8		2		9	11	4	
1		11	WATFORD	3-1	Neal 2 (2p), Rush	36690	7	12	1	6		10	3				2		9	11	4	5
1		18	Aston Villa	4-2	Hodgson, Dalglish, Kennedy, Rush	34568	7		1	6	10		3	4	8		2		9	11		
1		27	MANCHESTER CITY	5-2	Dalglish 3, Neal, Rush	43695	7	12	1	6	10		3	4	8		2		9	11		5
1		28	Sunderland	0-0		35041	7		1	6	10		3	4	8		2	5	9	11		
1	Jan	1	NOTTS COUNTY	5-1	Rush 3, Dalglish 2	33663	7		1	6	10	5	3	4	8		2		9	11		
1		3	ARSENAL	3-1	Rush, Souness, Dalglish	37713	7		1	6	10	5	3	4	8		2		9	11		
1		15	West Bromwich Albion	1-0	Rush	24401	7		1	6	10	5	3	4	8		2		9	11		
1		22	BIRMINGHAM CITY	1-0	Neal	30986	7		1	6	10	9	3	4	8		2			11		5
1	Feb	5	Luton Town	3-1	Rush, Kennedy, Souness	18434	7		1	6	10	5	3	4	8		2		9	11		12
1		12	IPSWICH TOWN	1-0	Dalglish	34976	7		1	6	10	5	3	4	8		2		9	11		12
1		26	Manchester United	1-1	Dalglish	57397	7		1				10	3	6	8	2		9	11	4	5
1	Mar	5	STOKE CITY	5-1	Dalglish 2, Neal, Johnston, Souness	30020	7		1	6			10	3	4	8	2		9	11		5
1		12	WEST HAM UNITED	3-0	Lee, Rush, og (Pike)	28511	7		1	6			10	3	4	8	2		9	11		5
1		19	EVERTON	0-0		44042	7		1	6	12	10	3	4	8		2		9	11		5
1		22	Brighton & Hove Albion	2-2	Rush 2	25022	7	12	1	6			10	3	11	8	2		9		4	5
1	Apr	2	SUNDERLAND	1-0	Souness	35821	7	9	1	6			10	3	4	8	2			11		5
1		4	Manchester City	4-0	Fairclough 2, Souness, Kennedy	35647	7	9	1	6			10	3	4	8	2			11		5
1		9	SWANSEA CITY	3-0	Rush, Lee, Fairclough	30010	7	12	1	6			10	3	4	8	2		9	11		5
1		12	Coventry City	0-0		15340	7		1	6			10	3	4	8	2		9	11		5
1		16	Southampton	2-3	Dalglish, Johnston	23578	7	9	1	6	12	10	3	4	8		2			11		5
1		23	NORWICH CITY	0-2		37022	7		1	6	9	10	3	4	8		2			11		5
1		30	Tottenham Hotspur	0-2		44907	7		1	6	10	8	3	5			2		9	11	4	
1	May	2	Nottingham Forest	0-1		25017	7		1	6	10	8	3	5			2	12	9	11	4	
1		7	ASTON VILLA	1-1	Johnston	39939	7		1	6	10	9	3	5	8		2			11	4	
1		14	Watford	1-2	Johnston	27173	7		1	6	9	10	3	5	8		2	12		11	4	

	Apps	Subs	Goals
Dalglish KM	42		18
Fairclough D	3	5	3
Grobbelaar BD	42		
Hansen AD	34		
Hodgson DJ	20	3	4
Johnston CP	30	3	7
Kennedy AP	42		3
Lawrenson MT	40		5
Lee S	40	2	3
McDermott T	0	2	
Neal PG	42		8
Nicol S	2		
Rush II	34		24
Souness GI	41		9
Thompson PB	24		
Whelan RA	26	2	2

One own goal

F.A. Cup

		Date	Opponent	Score	Scorers	Att																
R3	Jan	8	Blackburn Rovers	2-1	Hodgson, Rush	21967	7		1	6	10	5	3	4	8		2		9	11		
R4		29	STOKE CITY	2-0	Dalglish, Rush	36666	7		1	6	10	5	3	4	8		2		9	11		
R5	Feb	20	BRIGHTON & HOVE ALB.	1-2	Johnston	44868	7		1	6	10	12	3	4	8		2		9	11		5

F.L. Cup

		Date	Opponent	Score	Scorers	Att																
R2	Oct	5	Ipswich Town	2-1	Rush 2	19328	7		1	6			3	10	8		2		9	11	4	5
R2s		26	IPSWICH TOWN	2-0	Whelan, Lawrenson	17698	7		1	6	12		3	10	8		2		9	11	4	5
R3	Nov	10	ROTHERHAM UNITED	1-0	Johnston	20412			1	6	7	5	3	10	8		2		9	11	4	
R4		30	NORWICH CITY	2-0	Lawrenson, Fairclough	13235	7	12	1	6		5	3	10	8		2		9	11	4	5
R5	Jan	18	WEST HAM UNITED	2-1	Hodgson, Souness	23953	7		1	6	10	5	3	4	8		2		9	11		12
SF1	Feb	8	BURNLEY	3-0	Souness, Neal, Hodgson	33520	7		1	6	10	5	3	4	8		2		9	11		12
SF2		15	Burnley	0-1		20000	7		1	6		10	3	4	8		2		9	11		12
F	Mar	26	Manchester United	2-1	Kennedy, Whelan	100000	7	12	1	6		10	3	4	8		2		9	11		5

Final at Wembley Stadium, a.e.t.

European Cup

		Date	Opponent	Score	Scorers	Att																
R1.1	Sep	14	Dundalk	4-1	Whelan 2, Rush, Hodgson	16500	7		1	6	10		3		8		2		9	11	4	5
R1.2		29	DUNDALK	1-0	Whelan	12021	7		1	6		10	3		8	9	2			11	4	5
R2.1	Oct	19	HJK (Helsinki)	0-1		5722	7		1	6	10		3		8		2		9	11	4	5
R2.2	Nov	2	HJK (HELSINKI)	5-0	Kennedy 2, Dalglish, Johnston, Neal	16434	7		1	6		5	3	10	8		2		9	11	4	
QF1	Mar	2	Widzew Lodz	0-2		45531	7		1	6	12	10	3	4	8		2		9	11		5
QF2		16	WIDZEW LODZ	3-2	Neal (p), Rush, Hodgson	44494		12	1	6	7	10	3	4	8		2		9	11	14	5

F.A. Charity Shield

		Date	Opponent	Score	Scorers	Att																
	Aug	21	Tottenham Hotspur	1-0	Rush	82500	7		1	6	12		3	10	8		2		9	11	4	5

At Wembley Stadium

Liverpool 1983/84

Anfield

								Dalglish KM	Grobbelaar BD	Hansen AD	Hodgson DJ	Johnston CP	Kennedy AP	Lawrenson MT	Lee S	Neal PG	Nicol S	Robinson MJ	Rush IJ	Souness GJ	Wark J	Whelan RA
	Aug	27	Wolverhampton Wan.	1-1	Rush		26249	7	1	6		5	3	4	8	2		10	9	11		
		31	Norwich City	1-0	Souness		23271	7	1	6		5	3	4	8	2		10	9	11		
	Sep	3	NOTTM. FOREST	1-0	Rush		31376	7	1	6	12	5	3	4	8	2		10	9	11		
5		6	SOUTHAMPTON	1-1	Rush		26331	7	1	6		5	3	4	8	2		10	9	11		
4		10	Arsenal	2-0	Johnston, Dalglish		41880	7	1	6		5	3	4	8	2		10	9	11		
3		17	ASTON VILLA	2-1	Dalglish, Rush		34246	7	1	6		5	3	4	8	2		10	9	11		
4		24	Manchester United	0-1			56121	7	1	6		5	3	4	8	2	12	10	9	11		
6	Oct	1	SUNDERLAND	0-1			29534	7	1	6		5	3	4	8		2	10	9	11		
5		15	West Ham United	3-1	Robinson 3		32535	7	1	6	12	5	3	4	8	2		10	9	11		
2		22	Queen's Park Rangers	1-0	Nicol		27140	7	1	6		5	3	4	8	2	12	10	9	11		
2		29	LUTON TOWN	6-0	Rush 5, Dalglish		31940	7	1	6			3	4	8	2	5	10	9	11		
1	Nov	6	EVERTON	3-0	Rush, Robinson, Nicol		40375	7	1	6			3	4	8	2	5	10	9	11		
1		12	Tottenham Hotspur	2-2	Robinson, Rush		44348	7	1				3	4	8	2	5	10	9	11		
1		19	STOKE CITY	1-0	Rush		26529	7	1	6			3	4	8	2	5	10	9	11		
1		26	Ipswich Town	1-1	Dalglish		23880	7	1	6			3	4	8	2	5		9	11		10
1	Dec	3	BIRMINGHAM CITY	1-0	Rush		24791		1	6		7	3	4	8	2	5	10	9	11		12
		10	Coventry City	0-4			20649	7	1	6			3	4	8	2	5		9	11		10
		17	NOTTS COUNTY	5-0	Souness 2 (1p), Nicol, Rush, og (Hunt)		22436	7	1	6		10	3	4	8	2	5		9	11		
		26	West Bromwich Albion	2-1	Nicol, Souness		25094	7	1	6		10	3	4	8	2	5		9	11		
		27	LEICESTER CITY	2-2	Lee, Rush		33664	7	1	6	12	10	3	4	8	2	5		9	11		
		31	Nottingham Forest	1-0	Rush		29692	7	1	6		10	3	4	8	2	5		9	11		12
1	Jan	2	MANCHESTER UNITED	1-1	Johnston		44622	7	1	6	12	10	3	4	8	2	5		9	11		
1		14	WOLVERHAMPTON W.	0-1			23325		1	6		10	3	4	8	2	5	7	9	11		12
1		20	Aston Villa	3-1	Rush 3		19566		1	6		10	3	4	8	2	5	7	9	11		
1	Feb	1	WATFORD	3-0	Rush, Nicol, Whelan		20746		1	6		10	3	4	8	2	5	7	9			11
1		4	Sunderland	0-0			25646		1	6		10	3	4	8	2	5	7	9			11
1		11	ARSENAL	2-1	Kennedy, Neal		34642		1	6		10	3	4	8	2	5	7	9			11
1		18	Luton Town	0-0			14877		1	6	7	10	3	4	8	2			9	11		5
1		25	QUEEN'S PARK RANGERS	2-0	Rush, Robinson		32206		1	6		10	3	4	8	2		7	9	11		5
1	Mar	3	Everton	1-1	Rush		51245		1	6		10	3	4	8	2	12	7	9	11		5
1		10	TOTTENHAM HOTSPUR	3-1	Dalglish, Whelan, Lee		36718	7	1	6		10	3	4	8	2			9	11		5
1		16	Southampton	0-2			19998		1	6		10	3	4	8	2		11	12	9		5
1		31	Watford	2-0	Wark, Rush		21293	7	1	6			3	4	8	2			9	11	10	5
1	Apr	7	WEST HAM UNITED	6-0	Rush 2, Souness 2, Dalglish, Whelan		38359	7	1	6			3	4	8	2			9	11	10	5
1		14	Stoke City	0-2			24372	7	1	6		12	3	4	8	2			9	11	10	5
1		18	Leicester City	3-3	Whelan, Rush, Wark		27280	7	1	6			3	4	8	2			9	11	10	5
1		21	WEST BROMWICH ALB.	3-0	Souness, Dalglish, og (McNaught)		35320	7	1	6			3	4	8	2			9	11	10	5
1		28	IPSWICH TOWN	2-2	Kennedy, Rush		32069	7	1	6		11	3	4	8	2	12		9		10	5
1	May	5	Birmingham City	0-0			18817	7	1	6			3	4	8	2			9	11	10	5
1		7	COVENTRY CITY	5-0	Rush 4 (1p), Hansen		33393	7	1	6			3	4	8	2			9	11	10	5
1		12	Notts County	0-0			18745	7	1	6			3	4	8	2			9	11	10	5
1		15	NORWICH CITY	1-1	Rush		38837	7	1	6		10	3	4	8	2			9	11		5

		Apps	33	42	42	1	28	42	42	42	41	19	23	41	37	9	20
		Subs					4	1				4	1				3
		Goals	7		1		2	2		2	1	6	6	32	7	2	3

Two own goals

F.A. Cup

R3	Jan	6	NEWCASTLE UNITED	4-0	Rush 2, Robinson, Johnston		33566		1	6		10	3	4	8	2	5	7	9	11		
R4		29	Brighton & Hove Albion	0-2			19057		1	6		10	3	4	8	2	5	7	9	11		12

F.L. Cup

R2	Oct	5	Brentford	4-1	Rush 2, Robinson, Souness		17859	7	1	6		5	3	4	8		2	10	9	11		
R2s		25	BRENTFORD	4-0	Souness, Hodgson, Dalglish, Robinson		9092	7	1	6	9	5	3	4	8	2		10		11		
R3	Nov	8	Fulham	1-1	Rush		20142	7	1	6			3	4	8	2	5	10	9	11		
rep		22	FULHAM	1-1	Dalglish		15783	7	1	6		12	3	4	8	2	5	10	9	11		
rep2		29	Fulham	1-0	Souness		20905		1	6		7	3	4	8	2	5	10	9	11		12
R4	Dec	20	Birmingham City	1-1	Souness		17405	7	1	6		10	3	4	8	2	5		9	11		
rep		22	BIRMINGHAM CITY	3-0	Rush 2 (1p), Nicol		11638	7	1	6	12	10	3	4	8	2	5		9	11		
R5	Jan	17	Sheffield Wednesday	2-2	Nicol, Neal		49357		1	6		10	3	4	8	2	5	7	9	11		
rep		25	SHEFFIELD WEDNESDAY	3-0	Rush 2, Robinson		40485		1	6		10	3	4	8	2	5	7	9	11		
SF1	Feb	7	WALSALL	2-2	Whelan 2		31073		1	6	12	10	3		8	2	5	7	9			11
SF2		14	Walsall	2-0	Rush, Whelan		19591		1	6	7	10	3	4	8	2			9	11		5
F	Mar	25	Everton	0-0			100000		1	6			10	3	4	8	2		12	9	11	5
rep		28	Everton	1-0	Souness		52089	7	1	6		10	3	4	8	2			9	11		5

Final at Wembley Stadium, Final replay at Maine Road
R3, R3 replay and Final a.e.t.
G Gillespie played at 4 in SF1

European Cup

R1.1	Sep	14	OB (Odense)	1-0	Dalglish		30000	7	1	6		5	3	4	8	2		10	9	11		
R1.2		28	OB (ODENSE)	5-0	Robinson 2, Dalglish 2, og (Clausen)		14985	7	1	6	12	5	3	4	8		2	10	9	11		
R2.1	Oct	19	ATHLETIC BILBAO	0-0			33063	7	1	6		5	3	4	8	2		10	9	11		
R2.2	Nov	2	Athletic Bilbao	1-0	Rush		47500	7	1	6	12		3	4	8	2	5	10	9	11		
QF1	Mar	7	BENFICA	1-0	Rush		39096	12	1	6		10	3	4	8	2		7	9	11		5
QF2		21	Benfica	4-1	Whelan 2, Johnston, Rush		70000	7	1	6		10	3	4	8	2			9	11		5
SF1	Apr	11	DINAMO BUCHAREST	1-0	Lee		36941	7	1	6		10	3	4	8	2			9	11		5
SF2		25	Dinamo Bucharest	2-1	Rush 2		60000	7	1	6		10	3	4	8	2	12		9	11		5
F	May	30	Roma	1-1	Neal		69693	7	1	6		10	3	4	8	2	14		9	11		5

Final won on 4-2 penalties, a.e.t. Played at the Olympic Stadium, Rome

F.A. Charity Shield

	Aug	20	Manchester United	0-2			92000	7	1	6	13	12	3	4	8	2		10	9	11		

At Wembley Stadium
PB Thompson played at 5 (subbed)

122

Everton 1984/85

Goodison Park

			Date	Opponent	Score	Scorers	Att	Atkins IL	Bailey JA	Bracewell PW	Curran E	Danskin J	Gray AM	Harper A	Heath AP	Hughes DJ	Morrissey JJ	Mountfield DN	Oldroyd DR	Ratcliffe K	Reid P	Richardson K	Rimmer N	Sharp GM	Sheedy KM	Southall N	Steven TMcG	Stevens MG	Van Den Hauwe PWR	Wakenshaw RA	Walsh D	Wilkinson P
		Aug	25	TOTTENHAM HOTSPUR	1-4	Heath (p)	35596		3	10					12		8			5		4	6	11		9		1	7	2			
			27	West Bromwich Albion	1-2	Heath (p)	14062		3		7						8			5		4	6	11		9		1	10	2			
			31	Chelsea	1-0	Richardson	17734		3	10							8			5		4	6	11		9		1	7	2			
15		Sep	4	IPSWICH TOWN	1-1	Heath	20046		3	10	12						8			5		4	6	11		9		1	7	2			
13			8	COVENTRY CITY	2-1	Sharp, Steven	20026		3	10	12						8			5		4	6	11		9		1	7	2			
5			15	Newcastle United	3-2	Gray, Sheedy, Steven	29452		3	10				9			8			5		4	6				11	1	7	2			
6			22	SOUTHAMPTON	2-2	Mountfield, Sharp	22313		3	10							8			5		4	6			9	11	1	7	2			
6			29	Watford	5-4	Heath 2, Mountfield, Sharp, Steven	18335		3	10	12						8			5		4	6			9	11	1	7	2			
8		Oct	6	Arsenal	0-1		37049			10							8			5		4	6	11		9		1	7	2	3		
6			13	ASTON VILLA	2-1	Heath, Sharp	25043			10					11		8			5		4	6			9		1	7	2	3		
4			20	Liverpool	1-0	Sharp	45145			10					11		8			5		4	6			9		1	7	2	3		
2			27	MANCHESTER UNITED	5-0	Sheedy 2, Heath, Sharp, Stevens	40742			10				12		8			5		4	6			9	11	1	7	2	3			
1		Nov	3	LEICESTER CITY	3-0	Heath, Sheedy, Steven	27756			10				12		8			5		4	6			9	11	1	7	2	3			
1			10	West Ham United	1-0	Heath	24089			10						8			5		4	6			9	11	1	7	2	3			
1			17	STOKE CITY	4-0	Heath 2, Reid, Steven	26684			10						8			5		4	6			9	11	1	7	2	3			
1			24	Norwich City	2-4	Sharp, Sheedy	16477			10				12		8			5		4	6			9	11	1	7	2	3			
1		Dec	1	SHEFFIELD WEDNESDAY	1-1	Sharp (p)	35409			10				12		8			5		4	6			9	11	1	7	2	3			
1			8	Queen's Park Rangers	0-0		14338			10						8			5		4	6			9	11	1	7	2	3			
1			15	NOTTM. FOREST	5-0	Sharp 2, Reid, Sheedy, Steven	22453			10	12					8			5		4	6			9	11	1	7	2	3			
3			22	CHELSEA	3-4	Sharp 2 (1p), Bracewell	29867		3	10						8			5		4	6			9	11	1	7	2				
2			26	Sunderland	2-1	Mountfield 2	19714	2	3	10						8			5		4	6			9	11	1	7					
2			29	Ipswich Town	2-0	Sharp 2	16589		3	10	8								5		4	6			9	11	1	7		2			
2		Jan	1	LUTON TOWN	2-1	Steven 2	31641		3	10	8								5		4	6			9	11	1	7		2			
1			12	NEWCASTLE UNITED	4-0	Sheedy 2, Mountfield, Sharp	32156			10				8					5		4	6			9	11	1	7	2	3			
1		Feb	2	WATFORD	4-0	Stevens 2, Sheedy, Steven	34064			10	12			8					5		4	6			9	11	1	7	2	3			
1			23	Leicester City	2-1	Gray 2	17345			10				9	8				5		4	6				11	1	7	2	3			
1		Mar	2	Manchester United	1-1	Mountfield	51150			10	8			9					5		4	6				11	1	7	2	3			
1			16	Aston Villa	1-1	Richardson	22625			10				9	11				5		4		6		8		1	7	2	3			
1			23	ARSENAL	2-0	Gray, Sharp	36364							9	10				5		4	6	11		8		1	7	2	3			
1			30	Southampton	2-1	Richardson 2	18754			10				9					5		4	6	11		8		1	7	2	3			12
1		Apr	3	Tottenham Hotspur	2-1	Gray, Steven	48108			10				9	12				5		4	6			8	11	1	7	2	3			
1			6	SUNDERLAND	4-1	Gray 2, Sharp, Steven	35898		3	10				9	12				5		4	6			8	11	1	7	2				
1			16	WEST BROMWICH ALB.	4-1	Sharp 2 (1p), Atkins, Sheedy	29671	5		10				9	12						4	6			8	11	1	7	2	3			
1			20	Stoke City	2-0	Sharp, Sheedy	18344	5		10				9							4	6			8	11	1	7	2	3			
1			27	NORWICH CITY	3-0	Bracewell, Mountfield, Steven	32064			10				9	11				5		4		6		8		1	7	2	3			
1		May	4	Sheffield Wednesday	1-0	Gray	37381			10				9					5		4	6			8	11	1	7	2	3			
1			6	QUEEN'S PARK RANGERS	2-0	Mountfield, Sharp	50317			10				9					5		4	6			8	11	1	7	2	3			
1			8	WEST HAM UNITED	3-0	Mountfield 2, Gray	32606	4		10				9					5			6	12		8	11	1	7	2	3			
1			11	Nottingham Forest	0-1		18784	10							8				5	12	4		6			11	1	7	2	3			9
1			23	LIVERPOOL	1-0	Wilkinson	50947	10	3					9	7						4		6			11	1		2	5	12		8
1			26	Coventry City	1-4	Wilkinson	21596			10					2		5				4		6		9	11	1	7		3			8
1			28	Luton Town	0-2		11509		3			10		4		2	7					6	12			1				5	8	11	9
						Apps		6	15	37	4	1	21	10	17	2	1	37	0	40	36	14	0	36	29	42	40	37	31	1	1	4
						Subs					5		5	3					1			1	1							1		1
						Goals		1		2			9		11			10			2	4			21	11		12	3			2

F.A. Charity Shield

	Date	Opponent	Score	Scorers	Att																								
	Aug 18	Liverpool	1-0	og (Grobbelaar)	100000		3	10						8			5		4	6	11		9		1	7	2			

At Wembley Stadium

F.A. Cup

		Date	Opponent	Score	Scorers	Att																								
R3	Jan	4	Leeds United	2-0	Sharp (p), Sheedy	21211	12		10					8			5		4	6			9	11	1	7	2	3			
R4		26	DONCASTER ROVERS	2-0	Steven, Stevens	37535			10					8			5		4	6			9	11	1	7	2	3			
R5	Feb	16	TELFORD UNITED	3-0	Reid, Sheedy (p), Steven	47402			10					8	12		5		4	6			9	11	1	7	2	3			
R6	Mar	9	IPSWICH TOWN	2-2	Mountfield, Sheedy	36468			10	8			9				5		4	6				11	1	7	2	3			
rep		13	Ipswich Town	1-0	Sharp (p)	27737			10				9	11			5		4	6			8		1	7	2	3			
SF	Apr	13	Luton Town	2-1	Mountfield, Sheedy	45289			10				9				5		4	6			8	11	1	7	2	3			
F	May	18	Manchester United	0-1		100000			10				9				5		4	6			8	11	1	7	2	3			

SF at Villa Park, Final at Wembley Stadium

F.L. Cup

		Date	Opponent	Score	Scorers	Att																								
R2	Sep	26	Sheffield United	2-2	Mountfield, Sharp	16345		3	10						8			5		4	6			9	11	1	7	2			
R2s	Oct	10	SHEFFIELD UNITED	4-0	Bracewell, Heath, Mountfield, Sharp	18740			10					8			5		4	6	11		9		1	7	2	3			
R3		30	Manchester United	2-1	Sharp (p), og (Gidman)	50918			10					11	8			5		4	6			9		1	7	2	3			
R4	Nov	20	GRIMSBY TOWN	0-1		26298			10				12		8			5		4	6			9	11	1	7	2				

European Cup-Winners' Cup

		Date	Opponent	Score	Scorers	Att																								
R1.1	Sep	19	UC Dublin	0-0		10000		3	10	12					8			5		4	6			9	11	1	7	2			
R1.2	Oct	2	UC DUBLIN	1-0	Sharp	16277		3	10	11					8			5		4	6			9		1	7	2		12	
R2.1		24	Inter Bratislava	1-0	Bracewell	15000		3	10					11	8			5		4	6			9		1	7	2			
R2.2	Nov	7	INTER BRATISLAVA	3-0	Heath, Sharp, Sheedy	25007		3	10					12	8		13	5		4	6			9	11	1	7	2			
R3.1	Mar	6	FORTUNA SITTARD	3-0	Gray 3	25782			10	8			9					5		4	6	12			11	1	7	2	3		
R3.2		20	Fortuna Sittard	2-0	Reid, Sharp	20000	12			8				10				5		4	6	11		9		1	7	2	3	13	
SF1	Apr	10	Bayern Munich	0-0		67000			10					8				5		4	6	11		9		1	7	2	3		
SF2		24	BAYERN MUNICH	3-1	Gray, Sharp, Steven	49476			10				9					5		4	6			8	11	1	7	2	3		
F	May	15	Rapid Vienna	3-1	Gray, Sheedy, Steven	38500			10				9					5		4	6			8	11	1	7	2	3		

Final in Rotterdam

Liverpool 1985/86

Anfield

							Beglin JM	Dalglish KM	Gillespie GT	Grobbelaar BD	Hansen AD	Johnston CP	Kennedy AP	Lawrenson MT	Lee S	MacDonald KD	McMahon S	Molby J	Neal PG	Nicol S	Rush IJ	Walsh PAM	Wark J	Whelan RA
	Aug	17	ARSENAL	2-0	Whelan, Nicol	38261	11	7		1	6		3	4				10	2	8	9			5
		21	Aston Villa	2-2	Rush, Molby	20197	11			1	6	12	3	4				10	2	8	9		7	5
		24	Newcastle United	0-1		29670	11	7		1	6	12	3	4				10	2	8	9			5
4		26	IPSWICH TOWN	5-0	Rush 2, Nicol, Molby, Johnston	29383				1	6	7	3	4	11			10	2	8	9	12		5
8		31	West Ham United	2-2	Johnston, Whelan	19762				1	6	7	3	4	11			10	2	8	9			5
4	Sep	3	NOTTM. FOREST	2-0	Whelan 2	27135				1	6	7	3	4	11			10	2	8	9			5
2		7	WATFORD	3-1	Neal (p), Johnston, Rush	31395				1	6	7	3	4	11			10	2	8	9			5
4		14	Oxford United	2-2	Rush, Johnston	11474				1	6	7	3	4			11	10	2	8	9	12		5
2		21	Everton	3-2	Dalglish, Rush, McMahon	51509	3	7		1	6	8		4			11	10	12	2	9			5
2		28	TOTTENHAM HOTSPUR	4-1	Molby 2 (2p), Lawrenson, Rush	41521	3	7		1	6	8		4		12	11	10	2		9			5
2	Oct	5	Queen's Park Rangers	1-2	Walsh	24621	3			1	6	8		4			11	10	2		9	7		5
2		12	SOUTHAMPTON	1-0	McMahon	31070	3	7		1		8		4		12	11	6	2		9		10	5
2		19	Manchester United	1-1	Johnston	54492	3			1	6	8		4		12	11	10		2	9		7	5
2		26	LUTON TOWN	3-2	Walsh 2, Molby	31488	3	7		1	6	8		4			11	10		2		9		5
2	Nov	2	LEICESTER CITY	1-0	Rush	31718	3	12		1	6	8		4			11	10		2	9	7		5
2		9	Coventry City	3-0	Beglin, Walsh, Rush	16947	3			1	6	8		4			11	10	12	2	9	7		5
2		16	WEST BROMWICH ALB.	4-1	Nicol, Molby, Lawrenson, Walsh	28407	3	12		1	6	8		4			11	10		2	9	7		5
2		23	Birmingham City	2-0	Rush, Walsh	15062	3			1	6	8		4			11	10		2	9	7		5
2		30	CHELSEA	1-1	Molby (p)	38482	3			1	6	8		4			11	10		2	9	7		5
2	Dec	7	ASTON VILLA	3-0	Molby, Walsh. Johnston	29418	3			1	6	8		4	5	11		10		2	9	7		
2		14	Arsenal	0-2		35048	3			1	6	8		4	5	12	11	10		2	9	7		
2		21	NEWCASTLE UNITED	1-1	Nicol	30746	3	12		1	6	8		4	5		11			2	9	7	10	
2		26	Manchester City	0-1		35584	3	12		1	6	8		4		10	11			2	9	7		5
4		28	Nottingham Forest	1-1	MacDonald	27141	3	7		1	6	8		4	12	10		11		2	9			5
3	Jan	1	SHEFFIELD WEDNESDAY	2-2	Rush, Walsh	38964		7		1	6	8		4		3	11	10		2	9	12		5
3		12	Watford	3-2	Walsh 2, Rush	16967				1	6	8		4		3	11	10		2	9	7		5
3		18	WEST HAM UNITED	3-1	Molby (p), Rush, Walsh	41056			3	1	6	8		4				10		2	9	7	11	5
4	Feb	1	Ipswich Town	1-2	Whelan	20551	3		11	1	6	8		4	9			10		2		7	12	5
3		9	MANCHESTER UNITED	1-1	Wark	35004	3		11	1	6	8		4	2			10			9	7	12	5
3		22	EVERTON	0-2		45445	3		7	1	6	8		4	2	12	11	10			9			5
3	Mar	2	Tottenham Hotspur	2-1	Molby, Rush	16436	3		7	1	6	8		4	2		11	10			9			5
2		8	QUEEN'S PARK RANGERS	4-1	McMahon 2, Rush, Wark	26219	3	7		1	6	12		4	2		11	10			9		8	5
2		15	Southampton	2-1	Wark, Rush	19784	3		7	1	6	8		4	2			10			9		11	5
2		22	OXFORD UNITED	6-0	Rush 2, Molby 2(1p), Lawrenson, Whelan	37861	3	7	2	1	6	8		4			11			12	9			5
2		29	Sheffield Wednesday	0-0		37946	3		2	1	6	8					12	11	10		4	9	7	5
1		31	MANCHESTER CITY	2-0	McMahon 2	43316	3	7	2	1	6	8					11	10			4	9		5
1	Apr	12	COVENTRY CITY	5-0	Whelan 3, Molby, Rush	42729	3	7	2	1	6	8					12	10			4	9	11	5
1		16	Luton Town	1-0	Johnston	15390	3	7	2	1	6	8				12	11	10			4	9		5
1		19	West Bromwich Albion	2-1	Dalglish, Rush	22010	3	7		1	6	8		4			11	10		2		9		5
1		26	BIRMINGHAM CITY	5-0	Gillespie 3 (1p), Rush, Molby (p)	42021	3	7	2	1	6	8					11	10			4	9		5
1		30	Leicester City	2-0	Rush, Whelan	25799	3	7	2	1	6	8			12		11	10			4	9		5
1	May	3	Chelsea	1-0	Dalglish	43900	3	7	2	1	6	8			10		11				4	9		5

	Apps	Subs	Goals
Beglin JM	34		1
Dalglish KM	17	4	3
Gillespie GT	14		3
Grobbelaar BD	42		
Hansen AD	41		
Johnston CP	38	3	7
Kennedy AP	8	1	
Lawrenson MT	36	2	3
Lee S	13	7	
MacDonald KD	10		1
McMahon S	23	2	6
Molby J	39	1	14
Neal PG	11		1
Nicol S	33	3	4
Rush IJ	40	2	22
Walsh PAM	17		11
Wark J	7	3	3
Whelan RA	39		10

F.A. Cup

R3	Jan	4	NORWICH CITY	5-0	MacDonald, Walsh, McMahon, Whelan, Wark	29082				1	6	8		4		3	11	10		2	9	7	12	5
R4		26	Chelsea	2-1	Rush, Lawrenson	33625	3		11	1	6	8		4				10		2	9	7		5
R5	Feb	15	York City	1-1	Molby (p)	12443	3	7		1	6	8		4	2			10			9		5	
rep		18	YORK CITY	3-1	Wark, Molby, Dalglish	29362	3	7	11	1	6	12		4	2			10			9		8	5
R6	Mar	11	WATFORD	0-0		36775	3	7	8	1	6			4	2		11	10			9			5
rep		17	Watford	2-1	Molby (p), Rush	28097	3	7	2	1	6	8		4			11	10			9			5
SF	Apr	5	Southampton	2-0	Rush 2	44605	3	7	2	1	6	8					11	10			4	9	12	5
F	May	10	Everton	3-1	Rush 2, Johnston	98000	3	7		1	6	8		4		11		10		2	9			5

R5 replay, R6 replay and semi-final a.e.t.
SF at White Hart Lane, Final at Wembley Stadium

Played in R5: M Seagraves (at 11)

F.L. Cup

R2	Sep	24	OLDHAM ATHLETIC	3-0	McMahon 2, Rush	16150	3			1	6	10		4	8	12	11		2		9	7		5
R2s	Oct	9	Oldham Athletic	5-2	Whelan 2, Wark, Rush, MacDonald	7719	3	7		1	6			4		12	11		2		9		10	5
R3		29	BRIGHTON & HOVE ALB.	4-0	Walsh 3, Dalglish	15291	3	7		1	6	8		4			11	10		2		9		5
R4	Nov	26	MANCHESTER UNITED	2-1	Molby 2 (1p)	41291	3			1	6	8		4			11	10		2	9	7		5
R5	Jan	21	IPSWICH TOWN	3-0	Walsh, Whelan, Rush	19762	3		11	1	6	8		4				10		2	9	7	12	5
SF1	Feb	12	Queen's Park Rangers	0-1		15051	3			1	6	8		4				10			9		7	5
SF2	Mar	5	QUEEN'S PARK RANGERS	2-2	McMahon, Johnston	23863	3		7	1	6	8		4	2		11	10			9			5

Played in SF1: M Seagraves (at 11)

Everton 1986/87

Goodison Park

						Adams NJ	Aspinall WG	Clarke W	Harper A	Heath AP	Langley KJ	Marshall IP	Mimms RA	Mountfield DN	Pointon NG	Power PC	Ratcliffe K	Reid P	Richardson K	Sharp GM	Sheedy KM	Snodin I	Southall N	Steven TMcG	Stevens MG	Van Den Hauwe PWR	Watson D	Wilkinson P
	Aug	23	NOTTM. FOREST	2-0	Sheedy 2	35222				2	8	6		1			3	4		10	9	11			7			5	12
		25	Sheffield Wednesday	2-2	Langley, Sharp	33007				2	8	6		1			3	4			9	11			7			5	10
		30	Coventry City	1-1	Marshall	13662	10			2	8	6	12	1			3	4			9	11			7			5	
2	Sep	2	OXFORD UNITED	3-1	Harper, Langley, Steven (p)	26094	10			2	8	6		1			3	4			9	11			7			5	
5		6	QUEEN'S PARK RANGERS	0-0		30182	10			2	8	6	12	1			3	4			9	11			7			5	
3		13	Wimbledon	2-1	Sheedy, Sharp	11708				2	8	6		1	10		3	4			9	11			7			5	12
2		21	MANCHESTER UNITED	3-1	Heath, Sharp, Sheedy	26243	12				8	6		1	2		3	4			9	11			7			5	10
3		27	Tottenham Hotspur	0-2		28007	12				8	6		1	2		3	4			9	11			7			5	10
5	Oct	4	ARSENAL	0-1		30018	8	12				6		1	2		3	4			9	11			7			5	
7		11	Charlton Athletic	2-3	Sheedy 2	10564	7			2	10	6		1			3	4			9	11			8			5	12
6		18	Southampton	2-0	Steven (p), Wilkinson	18009		12		2	8	11		1	6		3	4			9				7			5	10
3		25	WATFORD	3-2	Mountfield 2, Steven (p)	28588	7			2	8	6			5		3	4			9			1	10				11
6	Nov	2	West Ham United	0-1		19094		12		2	8	6			5		3	4			9	11		1	7				10
8		8	CHELSEA	2-2	Steven (p), Sheedy	29748				2	8	6			5		3	4			9	11		1	7				10
7		15	Leicester City	2-0	Heath, Sheedy	13450	10	12		2	8	6			5		3	4			9	11		1	7				
5		23	LIVERPOOL	0-0		46655	10			2	8	6			5		3	4			9	11		1	7				12
4		29	Manchester City	3-1	Heath 2, Power	27097	10			2	8				5	3	6	4			9	11		1	7				12
3	Dec	6	NORWICH CITY	4-0	Heath, Power, Pointon, Steven (p)	26755				10	8					3	6	4			9	11		1	7	2		5	12
3		13	Luton Town	0-1		11151				10	8					3	6	4			9	11		1	7	2		5	12
4		20	WIMBLEDON	3-0	Heath, Sheedy, Steven	25562				10	8					3	6	4	12		9	11		1	7	2		5	
2		26	Newcastle United	4-0	Steven 2, Heath, Power	35225				10	8					3	6	4			9	11		1	7	2		5	12
2		28	LEICESTER CITY	5-1	Heath 2, Sheedy, Wilkinson, og (O'Neill)	39748		12		10	8					3	6	4				11		1	7	2		5	9
2	Jan	1	ASTON VILLA	3-0	Harper, Sheedy, Steven	40219		12		10	8					3	6	4				11		1	7	2		5	9
2		3	Queen's Park Rangers	1-0	Sharp	16636				10	8					3	6	4			9	11		1	7	2		5	
2		17	SHEFFIELD WEDNESDAY	2-0	Steven (p), Watson	33021				10	8					3	6	4			9	11	12	1	7	2		5	
2		25	Nottingham Forest	0-1		17009				10	8				5	12	3	4				11	6	1	7	2			9
1	Feb	7	COVENTRY CITY	3-1	Heath, Steven (p), Stevens	30408				12	8						11	4	6	9		10	1	7	2	3	5	
1		14	Oxford United	1-1	Wilkinson	11787				12	8						11	4	6			10	1	7	2	3	5	9
1		28	Manchester United	0-0		47421				8	9						11	4	6			10	1	7	2	3	5	12
2	Mar	8	Watford	1-2	Heath	14035			9		8						11	4	6			10	1	7	2	3	5	12
2		14	SOUTHAMPTON	3-0	Power, Watson, og (Wright)	26587			9	12	8						11	4	6			10	1	7	2	3	5	
2		21	CHARLTON ATHLETIC	2-1	Steven (p), Stevens	27309			9	12	8						11	4	6			10	1	7	2	3	5	
2		28	Arsenal	1-0	Clarke	36208			9	12	8						11	4	6			10	1	7	2	3	5	
1	Apr	4	Chelsea	2-1	Harper, og (McLaughlin)	21914			9	10	8					12	3	4	6			11	1	7	2		5	
1		11	WEST HAM UNITED	4-0	Clarke, Reid, Stevens, Watson	35746			9	10	8						3	4	6			11	1	7	2		5	
1		18	Aston Villa	1-0	Sheedy	31218			9	12	8						3	4				11	10	1	7	2		5	
1		20	NEWCASTLE UNITED	3-0	Clarke 3	43587			9	6	8					3	11	4					10	1	7	2		5	
1		25	Liverpool	1-3	Sheedy	44827			9		8						3	4	6			11	10	1	7	2		5	
1	May	2	MANCHESTER CITY	0-0		37548			9	12	8						11	4	6				10	1	7	2	3	5	
1		4	Norwich City	1-0	Van den Hauwe	22278					8						11	4	6	9			10	1	7	2	3	5	
1		9	LUTON TOWN	3-1	Steven 2 (2p), Sharp	44097				11	8							4	6		9		10	1	7	2	3	5	
1		11	TOTTENHAM HOTSPUR	1-0	Mountfield	28302	11				7	8			12			4	6		9		10	1		2	3	5	

						Apps	10	0	10	29	41	16	0	11	12	10	40	42	15	1	27	28	15	31	41	25	11	35	12
						Subs	2	6		7			2		1	2			1			1	1						10
						Goals			5	3	11	2	1		3	1	4		1		5	13			14	3	1	3	3

Three own goals

F.A. Charity Shield

	Aug	16	Liverpool	1-1	Heath	88231	12			2	8	6	5	1			3	4		10	9	11			7				13

F.A. Cup

R3	Jan	10	SOUTHAMPTON	2-1	Sharp 2	32320				10	8					3	6	4			9	11		1	7	2		5	
R4		31	Bradford City	1-0	Snodin	15519					8						11	4	6				10	1	7	2	3	5	9
R5	Feb	22	Wimbledon	1-3	Wilkinson	9924				13	8					12	11	4	6				10	1	7	2	3	5	9

F.L. Cup

R2	Sep	24	NEWPORT COUNTY	4-0	Wilkinson 2, Heath, Langley	11957	11				8	6		1	2		3	4			9				7			5	10
R2s	Oct	7	Newport County	5-1	Wilkinson 3, Sharp, og (Mullen)	7172	7	13		2		6		1		12	3	4			9	11			8			5	10
R3		28	SHEFFIELD WEDNESDAY	4-0	Wilkinson 2, Heath, Mountfield	24638				2	8	6			5		3	4			9	11		1	7				10
R4	Nov	19	Norwich City	4-1	Heath, Sharp, Sheedy, Steven (p)	17988	10			2	8	6			5		3	4			9	11		1	7				
R5	Jan	21	LIVERPOOL	0-1		53323				10	8				5	3	6	4			9	11	13	1	7	2			12

Full Members Cup

R1	Dec	3	NEWCASTLE UNITED	5-2	Sheedy, Sharp 3 (1p), Heath	7530	10			2	8					12	3	6	4		9	11			7			5	
R2	Mar	3	CHARLTON ATHLETIC	2-2	Wilkinson, Steven	7914	11			6	8	12					4	3					10	1	7		2	5	9

R2 lost 4-6 on penalties a.e.t.   J Ebbrell played at 13 in R2

Liverpool 1987/88

Anfield

							Ablett GI	Aldridge JW	Barnes JCB	Beardsley PA	Dalglish KM	Gillespie GT	Grobbelaar BD	Hansen AD	Hooper MD	Houghton RJ	Johnston CP	Lawrenson MT	MacDonald KD	McMahon S	Molby J	Nicol S	Spackman NJ	Venison B	Walsh PAM	Wark J	Watson AF	Whelan RA
	Aug	15	Arsenal	2-1	Aldridge, Nicol	54703		8	10	7		2	1	6			9			11		4		3	12			5
		29	Coventry City	4-1	Nicol 2, Aldridge (p), Beardsley	27509		8	10	7		2	1	6			9			11		4		3	12			5
	Sep	5	West Ham United	1-1	Aldridge (p)	29865		8	10	7		2	1	6						11		4	9	3				5
7		12	OXFORD UNITED	2-0	Aldridge, Barnes	42266		8	10	7		2	1	6						11		4	9	3	12	14		5
3		15	CHARLTON ATHLETIC	3-2	Aldridge (p), Hansen, McMahon	36637		8	10	7		2	1	6					12	11		4	9	3				5
3		20	Newcastle United	4-1	Nicol 3, Aldridge	23236		8	10	7		2	1	6					9	11		4	12	3				5
2		29	DERBY COUNTY	4-0	Aldridge 3 (2p), Beardsley	42405		8	10	7		2	1	6			9		14	11		4		3	12			5
2	Oct	3	PORTSMOUTH	4-0	Beardsley, McMahon, Aldridge, Whelan (p)	44357		8	10	7		2	1	6			9		14	11		4		3	12			5
1		17	QUEEN'S PARK RANGERS	4-0	Barnes 2, Aldridge (p), Johnston	43735		8	10	7		2	1	6			9		14	11		4		3	12			5
1		24	Luton Town	1-0	Gillespie	11997		8	10	7		2	1	6	9					11		4		3				5
1	Nov	1	EVERTON	2-0	McMahon, Beardsley	43760		8	10	7		2	1	6			9	3		11		4						5
		4	Wimbledon	1-1	Houghton	13452		8	10	7		2	1	6			12	9	3	11		4						5
2		15	Manchester United	1-1	Aldridge	47101		8	10	7		2	1	6				9	3	11		4						5
2		21	NORWICH CITY	0-0		37446		8	10	7		2	1	6	9		12	3		11		4						5
1		24	WATFORD	4-0	McMahon, Aldridge, Houghton, Barnes	32396		8	10	7		2	1	6	9			3		11		4	12		14			5
1		28	Tottenham Hotspur	2-0	McMahon, Johnston	47362		8				2	1	6	9		14	3		11		4	12		7			5
1	Dec	6	CHELSEA	2-1	Aldridge (p), McMahon	31211		8	10	7		2	1	6	9		12	3		11		4						5
1		12	Southampton	2-2	Barnes 2	19507	12	8	10	7		2	1	6	9			3		11		4						5
1		19	SHEFFIELD WEDNESDAY	1-0	Gillespie	35383		8	10	7		2	1	6	9		12			11		4		3				5
1		26	Oxford United	3-0	Aldridge, Barnes, McMahon	13627		8	10	7		2	1	6	9		12			11		4	14	3				5
1		28	NEWCASTLE UNITED	4-0	Aldridge 2 (1p), Houghton, McMahon	44637		8	10	7		2	1	6	9		12			11		4	14	3				5
1	Jan	1	COVENTRY CITY	4-0	Beardsley 2, Aldridge, Houghton	38790	12	8	10	7		2	1	6	9					11		4	14	3				5
1		16	ARSENAL	2-0	Aldridge, Beardsley	44294		8	10	7		2		6	1	9		3		11		4	12					5
1		23	Charlton Athletic	2-0	Beardsley, Barnes	28095		8	10	7		2		6	1	9	12			11		4	14	3				5
1	Feb	6	WEST HAM UNITED	0-0		42049	2	8	10	7			1	6		9	12			11		4	5	3				
1		13	Watford	4-1	Beardsley 2, Barnes, Aldridge	23838	2	8	10	7			1	6		9	12			11	14	4	5	3				
1		27	Portsmouth	2-0	Barnes 2	28117	2	8	10	7			1	6		9				11		4	5	3				
1	Mar	5	Queen's Park Rangers	1-0	Barnes	23171	2		10	7			1	6		9	8			11		4	5			3		
1		16	Derby County	1-1	Johnston	26367	3		10	7		2	1	6		9	8			11	12	4	5					
1		20	Everton	0-1		43930	3		10	7		2	1	6		9	8			11	12	4	5					
1		26	WIMBLEDON	2-1	Aldridge, Barnes	36464	3	8	10	7	12	2	1	6		9				11	14	4	5					
1	Apr	2	Nottingham Forest	1-2	Aldridge (p)	29188	3	8	10	12		2	1	6		14	9			11	7	4	5					
		4	MANCHESTER UNITED	3-3	Beardsley, McMahon, Gillespie	43497	3	8	10	7		2	1	6		9	12			11		4	5					
1		13	NOTTM. FOREST	5-0	Aldridge 2, Houghton, Gillespie, Beardsley	39535	3	8	10	7		2	1	6		9	12			11	14	4	5					
1		20	Norwich City	0-0		23681	3	8		7		2	1	6		9	10			11		4	5					
1		23	TOTTENHAM HOTSPUR	1-0	Beardsley	44798	3	8		7		2	1	6		9	10			11		4	5					
1		30	Chelsea	1-1	Barnes	35624		8	10	12			1	6		9	7			11		4	5				2	3
1	May	2	SOUTHAMPTON	1-1	Aldridge	37610	3	8	10	7		2	1	6		9	12			11		4	5					14
1		7	Sheffield Wednesday	5-1	Johnston 2, Beardsley 2, Barnes	35893	3		10	7		2	1	6		9	8			11	14	4	5					12
1		9	LUTON TOWN	1-1	Aldridge	30374	3	8	10		12	2	1			9	7		14	11		4	5					6

	Apps	15	36	38	36	0	35	38	39	2	26	18	10	0	40	1	40	19	18	1	0	2	26
	Subs	2			2	2					2	12	4	1		6		8		7	1		2
	Goals		26	15	15		4			1		5	5			9		6						1

F.A. Cup

R3	Jan	9	Stoke City	0-0		31979		8	10	7		2		6	1	9		3		11		4						5
R3		12	STOKE CITY	1-0	Beardsley	39147		8	10	7		2		6	1	9	12	3		11		4						5
R4		31	Aston Villa	2-0	Barnes, Beardsley	46324	3	8	10	7			1	6		9				11		4	5	2				
R5	Feb	21	Everton	1-0	Houghton	48270	3	8	10	7			1	6		9				11		4	5	2				
R6	Mar	13	Manchester City	4-0	Houghton, Beardsley, Johnston, Barnes	44047	3		10	7		2	1	6		9	8			11		4	5					
SF	Apr	9	Nottingham Forest	2-1	Aldridge 2 (1p)	51627	3	8	10	7		2	1	6		9				11		4	5					
F	May	14	Wimbledon	0-1		98203	3	8	10	7		2	1	6		9	14			11	12	4	5					

SF at Hillsborough, Final at Wembley Stadium

F.L. Cup

R2	Sep	23	Blackburn Rovers	1-1	Nicol	13924		8	10	7			1	6			9			11		4	2	3	12			5
R2s	Oct	6	BLACKBURN ROVERS	1-0	Aldridge	28994		8	10	7		2	1	6		9	12					4		3		11		5
R3		28	EVERTON	0-1		44071		8	10	7		2	1	6		9		3		11		4						5

Arsenal 1988/89

Highbury

								Adams TA	Bould SA	Caesar GC	Davis PV	Dixon LM	Groves P	Hayes M	Lukic J	Marwood B	Merson PC	O'Leary DA	Quinn NJ	Richardson K	Rocastle DC	Smith AM	Thomas ML	Winterburn N
	Aug	27	Wimbledon	5-1	Smith 3, Marwood, Merson		15723	6	5		8	2			1	11	10				7	9	4	3
	Sep	3	ASTON VILLA	2-3	Marwood, Smith		37417	6			8	2	12		1	11	10	5			7	9	4	3
		10	Tottenham Hotspur	3-2	Winterburn, Marwood, Smith		32621	6			8	2	12		1	11	10	5		13	7	9	4	3
5		17	SOUTHAMPTON	2-2	Marwood (p), Smith		31386	6			8	2		12	1	11	10	5		13	7	9	4	3
7		24	Sheffield Wednesday	1-2	Smith		17830	6			8	2	12		1	11	10	5			7	9	4	3
6	Oct	1	West Ham United	4-1	Smith 2, Thomas, Rocastle		27658	6	5		8	2	10	12	1	11					7	9	4	3
4		22	QUEEN'S PARK RANGERS	2-1	Adams, Smith		33202	6	5			2	12		1	11	10			8	7	9	4	3
3		25	Luton Town	1-1	Smith		10548	6	5			2			1	11	10			8	7	9	4	3
2		29	COVENTRY CITY	2-0	Thomas, Adams		31273	6	5			2	12	13	1	11	10			8	7	9	4	3
2	Nov	6	Nottingham Forest	4-1	Smith, Bould, Adams, Marwood		19038	6	5			2		12	1	11	10			8	7	9	4	3
2		12	Newcastle United	1-0	Bould		23807	6	5			2		10	1	11	12			8	7	9	4	3
2		19	MIDDLESBROUGH	3-0	Merson 2, Rocastle		32294	6	5			2		12	1	11	10			8	7	9	4	3
2		26	Derby County	1-2	Thomas		20209	6	5			2	12	11	1		10			8	7	9	4	3
2	Dec	4	LIVERPOOL	1-1	Smith		31867	6	5			2		12	1	11	10			8	7	9	4	3
2		10	Norwich City	0-0			23069	6	5			2		12	1	11	10			8	7	9	4	3
2		17	MANCHESTER UNITED	2-1	Thomas, Merson		37422	6	5			2			1	11	10			8	7	9	4	3
2		26	Charlton Athletic	3-2	Marwood 2 (1p), Merson		18439	6	5						1	11	10	2		8	7	9	4	3
1		31	Aston Villa	3-0	Smith, Rocastle, Groves		32486	6	5						1	11	10	2		8	7	9	4	3
1	Jan	2	TOTTENHAM HOTSPUR	2-0	Merson, Thomas		45129	6	5		13		12		1	11		2		8	7	9	4	3
1		14	Everton	3-1	Merson, Smith, Richardson		34825			6	4	2	12		1	11	10	5		8	7	9	13	3
1		21	SHEFFIELD WEDNESDAY	1-1	Merson		33487			6	4	2	12		1	11	10	5		8	7	9	13	3
1	Feb	4	WEST HAM UNITED	2-1	Groves, Smith		40137	6	13			2	11	12	1		10	5		8	7	9	4	3
1		11	Millwall	2-1	Marwood, Smith		21852	6	12			2			1	11	10	5		8	7	9	4	3
1		18	Queen's Park Rangers	0-0			20543	6	13			2			12	1	11	10	5		8	7	9	4	3
1		21	Coventry City	0-1			21429	6	5						12	1	11	10	2		8	7	9	4	3
1		25	LUTON TOWN	2-0	Groves, Smith		31026	6	5					10		1	11	12	2		8	7	9	4	3
1		28	MILLWALL	0-0			37524	6	5			13	10		1	11	12	2		8	7	9	4	3
1	Mar	11	NOTTM. FOREST	1-3	Smith		39639	6	5			13	10		1	11	12	2		8	7	9	4	3
1		21	CHARLTON ATHLETIC	2-2	Rocastle, Davis		30257	6			4	2	12		1	11	10	5		8	7	9	13	3
1		25	Southampton	3-1	Groves, Rocastle, Merson		19202	6			4	2	10		1	11	12	5		8	7	9		3
1	Apr	2	Manchester United	1-1	Adams		37977	6	10		4	2			1	11	12	5		8	7	9	13	3
1		8	EVERTON	2-0	Dixon, Quinn		37606	6	10			2			1	11	12	5	9	8	7		4	3
1		15	NEWCASTLE UNITED	1-0	Marwood		38023	6	10			2	13		1	11	12	5	9	8	7		4	3
1	May	1	NORWICH CITY	5-0	Smith 2, Winterburn, Thomas, Rocastle		28466	6	10			2		13	1		11	5	12	8	7	9	4	3
1		6	Middlesbrough	1-0	Hayes		21803	6	10			2	12	1			11	5		8	7	9	4	3
1		13	DERBY COUNTY	1-2	Smith		41012	6	10			2	12	13	1		11	5		8	7	9	4	3
1		17	WIMBLEDON	2-2	Winterburn, Merson		39132	6	13			2	12	11	1		10	5		8	7	9	4	3
1		26	Liverpool	2-0	Smith, Thomas		41718	6	10			2	12	13	1		11	5		8	7	9	4	3

	Apps	Subs	Goals
Adams TA	36		4
Bould SA	26	4	2
Caesar GC	2		
Davis PV	11	1	
Dixon LM	31	2	1
Groves P	6	15	1
Hayes M	3	14	1
Lukic J	38		
Marwood B	31		9
Merson PC	29	8	10
O'Leary DA	26	1	
Quinn NJ	2	2	
Richardson K	32		1
Rocastle DC	38		6
Smith AM	36		23
Thomas ML	33	4	7
Winterburn N	38		3

F.A. Cup

R3	Jan	8	West Ham United	2-2	Merson 2		22017	6	5			12		13		1	11	10	2		8	7	9	4	3
rep		11	WEST HAM UNITED	0-1			44124	6			13	2	12		1		11	10	5		8	7	9	4	3

F.L. Cup

R2	Sep	28	Hull City	2-1	Winterburn, Marwood		11450	6	5		8	2	10	13	1	11				12	7	9	4	3
R2s	Oct	12	HULL CITY	3-0	Smith 2, Merson		17885	6	5		8	2		13	1	11	10			12	7	9	4	3
R3	Nov	2	Liverpool	1-1	Rocastle		31961	6	5			2	12		1	11	10			8	7	9	4	3
rep		9	LIVERPOOL	0-0			54029	6	5			2			12	1	11	10			8	7	9	4	3
rep2		23	Liverpool	1-2	Merson		21708	6	5			2			12	1	11	10			8	7	9	4	3

R3 replay a.e.t. R3 replay 2 at Villa Park

Liverpool 1989/90

Anfield

							Ablett GI	Aldridge JW	Barnes JCB	Beardsley PA	Burrows D	Dalglish KM	Gillespie GT	Grobbelaar BD	Hansen AD	Houghton RJ	Hysen GI	Marsh MA	McMahon S	Molby J	Nicol S	Rosenthal R	Rush IJ	Staunton S	Tanner N	Venison B	Whelan RA
	Aug	19	MANCHESTER CITY	3-1	Barnes(p), Nicol, Beardsley	37628			10	7	3			1	6		2		11		4		9			8	5
		23	Aston Villa	1-1	Barnes	35796			10	7	3			1	6		2		11		4		9			8	5
		26	Luton Town	0-0		11124		12	10	7	3		8	1	6		2		11		4		9				5
5	Sep	9	Derby County	3-0	Rush, Barnes(p), Beardsley	20034			10	7	3		8	1	6		2		11		4		9				5
1		12	CRYSTAL PALACE	9-0	* see below	35779		12	10	7	3		8	1	6		2		11	14	4		9				5
2		16	NORWICH CITY	0-0		36885			10	7	3		8	1	6		2		11		4		9				5
1		23	Everton	3-1	Rush 2, Barnes	42453			10	7	3			1	6		2		11		4		9			8	5
1	Oct	14	Wimbledon	2-1	Beardsley, Whelan	13510			10	7	3			1	6		2		11		4			9		8	5
2		21	Southampton	1-4	Beardsley (p)	20501			10	7	3			1	6	12	2		11		4		9			8	5
1		29	TOTTENHAM HOTSPUR	1-0	Barnes	36550	6		10	7	3			1		8	2		11				9	12		4	5
2	Nov	4	COVENTRY CITY	0-1		36443	4		10	7	3			1	6	8	2		11	12			9				5
3		11	Queen's Park Rangers	2-3	Barnes 2 (1p)	18804			10	7	3			1	6	8	2		11	12	4		9				5
3		19	Millwall	2-1	Barnes, Rush	13547			10					1	6	8	2		11	4			9	3		7	5
1		26	ARSENAL	2-1	McMahon, Barnes	35983			10	12	4			1	6	8	2		11				9	3		7	5
1		29	Sheffield Wednesday	0-2		32732	4		10	7	12	2	1		8				11	6			9	3			5
1	Dec	2	Manchester City	4-1	Rush 2, Beardsley, McMahon	31641	4			7			6	1		8	2	12	11	10			9	3	14		5
2		9	ASTON VILLA	1-1	Beardsley	37436	4		10	7				1		8	2		11	6			9	3	12		5
2		16	Chelsea	5-2	Rush 2, Beardsley, Houghton, McMahon	31005	4			7				1	6	8	2		11	10	12		9			3	5
2		23	MANCHESTER UNITED	0-0		37426	4			7				1	6	8	2		11	10	12		9			3	5
1		26	SHEFFIELD WEDNESDAY	2-1	Molby, Rush	37488	6			7	12			1		8	2		11	10	4		9	14		3	5
1		30	CHARLTON ATHLETIC	1-0	Barnes	36678	7		10	12				1	6		2		14	11	4		9	8		3	5
1	Jan	1	Nottingham Forest	2-2	Rush 2	24518			10	7	8			1	6		2		11		4		9			3	5
1		13	LUTON TOWN	2-2	Barnes, Nicol	35312			10	7	12			1	6		2		11		4		9	8		3	5
1		20	Crystal Palace	2-0	Rush, Beardsley	29807			10	7				1	6		2		11		4		9	8		3	5
1	Feb	3	EVERTON	2-1	Barnes, Beardsley (p)	38730			10	7	8			1	6		2		11		4		9			3	5
1		10	Norwich City	0-0		20210			10	7	8			1	6		2		11		4		9			3	5
1	Mar	3	MILLWALL	1-0	Gillespie	36427			10	7	8		2	1	6	12			11				9			3	5
2		18	Manchester United	2-1	Barnes 2 (1p)	46629			10	7				1	6	8	2		11				9	4		3	5
2		21	Tottenham Hotspur	0-1		25656			10	7				1	6	8	2		11				9	4		3	5
1		31	SOUTHAMPTON	3-2	Barnes, Rush, og (Osman)	37027			10	7				1	6	8	2		11			14	9	4		3	5
1	Apr	3	WIMBLEDON	2-1	Rush, Gillespie	33319			10		3		4	1	6	8	2		11				9	7			5
1		11	Charlton Athletic	4-0	Rosenthal 3, Barnes	13982	4		10		3			1	6			14	11	12		9		7	8	2		5
1		14	NOTTM. FOREST	2-2	Rosenthal, McMahon	37265	12		10		3			1	6		2		11			8	9	4	7		5
		18	Arsenal	1-1	Barnes	33395	7		10		3			1	6		2		11	12	4	14	9	8			5
1		21	CHELSEA	4-1	Nicol 2, Rush, Rosenthal	38431	12		10		3		5	1	6		2		11	7	4	8	9				
1		28	QUEEN'S PARK RANGERS	2-1	Rush, Barnes(p)	37758			10		3		14	1	6	12	2		11	7	4	8	9		5		
1	May	1	DERBY COUNTY	1-0	Gillespie	38038	4		10			14	5	1		8	2		11	7		12	9	6	3		
1		5	Coventry City	6-1	Barnes 3, Rosenthal 2, Rush	23204	4		10				5	1			2		11	7		8	9	6	3		

Sep 12 scorers: Nicol 2, McMahon, Rush, Gillespie, Beardsley, Aldridge(p), Barnes, Hysen

Apps							13	0	34	27	23	0	11	38	31	16	35	0	37	12	21	5	36	18	2	25	34
Subs							2	2		2	3	1	2			3		2	1	5	2	3		2	2			
Goals								1	22	10			4			1	1		5	1	6	7	18				1

One own goal

F.A. Cup

R3	Jan	6	Swansea City	0-0		16098			10	7				1	6		2		11		4		9	8		3	5
rep		9	SWANSEA CITY	8-0	Rush 3, Barnes 2, Whelan, Beardsley, Nicol	29149			10	7				1	6		2		11		4		9	8		3	5
R4		28	Norwich City	0-0		23162			10	7				1	6		2		11		4		9	8		3	5
rep		31	NORWICH CITY	3-1	Nicol, Barnes, Beardsley (p)	29339			10	7	12			1	6		2		11		4		9	8		3	5
R5	Feb	17	SOUTHAMPTON	3-0	Rush, Beardsley, Nicol	35961			10	7	8			1	6	12	2		11		4		9			3	5
R6	Mar	11	Queen's Park Rangers	2-2	Barnes, Rush	21057			10	7			12	1	6	8	2		11				9	14		3	5
rep		14	QUEEN'S PARK RANGERS	1-0	Beardsley	38090			10	7				1	6	8	2		11		4		9			3	5
SF	Apr	8	Crystal Palace	3-4	Rush, McMahon, Barnes (p)	38389			10	7	3		4	1	6	8	2		11				9	14		12	5

SF at Villa Park, a.e.t

F.L. Cup

R2	Sep	19	WIGAN ATHLETIC	5-2	Rush 2, Beardsley, Barnes, Hysen	19231			10	7	3		8	1	6		2		11		4		9	12		14	5
R2s	Oct	4	WIGAN ATHLETIC	3-0	Staunton 3	17954				7	3			1	6	10	2		11	12	4		9	14		8	5
R3		25	Arsenal	0-1		40814	4		10	12	3			1		7			11	6			9			8	5

A Watson played at 2 in R3

F.A. Charity Shield

	Aug	12	Arsenal	1-0	Beardsley	63149			10	7	3			1	6		2		11		4		9			8	5

128

Arsenal 1990/91

Highbury

							Adams TA	Bould SA	Campbell KJ	Cole AA	Davis PV	Dixon LM	Groves P	Hillier D	Jonsson S	Limpar AE	Linighan A	Merson PC	O'Leary DA	Pates CG	Rocastle DC	Seaman DA	Smith AM	Thomas ML	Winterburn N
	Aug	25	Wimbledon	3-0	Merson, Smith, Groves	13776	6	5			8	2	12			11		10			7	1	9	4	3
		29	LUTON TOWN	2-1	Merson, Thomas	32723	6	5			8	2	12			11		10			7	1	9	4	3
	Sep	1	TOTTENHAM HOTSPUR	0-0		40009	6	5			8	2	12			11		10			7	1	9	4	3
5		8	Everton	1-1	Groves	29908	6	5			8	2	12			11		10			7	1	9	4	3
2		15	CHELSEA	4-1	Limpar, Dixon (p), Merson, Rocastle	40475	6	5	12		8	2	9			11	13	10			7	1		4	3
2		22	Nottingham Forest	2-0	Rocastle, Limpar	26013	6	5			8	2	9			11		10			7	1	12	4	3
2		29	Leeds United	2-2	Limpar 2	29885	6	5			8	2	12	13	4	11		10			7	1	9		3
2	Oct	6	NORWICH CITY	2-0	Davis 2	36737	6	5			8	2	12	13	4	11		10			7	1	9		3
2		20	Manchester United	1-0	Limpar	47232	6	5			8	2	12			11		10			7	1	9	4	3
2		27	SUNDERLAND	1-0	Dixon (p)	38485	6	5			8	2	12			11		10			7	1	9	4	3
2	Nov	3	Coventry City	2-0	Limpar 2	15283	6	5	12		8	2	7			11		10	13			1	9	4	3
2		10	Crystal Palace	0-0		28181	6	5	9		8	2	12			11		10	7			1	13	4	3
2		17	SOUTHAMPTON	4-0	Smith 2, Limpar, Merson	36229	6	5	12		8	2	7			11		10	13			1	9	4	3
2		24	Queen's Park Rangers	3-1	Merson, Smith, Campbell	18555	6	5	12		8	2	7			11		10	13			1	9	4	3
2	Dec	2	LIVERPOOL	3-0	Merson, Dixon (p), Smith	40419	6	5			8	2				11		10	7			1	9	4	3
1		8	Luton Town	1-1	Smith	12506	6	5			8	2	12			11		10	7			1	9	4	3
2		15	WIMBLEDON	2-2	Merson, Adams	30164	6	5			8	2	7			11		10	12			1	9	4	3
2		23	Aston Villa	0-0		22687		5			8	2	7			11	6	10			12	1	9	4	3
2		26	DERBY COUNTY	3-0	Smith 2, Merson	25558		5	12		8	2				11	6	10	13		7	1	9	4	3
1		29	SHEFFIELD UNITED	4-1	Smith 2, Dixon (p), Thomas	37810		5		12	8	2	7			11	6	10	13			1	9	4	3
1	Jan	1	Manchester City	1-0	Smith	30579		5			8	2	12	13		11	6	10	7			1	9	4	3
1		12	Tottenham Hotspur	0-0		34758		5			8	2	12	13		11	6	10	7			1	9	4	3
1		19	EVERTON	1-0	Merson	35349		5	12		8	2	6	13		11		10	7			1	9	4	3
1	Feb	2	Chelsea	1-2	Smith	28255		5	12		8	2	7	13		11	6	10				1	9	4	3
1		23	CRYSTAL PALACE	4-0	O'Leary, Merson, Smith, Campbell	42162		5	11		8	2					6	10	7	13	12	1	9	4	3
1	Mar	3	Liverpool	1-0	Merson	37221	6	5	11		12	2		8				10	7		13	1	9	4	3
1		17	LEEDS UNITED	2-0	Campbell 2	26208	6	5	11			2		8				10	7			1	9	4	3
1		20	NOTTM. FOREST	1-1	Campbell	34152	6	5	11		8	2	12			13		10	7			1	9	4	3
1		23	Norwich City	0-0		19102	6	5	10		8	2	12			11	13		7		4	1	9		3
1		30	Derby County	2-0	Smith 2	18397	6	5	4		8	2	12	13		11		10			7	1	9		3
1	Apr	3	ASTON VILLA	5-0	Campbell 2, Smith 2, Davis	41867	6	5	7		8	2	12	4		11		10				1	9	13	3
1		6	Sheffield United	2-0	Campbell, Smith	26920	6	5	7		8	2	12	4		11		10				1	9	13	3
1		9	Southampton	1-1	og (M Adams)	19691	6	5	7		8	2	10	4				12				1	9	13	3
1		17	MANCHESTER CITY	2-2	Campbell, Merson	38409	6	5	7		8	2	11				12		10	13		1	9	4	3
1		23	QUEEN'S PARK RANGERS	2-0	Dixon (p), Merson	42395	6	5	7		8	2	12	4		11		10	13			1	9		3
1	May	4	Sunderland	0-0		22606	6	5	7		8	2	11	4				10	12			1	9		3
1		6	MANCHESTER UNITED	3-1	Smith 3 (1p)	40229	6	5	7		8	2		4		11		10	12			1	9	13	3
1		11	COVENTRY CITY	6-1	Limpar 3, Smith, Groves, og (Peake)	41039	6	5	7		8	2	12	4		11	13	10				1	9		3

Apps	30	38	15	0	36	38	13	9	2	32	7	36	11	0	13	38	35	27	38
Subs			7	1	1		19	7		2	3	1	10	1	3		2	4	
Goals	1		9		3	5	3			11		13	1		2		22	2	

Two own goals

F.A. Cup

R3	Jan	5	SUNDERLAND	2-1	Smith, Limpar	35128		5			8	2	7			11	6	10	12			1	9	4	3
R4		27	LEEDS UNITED	0-0		30905		5	13		8	2	6	12		11		10	7			1	9	4	3
rep		30	Leeds United	1-1	Limpar	27763		5			8	2		7		11	6	10				1	9	4	3
rep2	Feb	13	LEEDS UNITED	0-0		30433		5	12		8	2	6			11	13	10	7			1	9	4	3
rep3		16	Leeds United	2-1	Merson, Dixon	27190		5	11		8	2					6	10	7			1	9	4	3
R5		27	Shrewsbury Town	1-0	Thomas	12536	6	5	11			2		8				10	7		12	1	9	4	3
R6	Mar	9	CAMBRIDGE UNITED	2-1	Campbell, Adams	42960	6	5	11		12	2		8				10	7			1	9	4	3
SF	Apr	14	Tottenham Hotspur	1-3	Smith	77893	6	5	7		8	2	12			11		10				1	9	4	3

R4 replay and replay 2 a.e.t. SF at Wembley Stadium

F.L. Cup

R2	Sep	25	Chester	1-0	Merson	4135	6	5	12		8	2	11	4				10			7	1	9		3
R2s	Oct	9	CHESTER	5-0	Groves 2, Smith, Adams, Merson	22902	6	5	13		8	2	11	4				10	12		7	1	9		3
R3		30	Manchester City	2-1	Groves, Adams	26825	6	5	12		8	2	7			11		10				1	9	4	3
R4	Nov	28	MANCHESTER UNITED	2-6	Smith 2	40884	6	5	12		8	2	7			11		10				1	9	4	3

Leeds United 1991/92

Elland Road

	Date	Opponent	Score	Scorers	Att	Agana PAO	Batty D	Cantona E	Chapman LR	Davison R	Dorigo AR	Fairclough CH	Hodge SB	Kamara C	Kelly GO	Lukic J	McAllister G	McClelland J	Newsome J	Shutt CS	Speed GA	Sterland M	Strachan GD	Varadi I	Wallace RS (Rod)	Wetherall D	Whitlow MW	Whyte CA
	Aug 20	NOTTM. FOREST	1-0	McAllister	29435		4		9		3	5				1	10	2			11		7		8			6
	24	SHEFFIELD WEDNESDAY	1-1	Hodge	30260		4		9		3	5	12			1	10	2			11	13	7		8			6
	28	Southampton	4-0	Speed 2, Strachan 2 (2p)	14711		4		9		3	5	12			1	10	2			11	13	7		8			6
6	31	Manchester United	1-1	Chapman	43778		4		9		3		12			1	10	5			11	2	7		8			6
6	Sep 3	ARSENAL	2-2	Chapman, Strachan (p)	28936		4		9		3		12			1	10	5			11	2	7		8	13		6
4	7	MANCHESTER CITY	3-0	Batty, Dorigo, Strachan (p)	28986		4		9		3		12			1	10	5			11	2	7		8			6
2	14	Chelsea	1-0	Shutt	23439		4		9		3		12			1	10	5		8	11	2	7					6
2	18	Coventry City	0-0		15483		4		9		3		12			1	10	5		8	11	2	7					6
2	21	LIVERPOOL	1-0	Hodge	32741		4		9		3		8			1	10	5			12	11	2					6
2	28	Norwich City	2-2	Dorigo, Speed	15828		4		9		3		8			1	10	5			12	11	2	7		13		6
2	Oct 1	Crystal Palace	0-1		18520		4		9		3		8			1	10	5			12	11	2	7		13		6
2	5	SHEFFIELD UNITED	4-3	Hodge 2, Sterland 2 (1p)	28694		4		9		3	12	7			1	10	5		8	11	2				13		6
2	19	Notts County	4-2	Chapman, Hodge, McAllister, Whyte	12970		4		9		3	5	10	13		1	12			8	11	2	7					6
1	26	OLDHAM ATHLETIC	1-0	og (Kilcline)	28135		4		9		3	5		13		1	10			12	11	2	7		8			6
2	Nov 2	Wimbledon	0-0		6348				9		3	5				1	10		12	4	11	2	7		8			6
1	16	QUEEN'S PARK RANGERS	2-0	Sterland, Wallace	27087		4		9		3	5				1	10				11	2	7	12	8			6
1	24	Aston Villa	4-1	Chapman 2, Sterland, Wallace	23713		4		9		3	5				1	10	11				2	7		8			6
1	30	EVERTON	1-0	Wallace	30059		4		9		3	5	12			1	10	13			11	2	7		8			6
1	Dec 7	Luton Town	2-0	Speed, Wallace	11550		4		9		3	5				1	10				11	2	7		8			6
1	14	TOTTENHAM HOTSPUR	1-1	Speed	31404		4		9		3					1	10	5			11	2	7		8			6
2	22	Nottingham Forest	0-0		27170		4		9		3				12	1	10	5			11	2	7		8			6
2	26	SOUTHAMPTON	3-3	Hodge 2, Speed	29053		4		9		3		7			1	10	5			11	2			8			6
2	29	MANCHESTER UNITED	1-1	Sterland (p)	32638		4		9		3	5	12			1	10				11	2	7		8			6
1	Jan 1	West Ham United	3-1	Chapman 2, McAllister	21766		4		9		3	5				1	10				11	2	7		8			6
1	12	Sheffield Wednesday	6-1	Chapman 3, Dorigo, Wallace, Whitlow	32228				9	13	3	5	4			1	10			7		2	7		8		12	6
1	18	CRYSTAL PALACE	1-1	Fairclough	27717		4			13	3	5	9			1	10				11	2	7		8		12	6
1	Feb 1	NOTTS COUNTY	3-0	Batty, Sterland, Wallace	27323		4				3	5	9		13	1	10				11	2	7		8		12	6
2	8	Oldham Athletic	0-2		18409		4	13			3	5	9			1	10				11	2	7		8		12	6
2	23	Everton	1-1	og (Keown)	19242		4	9			3	5				1	10			12	11	2	7		8			6
2	29	LUTON TOWN	2-0	Cantona, Chapman	28227	13	4	12	9		3	5				1	10				11	2	7		8			6
2	Mar 3	ASTON VILLA	0-0		29655	8	4	12	9			5				1	10	13			11	2	7				3	6
1	7	Tottenham Hotspur	3-1	McAllister, Newsome, Wallace	27622		4	12	9			5				1	10		13		11	2	7		8		3	6
1	11	Queen's Park Rangers	1-4	Speed	14641		4	12	9			5				1	10		2		11		7		8		3	6
1	14	WIMBLEDON	5-1	Chapman 3, Cantona, Wallace	26220		4	3	9			5				1	10		2	12	11		7					6
1	22	Arsenal	1-1	Chapman	27844		4	2	9		3	5				1	10				11		7					6
1	28	WEST HAM UNITED	0-0		31101		4	2	9		3	5	12			1	10		6		11		7		8			
2	Apr 4	Manchester City	0-4		30239		4	2	9		3	5				1	10				11		7		8			6
1	11	CHELSEA	3-0	Cantona, Chapman, Wallace	31363		4	12	9		3	5	2			1	10		13		11		7		8			6
2	18	Liverpool	0-0		35186		4	12	9		3	5	7			1	10		2		11				8			6
1	20	COVENTRY CITY	2-0	Fairclough, McAllister (p)	26582		4	12	9		3	5				1	10		2	13	11		7		8			6
1	26	Sheffield United	3-2	Newsome, Wallace, og (Gayle)	31084		4	12	9		3	5				1	10		2	13	11		7		8			6
1	May 2	NORWICH CITY	1-0	Wallace	33020		4	7	9		3	5	13			1	10		2		11		12		8			6

		Apps	1	40	6	38	0	38	30	12	0	0	42	41	16	7	6	41	29	35	2	34	0	3	41
		Subs	1		9		2			1	11	2	2		1	2	3	8		2	1	1		1	7	
		Goals		2	3	16		3	2	7				5			2	1	7	6	4		11		1	1

Three own goals

F.A. Cup

	Date	Opponent	Score		Att																							
R3	Jan 15	MANCHESTER UNITED	0-1		31819				9		3	5	4			1	10				11	2			8		13	6

A Williams played at 7: subbed

F.L. Cup

	Date	Opponent	Score	Scorers	Att																							
R2	Sep 24	Scunthorpe United	0-0		8392		4		9		3		8			1	10	5		12	11	2	7					6
R2s	Oct 8	SCUNTHORPE UNITED	3-0	Chapman, Speed, Sterland (p)	14558		4		9		3	13	7		12	1		5		8	11	2						6
R3	29	TRANMERE ROVERS	3-1	Chapman 2, Shutt	18266				9		3	5	4	12		1	10			8		2	7		11			6
R4	Dec 4	Everton	4-1	Wallace 2, Chapman, Speed	25467		4		9		3	5	12			1	10				11	2	7		8			6
R5	Jan 8	MANCHESTER UNITED	1-3	Speed	28886		4		9		3	5	13			1	10	12			11	2	7		8			6

A Williams played at 10 (subbed) in R2s and 13 in R3

Full Members Cup

	Date	Opponent	Score	Scorers	Att																							
R2	Oct 22	NOTTM FOREST	1-3	Wallace	6145		4				3	5		10		1				7	8	11	2		12			6

Also played: Snodin (9), Grayson (13)

130

Manchester United 1992/93

Old Trafford

						Blackmore CG	Bruce SR	Butt N	Cantona E	Dublin D	Ferguson D	Giggs RJ	Hughes LM	Ince PEC	Irwin JD	Kanchelskis A	McClair BJ	Pallister GA	Parker PA	Phelan MC	Robson B	Schmeichel PB	Sharpe LS	Wallace DL	Webb NJ
	Aug	15	Sheffield United	1-2	Hughes	28070	3	4			13	5	11	10	8	2	7	9	6		12		1			
		19	EVERTON	0-3		31901	3	4			13	5	11	10	8	2	7	9	6		12		1			
		22	IPSWICH TOWN	1-1	Irwin	31704	3	4			12	5	11	10		2	7	9	6		8		1			13
11		24	Southampton	1-0	Dublin	15623		4			7	5	11	10	8	3		9	6		2		1			
8		29	Nottingham Forest	2-0	Hughes, Giggs	19694	13	4			7	5	11	10	8	3	12	9	6		2		1			
6	Sep	2	CRYSTAL PALACE	1-0	Hughes	29736	2	4			7	5	11	10	8	3	12	9	6				1			
4		6	LEEDS UNITED	2-0	Kanchelskis, Bruce	31296	2	4				5	11	10	8	3	7	9	6				1			
3		12	Everton	2-0	McClair, Bruce (p)	30004	3	4				5	11	10	8	2	7	9	6				1			
4		19	Tottenham Hotspur	1-1	Giggs	33296	3	4				5	11	10	8	2	7	9	6				1		12	
4		26	QUEEN'S PARK RANGERS	0-0		33287	3	4				5	11	10	8	2	7	9	6				1		12	
6	Oct	3	Middlesbrough	1-1	Bruce (p)	24172	7	4				5	11	10	8	2	12	9	6	3	13		1			
5		18	LIVERPOOL	2-2	Hughes 2	33243	12	4				5	11	10	8	3	7	9	6	2			1			
7		24	Blackburn Rovers	0-0		20305	7	4				5	11	10	8	3	12	9	6	2			1			
7		31	WIMBLEDON	0-1		32622	4					5	11	10	8		7	9	6	2			12	1		
10	Nov	7	Aston Villa	0-1		39063	3	4				5	11	10	8			12	6	2		7	1	9		
8		21	OLDHAM ATHLETIC	3-0	McClair 2, Hughes	33497		4		13				11	10	8	3	9	6	2	12	7	1	5		
5		28	Arsenal	1-0	Hughes	29740		4						11	10	8	3	9	6	2		7	1	5		
5	Dec	6	MANCHESTER CITY	2-1	Ince, Hughes	35408		4		12				11	10	8	3	9	6	2		7	1	5		
3		12	NORWICH CITY	1-0	Hughes	34688		4		7				11	10	8	3	9	6	2			1	5		
4		19	Chelsea	1-1	Cantona	34496		4		7					10	8	3	12	9	6	2	5		1	11	
3		26	Sheffield Wednesday	3-3	McClair 2, Cantona	37708		4		7				11	10	8	3	12	9	6	2			1	5		
2		28	COVENTRY CITY	5-0	Giggs, Hughes, Cantona (p), Sharpe, Irwin	36025		4		7				11	10	8	3	12	9	6	2	13		1	5		
1	Jan	9	TOTTENHAM HOTSPUR	4-1	Cantona, Irwin, McClair, Parker	35648		4		7				11	10	8	3	12	9	6	2	13		1	5		
1		18	Queen's Park Rangers	3-1	Ince, Giggs, Kanchelskis	20142		4						11	10	8	3	7	9	6	2	12		1	5		
1		27	NOTTM. FOREST	2-0	Ince, Hughes	36085		4		7				11	10	8	3		9	6	2			1	5		
2		30	Ipswich Town	1-2	McClair	22007		4		7				11	10	8	3	12	9	6	2			1	5		
1	Feb	6	SHEFFIELD UNITED	2-1	McClair, Cantona	36156		4		7				11	10	8	3	12	9	6	2			1	5		
1		8	Leeds United	0-0		34166		4		7				11	10	8	3	12	9	6	2			1	5		
2		20	SOUTHAMPTON	2-1	Giggs 2	36257		4		7				11	10	8	3		9	6	2			1	5		
2		27	MIDDLESBROUGH	3-0	Giggs, Irwin, Cantona	36251		4		7				11	10	8	3		9	6	2			1	5		
1	Mar	6	Liverpool	2-1	Hughes, McClair	44374		4						11	10	8	3	7	9	6	2			1	5		
1		9	Oldham Athletic	0-1		17106		4			12			11	10	8	3	7	9	6	2			1	5		
1		14	ASTON VILLA	1-1	Hughes	36163		4		7				11	10	8	3		9	6	2			1	5		
2		20	Manchester City	1-1	Cantona	37136		4		7				11	10	8	3		9	6	2			1	5		
3		24	ARSENAL	0-0		37301		4		7				11	10	8	3		9	6	2		12	1	5		
2	Apr	5	Norwich City	3-1	Giggs, Kanchelskis, Cantona	20582		4		7				11		8	3	10	9	6	2		12	1	5		
1		10	SHEFFIELD WEDNESDAY	2-1	Bruce 2	40102		4		7				11	10	8	3		9	6	2		12	1	5		
1		12	Coventry City	1-0	Irwin	24410		4		7				11	10	8	3		9	6	2		12	1	5		
1		17	CHELSEA	3-0	Hughes, Cantona, og (Clarke)	40139		4		7				11	10	8	3	13	9	6	2		12	1	5		
1		21	Crystal Palace	2-0	Hughes, Ince	30115		4		7				11	10	8	3	5	9	6	2		12	1			
1	May	3	BLACKBURN ROVERS	3-1	Giggs, Ince, Pallister	40693		4		7				11	10	8	3	13	9	6	2		12	1	5		
1		9	Wimbledon	2-1	Ince, Robson	30115		4		11				12	10	8	3		9	6	2		7	1	5		

	Blackmore	Bruce	Butt	Cantona	Dublin	Ferguson	Giggs	Hughes	Ince	Irwin	Kanchelskis	McClair	Pallister	Parker	Phelan	Robson	Schmeichel	Sharpe	Wallace	Webb
Apps	12	42	0	21	3	15	40	41	41	40	14	41	42	31	5	5	42	27	0	0
Subs	2		1	1	1	4					13	1			6	9			2	1
Goals		5		9	1		9	15	6	5	3	9	1	1		1		1		

F.A. Cup

R3	Jan	5	BURY	2-0	Phelan, Gillespie	30668	12	4		7				10		3		9	6	2	11	13	1	5		
R4		23	BRIGHTON & HOVE ALB.	1-0	Giggs	33610		4					11		8	3		9	6	2	10			1	5	7	
R5	Feb	14	Sheffield United	1-2	Giggs	27150		4					11	10	8	3	7	9	6	2				1	5		

K Gillespie played at 8 in R3 and 12 in R4

F.L. Cup

R2	Sep	23	Brighton & Hove Albion	1-1	Wallace	16649		4						10	8	2	7	9	6						11	5
R2s	Oct	7	BRIGHTON & HOVE ALB.	1-0	Hughes	25405		4					11	10	8	3	5	9	6	2		7	1			
R3		28	Aston Villa	0-1		35964	7	4					5	11	10	8	3	12	9	6	2			1			

Played in R2: Walsh (1), Martin (3), D Beckham (12)

UEFA Cup

R1.1	Sep	16	TORPEDO MOSCOW	0-0		19998	5	4						10		2	7	9	6						11	8
R1.2		30	Torpedo Moscow	0-0		11357		4					11	10	8	2		9	6	12	3	13	1		7	5

Lost on penalties

Played in R1.1: Walsh (1), Martin (3, subbed), G Neville (12)

Manchester United 1993/94

Old Trafford

						Bruce SR	Butt N	Cantona E	Dublin D	Ferguson D	Giggs RJ	Hughes LM	Ince PEC	Irwin JD	Kanchelskis A	Keane RM	Martin LA	McClair BJ	McKee C	Neville GA	Pallister GA	Parker PA	Phelan MC	Robson B	Schmeichel PB	Sharpe LS	Thornley BL	Walsh G
	Aug	15	Norwich City	2-0	Giggs, Robson	19705	4					11	10	8	3	5	9					6	2		7	1		
		18	SHEFFIELD UNITED	3-0	Keane 2, Hughes	41949	4					11	10	8	3	5	9		12			6	2		7	1		
		21	NEWCASTLE UNITED	1-1	Giggs	41829	4					11	10	8	3	5	9		12			6	2		7	1	13	
1		23	Aston Villa	2-1	Sharpe 2	39624	4					7	10	8	3	5	9					6	2			1	11	
1		28	Southampton	3-1	Sharpe, Cantona, Irwin	16189	4		7			11	10	8	3	13	9		12			6	2			1	5	
1	Sep	1	WEST HAM UNITED	3-0	Sharpe, Bruce, Cantona (p)	44613	4		7			11		8	3	10	9		12			6	2		13	1	5	
1		11	Chelsea	0-1		37064	4		7			11		8	3		9		12			6	2		10	1	5	
1		19	ARSENAL	1-0	Cantona	44009	4		7			11	10	8	3		9		12			6	2			1	5	
1		25	SWINDON TOWN	4-2	Hughes 2, Kanchelskis, Cantona	44583	4		7			13	10	8	3	11	9		12			6	2			1	5	
1	Oct	2	Sheffield Wednesday	3-2	Hughes 2, Giggs	34548	4		7			11	10	8	3	12	9					6	2			1	5	
1		16	TOTTENHAM HOTSPUR	2-1	Keane, Sharpe	44655	4	13	8			11	10		3		9		12			6	2		7	1	5	
1		23	Everton	1-0	Sharpe	35455	4		7				10	8	3		9		11	2	9	6				1	5	
1		30	QUEEN'S PARK RANGERS	2-1	Cantona, Hughes	44663	4		7			11	10	8	3		9					6		2	6	1	5	
1	Nov	7	Manchester City	3-2	Cantona 2, Keane	35155	4		7			12	10	8	3	11	9					6	2			1	5	
1		20	WIMBLEDON	3-1	Pallister, Hughes, Kanchelskis	44748	4		7				10	8	3	11						6	2	12	9	1	5	
1		24	IPSWICH TOWN	0-0		43300	4		7		13	12	10	8	3	11						6	2		9	1	5	
1		27	Coventry City	1-0	Cantona	17009	4		7		9	11	10	8	3							6	2			1	5	
1	Dec	4	NORWICH CITY	2-2	Giggs, McClair	44694	4		7			11	10	8	3	5			9			6	2			1	12	
1		7	Sheffield United	3-0	Hughes, Sharpe, Cantona	26744	4		7			11	10	8	3		12		9			6	2			1	5	
1		11	Newcastle United	1-1	Ince	36332	4		7			11	10	8	3	13	12		9			6	2			1	5	
1		19	ASTON VILLA	3-1	Cantona 2, Ince	44499	4		7			12	10	8	3	11	9					6	2			1	5	
1		26	BLACKBURN ROVERS	1-1	Ince	44511	4		7		13	11	10	8	3		9		12			6	2			1	5	
1		29	Oldham Athletic	5-2	Giggs 2, Kanchelskis, Bruce, Cantona (p)	16708	4		7			11		8	3	10	9		12			6	2		13	1	5	
1	Jan	1	LEEDS UNITED	0-0		44724	4		7			11			3	5	10		9			6	2		8	1		
1		4	Liverpool	3-3	Bruce, Giggs, Irwin	42795	4		7			11		8	3	5	10		9			6	2			1		
1		15	Tottenham Hotspur	1-0	og (Calderwood)	31343	4		7			11	10	8	3	5	9		12			6	2			1		
1		22	EVERTON	1-0	Giggs	44750	4		7			11	10	8	3	5	9					6	2			1		
1	Feb	5	Queen's Park Rangers	3-2	Kanchelskis, Cantona, Giggs	21267	4		7			11	10	8	3	5	9					6	2			1		
1		26	West Ham United	2-2	Hughes, Ince	28382	4		7	12			10	8	3	5	11		9			6	2			1		13
1	Mar	5	CHELSEA	0-1		44745	4			12		11	10	8	3	5	7		9			6	2		13	1		
1		16	SHEFFIELD WEDNESDAY	5-0	Cantona 2, Giggs, Hughes, Ince	43669	4		7			11	10	8	3	5	9		12			6	2		13	1		
1		19	Swindon Town	2-2	Keane, Ince	18102	4		7			11	10	8	3		5		9			6	2			1		
1		22	Arsenal	2-2	Sharpe 2	36203	4		7			11	10	8	3		9		12			6	2			1	5	
1		30	LIVERPOOL	1-0	Ince	44751	4		7			12	10	8	3	11	9					6	2		13	1	5	
1	Apr	2	Blackburn Rovers	0-2		20866	4					11	10	8	3	7	9		12			6	2			1	5	
1		4	OLDHAM ATHLETIC	3-2	Giggs, Dublin, Ince	44686	4			12		11	10	8	2	7	5		9			6				1	3	
1		16	Wimbledon	0-1		28553	4			13		11	10	8	3	5			9						7	1	12	
1		23	MANCHESTER CITY	2-0	Cantona 2	44333	4		7			12	10	8	3	5	9					6	2			1	11	
1		27	Leeds United	2-0	Kanchelskis, Giggs	41127	4		7			11	10	8	3	5	9					6	2			1		
1	May	1	Ipswich Town	2-1	Cantona, Giggs	22478	4		7			11	10	8	3	5	9					6	2			1	12	13
		4	SOUTHAMPTON	2-0	Kanchelskis, Hughes	44705			7			11	10	8	2	5	9					6	4				3	1
		8	COVENTRY CITY	0-0		44717	4	7	10						3		13		9	11	2	6	12	8		5	1	

	Apps	Subs	Goals
Bruce SR	41		3
Butt N	0	1	
Cantona E	34		18
Dublin D	1	4	1
Ferguson D	1	2	
Giggs RJ	32	6	13
Hughes LM	36		11
Ince PEC	39		8
Irwin JD	42		2
Kanchelskis A	28	3	6
Keane RM	34	3	5
Martin LA	1		
McClair BJ	12	14	1
McKee C	1		
Neville GA	1		
Pallister GA	41		1
Parker PA	39		
Phelan MC	1	1	
Robson B	10	5	1
Schmeichel PB	40		
Sharpe LS	26	4	9
Thornley BL	0	1	
Walsh G	2	1	

One own goal

F.A. Cup

							Bruce	Butt	Cantona	Dublin	Ferguson	Giggs	Hughes	Ince	Irwin	Kanch	Keane	Martin	McClair	McKee	Neville	Pallister	Parker	Phelan	Robson	Schm	Sharpe	Thorn	Walsh
R3	Jan	9	Sheffield United	1-0	Hughes	22019	4		7			11	10	8	3	5	9					6	2			1			
R4		30	Norwich City	2-0	Keane, Cantona	21060	4		7			11	10	8	3	5	9		12			6	2			1			
R5	Feb	20	Wimbledon	3-0	Cantona, Ince, Irwin	27511	4		7	13		11	10	8	3	5	9		12			6	2			1			
R6	Mar	12	CHARLTON ATHLETIC	3-1	Kanchelskis 2, Hughes	44347	4		7			11	10	8	3	5	9					6	2			1			
SF	Apr	10	Oldham Athletic	1-1	Hughes	56399	4	12		9		11	10	8	3				7			6	2		13	1	5		
rep		13	Oldham Athletic	4-1	Irwin, Kanchelskis, Robson, Giggs	32211	4					11	10	8	3	5	9		12			6	2		7	1	13		
F	May	14	Chelsea	4-0	Cantona 2 (2p), Hughes, McClair	79634	4		7			11	10	8	3	5	9		13			6	2			1	12		

SF at Wembley Stadium, SF replay at Maine Road, Final at Wembley Stadium. Sealey played at 12 in game 4

F.L. Cup

R2	Sep	22	Stoke City	1-2	Dublin	23327	12			11	8		10		3	5		2	9			6		4	7	1	13		
R2s	Oct	6	STOKE CITY	2-0	Sharpe, McClair	41387	4					12	10		2	8	11	3	9			6			7	1	5		
R3		27	LEICESTER CITY	5-1	Bruce 2, McClair, Sharpe, Hughes	41344	4					12	10		13	8	11	3	9			6		2	7	1	5		
R4	Nov	30	Everton	2-0	Hughes, Giggs	34052	4		7		12	11	10	8	3	5						6	2		9	1			
R5	Jan	12	PORTSMOUTH	2-2	Giggs, Cantona	43794	4		7	12		11	10		3	5	13		9			6	2		8	1			
R5r		26	Portsmouth	1-0	McClair	24950	4		7				11		8	3	5	10	9			6	2			1			
SF1	Feb	13	SHEFFIELD WEDNESDAY	1-0	Giggs	43294	4		7			11	10	8	3	5	9					6	2			1			
SF2	Mar	2	Sheffield Wednesday	4-1	Hughes 2, McClair, Kanchelskis	34878	4					11	10	8	3	5	7		9			6	2			1			
F		27	Aston Villa	1-3	Hughes	77231	4		7			11	10	8	3	5	9		12			6	2				13		

Final at Wembley Stadium. Sealey played in the final in goal

European Cup

R1.1	Sep	15	Kispest-Honved	3-2	Keane 2, Cantona	9000	4		9			11		8	3		10					6	2	12	7	1	5		
R1.2		29	KISPEST-HONVED	2-1	Bruce 2	35781	4		9			11	10	8	3			12				6	2	13	7	1	5		
R2.1	Oct	20	GALATASARAY	3-3	Robson, Cantona, og (Hakan)	39396	4		9			11	10			5	2		6				12		7	1	3		
R2.2	Nov	3	Galatasaray	0-0		40000	4		9	13		11		8	3			10			12		5	2	7	1	6		

R2 lost on away goals

F.A. Charity Shield

	Aug	7	Arsenal	1-1	Hughes	66519	4		7			10	9	8	3	5	11					6	2		12	1			

At Wembley Stadium. Won on 5-4 on penalties after extra time.

132

Blackburn Rovers 1994/95

Ewood Park

								Atkins MN	Batty D	Berg H	Flowers TD	Gale AP	Gallacher KW	Hendry EC	Kenna JJ	Le Saux GP	Mimms RA	Newell MC	Pearce IA	Ripley SE	Shearer A	Sherwood TA	Slater RD	Sutton CR	Warhurst P	Wilcox JM	Witschge R	Wright AG
	Aug	20	Southampton	1-1	Shearer		14209			2	1	6		5		3				7	9	8	4	10		11		
		23	LEICESTER CITY	3-0	Berg, Shearer, Sutton		21050			2	1	6		5		3				13	7	9	8	4	10	12	11		
		27	COVENTRY CITY	4-0	Sutton 3, Wilcox		21657	12			1	6		5		3				13	7	9	8	4	10	2	11		
7		31	Arsenal	0-0			37629			2	1	6		5		3					7	9	8	4	10	12	11		
3	Sep	10	EVERTON	3-0	Shearer 2 (1p), Wilcox		26548	13		2	1	6		5		3				12	7	9	8	4	10		11		
2		18	Chelsea	2-1	Sutton, og (Johnsen)		17513	11		2	1	6		5		3					7	9	8	4	10	12			
2		24	ASTON VILLA	3-1	Shearer 2(1p), Sutton		22694	8		2	1	6		5		3					7	9	4		10	12	11		
2	Oct	1	Norwich City	1-2	Sutton		18146	8		2	1			5		3					7	9	4	12	10	6	11		
3		9	Newcastle United	1-1	Shearer (p)		34344	8		2	1			5		3					7	9	4		10	6	11		
2		15	LIVERPOOL	3-2	Sutton 2, Atkins		30263	8		2	1	4		5		3					7	9			10	6	11		
4		23	MANCHESTER UNITED	2-4	Hendry, Warhurst		30260	8		2	1	6		5		3				13	7	9		12	10	4	11		
4		29	Nottingham Forest	2-0	Sutton 2		22131	8		2	1			5		3				12	7	9	4		10	6	11		
2	Nov	2	Sheffield Wednesday	1-0	Shearer		24207			2	1	6		5		3					7	9	8		10	4	11		
2		5	TOTTENHAM HOTSPUR	2-0	Wilcox, Shearer (p)		26933			2	1	6		5		3					7	9			10	4	11		
2		19	Ipswich Town	3-1	Shearer, Sherwood, Sutton		17607	8			1	6				3				5	7	9	4	11	10	2			
1		26	QUEEN'S PARK RANGERS	4-0	Shearer 3 (1p), Sutton		21302	8		6	1					3				12	5	7	9	4	11	10	2		13
1	Dec	3	Wimbledon	3-0	Atkins, Shearer, Wilcox		12341	8		6	1			5		3					7	9	4		10	2	11		
1		10	SOUTHAMPTON	3-2	Shearer 2, Atkins		23372	8		6	1			5		3				13		7	9	4	12	10	2	11		
1		17	Leicester City	0-0			20559	8		2	1	6				3				5	7	9	4		10		11		
1		26	Manchester City	3-1	Atkins, Le Saux, Shearer		23387	8		2	1			5		3					7	9	4		10		11		
1		31	Crystal Palace	1-0	Sherwood		14232	8		2	1			5		3				6	7	9	4		10		11		
1	Jan	2	WEST HAM UNITED	4-2	Shearer 3(2p), Le Saux		25503	8		2	1	6		5		3				13		7	9	4		10	12	11		
1		14	NOTTM. FOREST	3-0	Warhurst, Wilcox, og (Chettle)		27510	8		2	1			5						12	6		9		7	10	4	11		3
1		22	Manchester United	0-1			43742	8		2	1			5		3				12	13		9	4		10	6	11		7
1		28	IPSWICH TOWN	4-1	Shearer 3 (1p), Sherwood		21325	12		2	1			5		3				13	6		9	8	7	10	4	11		
1	Feb	1	LEEDS UNITED	1-1	Shearer (p)		28561	8		2	1			5		3	12					6				10	7	11		
1		5	Tottenham Hotspur	1-3	Sherwood		28124	12		2				5				1	13	6	7	9	4		10	8	11		3
1		12	SHEFFIELD WEDNESDAY	3-1	Atkins, Shearer, Sherwood		22223	8		2				5				1		6		9	4	11	10	7			3
1		22	WIMBLEDON	2-1	Atkins, Shearer		20586	8		2				5		3		1	10	6	12	9	4	11		7			
1		25	NORWICH CITY	0-0			25579	8		2	1			5		3			10	6	7	9	4				12	11		
1	Mar	4	Aston Villa	1-0	Hendry		40114	8		2	1			5		3				6	7	9	4		10		11		
1		8	ARSENAL	3-1	Shearer 2 (1p), Le Saux		23452	8		2	1			5		3				13	6	7	9	4		10	12	11		
1		11	Coventry City	1-1	Shearer		18556	8		2	1			5		3				13	6	7	9	4	12	10	11		
1		18	CHELSEA	2-1	Shearer, Sherwood		25490	8		2	1			5	3						6	7	9	4		10				
1	Apr	1	Everton	2-1	Shearer, Sutton		37905	8		2	1			5	3	11					6	7	9	4		10				
1		4	Queen's Park Rangers	1-0	Sutton		16508	8		2	1			5	3	11					6	7	9	4		10				
1		15	Leeds United	1-1	Hendry		39426	8		2	1			5	3	11					6	7	9	4		10				
1		17	MANCHESTER CITY	2-3	Hendry, Shearer		27851	8	12	2	1			5	3	11					6	7	9	4		10				
1		20	CRYSTAL PALACE	2-1	Gallacher, Kenna		28005	8	4	5	1		11		2	3					6	7	9		12	10				
1		30	West Ham United	0-2			24202		4	2	1			5	3	6		12				7	9	8		10			11	
1	May	8	NEWCASTLE UNITED	1-0	Shearer		30545		4	2	1			5	3	11					6	7	9	8	12	10				
1		14	Liverpool	1-2	Shearer		40014		4	2	1			5	3	11					6	7	9	8		10				

	Apps	30	4	40	39	15	1	38	9	39	3	2	22	36	42	38	12	40	20	27	1	4
	Subs	4	1								1	10	6	1			6		7				1
	Goals			6			1	4	1	3					34	6		15	2	5		

Two own goals

F.A. Cup

| R3 | Jan | 8 | Newcastle United | 1-1 | Sutton | | 31721 | 8 | | 2 | 1 | | | 5 | | 3 | | | | 12 | | 7 | 9 | 4 | | 10 | 6 | 11 | | |
| rep | | 18 | NEWCASTLE UNITED | 1-2 | Sutton | | 22658 | 8 | | 2 | 1 | | | 5 | | 3 | | | | 13 | 6 | | 9 | | 7 | 10 | 4 | 11 | | 12 |

F.L. Cup

R2/1	Sep	20	BIRMINGHAM CITY	2-0	Sutton, Wilcox		14517	6		2	1			5		3				12	7			4	8	10	9	11		
R2/2	Oct	4	Birmingham City	1-1	Sutton		16275	8		2	1			5		3					7	9	4		10	6	11		
R3		26	COVENTRY CITY	2-0	Shearer 2		14538	8		2	1	6		5		3					7	9			10	4	11		
R4	Nov	30	LIVERPOOL	1-3	Sutton		30115			6	1	4		5		3				12	7	9	8		10	2	11		

UEFA Cup

| R1.1 | Sep | 13 | TRELLEBORGS FF | 0-1 | | | 13775 | 12 | | 2 | 1 | 6 | | 5 | | 3 | | | | | 7 | 9 | 8 | 4 | 10 | | 11 | | |
| R1.2 | | 27 | Trelleborgs FF | 2-2 | Shearer, Sutton | | 6730 | 8 | | 2 | 1 | | 6 | 5 | | 3 | | | | 12 | 7 | 9 | 4 | | 10 | 13 | 11 | | |

Played at 13 in R1/1: Makel

F.A. Charity Shield

| | Aug | 14 | Manchester United | 0-2 | | | 60402 | 4 | | 2 | 1 | 6 | | 5 | | 3 | | | | | 9 | 7 | | 8 | 10 | | 11 | | |

PL Thorne played at 12

Manchester United 1995/96

Old Trafford

						Beckham DRJ	Bruce SR	Butt N	Cantona E	Cole AA	Cooke TJ	Davies SI	Giggs RJ	Irwin JD	Keane RM	May D	McClair BJ	Neville GA	Neville PJ	O'Kane JA	Pallister GA	Parker PA	Pilkington KW	Prunier W	Schmeichel PB	Scholes P	Sharpe LS	Thornley BL
	Aug	19	Aston Villa	1-3	Beckham	34655	12		7						3	8		9	5	2	13	6	4			1	10	11	
		23	WEST HAM UNITED	2-1	Scholes, Keane	31966	11	4	7	12					3	8		9	2			6				1	10	5	13
		26	WIMBLEDON	3-1	Keane 2, Cole	32226	11	4	7		9		13	12	3	8			2			6				1	10	5	
3		28	Blackburn Rovers	2-1	Sharpe, Beckham	29843	11	4	7		9		13	12	3	8			2			6				1	10	5	
2	Sep	9	Everton	3-2	Sharpe 2, Giggs	39496	11	4	7		9		13	12	3	8			2			6				1	10	5	
2		16	BOLTON WANDERERS	3-0	Scholes 2, Giggs	32812	10	4	7			8	12	11							3	6	2			1	9	5	
1		23	Sheffield Wednesday	0-0		34101	10	4	7			12	8	11	3		5					6	2			1	9		
3	Oct	1	LIVERPOOL	2-2	Butt, Cantona (p)	34934	13	4	10	7	9			11		8			2	3		6				1	12	5	
2		14	MANCHESTER CITY	1-0	Scholes	35707	8	4	7		9			11		5		12	2	3		6				1	10	13	
2		21	Chelsea	4-1	Scholes 2, Giggs, McClair	30192		4	8	7	9			11	3	5		12	2			6				1	10		
2		28	MIDDLESBROUGH	2-0	Pallister, Cole	36580		4	8	7	9			11	3	5		12	2			6				1	10		
2	Nov	4	Arsenal	0-1		38317	14	4	8	7	9			11	3	5		13	2			6				1	10	12	
2		18	SOUTHAMPTON	4-1	Giggs 2, Scholes, Cole	39301	5	4	8	7	9			11	3			13	2	12		6				1	10	14	
2		22	Coventry City	4-0	McClair 2, Irwin, Beckham	23344	5	4	10	7	9			11	3		14	8	2	12		6				1		13	
2		27	Nottingham Forest	1-1	Cantona (p)	29263	10	4	5	7	9			11	3			8	2			6				1	12	13	
2	Dec	2	CHELSEA	1-1	Beckham	42019	11	4		7	9	12			3		6	8	2					1			10	5	
2		9	SHEFFIELD WEDNESDAY	2-2	Cantona 2	41849	11	4		7	9	13	12				6	8	2	3				1			10	5	
2		17	Liverpool	0-2		40546	10	4		7	9			11	3		6	8	2							1	12	5	
2		24	Leeds United	1-3	Cole	39801	11	4	10	7	9				3	5	14	8	2	13			6			1	12		
2		27	NEWCASTLE UNITED	2-0	Cole, Keane	42024	5		10	7	9			11	3	8	4	12	6	2						1			
2		30	QUEEN'S PARK RANGERS	2-1	Cole, Giggs	41890	8		10	7	9			11	2	5		13	6	3			12		4	1		14	
2	Jan	1	Tottenham Hotspur	1-4	Cole	32852	8		10	7	9			11		5		12	4	3			2	14	6	1		13	
2		13	ASTON VILLA	0-0		42667			10	7	9			11	2	8			6	3						1	12	5	
2		22	West Ham United	1-0	Cantona	24197	12	4	10	7	9			11	3	8			2	6						1		5	
2	Feb	3	Wimbledon	4-2	Cantona 2 (1p), Cole, og (Perry)	25423	12	4	10	7	9			11	2	8			6	3						1		5	
2		10	BLACKBURN ROVERS	1-0	Sharpe	42681	10			7	9			11	2	8	4			3		6				1		5	
2		21	EVERTON	2-0	Keane, Giggs	42459	12	4	10	7	9			11	2	8				3		6				1		5	
2		25	Bolton Wanderers	6-0	Scholes 2, Beckham, Bruce, Cole, Butt	21381	5	4	10	7	9			11	2	8		12		3		6				1	13		
2	Mar	4	Newcastle United	1-0	Cantona	36584		4	10	7	9			11	2	8			6	3						1		5	
1		16	Queen's Park Rangers	1-1	Cantona	18817	10	4	12	7	9			11	3	5	6	8	2							1	13	14	
2		20	ARSENAL	1-0	Cantona	50028		4	10	7	9			11		8	6		2	3						1	12	5	
1		24	TOTTENHAM HOTSPUR	1-0	Cantona	50508	13	4	10	7	9			11		8	6	12	2	3						1		5	
1	Apr	6	Manchester City	3-2	Cole, Giggs, Cantona (p)	29688	8	4	10	7	9			11	2	5	13		6	3						1		12	
1		8	COVENTRY CITY	1-0	Cantona	50332	4		10	7	9			11	2		6	8	5							1		3	
1		13	Southampton	1-3	Giggs	15262	6	4	10	7	9			11	2	8	13		5							1	12	3	
1		17	LEEDS UNITED	1-0	Keane	48382	10	4		7	9			11	2	5	14	8		3		6				1	12	13	
1		28	NOTTM. FOREST	5-0	Beckham 2, Scholes, Giggs, Cantona	53926	10			7				11	2	8	4		12	3		6				1	9	5	
1	May	5	Middlesbrough	3-0	May, Cole, Giggs	29922	8		10	7	12			11	2	5	4			3		6				1	9		

	Apps	Subs	Goals
Beckham DRJ	26	7	7
Bruce SR	30		1
Butt N	31	1	2
Cantona E	30		14
Cole AA	32	2	11
Cooke TJ	1	3	
Davies SI	1	5	
Giggs RJ	30	3	11
Irwin JD	31		1
Keane RM	29	5	6
May D	11	10	1
McClair BJ	12	1	3
Neville GA	30	3	
Neville PJ	21	1	
O'Kane JA	0	1	
Pallister GA	21		1
Parker PA	5	1	
Pilkington KW	2	1	
Prunier W	2		
Schmeichel PB	36		
Scholes P	16	10	10
Sharpe LS	21	10	4
Thornley BL	0	1	

One own goal

F.A. Cup

R3	Jan	6	SUNDERLAND	2-2	Butt, Cantona	41563	10	4	8	7	9			11	3	5			2	12		6		1				13	
rep		16	Sunderland	2-1	Scholes, Cole	21378		4	10	7	9			11	3	8			6	5			2			1	13	12	
R4		27	Reading	3-0	Giggs, Parker, Cantona	14780		4	10	7	9			11	3	8			2	6			12			1		5	
R5	Feb	18	MANCHESTER CITY	2-1	Sharpe, Cantona (p)	42692		4	10	7	9			11	2	8				3		6				1		5	
R6	Mar	11	SOUTHAMPTON	2-0	Cantona, Sharpe	45446		4	10	7	9			11	3	8			6	2						1		5	
SF		31	Chelsea	2-1	Cole, Beckham	38421	8		10	7	9			11		4	6		5	2						1		3	
F	May	11	Liverpool	1-0	Cantona	79007	8		10	7	9			11	2	5	4		12	3		6				1	13		

SF at Villa Park, Final at Wembley Stadium

F.L. Cup

R2	Sep	20	YORK CITY	0-3		29049	8	13				12	10	11	3			9		7		6	2	1				5	
R2s	Oct	3	York City	3-1	Scholes 2, Cooke	9386	8	4		7	9	5		11		13			2	12		6				1	10	3	

McGibbon played at 4 in R2

UEFA Cup

R1.1	Sep	12	Rotor Volgograd	0-0		40000	10	4	7				12	11	3	8			2			6	13			1	9	5	
R1.2		26	ROTOR VOLGOGRAD	2-2	Scholes, Schmeichel	29724	10	4	7		9	13		11		8			2	3		6				1	12	5	

Lost on away goals

Manchester United 1996/97

Old Trafford

	Date		Opponent	Score	Scorers	Att	Beckham DRJ	Butt N	Cantona E	Casper CM	Clegg MJ	Cole AA	Cruyff J	Giggs RJ	Irwin JD	Johnsen JR	Keane RM	May D	McClair BJ	Neville GA	Neville PJ	O'Kane JA	Pallister GA	Poborsky K	Schmeichel PB	Scholes P	Solskjaer OG	Thornley BL	Van der Gouw R
	Aug	17	Wimbledon	3-0	Beckham, Cantona, Irwin	25786	10	8	7					11	2	12	5	4	13		3		6		1	9			
		21	EVERTON	2-2	Cruyff, og (Unsworth)	54943	10	8	7				9	11	2			4	12		3		6	5	1				
		25	BLACKBURN ROVERS	2-2	Cruyff, Solskjaer	54178	10		7				9	11	2	5		4	8	12	3		6		1		13		
7	Sep	4	Derby County	1-1	Beckham	18025	10	8	7				9	11	3	5		4		2			6		1	12	13		
5		7	Leeds United	4-0	Butt, Cantona, Poborsky, og (Martyn)	39694	10	8	7			14	9	11	3	6		4	12	2				5	1		13		
1		14	NOTTM. FOREST	4-1	Cantona 2 (1p), Giggs, Solskjaer	54984	10	8	7				13		3	4			12	2			6	5	1		9		
4		21	Aston Villa	0-0		39339	10		7				13	9	11	3	4	5		2			6	12			8		1
3		29	TOTTENHAM HOTSPUR	2-0	Solskjaer 2	54943	10	8	7					13	11	3		4		2			6	5	1	12	9		
4	Oct	12	LIVERPOOL	1-0	Beckham	55128	10	8	7					11	13	3	6	4		2				5	1	12	9		
5		20	Newcastle United	0-5		36579	10	8	7					13		3	5		4	14	2		6	11	1	12	9		
5		26	Southampton	3-6	Beckham, May, Scholes	15256	10	8						11			5	4	14	2	3		6		1	9	13		
6	Nov	2	CHELSEA	1-2	May	55198	10	8	7						2	6	5	4			3			12	1	9	11		
6		16	ARSENAL	1-0	og (Winterburn)	55210	10	8	7					11		6		4		2	3			5	1		9		
7		23	Middlesbrough	2-2	Keane, May	30063	10	8	7	2			12			6	5	4	13			3			1	9		11	
5		30	LEICESTER CITY	3-1	Butt 2, Solskjaer	55196	10	8	7				9	11	3		5	4		2			6	13	1		12		
6	Dec	8	West Ham United	2-2	Beckham, Solskjaer	25045	10		7					11	3	2		4	5		12		6	8	1		9		
6		18	Sheffield Wednesday	1-1	Scholes	37671	13	8	7					11	3	5		4		2	12		6		1	9	10		
4		21	SUNDERLAND	5-0	Solskjaer 2, Cantona 2 (1p), Butt	55081		8	7					11	5			4	13	2	3		6	12	1	10	9	14	
3		26	Nottingham Forest	4-0	Beckham, Butt, Cole, Solskjaer	29032	10	8	7			14		11	3	6		4	13	2				12	1	5	9		
2		28	LEEDS UNITED	1-0	Cantona (p)	55256	10	12	7				13		11	3	6	5	4	2					1	8	9		
3	Jan	1	ASTON VILLA	0-0		55133	10	8	7				13		11	3	6	5	4	2					1	12	9		
2		12	Tottenham Hotspur	2-1	Beckham, Solskjaer	33026	10		7	14			13		11		3	5	4	2			6	12	1	8	9		
2		18	Coventry City	2-0	Giggs, Solskjaer	23080		7	12				11	3	4	5			2			6	10	1	8	9			
1		29	WIMBLEDON	2-1	Cole, Giggs	55314	10		7		2	12		11	3		5		4				6		1	8	9		
1	Feb	1	SOUTHAMPTON	2-1	Cantona, Pallister	55269	10		7		2	13		11	3	12	5		4				6	8	1		9		
1		19	Arsenal	2-1	Cole, Solskjaer	38172	10	12				9		11	3	4	5			13	2		6	8	1		7		
1		22	Chelsea	1-1	Beckham	28324	10					9	13	11	3	4	5				2		6		1		7		
1	Mar	1	COVENTRY CITY	3-1	Cole, Poborsky, og (Breen)	55230	10		7			9	8	11	3	13		4	14	2	12		6	5	1				
1		8	Sunderland	1-2	og (Melville)	22204	10		7			13	11		3	6		4	9	2	5			8	1		12		
1		15	SHEFFIELD WEDNESDAY	2-0	Cole, Poborsky	55267	10	5	7			9		11	3			4		2			6	13	1	12	8		
1		22	Everton	2-0	Cantona, Solskjaer	40079	10	8	7					11	2	12	5	4	13		3		6		1		9		
1	Apr	5	DERBY COUNTY	2-3	Cantona, Solskjaer	55243	10	8	7			9		11	12	4	5			2	3		6		1	13	14		
1		12	Blackburn Rovers	3-2	Cantona, Cole, Scholes	30476	12	8	7			9				4	5			2	3		6			10	11		1
1		19	Liverpool	3-1	Pallister 2, Cole	40892	10	8	7			9				4	5		12	2	3		6	1		11			
1	May	3	Leicester City	2-2	Solskjaer 2	21068	12	8	7			9				4	5			2	3		6		1		10		
1		5	MIDDLESBROUGH	3-3	Keane, G Neville, Solskjaer	54489	10		7			9			3	5	8	4		2			6		1	12	11		
1		8	NEWCASTLE UNITED	0-0		55236	10		7			9				6	5	4	13	2	3			8	1	11	12		
1		11	WEST HAM UNITED	2-0	Cruyff, Solskjaer	55249	10	8	7		14		12		2	6		4	13		3			5	1	11	9		

	Apps	Subs	Goals
Beckham	33	3	8
Butt	24	2	5
Cantona	36		11
Casper	0	2	
Clegg	3	1	
Cole	10	10	7
Cruyff	11	5	3
Giggs	25	1	3
Irwin	29	2	1
Johnsen	26	5	
Keane	21		2
May	28	1	3
McClair	4	15	
G Neville	30	1	1
P Neville	15	3	
O'Kane	1		
Pallister	27		3
Poborsky	15	7	3
Schmeichel	36		
Scholes	16	8	3
Solskjaer	25	8	18
Thornley	1	1	
Van der Gouw	2		

Five own goals

F.A. Cup

	Date		Opponent	Score	Scorers	Att																						
R3	Jan	5	TOTTENHAM HOTSPUR	2-0	Beckham, Scholes	52495	10		7				9		11	3	6	5	4	12	2			1	8	13		
R4		25	WIMBLEDON	1-1	Scholes	53342			7	4	2	13		11	3		5		8	6				10	1	9	12		
rep	Feb	4	Wimbledon	0-1		25601	10		7				9		11	3	4	5		12	2		6	8	1		13		

F.L. Cup

	Date		Opponent	Score	Scorers	Att																						
R3	Oct	23	SWINDON TOWN	2-1	Poborsky, Scholes	49305				6							5	4	9	2	3			11		10		7	1
R4	Nov	27	Leicester City	0-2		20428				6	3		7				5	4	8			2		10		9		11	1

Cooke played at 13 in R4
S Davies played at 12 in R3 and 14 in R4
Appleton played at 8 (subbed) in R3 and 12 in R4

Champions League

	Date		Opponent	Score	Scorers	Att																						
CL	Sep	11	Juventus	0-1		50000	10	8	7				13	9	11	3	4			14	2		6	5	1		12		
CL		25	RAPID VIENNA	2-0	Beckham, Solskjaer	51831	10	13	7				14		11	3	4	5	12		2		6	8	1		9		
CL	Oct	16	Fenerbahce	2-0	Beckham, Cantona	26200	10	8	7					11		3	5		4		2		6	12	1		9		
CL		30	FENERBAHCE	0-1		53297	10	8	7					11		3	6	5	4	2	12			9	1	13	14		
CL	Nov	20	JUVENTUS	0-1		53529	10	8	7					13	11		6	5	4	12	2	3			1		9		
CL	Dec	4	Rapid Vienna	2-0	Cantona, Giggs	45000	10	8	7	12				11	3			5	4	13	2		6	14	1		9		
QF1	Mar	5	PORTO	4-0	Cantona, Cole, Giggs, May	53415	10		7			9		11	3	5		4		2			6		1		8		
QF2		19	Porto	0-0		40000	10	8	7						3	11	5	4		2	12		6	14	1	13	9		
SF1	Apr	9	Borussia Dortmund	0-1		48500	10	8	7			12		11	3	4	5			2			6			13	9		1
SF2		23	BORUSSIA DORTMUND	0-1		53606	10	8	7			9			13		5		4	2	3		6		1	12	11		

F.A. Charity Shield

	Date		Opponent	Score	Scorers	Att																						
	Aug	11	Newcastle United	4-0	Cantona, Butt, Beckham, Keane	73214	8	10	7				13	11	2		5	4		12	3		6	14	1	9			

At Wembley Stadium

135

Arsenal 1997/98

Highbury

						Adams TA	Anelka N	Bergkamp DNM	Boa Morte PL	Bould SA	Dixon LM	Garde R	Grimandi G	Hughes SJ	Keown MR	Manninger A	Marshall SR	Mendez Rodriguez A	Overmars M	Parlour R	Petit E	Platt DA	Seaman DA	Upson MJ	Vernazza PAP	Vieira P	Winterburn N	Wreh C	Wright IE
	Aug	9	Leeds United	1-1	Wright	37993			10		5		2	6	13					11	7	9	12	1			4	3		8
		11	COVENTRY CITY	2-0	Wright 2	37324			10				2	6	13		5			11	7	9	12	1			4	3		8
		23	Southampton	3-1	Bergkamp 2, Overmars	15246			10	14	5		2	6				13		11	7	9	12	1			4	3		8
3		27	Leicester City	3-3	Bergkamp 3	21089		14	10		5	2		6	13					11	7	9	12	1			4	3		8
5		30	TOTTENHAM HOTSPUR	0-0		38102		13	10		5	2		6						11	7	9	12	1			4	3		8
4	Sep	13	BOLTON WANDERERS	4-1	Wright 3, Parlour	38138		13	10	14	5	2		6						11	7	9	12	1			4	3		8
2		21	Chelsea	3-2	Bergkamp 2, Winterburn	31290	6		10	13	5	2		12						11	7	9		1			4	3		8
1		24	WEST HAM UNITED	4-0	Overmars 2, Bergkamp, Wright (p)	38012	6	14	10		5	2		12						11	7	9	13	1			4	3		8
1		27	Everton	2-2	Overmars, Wright	35457	6		10	14	5		12	2						11	7	9	13	1			4	3		8
1	Oct	4	BARNSLEY	5-0	Bergkamp 2, Parlour, Platt, Wright	38049	6	13	10	14	5	2								11	7	9	12	1			4	3		8
1		18	Crystal Palace	0-0		26180	6		10	11	5			2				13			7	9	12	1			4	3		8
2		26	ASTON VILLA	0-0		38061	6	13	10	11	5	2									7	9	12	1			4	3		8
2	Nov	1	Derby County	0-3		30004	6	10		12	5	2									7	9	11	1			4	3	13	8
2		9	MANCHESTER UNITED	3-2	Anelka, Platt, Vieira	38205	6	10			12	2		5						11	7		9	1			4	3	13	8
3		22	Sheffield Wednesday	0-2		34373	6					2		5	12	4		13	10	11	7		9	1				3	14	8
5		30	LIVERPOOL	0-1		38094	6		10			2			12	7	5			11		9		1				3	13	8
4	Dec	6	Newcastle United	1-0	Wright	36751	6		10			2				5				11	7	9	4	1				3		8
5		13	BLACKBURN ROVERS	1-3	Overmars	38147	6		10	13		2				5				11	7	9	4	1			12	3		8
6		26	LEICESTER CITY	2-1	Platt, og (Walsh)	38023		13	10		5	2			12	6				11	7		9	1			4	3		8
6		28	Tottenham Hotspur	1-1	Parlour	29601		8	10		5	2			12	13	6			11	7	9		1			4	3		
5	Jan	10	LEEDS UNITED	2-1	Overmars 2	38018			10		5	2				6				11	7	9		1			4	3		8
5		17	Coventry City	2-2	Anelka, Bergkamp	22777		8	10	13	5	2		12		6					7	9		1	11		4	3		
5		31	SOUTHAMPTON	3-0	Adams, Anelka, Bergkamp	38056	6	8	10		5			2	4		1			11	7	9	12					3	13	
5	Feb	8	CHELSEA	2-0	Hughes 2	38083	6	8	10		5	14		2	4		1			11	7	9	13					3		12
2		21	CRYSTAL PALACE	1-0	Grimandi	38094		8		11		2		6	9	5	1				7				3	10	4			
2	Mar	2	West Ham United	0-0		25717	6	8		13		2			10	5	1			11		9	7		3		4	12		
2		11	Wimbledon	1-0	Wreh	22291	6		10	14		2	12		13	5	1			11	7	9					4	3	8	
2		14	Manchester United	1-0		55174	6	13	10			2	12			5	1			11	7	9					4	3	8	
2		28	SHEFFIELD WEDNESDAY	1-0	Bergkamp	38087	6	14	10			2	12	13	9	5				11	7			1			4	3	8	
2		31	Bolton Wanderers	1-0	Wreh	25000	6	8			12			2	13	5				11	7	9	14	1			4	3	10	
2	Apr	11	NEWCASTLE UNITED	3-1	Anelka 2, Vieira	38102	6	8		14	5		2		13					11	7	9	12	1			4	3	10	
2		13	Blackburn Rovers	4-1	Parlour 2, Anelka, Bergkamp	28212	6	8	10		5		2		13					11	7	9	12	1			4	3		
1		18	WIMBLEDON	5-0	Adams, Bergkamp, Overmars, Petit, Wreh	38024	6	8	10			13	2							11	7	9	12	1	5		4	3	14	
1		25	Barnsley	2-0	Bergkamp, Overmars	18691	6	8	10			2				5				11		9	7	1			4	3	12	
1		29	DERBY COUNTY	1-0	Petit	38121	6	8	10			2				5				11	7	9	12	1			4	3	13	
1	May	3	EVERTON	4-0	Overmars 2, Adams, og (Bilic)	38269	6	8				2	12			5				11	7	9	14	1			4	3	10	13
1		6	Liverpool	0-4		44417		13			11	5	2		6	9		1	14		7		4		3		12		10	8
1		10	Aston Villa	0-1		39372	6	10							2	5				11	7	9	12	1			4	3	13	8

Feb 21: GG McGowan played at 12
Dec 28: I Rankin played at 14

	Apps	26	16	28	4	21	26	6	16	7	18	7	1	1	32	34	32	11	31	5	1	31	35	7	22
	Subs		10		11	3	2	4	6	10		2	2					20			2	1	9	2	
	Goals	3	6	16					1	2					12	5	2	3				2	1	3	10

Two own goals

F.A. Cup

R3	Jan	3	Port Vale	0-0		37471		8	10	13	5			2	14	6				11	7	9		1			4	3	12	
rep		14	Port Vale	1-1	Bergkamp	14964		13	10	14	5	2		12	9	6				11	7			1			4	3		8
R4		24	Middlesbrough	2-1	Overmars, Parlour	28264	6	8	10		5	2		12			1			11	7	9					4	3		
R5	Feb	15	CRYSTAL PALACE	0-0		37164		8	10		5	2		6	4		1			11	7	9	12				13	3	14	
rep		25	Crystal Palace	2-1	Anelka, Bergkamp	15674	6	8	10	11		2			9	5	1			13		7			3		4			
R6	Mar	8	WEST HAM UNITED	1-1	Bergkamp (p)	38077	6	8	10			2				5	1			11	7	9					4	3	12	
rep		17	West Ham United	1-1	Anelka	25859	6	8	10	13		2	7		14	5	1			11		9					4	3	12	
SF	Apr	5	Wolverhampton Wanderers	1-0	Wreh	39372	6	8				12			2	14	5			11	7	9	13	1			4	3	10	
F	May	16	Newcastle United	2-0	Anelka, Overmars	79183	6	8							2	5				11	7	9	12	1			4	3	10	

R3 replay and R6 replay both won 4-3 on penalties a.e.t
SF at Villa Park, Final at Wembley Stadium
J Crowe played at 12 in R5 replay

F.L. Cup

R3	Oct	14	BIRMINGHAM CITY	4-1	Boa Morte 2, Mendez, Platt	27097			8		2		4	10		1	5	11			7		3	6			9			
R4	Nov	18	COVENTRY CITY	1-0	Bergkamp	30199		9	10		5	2			11	6	1	12	8		7		4		3			13		
R5	Jan	6	West Ham United	2-1	Overmars, Wright	24770			10		5			2	13	6				11	7	9		1			4	3	12	8
SF1		28	CHELSEA	2-1	Hughes, Overmars	38114	6	8	10		5			2	4		1			11	7	9	12					3		
SF2	Feb	18	Chelsea	1-3	Bergkamp	34330	6	8	10					2	5	12		1		11	7	9	13				4	3		

R4 a.e.t.
J Crowe played at 12 in game 1. Muntasser played at 13

UEFA Cup

R1.1	Sep	16	PAOK (Thessaloniki)	0-1		42000	6	10		14	5	2								11	7	9	12	1			4	3	13	8
R1.2		30	PAOK (THESSALONIKI)	1-1	Bergkamp	37982	6	12	10		5	2								11	7	9	13	1			4	3		8

Manchester United 1998/99

Old Trafford

						Beckham DRI	Berg H	Blomqvist LJ	Brown WM	Butt N	Cole AA	Cruyff J	Curtis JCK	Giggs RJ	Greening J	Irwin JD	Johnsen JR	Keane RM	May D	Neville GA	Neville PJ	Schmeichel PB	Scholes P	Sheringham EP	Solskjaer OG	Stam J	Van der Gouw R	Yorke D
	Aug	15	LEICESTER CITY	2-2	Sheringham, Beckham	55052	7	13			5	9			11		3	4	8		2	1	10	12		6		
		22	West Ham United	0-0		25912	7	4			5	9			11		3	6	8		2	12	1		13	6			10
	Sep	9	CHARLTON ATHLETIC	4-1	Solskjaer 2, Yorke 2	55147	7	12	11			13					3	4	5		2	1	8	14	9	6			10
5		12	COVENTRY CITY	2-0	Yorke, Johnsen	55193	7	12	14		13				11			4	5		2	3	1	8		9	6			10
10		20	Arsenal	0-3		38142	7	4	11		5				9		3		8		2		1			6			10
3		24	LIVERPOOL	2-0	Irwin (p), Scholes	55181	7				12	13			11		3		5		4	2	1	8		9	6			10
2	Oct	3	Southampton	3-0	Yorke, Cole, Cruyff	15251			11	12	5	9	14				3		8		4	2			13		6	1	10
2		17	WIMBLEDON	5-1	Cole 2, Giggs, Beckham, Yorke	55265	7		11	2		9	13	12	8				5		4	3			14		6	1	10
2		24	Derby County	1-1	Cruyff	30867	7		13	2	5	9	14		11				8		4	3	1	12			6		10
2		31	Everton	4-1	Yorke, Cole, Blomqvist, og (Short)	40087	7		11	2		9					12		5		4	3	1	8			6		10
3	Nov	8	NEWCASTLE UNITED	0-0		55174	7		11	2	14	9					3	12	5		4		1	8			13	6	10
2		14	BLACKBURN ROVERS	3-2	Scholes 2, Yorke	55198	7		11		5	9	12	3					14		4	2	1	8			13	6	10
2		21	Sheffield Wednesday	1-3	Cole	39475	7		11	12	14	9					3		5		4	2	1	8			13	6	10
2		29	LEEDS UNITED	3-2	Solskjaer, Keane, Butt	55172		12		2	5	9			14				8		4	3	1	7	13	11	6		10
2	Dec	5	Aston Villa	1-1	Scholes	39241	7		11	2	12	9			13		3		5		4		1	8			6		10
		12	Tottenham Hotspur	2-2	Solskjaer 2	36058	7	12	14		5	13			11			3	8		4	2	1			10	9	6		
2		16	CHELSEA	1-1	Cole	55159	13		11	2	5	9			14		3		8		4		1	7	12		6		10
3		19	MIDDLESBROUGH	2-3	Butt, Scholes	55152	7				5	9			11		3	6	8		4	2	1	13	10	12			
3		26	NOTTM. FOREST	3-0	Johnsen 2, Giggs	55216	7	4	14		5				11	12	3	6	8			2	1	9	10	13			
3		29	Chelsea	0-0		34741	7				5	9			11		3	4	8		2		1	10	12		6		
3	Jan	10	WEST HAM UNITED	4-1	Yorke, Cole 2, Solskjaer	55180		4	11	2	5	9	14		7		3	12	8							13	6	1	10
2		16	Leicester City	6-2	Yorke 3, Cole 2, Stam	22091	7	4	11	2		9			8		3		5			12	1				6		10
1		31	Charlton Athletic	1-0	Yorke	20043	7	4			5	9			11		3				2	1	12			13	6		10
1	Feb	3	DERBY COUNTY	1-0	Yorke	55174			12		5				11		3	4	8		2	1	7			9	6		10
1		6	Nottingham Forest	8-1	Yorke 2, Cole 2, Solskjaer 4	30025	7		11		14	9		12				4	5		2	3	1	8		13	6		10
1		17	ARSENAL	1-1	Cole	55171	7		11		5	9			12			4	8		2	3	1	13			6		10
1		20	Coventry City	1-0	Giggs	22594	7	12				9			11		3	4	5		2	14	1	8		13	6		10
1		27	SOUTHAMPTON	2-1	Keane, Yorke	55316	7	4			5	14			11		12	6	13		2	3	1	8		9			10
1	Mar	13	Newcastle United	2-1	Cole 2	36776	7	4				9			11		3	14	5		2	13	1	8			6	12	10
1		21	EVERTON	3-1	Solskjaer, G Neville, Beckham	55182	7	4			8	9		14		12		5			2	3	1		13	11	6		10
1	Apr	3	Wimbledon	1-1	Beckham	26121	7	4	11			9					3	6	5		2		1	8			12		10
1		17	SHEFFIELD WEDNESDAY	3-0	Solskjaer, Sheringham, Scholes	55270			11	4	5					13	14		8	12	2	3		7	10	9	6	1	
2		25	Leeds United	1-1	Cole	40255	7		11	6	5	9					3		8	4	2	12	1	13	14				10
1	May	1	ASTON VILLA	2-1	og (Watson), Beckham	55189	7		11	12	5						3	6		4	2	13	1	8	9				10
2		5	Liverpool	2-2	Yorke, Irwin (p)	44702	7				12	9					3	4	5		2	13	1	8			6		10
1		9	Middlesbrough	1-0	Yorke	34655	7				12	14					3		5	4	2	13	1	8	9		6		10
1		12	Blackburn Rovers	0-0		30436	7				5	9			11		3	4		12	2	8	1	13	14		6		10
1		16	TOTTENHAM HOTSPUR	2-1	Beckham, Cole	55189	7				12	13			11		3	6	5	4	2	14	1	8	9				10

Apps	33	10	20	11	22	26	0	1	20	0	26	19	33	4	34	19	34	24	7	9	30	4	32
Subs	1	6	5	3	9	6	5	3	4	3	3	3	2	2		9		7	10	10		1	
Goals	6		1		2	17	2		3		2	3	2		1			6	2	12	1		18

Two own goals

F.A. Charity Shield

| | Aug | 9 | Arsenal | 0-3 | | 67342 | 7 | 13 | | | 5 | 9 | 15 | | 11 | | 3 | 4 | 8 | | 2 | 14 | 1 | 10 | 16 | 12 | 6 | | |

Played at Wembley Stadium

F.A. Cup

R3	Jan	3	MIDDLESBROUGH	3-1	Irwin (p), Cole, Giggs	52232		4	11	2	5	9			7		3		8			12	1		13	14	6		10
R4		24	LIVERPOOL	2-1	Yorke, Solskjaer	54591	7	4			5	9			11		3	13	8		2		1	14		12	6		10
R5	Feb	14	FULHAM	1-0	Cole	54798	7	4	13		5	9				12	3		14		2	11	1			8	6		10
R6	Mar	7	CHELSEA	0-0		54587	7	4	11	6		14					3		8		2	5	1	10	13	9			12
rep		10	Chelsea	2-0	Yorke 2	33075	7	4	14			9			11		3		5		2	12	1	8			13	6		10
SF	Apr	11	Arsenal	0-0		39217	7				5	9			11		3		4	8	2	12	1	13			14	6		10
rep		14	Arsenal	2-1	Beckham, Giggs	30223	7		11		5				14			4	8		2	3	1	13	10	9	6		12
F	May	22	Newcastle United	2-0	Scholes, Sheringham	79101	7					9			11			6	5	4	2	3	1	8	12	10	13		14

SF and SF replay at Villa Park, Final at Wembley Stadium

F.L. Cup

R3	Oct	28	BURY	2-0	Solskjaer, Nevland	52495		4		12					11	3			9			6		8		14		10	1	
R4	Nov	11	NOTTINGHAM FOREST	2-1	Solskjaer 2	37237		4			5		9	3		7						6					10			1
R5	Dec	2	Tottenham Hotspur	1-3	Sheringham	35702	12	4	14			5			3	11	7		6					8		10	9		1	

R3 a.e.t.

Clegg played at 2 in all three games, subbed in R3
Mulryne played at 5 (subbed) in R3 and 8 in R4
Nevland played at 13 in R3, Notman played at 13 in R5
M Wilson played at 7 (subbed) in game 1 and 11 in game 2
Wallwork played at 12 in R4

Champions League

QR1	Aug	12	LKS LODZ	2-0	Cole, Giggs	50906	7				5	9			11		3	4	8		2		1	10		12	6		
QR2		26	LKS Lodz	0-0		8000	7				5				11		3	4	8		2	1	9	10	12	6			
CL	Sep	16	BARCELONA	3-3	Beckham, Scholes, Giggs	53601	7	4	14		13				11		3		5		2	12	1	8		9	6		10
CL		30	Bayern Munich	2-2	Scholes, Yorke	53000	7		11				12				3		5		4	2	1	8	9		6		10
CL	Oct	21	Brondby	6-2	Keane, Cole, Yorke, Giggs 2, Solskjaer	40530			11	2		9	12		7				5		4	3	1	8		13	6		10
CL	Nov	4	BRONDBY	5-0	P Neville, Beckham, Cole, Yorke, Scholes	53250	7		11	12		9	14				2		5		4	3	1	8		13	6		10
CL		25	Barcelona	3-3	Cole, Yorke 2	67648	7		11	2	12	9					3		5		4		1	8			6		10
CL	Dec	9	BAYERN MUNICH	1-1	Keane	54434	7				2	13	9		11		3	12	5		4		1	8			6		10
QF1	Mar	3	INTERNAZIONALE	2-0	Yorke 2	54430	7	12			13	9			11		3	4	5		2		1	8			6		10
QF2		17	Internazionale	1-1	Scholes	79528	7	4				9			11		3	5	8		2	13	1	12			6		10
SF1	Apr	7	JUVENTUS	1-1	Giggs	54487	7	4				9			11		3	12	5		2		1	8	13		6		10
SF2		21	Juventus	3-2	Keane, Cole, Yorke	64500	7				5	9					3	4	8		2		1				6		10
F	May	26	Bayern Munich	2-1	Sheringham, Solskjaer	90000	8		11		5	9			7		3	4			2		1		13	12	6		10

Final in Barcelona

M Wilson played at 14 on Oct 21

Manchester United 1999/2000

Old Trafford

						Beckham DRJ	Berg H	Bosnich MJ	Butt N	Clegg MJ	Cole AA	Cruyff J	Culkin NJ	Curtis JCK	Fortune Q	Giggs RJ	Greening J	Higginbotham DJ	Irwin JD	Johnsen JR	Keane RM	May D	Neville GA	Neville PJ	Scholes P	Sheringham EP	Silvestre MS	Solskjaer OG	Stam J	Taibi M	Van der Gouw R	Wallwork R	Wilson MA	Yorke D
	Aug	8	Everton	1-1	Yorke	39141	7	4	1	12		9								3		5			2	8			11	6					10
		11	SHEFFIELD WEDNESDAY	4-0	Scholes, Yorke, Cole, Solskjaer	54941	7	4	1	12		9					11			3		5			2	8	13		14	6					10
		14	LEEDS UNITED	2-0	Yorke 2	55187	7	4	1	13		9					11			3		5			2	8	14			6	12				10
1		22	Arsenal	2-1	Keane 2	38147	7	4		13		9	12				11			3		5			2	8	14			6	1				10
1		25	Coventry City	2-1	Scholes, Yorke	22022	7	4		5				12			11			3		8			2	13	9		14	6	1				10
1		30	NEWCASTLE UNITED	5-1	Cole 4, Giggs	55190	7	4		5	12	9					14	11						2	3	8	13			6	1					10
1	Sep	11	Liverpool	3-2	og 2 (Carragher 2), Cole	44929	7	4		5	12	9					11								2	8		3		6	1		13		10
1		18	WIMBLEDON	1-1	Cruyff	55189		4					13	12			8			2					5	7		9	3	11	6	1				10
1		25	SOUTHAMPTON	3-3	Sheringham, Yorke 2	55249	7	4		5										2					8	9	3	11	6	1				10
2	Oct	3	Chelsea	0-5		34909	7	4		5		9								2					11	8	14	3	13	6	1		12		10
2		16	WATFORD	4-1	Yorke, Cole 2, Irwin (p)	55188	7		1	5		9					11	14		2		12			3	8		4	13	6					10
3		23	Tottenham Hotspur	1-3	Giggs	36072	7		1			9					11	12		2		5			3	8		4	13	6					10
2		30	ASTON VILLA	3-0	Scholes, Cole, Keane	55211	7		1			9	14				11			2		5			3	8		4	13	6			12		10
1	Nov	6	LEICESTER CITY	2-0	Cole 2	55191		12	1			9					11		3			5	13		2	8		4	7	6					10
1		20	Derby County	2-1	Butt, Cole	33370	7	12		5		9					11					8		2	3			4	13	6	1				10
1	Dec	4	EVERTON	5-1	Irwin (p), Solskjaer 4	55193			1	5		14					11			3		8		2	13	7	9	4	10	6		12			
1		18	West Ham United	4-2	Yorke 2, Giggs 2	26037	7			13							11			3		5		2	12	8	9	4		6	1				10
2		26	BRADFORD CITY	4-0	Fortune, Yorke, Cole, Keane	55188			1	5		14				11						8		2	3	7	9	4	10	6			12		13
2		28	Sunderland	2-2	Keane, Butt	41269	7		1	5		9					11			3		8		2		14		12	4	13	6					10
2	Jan	24	ARSENAL	1-1	Sheringham	58293	7		1	5		9					11			3		8		2	12		13	4		6					10
1		29	MIDDLESBROUGH	1-0	Beckham	61267	7		1	5		14					11			3		8		2		12	9	4	13	6					10
1	Feb	2	Sheffield Wednesday	1-0	Sheringham	39640	7		1	5							11			3		8		2		12	9	4		6					10
1		5	COVENTRY CITY	3-2	Cole 2, Scholes	61380	7		1	13		9	12									5		2	3	8	10	4	11	6					
1		12	Newcastle United	0-3		36470	7		1	12		9					11			3		8		2		8	10	4	13	6					
1		20	Leeds United	1-0	Cole	40160			1	5		9					11			3		8		2		7	12	4		6					10
		26	Wimbledon	2-2	Cruyff, Cole	26129	7	12	1	5		9	8				11							2	3		10	4	13	6					
1	Mar	4	LIVERPOOL	1-1	Solskjaer	61592	7					5					12			11		3		8	2		13	4	9	6	1				10
		11	DERBY COUNTY	3-1	Yorke 3	61619	7	6	1	13					11					5		2	3	8		4	9			6				12	
		18	Leicester City	2-0	Beckham, Yorke	22170	7	4	1	13		9					11			3		5		2		8	12			6					10
		25	Bradford City	4-0	Yorke 2, Scholes, Beckham	18276	7	6	1			9					11					5		2	3	8		4	13					12		10
1	Apr	1	WEST HAM UNITED	7-1	* see below	61611	7		1	12		9					11			3		5		2		8	14	4	13	6					10
		10	Middlesbrough	4-3	Giggs, Cole, Scholes, Fortune	34775	7	4	1	13		9				14	11			3		5		2		8		12		6					
		15	SUNDERLAND	4-0	Solskjaer 2, Butt, Berg	61612	14	13	1	5						11						8		2	3	7	9	4	10	6		12			
		22	Southampton	3-1	Beckham, og (Benali), Solskjaer	15245	7			5		9					11				12	8		2	3		14	4	10	6	1				13
		24	CHELSEA	3-2	Yorke 2, Solskjaer	61593	7	12		5			14				11				6	8		2	3	13		4	9		1				10
		29	Watford	3-2	Yorke, Giggs, Cruyff	20250		4		5			13				11	7	12		6			2		9	3	10			1		8	14	
1	May	6	TOTTENHAM HOTSPUR	3-1	Solskjaer, Beckham, Sheringham	61629	7	13		5		14					11	12	3					2	8	9	4	10	6	1				
1		14	Aston Villa	1-0	Sheringham	39217		6				13					11			5	3			2	7	9	4	8			1	12			10

Apr 1 scorers: Scholes 3(1p), Irwin (p), Cole, Beckham, Solskjaer

	Apps	30	16	23	21	0	23	1	0	0	4	30	1	2	25	2	28	0	22	25	27	15	30	15	33	4	11	0	1	29
	Subs	1	6		11	2	5	7	1	1	2		3	1		1	1		4	4	12	1	13			3	5	2	3	
	Goals	6	1		3		19	3			2	6			3		5				9	5		12							20

Three own goals

Club World Championship

Jan	6	Nexaca	1-1	Yorke	26000	7		1	5		9					11			3		8		2	12			14	4	13	6					10
	8	Vasco da Gama	1-3	Butt	5000			1	5							12			14	11			3		8		2	7		13	4	9	6			10
	11	South Melbourne	2-0	Fortune 2	25000	13	4				9	8				11		7	3					2				10				1	6	5	

All games played in Rio. Did not qualify for final.   Rachubka played at 12 on Jan 11

FA Cup: Did not enter

F.L. Cup

| R3 | Oct | 13 | Aston Villa | 0-3 | | 33815 | | 1 | | 2 | | 9 | | 4 | | | 7 | 3 | | | | | | | | | | 10 | | | 5 | | | | |

Also played: Chadwick (11), Healy (12), O'Shea (6), Twiss (8, subbed), Wellens (13)

Champions League

CL	Sep	14	CROATIA ZAGREB	0-0		53250	7	4			2	9					12	11							3	8	13			6	1		5			10
CL		22	Sturm Graz	3-0	Keane, Yorke, Cole	16480	7	4				9	11							2		5			3	8	14		13	6	1		12			10
CL		29	OLYMPIQUE MARSEILLE	2-1	Cole, Scholes	53993	7	4		5	13	9				14				2					3	8	12		11	6	1					10
CL	Oct	19	Olympique Marseille	0-1		57745	7	4	1			9					11			2		5			3	8			12	6						10
CL		27	Croatia Zagreb	2-1	Beckham, Keane	38000	7	4	1			9	13				11	12		3		5			3	8			14	6						
CL	Nov	2	STURM GRAZ	2-1	Solskjaer, Keane	53745		6	1			9	13				11	7	12	3		5	4	2	14		10					8				
C2		23	Fiorentina	0-2		40000	7	4	1			9					11			3		5		2	12	8	13		14	6						10
C2	Dec	8	VALENCIA	3-0	Keane, Solskjaer, Scholes	54606	7			12		9					11			3		5	4	2		8			10	6	1					13
C2	Mar	1	GIRONDINS BORDEAUX	2-0	Giggs, Sheringham	59786	7			5		9				12	11			3		8		2	13		10	4	14	6	1					
C2		7	Girondins Bordeaux	2-1	Keane, Solskjaer	33100	7	13		5		9					11			3		8		2		10	4	12	6		1					14
C2		15	FIORENTINA	3-1	Cole, Keane, Yorke	59926	7	4	1			9					11			3		5		2		8				6						10
C2		21	Valencia	0-0		48432		4	1	5			12		11					3		8		2	7	9		10	6							
QF1	Apr	4	Real Madrid	0-0		64119	7	4	1	13		9					11			3		5		2		8	14	12		6						10
QF2		19	REAL MADRID	2-3	Beckham, Scholes (p)	59178	7	4				9					11			3		5		2		8	14	12	13	6	1					10

F.A. Charity Shield

| Aug | 1 | Arsenal | 1-2 | Yorke | 70185 | 7 | 4 | 1 | | 5 | | 9 | 11 | | | | | | 3 | | | 13 | | 2 | 8 | 12 | | 14 | 6 | | | | | | 10 |

Played at Wembley Stadium

World Club Championship

| Nov | 30 | Palmeiras | 1-0 | Keane | 53372 | 7 | | 1 | 5 | | | | | | | 11 | | | 3 | | 8 | | 2 | | 10 | 13 | 4 | 9 | 6 | | | | | | 12 |

Played in Tokyo

European Super Cup

| Aug | 27 | Lazio | 0-1 | | 14461 | 7 | 4 | | | | 9 | 13 | | 12 | | | 14 | | | | 5 | | 2 | 3 | 8 | 10 | | 11 | 6 | 1 | | | | | |

Played in Monaco

Manchester United 2000/01

Old Trafford

	Date		Opponent	Score	Scorers	Att	Barthez FA	Beckham DRJ	Brown WM	Butt N	Chadwick LH	Cole AA	Djordjic B	Fortune Q	Giggs RJ	Goram AL	Greening J	Healy DJ	Irwin JD	Johnsen JR	Keane RM	May D	Neville GA	Neville PJ	Rachubka P	Scholes P	Sheringham EP	Silvestre MS	Solskjaer OG	Stam J	Stewart MJ	Van der Gouw R	Wallwork R	Yorke D
	Aug	20	NEWCASTLE UNITED	2-0	Johnsen, Cole	67477	1	7				9			11					4	5		2	3		8	10		13	6			12	14
		22	Ipswich Town	1-1	Beckham	22007	1	7				13			11						5		2	3		8	14	12	9	6			4	10
		26	West Ham United	2-2	Beckham, Cole	25998	1	7				9			11						5		4	2		8	10	3		6				
1	Sep	5	BRADFORD CITY	6-0	Cole,Fortune 2,Sheringham 2,Beckham	67447	1	8		5		9		11				7			4		2	12		13	10	3	14			6		
		9	SUNDERLAND	3-0	Scholes 2, Sheringham	67503	1	7		5		9			11				12	4			2			8	10	3	13	6				
		16	Everton	3-1	Butt, Giggs, Solskjaer	38541	1	7	6	5					11					2			4	13		8	9	3	10			12		14
		23	CHELSEA	3-3	Scholes, Sheringham, Beckham	67568		7	12	14		9			11				2		6	5	4			8	10	3	13	1				
2	Oct	1	Arsenal	0-1		38146	1	7				9			11				2	6	5		4			8	10	3	13					12
		14	Leicester City	3-0	Sheringham 2, Solskjaer	22132	1		4	5					11	12			2	6	8						9	3	7					10
		21	LEEDS UNITED	3-0	Yorke, Beckham, og (Jones)	67523	1	13	12	5				7							6	8	4	2		11		3	9					10
		28	SOUTHAMPTON	5-0	Cole 2, Sheringham 3	67581	1	7	6	5		9			11				2				4	3		8	10		13				12	14
1	Nov	4	Coventry City	2-1	Cole, Beckham	21077	1	7	6			9			11				3				5	4	2	8	10		12					13
		11	MIDDLESBROUGH	2-1	Butt, Sheringham	67576	1	7	6	5	14				11								8	4	2	11	13	3	9				12	10
		18	Manchester City	1-0	Beckham	34429	1	7	6	5					12				3				8	4	2	11	9							10
		25	Derby County	3-0	Sheringham, Butt, Yorke	32910	1		6	5	7		13						2				8	4		11	9	3	14		12			10
1	Dec	2	TOTTENHAM HOTSPUR	2-0	Scholes, Solskjaer	67583	1	7	6	5					12								8	4	2	11	9	3	13					10
		9	Charlton Athletic	3-3	Giggs, Solskjaer, Keane	20043		7	6	5	11				9		13				8		4	2		14	12	3	10		1			
		17	LIVERPOOL	0-1		67533	1	7	6	5	12				11		13		2				8	4		10		3	9					
		23	IPSWICH TOWN	2-0	Solskjaer 2	67597	1	7	6					11	9		12	14					5	4	2	8		3	10			13		
		26	Aston Villa	1-0	Solskjaer	40889	1	7	6	5					11				2				8	4	13	10		3	9			12		
		30	Newcastle United	1-1	Beckham (p)	52134	1	7	6	5	13				11								8	4	2	14		3	9				12	10
1	Jan	1	WEST HAM UNITED	3-1	Solskjaer, og (S Pearce), Yorke	67603	1	7	6	13					11		14						5	4	2	8		3	9				12	10
		13	Bradford City	3-0	Sheringham, Giggs, Chadwick	20551	1	7	13		12	14			11				2				8	4	5		9	3	10	6				
		20	ASTON VILLA	2-0	G Neville, Sheringham	67533	1				5	12	13		11		7		2				8	4	3		9		10	6				
		31	Sunderland	1-0	Cole	47250	1	7	4	13		9			11								5	2	12	8	10	3	14	6				
1	Feb	3	EVERTON	1-0	og (S Watson)	67528	1	7	4		11	9			13				2					5		8	14	3		6			12	10
		10	Chelsea	1-1	Cole	34960		7	4			9			11								5	2			8	3	10	6	1			
		25	ARSENAL	6-1	Yorke 3, Keane, Solskjaer, Sheringham	67535	1	7	4	5	12										8		2			11	13	3	9	6				10
1	Mar	3	Leeds United	1-1	Chadwick	40055	1	7	4	5	12						3						2	11		8	9		10	6				13
		17	LEICESTER CITY	2-0	Yorke, Silvestre	67539			5	13				7			3		8		4	2	1	11	9	12	10	6					14
		31	Liverpool	0-2		44806	1	7	6	5	14				11		3						8	4	2	13	9	12						10
1	Apr	10	CHARLTON ATHLETIC	2-1	Cole, Solskjaer	67505	1		6	5		9			11		2						8	4	12	7	14	3	13					10
		14	COVENTRY CITY	4-2	Yorke 2, Giggs, Scholes	67637		13	4	5		9			11	1							8	2		7		3	14	6		12		10
		21	MANCHESTER CITY	1-1	Sheringham (p)	67535	1	7	2	13	11				14								5	4	3	8	9	12	10	6				
		28	Middlesbrough	2-0	P Neville, Beckham	34417		7	2	5	12	13		11	14				4					3		9		10	6	8	1			
1	May	5	DERBY COUNTY	0-1		67526	1	7		5	11	9			14				2	4				3			10	13			8	12	6	
		13	Southampton	1-2	Giggs	15246			6		7			11	9	1			2	4		13	3								8	12	5	10
		19	Tottenham Hotspur	1-3	Scholes	36078				5		9	12		11				2	6		4		7		8	10	3			1			
						Apps	30	29	25	24	6	15	0	6	24	2	3	0	20	11	28	1	32	24	1	28	23	25	19	15	3	5	4	15
						Subs		2	3	4	10	4	1	1	7		4	1	1			1		5		4	6	5	12			5	8	7
						Goals		9		3	2	9		2	5					1	2			1		6	15	1	10					9

Played on Aug 26 at 12: H Berg

Three own goals

F.A. Charity Shield

	Date		Opponent	Score		Att																											
	Aug	13	Chelsea	0-2		65148	1	7				13		15	11				3	4	5		2			8	9	6	10	12					14

Played at the Millennium Stadium, Cardiff

F.A. Cup

	Date		Opponent	Score	Scorers	Att																											
R3	Jan	7	Fulham	2-1	Sheringham, Solskjaer	19178		7	6	5	13				11								8	4	2		14	3	9			1	12	10
R4		28	WEST HAM UNITED	0-1		67029	1	7		5		9			11						2		8	4			10	3	12	6				13

F.L. Cup

	Date		Opponent	Score	Scorers	Att																											
R3	Oct	31	Watford	3-0	Solskjaer 2, Yorke	18871			6		7			11			8								3	13		9				12	1	5	10
R4	Nov	28	Sunderland	1-2	Yorke	47543				7				11			8	14		6					3			9				13	1	5	10

R4 a.e.t. Played in both games: Clegg (at 2), O'Shea (4). Webber played at 12 in R4

Champions League

	Date		Opponent	Score	Scorers	Att																											
CL	Sep	13	ANDERLECHT	5-1	Cole 3, Irwin (p), Sheringham	62749	1	7				9			11				2	6	5		4	12		8	10	3	14					13
CL		19	Dinamo Kiev	0-0		60000		7		5		9			11				2	6	8		4				13	3	12		1			10
CL		26	PSV (Eindhoven)	1-3	Scholes (p)	33500	1	14	6	5					13		7				8		4	2		11		3	9				12	10
CL	Oct	18	PSV (EINDHOVEN)	3-1	Sheringham, Scholes, Yorke	66316	1	7	12	13		9			11				2	6	5		4			8	10	3						14
CL		24	Anderlecht	1-2	Irwin (p)	28000	1	7	13	5		9			11				2	6			4			8		3	12					10
CL	Nov	8	DINAMO KIEV	1-0	Sheringham	66776	1	7	6	5		9		13	11				3		8		4	2			10	14						12
C2		21	PANATHINAIKOS	3-1	Sheringham, Scholes 2	65024	1	7	6	5											8		4	2		11	9	3						10
C2	Dec	6	Sturm Graz	2-0	Scholes, Giggs	16500	1	7	6	5					13				2				8	4	12	11	9	3	14					10
C2	Feb	14	Valencia	0-0		51000	1	7	4	12		9			11						5		2			8	10	3	13	6				
C2		20	VALENCIA	1-1	Cole	66715	1	7	4	13		9			11						5		2			8	10	3	12	6				
C2	Mar	7	Panathinaikos	1-1	Scholes	27231	1	7	4		12	9									5		2	11		8	13	3	14	6				10
C2		13	STURM GRAZ	3-0	Butt, Sheringham, Keane	66404	1			5	7						12		2		8		4			11	9	3	10	6				
QF1	Apr	3	BAYERN MUNICH	0-1		66584	1	7	4			9			11						5		2			8		3	10	6				12
QF2		18	Bayern Munich	1-2	Giggs	60000	1		4	5	12	9			11						8		2			7	14	3	13	6				10

Arsenal 2001/02

Highbury

						Adams TA	Aliadiere J	Bergkamp DNM	Campbell SJ	Cole A	Dixon LM	Edu	Grimandi G	Henry T	Jeffers F	Kanu N	Keown MR	Lauren	Ljungberg KF	Luzhny O	Parlour R	Pires R	Seaman DA	Stepanovs I	Taylor SJ	Upson MJ	Van Bronckhorst GC	Vieira P	Wiltord S	Wright RI
Aug	18	Middlesbrough	4-0	Henry, Pires (p), Bergkamp 2	31557	6		14	5	3			12	10				2	8		7	11	1					13	4	9	
	21	LEEDS UNITED	1-2	Wiltord	38062	6		12	5	3				10	14				2	8		7	11	1					13	4	9	
	25	LEICESTER CITY	4-0	Ljungberg, Wiltord, Henry, Kanu	37909	6		10	5	3				12	13		14		2	8			7	1					11	4	9	
4 Sep	8	Chelsea	1-1	Henry	40855	6		8	12	3			4	10			13	5	2	14			7	1					11		9	
1	15	Fulham	3-1	Ljungberg, Henry, Bergkamp	20805			12	6	3			13	10	9			5	2	8		7	11	1					4	14		
2	22	BOLTON WANDERERS	1-1	Jeffers	38014	6		8		3			5	10	14					2		7	13	1				12	11	4	9	
1	29	Derby County	2-0	Henry 2 (1p)	29200					3			14	10	9	13	5	2	8	12		7						6	11	4		1
2 Oct	13	Southampton	2-0	Henry, Pires	29759			13	5	3			14	10					2	8		12	7					6	11	4	9	1
1	20	BLACKBURN ROVERS	3-3	Henry, Pires, Bergkamp	38108			10					8	9		12	5	2				7	11					6	3	4	13	1
3	27	Sunderland	1-1	Kanu	48029			13	6					12		10	5	2	8			7						3	11	4	9	1
5 Nov	4	CHARLTON ATHLETIC	2-4	Henry 2 (1p)	38010			10		3			6	9			5	2	8				7						11	4	12	1
5	17	Tottenham Hotspur	1-1	Pires	36049			10	8	3				8			12	5	2			7	11							4	9	1
3	25	MANCHESTER UNITED	3-1	Ljungberg, Henry 2	38174			12	5	3			13	10		9			2	8		7	11			1	6		4			
2 Dec	1	Ipswich Town	2-0	Ljungberg, Henry (p)	24666			13	5	3	12			10		9			2	8		7	11			1	6	14	4			
2	9	ASTON VILLA	3-2	Wiltord, Henry 2	38074			10	5	3				9		14	12	2	8			7	11			1	6		4	13		
2	15	West Ham United	1-1	Cole	34523			10	6	3	12	8	9			13	5	2					11						4	7		
3	18	NEWCASTLE UNITED	1-3	Pires	38012			12	6	3				10			9	5	2			8	11			1			13	4	7	
2	23	Liverpool	2-1	Ljungberg, Henry (p)	44297				6	3				10			9	5	2	8	13	4	7			1	12	11			14	
2	26	CHELSEA	2-1	Campbell, Wiltord	38079			14	6	3				10			9	5	2	8		7	11			1		12	4	13	1	
1	29	MIDDLESBROUGH	2-1	Cole, Pires	37948			13	6	3			14	10		9	5		8	2		7							11	4	12	
4 Jan	13	LIVERPOOL	1-1	Ljungberg	38132			14	6		12		8	10		9	5		11	2			7			1	3		4	13		
4	20	Leeds United	1-1	Pires	40143			10	6	3	12			9			5		8	2		7	11						13	4	14	1
2	23	Leicester City	3-1	Wiltord, Henry, Van Bronckhorst	21344			10	6	3				12	9		5			2		7	11					13	8	4	14	1
2	30	Blackburn Rovers	3-2	Henry, Bergkamp 2	25893			10	6	3				14	9		5		2	8			11					12	13	4	7	1
3 Feb	2	SOUTHAMPTON	1-1	Wiltord	38024			10	5	3		14	12	9					2	8		11						6	13	4	7	1
4	10	Everton	1-0	Wiltord	30859				5		12		8	10					2	7				6			3	11	4	9	1
2	23	FULHAM	4-1	Lauren, Vieira, Henry 2	38029		13		5		12		14	10				7	2	8	11	1	6						3	4	9	
2 Mar	2	Newcastle United	2-0	Campbell, Bergkamp	52067			10	5		2	12	8			13		7		3		11	1	6					4	9		
1	5	DERBY COUNTY	1-0	Pires	37878			10	5		12	13		9				2		3	8	11	1	6					4	7		
2	17	Aston Villa	2-1	Pires, Edu	41520			10	5		12	8	13			14		3	7	2		11	1	6					4	9		
3	30	SUNDERLAND	3-0	Vieira, Wiltord, Bergkamp	38047	6		10	5	3		8	12	9	13	14			11	2			1						4	7		
1 Apr	1	Charlton Athletic	3-0	Ljungberg, Henry 2	26339			10	6	3	2	13	8	9			5		11	12			1						4	7		
1	6	TOTTENHAM HOTSPUR	2-1	Lauren (p), Ljungberg	38186	6		10	5		12	8		9		13		2	11	3	14		1						4	7		
1	21	IPSWICH TOWN	2-0	Ljungberg 2	38058	6		10		3			8	13	9		12	5	2	11		7	1						4			
1	24	WEST HAM UNITED	2-0	Ljungberg, Kanu	38038	6		10		3	14	8	13	9			12	5	2	11			1						4			
1	29	Bolton Wanderers	2-0	Ljungberg, Wiltord	27351	6			10	13	3	12	8					14	5	2	11		7	1						4	9	
1 May	8	Manchester United	1-0	Wiltord	67580				6	3	12	8						10	5	2	11		7	1						4	9	
1	11	EVERTON	4-3	Henry 2, Bergkamp, Jeffers	38254			10		3	2	11	4	9	14					5	8			6	12				13	7	1	

	Apps	Subs	Goals
Adams TA	10		
Aliadiere J	0	1	
Bergkamp DNM	22	11	9
Campbell SJ	29	2	2
Cole A	29		2
Dixon LM	3	10	
Edu	8	6	1
Grimandi G	11	15	
Henry T	31	2	24
Jeffers F	2	4	2
Kanu N	9	14	3
Keown MR	21	1	
Lauren	27		2
Ljungberg KF	24	1	12
Luzhny O	15	3	
Parlour R	25	2	1
Pires R	27	1	9
Seaman DA	17		
Stepanovs I	6		
Taylor SJ	9	1	
Upson MJ	10	4	
Van Bronckhorst GC	13	8	1
Vieira P	35	1	2
Wiltord S	23	10	10
Wright RI	12		

F.A. Cup

R3	Jan	5	Watford	4-2	Ljungberg, Henry, Bergkamp, Kanu	20105			13	6	3				10		9	5		8	2		7			1				11	4	12	
R4		27	LIVERPOOL	1-0	Bergkamp	38092			10	6	3				13	9		5			2		14	11					12	8	4	7	1
R5	Feb	16	GILLINGHAM	5-2	Adams, Parlour, Wiltord 2, Kanu	38003	6			5		2	11	12	14	10	9				8	13								4	7	1	
R6	Mar	9	Newcastle United	1-1	Edu	51027			13	5		2	11	8			10		3	7			12		6					4	9	1	
rep		23	NEWCASTLE UNITED	3-0	Campbell, Pires, Bergkamp	38073	6		10	5	3	13	8	14		12				7	2		11							4	9	1	
SF	Apr	14	Middlesbrough	1-0	og (Festa)	61168			10		6	12	8		9				14	5	2	11	3	13						4	7	1	
F	May	4	Chelsea	2-0	Parlour, Ljungberg	73963	6		10	5	3			14			9		13	12	2	11		8		1				4	7		

SF at Old Trafford, Final at the Millennium Stadium, Cardiff Juan played at 3 in R5

F.L. Cup

R3	Nov	5	MANCHESTER UNITED	4-0	Wiltord 3 (1p), Kanu (p)	30693							8	4			10				2	7			5				3		9	1	
R4		27	GRIMSBY TOWN	2-0	Edu, Wiltord	16917		13	10				8					5							6	1			11		9		
R5	Dec	11	Blackburn Rovers	0-4		13278			13				11	4			10	5							14	1	6	3		9			

Played in R3: Tavlaridis (6), Pennant (11, subbed), Halls (12), Itonga (13), Ricketts (14)
Played in R4: Tavlaridis (2), Juan (3), Inamoto (4, subbed), Pennant (7, subbed), Halls (12), Svard (14)
Played in R5: Tavlaridis (2, subbed), Pennant (7, subbed), Inamoto (8, subbed), Halls (12)

Champions League

CL	Sep	11	RCD Mallorca	0-1		22000				6	3				10	13	14	5	2	8		12	7	1					11	4	9		
CL		19	SCHALKE 04	3-2	Ljungberg, Henry 2 (1p)	35361			12					6	10			5	2	8			7	11	1				13	3	4	9	
CL		26	Panathinaikos	0-1		17200					3				10	14	13	5	2	8			7	11	1				6	12	4	9	
CL	Oct	16	PANATHINAIKOS	2-1	Henry 2 (1p)	35432			13	5	3				14	10				2	8		12	7					6	11	4	9	
CL		24	RCD MALLORCA	3-1	Henry, Pires, Bergkamp	34764			10	6					8	9		12	5	2	7		13	11					3	4	14	1
CL		30	Schalke 04	1-3	Wiltord	52500				5	3		8	4			10	12		2	7	11			13		6				9	1	
C2	Nov	21	Deportivo (La Coruna)	0-2		35800				5	3			14			10		13	2	8			7					12	6	11	4	9	1
C2	Dec	4	JUVENTUS	3-1	Ljungberg 2, Henry	35421			13	5	3				14	10		9	12	2	8		7	11					1	6		4	9	
C2	Feb	19	Bayer Leverkusen	1-1	Pires	22200				5			13	12	10			9		2			8	11	1	6				3	4	7	
C2		27	BAYER LEVERKUSEN	4-1	Vieira, Henry, Pires, Bergkamp	35019			10	5		2	14	8	9					3			11	1	6					4	7		
C2	Mar	12	DEPORTIVA (LA CORUNA)	0-2		35392			10	5					8	9		12		2	13	3		11	1	6				4	7		
C2		20	Juventus	0-1		8652				5	12	2	8		10		9		3	7	6		11	1						4	13		

Inamoto played at 14 on Sep 19 and 12 on Feb 27
Pennant played at 14 on Oct 30 and 13 on Feb 27

Manchester United 2002/03

Old Trafford

Due to the complexity and density of this statistical table (league appearances, goals, and player lineups across all competitions), a full cell-by-cell transcription is not reproduced here. Key structural elements:

League (Premier League)

Columns of players (by surname, initials): Barthez FA, Beckham DRJ, Blanc LR, Brown WM, Butt N, Carroll RE, Chadwick LH, Ferdinand RG, Fortune CD, Giggs RJ, Keane RM, Lopez R, May D, Neville GA, Neville PJ, O'Shea JF, Pugh DA, Richardson KE, Roche LP, Scholes P, Silvestre MS, Solskjaer OG, Stewart MJ, Van Nistelrooy RJM, Veron JS.

Date	Opponent	Score	Scorers	Att
Aug 17	WEST BROMWICH ALB.	1-0	Solskjaer	67645
23	Chelsea	2-2	Beckham, Giggs	41541
31	Sunderland	1-1	Giggs	47586
Sep 3	MIDDLESBROUGH	1-0	Van Nistelrooy (p)	67464
11	BOLTON WANDERERS	0-1		67623
14	Leeds United	0-1		39622
21	TOTTENHAM HOTSPUR	1-0	Van Nistelrooy (p)	67611
28	Charlton Athletic	3-1	Van Nistelrooy, Giggs, Scholes	26630
Oct 7	EVERTON	3-0	Van Nistelrooy (p), Scholes 2	67629
19	Fulham	1-1	Solskjaer	18103
26	ASTON VILLA	1-1	Forlan	67619
Nov 2	SOUTHAMPTON	2-1	P Neville, Forlan	67691
9	Manchester City	1-3	Solskjaer	34649
17	West Ham United	1-1	Van Nistelrooy	35049
23	NEWCASTLE UNITED	5-3	Van Nistelrooy 3, Solskjaer, Scholes	67619
Dec 1	Liverpool	2-1	Forlan 2	44250
7	ARSENAL	2-0	Veron, Scholes	67650
14	WEST HAM UNITED	3-0	og (Schemmel), Veron, Solskjaer	67555
22	Blackburn Rovers	0-1		30475
26	Middlesbrough	1-3	Giggs	34673
28	BIRMINGHAM CITY	2-0	Beckham, Forlan	67640
Jan 1	SUNDERLAND	2-1	Beckham, Scholes	67609
11	West Bromwich Albion	3-1	Van Nistelrooy, Solskjaer, Scholes	27129
18	CHELSEA	2-1	Forlan, Scholes	67606
Feb 1	Southampton	2-0	Van Nistelrooy, Giggs	32085
4	Birmingham City	1-0	Van Nistelrooy	29475
9	MANCHESTER CITY	1-1	Van Nistelrooy	67646
22	Bolton Wanderers	1-1	Solskjaer	27409
Mar 5	LEEDS UNITED	2-1	og (Radebe), Silvestre	67135
15	Aston Villa	1-0	Beckham	42602
22	FULHAM	3-0	Van Nistelrooy 3 (1p)	67706
Apr 5	LIVERPOOL	4-0	Van Nistelrooy 2 (2p), Solskjaer, Giggs	67639
12	Newcastle United	6-2	Van Nistelrooy (p), Solskjaer, Giggs, Scholes 3	52164
16	Arsenal	2-2	Van Nistelrooy, Giggs	38164
19	BLACKBURN ROVERS	3-1	Van Nistelrooy, Scholes 2	67626
27	Tottenham Hotspur	2-0	Van Nistelrooy, Scholes	36073
May 3	CHARLTON ATHLETIC	4-1	Beckham, Van Nistelrooy 3	67721
11	Everton	2-1	Beckham, Van Nistelrooy (p)	40168

Apps/Subs/Goals totals row at bottom. Two own goals.

F.A. Cup

Rd	Date	Opponent	Score	Scorers	Att
R3	Jan 4	PORTSMOUTH	4-1	Beckham, Van Nistelrooy 2 (2p), Scholes	67222
R4	26	WEST HAM UNITED	6-0	Van Nistelrooy 2, Solskjaer, Giggs 2, P Neville	67181
R5	Feb 15	ARSENAL	0-2		67209

F.L. Cup

Rd	Date	Opponent	Score	Scorers	Att
R3	Nov 5	LEICESTER CITY	2-0	Beckham (p), Richardson	47848
R4	Dec 3	Burnley	2-0	Solskjaer, Forlan	22034
R5	17	CHELSEA	1-0	Forlan	57985
SF1	Jan 7	BLACKBURN ROVERS	1-1	Scholes	62740
SF2	22	Blackburn Rovers	3-1	Van Nistelrooy (p), Scholes 2	29048
F	Mar 2	Liverpool	0-2		74500

Final at the Millennium Stadium, Cardiff. Nardiello played at 7 game 1 (subbed)

Champions League

Rd	Date	Opponent	Score	Scorers	Att
Q3	Aug 14	Zalaegerszeg	0-1		40000
Q3	27	ZALAEGERSZEG	5-0	Beckham, Van Nistelrooy 2(1p), Solskjaer, Scholes	66814
CL	Sep 18	MACCABI HAIFA	5-2	Veron, Van Nistelrooy, Solskjaer, Giggs, Forlan(p)	63439
CL	24	Bayer Leverkusen	2-1	Van Nistelrooy 2	22500
CL	Oct 1	OLYMPIAKOS (PEIRAIA)	4-0	Giggs 2, Veron, Solskjaer	66902
CL	23	Olympiakos (Peiraia)	3-2	Blanc, Veron, Scholes	14000
CL	29	Maccabi Haifa	0-3		23000
CL	Nov 13	BAYER LEVERKUSEN	2-0	Veron, Van Nistelrooy	66185
C2	26	Basle	3-1	Van Nistelrooy 2, Solskjaer	29501
C2	Dec 11	DEPORTIVO (LA CORUNA)	2-0	Van Nistelrooy	67014
C2	Feb 19	JUVENTUS	2-1	Brown, Van Nistelrooy	66703
C2	25	Juventus	3-0	Van Nistelrooy, Giggs 2	59111
C2	Mar 12	BASLE	1-1	G Neville	66870
C2	18	Deportivo (La Coruna)	0-2		25000
QF1	Apr 8	Real Madrid	1-3	Van Nistelrooy	75000
QF2	23	REAL MADRID	4-3	og (Helguera), Beckham 2, Van Nistelrooy	66708

Fletcher played at 7 on Mar 18 and 14 on Apr 23
Lynch played at 2 and Webber at 14 on Mar 18
Nardiello played at 12 and Timm played at 13 on Oct 29

Arsenal 2003/04

Highbury

						Aliadiere J	Bentley DM	Bergkamp DNM	Campbell SJ	Clichy G	Cole A	Cygan P	Edu	Henry T	Hoyte JR	Kanu N	Keown MR	Lauren	Lehmann J	Ljungberg KF	Parlour R	Pires R	Reyes JA	Silva GA	Toure HK	Vieira P	Wiltord S
	Aug	16	EVERTON	2-1	Henry (p), Pires	38014				6		3		10				12	2	1	7	13	11		8	5	4	9
		24	Middlesbrough	4-0	Silva, Henry, Wiltord 2	29450			13	6		3		14	10				2	1	7	12	11		8	5	4	9
		27	ASTON VILLA	2-0	Campbell, Henry	38010			13	6		3			10				2	1	7	12	11		8	5	4	9
1		31	Manchester City	2-1	Ljungberg, Wiltord	46436			13			3		14	10		6		2	1	7	12	11		8	5	4	9
1	Sep	13	PORTSMOUTH	1-1	Henry (p)	38052			10	6		3		8	9				2	1	12	7	11			5	4	13
1		21	Manchester United	0-0		67639			10			3		12	9		6		2	1	11	7			8	5	4	
1		26	NEWCASTLE UNITED	3-2	Silva, Henry 2 (1p)	38112						3	12	13	10		6		2	1	11	7	14		8	5	4	9
1	Oct	4	Liverpool	2-1	og (Hyypia), Pires	44374	9			6		3		4	10				2	1		7	11		8	5		12
1		18	CHELSEA	2-1	Henry, Edu	38172			13	6		3	14	4	10		12		2	1		7	11		8	5		9
1		26	Charlton Athletic	1-1	Henry	26660				10	6	3			9		12		2	1	7	4	11		8	5		13
1	Nov	1	Leeds United	4-1	Silva, Henry 2, Pires	36491	13		10	6		3		12	9				2	1	7	4	11		8	5		
1		8	TOTTENHAM HOTSPUR	2-1	Ljungberg, Pires	38101			13	6		3	12	14	10		9		2	1	7	4	11		8	5		
1		22	Birmingham City	3-0	Bergkamp, Ljungberg, Pires	29588	13		10	6	11	3	5	4	9	12	14			1	7		8			2		
2		30	FULHAM	0-0		38063	12		10	6		3	5	4	9		13			1	7		11		8	2		
2	Dec	6	Leicester City	1-1	Silva	32108	9		10	6	14	3	5	4				12		1	7		11		8	2		13
1		14	BLACKBURN ROVERS	1-0	Bergkamp	37677			10	6		3	5	12	9					1	7		13	11		8	2	4	
1		20	Bolton Wanderers	1-1	Pires	28003			10	6	3		5		9					1	7		12	11		8	2	4	
2		26	WOLVERHAMPTON W.	3-0	og (Craddock), Henry 2	38003	13		10	6	3		5	12	9					1	7		8	11			2	4	
2		29	Southampton	1-0	Pires	32151			10	6	3		5	12	9		13		14	1	7		8	11			2	4	
2	Jan	7	Everton	1-1	Kanu	38726				6		3	5	14	10		9		12	1	7		8	11		13	2	4	
1		10	MIDDLESBROUGH	4-1	Henry, og (Queudrue), Ljungberg, Pires	38117	10			6		3	5	14	9		13		2	1	7		12	11		8		4	
1		18	Aston Villa	2-0	Henry 2 (1p)	39380				6		3	5	14	10		9		2	1	7		12	11		8	13	4	
1	Feb	1	MANCHESTER CITY	2-1	og (Tarnat), Henry	38103			10	6		3	14	12	9				2	1	7		4	11	13	8	5		
1		7	Wolverhampton Wan.	3-1	Toure, Henry, Bergkamp	29392			10	6		3		11	9				2	1			7	12	8	5	4		
1		10	SOUTHAMPTON	2-0	Henry 2	38007				6	12	3			9				2	1			7	11	10	8	5	4	
1		21	Chelsea	2-1	Vieira, Edu	41847			10	6	3			7	9				2	1	12			11		8	5	4	
1		28	CHARLTON ATHLETIC	2-1	Henry, Pires	38137			10	6		3	14	8	9				2	1	7			11	13	12	5	4	
1	Mar	13	Blackburn Rovers	2-0	Henry, Pires	28627				6	12	3	13	7	9				2	1				11	10	8	5	4	
1		20	BOLTON WANDERERS	2-1	Bergkamp, Pires	38053			10	6		3	13	7	9				2	1	12			11		8	5	4	
1		28	MANCHESTER UNITED	1-1	Henry	38184			14	6	3		12	8	9				2	1	7			11	10	13	5	4	
1	Apr	9	LIVERPOOL	4-2	Henry 3, Pires	38119			10	6		3		13	9			12	2	1	7			11		8	5	4	
1		11	Newcastle United	0-0		52141			14	6	12	3		11	9				2	1				13	10	8	5	4	7
1		16	LEEDS UNITED	5-0	Henry 4 (1p), Pires	38094			10	6	3			12	9				2	1		14	11		8	5	4	7
1		25	Tottenham Hotspur	2-2	Vieira, Pires	36097			10	6		3		12	9				2	1			7	11	13	8	5	4	
1	May	1	BIRMINGHAM CITY	0-0		38061	14		10	6		3			9				13	2	1	7		12	11	8	5	4	
1		4	Portsmouth	1-1	Reyes	20140	12	11		6		3			9		14	13	2	1	7			8		10	5	4	
1		9	Fulham	1-0	Reyes	18102	13			6	14	3			9				2	1	7		8	12	11	10	5	4	
1		15	LEICESTER CITY	2-1	Vieira, Henry	38419			10	6		3		14	9				12	2	1	7		11	13	8	5	4	

Apps	3	1	21	35	7	32	10	13	37	0	3	3	30	38	27	16	33	7	29	36	29	8
Subs	7		7		5		8	17		1	7	7	2		3	9	3	6	3	1		4
Goals			4	1				2	30		1				4		14	2	4	1	3	3

Four own goals

F.A. Community Shield

	Aug	10	Manchester United	1-1	Henry	59293			10	6		3		13	9				2	1	11	7	12		8	5	4	14

Lost 3-4 on penalties a.e.t. At the Millennium Stadium, Cardiff. Also played: Jeffers (15), Van Bronckhorst (16)

F.A. Cup

R3	Jan	4	Leeds United	4-1	Toure, Henry, Pires, Edu	32207				6		3		11	10		9	5	2	1	7	12	13		8	14	4	
R4		24	MIDDLESBROUGH	4-1	Bergkamp, Ljungberg 2, Bentley	37256		13	10	6	12	3		8					2	1	9	7	11			5	4	
R5	Feb	15	CHELSEA	2-1	Reyes 2	38136			10	6	13	3		12					2	1		7	11	9	8	5	4	
R6	Mar	6	Portsmouth	5-1	Toure, Henry 2, Ljungberg 2	20137		13		6	12	3		11	9		14		2	1	7			10	8	5	4	
SF	Apr	3	Manchester United	0-1		39939	9		10	6	3			8	14		12		2	1	7		11	13		5	4	

SF at Villa Park

F.L. Cup

R3	Oct	28	ROTHERHAM UNITED	1-1	Aliadiere	27451	10				3		5	4		2	9											7
R4	Dec	2	WOLVERHAMPTON W.	5-1	Aliadiere 2, Kanu, Wiltord, Fabregas	28161	10	11			3					2	9									4		7
R5		16	West Bromwich Albion	2-0	Kanu, Aliadiere	20369	10	11			3				8		9	5	2			4						7
SF1	Jan	20	MIDDLESBROUGH	0-1		31070		11			3		5	4			9	6				7			8	2		
SF2	Feb	3	Middlesbrough	1-2	Edu	28781		10				11	3	5	8			6				7		9		2	4	

R3 won 9-8 on penalties a.e.t.

Also played: Stack in goal (all games). Tavlaridis (at 6 in R3, 5 in R4, 6 in R5)
Fabregas (at 8 (subbed) in R3, 8 in R4, 12 in R5). Thomas (at 11 (subbed) in R3, 13 in R5, 12 in SF1)
Spicer (at 12 in R3). Owusu-Abeyie (at 13 in R3, 10 in SF1 (subbed) and 12 in SF2)
Smith (at 14 in R3 and R4, 13 in SF1). Simek (at 6 in R4).
Skulason (2 at 12), Papadopulos (2, at 13)

Champions League

CL	Sep	17	INTERNAZIONALE	0-3		34393			12	6		3			10	14			2	1	7	13	11		8	5	4	9
CL		30	Lokomotiv Moscow	0-0		27000						3		4	10		6	2	1			7	11		8	5		9
CL	Oct	21	Dinamo Kiev	1-2	Henry	60000				6		3		4	10	14			2	1	13	7	11		8	5	12	9
CL	Nov	5	DINAMO KIEV	1-0	Cole	34419			10	6		3		14	9		12		2	1	7	4	11		8	5		13
CL		25	Internazionale	5-1	Henry 2, Ljungberg, Pires, Edu	44884	13			6		3	5	8	10		9			1	7	4	11		12	2		
CL	Dec	10	LOKOMOTIV MOSCOW	2-0	Ljungberg, Pires	35343			10	6		3	5		9		12			1	7		11		8	2	4	
R1.1	Feb	24	RC Celta Vigo	3-2	Pires, Edu 2	21000		13		6	3		12	8	9		14		2	1	7			11	10		5	4	
R1.2	Mar	10	RC Celta Vigo	2-0	Henry 2	35402			10	6		3		8	9		13		2	1	7			11	14	12	5	4	
QF1		24	Chelsea	1-1	Pires	40778			10	6		3		8	9				2	1	7			11	12	13	5	4	
QF2	Apr	6	CHELSEA	1-2	Reyes	35486			12	6		3		8	9				2	1	7			11	10		5	4	

142

Chelsea 2004/05

Stamford Bridge

	Date		Opponent	Score	Scorers	Att	Babayaro C	Bridge WM	Carvalho AR	Cech P	Cole JJ	Cudicini C	De Oliveira FV	Drogba DYT	Duff DA	Ferreira RP	Forssell MK	Gallas W	Geremi	Gudjohnsen ES	Huth R	Jarosik J	Johnson GMcL	Kezman M	Lampard FJ	Makelele C	Morais N	Mutu A	Parker SM	Robben A	Smertin A	Terry JG	Tiago Mendes C	Watt SM
	Aug	15	MANCHESTER UNITED	1-0	Gudjohnsen	41813	3	14	1					9		2		6	11	10					12	8	4			13			7	5	
		21	Birmingham City	1-0	Cole	28559	3	6	1		14			9		2			11	10					13	8	4						7	5	12
		24	Crystal Palace	2-0	Drogba, Tiago	24953	3			1	11			9		2		6	14	12					10	8	4		13					5	7
2		28	SOUTHAMPTON	2-1	og (Beattie), Lampard (p)	40864		3	6	1	11			9	14	2				12	10				13	8	4							5	7
2	Sep	11	Aston Villa	0-0		36691	3		6	1	11			9		2				13					10	8	4		14				12	5	7
2		19	TOTTENHAM HOTSPUR	0-0		42246		3	6	1	11			9	14	2				10					13	8	4						12	5	7
2		25	Middlesbrough	1-0	Drogba	32341			6	1				9	11	2		3		10	14				13	8	4						7	5	12
2	Oct	3	LIVERPOOL	1-0	Cole	42028			6	1	13			9	11	2		3	14	10						8	4						7	5	12
2		16	Manchester City	0-1		45047		12	6	1	14				11	2		3	13	9					10	8	4						5	7	
2		23	BLACKBURN ROVERS	4-0	Gudjohnsen 3 (1p), Duff	41546		3	6	1	11				10					9			2		13	8					4	14	7	5	12
2		30	West Bromwich Albion	4-1	Gallas, Lampard, Gudjohnsen, Duff	27399		3	12	1	11				10	2		6		9					8	4						14	7	5	13
1	Nov	6	EVERTON	1-0	Robben	41965	3		6	1					10	2				9		13		14	12	8	4				11		5	7	
1		13	Fulham	4-1	Gallas, Lampard, Tiago, Robben	21877			6	1					10	2		3		9	13				14	8	4				11		7	5	12
1		20	BOLTON WANDERERS	2-2	Tiago, Duff	42203			6	1					10	2		3		9				12	13	8	4				11			5	7
1		27	Charlton Athletic	4-0	Terry 2, Gudjohnsen, Duff	26355	14		6	1				12	10	2		3	13	9						8	4				11			5	7
1	Dec	4	NEWCASTLE UNITED	4-0	Lampard,Drogba,Kezman(p),Robben	42328		12	6	1				14	10	2		3		9					13	8	4				11			5	7
1		12	Arsenal	2-2	Terry, Gudjohnsen	38153		12	6	1				13	10	2		3		9						8	4				14	11		5	7
1		18	NORWICH CITY	4-0	Lampard, Drogba, Duff, Robben	42071		3		1				13	10	2		6		9					14	8	4				12	11		5	7
1		26	ASTON VILLA	1-0	Duff	41950		3		1				12	10	2		6		9						8	4	14				11	13	5	7
1		28	Portsmouth	2-0	Cole, Robben	20210				1	12			9		3		6	14	13						8	4					11	7	5	
1	Jan	1	Liverpool	1-0	Cole	43886				1	13			12	10	3		6		9					2	14	8	4				11		5	7
1		4	MIDDLESBROUGH	2-0	Drogba 2	40982				1	7			9		3		6							12	14	8	4				11	3	5	13
1		15	Tottenham Hotspur	2-0	Lampard 2 (1p)	36105				1	14			9	10	3		6		13			12	2		8	4				11	7	5	
1		22	PORTSMOUTH	3-0	Drogba 2, Robben	42267		3		1	7			9	10	2		6		12					14	8	4				11		5	13
1	Feb	2	Blackburn Rovers	1-0	Robben	23414		3		1	13				10	2		6		9	14				12	8	4				11		5	7
1		6	MANCHESTER CITY	0-0		42093		3		1	12				11	2		6		9		7			10	8	4						5	13
1		12	Everton	1-0	Gudjohnsen	40270		3	14	1	10				11	2		6		9		13	12			8	4							5	7
1	Mar	5	Norwich City	3-1	Kezman, Carvalho, Cole	24506			6	1	10			9	11	3				13		14	2	12	8	4							5	7
1		15	WEST BROMWICH ALB.	1-0	Robben	41713				1	7			9	11	2		3		10	6	13			12	8	4					14	5		
1		19	CRYSTAL PALACE	4-1	Lampard, Kezman 2, Cole	41667			6	1	7			9	11	3				10			2		13	8	4					14		5	12
1	Apr	2	Southampton	3-1	Lampard, Gudjohnsen 2	31949				1	7			13	11			3		9		6	14	2	10	8	4							5	12
1		9	BIRMINGHAM CITY	1-1	Drogba	42031				1	10			9	11			3		13	6	12	2	9	8							4	5	7	
1		20	ARSENAL	0-0		41621		6		1	7			9	11			3		10		13	2	14		8	4							5	12	
1		23	FULHAM	3-1	Lampard, Gudjohnsen, Cole	42081		6		1	7			9	11					10	3	12	2		14	8	4				13			5	14	
1		30	Bolton Wanderers	2-0	Lampard 2	27653		6		1	14			9				3	2	10	13	11				8	4						12	5	7	
1	May	7	CHARLTON ATHLETIC	1-0	Makelele	42065		6		1		1						14	3	11	9	13	2			8	4							5	7	
1		10	Manchester United	3-1	Gudjohnsen, Tiago, Cole	67832			6		10	1						3	11	9	5	12				8	4	13							7	
1		14	Newcastle United	1-1	Lampard (p)	52326			6		10	1	12						2	9	5	11	3			8	4	13							7	14

May 10: APSA Grant played at 14
May 7: LJ Pidgeley played at 12

	Apps	3	12	22	35	19	3	0	18	28	29	0	28	6	30	6	3	13	6	38	36	0	0	1	14	11	36	21	0
	Subs	1	3	3		9		1	8	2		1		7	7	4	11	4	19			2	2	3	4	5		13	1	
	Goals			1		8			10	6		2			12				4	13	1				7		3	4		

One own goal

F.A. Cup

R3	Jan	8	SCUNTHORPE UNITED	3-1	Kezman, Gudjohnsen, Crosby (og)	40019					8	1		9		12			4	11		13	2	10			6				14	3			7	5
R4		30	BIRMINGHAM CITY	2-0	Terry, Huth	40379		3			8	1		12	11					9	6	4	2	10	13							14	7	5		
R5	Feb	20	Newcastle United	0-1		45740		3	6		10	1			14			5	11	13		4	2	9	12						8			7		

F.L. Cup

R3	Oct	27	WEST HAM UNITED	1-0	Kezman	41774	3		6		10	1			13	2		5	4	14				9	12						8	11			7	
R4	Nov	10	Newcastle United	2-0	Gudjohnsen, Robben	38055		3			10	1			11	7			6	12			2	9	13						8	14			5	4
R5		30	Fulham	2-1	Duff, Lampard	14531		3	6		14	1		9	10					12			2		13	4					8	11	7	5		
SF1	Jan	12	MANCHESTER UNITED	0-0		41492			6	1	10			9	11	2		3		13		7		14	12	8	4					5				
SF2		26	Manchester United	2-1	Lampard, Duff	67000		3		1	10			13	11	2		6		9		14			12	8	4								5	7
F	Feb	27	Liverpool	3-2	og (Gerrard), Drogba, Kezman	71622		3		1	14			9	10	2		6		12		13				8	4					11			5	7

R4 a.e.t. Final at Millennium Stadium Cardiff, a.e.t.

Champions League

CL	Sep	14	Paris Saint-Germain	3-0	Terry, Drogba 2	40263		3		1	11			9	12	2		6	14	10					13	8	4								5	7	
CL		29	PORTO	3-1	Terry, Smertin, Drogba	39237			6	1				9	11	2		3	12	10					13	8	4							7	5	14
CL	Oct	20	CSKA MOSCOW	2-0	Terry, Gudjohnsen	33945		3		1	14				11	2		6		9					10	8	4				12		7	5	13
CL	Nov	2	CSKA Moscow	1-0	Robben	28000			6	1					11	12		3		9			2	13	8	4					10	7		5	14
CL		24	PARIS SAINT-GERMAIN	0-0		39626	3	6		10	1			13	14			5		12			2	9	8						4	11	7			
CL	Dec	7	Porto	1-2	Duff	42409	11	6		1				9	10	2		3							13	8					4	14	7	5	12
R1.1	Feb	23	Barcelona	1-2	og (Belletti)	89000			6	1	10			9	11	2		3		14		13				8	4						12	5	7	
R1.2	Mar	8	BARCELONA	4-2	Terry, Lampard, Gudjohnsen, Duff	41315			6	1	7			9	11	2		3		10	14			12	10	8	4						5	13	
QF1	Apr	6	BAYERN MUNICH	4-2	og (Lucio), Lampard 2, Drogba	40253			6	1	7			9	11		14	3		10	12		2			8	4							5	13	
QF2		12	Bayern Munich	2-3	Lampard, Drogba	59000			6	1	7			9	11			3	13	10	2					8	4	12						5	14	
SF1		27	LIVERPOOL	0-0		40497			6	1	11			9				3		10			2	13		8	4					12		5	7	
SF2	May	3	Liverpool	0-1		42529			6	1	11			9				3	2	10	12				13	8	4					14		5	7	

143

Chelsea 2005/06

Stamford Bridge

							Carvalho AR	Cech P	Cole CM	Cole JJ	Crespo HJ	Cudicini C	Del Horno A	Diarra L	Drogba DYT	Duff DA	Essien M	Ferreira RP	Gallas W	Geremi	Gudjohnsen ES	Huth R	Johnson GMcL	Lampard FJ	Makelele C	Maniche	Pidgeley LJ	Robben A	Smith JD	Terry JG	Wright-Phillips SC
	Aug	14	Wigan Athletic	1-0	Crespo	23575		1		13	14		3		9	11		2	6		10			8	4			7		5	12
		21	ARSENAL	1-0	Drogba	42136		1			9		3		13	11	14	2	6		10			8	4			7		5	12
		24	WEST BROMWICH ALB.	4-0	Lampard 2, Drogba, J Cole	41201				11	13	1	3		9	12	10		6				2	8	4			14		5	7
1		27	Tottenham Hotspur	2-0	Del Horno, Duff	36077		1		7	13		3		9	11	10	2	6				14	8	4					5	12
1	Sep	10	SUNDERLAND	2-0	Drogba, Geremi	41969		1		12	9		3		13	14	4		6	2	10			8				11		5	7
1		17	Charlton Athletic	2-0	Robben, Crespo	27111	6	1		12	9				13	11	10	2	3					8	4			7		5	14
1		24	ASTON VILLA	2-1	Lampard 2 (1p)	42146	6	1			9				14	11	10	2	3		13			8	4			7		5	12
1	Oct	2	Liverpool	4-1	Lampard (p), Duff, Geremi, J Cole	44235	6	1		7			3		9	11	10		2	14		12		8	4			13		5	
1		15	BOLTON WANDERERS	5-1	Lampard 2, Drogba 2, Gudjohnsen	41775	6	1	13	11			3		9		10	14	2		12			8	4					5	7
1		23	Everton	1-1	Lampard	36042		1		11	13		3		9		10		2		12	6		8	4			14		5	7
1		29	BLACKBURN ROVERS	4-2	Lampard 2(1p), Drogba, og(Khizanishvili)	41553	6	1		11	13		3		9		10		2		14			8	4			12		5	7
1	Nov	6	Manchester United	0-1		67864		1	12	7			3		9	11	10	2	6		14			8	4					5	13
1		19	NEWCASTLE UNITED	3-0	Duff, Crespo, J Cole	42468	6	1		7	9		3			11	13		12		10		2	8	4					5	14
1		26	Portsmouth	2-0	Lampard (p), Crespo	20182	6	1	13	7	9					11	4	2	3	12	10			8						5	14
1	Dec	3	MIDDLESBROUGH	1-0	Terry	41666	6	1	13				3		9	11	4		2	14	10			8				7		5	12
1		10	WIGAN ATHLETIC	1-0	Terry	42060	6			10	9	1	3		14	11	4		2	13	12			8				7		5	
1		18	Arsenal	2-0	Robben, J Cole	38347	6	1		11					9		10	2	3	12		13		8	4			7		5	
1		26	FULHAM	3-2	Gallas, Lampard, Crespo	42313		1		10	9				12			2	3	14	13	6		8	4			11		5	7
1		28	Manchester City	1-0	J Cole	46587		1		7	12		3		9	11	8	13	6	2	10				4			14		5	
1		31	BIRMINGHAM CITY	2-0	Robben, Crespo	40652	6	1		11	9				14		4	2	3		10			8	12			7		5	13
1	Jan	2	West Ham United	3-1	Lampard, Drogba, Crespo	34758	6	1			13		3		9	11	10			2	12			8	4			7		5	14
1		15	Sunderland	2-1	Robben, Crespo	32420	6	1	12	11	9		3			14			2		10	13		8	4			7		5	
1		22	CHARLTON ATHLETIC	1-1	Gudjohnsen	41355	6	1	12	7	9		3			11			2		10			8	4	14				5	13
1	Feb	1	Aston Villa	1-1	Robben	38562	6	1		11	9					14			3		10	13	2	8	4	12		7		5	
1		5	LIVERPOOL	2-0	Gallas, Crespo	42316	6	1		10	9			3	12		13	10		2		14		8	4			7		5	
1		11	Middlesbrough	0-3		31037	6	1	12	11	9						4		3	2	10			8		13				5	14
1		25	PORTSMOUTH	2-0	Robben, Lampard	42254		1		10			3		9	12	4	2			14	6		8	13			11		5	7
1	Mar	4	West Bromwich Albion	2-1	Drogba, J Cole	26581		1		14					9	11	8	2	3	13	10	6			4			7		5	12
1		11	TOTTENHAM HOTSPUR	2-1	Gallas, Essien	42243		1		11	9				12	14	10	2	3			6		8	4	13				5	7
1		19	Fulham	0-1		22486	12	1		11	9				13	14	10	2	3			6		8	4					5	7
1		25	MANCHESTER CITY	2-0	Drogba 2	42321	6	1		7	13		3		9	11	14	2			10			8	4					5	12
1	Apr	1	Birmingham City	0-0		26364	6	1		14	12		3		9	11	13	2			10			8	4			7		5	
1		9	WEST HAM UNITED	4-1	Terry, Gallas, Drogba, Crespo	41919	14	1		12	10		3		9		11		2					8	4	7		13		5	
1		15	Bolton Wanderers	2-0	Terry, Lampard	27266		1		7	10		3		9		11	12	6	2		13		8	4			14		5	
1		17	EVERTON	3-0	Lampard, Drogba, Essien	41765		1		13	10	12	3		9		11		6	2				8	4			7		5	14
1		29	MANCHESTER UNITED	3-0	Gallas, J Cole, Carvalho	42219	6	1		11	14				9	12	10	2	3					8	4	13		7		5	
1	May	2	Blackburn Rovers	0-1		20243	6		12	14	9	1	3	4		13			5	2	10			8		11					7
1		7	Newcastle United	0-1		52309	6		14	9				4		11		2	3				5	8				10	1	7	13	12

	Apps	Subs	Goals
Carvalho AR	22	2	1
Cech P	34		
Cole CM	0	9	
Cole JJ	26	8	7
Crespo HJ	20	10	10
Cudicini C	3	1	
Del Horno A	25		1
Diarra L	2	1	
Drogba DYT	20	9	12
Duff DA	18	10	3
Essien M	27	4	2
Ferreira RP	18	3	
Gallas W	33	1	5
Geremi	8	7	2
Gudjohnsen ES	16	10	2
Huth R	7	6	
Johnson GMcL	4		
Lampard FJ	35		16
Makelele C	29	2	
Maniche	3	5	
Pidgeley LJ	1		
Robben A	21	7	6
Smith JD	0	1	
Terry JG	36		4
Wright-Phillips SC	10	17	

One own goal

F.A. Community Shield

Aug	7	Arsenal	2-1	Drogba 2	58014		1		16	14			3	9	11		2	6	13	10			8	4			7		5	12

At the Millennium Stadium, Cardiff

Tiago Mendes played at 15

F.A. Cup

R3	Jan	6	HUDDERSFIELD TOWN	2-1	Gudjohnsen, C Cole	41650	6		9	8		1	12	4		11			13			10	5	2				14			7
R4		28	Everton	1-1	Lampard	29742		12	11	9	1		3			13				6			14	2	8	4	10		7		5	
rep	Feb	8	EVERTON	4-1	Terry, Robben, Lampard (p), Crespo	39301				14	9	1				4		3	12	10	6	2		8				13		11	5	7
R5		19	COLCHESTER UNITED	3-1	Ferreira, J Cole 2	41810	6			13	14	1		4	9	11	10	2				5	3	12		8						7
R6	Mar	22	NEWCASTLE UNITED	1-0	Terry	42279	6			7	13	1	3		9	11	12		2	10				8	4					5	14
SF	Apr	22	Liverpool	1-2	Drogba	64575				12	10	1	3		9	14	11	7	6	2				8	4			13		5	

SF at Old Trafford

WM Bridge played at 3 (subbed) in R3

F.L. Cup

R3	Oct	26	Charlton Athletic	1-1	Terry	42198				13	9	1			14		8	2		4	10	6		12				11		5	7

Lost 4-5 on penalties a.e.t.

WM Bridge played at 3 (subbed)

Champions League

CL	Sep	13	ANDERLECHT	1-0	Lampard	29575	6	1		14					9	11	10	2	3				13	8	4			7		5	12
CL		28	Liverpool	0-0		42743	6	1			14				9	11	10	2	3				13	8	4			7		5	12
CL	Oct	19	REAL BETIS BALOMPIE	4-0	Drogba, Crespo, J Cole, Carvalho	36457	6			11	14		3	12	9		10		2		13			8	4					5	7
CL	Nov	1	Real Betis Balompie	0-1		55000	6	1		11					13	12	10	2	3		9			8	4			7		5	14
CL		23	Anderlecht	2-0	Crespo, Carvalho	21845	6	1	13	7	9		3	12		14	10			2				8						5	
CL	Dec	6	LIVERPOOL	0-0		41598	6	1	13					12	9	11	4	2	3		10			8				7		5	14
R1.1	Feb	22	BARCELONA	1-2	Motta (og)	39521	6	1		11	9		3		13			2		14	10			8	4			7		5	12
R1.2	Mar	7	Barcelona	1-1	Lampard (p)	98436	6	1		10	12				9	11		2	3					14	13	8	4			7	5

144

Manchester United 2006/07

Old Trafford

						Brown W	Carrick M	Dong Fangzhuo	Eagles C	Evra P	Ferdinand R	Fletcher D	Giggs R	Heinze G	Kuszczak T	Larsson H	Lee K	Neville G	O'Shea J	Park J	Richardson K	Ronaldo C	Rooney W	Saha L	Scholes P	Silvestre M	Smith A	Solskjaer O	Van der Sar E	Vidic N
Aug	20	FULHAM	5-1	Saha, og (Pearce), Rooney 2, Ronaldo	75115	6				3	5		11					2	4	14		7	10	9	8	12		13	1	
	23	Charlton Athletic	3-0	Fletcher, Saha, Solskjaer	25422	2	13			3	5	7	11						4	8		10		9		6		12	1	
	26	Watford	2-1	Silvestre, Giggs	19453	2	4				5	8	11						3	12	13	7		9		6		10	1	
1	Sep 9	TOTTENHAM HOTSPUR	1-0	Giggs	75453	6	8			3	5	14	11					2	4	13	10	7		9		12			1	
2	17	ARSENAL	0-1		75595	6	13			12	5	7			1			2	4			11	10	9	8	3		14		
3	23	Reading	1-1	Ronaldo	24098		4				5	7		3				2	12		11	9	10	13	8			14	1	6
1	Oct 1	NEWCASTLE UNITED	2-0	Solskjaer 2	75664	6	4			12	5	7		3				2				11	10		8			9	1	6
1	14	Wigan Athletic	3-1	Vidic, Saha, Solskjaer	20631	2	8			3	5		12						4			10	9	11				7	1	6
1	22	LIVERPOOL	2-0	Scholes, Ferdinand	75828	13	4			3	5	7	11					2	12			10	9		8				1	6
1	28	Bolton Wanderers	4-0	Rooney 3, Ronaldo	27229		4			3	5	13	11	14				2	12			7	10	9	8				1	6
1	Nov 4	PORTSMOUTH	3-0	Saha (p), Ronaldo, Vidic	76004		4			3	5	14	11					2	12			7	10	9	8	13			1	6
1	11	Blackburn Rovers	1-0	Saha	26162		4			3	5	14	11					2	12			7	10	9	8	13			1	6
1	18	Sheffield United	2-1	Rooney 2	32584		4			3	5		11	12				2				7	10	9	8				1	6
1	26	CHELSEA	1-1	Saha	75948		4				5	13	11	3				2	12			7	10	9	8				1	6
1	29	EVERTON	3-0	Ronaldo, Evra, O'Shea	75723	12	8			3	5	7		13				2	4		9	11	10			6			1	
1	Dec 2	Middlesbrough	2-1	Saha (p), Fletcher	31238	13					5	4	11	3				2	12			7	10	9	8				1	6
1	9	MANCHESTER CITY	3-1	Rooney, Saha, Ronaldo	75858					5			11	3				2	12			7	10	9	8				1	6
1	17	West Ham United	0-1		34966		4			5			11	3				2	12	14		7	10	9	8			13	1	6
1	23	Aston Villa	3-0	Ronaldo 2, Scholes	42551					3	5	4	11					2	12	10		7	13	9	8	14			1	6
1	26	WIGAN ATHLETIC	3-1	Ronaldo 2, Solskjaer	76018	2				3		7		14					4	11	13	12	10		8	5		9	1	6
1	30	READING	3-2	Solskjaer, Ronaldo 2	75910	2	8				5	14	12	3				2	4	11	13	7	10			6		9	1	
1	Jan 1	Newcastle United	2-2	Scholes 2	52302		13			3	5	4	11					2		12		7	10	9	8				1	6
1	13	ASTON VILLA	3-1	Park, Carrick, Ronaldo	76073		4			3	5					9		2	12	11		7	10	13	8			14	1	6
1	21	Arsenal	1-2	Rooney	60128		4			3	5		11	13		9		2				7	10	12	8				1	6
1	31	WATFORD	4-0	Ronaldo (p), og (Doyley), Larsson, Rooney	76032	12	8			5		3	1	14		2	4		11	7	10			13		9		6	
1	Feb 4	Tottenham Hotspur	4-0	Ronaldo (p), Vidic, Scholes, Giggs	36146		4			3	5		11			9		2	12	14		7	10	13	8				1	6
1	10	CHARLTON ATHLETIC	2-0	Park, Fletcher	75883					3	5	7	11		1	13		2		4	12		10	9	8					6
1	24	Fulham	2-1	Giggs, Ronaldo	24459	2	4			3	5		11			9			12			7	10	13	8	14			1	6
1	Mar 3	Liverpool	1-0	O'Shea	44403		4			3	5		11			9		2	12			7	10	13	8	14			1	6
1	17	BOLTON WANDERERS	4-1	Park 2, Rooney 2	76058	12	8			5		9	3	1				2	4	11	13	7	10			14				6
1	31	BLACKBURN ROVERS	4-1	Scholes, Carrick, Park, Solskjaer	76098	2	4			5		9	3						12	11		7		8				14	13	1	6
1	Apr 7	Portsmouth	1-2	O'Shea	20223	4	6			5		7	12	3					2		11	9	10		8			14	13	1	6
1	17	SHEFFIELD UNITED	2-0	Carrick, Rooney	75540	5	4			3		6	11	2	1					12	7	10		8		9	13		
1	21	MIDDLESBROUGH	1-1	Richardson	75967	6	4				5	13	12	3				2		11	7	10		8		9	14	1	
1	28	Everton	4-2	O'Shea, og (P Neville), Rooney, Eagles	39682	6	4		14	3		11	5					2		13	12	10		8		9	7	1	
1	May 5	Manchester City	1-0	Ronaldo (p)	47244	2	4				5	13	11	3					12		7	10		8		9		1	6
1	9	Chelsea	0-0		41794	5	13	10	7		8		3	1		2		4		11		12				6	9		
1	13	WEST HAM UNITED	0-1		75927	6	4			3		8	14	5				2		11	12	10		13		9	7	1	

Apps	17	29	1	1	22	33	16	25	17	6	5	1	24	16	8	8	31	33	18	29	6	6	9	32	25
Subs	5	4		1	2		8	5	5		2			16	6	7	3	2	6	1	8	3	10		
Goals		3		1	1	1	3	4			1			4	5	1	17	14	8	6	1		7		3

Three own goals

F.A. Cup

R3	Jan 7	ASTON VILLA	2-1	Larsson, Solskjaer	74924	6	8			3	5	12	11			1	9		2	13	4		7	10				14			
R4	27	PORTSMOUTH	2-1	Rooney 2	71137		4			7		3	5	13	11		1	9	2		4		12			8			10		6
R5	Feb 17	READING	1-1	Carrick	70608	2	4			12		8			3	1	13				11		7		9	14	5		10		6
rep	27	Reading	3-2	Heinze, Saha, Solskjaer	23821	6				5	8		3					4	7	11	13	12	9		2			10	1	
R6	Mar 10	Middlesbrough	2-2	Rooney, Ronaldo (p)	33308		8				5		11	3	1	9		2	4			7	10							6
rep	19	MIDDLESBROUGH	1-0	Ronaldo (p)	71325	2	4				5		13	3	1				13	12	8		7	10			9				6
SF	Apr 14	Watford	4-1	Rooney 2, Ronaldo, Richardson	37425	6	4			2	5	12	11	3						13	7	10		8		9	14	1	
F	May 19	Chelsea	0-1		89826	2	4				5	10	11	3					12			7	9		8		13	14	1	6

SF at Villa Park, Final at Wembley Stadium, a.e.t.

F.L. Cup

| R3 | Oct 25 | Crewe Alexandra | 2-1 | Solskjaer, Lee | 10046 | 5 | | | | | | 3 | 1 | | 12 | | | | 11 | | | | | | | | 6 | 9 | 10 | | |
| R4 | Nov 7 | Southend United | 0-1 | | 11532 | 5 | | | 14 | | 8 | | 3 | 1 | 12 | | 2 | | 11 | 7 | 10 | | | | | 6 | 9 | | |

R3 a.e.t.

Played in R3: Gray (at 2, subbed), D Jones (4), Marsh (7, subbed by Barnes, 13, who was then subbed by Shawcross, 14), R Jones (8)

Played in R4: D Jones (4, subbed by Shawcross, 13)

Champions League

CL	Sep 13	CELTIC	3-2	Saha 2 (1p), Solskjaer	74031	6	4				5	7	11					2	12		13		10	9	8	3		14	1	
CL	26	Benfica	1-0	Saha	61000		4				5	13		3				2	11			7	10	9	8		12		1	6
CL	Oct 17	FC COPENHAGEN	3-0	Scholes, O'Shea, Richardson	72020	5	4			3		7						2			13	11	10	9	8		14	12	1	6
CL	Nov 1	FC Copenhagen	0-1		40308	5	8			12	13	11		2					4			7	10		14	3		9	1	6
CL	21	Celtic	0-1		60632		4			12	5		11	3				2	13			7	10	9	8				1	6
CL	Dec 6	BENFICA	3-1	Vidic, Giggs, Saha	74955		4			3	5	14	11	12				2				7	10	9	8			13	1	6
R1.1	Feb 20	Lille	1-0	Giggs	31680		4			3	5		11			9		2	13			7	10	12	8				1	6
R1.2	Mar 7	LILLE	1-0	Larsson	75182		8				5					9		2	4	14	12	7		11	3	13			1	6
QF1	Apr 4	Roma	1-2	Rooney	75000	2	4			5	12	11	3					6				7	10	13	8			9	1	
QF2	10	ROMA	7-1	Carrick 2, Smith, Rooney, Ronaldo 2, Evra	74476	2	4			12	5	8	11	6					3		14	7	10				9	13	1	
SF1	24	AC MILAN	3-2	Rooney 2, Ronaldo	73820	6	4			3		7	11	5					2			9	10		8				1	
SF2	May 2	AC Milan	0-3		67500	5	4					7	11	3					2			9	10	12	8				1	6

PLAYERS WITH ONE LEAGUE APPEARANCE OR MORE IN CHAMPIONSHIP WINNING SEASONS

		D.o.B.	Birthplace	Died	No.	First	Last	Club	Apps	Subs	Gls	Int
Ablett GI	Gary	19/11/1965	Liverpool		2	1988	1990	Liverpool	28	4	0	
Adams NJ	Neil	23/11/1965	Stoke-on-Trent		1	1987		Everton	10	2	0	
Adams TA	Tony	10/10/1966	Romford		4	1989	2002	Arsenal	102	0	8	e
Adamson J	Jimmy	04/04/1929	Ashington		1	1960		Burnley	42	0	1	
Agana PAO	Tony	02/10/1963	Bromley		1	1992		Leeds United	1	1	0	
Aitken A	Andy 'Daddler'	27/04/1877	Ayr	1955	2	1905	1907	Newcastle United	31	0	2	s
Aitkenhead WCA	Wattie	21/05/1877	Maryhill	1966	2	1912	1914	Blackburn Rovers	46	0	22	s
Aldridge JW	John	18/09/1958	Liverpool		2	1988	1990	Liverpool	36	2	27	r
Aliadiere J	Jeremie	30/03/1983	Rambouillet, France		2	2002	2004	Arsenal	3	8	0	
Allan SJE	Jack	28/12/1886	Wallsend	1919	1	1909		Newcastle United	9	0	5	
Allen AR	Reg	03/05/1919	Marylebone	1976	1	1952		Manchester Utd.	33	0	0	
Allen JWA	Jack	31/01/1903	Newburn	1957	2	1929	1930	Sheffield Wed.	76	0	66	
Allen LW	Les	04/09/1937	Dagenham		1	1961		Tottenham H	42	0	23	
Almond J	Jack	06/11/1876	Darlington	1912	1	1898		Sheffield Utd.	20	0	8	
Anderson AL	Andrew		Glasgow		1	1909		Newcastle United	19	0	3	
Anderson GA	George	1889	Haydon Bridge	1954	1	1913		Sunderland	2	0	0	
Anderson J	Joe	1895	Bishopton		1	1921		Burnley	41	0	25	
Anderson VA	Viv	29/08/1956	Nottingham		1	1978		Nottm. Forest	37	0	3	e
Anderson WJ	Willie	24/01/1947	Liverpool		1	1967		Manchester Utd.	0	1	0	
Anelka N	Nicolas	14/03/1979	Versailles, France		1	1998		Arsenal	16	10	6	fr
Angus J	Jack				1	1891		Everton	11	0	0	
Angus J	John	02/09/1938	Warkworth		1	1960		Burnley	41	0	0	e
Anthony W	Walter	21/11/1879	Basford	1950	2	1912	1914	Blackburn Rovers	28	0	1	
Appleyard W	Bill	16/11/1878	Caistor	1958	2	1905	1907	Newcastle United	51	0	30	
Armstrong G	George	09/08/1944	Hebburn	2000	1	1971		Arsenal	42	0	7	
Armstrong K	Ken	03/06/1924	Bradford	1984	1	1955		Chelsea	39	0	1	e
Arrowsmith AW	Alf	11/12/1942	Manchester	2005	2	1964	1966	Liverpool	23	2	16	
Ashcroft CT	Charlie	03/07/1926	Chorley		1	1947		Liverpool	2	0	0	
Ashcroft J	Jimmy	12/09/1878	Liverpool	1943	1	1912		Blackburn Rovers	8	0	0	e
Aspinall WG	Warren	13/09/1967	Wigan		1	1987		Everton	0	6	0	
Aston CL	Charlie	1875	Bilston	1931	2	1899	1900	Aston Villa	16	0	0	
Aston J (snr)	John	03/09/1921	Prestwich	2003	1	1952		Manchester Utd.	18	0	4	e
Aston J (jnr)	John	28/06/1947	Manchester		2	1965	1967	Manchester Utd.	27	4	5	
Athersmith WC	Charlie	10/05/1872	Bloxwich	1910	5	1894	1900	Aston Villa	136	0	34	e
Atkins IL	Ian	16/01/1957	Birmingham		1	1985		Everton	6	0	1	
Atkins MN	Mark	14/08/1968	Doncaster		1	1995		Blackburn Rovers	30	4	6	
Auld JR	John	07/01/1862	Lugar	1932	3	1892	1895	Sunderland	55	0	4	s
Babayaro C	Celestine	29/08/1978	Kaduna, Nigeria		1	2005		Chelsea	3	1	0	ng
Bache JW	Joe	08/02/1880	Stourbridge	1960	1	1910		Aston Villa	32	0	20	e
Bailey AD	Tony	23/09/1946	Burton-on-Trent		1	1972		Derby County	1	0	0	
Bailey JA	John	01/04/1957	Liverpool		1	1985		Everton	15	0	0	
Bailey RN	Roy	26/05/1932	Epsom	1993	1	1962		Ipswich Town	37	0	0	
Baily EF	Eddie	06/08/1925	Clapton		1	1951		Tottenham H	40	0	12	e
Bain D	David	05/08/1900	Rutherglen		1	1928		Everton	2	0	0	
Baird J	John	1870	Alexandria	1905	1	1894		Aston Villa	29	0	0	
Baker A	Alf	27/04/1898	Ilkeston	1955	1	1931		Arsenal	1	0	0	e
Baker PRB	Peter	10/12/1931	Hampstead		1	1961		Tottenham H	41	0	1	
Ball AJ	Alan	12/05/1945	Farnworth		1	1970		Everton	37	0	10	e
Balmer J	Jack	06/02/1916	Liverpool	1984	1	1947		Liverpool	39	0	24	
Bamber J	Jack	11/04/1895	Peasley Cross	1971	2	1922	1923	Liverpool	12	0	0	e
Bannister J	Jimmy	20/09/1880	Leyland		1	1908		Manchester Utd.	36	0	5	
Barber AW	Arthur				1	1939		Everton	2	0	0	
Barkas E	Ned	21/01/1901	Wardley Colliery	1962	3	1924	1926	Huddersfield T	35	0	0	
Barkas S	Sam	29/12/1909	Wardley Colliery	1989	1	1937		Manchester City	30	0	0	e
Barlow H	Bert	22/07/1916	Kilnhurst	2004	2	1949	1950	Portsmouth	31	0	9	
Barnes JCB	John	07/11/1963	Kingston, Jamaica		2	1988	1990	Liverpool	72	0	37	e
Barnes W	Walley	16/01/1920	Brecon	1975	1	1948		Arsenal	35	0	0	w
Barrett C	Colin	03/08/1952	Stockport		1	1978		Nottm. Forest	33	2	1	
Barron GW	George	01/10/1883	Darlington		1	1903		Sheffield Wed.	1	0	0	
Barthez FA	Fabien	28/06/1971	Lavelanet, France		2	2001	2003	Manchester Utd.	60	0	0	fr
Bartlett WJ	Billy	13/04/1878	Newcastle	1939	1	1904		Sheffield Wed.	4	0	0	
Barton KR	Ken	20/09/1937	Caernarvon	1982	1	1961		Tottenham H	1	0	0	
Basnett A	Alf	10/04/1893	St Helens	1966	1	1921		Burnley	15	0	0	
Bastin CS	Cliff	14/03/1912	Exeter	1991	5	1931	1938	Arsenal	196	0	109	e
Bates MJ	Mick	19/09/1947	Armthorpe		2	1969	1974	Leeds United	12	2	2	
Batty D	David	02/12/1968	Leeds		1	1992		Leeds United	40	0	2	e
					1	1995		Blackburn Rovers	4	1	0	
Baxter W	Billy	21/09/1924	Leven	2002	1	1954		Wolves	5	0	0	
Baxter WA	Bill	23/04/1939	Edinburgh		1	1962		Ipswich Town	40	0	0	
Beadles GH	Harry	28/09/1897	Llanllwchaiarn	1958	2	1922	1923	Liverpool	15	0	6	w
Beardsley PA	Peter	18/01/1961	Longbenton		2	1988	1990	Liverpool	63	4	25	e
Beasley AE	Pat	27/07/1913	Stourbridge	1986	2	1934	1935	Arsenal	43	0	16	e
Beckham DRJ	David	02/05/1975	Leytonstone		6	1996	2003	Manchester Utd.	178	18	42	e
Bedingfield F	Frank	1877	Sunderland	1904	1	1899		Aston Villa	1	0	1	
Beech GC	Jack		Sheffield		2	1903	1904	Sheffield Wed.	7	0	0	
Beeson GW	George	31/08/1906	Clay Cross	1999	1	1930		Sheffield Wed.	2	0	0	
Beglin JM	Jim	29/07/1963	Waterford		1	1986		Liverpool	34	0	1	r
Belfitt RM	Rod	30/10/1945	Doncaster		1	1969		Leeds United	6	2	3	
Bell A	Alex	1882	Cape Town, South Af.	1934	2	1908	1911	Manchester Utd.	62	0	1	s
					1	1914		Blackburn Rovers	8	0	0	
Bell C	Colin	26/02/1946	Hesleden		1	1968		Manchester City	35	0	14	e
Bell RC	Robert 'Bunny'	10/04/1911	Birkenhead	1988	1	1939		Everton	4	0	3	

146

		D.o.B.	Birthplace	Died	No.	First	Last	Club	Apps	Subs	Gls	Int
Bennett LD	Les	10/01/1918	Wood Green	1999	1	1951		Tottenham H	25	0	7	
Bennett R	Ron	08/05/1927	Hinckley	1997	1	1950		Portsmouth	2	0	1	
Bennett W	Walter	1874	Mexborough	1908	1	1898		Sheffield Utd.	26	0	12	e
Bent G	Geoff	27/09/1932	Salford	1958	2	1956	1957	Manchester Utd.	10	0	0	
Bentham SJ	Stan	17/03/1915	Leigh	2002	1	1939		Everton	41	0	9	
Bentley A	Alf	1886	Alfreton	1940	1	1920		West Bromwich A.	24	0	15	
Bentley DM	David	27/08/1984	Peterborough		1	2004		Arsenal	1	0	0	
Bentley TFR	Roy	17/05/1924	Shirehampton		1	1955		Chelsea	41	0	22	e
Benwell LA	Lou	1870	Birmingham	1929	1	1894		Aston Villa	1	0	0	
Berg H	Henning	01/09/1968	Eidsvell, Norway		1	1995		Blackburn Rovers	40	0	1	no
					3	1999	2001	Manchester Utd.	26	13	1	
Bergkamp DNM	Dennis	18/05/1969	Amsterdam, Holland		3	1998	2004	Arsenal	71	18	29	ho
Berry RJ	Johnny	01/06/1926	Aldershot	1994	3	1952	1957	Manchester Utd.	110	0	18	e
Berry WA	Bill	1884	Monkwearmouth		1	1908		Manchester Utd.	3	0	1	
Best G	George	22/05/1946	Belfast	2005	2	1965	1967	Manchester Utd.	83	0	20	n
Best R	Bobby	12/09/1891	Mickley	1947	1	1913		Sunderland	3	0	0	
Biggs AG	Arthur	26/05/1915	Wootton	1996	1	1938		Arsenal	2	0	0	
Bingham WL	Billy	05/08/1931	Belfast		1	1963		Everton	23	0	5	n
Binks S	Sid	25/07/1899	Bishop Auckland	1978	2	1925	1926	Huddersfield T	4	0	1	
Birch B	Brian	18/11/1931	Salford		1	1952		Manchester Utd.	2	0	0	
Birchenough F	Frank	1898	Crewe		1	1921		Burnley	2	0	0	
Birkett RJE	Ralph	09/01/1913	Newton Abbot	2002	2	1934	1935	Arsenal	19	0	7	e
Blackburn R	Robert	1885	Edinburgh		1	1907		Newcastle United	3	0	0	
Blacklaw AS	Adam	02/09/1937	Aberdeen		1	1960		Burnley	41	0	0	s
Blackmore CG	Clayton	23/09/1964	Neath		1	1993		Manchester Utd.	12	2	0	w
Blair J	John		Glasgow		1	1898		Sheffield Utd.	1	0	0	
Blanc LR	Laurent	19/11/1965	Ales, France		1	2003		Manchester Utd.	15	4	0	fr
Blanchflower J	Jackie	07/03/1933	Belfast	1998	3	1952	1957	Manchester Utd.	30	0	3	n
Blanchflower RD	Danny	10/02/1926	Belfast	1993	1	1961		Tottenham H	42	0	6	n
Blanthorne R	Bob	08/01/1884	Rock Ferry	1965	1	1909		Newcastle United	1	0	0	
Blenkinsop E	Ernie	20/04/1902	Cudworth	1969	2	1929	1930	Sheffield Wed.	78	0	1	e
Blomqvist LJ	Jesper	05/02/1974	Tavelsjo, Sweden		1	1999		Manchester Utd.	20	5	1	sw
Blott SP	Prince	01/01/1886	Holloway	1969	1	1911		Manchester Utd.	1	0	0	
Blunstone F	Frank	17/10/1934	Crewe		1	1955		Chelsea	23	0	3	e
Boa Morte PL	Luis	04/08/1977	Lisbon, Portugal		1	1998		Arsenal	4	11	0	pt
Bocking W	Bill	11/06/1902	Stockport	1985	1	1932		Everton	10	0	0	
Boersma P	Phil	24/09/1949	Kirkby		2	1973	1976	Liverpool	20	2	7	
Bond JE	Ernie	04/05/1929	Preston		1	1952		Manchester Utd.	19	0	4	
Book AK	Tony	04/09/1934	Bath		1	1968		Manchester City	42	0	1	
Boot LGW	Leonard	04/11/1899	West Bromwich	1937	2	1924	1925	Huddersfield T	10	0	0	
Booth C	Colin	30/12/1934	Manchester		2	1958	1959	Wolves	26	0	9	
Bosnich MJ	Mark	13/01/1972	Fairfield, Australia		1	2000		Manchester Utd.	23	0	0	au
Bould SA	Steve	16/11/1962	Stoke-on-Trent		3	1989	1998	Arsenal	85	7	2	e
Boulton CD	Colin	12/09/1945	Cheltenham		2	1972	1975	Derby County	84	0	0	
Boulton FP	Frank	12/08/1917	Chipping Sodbury	1987	1	1938		Arsenal	15	0	0	
Bourne JA	Jeff	19/06/1948	Linton, Derbyshire		1	1975		Derby County	7	10	2	
Bowden ER	Ray	13/09/1909	Looe	1998	4	1933	1938	Arsenal	73	0	30	e
Bowen DL	David	07/06/1928	Nantyffyllon	1995	1	1953		Arsenal	2	0	0	w
Bowler GC	Gerry	08/06/1919	Derry	2006	1	1949		Portsmouth	2	0	0	i
Bowles S	Stan	24/12/1948	Manchester		1	1968		Manchester City	4	0	2	e
Bowman T	Tommy	26/10/1873	Tarbolton	1958	2	1899	1900	Aston Villa	61	0	2	
Bowser S	Sid	06/04/1891	Handsworth	1961	1	1920		West Bromwich A.	41	0	10	e
Bowyer I	Ian	06/06/1951	Little Sutton		1	1978		Nottm. Forest	26	3	4	
Boyd JM	Jimmy	29/04/1907	Glasgow	1991	1	1927		Newcastle United	2	0	0	s
Boyes WE	Wally	05/01/1913	Killamarsh	1960	1	1939		Everton	36	0	4	e
Boyle TW	Tommy	29/01/1888	Hoyland	1940	1	1921		Burnley	38	0	7	e
Brabrook P	Peter	08/11/1937	Greenwich		1	1955		Chelsea	3	0	0	e
Bracewell PW	Paul	19/07/1962	Heswall		1	1985		Everton	37	0	2	e
Bradley JE	Jimmy	1881	Goldenhill	1954	1	1906		Liverpool	31	0	0	
Bradshaw AE	Albert				1	1898		Sheffield Utd.	1	0	0	
Bradshaw W	Billy	1884	Padiham		2	1912	1914	Blackburn Rovers	63	0	6	e
Brady A	Alec	02/04/1865	Cathcart	1913	1	1891		Everton	21	0	9	
Brain J	Jimmy	11/09/1900	Bristol	1971	1	1931		Arsenal	16	0	4	
Bray J	Jackie	22/04/1909	Oswaldtwistle	1982	1	1937		Manchester City	40	0	2	e
Bremner DG	Des	07/09/1952	Aberchider		1	1981		Aston Villa	42	0	2	s
Bremner GH	Gordon	12/11/1917	Glasgow		1	1938		Arsenal	2	0	1	
Bremner WJ	Billy	09/12/1942	Stirling	1997	2	1969	1974	Leeds United	84	0	16	s
Brennan JSA	Shay	06/05/1937	Manchester	2000	2	1965	1967	Manchester Utd.	58	0	0	r
Bridge WM	Wayne	05/08/1980	Southampton		1	2005		Chelsea	12	3	0	e
Brittan C	Colin	02/06/1927	Bristol		1	1951		Tottenham H	8	0	0	
Britton CS	Cliff	29/08/1909	Hanham	1975	1	1939		Everton	1	0	0	e
Broadbent PF	Peter	15/05/1933	Elvington		3	1954	1959	Wolves	116	0	49	e
Bromilow TG	Tom	07/10/1894	Liverpool	1959	2	1922	1923	Liverpool	81	0	5	e
Brook EF	Eric	27/11/1907	Mexborough	1965	1	1937		Manchester City	42	0	20	e
Broomfield HC	Herbert	11/12/1878	Audlem		1	1908		Manchester Utd.	9	0	0	
Brophy T	Tom	08/01/1897	St Helens		1	1921		Burnley	3	0	0	
Brown AA	Albert	1862	Aston	1930	1	1894		Aston Villa	6	0	2	
Brown AD	Sandy	24/03/1939	Grangemouth		1	1970		Everton	31	5	0	
Brown G	George	22/06/1903	Mickley	1948	3	1924	1926	Huddersfield T	95	0	63	e
Brown H	Harry	1883	Northampton	1934	1	1907		Newcastle United	22	0	8	
Brown JH	Jack	18/03/1899	Worksop	1962	2	1929	1930	Sheffield Wed.	83	0	0	e
Brown W	William	10/05/1897	Cambuslang		2	1915	1928	Everton	6	0	0	
Brown WDF	Bill	08/10/1931	Arbroath	2004	1	1961		Tottenham H	41	0	0	s
Brown WM	Wes	13/10/1979	Manchester		4	1999	2007	Manchester Utd.	75	11	0	e
Bruce SR	Steve	31/12/1960	Corbridge		3	1993	1996	Manchester Utd.	113	0	9	

		D.o.B.	Birthplace	Died	No.	First	Last	Club	Apps	Subs	Gls	Int
Buchan CM	Charlie	22/09/1891	Plumstead	1960	1	1913		Sunderland	36	0	27	e
Buckley CS	Chris	09/09/1886	Urmston	1974	1	1910		Aston Villa	37	0	1	
Burgess H	Herbert	25/02/1883	Openshaw	1954	1	1908		Manchester Utd.	27	0	0	e
Burgess H	Harry	20/08/1904	Alderley Edge	1957	1	1930		Sheffield Wed.	39	0	19	e
Burgess WAR	Ron	09/04/1917	Cwm	2005	1	1951		Tottenham H	35	0	2	w
Burns K	Kenny	23/09/1953	Glasgow		1	1978		Nottm. Forest	41	0	4	s
Burridge BJH	Bert	11/03/1898	Beamish	1977	2	1929	1930	Sheffield Wed.	4	0	0	
Burrows D	David	25/10/1968	Dudley		1	1990		Liverpool	23	3	0	
Burton GF	Frank	1868	Aston	1935	3	1894	1897	Aston Villa	26	0	1	
Burton HA	Harry	1881	West Bromwich	1923	1	1904		Sheffield Wed.	26	0	0	
Bush WT	Tom	22/02/1914	Hodnet	1969	1	1947		Liverpool	3	0	0	
Butler EAE	Ernie	13/05/1919	Box	2002	2	1949	1950	Portsmouth	84	0	0	
Butler JH	Joe	1879	Horschay	1941	1	1913		Sunderland	32	0	0	
Butt N	Nicky	21/01/1975	Manchester		8	1993	2003	Manchester Utd.	136	33	15	e
Byrne G	Gerry	29/08/1938	Liverpool		2	1964	1966	Liverpool	75	0	1	e
Byrne RW	Roger	08/09/1929	Manchester	1958	3	1952	1957	Manchester Utd.	99	0	10	e
Caesar GC	Gus	05/03/1966	Tottenham		1	1989		Arsenal	2	0	0	
Cain R	Bob	13/02/1866	Slamannan		1	1898		Sheffield Utd.	30	0	0	
Callaghan IR	Ian	10/04/1942	Liverpool		5	1964	1977	Liverpool	198	1	20	e
Cameron WS	William 'Kilty'	1884	Mossend	1958	1	1912		Blackburn Rovers	13	0	1	
Campbell JJ	Johnny	1871	Glasgow	1947	2	1896	1897	Aston Villa	55	0	39	s
Campbell JM	Johnny	19/02/1870	Renton	1906	3	1892	1895	Sunderland	81	0	83	
Campbell KJ	Kevin	04/02/1970	Lambeth		1	1991		Arsenal	15	7	9	
Campbell SJ	Sol	18/09/1974	Newham		2	2002	2004	Arsenal	64	2	3	e
Campbell WC					1	1891		Everton	13	0	1	
Cantona E	Eric	24/05/1966	Paris, France		1	1992		Leeds United	6	9	3	fr
					4	1993	1997	Manchester Utd.	121	1	52	
Cantwell NEC	Noel	28/12/1932	Cork	2005	2	1965	1967	Manchester Utd.	6	0	1	r
Carberry LJ	Larry	18/01/1936	Liverpool		1	1962		Ipswich Town	42	0	0	
Carey JJ	Johnny	23/02/1919	Dublin	1995	1	1952		Manchester Utd.	38	0	3	ir
Carlin J	John	1880	Liverpool		1	1906		Liverpool	14	0	6	
Carney LF	Len	30/05/1915	Liverpool	1996	1	1947		Liverpool	2	0	1	
Carr EM	Eddie	03/10/1917	Wheatley Hill	1998	1	1938		Arsenal	11	0	7	
Carr J	Jack	1876	Seaton Burn	1948	3	1905	1909	Newcastle United	64	0	0	e
Carrick M	Michael	28/07/1981	Wallsend		1	2007		Manchester Utd.	29	4	3	e
Carroll RE	Roy	30/09/1977	Enniskillen		1	2003		Manchester Utd.	8	2	0	n
Carter HS	Raich	21/12/1913	Sunderland	1994	1	1936		Sunderland	39	0	31	e
Cartlidge A	Arthur	12/06/1880	Stoke-on-Trent	1940	1	1910		Aston Villa	35	0	0	
Cartwright S	Sidney	16/07/1910	Kiveton Park	1988	1	1938		Arsenal	6	0	2	
Carvalho AR	Ricardo	18/05/1978	Amarante, Portugal		2	2005	2006	Chelsea	44	5	2	pt
Case JR	Jimmy	18/05/1954	Liverpool		4	1976	1980	Liverpool	125	3	17	
Caskie J	Jimmy	30/01/1914	Glasgow	1977	1	1939		Everton	5	0	1	
Casper CM	Chris	28/04/1975	Burnley		1	1997		Manchester Utd.	0	2	0	
Cassidy JA	Jim		Lurgan		1	1937		Manchester City	1	0	0	
Cassidy L	Laurie	10/03/1923	Manchester		1	1952		Manchester Utd.	1	0	0	
Cawthorne H	Harry	1900	Darnall	1967	3	1924	1926	Huddersfield T	42	0	1	
Cech P	Petr	20/05/1982	Plzen, Czech Republic		2	2005	2006	Chelsea	69	0	0	cz
Chadwick LH	Luke	18/11/1980	Cambridge		2	2001	2003	Manchester Utd.	6	11	2	
Chadwick WE	Edgar	14/06/1869	Blackburn	1942	1	1891		Everton	22	0	10	e
Chambers H	Harry	17/11/1896	Willington Quay	1949	2	1922	1923	Liverpool	71	0	41	e
Chandler A	Bert	15/01/1897	Carlisle	1963	1	1927		Newcastle United	4	0	0	
Chapman GR	George	23/10/1886	Broxburn		2	1912	1914	Blackburn Rovers	42	0	18	
Chapman H	Harry	1879	Kiveton Park	1916	2	1903	1904	Sheffield Wed.	66	0	28	
Chapman LR	Lee	05/12/1959	Lincoln		1	1992		Leeds United	38	0	16	
Charlton J	Jack	08/05/1935	Ashington		1	1969		Leeds United	41	0	3	e
Charlton R	Bobby	11/10/1937	Ashington		3	1957	1967	Manchester Utd.	97	0	32	e
Chatham RH	Ray	20/07/1924	Wolverhampton	1999	1	1954		Wolves	1	0	0	
Chatt RS	Bob	1870	Barnard Castle	1935	3	1894	1897	Aston Villa	41	0	9	
Checkland FJ	Frank	31/07/1895	Seaforth	1960	1	1922		Liverpool	5	0	0	
Chedgzoy S	Sam	27/01/1890	Ellesmere Port	1967	1	1915		Everton	30	0	2	e
Cheetham RAJ	Roy	21/12/1939	Eccles		1	1968		Manchester City	2	1	0	
Chenhall JC	John	23/07/1927	Bristol		1	1953		Arsenal	13	0	0	
Cherry TJ	Trevor	23/02/1948	Huddersfield		1	1974		Leeds United	37	1	1	e
Chilton AC	Allenby	16/09/1918	South Hylton	1996	1	1952		Manchester Utd.	42	0	0	e
Chorlton T	Tom	1882	Heaton Mersey	1952	1	1906		Liverpool	6	0	1	
Clamp HE	Eddie	14/09/1934	Coalville	1995	3	1954	1959	Wolves	69	0	13	e
Clark AW	Archie	04/04/1902	Shoreham, Kent	1967	1	1932		Everton	39	0	1	
Clark FA	Frank	09/09/1943	Rowlands Gill		1	1978		Nottm. Forest	12	1	1	
Clark GV	Gordon	15/06/1913	Gainsborough	1997	1	1937		Manchester City	13	0	0	
Clark JMcNC	Jimmy	1913	Glasgow		1	1936		Sunderland	28	0	0	
Clark JR	Bob	06/02/1903	Newburn	1977	1	1927		Newcastle United	17	0	4	
Clarke AJ	Allan	31/07/1946	Willenhall		1	1974		Leeds United	34	0	13	e
Clarke HA	Harry	23/02/1923	Woodford	2000	1	1951		Tottenham H	42	0	0	e
Clarke I	Ike	09/01/1915	Tipton	2002	2	1949	1950	Portsmouth	61	0	31	
Clarke W	Wayne	28/02/1961	Wolverhampton		1	1987		Everton	10	0	5	
Clay JH	John	22/11/1946	Stockport		1	1968		Manchester City	1	1	0	
Clayton G	Gordon	03/11/1936	Wednesbury	1991	1	1957		Manchester Utd.	2	0	0	
Clegg MJ	Michael	03/07/1977	Ashton-under-Lyne		2	1997	2000	Manchester Utd.	3	3	0	
Clemence RN	Ray	05/08/1948	Skegness		5	1973	1980	Liverpool	208	0	0	e
Clempson F	Frank	27/05/1930	Salford	1970	1	1952		Manchester Utd.	8	0	2	
Clennell J	Joe	19/02/1889	New Silksworth	1965	2	1912	1914	Blackburn Rovers	22	0	10	
					1	1915		Everton	36	0	14	
Clichy G	Gael	26/02/1985	Paris, France		1	2004		Arsenal	7	5	0	
Cockburn H	Henry	14/09/1921	Ashton-under-Lyne	2004	1	1952		Manchester Utd.	38	0	2	e
Coggins WH	Billy	16/09/1901	Bristol	1958	1	1932		Everton	1	0	0	

		D.o.B.	Birthplace	Died	No.	First	Last	Club	Apps	Subs	Gls	Int
Cohen A	Avi	14/11/1956	Tel Aviv, Israel		1	1980		Liverpool	3	1	1	is
Cole A	Ashley	20/12/1980	Stepney		2	2002	2004	Arsenal	61	0	2	e
Cole AA	Andy	15/10/1971	Nottingham		1	1991		Arsenal	0	1	0	e
					5	1996	2001	Manchester Utd.	106	27	63	
Cole CM	Carlton	12/11/1983	Croydon		1	2006		Chelsea	0	9	0	
Cole JJ	Joe	08/11/1981	Islington		2	2005	2006	Chelsea	45	17	15	e
Coleman AG	Tony	02/05/1945	Great Crosby		1	1968		Manchester City	38	0	8	
Coleman E	Tim	04/01/1908	Blidworth	1984	2	1933	1934	Arsenal	39	0	25	
Collett E	Ernie	17/11/1914	Sheffield	1980	1	1938		Arsenal	5	0	0	
Colman E	Eddie	01/11/1936	Salford	1958	2	1956	1957	Manchester Utd.	61	0	1	
Common A	Alf	25/05/1880	Millfield, Co. Durham	1946	1	1902		Sunderland	4	0	2	e
Compton DCS	Denis	23/05/1918	Hendon	1997	2	1938	1948	Arsenal	21	0	7	
Compton JF	John	27/08/1937	Poplar		1	1962		Ipswich Town	39	0	0	
Compton LH	Les	12/09/1912	Woodford	1984	4	1933	1948	Arsenal	53	0	2	e
Connelly JM	John	18/07/1938	St Helens		1	1960		Burnley	34	0	20	e
					2	1965	1967	Manchester Utd.	48	0	17	
Conner J	Jack	27/12/1891	Rutherglen		1	1913		Sunderland	2	0	0	
Connor DR	Dave	27/10/1945	Wythenshawe		1	1968		Manchester City	10	3	1	
Connor J	Jimmy	01/06/1909	Renfrew	1980	1	1936		Sunderland	42	0	7	s
Connor JE	Edward	1884	Weaste	1955	1	1911		Manchester Utd.	7	0	1	
Cook AF	Arthur	1889	Stafford	1930	1	1920		West Bromwich A.	7	0	0	
Cook GW	Billy	27/02/1895	Evenwood	1980	3	1924	1926	Huddersfield T	79	0	32	
Cook W	Billy	20/01/1909	Coleraine	1993	1	1939		Everton	40	0	5	i
Cooke TJ	Terry	05/08/1976	Marston Green		1	1996		Manchester Utd.	1	3	0	
Cooper T	Terry	12/07/1944	Brotherton		2	1969	1974	Leeds United	35	2	1	e
Cope HW	Horace	24/05/1899	Treeton	1961	2	1931	1933	Arsenal	5	0	0	
Cope R	Ron	05/10/1934	Crewe		1	1957		Manchester Utd.	2	0	0	
Copping W	Wilf	17/08/1909	Middlecliffe	1980	2	1935	1938	Arsenal	69	0	0	e
Cormack PB	Peter	17/07/1946	Edinburgh		2	1973	1976	Liverpool	46	1	9	s
Coulton F	Frank	1862	Walsall	1929	1	1894		Aston Villa	1	0	0	
Cowan, James	Jimmy	17/10/1868	Jamestown	1918	5	1894	1900	Aston Villa	141	0	9	s
Cowan, John	John	1870	Dumbarton	1937	3	1896	1899	Aston Villa	47	0	20	
Cowans GS	Gordon	27/10/1958	Cornforth		1	1981		Aston Villa	42	0	5	e
Cowell A	Arthur	20/05/1886	Lower Darwen	1959	2	1912	1914	Blackburn Rovers	69	0	0	e
Cowell W	Billy	07/12/1902	Acomb, Northumberland	1999	1	1924		Huddersfield T	2	0	0	
Cox FJA	Freddie	01/11/1920	Reading	1973	1	1953		Arsenal	9	0	1	
Cox G	George	23/08/1911	Warnham	1985	1	1934		Arsenal	2	0	0	
Cox J	Jack	21/12/1877	Blackpool	1955	2	1901	1906	Liverpool	60	0	18	e
Crabtree JJ	Jimmy	1895	Clitheroe	1965	1	1914		Blackburn Rovers	10	0	0	
Crabtree JW	Jimmy	23/12/1871	Burnley	1908	4	1896	1900	Aston Villa	101	0	5	e
Craggs J	Jack	1880	Trimdon Grange		1	1902		Sunderland	6	0	2	
Crawford R	Ray	13/07/1936	Portsmouth		1	1962		Ipswich Town	41	0	33	e
Crawshaw P	Percy	1879	Sheffield		1	1903		Sheffield Wed.	1	0	0	
Crawshaw TH	Tommy	27/12/1872	Sheffield	1960	2	1903	1904	Sheffield Wed.	65	0	2	e
Crayston WJ	Jack	09/10/1910	Grange-over-Sands	1992	2	1935	1938	Arsenal	68	0	7	e
Crerand PT	Pat	19/02/1939	Glasgow		2	1961	1967	Manchester Utd.	78	0	6	s
Crespo HJ	Hernan	06/07/1975	Florida, Argentina		1	2006		Chelsea	20	10	10	ar
Cresswell W	Warney	05/11/1897	South Shields	1973	2	1928	1932	Everton	76	0	0	e
Cringan W	Billy	15/05/1890	Muirkirk	1958	1	1913		Sunderland	10	0	0	s
Crisp J	Jack	27/11/1896	Hamstead	1939	1	1920		West Bromwich A.	38	0	8	
Critchley E	Ted	31/12/1904	Ashton-under-Lyne	1996	2	1928	1932	Everton	77	0	14	
Crompton J	Jack	18/12/1921	Chorlton		2	1952	1956	Manchester Utd.	10	0	0	
Crompton R	Bob	26/09/1879	Blackburn	1941	2	1912	1914	Blackburn Rovers	66	0	0	e
Cross B	Benny	23/08/1898	Birkenhead	1984	1	1921		Burnley	37	0	14	
Crumley RJ	Bob		Lochee		1	1905		Newcastle United	1	0	0	
Cruyff J	Jordi	09/02/1974	Amsterdam, Holland		3	1997	2000	Manchester Utd.	12	17	8	ho
Cudicini C	Carlo	06/09/1973	Milan, Italy		2	2005	2006	Chelsea	6	1	0	
Cuggy F	Frank	16/06/1889	Walker	1965	1	1913		Sunderland	32	0	1	e
Culkin NJ	Nick	06/07/1978	York		1	2000		Manchester Utd.	0	1	0	
Cummings TS	Tommy	12/09/1928	Castledown		1	1960		Burnley	23	0	0	
Cunliffe JN	Jimmy 'Nat'	05/07/1912	Blackrod	1986	1	1939		Everton	7	0	3	e
Cunningham J	John	1873	Glasgow	1910	1	1898		Sheffield Utd.	24	0	7	
Cunningham W	Willie	27/10/1899	Radcliffe		1	1922		Liverpool	5	0	0	
Curran E	Terry	20/03/1955	Kinsley		1	1985		Everton	4	5	0	
Curry JJ	Joseph	1887	Newcastle		1	1911		Manchester Utd.	5	0	0	
Curry T	Tom	01/09/1894	South Shields	1958	1	1927		Newcastle United	5	0	0	
Curtis DP	Dermot	26/08/1932	Dublin		1	1962		Ipswich Town	4	0	0	r
Curtis JCK	John	03/09/1978	Nuneaton		2	1999	2000	Manchester Utd.	1	4	0	
Cygan P	Pascal	19/04/1974	Lens, France		1	2004		Arsenal	10	8	0	
Dale W	Billy	17/02/1905	Manchester	1987	1	1937		Manchester City	36	0	0	
Dalglish KM	Kenny	04/03/1951	Dalmarnock		8	1979	1990	Liverpool	218	7	78	s
Dalton E	Edward		Manchester		1	1908		Manchester Utd.	1	0	0	
Daniel PA	Peter	22/12/1946	Ripley		1	1975		Derby County	37	0	3	
Daniel WR	Ray	02/11/1928	Swansea	1997	1	1953		Arsenal	41	0	5	w
Danskin J	Jason	28/12/1967	Winsford		1	1985		Everton	1	0	0	
D'Arcy FA	Frank	08/12/1946	Liverpool		1	1970		Everton	0	5	0	
Davidson RT	Bobby	27/04/1913	Lochgelly	1988	2	1935	1938	Arsenal	16	0	4	
Davies AL	Arthur	03/01/1905	New Brighton	1940	1	1928		Everton	10	0	0	
Davies JO	Jack	1881	Liverpool		1	1901		Liverpool	1	0	0	
Davies R	Roger	25/10/1950	Wolverhampton		1	1975		Derby County	39	1	12	
Davies SI	Simon	23/04/1974	Winsford		1	1996		Manchester Utd.	1	5	0	w
Davies W	Bill 'Tinker'	13/04/1882	Wrexham	1966	1	1912		Blackburn Rovers	11	0	2	w
Davis H	Harry	1879	Wombwell	1962	2	1903	1904	Sheffield Wed.	58	0	18	e
Davis H	Bert	11/08/1906	Bradford	1981	1	1936		Sunderland	25	0	10	
Davis PV	Paul	09/12/1961	Dulwich		2	1989	1991	Arsenal	47	2	4	

149

		D.o.B.	Birthplace	Died	No.	First	Last	Club	Apps	Subs	Gls	Int
Davison R	Bobby	17/07/1959	South Shields		1	1992		Leeds United	0	2	0	
Dawson AD	Alex	21/02/1940	Aberdeen		1	1957		Manchester Utd.	3	0	3	
Dawson J	Jerry	18/03/1888	Holme-in-Cliviger	1970	1	1921		Burnley	39	0	0	e
Dawson JEIB	Jimmy	21/12/1927	Stoneyburn	2005	1	1950		Portsmouth	1	0	0	
Dawson PH	Percy	29/11/1890	Cullercoats		1	1914		Blackburn Rovers	8	0	3	
Deacy ES	Eamonn	01/10/1958	Galway		1	1981		Aston Villa	5	4	0	r
Dean WR	Bill 'Dixie'	22/01/1907	Birkenhead	1980	2	1928	1932	Everton	77	0	105	e
Deeley NV	Norman	30/11/1933	Wednesbury		3	1954	1959	Wolves	85	0	40	e
Delapenha LL	Lindy	20/05/1927	Kingston, Jamaica		2	1949	1950	Portsmouth	7	0	0	
Del Horno A	Asier	19/01/1981	Barakaldo, Spain		1	2006		Chelsea	25	0	1	sp
Dennis HT	Harold	1903	Newark		1	1926		Huddersfield T	1	0	0	
Dennison H	Harry	04/11/1894	Bradford		1	1912		Blackburn Rovers	1	0	0	
De Oliveira FV	Filipe	27/05/1984	Braga, Portugal		1	2005		Chelsea	0	1	0	
Devey JHG	Jack	26/12/1866	Birmingham	1940	5	1894	1900	Aston Villa	143	0	87	e
Devey W	Will	12/04/1865	Perry Barr	1948	1	1894		Aston Villa	4	0	0	
Devlin WA	Bill	30/07/1899	Bellshill	1972	1	1926		Huddersfield T	4	0	4	
Dewhurst F	Fred	16/12/1863	Fulwood	1895	2	1889	1890	Preston NE	22	0	12	e
Diarra L	Lassana	10/03/1985	Paris, France		1	2006		Chelsea	2	1	0	
Dickinson JW	Jimmy	24/04/1925	Alton	1982	2	1949	1950	Portsmouth	81	0	0	e
Dicks AV	Alan	29/08/1934	Kennington		1	1955		Chelsea	1	0	0	
Ditchburn EG	Ted	24/10/1921	Gillingham	2005	1	1951		Tottenham H	42	0	0	e
Dixon LM	Lee	17/03/1964	Manchester		4	1989	2002	Arsenal	98	14	6	e
Djordjic B	Bojan	06/02/1982	Belgrade, Yugoslavia		1	2001		Manchester Utd.	0	1	0	
Dodds JT	Jack	1885	Hexham		1	1907		Newcastle United	4	0	0	
Dodgin W	Bill	04/11/1931	Wardley	2000	1	1953		Arsenal	1	0	0	
Doherty JH	John	12/03/1935	Manchester		2	1956	1957	Manchester Utd.	19	0	4	
Doherty PD	Peter	05/06/1913	Magherafelt	1990	1	1937		Manchester City	41	0	30	i
Doig JE	Ned	29/10/1866	Letham	1919	4	1892	1902	Sunderland	118	0	0	s
					1	1906		Liverpool	8	0	0	
Dominy AA	Art	11/02/1893	South Stoneham	1974	1	1928		Everton	1	0	0	
Dong Fangzhuo		23/01/1985	Dalian, China		1	2007		Manchester Utd.	1	0	0	ch
Done CC	Cyril	21/10/1920	Liverpool	1993	1	1947		Liverpool	17	0	10	
Donnelly A	Tony	1886	Middleton	1947	1	1911		Manchester Utd.	15	0	0	
Donnelly R	Robert		Craigneuk		1	1937		Manchester City	7	0	1	
Dorigo AR	Tony	31/12/1965	Melbourne, Australia		1	1992		Leeds United	38	0	3	e
Dorrell W	Billy	1873	Coventry	1953	1	1896		Aston Villa	2	0	1	
Dougal PG	Peter	21/03/1909	Denny	1974	2	1934	1935	Arsenal	13	0	1	
Douglas GH	George	18/08/1893	Stepney	1979	1	1921		Burnley	2	0	0	
Dowd HW	Harry	04/07/1938	Salford		1	1968		Manchester City	7	0	0	
Downie ALB	Alex	08/10/1876	Glasgow	1953	1	1908		Manchester Utd.	10	0	0	
Downie JD	Johnny	19/07/1925	Lanark		1	1952		Manchester Utd.	31	0	11	
Doyle D	Dan	16/09/1864	Paisley	1918	1	1891		Everton	20	0	0	s
Doyle M	Mike	25/11/1946	Manchester		1	1968		Manchester City	37	1	5	e
Drake EJ	Ted	16/08/1912	Southampton	1995	3	1934	1938	Arsenal	78	0	66	e
Drogba DYT	Didier	11/03/1978	Abidjan, Ivory Coast		2	2005	2006	Chelsea	38	17	22	iv
Drummond G	Geordie	1865	Edinburgh	1914	2	1889	1890	Preston NE	30	0	11	
Drury GB	George	22/01/1914	Hucknall	1972	1	1938		Arsenal	11	0	0	
Dublin D	Dion	22/04/1969	Leicester		2	1993	1994	Manchester Utd.	4	8	2	e
Duckworth R	Dick		Blackburn		2	1908	1911	Manchester Utd.	57	0	2	
Duff DA	Damien	02/03/1979	Ballyboden		2	2005	2006	Chelsea	46	12	9	r
Duffy CF	Chris	1885	Jarrow		1	1907		Newcastle United	7	0	1	
Duncan ASM	Scott	02/11/1888	Dumbarton	1976	1	1909		Newcastle United	14	0	2	
Dunlop A	Albert	21/04/1932	Liverpool	1990	1	1963		Everton	4	0	0	
Dunlop W	Billy		Annbank		2	1893	1895	Sunderland	23	0	1	
Dunlop WTP	Billy	14/07/1871	Hurlford	1945	2	1901	1906	Liverpool	63	0	0	s
Dunn J	Jimmy	25/11/1900	Glasgow	1963	1	1932		Everton	22	0	10	s
Dunne AP	Tony	24/07/1941	Dublin		2	1965	1967	Manchester Utd.	82	0	0	r
Dunne J	Jimmy	03/09/1905	Ringsend	1949	2	1934	1935	Arsenal	22	0	9	ir
Dunne PAJ	Pat	09/02/1943	Dublin		1	1965		Manchester Utd.	37	0	0	r
Dunning JW	Willie	02/01/1865	Arthurlie	1902	1	1894		Aston Villa	28	0	0	
Duns L	Len	28/09/1916	Newcastle	1989	1	1936		Sunderland	17	0	5	
Duquemin LS	Len	17/07/1924	Cobo, Guernsey	2003	1	1951		Tottenham H	33	0	14	
Durandt CM	Cliff	16/04/1940	Johannesburg, S. Af.	2002	1	1959		Wolves	1	0	0	
Durban WA	Alan	07/07/1941	Bridgend		1	1972		Derby County	31	0	6	w
Dwyer NM	Noel	30/10/1934	Dublin	1993	1	1958		Wolves	5	0	0	r
Dyson TK	Terry	29/11/1934	Malton		1	1961		Tottenham H	40	0	12	
Eagles CM	Mark	19/11/1985	Hemel Hempstead		1	2007		Manchester Utd.	1	1	1	
Easdale J	John	16/01/1919	Dumbarton		1	1947		Liverpool	2	0	0	
Eastham H	Harry	30/06/1917	Blackpool	1998	1	1947		Liverpool	19	0	0	
Easton W	Bill	10/10/1904	Newcastle	1960	1	1928		Everton	3	0	1	
Edmonds H	Hugh	1884	Chryston		1	1911		Manchester Utd.	13	0	0	
Edwards D	Duncan	01/10/1936	Dudley	1958	2	1956	1957	Manchester Utd.	67	0	8	e
Edwards J	Jack		Preston	1960	1	1889		Preston NE	4	0	3	
Edwards RH	Bobby	22/05/1931	Guildford		1	1955		Chelsea	1	0	0	
Ekner DH	Dan	05/02/1927	Sweden	1975	1	1950		Portsmouth	5	0	0	
Elder AR	Alex	25/04/1941	Lisburn		1	1960		Burnley	34	0	0	n
Elder J	Jimmy	05/03/1928	Scone		1	1950		Portsmouth	1	0	0	
Ellam R	Roy	13/01/1943	Hemsworth		1	1974		Leeds United	3	1	0	
Elliott J	Jack				1	1891		Everton	1	0	0	
Elliott JAE	James	20/10/1869	Middlesbrough	1899	2	1894	1896	Aston Villa	13	0	0	
Elsworthy JT	John	26/07/1931	Nantyderry		1	1962		Ipswich Town	41	0	2	
Essien M	Michael	03/12/1982	Accra, Ghana		1	2006		Chelsea	27	4	2	gh
Evans AJ	Albert	1874	Barnard Castle	1966	3	1897	1900	Aston Villa	70	0	0	
Evans AJ	Allan	12/10/1956	Polbeth		1	1981		Aston Villa	39	0	7	s
Evra P	Patrice	15/05/1981	Dakar, Senegal		1	2007		Manchester Utd.	22	2	1	fr

		D.o.B.	Birthplace	Died	No.	First	Last	Club	Apps	Subs	Gls	Int
Eyre E	Edmund	1884	Worksop	1943	1	1910		Aston Villa	13	0	2	
Eyre IJ	Isaac	1875	Heeley		1	1904		Sheffield Wed.	1	0	0	
Fagan W	Willie	20/02/1917	Inveresk	1992	1	1947		Liverpool	18	0	7	
Fairclough CH	Chris	12/04/1964	Nottingham		1	1992		Leeds United	30	1	2	
Fairclough D	David	05/01/1957	Liverpool		5	1976	1983	Liverpool	32	28	20	
Farquhar JW	Billy	1879	Elgin		1	1902		Sunderland	13	0	0	
Felton W	Billy	01/08/1900	Heworth	1977	1	1929		Sheffield Wed.	3	0	0	e
Ferdinand RG	Rio	07/11/1978	Peckham		2	2003	2007	Manchester Utd.	60	1	1	e
Ferguson D	Darren	09/02/1972	Glasgow		2	1993	1994	Manchester Utd.	16	2	0	
Ferguson M	Matthew	1873	Bellshill	1902	1	1902		Sunderland	29	0	0	
Fern TE	Tommy	01/04/1886	Measham	1966	1	1915		Everton	36	0	0	
Ferns P	Phil	14/11/1937	Liverpool		1	1964		Liverpool	18	0	0	
Ferreira RP	Paulo	18/01/1979	Cascais, Portugal		2	2005	2006	Chelsea	47	3	0	pt
Ferrier HR	Harry	20/05/1920	Ratho	2002	2	1949	1950	Portsmouth	82	0	0	
Ferrier R	Bob	1874	Dumbarton	1947	2	1903	1904	Sheffield Wed.	64	0	0	
Fields AG	Alf	15/11/1918	Canning Town		1	1948		Arsenal	6	0	0	
Finlayson MJ	Malcolm	14/06/1930	Bowhill		2	1958	1959	Wolves	76	0	0	
Fitzpatrick JHN	John	18/08/1946	Aberdeen		2	1965	1967	Manchester Utd.	5	0	0	
Fleetwood T	Tom	06/12/1888	Toxteth Park	1945	1	1915		Everton	35	0	2	
Fleming G	George	20/05/1869	Bannockburn		1	1906		Liverpool	4	0	0	
Fletcher DB	Darren	01/02/1984	Edinburgh		1	2007		Manchester Utd.	16	8	3	s
Flewin R	Reg	28/11/1920	Portsmouth		2	1949	1950	Portsmouth	63	0	0	
Flowers R	Ron	28/07/1934	Edlington		3	1954	1959	Wolves	74	0	3	e
Flowers TD	Tim	03/02/1967	Kenilworth		1	1995		Blackburn Rovers	39	0	0	e
Forbes AR	Alex	21/01/1925	Dundee		2	1948	1953	Arsenal	44	0	3	s
Forlan CD	Diego	19/05/1979	Montevideo, Uruguay		1	2003		Manchester Utd.	7	18	6	uy
Forshaw R	Dick	20/08/1895	Preston		2	1922	1923	Liverpool	84	0	36	
					1	1928		Everton	23	0	5	
Forssell MK	Mikael	15/03/1981	Steinfurt, Germany		1	2005		Chelsea	0	1	0	fi
Fortune Q	Quinton	21/05/1977	Cape Town, S. Af.		3	2000	2003	Manchester Utd.	15	7	4	sa
Foulke WH	Willie	12/04/1874	Dawley	1916	1	1898		Sheffield Utd.	29	0	0	e
Foulkes WA	Bill	05/01/1932	Prescot		4	1956	1967	Manchester Utd.	140	0	4	e
Freeman BC	Bert	1885	Handsworth	1955	1	1921		Burnley	3	0	0	e
Freeman RH	Raymond		Droitwich		1	1937		Manchester City	1	0	0	
French PA	Archibald				1	1898		Sheffield Utd.	1	0	0	
Froggatt J	Jack	17/11/1922	Sheffield	1993	2	1949	1950	Portsmouth	80	0	30	e
Furnell J	Jim	23/11/1937	Clitheroe		1	1960		Burnley	1	0	0	
					1	1964		Liverpool	2	0	0	
Gabriel J	Jimmy	16/10/1940	Dundee		1	1963		Everton	40	0	5	s
Gale AP	Tony	19/11/1959	Westminster		1	1995		Blackburn Rovers	15	0	0	
Gallacher HK	Hughie	02/02/1903	Bellshill	1957	1	1927		Newcastle United	38	0	36	s
Gallacher KW	Kevin	23/11/1966	Clydebank		1	1995		Blackburn Rovers	1	0	1	s
Gallacher P	Patsy	21/08/1909	Bridge of Weir	1992	1	1936		Sunderland	37	0	19	s
Gallas W	William	17/08/1977	Asnieres, France		2	2005	2006	Chelsea	61	1	7	fr
Galt JH	Jimmy	11/08/1885	Saltcoats	1935	1	1915		Everton	32	0	2	s
Garbutt WT	Billy	09/01/1883	Stockport	1964	1	1912		Blackburn Rovers	1	0	0	
Garde R	Remi	03/04/1966	L'Arbresle, France		1	1998		Arsenal	6	4	0	fr
Gardner A	Alec	1877	Leith	1952	3	1905	1909	Newcastle United	77	0	2	
Garfield JH	James	1875	Canterbury	1949	1	1900		Aston Villa	1	0	1	
Garraty W	Billy	06/10/1878	Saltley	1931	2	1899	1900	Aston Villa	42	1	33	e
Garside JA	Jimmy	1885	Manchester		1	1906		Liverpool	4	0	0	
Gaskell JD	David	05/10/1940	Wigan		2	1965	1967	Manchester Utd.	10	0	0	
Edu	Edu	15/05/1978	Sao Paulo, Brazil		2	2002	2004	Arsenal	21	23	3	br
Gaudie R	Ralph	1875	Guisborough		1	1898		Sheffield Utd.	6	0	2	
Gaudie R	Richard	1874	Sheffield	1938	1	1899		Aston Villa	5	0	1	
Geary F	Fred	23/01/1868	Hyson Green	1955	1	1891		Everton	22	0	20	e
Geddis D	David	12/03/1958	Carlisle		1	1981		Aston Villa	8	1	4	
Gee CW	Charlie	06/04/1909	Reddish	1981	2	1932	1939	Everton	40	0	0	e
Gemmell J	Jimmy	17/11/1880	Glasgow		1	1902		Sunderland	31	0	10	
Gemmill A	Archie	24/03/1947	Paisley		2	1972	1975	Derby County	81	0	3	s
					1	1978		Nottm. Forest	32	2	3	
George FC	Charlie	10/10/1950	Islington		1	1971		Arsenal	17	0	5	e
George W	Billy	29/06/1874	Atcham	1933	3	1899	1910	Aston Villa	67	0	0	e
Gerrish WWW	Billy	1884	Bristol	1916	1	1910		Aston Villa	36	0	14	
Gibbons L	Len	22/11/1930	Wirral		1	1954		Wolves	1	0	0	
Gibson CJ	Colin	06/04/1960	Bridport		1	1981		Aston Villa	19	2	0	
Gibson TRD	Don	12/05/1929	Manchester		1	1952		Manchester Utd.	17	0	0	
Gibson W	Will	1869	Cambuslang	1911	2	1892	1893	Sunderland	50	0	3	
Gibson WK	William	1876	Ireland		1	1902		Sunderland	1	0	0	i
Gibson WM	Willie	21/07/1898	Larkhall		1	1927		Newcastle United	32	0	0	
Giggs RJ	Ryan	29/11/1973	Cardiff		9	1993	2007	Manchester Utd.	258	31	62	w
Giles MJ	Johnny	06/01/1940	Cabra		2	1969	1974	Leeds United	49	0	10	r
Gilhespy TWC	Cyril	18/02/1898	Fencehouses	1985	2	1922	1923	Sunderland	12	0	3	
Gillan JS	James	1870	Derby	1944	1	1894		Aston Villa	3	0	0	
Gillespie GT	Gary	05/07/1960	Bonnybridge		3	1986	1990	Liverpool	60	2	11	s
Gillespie J	James		Scotland	1932	2	1893	1895	Sunderland	49	0	24	s
Gillespie JW	John		Scotland		1	1893		Sunderland	5	0	0	
Gillick T	Torry	19/05/1915	Airdrie	1971	1	1939		Everton	40	0	14	s
Gladwin CE	Charlie	09/12/1887	Worksop	1952	1	1913		Sunderland	27	0	0	
Glover JW	John	28/10/1876	West Bromwich	1955	1	1901		Liverpool	11	0	0	
Goddard AM	Arthur	1876	Heaton Norris		1	1906		Liverpool	38	0	7	
Goddard G	George	20/12/1903	Gomshall	1987	1	1936		Sunderland	3	0	1	
Goldie WG	Billy	22/01/1878	Hurlford	1952	1	1901		Liverpool	34	0	2	
Goodall AL	Archie	19/06/1864	Belfast	1929	1	1889		Preston NE	2	0	1	i
Goodall FR	Roy	31/12/1902	Dronfield	1982	3	1924	1926	Huddersfield T	81	0	2	e

		D.o.B.	Birthplace	Died	No.	First	Last	Club	Apps	Subs	Gls	Int
Goodall J	John	19/06/1863	Westminster	1942	1	1889		Preston NE	21	0	20	e
Goodchild G	George	1875	Ryhope		1	1895		Sunderland	1	0	0	
Goodwin F	Freddie	28/06/1933	Heywood		2	1956	1957	Manchester Utd.	14	0	0	
Goram AL	Andy	13/04/1964	Bury		1	2001		Manchester Utd.	2	0	0	s
Gordon JB	Jack	1863	Port Glasgow		2	1889	1890	Preston NE	42	0	15	
Gordon P	Patrick	1864	Renton		1	1891		Everton	3	0	0	
Goring H	Peter	02/01/1927	Bishop's Cleeve	1994	1	1953		Arsenal	29	0	10	
Gorman J	Jimmy	1882	Middlesbrough		1	1906		Liverpool	1	0	0	
Gosnell AA	Bert	10/02/1880	Colchester	1972	3	1905	1909	Newcastle United	56	0	7	e
Gow DR	Donald	08/02/1868	Blair	1945	2	1892	1895	Sunderland	23	0	0	s
Graham G	George	30/11/1944	Bargeddie		1	1971		Arsenal	36	2	11	s
Graham J	Johnny	23/02/1857	Ayr	1927	2	1889	1890	Preston NE	39	0	0	s
Graham R	Bobby	22/11/1944	Motherwell		1	1966		Liverpool	1	0	0	
Graham S	Sam	07/04/1878	Galston		1	1905		Newcastle United	3	0	0	
Graham W	Willie		Ayr		1	1889		Preston NE	5	0	0	
Grant APSA	Anthony	04/06/1987	Lambeth		1	2005		Chelsea	0	1	0	
Gray AM	Andy	30/11/1955	Glasgow		1	1985		Everton	21	5	9	s
Gray E	Eddie	17/11/1948	Glasgow		2	1969	1974	Leeds United	40	1	5	s
Gray FJS	Frederick	15/07/1869	Rugeley		1	1890		Preston NE	1	0	1	
Gray FT	Frank	27/10/1954	Glasgow		1	1974		Leeds United	3	3	0	s
Greaves ID	Ian	26/05/1932	Crompton		2	1956	1957	Manchester Utd.	18	0	0	
Greenhalgh N	Norman	10/08/1914	Bolton	1995	1	1939		Everton	42	0	1	
Greenhoff J	Jimmy	19/06/1946	Barnsley		1	1969		Leeds United	3	0	0	
Greening J	Jonathan	02/01/1979	Scarborough		3	1999	2001	Manchester Utd.	4	10	0	
Greenwood R	Ron	11/11/1921	Worsthorne	2006	1	1955		Chelsea	21	0	0	
Gregg H	Harry	25/10/1932	Derry		1	1967		Manchester Utd.	2	0	0	n
Gregg RE	Bob	04/02/1904	Ferryhill	1991	2	1929	1930	Sheffield Wed.	35	0	7	
Gregory H	Howard	06/04/1893	Aston Manor	1954	1	1920		West Bromwich A.	34	0	12	
Grenyer A	Alan	31/08/1892	North Shields	1953	1	1915		Everton	14	0	1	
Griffiths H	Harry	02/01/1886	Middlesbrough		1	1906		Liverpool	1	0	0	
Griffiths JA	Jeremiah	1872	Birmingham	1940	2	1896	1897	Aston Villa	2	0	0	
Griffiths PH	Philip	25/10/1905	Tylorstown	1978	1	1932		Everton	7	0	3	w
Griffiths WM	Mal	08/03/1919	Merthyr Tydfil	1969	1	1938		Arsenal	9	0	5	w
Grimandi G	Gilles	11/11/1970	Gap, France		2	1998	2002	Arsenal	27	21	1	
Grobbelaar BD	Bruce	06/10/1957	Durban, South Africa		6	1982	1990	Liverpool	244	0	0	zm
Groves P	Perry	19/04/1965	Bow		2	1989	1991	Arsenal	19	34	7	
Groves W	Willie	1869	Leith	1908	1	1894		Aston Villa	22	0	3	s
Gudjohnsen ES	Eidur	15/09/1978	Reykjavik, Iceland		2	2005	2006	Chelsea	46	17	14	ic
Gurney R	Bobby	13/10/1907	Silksworth	1994	1	1936		Sunderland	39	0	31	e
Guttridge WH	Bill	04/03/1931	Darlaston		1	1954		Wolves	2	0	0	
Haggart W	William	1874	Edinburgh	1934	1	1899	1900	Aston Villa	2	0	0	
Hall AE	Bert	1882	Wordsley	1957	1	1910		Aston Villa	25	0	6	e
Hall AW	Alex	06/11/1908	East Calder	1991	1	1936		Sunderland	38	0	0	
Hall BW	Brian	22/01/1946	Glasgow		2	1973	1976	Liverpool	29	5	4	
Hall T	Tom	04/09/1891	Newburn		1	1913		Sunderland	20	0	7	
Hall W	Wilf	14/10/1934	Haydock		1	1962		Ipswich Town	5	0	0	
Halley G	George	29/10/1887	Cronberry		1	1921		Burnley	26	0	0	
Halse HJ	Harold	01/01/1886	Leytonstone	1949	2	1908	1911	Manchester Utd.	29	0	13	e
Hampson W	Billy	26/08/1884	Radcliffe	1966	1	1927		Newcastle United	2	0	0	
Hampton JH	Harry	21/04/1885	Wellington, Shropshire	1963	1	1910		Aston Villa	32	0	26	e
Hancocks J	Johnny	30/04/1919	Oakengates	1994	1	1954		Wolves	42	0	25	e
Hannah AB	Andrew	17/09/1864	Renton	1940	1	1891		Everton	20	0	0	s
Hannah D	Davy	28/04/1867	Raffrey	1936	3	1892	1895	Sunderland	39	0	7	
Hannah J	Jimmy	1868	Glasgow		3	1892	1895	Sunderland	78	0	47	s
Hansen AD	Alan	13/06/1955	Sauchie		8	1979	1990	Liverpool	294	0	7	s
Hapgood EA	Eddie	27/09/1908	Bristol	1973	5	1931	1938	Arsenal	191	0	1	e
Hardy HJ	Harry	14/01/1895	Stockport	1969	1	1928		Everton	6	0	0	e
Hardy S	Sam	26/08/1883	Newbold	1966	1	1906		Liverpool	30	0	0	e
Hare CB	Charlie	1871	Birmingham	1934	1	1894		Aston Villa	10	0	7	
Hargreaves L	Len	07/03/1906	Kimberworth	1980	1	1929		Sheffield Wed.	2	0	1	
Harley J	Jim	02/02/1917	Methil	1989	1	1947		Liverpool	17	0	0	
Harper A	Alan	01/11/1960	Liverpool		2	1985	1987	Everton	39	10	3	
Harper EC	Ted	22/08/1901	Sheerness	1959	1	1929		Sheffield Wed.	6	0	5	e
Harper W	Bill	19/01/1897	Tarbrax	1989	1	1931		Arsenal	19	0	0	s
Harris B	Brian	16/05/1935	Bebington		1	1963		Everton	24	0	1	
Harris EJ	Edward	1872	Willenhall	1940	1	1896		Aston Villa	1	0	0	
Harris G	Gordon	02/06/1940	Worksop		1	1960		Burnley	2	0	0	e
Harris GW	Gerry	08/10/1935	Claverley		2	1958	1959	Wolves	79	0	1	
Harris J	Joe	19/03/1896	Glasgow	1933	1	1927		Newcastle United	9	0	0	s
Harris J	John	30/06/1917	Glasgow	1988	1	1955		Chelsea	31	0	0	
Harris PP	Peter	19/12/1925	Portsmouth	2003	2	1949	1950	Portsmouth	80	0	33	e
Harrison G	George	18/07/1892	Church Gresley	1939	1	1915		Everton	26	0	4	e
Hart H	Hunter	11/03/1897	Glasgow		1	1928		Everton	41	0	1	
Harvey D	David	07/02/1948	Leeds		1	1974		Leeds United	39	0	0	s
Harvey J	John		Scotland		2	1893	1895	Sunderland	27	0	5	
Harvey JC	Colin	16/11/1944	Liverpool		1	1970		Everton	35	0	3	e
Hastings AC	Alex	17/03/1912	Falkirk	1988	1	1936		Sunderland	31	0	0	s
Hatfield SE	Ernie	16/01/1902	Basford		1	1929		Sheffield Wed.	1	0	0	
Hatton SEO	Sid	22/01/1892	West Bromwich	1961	1	1920		West Bromwich A.	1	0	0	
Hawksworth A	Anthony	15/01/1938	Sheffield		1	1957		Manchester Utd.	1	0	0	
Hayes JV	Vince	1879	Miles Platting		1	1911		Manchester Utd.	1	0	20	
Hayes M	Martin	21/03/1966	Walthamstow		1	1989		Arsenal	3	14	1	
Haynes AE	Alfred	04/04/1907	Oxford	1953	3	1931	1934	Arsenal	9	0	0	
Heale JA	Jimmy	19/09/1914	Bristol	1997	1	1937		Manchester City	10	0	6	
Healy DJ	David	05/08/1979	Downpatrick		1	2001		Manchester Utd.	0	1	0	n

		D.o.B.	Birthplace	Died	No.	First	Last	Club	Apps	Subs	Gls	Int
Heath AP	Adrian	11/01/1961	Stoke-on-Trent		2	1985	1987	Everton	58	0	22	
Heaton C	Charles	1868	Preston		1	1890		Preston NE	2	0	1	
Hector KJ	Kevin	02/11/1944	Leeds		2	1972	1975	Derby County	80	0	25	e
Hedley GA	George	20/07/1876	South Bank	1942	1	1898		Sheffield Utd.	2	0	0	e
Heighway SD	Steve	25/11/1947	Dublin		5	1973	1980	Liverpool	144	9	22	r
Heinze GI	Gabriel	19/04/1978	Crespo, Argentina		1	2007		Manchester Utd.	17	5	0	ar
Hemmingfield WE	Bill	1875	Wortley	1953	1	1904		Sheffield Wed.	6	0	1	
Henderson JG	Jackie	17/01/1932	Bishopbriggs	2005	2	1958	1959	Wolves	9	0	3	s
Hendry ECJ	Colin	07/12/1965	Keith		1	1995		Blackburn Rovers	38	0	4	s
Hendry WH	Billy	1864	Newport-on-Tay	1901	1	1890		Preston NE	1	0	0	
Hennessey WT	Terry	01/09/1942	Llay		1	1972		Derby County	17	1	0	w
Henry RP	Ron	17/08/1934	Shoreditch		1	1961		Tottenham H	42	0	0	e
Henry T	Thierry	17/08/1977	Paris, France		2	2002	2004	Arsenal	68	2	54	fr
Herd A	Alex	08/11/1911	Bowhill	1982	1	1937		Manchester City	32	0	15	
Herd DG	David	15/04/1934	Hamilton		2	1965	1967	Manchester Utd.	65	0	36	s
Heslop GW	George	01/07/1940	Wallsend	2006	1	1963		Everton	1	0	0	
					1	1968		Manchester City	41	0	1	
Hewitt J	Joe	03/05/1881	Chester	1971	1	1902		Sunderland	5	0	1	
					1	1906		Liverpool	37	0	23	
Hibbitt TA	Terry	01/12/1947	Bradford	1994	1	1969		Leeds United	9	3	3	
Higginbotham DJ	Danny	29/12/1978	Manchester		1	2000		Manchester Utd.	2	1	0	
Higgins A	Sandy	04/11/1885	Kilmarnock	1939	2	1907	1909	Newcastle United	27	0	5	s
Higham P	Peter	08/11/1930	Wigan		1	1950		Portsmouth	1	0	0	
Hill FR	Frank	21/05/1906	Forfar	1993	3	1933	1935	Arsenal	66	0	4	s
Hill H	Harold	24/09/1899	Blackwell, Derbyshire	1969	1	1929		Sheffield Wed.	1	0	0	
Hillier D	David	19/12/1969	Blackheath		1	1991		Arsenal	9	7	0	
Hince PF	Paul	02/03/1945	Manchester		1	1968		Manchester City	6	0	2	
Hindmarsh JW	Billy	26/12/1919	Crook	1994	2	1949	1950	Portsmouth	44	0	0	
Hinton AT	Alan	06/10/1942	Wednesbury		2	1972	1975	Derby County	46	5	17	e
Hobson HB	Bert	1890	Tow Law	1963	1	1913		Sunderland	3	0	0	
Hobson RGE	George		Leeds		1	1926		Huddersfield T	2	0	0	
Hodge J	Jimmy	05/07/1891	Stenhousemuir	1970	1	1911		Manchester Utd.	2	0	0	
Hodge SB	Steve	25/10/1962	Nottingham		1	1992		Leeds United	12	11	7	e
Hodgetts D	Denny	28/11/1863	Birmingham	1945	2	1894	1896	Aston Villa	47	0	15	e
Hodgson DJ	David	06/08/1960	Gateshead		2	1983	1984	Liverpool	21	7	4	
Hodkinson JC	Joe	1889	Lancaster	1954	1	1914		Blackburn Rovers	33	0	2	e
Hofton LB	Leslie	1888	Sheffield		1	1911		Manchester Utd.	9	0	0	
Hogg R	Robert	1877	Whitburn	1963	1	1902		Sunderland	29	0	5	
Hogg W	Billy	29/05/1879	Newcastle	1937	1	1902		Sunderland	28	0	10	e
Holden RH	Dick	1885	Middleton	1971	2	1908	1911	Manchester Utd.	34	0	0	
Holley GH	George	25/11/1885	Seaham Harbour	1942	1	1913		Sunderland	30	0	12	e
Hollowbread JF	John	02/01/1934	Enfield		1	1961		Tottenham H	1	0	0	
Holmes R	Bob	23/06/1867	Preston	1955	2	1889	1890	Preston NE	40	0	0	e
Holt J	Johnny	10/04/1865	Church		1	1891		Everton	21	0	1	e
Holton CC	Cliff	29/04/1929	Oxford	1996	1	1953		Arsenal	21	0	19	
Homer TP	Thomas		Birmingham		1	1911		Manchester City	7	0	6	
Hooper AH	Arthur		Brierley Hill		1	1911		Manchester Utd.	2	0	0	
Hooper M	Mark	14/07/1901	Darlington	1974	2	1929	1930	Sheffield Wed.	84	0	33	
Hooper MD	Mike	10/02/1964	Bristol		1	1988		Liverpool	2	0	0	
Hopkin F	Fred	23/09/1895	Dewsbury	1970	2	1922	1923	Liverpool	82	0	1	
Hornby CF	Cecil	25/04/1907	West Bromwich	1964	1	1936		Sunderland	8	0	2	
Horne DT	Des	12/12/1939	Johannesburg, S. Af.		1	1959		Wolves	8	0	3	
Horne SF	Stan	17/12/1944	Clanfield		1	1968		Manchester City	4	1	0	
Houghton H	Harold	26/08/1906	Liverpool	1986	1	1928		Everton	1	0	0	
Houghton RJ	Ray	09/01/1962	Glasgow		2	1988	1990	Liverpool	42	5	6	r
Hounsfield RE	Reginald	14/08/1882	Sheffield		1	1903		Sheffield Wed.	2	0	0	
Houston J	Johnny	17/05/1889	Belfast		1	1915		Everton	1	0	0	i
Howard H	Harry	1871	Rotherham		1	1898		Sheffield Utd.	3	0	0	
Howarth HR	Horace		Liverpool		1	1915		Everton	1	0	0	
Howarth RH	Bob	20/06/1865	Preston	1938	2	1889	1890	Preston NE	39	0	0	e
Howell R	Rabbi	12/10/1867	Wincobank	1937	1	1898		Sheffield Utd.	24	0	0	e
					1	1901		Liverpool	2	0	0	
Howells R	Ron	03/08/1935	Ferndale		1	1958		Wolves	2	0	0	
Howie J	Jimmy	19/03/1878	Galston	1962	3	1905	1909	Newcastle United	88	0	26	s
Hoyland GA	George				1	1904		Sheffield Wed.	1	0	0	
Hoyte JR	Justin	20/11/1984	Waltham Forest		1	2004		Arsenal	0	1	0	
Hudspeth FC	Frank	20/04/1890	Percy Main	1963	1	1927		Newcastle United	42	0	3	e
Hughes DJ	Darren	06/10/1965	Prescot		1	1985		Everton	2	0	0	
Hughes EW	Emlyn	28/08/1947	Barrow	2004	4	1973	1979	Liverpool	140	0	10	e
Hughes L	Laurie	02/03/1924	Waterloo, Lancashire		1	1947		Liverpool	30	0	0	e
Hughes LM	Mark	01/11/1963	Wrexham		2	1993	1994	Manchester Utd.	77	0	26	w
Hughes SJ	Stephen	18/09/1976	Reading		1	1998		Arsenal	7	10	2	
Hulme A	Aaron	1883	Manchester	1933	1	1908		Manchester Utd.	1	0	0	
Hulme JHA	Joe	26/08/1904	Stafford	1991	5	1931	1938	Arsenal	103	0	49	e
Humphreys G	Gerry	14/01/1946	Llandudno		1	1970		Everton	1	0	0	
Hunt GS	George	22/02/1910	Barnsley	1996	1	1938		Arsenal	18	0	3	e
Hunt R	Roger	20/07/1938	Golborne		2	1964	1966	Liverpool	78	0	61	e
Hunter GC	George	16/08/1886	Peshawar, India	1934	1	1910		Aston Villa	32	0	1	
Hunter JB	John 'Sailor'	06/04/1878	Johnstone	1966	1	1901		Liverpool	8	0	3	s
Hunter N	Norman	29/10/1943	Eighton Banks		2	1969	1974	Leeds United	84	0	0	e
Hunter TJ	Jack	1877	Liverpool		1	1901		Liverpool	2	0	0	
Hurst JW	John	06/02/1947	Blackpool		1	1970		Everton	42	0	5	
Husband J	Jimmy	15/10/1947	Newcastle		1	1970		Everton	30	0	6	
Huth R	Robert	18/08/1984	Berlin, Germany		2	2005	2006	Chelsea	13	10	0	ge
Hysen GI	Glenn	30/10/1959	Gothenburg, Sweden		1	1990		Liverpool	35	0	1	sw

		D.o.B.	Birthplace	Died	No.	First	Last	Club	Apps	Subs	Gls	Int
Hyslop T	Tommy	22/09/1874	Mauchline	1936	1	1895		Sunderland	12	0	7	s
Ince PEC	Paul	21/10/1967	Ilford		2	1993	1994	Manchester Utd.	80	0	14	e
Inglis J	Jock				2	1889	1890	Preston NE	3	0	2	
Innerd W	Wilf	1878	Newcastle		1	1905		Newcastle United	1	0	0	
Irvine RW	Bobby	29/04/1900	Lisburn	1979	1	1928		Everton	9	0	3	i
Irwin CT	Colin	09/02/1957	Liverpool		1	1980		Liverpool	7	1	2	
Irwin JD	Denis	31/10/1965	Cork		7	1993	2001	Manchester Utd.	213	6	14	r
Islip E	Ernie	31/10/1892	Parkwood Springs	1941	1	1924		Huddersfield T	3	0	0	
Jack DBN	David	03/04/1898	Bolton	1958	3	1931	1934	Arsenal	83	0	54	e
Jackson A	Alan	22/08/1938	Swadlincote		2	1958	1959	Wolves	4	0	1	
Jackson AS	Alex	12/05/1905	Renton	1946	1	1926		Huddersfield T	39	0	16	s
Jackson G	George	14/01/1911	Liverpool	2002	1	1939		Everton	2	0	0	
Jackson RW	Dicky	1878	Middlesbrough		1	1902		Sunderland	32	0	3	
Jackson TA	Tommy	03/11/1946	Belfast		1	1970		Everton	14	1	0	n
James AW	Alex	14/09/1901	Mossend	1953	4	1931	1935	Arsenal	132	0	15	s
Jardine D	David				1	1891		Everton	10	0	0	
Jarosik J	Jiri	27/10/1977	Usti Nad Lebem, Czech		1	2005		Chelsea	3	11	0	cz
Jarvis TR	Richard	1885		1924	1	1904		Sheffield Wed.	1	0	0	
Jefferis F	Frank	03/07/1884	Fordingbridge	1938	1	1915		Everton	18	0	4	e
Jeffers F	Francis	25/01/1981	Liverpool		1	2002		Arsenal	2	4	2	e
Jenkinson TJ	Thomas				1	1898		Sheffield Utd.	2	0	0	
Jephcott AC	Claude	31/10/1890	Smethwick	1950	1	1920		West Bromwich A.	21	0	5	
Jobey G	George	1885	Heddon	1962	2	1907	1909	Newcastle United	11	0	1	
Johanneson AL	Albert	12/03/1940	Johannesburg, S. Af.	1995	1	1969		Leeds United	0	1	1	
John RF	Bob	03/02/1900	Barry Dock	1982	4	1931	1935	Arsenal	117	0	3	w
Johnsen JR	Ronny	10/06/1969	Sandefjord, Norway		4	1997	2001	Manchester Utd.	58	9	4	no
Johnson DE	David	23/10/1951	Liverpool		4	1977	1982	Liverpool	92	16	44	e
Johnson G	George	1871	West Bromwich	1934	2	1899	1900	Aston Villa	33	0	14	
Johnson GMcL	Glen	23/08/1984	Greenwich		2	2005	2006	Chelsea	17	4	0	e
Johnson RK	Dick	1895	Gateshead	1933	1	1923		Liverpool	37	0	14	
Johnson TCF	Tommy	19/08/1901	Dalton-in-Furness	1973	1	1932		Everton	41	0	22	e
Johnson WH	Harry	1876	Ecclesfield	1940	1	1898		Sheffield Utd.	10	0	2	e
Johnston CP	Craig	25/06/1960	Johannesburg, S. Af.		5	1982	1988	Liverpool	127	24	27	
Johnston H	Harry	1871	Glasgow	1936	1	1895		Sunderland	29	0	2	
Johnston J	James	1886	Rothesay	1953	2	1912	1914	Blackburn Rovers	7	0	0	
Johnston R	Bert	02/06/1909	Falkirk	1968	1	1936		Sunderland	10	0	0	s
Johnston WG	Billy	16/01/1901	Edinburgh	1964	1	1924		Huddersfield T	8	0	0	
Johnstone W	William				1	1890		Preston NE	2	0	0	
Johnstone W	Bill	18/05/1900	Fife		1	1931		Arsenal	2	0	1	
Jones B	Bryn	14/02/1912	Penyard	1985	1	1948		Arsenal	7	0	1	w
Jones C	Cliff		Rotherham		1	1921		Burnley	31	0	0	
Jones C	Charlie	12/12/1899	Troedyrhiw	1966	3	1931	1934	Arsenal	69	0	1	w
Jones CMN	Chris	19/11/1945	Altrincham		1	1968		Manchester City	2	0	0	
Jones CW	Cliff	07/02/1935	Swansea		1	1961		Tottenham H	29	0	15	w
Jones G	Gwyn	20/03/1935	Llandwrog		2	1958	1959	Wolves	6	0	0	
Jones JP	Joey	04/03/1955	Llandudno		2	1976	1977	Liverpool	52	0	3	w
Jones LJ	Les	01/07/1911	Aberdare	1981	1	1938		Arsenal	28	0	3	w
Jones M	Mark	15/06/1933	Barnsley	1958	3	1952	1957	Manchester Utd.	74	0	1	
Jones MD	Mick	24/04/1945	Worksop		2	1969	1974	Leeds United	68	3	28	e
Jones TG	Tommy 'TG'	12/10/1917	Connah's Quay	2004	1	1939		Everton	39	0	0	w
Jones TJ	Tommy	06/12/1909	Tonypandy		1	1930		Sheffield Wed.	1	0	0	w
Jones WH	Bill	13/05/1921	Macclesfield		1	1947		Liverpool	26	0	2	e
Jonsson S	Siggi	27/09/1966	Akranes, Iceland		1	1991		Arsenal	2	0	0	ic
Jordan J	Joe	15/12/1951	Carluke		1	1974		Leeds United	25	8	7	s
Joy B	Bernard	29/10/1911	Fulham	1984	1	1938		Arsenal	26	0	0	e
Kamara C	Chris	25/12/1957	Middlesbrough		1	1992		Leeds United	0	2	0	
Kanchelskis A	Andrei	23/01/1969	Kirowograd, Ukraine		2	1993	1994	Manchester Utd.	42	16	9	un
Kanu N	Nwankwo	01/08/1976	Owerri, Nigeria		2	2002	2004	Arsenal	12	21	4	ng
Kay AH	Tony	13/05/1937	Sheffield		1	1963		Everton	19	0	1	e
Kaye GH	Harry	19/04/1919	Liverpool	1992	1	1947		Liverpool	1	0	0	
Kean FW	Fred	10/12/1898	Sheffield	1973	1	1929		Sheffield Wed.	4	0	0	e
Keane RM	Roy	10/08/1971	Cork		7	1994	2003	Manchester Utd.	192	8	22	r
Kearns JH	John	1880	Nuneaton	1949	1	1910		Aston Villa	10	0	0	
Keegan JK	Kevin	14/02/1951	Armthorpe		3	1973	1977	Liverpool	120	0	37	e
Keizer GP	Gerry	18/08/1910	Amsterdam, Holland	1980	1	1931		Arsenal	12	0	0	ho
Kelly EP	Eddie	07/02/1951	Glasgow		1	1971		Arsenal	21	2	4	
Kelly GO	Gary	09/07/1974	Drogheda		1	1992		Leeds United	0	2	0	r
Kelly J	Jerry	1900	Hamilton		1	1928		Everton	40	0	1	
Kelly JPV	Phil	10/07/1939	Dublin		1	1959		Wolves	1	0	0	r
Kelly R	Bob	16/11/1893	Ashton-in-Makerfield	1969	1	1921		Burnley	37	0	20	e
Kelsey AJ	Jack	19/11/1929	Llansamlet	1992	1	1953		Arsenal	25	0	0	w
Kelsey WJ	Billy	1888	Boldon		1	1907		Newcastle United	2	0	0	
Kelso RR	Bob	02/10/1865	Cardross	1942	1	1890		Preston NE	20	0	0	s
Kendall H	Howard	22/05/1946	Ryton-on-Tyne		1	1970		Everton	36	0	4	
Kenna JJ	Jeff	27/08/1970	Dublin		1	1995		Blackburn Rovers	9	0	1	r
Kennedy AP	Alan	31/08/1954	Sunderland		6	1979	1986	Liverpool	198	2	12	e
Kennedy R	Bobby	23/06/1937	Motherwell		1	1968		Manchester City	4	2	0	
Kennedy R	Ray	28/07/1951	Seaton Delaval		1	1971		Arsenal	41	0	19	e
					5	1976	1982	Liverpool	167	1	34	
Kenyon RN	Roger	04/01/1949	Blackpool		1	1970		Everton	8	1	0	
Keown MR	Martin	24/07/1966	Oxford		3	1998	2004	Arsenal	42	8	0	e
Kettle B	Brian	22/04/1956	Prescot		2	1976	1977	Liverpool	3	0	0	
Kezman M	Mateja	12/04/1979	Belgrade, Yugoslavia		1	2005		Chelsea	6	19	4	sm
Kirchen AJ	Alf	26/04/1913	Shouldham	1999	2	1935	1938	Arsenal	26	0	8	e
Kirkaldy JW	James	08/11/1885	Newcastle		1	1907		Newcastle United	3	0	1	

		D.o.B.	Birthplace	Died	No.	First	Last	Club	Apps	Subs	Gls	Int
Kirkwood D	David				1	1891		Everton	19	0	1	
Kirsopp WHJ	Billy	21/04/1892	Liverpool	1978	1	1915		Everton	16	0	9	
Kuszczak T	Tomasz	20/03/1982	Krosno Odrzanskie, Pol		1	2007		Manchester Utd.	6	0	0	po
Labone BL	Brian	23/01/1940	Liverpool	2006	2	1963	1970	Everton	74	0	0	e
Lacey W	Billy	20/09/1889	Wexford	1969	2	1922	1923	Liverpool	69	0	2	i
Lambert J	Jack	22/05/1902	Greasbrough	1940	3	1931	1934	Arsenal	49	0	53	
Lambert R	Ray	18/07/1922	Bagillt		1	1947		Liverpool	36	0	0	w
Lampard FJ	Frank	20/06/1978	Romford		2	2005	2006	Chelsea	73	0	29	e
Lane F	Frankie	20/07/1948	Wallasey		1	1973		Liverpool	1	0	0	
Lane JW	Jack	29/05/1898	Birmingham	1984	1	1921		Burnley	1	0	0	
Langley A	Ambrose	10/03/1870	Horncastle	1937	2	1903	1904	Sheffield Wed.	42	0	6	
Langley KJ	Kevin	24/05/1964	St Helens		1	1987		Everton	16	0	2	
Larsson H	Henrik	20/09/1971	Helsingborg		1	2007		Manchester Utd.	5	2	1	sw
Latham G	George	01/01/1881	Newtown	1939	1	1906		Liverpool	5	0	0	w
Latheron EG	Eddie	1887	Grangetown	1917	2	1912	1914	Blackburn Rovers	57	0	20	e
Latta A	Alex	1867	Dumbarton	1928	1	1891		Everton	10	0	4	s
Lauren	Lauren	19/01/1977	Lodhji Kribi, Cameroon		2	2002	2004	Arsenal	57	2	2	cm
Law D	Denis	24/02/1940	Aberdeen		2	1965	1967	Manchester Utd.	72	0	51	s
Lawler C	Chris	20/10/1943	Liverpool		3	1964	1973	Liverpool	88	0	8	e
Lawrence J	Jimmy	16/02/1885	Glasgow	1934	3	1905	1909	Newcastle United	100	0	0	s
Lawrence TJ	Tommy	14/05/1940	Dailly		2	1964	1966	Liverpool	82	0	0	s
Lawrenson MT	Mark	02/06/1957	Preston		5	1982	1988	Liverpool	165	7	10	r
Lawson FIA	Ian	24/03/1939	Ouston		1	1960		Burnley	8	0	3	
Lawton T	Tommy	06/10/1919	Bolton	1996	1	1939		Everton	38	0	34	e
Layton AED	Arthur	1885	Gornal	1959	1	1910		Aston Villa	4	0	0	
Layton W	Willie	1875	Gornal	1944	2	1903	1904	Sheffield Wed.	63	0	0	
Leach T	Tommy 'Tony'	23/09/1903	Wincobank	1968	2	1929	1930	Sheffield Wed.	76	0	2	e
Leadbetter JH	Jimmy	15/07/1928	Edinburgh	2006	1	1962		Ipswich Town	41	0	8	
Lee FH	Francis	29/04/1944	Westhoughton		1	1968		Manchester City	31	0	16	e
					1	1975		Derby County	34	0	12	
Lee KC	Kieran	22/06/1988	Stalybridge		1	2007		Manchester Utd.	1	0	0	
Lee S	Sammy	07/02/1959	Liverpool		6	1979	1986	Liverpool	137	4	8	e
Lehmann J	Jens	10/11/1969	Essen, Germany		1	2004		Arsenal	38	0	0	ge
Leigh WH	Walter	1874	Yardley	1938	1	1899		Aston Villa	1	0	0	
Le Saux GP	Graeme	17/10/1968	Harrow		1	1995		Blackburn Rovers	39	0	3	e
Lewis E	Eddie	03/01/1935	Manchester		1	1956		Manchester Utd.	4	0	1	
Lewis H	Harry	19/12/1896	Birkenhead	1976	1	1922		Liverpool	19	0	1	
Lewis JL	Jim	26/06/1927	Hackney		1	1955		Chelsea	17	0	6	
Lewis RJ	Reg	07/03/1920	Bilston	1997	2	1938	1948	Arsenal	32	0	16	
Liddell G	Gary	27/08/1954	Bannockburn		1	1974		Leeds United	0	1	0	
Liddell R	Robert	1877	Blaydon		2	1907	1909	Newcastle United	6	0	1	
Liddell WB	Billy	10/01/1922	Townhill	2001	1	1947		Liverpool	34	0	7	s
Lill MJ	Mickey	03/08/1936	Barking	2004	2	1958	1959	Wolves	19	0	13	
Limpar AE	Anders	24/09/1965	Solna, Sweden		1	1991		Arsenal	32	2	11	sw
Lindsay A	Alec	27/02/1948	Bury		3	1973	1977	Liverpool	44	0	4	e
Lindsay JJ	James	16/10/1891	Johnstone		1	1921		Burnley	8	0	2	
Linighan A	Andy	18/06/1962	Hartlepool		1	1991		Arsenal	7	3	0	
Linkson OHS	Oscar	1888	Barnet	1916	1	1911		Manchester Utd.	7	0	0	
Lishman DJ	Doug	14/09/1923	Birmingham	1994	1	1953		Arsenal	39	0	22	
Livingstone GT	Geordie	05/05/1876	Dumbarton	1950	1	1911		Manchester Utd.	10	0	0	s
Ljungberg KF	Freddie	16/04/1977	Halmstad, Sweden		2	2002	2004	Arsenal	51	4	16	sw
Lloyd LV	Larry	06/10/1948	Bristol		1	1973		Liverpool	42	0	2	e
					1	1978		Nottm. Forest	26	0	0	
Lochhead A	Alex	1869	Johnstone		1	1891		Everton	1	0	0	s
Logan J	Jimmy	24/06/1870	Troon	1896	1	1892		Sunderland	2	0	0	s
					1	1894		Aston Villa	4	0	1	
Logan JL	James	1885	Barrhead	1948	1	1910		Aston Villa	16	0	0	
Logan N	Neil		Burnbank		1	1898		Sheffield Utd.	5	0	4	
Logie JT	Jimmy	23/11/1919	Edinburgh	1984	2	1948	1953	Arsenal	71	0	18	s
Longworth E	Ephraim	02/10/1887	Halliwell	1968	2	1922	1923	Liverpool	67	0	0	e
Lopez R	Ricardo	30/12/1971	Madrid, Spain		1	2003		Manchester Utd.	0	1	0	sp
Lorimer PP	Peter	14/12/1946	Dundee		2	1969	1974	Leeds United	62	4	21	s
Loughlin J	Jimmy	09/10/1905	Darlington		1	1927		Newcastle United	4	0	0	
Low HF	Harry	1882	Aberdeen	1920	1	1913		Sunderland	37	0	4	
Low J	Jimmy	09/03/1894	Kilbirnie		1	1927		Newcastle United	2	0	1	
Lowe H	Harry	19/02/1907	Skelmersdale	1975	1	1932		Everton	1	0	0	
Lucas T	Tommy	20/09/1895	St Helens	1953	2	1922	1923	Liverpool	28	0	2	e
Lukic J	John	11/12/1960	Chesterfield		1	1989		Arsenal	38	0	0	
					1	1992		Leeds United	42	0	0	
Luzhny O	Oleg	05/08/1968	Kiev, Ukraine		1	2002		Arsenal	15	3	0	un
Lyall J	Jack	16/04/1881	Dundee	1944	2	1903	1904	Sheffield Wed.	66	0	0	s
Lyons AT	Tommy	05/07/1885	Littleworth	1938	1	1910		Aston Villa	35	0	0	
McAllister A	Sandy	1878	Kilmarnock	1918	1	1902		Sunderland	34	0	1	
McAllister G	Gary	25/12/1964	Motherwell		1	1992		Leeds United	41	1	5	s
Macaulay AR	Archie	30/07/1915	Falkirk	1993	1	1948		Arsenal	40	0	0	s
McClair BJ	Brian	08/12/1963	Airdrie		4	1993	1997	Manchester Utd.	69	40	13	s
McClarence JP	Joe	1885	Newcastle		2	1905	1907	Newcastle United	11	0	6	
McClellan SB	Sid	11/06/1925	Bromley	2000	1	1951		Tottenham H	7	0	3	
McClelland J	John	07/12/1955	Belfast		1	1992		Leeds United	16	2	0	n
McClure JH	Joe	03/11/1907	Cockermouth	1973	1	1932		Everton	7	0	0	
McCombie A	Andy	30/06/1876	Inverness	1952	1	1902		Sunderland	26	0	1	s
					3	1905	1909	Newcastle United	58	0	0	
McCracken WR	Billy	29/01/1883	Belfast	1979	3	1905	1909	Newcastle United	65	0	2	i
McCreadie A	Andrew	19/11/1870	Girvan		1	1895		Sunderland	27	0	8	s
McCullough K	Keiller	25/03/1905	Larne		1	1937		Manchester City	2	0	0	i

		D.o.B.	Birthplace	Died	No.	First	Last	Club	Apps	Subs	Gls	Int
McDermott T	Terry	08/12/1951	Kirkby		6	1976	1983	Liverpool	131	9	35	e
MacDonald KD	Kevin	22/11/1960	Inverness		2	1986	1988	Liverpool	10	8	1	
McDonald TH	Tommy	25/09/1895	Inverness	1969	1	1927		Newcastle United	41	0	17	
McDowall LJ	Les	25/10/1912	Gunga Pur, India	1991	1	1936		Sunderland	1	0	0	
McEleny CR	Charlie	03/03/1873	Raymoghy	1908	1	1900		Aston Villa	1	0	0	
McFarland RL	Roy	05/04/1948	Liverpool		2	1972	1975	Derby County	42	0	4	e
McGhie A	Alex		Liverpool		1	1914		Blackburn Rovers	9	0	3	
McGillivray J	Jimmy	1889	Broughton		1	1908		Manchester Utd.	1	0	0	
McGlen W	Bill	27/04/1921	Bedlington	1999	1	1952		Manchester Utd.	2	0	0	
McGovern JP	John	28/10/1949	Montrose		1	1972		Derby County	39	1	3	
					1	1978		Nottm. Forest	31	0	4	
McGowan GG	Gavin	16/01/1976	Blackheath		1	1998		Arsenal	0	1	0	
McGrory R	Bob	17/10/1895	Bishopton	1954	1	1921		Burnley	3	0	0	
McGuigan A	Andy	24/02/1878	Newton Stewart	1948	1	1901		Liverpool	13	0	5	
McGuinness W	Wilf	25/10/1937	Manchester		2	1956	1957	Manchester Utd.	16	0	1	e
McIlroy J	Jimmy	25/10/1931	Lambeg		1	1960		Burnley	32	0	6	n
McIntyre EP	Teddy	1881	Newcastle	1928	1	1905		Newcastle United	2	0	0	
Mackay DC	Dave	14/11/1934	Musselburgh		1	1961		Tottenham H	37	0	4	s
McKay K	Kenny	1877	Wishaw		1	1898		Sheffield Utd.	25	0	5	
McKay R	Bobby	02/09/1900	Govan		1	1927		Newcastle United	25	0	10	s
McKee C	Colin	22/08/1973	Glasgow		1	1994		Manchester Utd.	1	0	0	
MacKenzie RR	Roddie	22/05/1901	Inverness		1	1927		Newcastle United	38	0	2	
Mackey TS	Tom	22/10/1908	Cassop	1969	1	1930		Sheffield Wed.	1	0	0	
McKinlay D	Donald	25/07/1891	Newton Mearns	1959	2	1922	1923	Liverpool	71	0	6	s
McLatchie CC	Colin	02/11/1876	New Cumnock	1952	1	1902		Sunderland	25	0	4	
McLean D	Duncan	12/09/1869	Dumbarton		1	1891		Everton	5	0	0	s
McLeod JS	John	20/04/1912	Gorbals		1	1937		Manchester City	3	0	2	
McLeod T	Tommy	26/12/1920	Musselburgh	1999	1	1947		Liverpool	3	0	0	
McLintock F	Frank	28/12/1939	Glasgow		1	1971		Arsenal	42	0	5	s
McMahon S	Steve	20/08/1961	Liverpool		3	1986	1990	Liverpool	100	1	20	e
McNab A	Sandy	27/12/1911	Glasgow	1962	1	1936		Sunderland	13	0	1	s
McNab JS	Jock	17/04/1894	Cleland	1949	2	1922	1923	Liverpool	68	0	3	s
McNab R	Bob	20/07/1943	Huddersfield		1	1971		Arsenal	40	0	0	e
McNaught K	Ken	11/01/1955	Kirkcaldy		1	1981		Aston Villa	42	0	0	
McNeal R	Bobby	15/01/1891	Hobson Village	1956	1	1920		West Bromwich A.	42	0	2	e
McNeill R	Robert				1	1895		Sunderland	22	0	0	
McNichol J	Johnny	20/08/1925	Kilmarnock		1	1955		Chelsea	40	0	14	
McNulty T	Tom	30/12/1929	Salford	1979	1	1952		Manchester Utd.	24	0	0	
Maconnachie JSJ	Jock	08/05/1885	Aberdeen	1956	1	1915		Everton	28	0	0	
McPherson IB	Ian	26/07/1920	Glasgow	1983	1	1948		Arsenal	29	0	5	
McPherson L	Lacky	11/07/1900	Denistoun		1	1932		Everton	3	0	0	
McQueen G	Gordon	26/06/1952	Kilbirnie		1	1974		Leeds United	36	0	0	s
McShane H	Harry	08/04/1920	Holytown		1	1952		Manchester Utd.	12	0	1	
McWilliam P	Peter	22/09/1878	Inveravon	1951	3	1905	1909	Newcastle United	85	0	6	s
Madeley PE	Paul	20/09/1944	Beeston, West Yorks		2	1969	1974	Leeds United	70	0	5	e
Magee TP	Tommy	06/05/1899	Widnes	1974	1	1920		West Bromwich A.	24	0	7	e
Maitland AE	Alf	08/10/1896	Leith	1981	1	1927		Newcastle United	36	0	0	
Makelele C	Claude	18/02/1973	Kinshasa, DR Congo		2	2005	2006	Chelsea	65	2	1	fr
Makepeace JWH	Harry	22/08/1881	Middlesbrough	1952	1	1915		Everton	23	0	1	e
Malcolm KC	Ken	25/07/1926	Aberdeen		1	1962		Ipswich Town	3	0	0	
Male CG	George	08/05/1910	Plaistow	1998	6	1931	1948	Arsenal	161	0	0	e
Malloch JM	Jock	02/11/1877	Lochee		2	1903	1904	Sheffield Wed.	58	0	3	
Mann CJ	Christopher	1877	West Smethwick	1934	1	1900		Aston Villa	7	0	0	
Manninger A	Alex	04/06/1977	Salzburg, Austria		1	1998		Arsenal	7	0	0	as
Mapson J	Johnny	02/05/1917	Birkenhead	1999	1	1936		Sunderland	7	0	0	
Marchi AV	Tony	21/01/1933	Edmonton		1	1961		Tottenham H	6	0	0	
Marden RJ	Ben	10/02/1927	Fulham	2000	1	1953		Arsenal	8	0	4	
Marinello P	Peter	20/02/1950	Edinburgh		1	1971		Arsenal	1	2	0	
Marrison T	Tom	01/01/1885	Rotherham	1926	1	1903		Sheffield Wed.	1	0	1	
Marsden W	Billy	10/11/1901	Silksworth	1983	2	1929	1930	Sheffield Wed.	79	0	4	e
Marsh MA	Mike	21/07/1969	Liverpool		1	1990		Liverpool	0	2	0	
Marshall IP	Ian	20/03/1966	Liverpool		1	1987		Everton	0	2	1	
Marshall J	Jimmy	03/01/1908	Avonbridge	1977	1	1935		Arsenal	4	0	0	s
Marshall RS	Bobby	03/04/1903	Hucknall	1966	1	1937		Manchester City	38	0	0	
Marshall SR	Scott	01/05/1973	Edinburgh		1	1998		Arsenal	1	2	0	
Marshall WF	Billy	11/07/1936	Belfast		1	1960		Burnley	1	0	0	
Martin GS	George	14/07/1899	Bothwell	1972	2	1928	1932	Everton	12	0	3	
Martin H	Harry	05/12/1891	Selston	1974	1	1913		Sunderland	38	0	5	e
Martin LA	Lee	05/02/1968	Hyde		1	1994		Manchester Utd.	1	0	0	
Marwood B	Brian	05/02/1960	Seaham		1	1989		Arsenal	31	0	9	e
Mason RH	Bobby	22/03/1936	Tipton		2	1958	1959	Wolves	54	0	20	
Matthews RW	Billy	04/04/1897	Plas Bennion	1987	1	1922		Liverpool	7	0	4	w
May D	David	24/06/1970	Oldham		6	1996	2003	Manchester Utd.	44	11	4	
Meagan MK	Mick	29/05/1934	Dublin		1	1963		Everton	32	0	0	r
Mearns FC	Fred	31/03/1879	Sunderland	1931	1	1902		Sunderland	2	0	0	
Medley LD	Les	03/09/1920	Edmonton	2001	1	1951		Tottenham H	35	0	11	e
Medwin TC	Terry	25/09/1932	Swansea		1	1961		Tottenham H	14	0	5	w
Meehan P	Peter	28/02/1874	Broxburn	1915	1	1895		Sunderland	19	0	1	
Melia JJ	Jimmy	01/11/1937	Liverpool		1	1964		Liverpool	24	0	4	e
Mellors RD	Dick	17/03/1905	Mansfield	1960	1	1930		Sheffield Wed.	1	0	0	
Mendez Rodriguez A	Alberto	24/10/1974	Nuremburg, Germany		1	1998		Arsenal	1	2	0	
Menzies AW	Alexander	25/11/1882	Blantyre		1	1908		Manchester Utd.	6	0	0	s
Mercer J	Joe	09/08/1914	Ellesmere Port	1990	1	1939		Everton	41	0	0	e
					2	1948	1953	Arsenal	68	0	2	
Mercer WH	Billy	1892	Prescot	1956	2	1925	1926	Huddersfield T	40	0	0	

		D.o.B.	Birthplace	Died	No.	First	Last	Club	Apps	Subs	Gls	Int
Meredith TG	Trevor	25/12/1936	Bridgnorth		1	1960		Burnley	7	0	3	
Meredith WH	Billy	28/07/1874	Chirk	1958	2	1908	1911	Manchester Utd.	72	0	15	w
Merson PC	Paul	20/03/1968	Harlesden		2	1989	1991	Arsenal	65	9	23	e
Meston SW	Sammy	30/05/1902	Southampton	1953	1	1928		Everton	1	0	0	
Middleton J	John	24/12/1956	Skegness		1	1978		Nottm. Forest	5	0	0	
Middleton MY	Matt	24/10/1907	Boldon Colliery	1979	1	1936		Sunderland	9	0	0	
Miles A	Freddie	1884	Aston	1926	1	1910		Aston Villa	27	0	0	
Millar J	Jimmy	02/03/1870	Annbank	1907	4	1892	1902	Sunderland	107	0	49	s
Miller BG	Brian	19/01/1937	Hapton		1	1960		Burnley	42	0	3	e
Millership W	Walter	08/06/1910	Warsop Vale	1978	1	1930		Sheffield Wed.	6	0	1	
Milligan GH	George	31/08/1917	Failsworth	1983	1	1939		Everton	1	0	0	
Mills-Roberts RH	Robert	05/08/1862	Penmachno	1935	1	1889		Preston NE	2	0	0	w
Milne G	Gordon	29/03/1937	Preston		2	1964	1966	Liverpool	70	0	10	e
Milne JV	Jackie	25/03/1911	Stirling		1	1938		Arsenal	16	0	4	s
Milton A	Albert	1885	High Green	1917	1	1913		Sunderland	27	0	0	
Milton CA	Arthur	10/03/1928	Bristol		1	1953		Arsenal	25	0	7	e
Milward A	Alf	12/09/1870	Great Marlow	1941	1	1891		Everton	22	0	11	e
Mimms RA	Bobby	12/10/1963	York		1	1987		Everton	11	0	0	
					1	1995		Blackburn Rovers	3	1	0	
Minshull R	Ray	15/07/1920	Bolton	2005	1	1947		Liverpool	6	0	0	
Mitchell FWG	Frank	25/05/1890	Elgin		1	1915		Everton	2	0	0	
					1	1922		Liverpool	3	0	0	
Moger HH	Harry	1879	Southampton		2	1908	1911	Manchester Utd.	54	0	0	
Moir I	Ian	30/06/1943	Aberdeen		1	1965		Manchester Utd.	1	0	0	
Molby J	Jan	04/07/1963	Kolding, Denmark		3	1986	1990	Liverpool	52	11	15	de
Mooney EP	Peter	22/03/1897	Walker		1	1927		Newcastle United	3	0	0	
Moorwood TL	Len	21/09/1888	Wednesbury	1976	1	1920		West Bromwich A.	3	0	0	
					1	1921		Burnley	1	0	0	
Morais N	Nuno	29/01/1984	Penafiel, Portugal		1	2005		Chelsea	0	2	0	
Moralee MW	Matt	04/03/1878	Newcastle	1962	2	1903	1904	Sheffield Wed.	2	0	0	
Moran DW	Doug	29/07/1934	Musselburgh		1	1962		Ipswich Town	42	0	14	
Moran R	Ronnie	28/02/1934	Liverpool		1	1964		Liverpool	35	0	1	
Mordue J	Jackie	13/12/1886	Edmondsley	1957	1	1913		Sunderland	35	0	15	e
Morley WA	Tony	26/08/1954	Ormskirk		1	1981		Aston Villa	42	0	10	e
Morren T	Tom	1875	Middlesbrough	1929	1	1898		Sheffield Utd.	26	0	2	e
Morris F	Fred	27/08/1893	Tipton	1962	1	1920		West Bromwich A.	39	0	37	e
Morrison TK	Tom	21/07/1904	Kilmarnock		1	1936		Sunderland	21	0	0	s
Morrissey JJ	Johnny	18/04/1940	Liverpool		2	1963	1970	Everton	69	0	16	
Morrissey JJ	John	08/03/1965	Liverpool		1	1985		Everton	1	0	0	
Mortimer DG	Dennis	05/04/1952	Liverpool		1	1981		Aston Villa	42	0	4	
Morton D	David				1	1898		Sheffield Utd.	2	0	0	
Morton H	Harry	07/01/1909	Chadderton	1974	1	1939		Everton	1	0	0	
Moss AJ	Arthur	14/11/1887	Crewe	1930	1	1910		Aston Villa	1	0	0	
Moss F	Frank	05/11/1909	Leyland	1970	3	1933	1935	Arsenal	111	0	1	e
Mosscrop E	Eddie	16/06/1892	Southport	1980	1	1921		Burnley	14	0	1	e
Mountfield DN	Derek	02/11/1962	Liverpool		2	1985	1987	Everton	49	1	13	
Mulhearn KJ	Ken	16/10/1945	Liverpool		1	1968		Manchester City	33	0	0	
Mullen J	Jimmy	06/01/1923	Newcastle	1987	3	1954	1959	Wolves	92	0	15	e
Murphy P	Peter	07/03/1922	Hartlepool	1975	1	1951		Tottenham H	25	0	9	
Murray DB	David	1882	Busby	1915	1	1906		Liverpool	3	0	0	
Murray JR	Jimmy	11/10/1935	Elvington		2	1958	1959	Wolves	69	0	50	
Murray JW	John	24/04/1865	Strathblane	1922	1	1892		Sunderland	22	0	0	s
Murray W	Bill	10/03/1901	Aberdeen	1961	1	1936		Sunderland	21	0	0	
Murray WB	Willie	1883	Forres		1	1902		Sunderland	7	0	2	
Mutu A	Adrian	08/01/1979	Calinesti, Romania		1	2005		Chelsea	0	2	0	ro
Neal PG	Phil	20/02/1951	Irchester		8	1976	1986	Liverpool	304	2	31	e
Needham DW	Dave	21/05/1949	Leicester		1	1978		Nottm. Forest	16	0	4	
Needham E	Ernest	21/01/1873	Whittington Moor	1936	1	1898		Sheffield Utd.	29	0	8	e
Neilson R	Dick	01/04/1916	Blackhall	2005	1	1937		Manchester City	2	0	1	
Nelson AN	Andy	05/07/1935	Custom House		1	1962		Ipswich Town	42	0	0	
Nelson S	Sammy	01/04/1949	Belfast		1	1971		Arsenal	2	2	0	n
Nesbitt W	Billy	22/11/1891	Portsmouth, Lancs	1972	1	1921		Burnley	40	0	5	
Ness HM	Harry	1885	Scarborough	1957	1	1913		Sunderland	13	0	0	
Neville GA	Gary	18/02/1975	Bury		8	1994	2007	Manchester Utd.	192	9	3	e
Neville PJ	Phil	21/01/1977	Bury		6	1996	2003	Manchester Utd.	123	30	2	e
Newell MC	Mike	27/01/1965	Liverpool		1	1995		Blackburn Rovers	2	10	0	
Newsome J	Jon	06/09/1970	Sheffield		1	1992		Leeds United	7	3	2	
Newton HA	Henry	18/02/1944	Nottingham		1	1975		Derby County	35	1	3	
Newton KR	Keith	23/06/1941	Manchester	1998	1	1970		Everton	12	0	0	e
Nicholson B	Ben	1884	Ashington		1	1907		Newcastle United	1	0	0	
Nicholson WE	Bill	26/01/1919	Scarborough	2004	1	1951		Tottenham H	41	0	1	e
Nicol S	Steve	11/12/1961	Irvine		5	1983	1990	Liverpool	115	9	22	s
Nieuwenhuys B	Berry	05/11/1911	Boksburg, South Africa	1984	1	1947		Liverpool	15	0	5	
Nish DJ	David	26/09/1947	Burton-on-Trent		1	1975		Derby County	38	0	2	e
Geremi	Geremi	20/12/1978	Bafoussam, Cameroon		2	2005	2006	Chelsea	14	14	2	cm
Noble R	Bobby	18/12/1945	Manchester		1	1967		Manchester Utd.	29	0	0	
Noon MT	Michael	1876	Burton-on-Trent	1939	1	1900		Aston Villa	15	0	0	
Norman M	Maurice	08/05/1934	Mulbarton		1	1961		Tottenham H	41	0	4	e
Nuttall TAB	Tommy	1889	Bolton		1	1915		Everton	5	0	0	
Oakes AA	Alan	07/09/1942	Winsford		1	1968		Manchester City	41	0	2	
Oakes DJ	Don	08/10/1928	St Asaph	1977	1	1953		Arsenal	2	0	1	
O'Connell SCP	Seamus	01/01/1930	Carlisle		1	1955		Chelsea	10	0	7	
O'Donnell J	Jack	25/03/1897	Gateshead		1	1928		Everton	42	0	1	
Ogley A	Alan	04/02/1946	Darton		1	1968		Manchester City	2	0	0	
O'Grady M	Mike	11/10/1942	Leeds		1	1969		Leeds United	38	0	8	e

		D.o.B.	Birthplace	Died	No.	First	Last	Club	Apps	Subs	Gls	Int
Ogrizovic S	Steve	12/09/1957	Mansfield		1	1980		Liverpool	1	0	0	
O'Hare J	John	24/09/1946	Renton		1	1972		Derby County	40	0	13	s
					1	1978		Nottm. Forest	10	0	0	
O'Kane JA	John	15/11/1974	Nottingham		2	1996	1997	Manchester Utd.	1	1	0	
Oldroyd DR	Darren	01/11/1966	Ormskirk		1	1985		Everton	0	1	0	
O'Leary DA	David	02/05/1958	Stoke Newington		2	1989	1991	Arsenal	37	10	1	r
Maniche	Maniche	11/11/1977	Lisbon, Portugal		1	2006		Chelsea	3	5	0	pt
Oliver JS	Sid	1867	Southwick, Co. Durham		1	1892		Sunderland	3	0	0	
O'Neill MHM	Martin	01/03/1952	Kilrea		1	1978		Nottm. Forest	38	2	8	n
Orr J	Johnny	1888	Leith		2	1912	1914	Blackburn Rovers	24	0	11	
Orr R	Ronald	06/08/1880	Bartonholm		1	1905	1907	Newcastle United	39	0	13	s
O'Shea JF	John	30/04/1981	Waterford		2	2003	2007	Manchester Utd.	42	22	4	r
Overmars M	Marc	29/03/1973	Emst, Holland		1	1998		Arsenal	32	0	12	ho
Owen AW	Aled	07/01/1934	Brynteg		1	1962		Ipswich Town	1	0	0	
Paisley R	Bob	23/01/1919	Hetton-le-Hole	1996	1	1947		Liverpool	33	0	0	
Pallister GA	Gary	30/06/1965	Ramsgate		4	1993	1997	Manchester Utd.	131	0	6	e
Palmer W	Bill	1888	Barnsley		1	1915		Everton	17	0	1	
Pardoe G	Glyn	01/06/1946	Winsford		1	1968		Manchester City	41	0	0	
Park J-S	Ji-Sung	25/02/1981	Seoul, South Korea		1	2007		Manchester Utd.	8	6	5	sr
Park O	Ossie	07/02/1905	Darlington		1	1927		Newcastle United	5	0	0	
Parker AH	Alex	02/08/1935	Irvine		1	1963		Everton	33	0	2	s
Parker HC	Cliff	06/09/1913	Denaby	1983	2	1949	1950	Portsmouth	8	0	0	
Parker PA	Paul	04/04/1964	West Ham		3	1993	1996	Manchester Utd.	75	2	1	e
Parker RN	Bobby	27/03/1891	Possilpark	1950	1	1915		Everton	35	0	36	
Parker SM	Scott	13/10/1980	Lambeth		1	2005		Chelsea	1	3	0	e
Parker TR	Tom	19/11/1897	Woolston	1987	2	1931	1933	Arsenal	46	0	0	e
Parkin R	Ray	28/01/1911	Crook	1971	2	1933	1934	Arsenal	10	0	0	
Parkinson J	Jack	13/09/1883	Bootle	1942	1	1906		Liverpool	9	0	7	e
Parlour R	Ray	07/03/1973	Romford		3	1998	2004	Arsenal	75	11	5	e
Parry CF	Charlie	1870	Llansillin	1922	1	1891		Everton	13	0	0	
Parry E	Ted	09/12/1892	Colwyn Bay	1976	1	1922		Liverpool	7	0	0	w
Parry MP	Maurice	07/11/1877	Trefonen	1935	2	1901	1906	Liverpool	44	0	1	w
Parsons EG	Eric 'Rabbit'	09/11/1923	Worthing		1	1955		Chelsea	42	0	11	
Pates CG	Colin	10/08/1961	Carshalton		1	1991		Arsenal	0	1	0	
Pauls CA	Charles	1868	Preston		1	1890		Preston NE	3	0	0	
Pearce IA	Ian	07/05/1974	Bury St Edmunds		1	1995		Blackburn Rovers	22	6	0	
Pearson HP	Hubert	1886	Kettlebrook	1955	1	1920		West Bromwich A.	39	0	0	
Pearson SC	Stan	11/01/1919	Salford	1997	1	1952		Manchester Utd.	41	0	22	e
Pegg D	David	20/09/1935	Doncaster	1958	2	1956	1957	Manchester Utd.	72	0	15	e
Pennington J	Jesse	23/08/1883	West Bromwich	1970	1	1920		West Bromwich A.	37	0	0	e
Percival J	Jack	16/05/1913	Pittington	1979	1	1937		Manchester City	42	0	1	
Perkins WH	Bill	26/01/1876	Wellingborough		1	1901		Liverpool	34	0	0	
Petit E	Emmanuel	22/09/1970	Dieppe, France		1	1998		Arsenal	32	0	2	fr
Phelan MC	Mike	24/09/1962	Nelson		2	1993	1994	Manchester Utd.	6	7	0	e
Phillips EJ	Ted	21/08/1933	Leiston		1	1962		Ipswich Town	40	0	28	
Phillips HL	Len	11/09/1922	Shoreditch		2	1949	1950	Portsmouth	74	0	16	e
Picken JB	John	1880	Hurlford	1952	2	1908	1911	Manchester Utd.	22	0	5	
Pickett RA	Reg	06/01/1927	India		1	1950		Portsmouth	14	0	1	
					1	1962		Ipswich Town	3	0	0	
Pidgeley LJ	Lenny	07/02/1984	Twickenham		2	2005	2006	Chelsea	1	1	0	
Pilkington B	Brian	12/02/1933	Leyland		1	1960		Burnley	41	0	9	e
Pilkington KW	Kevin	08/03/1974	Hitchin		1	1996		Manchester Utd.	2	1	0	
Pires R	Robert	29/10/1973	Reims, France		2	2002	2004	Arsenal	60	4	23	fr
Platt DA	David	10/06/1966	Chadderton		1	1998		Arsenal	11	20	3	e
Platt EH	Ted	26/03/1921	Wolstanton	1996	1	1953		Arsenal	3	0	0	
Poborsky K	Karel	30/03/1972	Jindrichuv-Hradec, Cze		1	1997		Manchester Utd.	15	7	3	cz
Pointer R	Ray	10/10/1936	Cramlington		1	1960		Burnley	42	0	19	e
Pointon NG	Neil	28/11/1964	Church Warsop		1	1987		Everton	10	2	1	
Polk S	Stan	28/10/1921	Liverpool		1	1947		Liverpool	6	0	0	
Porteous G	George		Glasgow		1	1914		Blackburn Rovers	1	0	0	
Porteous TS	Tom	1865	Newcastle	1919	2	1892	1893	Sunderland	55	0	0	e
Powell S	Steve	20/09/1955	Derby		2	1972	1975	Derby County	14	4	2	
Power PC	Paul	30/10/1953	Manchester		1	1987		Everton	40	0	4	
Pratt D	David	05/03/1896	Lochore		1	1923		Liverpool	7	0	0	
Preedy CJF	Charlie	11/01/1900	Neemuch, India	1978	2	1931	1933	Arsenal	12	0	0	
Priday RH	Bob	29/03/1925	Cape Town, S. Af.	1998	1	1947		Liverpool	9	0	2	
Priest AE	Fred	1875	Darlington	1922	1	1898		Sheffield Utd.	28	0	4	e
Prior G	George		Edinburgh		1	1902		Sunderland	5	0	0	
Pritchard RT	Roy	09/05/1925	Dawley	1993	1	1954		Wolves	27	0	0	
Proctor BJ	Benjamin				1	1912		Blackburn Rovers	1	0	0	
Prunier W	William	14/08/1967	Montreuil, France		1	1996		Manchester Utd.	2	0	0	fr
Pudan AE	Dick	1881	East Ham	1957	1	1909		Newcastle United	3	0	0	
Pugh DA	Danny	19/10/1982	Manchester		1	2003		Manchester Utd.	0	1	0	
Quinn NJ	Niall	06/10/1966	Dublin		1	1989		Arsenal	2	1	1	r
Rachubka PS	Paul	21/05/1981	San Luis Obispo, USA		1	2001		Manchester Utd.	1	0	0	
Radford J	John	22/02/1947	Hemsworth		1	1971		Arsenal	41	0	15	e
Raisbeck AG	Alex	26/12/1878	Wallacestone	1949	2	1901	1906	Liverpool	67	0	2	s
Raitt D	David		Buckhaven		1	1928		Everton	6	0	0	
Ramsden B	Barney	08/11/1917	Sheffield	1976	1	1947		Liverpool	23	0	0	
Ramsey AE	Alf	22/01/1920	Dagenham	1999	1	1951		Tottenham H	40	0	4	e
Randall CE	Charles	1882	Burnopfield	1916	1	1909		Newcastle United	1	0	0	
Randle WW	Walter	1870	Aston	1931	1	1894		Aston Villa	1	0	0	
Rankin I	Isaiah	22/05/1978	Edmonton		1	1998		Arsenal	0	1	0	
Ratcliffe K	Kevin	12/11/1960	Mancot		2	1985	1987	Everton	82	0	0	w
Raw H	Harry	06/07/1903	Tow Law	1965	1	1926		Huddersfield T	2	0	0	

Name	First	D.o.B.	Birthplace	Died	No.	First	Last	Club	Apps	Subs	Gls	Int
Raybould SF	Sam	1875	Chesterfield	1949	2	1901	1906	Liverpool	56	0	26	
Reaney P	Paul	22/10/1944	Fulham		2	1969	1974	Leeds United	78	0	1	e
Redman W	Bill	29/01/1928	Manchester	1994	1	1952		Manchester Utd.	18	0	0	
Reed FWM	Fred	1894	Scotswood	1967	1	1920		West Bromwich A.	1	0	0	
Regan RH	Bobby		Falkirk		1	1937		Manchester City	4	0	0	
Reid JDJ	Duggie	03/10/1917	Mauchline	2002	2	1949	1950	Portsmouth	56	0	33	
Reid P	Peter	20/06/1956	Huyton		2	1985	1987	Everton	51	1	3	e
Reyes JA	Jose Antonio	01/09/1983	Utrera, Spain		1	2004		Arsenal	7	6	2	sp
Reynolds J	Jack 'Baldy'	1869	Blackburn	1917	3	1894	1897	Aston Villa	72	0	11	ei
Rice PJ	Pat	17/03/1949	Belfast		1	1971		Arsenal	41	0	0	n
Richardson GE	Ted	04/07/1902	Easington		2	1924	1925	Huddersfield T	6	0	0	
Richardson GEH	George	04/12/1891	Seaham Harbour	1969	1	1924		Huddersfield T	2	0	0	
Richardson J	Jimmy	1885	Glasgow	1951	1	1913		Sunderland	18	0	11	
Richardson K	Kevin	04/12/1962	Newcastle		2	1985	1987	Everton	15	1	4	e
					1	1989		Arsenal	32	2	1	
Richardson KE	Kieran	21/10/1984	Greenwich		2	2003	2007	Manchester Utd.	8	9	1	e
Richardson S	Sammy	11/08/1894	Great Bridge	1960	1	1920		West Bromwich A.	40	0	0	
Ridley J	James		Tyneside		1	1909		Newcastle United	5	0	1	
Rigby A	Arthur	07/06/1900	Chorlton	1960	1	1932		Everton	3	0	0	e
Rimmer EJ	Ellis	02/01/1907	Birkenhead	1965	2	1929	1930	Sheffield Wed.	74	0	22	e
Rimmer JJ	Jimmy	10/02/1948	Southport		1	1981		Aston Villa	42	0	0	e
Rimmer N	Neill	13/11/1967	Liverpool		1	1985		Everton	0	1	0	
Rioch BD	Bruce	06/09/1947	Aldershot		1	1975		Derby County	42	0	15	s
Ripley SE	Stuart	20/11/1967	Middlesbrough		1	1995		Blackburn Rovers	36	1	0	e
Robben A	Arjen	23/01/1984	Groningen, Holland		2	2005	2006	Chelsea	35	11	13	ho
Roberts C	Charlie	06/04/1883	Rise Carr	1939	2	1908	1911	Manchester Utd.	65	0	3	e
Roberts H	Herbie	19/02/1905	Oswestry	1944	5	1931	1938	Arsenal	155	0	2	e
Roberts J	Jas	07/01/1891	Mold		1	1915		Everton	1	0	0	w
Roberts JG	John	11/09/1946	Abercynon		1	1971		Arsenal	18	0	0	w
Robertson AS	Sandy	1860	Edinburgh	1927	2	1889	1890	Preston NE	28	0	3	
Robertson HR	Hope		Whiteinch		1	1891		Everton	3	0	1	
Robertson JN	John	20/01/1953	Uddingston		1	1978		Nottm. Forest	42	0	12	s
Robertson JT	Jack	1877	Newton Mearns		1	1901		Liverpool	25	0	0	
Robertson T	Tommy	1873	Renton		1	1901		Liverpool	34	0	9	s
Robertson WG	Bill	13/11/1928	Glasgow	1973	1	1955		Chelsea	26	0	0	
Robinson A	Alfred	1888	Manchester		2	1912	1914	Blackburn Rovers	58	0	0	
Robinson MJ	Michael	12/07/1958	Leicester		1	1984		Liverpool	23	1	6	r
Robinson RS	Robbie	01/10/1879	Sunderland		1	1906		Liverpool	34	0	11	
Robson B	Bryan	11/01/1957	Witton Gilbert		2	1993	1994	Manchester Utd.	15	14	2	e
Robson J	Jimmy	23/01/1939	Pelton		1	1960		Burnley	38	0	18	
Robson JD	John	15/07/1950	Consett	2004	1	1972		Derby County	41	0	2	
Rocastle DC	David	02/05/1967	Lewisham	2001	2	1989	1991	Arsenal	51	3	8	e
Roche LP	Lee	28/10/1980	Bolton		1	2003		Manchester Utd.	0	1	0	
Rodger C	Colin	1911	Ayr		1	1937		Manchester City	9	0	7	
Rodgerson R	Ralph	25/12/1913	Sunderland	1972	1	1936		Sunderland	3	0	0	
Rogers E	Tim	15/10/1909	Chirk	1996	1	1935		Arsenal	5	0	2	
Rogers JH	Joe	1915	Normanton		1	1937		Manchester City	2	0	0	
Ronaldo CdosS	Cristiano	05/02/1985	Madeira, Portugal		1	2007		Manchester Utd.	31	3	17	pt
Rooke RL	Ronnie	07/12/1911	Guildford	1985	1	1948		Arsenal	42	0	33	
Rookes PW	Phil	23/04/1919	Dulverton	2003	2	1949	1950	Portsmouth	28	0	0	
Rooney WF	Walter	31/03/1902	Liverpool	1963	1	1928		Everton	4	0	0	
Rooney WM	Wayne	24/10/1985	Liverpool		1	2007		Manchester Utd.	33	2	14	e
Roper DGB	Don	14/12/1922	Botley	2001	2	1948	1953	Arsenal	81	0	24	
Rosenthal R	Ronny	11/10/1963	Haifa, Israel		1	1990		Liverpool	5	3	7	is
Ross JD	Jimmy	28/03/1866	Edinburgh	1902	2	1889	1890	Preston NE	42	0	38	
Ross NJ	Nick	02/01/1863	Edinburgh	1894	1	1890		Preston NE	20	0	22	
Rowley JF	Jack	07/10/1918	Wolverhampton	1998	1	1952		Manchester Utd.	40	0	30	e
Royle J	Joe	08/04/1949	Norris Green		1	1970		Everton	42	0	23	e
Ruddlesdin H	Herrod	1877	Birdwell	1910	2	1903	1904	Sheffield Wed.	64	0	2	e
Rush IJ	Ian	20/10/1961	St Asaph		5	1982	1990	Liverpool	183	0	113	w
Russell D	Dave	1862	Beith	1918	2	1889	1890	Preston NE	39	0	4	
Russell G	George	1869	Ayrshire	1930	1	1894		Aston Villa	5	0	0	
Russell JW	Jim	14/09/1916	Edinburgh	1994	1	1936		Sunderland	1	0	0	
Rutherford J	Jock	12/10/1884	Percy Main	1963	3	1905	1909	Newcastle United	89	0	25	e
Ryalls J	Joe	1881	Sheffield		2	1903	1904	Sheffield Wed.	2	0	0	
Ryan J	Jimmy	12/05/1945	Stirling		1	1967		Manchester Utd.	4	1	0	
Sadler D	David	05/02/1946	Yalding		2	1965	1967	Manchester Utd.	41	1	6	e
Sagar E	Ted	07/02/1910	Campsall	1986	2	1932	1939	Everton	82	0	0	e
Saha L	Louis	08/08/1978	Paris, France		1	2007		Manchester Utd.	18	6	8	fr
St John I	Ian	07/06/1938	Motherwell		2	1964	1966	Liverpool	81	0	31	s
Sambrook JH	Jack	10/03/1899	Wednesfield	1973	1	1923		Liverpool	2	0	0	
Sammels JC	Jon	23/07/1945	Ipswich		1	1971		Arsenal	13	2	1	
Satterthwaite CO	Charlie	1877	Cockermouth	1948	1	1901		Liverpool	22	0	5	
Saul FL	Frank	23/08/1943	Canvey Island		1	1961		Tottenham H	6	0	3	
Saunders DW	Derek	06/01/1928	Ware		1	1955		Chelsea	42	0	1	
Scanlon AJ	Albert	10/10/1935	Manchester		2	1956	1957	Manchester Utd.	11	0	3	
Scarth JW	Jimmy	26/08/1926	North Shields	2000	1	1951		Tottenham H	1	0	0	
Schmeichel PB	Peter	18/11/1963	Gladsaxe, Denmark		5	1993	1999	Manchester Utd.	188	0	0	de
Scholes P	Paul	16/11/1974	Salford		7	1996	2007	Manchester Utd.	171	36	54	e
Scott AS	Alex	22/11/1936	Falkirk	2001	1	1963		Everton	17	0	4	s
Scott E	Elisha	24/08/1893	Belfast	1959	2	1922	1923	Liverpool	81	0	0	i
Scott J	Jock				3	1892	1895	Sunderland	50	0	16	
Scott J	Johnny	22/12/1933	Belfast	1978	1	1956		Manchester Utd.	1	0	0	n
Scott L	Laurie	23/04/1917	Sheffield	1999	1	1948		Arsenal	39	0	0	e
Scott W	Walter	1886	Worksop	1955	1	1913		Sunderland	4	0	0	

		D.o.B.	Birthplace	Died	No.	First	Last	Club	Apps	Subs	Gls	Int
Scoular J	Jimmy	11/01/1925	Livingston	1998	2	1949	1950	Portsmouth	78	0	0	s
Seaman DA	David	19/09/1963	Rotherham		3	1991	2002	Arsenal	86	0	0	e
Seddon WC	Bill	28/07/1901	Clapton	1993	1	1931		Arsenal	18	0	0	
Seed JM	Jimmy	25/03/1895	Blackhill	1966	2	1929	1930	Sheffield Wed.	71	0	17	e
Seith R	Bobby	09/03/1932	Coatbridge		1	1960		Burnley	27	0	0	
Setters ME	Maurice	16/12/1936	Honiton		1	1965		Manchester Utd.	5	0	0	
Seymour GS	Stan	16/05/1893	Kelloe	1978	1	1927		Newcastle United	42	0	18	
Sharp A	Bert	1876	Hereford	1941	1	1899		Aston Villa	4	0	0	
Sharp GM	Graeme	16/10/1960	Glasgow		2	1985	1987	Everton	63	0	26	s
Sharp J	Jack	15/02/1878	Hereford	1938	1	1899		Aston Villa	8	0	4	e
Sharpe LS	Lee	27/05/1971	Halesowen		3	1993	1996	Manchester Utd.	74	14	14	e
Sharples GFV	George	20/09/1943	Ellesmere Port		1	1963		Everton	2	0	0	
Shaw A	Arthur	09/04/1924	Limehouse		1	1953		Arsenal	25	0	0	
Shaw GE	George	13/10/1899	Swinton	1973	3	1924	1926	Huddersfield T	24	0	0	e
Shaw GR	Gary	21/01/1961	Birmingham		1	1981		Aston Villa	40	0	18	
Shaw HV	Harry	22/05/1905	Hednesford	1984	1	1936		Sunderland	1	0	0	
Shea DH	Danny	06/11/1887	Wapping	1960	1	1914		Blackburn Rovers	36	0	27	e
Shearer A	Alan	13/08/1970	Newcastle		1	1995		Blackburn Rovers	42	0	34	e
Sheedy KM	Kevin	21/10/1959	Builth Wells		1	1982		Liverpool	0	2	0	r
					2	1985	1987	Everton	57	0	24	
Sheldon J	Jackie	11/02/1888	Clay Cross	1941	1	1911		Manchester Utd.	5	0	0	
Shepherd A	Albert	10/12/1885	Great Lever	1929	1	1909		Newcastle United	14	0	11	e
Sheringham EP	Teddy	02/04/1966	Highams Park		3	1999	2001	Manchester Utd.	45	28	22	e
Sherwood TA	Tim	06/02/1969	St Albans		1	1995		Blackburn Rovers	38	0	6	e
Shilton PL	Peter	18/09/1949	Leicester		1	1978		Nottm. Forest	37	0	0	e
Shone D	Danny	27/04/1892	Wirral	1974	2	1922	1923	Liverpool	16	0	6	
Short J	Jack	18/02/1928	Great Houghton	1976	1	1954		Wolves	26	0	0	
Shorthouse WH	Bill	27/05/1922	Bilston		1	1954		Wolves	40	0	0	
Showell GW	George	09/02/1934	Bilston		2	1958	1959	Wolves	15	0	3	
Shutt CS	Carl	10/10/1961	Sheffield		1	1992		Leeds United	6	8	1	
Sidebottom G	Geoff	29/12/1936	Mapplewell		1	1959		Wolves	3	0	0	
Sidey NW	Norman	31/05/1907	Nunhead	1969	4	1933	1938	Arsenal	23	0	0	
Sidlow C	Cyril	26/11/1915	Colwyn Bay	2005	1	1947		Liverpool	34	0	0	w
Sillett RPT	Peter	01/02/1933	Southampton	1998	1	1955		Chelsea	21	0	6	e
Silva GA	Gilberto	07/10/1976	Lagoa da Prata, Brazil		1	2004		Arsenal	29	3	4	br
Silvestre MS	Mikael	09/08/1977	Chambray-les-Tours, Fr		4	2000	2007	Manchester Utd.	95	14	3	fr
Simpson G	George	1883	Jarrow		2	1903	1904	Sheffield Wed.	25	0	7	
Simpson J	Jock	25/12/1886	Pendleton	1959	2	1912	1914	Blackburn Rovers	69	0	4	e
Simpson PF	Peter	13/01/1945	Gorleston		1	1971		Arsenal	25	0	0	
Simpson RH	Bobby	1889	Redcar		1	1915		Everton	9	0	0	
Simpson VS	Vivian	1883	Sheffield	1918	2	1903	1904	Sheffield Wed.	10	0	2	
Sims DN	Nigel	09/08/1931	Coton-in-Elms		1	1954		Wolves	8	0	0	
Sinclair TS	Thomas		Glasgow		1	1907		Newcastle United	3	0	0	
Slater RD	Robbie	22/11/1964	Ormskirk		1	1995		Blackburn Rovers	12	6	0	au
Slater WJ	Bill	29/04/1927	Clitheroe		3	1954	1959	Wolves	80	0	3	e
Sloan JW	Paddy	30/04/1920	Lurgan	1993	1	1948		Arsenal	3	0	0	ir
Small J	Jack	29/10/1889	South Bank	1946	1	1913		Sunderland	1	0	0	
Smalley RE	Robert			1947	1	1891		Everton	1	0	0	
Smellie RJ	Robert	15/10/1865	Dalziel		1	1893		Sunderland	23	0	0	s
Smelt L	Len	10/12/1885	Rotherham	1933	1	1921		Burnley	39	0	0	
Smertin A	Alexei	01/05/1975	Barnaul, Russia		1	2005		Chelsea	11	5	0	ru
Smith A	Alan	28/10/1980	Rothwell		1	2007		Manchester Utd.	6	3	0	e
Smith AM	Alan	21/11/1962	Birmingham		2	1989	1991	Arsenal	71	2	46	e
Smith AW	Andy	1890	Birmingham	1968	1	1920		West Bromwich A.	29	0	7	
Smith AWT	Bertie	22/04/1900	Camberwell	1957	2	1924	1926	Huddersfield T	9	0	1	
Smith J	Jock	1866	Ayrshire	1911	1	1892		Sunderland	14	0	1	
Smith J	Joe	17/04/1890	Darby End	1956	1	1920		West Bromwich A.	40	0	0	e
Smith J	John	04/01/1939	Shoreditch	1988	1	1961		Tottenham H	1	0	0	
Smith JD	Jimmy	07/01/1987	Woodford		1	2006		Chelsea	0	1	0	
Smith JL	Les	24/12/1927	Halesowen		1	1954		Wolves	4	0	1	
Smith L	Lionel	23/08/1920	Mexborough	1980	2	1948	1953	Arsenal	32	0	0	e
Smith N	Norman	15/12/1897	Newburn	1978	1	1925		Huddersfield T	1	0	0	
Smith PJ	Percy	1880	Burbage Spring	1959	2	1912	1914	Blackburn Rovers	64	0	4	
Smith RA	Bobby	22/02/1933	Lingdale		1	1955		Chelsea	4	0	0	e
					1	1961		Tottenham H	36	0	28	
Smith S	Steve	14/01/1874	Abbots Bromley	1935	5	1894	1900	Aston Villa	99	0	16	e
Smith T	Tommy	05/04/1945	Liverpool		4	1966	1977	Liverpool	115	0	5	e
Smith WH	Billy	23/05/1895	Tantobie	1951	3	1924	1926	Huddersfield T	108	0	28	e
Smith WS	William	22/10/1903	South Shields		1	1930		Sheffield Wed.	4	0	0	
Snodin I	Ian	15/08/1963	Thrybergh		1	1987		Everton	15	1	0	
Solskjaer OG	Ole Gunnar	26/02/1973	Kristiansund, Norway		6	1997	2007	Manchester Utd.	106	61	68	no
Souness GJ	Graeme	06/05/1953	Edinburgh		5	1979	1984	Liverpool	194	1	30	s
Southall N	Neville	16/09/1958	Llandudno		2	1985	1987	Everton	73	0	0	w
Soye J	Jimmy	14/04/1885	Govan		1	1907		Newcastle United	1	0	0	
Spackman NJ	Nigel	02/12/1960	Romsey		1	1988		Liverpool	19	8	0	
Speed GA	Gary	08/09/1969	Mancot		1	1992		Leeds United	41	0	7	w
Speedie FB	Finlay	18/08/1880	Dumbarton	1953	1	1907		Newcastle United	27	0	10	s
Spence JW	Bill	10/01/1926	Hartlepool		1	1950		Portsmouth	16	0	0	
Spence MB	Bonwell	21/02/1899	Ferryhill	1982	2	1925	1926	Huddersfield T	5	0	0	
Spencer CW	Charlie	04/12/1899	Washington	1953	1	1927		Newcastle United	34	0	0	e
Spencer H	Howard	23/08/1875	Edgbaston	1940	4	1896	1900	Aston Villa	95	0	1	e
Spicer EW	Eddie	20/09/1922	Liverpool	2004	1	1947		Liverpool	10	0	0	
Spiksley F	Fred	25/01/1870	Gainsborough	1948	1	1903		Sheffield Wed.	32	0	8	e
Sprake G	Gary	03/04/1945	Winch Wen		1	1969		Leeds United	42	0	0	w
Stacey GW	George	1887	Thorpe Hesley		2	1908	1911	Manchester Utd.	54	0	1	

Name	First	D.o.B.	Birthplace	Died	No.	First	Last	Club	Apps	Subs	Gls	Int
Stam J	Jaap	17/07/1972	Kampen, Holland		3	1999	2001	Manchester Utd.	78	0	1	ho
Staunton S	Steve	19/01/1969	Drogheda		1	1990		Liverpool	18	2	0	r
Steele DM	David	26/07/1894	Carluke	1964	3	1924	1926	Huddersfield T	88	0	0	s
Stein J	Jimmy	07/11/1907	Coatbridge		1	1932		Everton	37	0	9	
Stepanovs I	Igors	21/01/1976	Ogre, Latvia		1	2002		Arsenal	6	0	0	la
Stephen JF	Jimmy	23/08/1922	Fettercairn		1	1950		Portsmouth	1	0	0	s
Stephenson C	Clem	06/02/1890	Seaton Delaval	1961	3	1924	1926	Huddersfield T	105	0	20	e
Stephenson RA	Roy	27/05/1932	Crook	2000	1	1962		Ipswich Town	41	0	7	
Stepney AC	Alex	18/09/1942	Mitcham		1	1967		Manchester Utd.	35	0	0	e
Sterland M	Mel	01/10/1961	Sheffield		1	1992		Leeds United	29	2	6	e
Steven TMcG	Trevor	21/09/1963	Berwick-on-Tweed		2	1985	1987	Everton	81	0	26	e
Stevens D	Dennis	30/11/1933	Dudley		1	1963		Everton	42	0	7	
Stevens MG	Gary	27/03/1963	Barrow		2	1985	1987	Everton	62	0	6	e
Stevenson AE	Alex	09/08/1912	Dublin	1985	1	1939		Everton	36	0	11	ir
Stevenson W	Willie	26/10/1939	Leith		2	1964	1966	Liverpool	79	0	6	
Stewart DS	David	11/03/1947	Glasgow		1	1974		Leeds United	3	0	0	s
Stewart J	Jimmy	1883	Gateshead	1957	2	1903	1904	Sheffield Wed.	11	0	1	e
					1	1909		Newcastle United	25	0	8	
Stewart MJ	Michael	26/02/1981	Edinburgh		2	2001	2003	Manchester Utd.	3	1	0	s
Stiles NP	Nobby	18/05/1942	Manchester		2	1965	1967	Manchester Utd.	78	0	3	e
Stockill RR	Reg	24/11/1913	York	1995	1	1933		Arsenal	4	0	3	
Stockin R	Ron	27/06/1931	Birmingham		1	1954		Wolves	6	0	0	
Storey PE	Peter	07/09/1945	Farnham		1	1971		Arsenal	40	0	2	e
Storton TG	Trevor	26/11/1949	Keighley		1	1973		Liverpool	4	0	0	
Strachan GD	Gordon	09/02/1957	Edinburgh		1	1992		Leeds United	35	1	4	s
Strange AH	Alf	02/04/1900	Marehay	1978	2	1929	1930	Sheffield Wed.	83	0	8	e
Strong GH	Geoff	19/09/1937	Newcastle		1	1966		Liverpool	21	1	5	
Stuart EA	Eddie	12/05/1931	Johannesburg, S. Af.		3	1954	1959	Wolves	90	0	0	
Stubbins A	Albert	13/07/1919	Wallsend	2002	1	1947		Liverpool	36	0	24	
Stubbs FL	Frank	13/04/1878	Woodhouse Eaves	1944	1	1903		Sheffield Wed.	1	0	0	
Stubbs LL	Les	18/02/1929	Great Wakering		1	1955		Chelsea	27	0	5	
Summerbee MG	Mike	15/12/1942	Cheltenham		1	1968		Manchester City	41	0	14	e
Suttie T	Tommy	1883	Lochgelly		1	1912		Blackburn Rovers	7	0	0	
Sutton CR	Chris	10/03/1973	Nottingham		1	1995		Blackburn Rovers	40	0	15	e
Swain KM	Kenny	28/01/1952	Birkenhead		1	1981		Aston Villa	42	0	0	
Swift FV	Frank	26/12/1913	Blackpool	1958	1	1937		Manchester City	42	0	0	e
Swinbourne RH	Roy	25/08/1929	Barnburgh		1	1954		Wolves	40	0	24	
Swindin GH	George	04/12/1914	Campsall	2005	3	1938	1953	Arsenal	73	0	0	
Taibi M	Massimo	18/02/1970	Palermo, Italy		1	2000		Manchester Utd.	4	0	0	
Tanner N	Nick	24/05/1965	Kingswood		1	1990		Liverpool	2	2	0	
Taylor D	David	29/09/1883	Govan	1949	1	1921		Burnley	11	0	0	
Taylor EH	Ted	07/03/1887	Liverpool	1956	3	1924	1926	Huddersfield T	74	0	0	e
					1	1928		Everton	26	0	0	
Taylor PH	Phil	18/09/1917	Bristol		1	1947		Liverpool	35	0	1	e
Taylor SJ	Stuart	28/11/1980	Romford		1	2002		Arsenal	9	1	0	
Taylor T	Tommy	29/01/1932	Barnsley	1958	2	1956	1957	Manchester Utd.	65	0	47	e
Taylor W	Bill	1886	Southwell	1966	1	1921		Burnley	2	0	0	
Temple DW	Derek	13/11/1938	Liverpool		1	1963		Everton	5	0	1	e
Templeton RB	Bobby	22/06/1879	Coylton	1919	2	1899	1900	Aston Villa	12	0	4	s
					1	1905		Newcastle United	10	0	0	
Terry JG	John	07/12/1980	Barking		2	2005	2006	Chelsea	72	0	7	e
Thackeray F	Fred	1878	Sheffield		1	1903		Sheffield Wed.	5	0	0	
Thickett H	Harry	28/03/1873	Hexthorpe	1920	1	1898		Sheffield Utd.	29	0	0	e
Thomas ML	Michael	24/08/1967	Lambeth		2	1989	1991	Arsenal	60	8	9	e
Thomas RJ	Rod	11/01/1947	Glyncorrwg		1	1975		Derby County	22	0	0	w
Thompson L	Len	18/02/1901	Sheffield		1	1931		Arsenal	2	0	0	
Thompson P	Peter	27/11/1942	Carlisle		2	1964	1966	Liverpool	82	0	11	e
Thompson PB	Phil	21/01/1954	Liverpool		7	1973	1983	Liverpool	218	2	2	e
Thompson R	Bob	27/02/1890	Newcastle	1958	1	1915		Everton	33	0	0	
Thompson WG	Bill	10/08/1921	Glasgow	1988	2	1949	1950	Portsmouth	12	0	2	
Thomson CB	Charlie	12/06/1878	Prestonpans	1936	1	1913		Sunderland	35	0	1	s
Thomson CM	Charlie	11/12/1910	Glasgow	1984	1	1936		Sunderland	42	0	1	s
Thomson CR	Chick	02/03/1930	Perth		1	1955		Chelsea	16	0	0	
Thomson E	Ernest	1884			1	1908		Manchester Utd.	3	0	0	
Thomson GM	George	19/10/1936	Edinburgh		1	1963		Everton	19	0	0	
Thomson JR	Jock	06/07/1906	Thornton	1979	2	1932	1939	Everton	65	0	0	s
Thomson R	Bobby	21/11/1939	Menstrie		1	1964		Liverpool	2	0	0	
Thomson S	Sammy	14/02/1862	Lugar	1943	2	1889	1890	Preston NE	34	0	10	s
Thornley BL	Ben	21/04/1975	Bury		3	1994	1997	Manchester Utd.	1	3	0	
Thorpe JH	Jimmy	16/09/1913	Jarrow	1936	1	1936		Sunderland	26	0	0	
Tiago Mendes C	Cardoso	02/05/1981	Viana do Castelo, P'tugal		1	2005		Chelsea	21	13	4	pt
Tickridge S	Sid	10/04/1923	Stepney	1997	1	1951		Tottenham H	1	0	0	
Tilson SF	Fred	19/04/1904	Barnsley	1972	1	1937		Manchester City	23	0	15	e
Tinsley WE	Walter	10/08/1891	Ironville	1966	1	1913		Sunderland	7	0	3	
Todd C	Colin	12/12/1948	Chester-le-Street		2	1972	1975	Derby County	79	0	2	e
Toseland E	Ernie	17/03/1905	Northampton	1987	1	1937		Manchester City	42	0	7	
Toshack JB	John	22/03/1949	Cardiff		3	1973	1977	Liverpool	79	0	39	w
Toure HK	Kolo	19/03/1981	Ivory Coast		1	2004		Arsenal	36	1	1	iv
Trainer J	Jimmy	07/01/1863	Wrexham	1915	2	1889	1890	Preston NE	42	0	0	w
Tranter GH	George	1887	Quarry Bank	1940	1	1910		Aston Villa	28	0	0	
Trentham DH	Douglas	02/11/1917	Chirbury	2003	1	1939		Everton	1	0	1	
Trim RF	Reg	01/10/1913	Portsmouth	1997	1	1935		Arsenal	1	0	0	
Trotter JW	Jimmy	25/11/1899	Easington	1984	1	1929		Sheffield Wed.	6	0	1	
Troughear W	Billy	1885	Workington	1955	1	1913		Sunderland	6	0	0	
Troup A	Alec	04/05/1895	Forfar	1951	1	1928		Everton	42	0	10	s

		D.o.B.	Birthplace	Died	No.	First	Last	Club	Apps	Subs	Gls	Int
Turnbull A	Sandy		Hurlford	1917	2	1908	1911	Manchester Utd.	65	0	43	
Turnbull JMcL	Jimmy	23/05/1884	Bannockburn		1	1908		Manchester Utd.	26	0	10	
Uphill EDH	Dennis	11/08/1931	Bath		1	1951		Tottenham H	2	0	1	
Upson MJ	Matthew	18/04/1979	Diss		2	1998	2002	Arsenal	15	4	0	e
Urwin T	Tommy	05/02/1896	Haswell	1968	1	1927		Newcastle United	39	0	4	e
Van Bronckhorst GC	Giovanni	05/02/1975	Rotterdam, Holland		1	2002		Arsenal	13	8	1	ho
Van Den Hauwe PWR	Pat	16/12/1960	Dendermonde, Belgium		2	1985	1987	Everton	42	0	1	w
Van der Gouw R	Raimond	24/03/1963	Oldenzaal, Holland		4	1997	2001	Manchester Utd.	22	9	0	
Van der Sar E	Edwin	29/10/1970	Leiden, Holland		1	2007		Manchester Utd.	32	0	0	ho
Van Nistelrooy RJM	Ruud	01/07/1976	Oss, Holland		1	2003		Manchester Utd.	33	1	25	ho
Varadi I	Imre	08/07/1959	Paddington		1	1992		Leeds United	2	1	0	
Veall RJ	Ray	16/03/1943	Skegness		1	1963		Everton	11	0	1	
Veitch CCMcK	Colin	22/05/1881	Newcastle	1938	3	1905	1909	Newcastle United	87	0	26	e
Venison B	Barry	16/08/1964	Consett		2	1988	1990	Liverpool	43	0	0	e
Vernazza PAP	Paolo	01/11/1979	Islington		1	1998		Arsenal	1	0	0	
Vernon TR	Roy	14/04/1937	Prestatyn	1993	1	1963		Everton	41	0	24	w
Veron JS	Juan Sebastian	09/03/1975	La Plata, Argentina		1	2003		Manchester Utd.	21	4	2	ar
Vidic N	Nemanja	21/10/1981	Subotica, Serbia		1	2007		Manchester Utd.	25	0	3	sm
Vieira P	Patrick	23/06/1976	Dakar, Senegal		3	1998	2004	Arsenal	95	3	7	fr
Viollet DS	Dennis	20/09/1933	Manchester	1999	2	1956	1957	Manchester Utd.	61	0	36	e
Virr AE	Albert	1902	Liverpool	1959	1	1928		Everton	39	0	1	
Wade SJ	Joe	07/07/1921	Shoreditch	2005	2	1948	1953	Arsenal	43	0	0	
Wadsworth H	Harold	01/10/1898	Bootle	1975	2	1922	1923	Liverpool	4	0	0	
Wadsworth SJ	Sam	13/09/1896	Darwen	1961	3	1924	1926	Huddersfield T	108	0	0	e
Wadsworth W	Walter	07/10/1890	Bootle	1951	2	1922	1923	Liverpool	75	0	2	
Wakenshaw RA	Robbie	22/12/1965	Ponteland		1	1985		Everton	1	1	0	
Walker J	John	31/05/1874	Coatbridge	1940	1	1901		Liverpool	29	0	7	s
Walker JMcI	Jim	10/06/1947	Northwich		1	1972		Derby County	3	3	1	
Walker T	Tommy	04/03/1902	Cross Colls	1973	2	1929	1930	Sheffield Wed.	75	0	0	
Wall G	George	20/02/1885	Boldon Colliery	1962	2	1908	1911	Manchester Utd.	62	0	24	e
Wallace CW	Charlie	20/01/1885	Southwick, Co. Durham	1970	1	1910		Aston Villa	38	0	7	e
Wallace DL	Danny	21/01/1964	Greenwich		1	1993		Manchester Utd.	0	2	0	e
Wallace GH	Gordon	13/06/1944	Glasgow		1	1964		Liverpool	1	0	0	
Wallace RS	Rod	02/10/1969	Greenwich		1	1992		Leeds United	34	0	11	
Wallwork R	Ronnie	10/09/1977	Manchester		2	2000	2001	Manchester Utd.	4	13	0	
Walmsley A	Albert	21/10/1885	Blackburn		2	1912	1914	Blackburn Rovers	74	0	1	
Walsh D	Derek	24/10/1967	Hamilton		1	1985		Everton	1	0	0	
Walsh G	Gary	21/03/1968	Wigan		1	1994		Manchester Utd.	2	1	0	
Walsh PAM	Paul	01/10/1962	Plumstead		2	1986	1988	Liverpool	18	10	11	e
Walter JD	Joe	16/08/1895	Eastville	1995	2	1924	1925	Huddersfield T	33	0	1	
Walters J	Joe	1886	Stourbridge	1923	1	1910		Aston Villa	14	0	6	
Walters WE	Sonny	05/09/1924	Edmonton	1970	1	1951		Tottenham H	40	0	15	
Walton JA	Johnny	21/03/1928	Horwich	1979	1	1952		Manchester Utd.	2	0	0	
Wareing W	Billy		Southport		1	1915		Everton	8	0	0	
Warhurst P	Paul	26/09/1969	Stockport		1	1995		Blackburn Rovers	20	7	2	
Wark J	John	04/08/1957	Glasgow		3	1984	1988	Liverpool	16	3	5	s
Waterhouse F	Frank	1889	Langley Green		1	1920		West Bromwich A.	2	0	0	
Watkins AE	Fred	1878	Llanwnog	1957	1	1900		Aston Villa	1	0	0	w
Watkinson WW	Billy	16/03/1922	Prescot	2001	1	1947		Liverpool	6	0	1	
Watson AF	Alex	05/04/1968	Liverpool		1	1988		Liverpool	2	0	0	
Watson D	Dave	20/11/1961	Liverpool		1	1987		Everton	35	0	3	e
Watson J	Jimmy	04/10/1877	Motherwell	1915	1	1902		Sunderland	33	0	0	s
Watson TG	Gordon	01/03/1914	Wolsingham	2001	1	1939		Everton	16	0	0	
Watson W	Billy	11/09/1890	Birkdale	1955	1	1921		Burnley	42	0	2	e
Watson W	Billy	31/12/1893	Bolton-on-Dearne	1962	3	1924	1926	Huddersfield T	123	0	0	
Watt SM	Steve	01/05/1985	Aberdeen		1	2005		Chelsea	0	1	0	
Watts C	Charlie	1872	Middlesbrough	1924	1	1905		Newcastle United	4	0	0	
Weaver W	Walter	09/11/1898	Birkenhead	1965	1	1921		Burnley	27	0	2	
Webb NJ	Neil	30/07/1963	Reading		1	1993		Manchester Utd.	0	1	0	e
Webster C	Colin	17/07/1932	Cardiff	2001	2	1956	1957	Manchester Utd.	20	0	7	w
Webster R	Ron	21/06/1943	Belper		2	1972	1975	Derby County	62	0	2	
Weldon A	Tony	12/11/1900	Croy	1953	1	1928		Everton	38	0	7	
Welford JW	Jimmy	27/03/1869	Barnard Castle	1945	3	1894	1897	Aston Villa	53	0	1	
Weller LC	Louis	07/05/1887	Stoke-on-Trent	1952	1	1915		Everton	6	0	0	
West A	Alf	15/12/1881	Nottingham	1944	1	1906		Liverpool	37	0	3	
West EJ	Enoch 'Knocker'	31/03/1886	Hucknall Torkard	1965	1	1911		Manchester Utd.	35	0	19	
West G	Gordon	24/04/1943	Darfield		2	1963	1970	Everton	80	0	0	e
Wetherall D	David	14/03/1971	Sheffield		1	1992		Leeds United	0	1	0	
Whalley A	Arthur	17/02/1886	Rainford	1952	1	1911		Manchester Utd.	15	0	0	
Whelan RA	Ronnie	25/09/1961	Dublin		6	1982	1990	Liverpool	176	8	27	r
Whelan WA	Liam	01/04/1935	Dublin	1958	2	1956	1957	Manchester Utd.	52	0	30	r
Wheldon GF	Fred	01/11/1869	Langley Green	1924	3	1897	1900	Aston Villa	97	0	45	e
White H	Henry				1	1898		Sheffield Utd.	6	0	0	
White JA	John	28/04/1937	Musselburgh	1964	1	1961		Tottenham H	42	0	13	s
White TA	Tommy	29/07/1908	Pendleton	1967	2	1928	1932	Everton	24	0	20	e
White WH	Billy	13/10/1936	Liverpool	2000	1	1960		Burnley	6	0	2	
Whitefoot J	Jeff	31/12/1933	Cheadle		2	1952	1956	Manchester Utd.	18	0	0	
Whitehouse J	Jimmy	1873	Birmingham	1934	1	1897		Aston Villa	22	0	0	
Whitehouse JC	Jack	04/03/1897	Smethwick	1948	1	1929	1930	Sheffield Wed.	10	0	1	
Whitehurst W	Walter	07/06/1934	Manchester		1	1956		Manchester Utd.	1	0	0	
Whiteside KD	Kerr	1887	Scotland		1	1908		Manchester Utd.	1	0	0	
Whitham M	Mick	06/11/1867	Ecclesfield	1924	1	1898		Sheffield Utd.	1	0	0	e
Whitlow MW	Mike	13/01/1968	Northwich		1	1992		Leeds United	3	7	1	
Whitson TT	Tony	1885	Cape Town, South Af.	1945	1	1909		Newcastle United	30	0	0	
Whittle A	Alan	10/03/1950	Liverpool		1	1970		Everton	15	0	11	

		D.o.B.	Birthplace	Died	No.	First	Last	Club	Apps	Subs	Gls	Int
Whittle R	Richard				1	1889		Preston NE	1	0	1	
Whyte CA	Chris	02/09/1961	Islington		1	1992		Leeds United	41	0	1	
Wicks SM	Stan	11/07/1928	Reading	1983	1	1955		Chelsea	21	0	1	
Wignall F	Frank	21/08/1939	Blackrod		1	1963		Everton	1	0	1	e
					1	1972		Derby County	10	1	5	
Wilcox JM	Jason	15/07/1971	Farnworth		1	1995		Blackburn Rovers	27	0	5	e
Wilkes A	Albert	1874	Birmingham	1936	2	1899	1900	Aston Villa	32	0	2	e
Wilkes TH	Tom	19/06/1874	Alcester	1921	3	1896	1899	Aston Villa	41	0	0	
Wilkinson J	Jack	13/06/1902	Wath-on-Dearne	1979	2	1929	1930	Sheffield Wed.	7	0	0	
Wilkinson P	Paul	30/10/1964	Grimoldby		2	1985	1987	Everton	16	11	5	
Willemse SB	Stan	23/08/1924	Brighton		1	1955		Chelsea	36	0	1	
Williams BD	Ben	29/10/1900	Penrhiwceiber	1968	1	1932		Everton	33	0	0	w
Williams BF	Bert	31/01/1920	Bradley, Staffordshire		1	1954		Wolves	34	0	0	e
Williams G	Gary	17/06/1960	Wolverhampton		1	1981		Aston Villa	21	1	0	
Williams H	Harry	1883	Farnworth		1	1908		Manchester Utd.	1	0	0	
Williams JJ	Joey	04/06/1902	Rotherham		2	1925	1926	Huddersfield T	58	0	6	
					1	1931		Arsenal	9	0	2	
Willis A	Arthur	02/02/1920	Denaby	1987	1	1951		Tottenham H	39	0	0	e
Willis DL	David	1881	Byker	1949	1	1909		Newcastle United	20	0	1	
Wills T	Thomas		Kilmarnock	1912	1	1905		Newcastle United	2	0	0	
Wilshaw DJ	Dennis	11/03/1926	Stoke-on-Trent	2004	2	1954	1958	Wolves	51	0	29	e
Wilson AA	Alex	29/10/1908	Wishaw	1971	3	1934	1938	Arsenal	24	0	0	
Wilson AMcC	Andy	10/12/1880	Irvine	1945	2	1903	1904	Sheffield Wed.	63	0	22	s
Wilson C	Charlie	1877	Stockport		1	1901		Liverpool	25	0	1	
Wilson C	Charlie	30/03/1895	Atherstone	1971	3	1924	1926	Huddersfield T	73	0	44	
Wilson C	Charlie	20/07/1905	Heeley	1985	2	1929	1930	Sheffield Wed.	12	0	1	
Wilson GW	George	1884	Lochgelly	1960	1	1909		Newcastle United	28	0	5	s
Wilson H	Hughie	18/03/1869	Mauchline	1940	3	1892	1895	Sunderland	76	0	21	s
Wilson MA	Mark	09/02/1979	Scunthorpe		1	2000		Manchester Utd.	1	2	0	
Wilson RP	Bob	30/10/1941	Chesterfield		1	1971		Arsenal	42	0	0	s
Wilson T	Tommy	16/04/1896	Seaham	1948	3	1924	1926	Huddersfield T	122	0	0	e
Wilson TC	Tom	20/10/1877	Preston	1940	1	1908		Manchester Utd.	1	0	0	
Wilson W	Willie	07/09/1900	Port Seaton		1	1927		Newcastle United	42	0	0	
Wiltord S	Sylvain	10/05/1974	Neuilly-sur-Marne, France		2	2002	2004	Arsenal	31	14	13	fr
Winterburn N	Nigel	11/12/1963	Nuneaton		3	1989	1998	Arsenal	111	1	4	e
Withe P	Peter	30/08/1951	Toxteth		1	1978		Nottm. Forest	40	0	12	e
					1	1981		Aston Villa	36	0	20	
Withers CF	Charlie	06/09/1922	Edmonton	2005	1	1951		Tottenham H	4	0	0	
Witschge R	Richard	20/09/1969	Amsterdam, Holland		1	1995		Blackburn Rovers	1	0	0	ho
Wood RE	Ray	11/06/1931	Hebburn	2002	2	1956	1957	Manchester Utd.	80	0	0	e
Woodcock AS	Tony	06/12/1955	Eastwood		1	1978		Nottm. Forest	36	0	11	e
Woolley A	Albert	1870	Hockley	1896	1	1894		Aston Villa	14	0	8	
Wreh C	Christopher	14/05/1975	Monrovia, Liberia		1	1998		Arsenal	7	9	3	li
Wright AG	Alan	28/09/1971	Ashton-under-Lyne		1	1995		Blackburn Rovers	4	1	0	
Wright AM	Alex	18/10/1925	Kirkcaldy		1	1951		Tottenham H	2	0	1	
Wright IE	Ian	03/11/1963	Woolwich		1	1998		Arsenal	22	2	10	e
Wright RI	Richard	05/11/1977	Ipswich		1	2002		Arsenal	12	0	0	e
Wright TJ	Tommy	21/10/1944	Liverpool		1	1970		Everton	42	0	1	e
Wright WA	Billy	06/02/1924	Ironbridge	1994	3	1954	1959	Wolves	116	0	0	e
Wright WP	Bill		Seaforth		1	1915		Everton	2	0	0	
Wright-Phillips SC	Shaun	25/10/1981	Greenwich		1	2006		Chelsea	10	17	0	e
Wylie TG	Tom	1872	Maybole		1	1891		Everton	4	0	4	s
Yeats R	Ron	15/11/1937	Aberdeen		2	1964	1966	Liverpool	78	0	3	s
Yeuell JH	Jasper	23/03/1925	Bilston	2003	2	1949	1950	Portsmouth	12	0	0	
Yorath TC	Terry	27/03/1950	Cardiff		1	1974		Leeds United	23	5	2	w
Yorke D	Dwight	03/11/1971	Canaan, Tobago		3	1999	2001	Manchester Utd.	76	10	47	tt
Young A	Alex	03/02/1937	Loanhead		1	1963		Everton	42	0	22	s
Young NJ	Neil	17/02/1944	Manchester		1	1968		Manchester City	40	0	19	

TOP SIX CLUBS AT END OF DECEMBER AND END OF SEASON

	home: p w d l f a	away: w d l f a	tots: f a pts		home: p w d l f a	away: w d l f a	tots: f a pts av/dif
1888/89							
Preston North End	18 9 1 0 35 6	6 2 0 29 6	64 12 33	Preston North End	22 10 1 0 39 7	8 3 0 35 8	74 15 40 4.9333
Aston Villa	16 8 0 0 36 12	2 4 2 12 15	48 27 24	Aston Villa	22 10 0 1 44 16	2 5 4 17 27	61 43 29 1.4186
Wolverhampton Wan.	16 6 2 1 24 13	2 2 3 15 15	39 28 20	Wolverhampton Wan.	22 8 2 1 31 14	4 2 5 20 23	51 37 28 1.3784
Blackburn Rovers	16 5 3 0 35 18	2 2 4 17 17	52 35 19	Blackburn Rovers	22 7 4 0 44 22	3 2 6 22 23	66 45 26 1.4666
West Bromwich Alb.	17 5 1 2 20 18	4 0 5 14 18	34 36 19	Bolton Wanderers	22 6 0 5 35 30	4 2 5 28 29	63 59 22 1.0677
Accrington	17 4 3 0 21 10	1 4 5 20 29	41 39 17	West Bromwich Alb.	22 6 2 3 25 24	4 0 7 15 22	40 46 22 0.8695
1889/90							
Preston North End	17 6 1 2 32 9	5 1 2 26 16	58 25 24	Preston North End	22 8 1 2 41 12	7 2 2 30 18	71 30 33 2.3666
Everton	16 5 2 1 25 14	5 1 2 20 16	45 30 23	Everton	22 8 2 1 40 15	6 1 4 25 25	65 40 31 1.6250
Blackburn Rovers	16 8 0 2 51 18	2 2 2 14 11	65 29 22	Blackburn Rovers	22 9 0 2 59 18	3 3 5 19 23	78 41 27 1.9024
Wolverhampton Wan.	17 4 3 1 21 11	4 2 3 19 14	40 25 21	Wolverhampton Wan.	22 6 3 2 28 14	4 2 5 23 24	51 38 25 1.3421
Derby County	15 6 2 0 22 9	1 1 5 10 30	32 39 17	West Bromwich Alb.	22 8 1 2 37 20	3 2 6 10 30	47 50 25 0.9400
Aston Villa	18 5 2 2 26 13	1 2 6 12 28	38 41 16	Accrington	22 6 4 1 33 25	3 2 6 20 31	53 56 24 0.9464
1890/91							
Everton	18 7 0 1 30 9	5 1 4 22 14	52 23 25	Everton	22 9 0 2 39 12	5 1 5 24 17	63 29 29 2.1724
Notts County	18 8 1 1 29 11	1 3 4 10 15	39 26 22	Preston North End	22 7 3 1 30 5	5 0 6 14 18	44 23 27 1.9130
Wolverhampton Wan.	18 7 1 2 19 8	3 1 4 12 26	31 34 22	Notts County	22 9 1 1 33 11	2 3 6 19 24	52 35 26 1.4857
Blackburn Rovers	16 6 1 1 20 10	3 1 4 19 21	39 31 20	Wolverhampton Wan.	22 8 1 2 23 8	4 1 6 16 42	39 50 26 0.7800
Bolton Wanderers	16 6 0 2 26 13	2 1 5 8 16	34 29 17	Bolton Wanderers	22 9 0 2 36 14	3 1 7 11 20	47 34 25 1.3823
Preston North End	14 5 2 1 19 4	2 0 4 7 8	26 12 16	Blackburn Rovers	22 7 1 3 29 19	4 1 6 23 24	52 43 24 1.2093
1891/92							
Bolton Wanderers	19 7 2 1 23 11	5 0 4 12 15	35 26 26	Sunderland	26 13 0 0 55 11	8 0 5 38 25	93 36 42 2.5833
Preston North End	17 8 0 1 30 7	4 1 3 10 12	40 19 25	Preston North End	26 12 0 1 42 8	6 1 6 19 23	61 31 37 1.9677
Sunderland	16 8 0 0 35 6	4 0 4 23 19	58 25 24	Bolton Wanderers	26 9 2 2 29 14	8 0 5 22 23	51 37 36 1.3783
Aston Villa	17 7 0 2 39 14	4 0 4 16 18	55 32 22	Aston Villa	26 10 0 3 63 23	5 0 8 26 33	89 56 30 1.5892
Blackburn Rovers	19 5 3 1 27 16	2 2 6 17 31	44 47 19	Everton	26 8 2 3 32 22	4 2 7 17 27	49 49 28 1.0000
Wolverhampton Wan.	20 6 2 2 26 12	1 1 8 14 26	40 38 17	Wolverhampton Wan.	26 8 2 3 34 15	3 2 8 25 31	59 46 26 1.2826
1892/93							
Preston North End	19 9 0 0 24 6	5 1 4 14 15	38 21 29	Sunderland	30 13 2 0 58 17	9 2 4 42 19	100 36 48 2.7777
Sunderland	16 7 1 0 27 6	5 0 3 27 11	54 17 25	Preston North End	30 11 2 2 34 10	6 1 8 23 29	57 39 37 1.4615
Aston Villa	21 7 1 1 28 15	4 0 8 20 29	48 44 23	Everton	30 9 3 3 44 17	7 1 7 30 34	74 51 36 1.4509
Sheffield Wed.	18 6 2 1 25 17	4 0 5 16 17	41 34 22	Aston Villa	30 12 1 2 50 24	4 2 9 23 38	73 62 35 1.1774
Wolverhampton Wan.	20 8 2 1 24 11	0 2 7 12 32	36 43 20	Bolton Wanderers	30 12 1 2 43 21	1 5 9 13 34	56 55 32 1.0181
Bolton Wanderers	19 6 1 1 26 12	1 4 6 10 19	36 31 19	Burnley	30 10 2 3 37 15	3 2 10 14 29	51 44 30 1.1590
1893/94							
Aston Villa	22 9 1 0 36 6	5 3 4 22 22	58 28 32	Aston Villa	30 12 2 1 49 13	7 4 4 35 29	84 42 44 2.0000
Burnley	20 10 0 0 31 6	2 2 6 15 27	46 33 26	Sunderland	30 11 3 1 46 14	6 1 8 26 30	72 44 38 1.6363
Wolverhampton Wan.	21 9 1 2 29 19	3 1 5 11 21	40 40 26	Derby County	30 9 2 4 47 32	7 2 6 26 30	73 62 36 1.1774
Blackburn Rovers	19 8 0 1 26 11	3 2 5 14 21	40 32 24	Blackburn Rovers	30 13 0 2 48 15	3 2 10 21 38	69 53 34 1.3018
West Bromwich Alb.	22 5 4 2 27 20	5 0 6 26 27	53 47 24	Burnley	30 13 0 2 43 17	2 4 9 18 34	61 51 34 1.1960
Nottingham Forest	18 6 2 2 24 19	3 1 4 14 16	38 25 21	Everton	30 11 1 3 63 23	4 2 9 27 34	90 57 33 1.5789
1894/95							
Aston Villa	20 9 0 1 36 7	4 1 5 18 16	54 23 27	Sunderland	30 13 2 0 51 14	8 3 4 29 23	80 37 47 2.1621
Everton	16 7 1 0 28 7	5 2 1 24 16	52 23 27	Everton	30 12 2 1 47 18	6 4 5 35 32	82 50 42 1.6400
Sunderland	17 9 0 0 36 6	3 2 3 11 12	47 18 26	Aston Villa	30 12 2 1 51 12	5 3 7 31 31	82 43 39 1.9069
Blackburn Rovers	20 7 3 1 26 13	2 2 5 13 21	39 34 23	Preston North End	30 9 3 3 32 14	6 2 7 30 32	62 46 35 1.3478
Preston North End	20 5 2 2 15 9	4 2 5 18 20	33 29 22	Blackburn Rovers	30 9 5 1 40 15	2 5 8 19 34	59 49 32 1.2040
Burnley	19 6 1 2 19 11	3 2 5 13 14	32 25 21	Sheffield United	30 10 2 3 33 17	4 2 9 24 38	57 55 32 1.0363
1895/96							
Derby County	18 10 0 0 37 8	3 2 3 16 14	53 22 28	Aston Villa	30 14 1 0 47 17	6 4 5 31 28	78 45 45 1.7333
Everton	19 8 2 1 31 12	4 1 3 17 13	48 25 27	Derby County	30 12 2 1 42 13	5 5 5 26 22	68 35 41 1.9428
Aston Villa	19 9 1 0 32 12	3 2 4 17 17	49 29 27	Everton	30 10 4 1 40 17	6 3 6 26 26	66 43 39 1.5348
Stoke City	21 9 0 1 32 7	3 0 8 9 22	41 29 24	Bolton Wanderers	30 12 2 1 34 14	4 3 8 15 23	49 37 37 1.3243
Sunderland	18 5 3 0 15 8	3 2 5 11 14	26 22 21	Sunderland	30 10 5 0 36 14	5 2 8 16 27	52 41 37 1.2682
Bolton Wanderers	19 5 1 1 13 8	4 1 7 14 17	27 25 20	Stoke	30 12 0 3 43 11	3 0 12 13 36	56 47 30 1.1914
1896/97							
Aston Villa	17 5 2 1 17 9	6 2 1 22 12	39 21 26	Aston Villa	30 10 3 2 36 16	11 2 2 37 22	73 38 47 1.9210
Bolton Wanderers	17 5 2 0 14 3	4 2 4 14 13	28 16 22	Sheffield United	30 6 4 5 22 16	7 6 2 20 13	42 29 36 1.4482
Derby County	18 8 1 2 40 18	1 2 4 7 12	47 30 21	Derby County	30 10 2 3 45 22	6 2 7 25 28	70 50 36 1.4000
Liverpool	20 5 3 1 18 6	3 2 6 14 20	32 26 21	Preston North End	30 8 4 3 35 21	3 8 4 20 19	55 40 34 1.3750
Sheffield United	15 4 4 1 12 6	3 2 1 10 7	22 13 20	Liverpool	30 7 6 2 25 10	5 3 7 21 28	46 38 33 1.2105
Preston North End	16 6 2 1 25 15	1 4 2 10 9	35 24 20	Sheffield Wed.	30 9 4 2 29 11	1 7 7 13 26	42 37 31 1.1351
1897/98							
Aston Villa	19 9 0 0 34 15	1 4 5 10 18	44 33 24	Sheffield United	30 9 4 2 27 14	8 4 3 29 17	56 31 42 1.8064
Sheffield United	17 4 3 1 17 12	4 4 1 18 10	35 22 23	Sunderland	30 12 2 1 27 8	4 3 8 16 22	43 30 37 1.4333
Wolverhampton Wan.	19 6 4 1 22 10	2 2 4 11 14	33 24 22	Wolverhampton Wan.	30 10 4 1 36 14	4 3 8 21 27	57 41 35 1.3902
West Bromwich Alb.	18 6 4 0 18 8	2 2 4 12 17	30 25 22	Everton	30 11 3 1 33 12	2 6 7 15 27	48 39 35 1.2307
Sheffield Wed.	18 8 0 2 26 7	1 3 4 7 13	33 20 21	Sheffield Wed.	30 12 0 3 39 15	3 3 9 12 27	51 42 33 1.2142
Everton	16 6 1 1 19 8	2 3 3 9 16	28 24 20	Aston Villa	30 12 1 2 47 21	2 4 9 14 30	61 51 33 1.1960
1898/99							
Aston Villa	18 9 2 0 30 8	3 1 3 10 9	40 17 27	Aston Villa	34 15 2 0 58 13	4 5 8 18 27	76 40 45 1.9000
Everton	20 9 0 2 19 5	2 4 3 11 15	30 20 26	Liverpool	34 12 3 2 29 10	7 2 8 20 23	49 33 43 1.4848
Burnley	20 7 2 1 24 11	3 4 3 11 15	35 26 26	Burnley	34 11 5 1 32 15	4 4 9 13 32	45 47 39 0.9574
Notts County	19 5 5 1 25 16	2 4 2 6 7	31 23 23	Everton	34 10 2 5 25 13	5 6 6 23 28	48 41 38 1.1707
Liverpool	20 5 2 1 14 7	5 1 6 15 15	29 22 23	Notts County	34 9 6 2 33 20	3 7 7 14 31	47 51 37 0.9215
Bury	19 5 3 1 18 9	4 1 5 10 17	28 26 22	Blackburn Rovers	34 9 5 3 41 23	5 3 9 19 29	60 52 36 1.1538
1899/1900							
Sheffield United	21 8 3 0 29 6	6 4 0 15 9	44 15 35	Aston Villa	34 12 4 1 45 18	10 2 5 32 17	77 35 50 2.2000
Aston Villa	20 8 2 1 30 11	5 1 3 18 10	48 21 29	Sheffield United	34 11 5 1 40 11	7 7 3 23 22	63 33 48 1.9090
Wolverhampton Wan.	18 5 1 2 15 7	4 4 2 11 11	26 18 23	Sunderland	34 12 4 1 45 18	10 2 5 32 17	77 35 50 2.2000
Wolverhampton Wan.	18 5 1 2 15 7	4 4 2 11 11	26 18 23	Sunderland	34 12 3 2 27 9	7 1 9 23 26	50 35 41 1.4285
Sunderland	18 5 1 1 13 3	5 1 5 16 15	29 18 22	Wolverhampton Wan.	34 8 5 4 28 16	7 5 5 20 21	48 37 39 1.2972
Stoke City	21 7 2 2 18 11	2 2 6 8 16	26 27 22	Newcastle United	34 10 5 2 34 15	3 5 9 19 28	53 43 36 1.2325
Bury	18 8 1 1 21 10	1 2 5 8 15	29 25 21	Derby County	34 11 2 4 32 15	3 6 8 13 28	45 43 36 1.0465

164

1900/01																														
Nottingham Forest	20	8	3	1	23	7	3	2	3	12	7	35	14	27	Liverpool	34	12	2	3	36	13	7	5	5	23	22	59	35	45	1.6857
Aston Villa	22	7	3	2	28	12	2	4	4	11	16	39	28	25	Sunderland	34	12	3	2	43	11	3	10	4	14	15	57	26	43	2.1923
Newcastle United	18	6	2	0	13	5	3	4	3	11	12	24	17	24	Notts County	34	13	2	2	39	18	5	2	10	15	28	54	46	40	1.1739
Bury	19	7	2	1	22	5	2	3	4	12	14	34	19	23	Nottingham Forest	34	10	4	3	32	14	6	3	8	21	22	53	36	39	1.4722
Notts County	21	7	1	1	19	9	3	2	7	10	22	29	31	23	Bury	34	11	3	3	31	10	5	4	8	22	27	53	37	39	1.4324
Sunderland	18	5	3	1	17	5	2	5	2	9	10	26	15	22	Newcastle United	34	10	5	2	27	13	4	5	8	15	24	42	37	38	1.1351
1901/02																														
Aston Villa	19	7	3	1	20	7	3	1	4	8	6	28	13	24	Sunderland	34	12	3	2	32	14	7	3	7	18	21	50	35	44	1.4285
Everton	19	7	2	1	22	7	3	2	4	14	17	36	24	24	Everton	34	11	2	4	31	11	6	5	6	22	24	53	35	41	1.5142
Sunderland	18	6	1	1	17	9	4	3	3	12	14	29	23	24	Newcastle United	34	11	3	3	41	14	3	6	8	7	20	48	34	37	1.4117
Wolverhampton Wan.	20	7	3	0	19	6	1	2	7	9	26	28	32	21	Blackburn Rovers	34	12	2	3	36	16	3	4	10	16	32	52	48	36	1.0833
Derby County	16	6	3	0	15	5	1	3	3	4	9	19	14	20	Nottingham Forest	34	11	4	2	32	13	2	5	10	11	30	43	43	35	1.0000
Bury	17	5	2	0	14	3	2	3	5	11	16	25	19	19	Derby County	34	11	5	1	26	10	2	4	11	13	31	39	41	35	0.9512
1902/03																														
Sheffield United	19	6	0	4	20	13	5	2	2	12	8	32	21	24	Sheffield Wed.	34	12	3	2	31	7	7	1	9	23	29	54	36	42	1.5000
West Bromwich Alb.	18	7	0	2	23	12	4	2	3	12	11	35	23	24	Aston Villa	34	11	3	3	43	18	8	0	9	18	22	61	40	41	1.5250
Derby County	18	8	1	0	24	7	3	1	5	10	16	34	23	24	Sunderland	34	10	5	2	27	11	6	4	7	24	25	51	36	41	1.4166
Notts County	19	5	4	1	12	7	4	2	3	10	14	22	21	24	Sheffield United	34	11	0	6	36	22	6	5	6	22	22	58	44	39	1.3181
Sheffield Wed.	19	5	1	2	12	4	6	0	5	19	19	31	23	23	Liverpool	34	11	3	3	48	21	6	1	10	20	28	68	49	38	1.3877
Liverpool	18	7	1	1	35	12	3	1	5	11	16	46	28	22	Stoke	34	11	2	4	29	11	4	5	8	17	27	46	38	37	1.2105
1903/04																														
Sheffield United	19	7	3	1	32	17	5	1	2	13	11	45	28	28	Sheffield Wed.	34	14	3	0	34	10	6	4	7	14	18	48	28	47	1.7142
Aston Villa	19	8	0	1	24	8	2	4	4	18	22	42	30	24	Manchester City	34	10	4	3	35	19	9	2	6	36	26	71	45	44	1.5777
Manchester City	18	6	1	2	19	12	5	1	3	18	15	37	27	24	Everton	34	13	0	4	36	12	6	5	6	23	20	59	32	43	1.8437
Sheffield Wed.	17	5	2	0	11	4	3	4	3	10	10	21	14	22	Newcastle United	34	12	3	2	31	13	6	3	8	27	32	58	45	42	1.2888
Sunderland	18	7	1	1	23	7	3	1	5	13	21	36	28	22	Aston Villa	34	13	1	3	41	16	4	6	7	29	32	70	48	41	1.4583
Wolverhampton Wan.	18	7	2	0	16	8	3	0	6	11	25	27	33	22	Sunderland	34	12	3	2	41	15	5	2	10	22	34	63	49	39	1.2857
1904/05																														
Sheffield United	21	9	0	1	26	10	4	2	5	17	23	43	33	28	Newcastle United	34	14	1	2	41	12	9	1	7	31	21	72	33	48	2.1818
Everton	20	7	2	1	22	7	5	1	4	18	15	40	22	27	Everton	34	14	2	1	36	11	7	3	7	27	25	63	36	47	1.7500
Newcastle United	18	7	1	0	22	6	5	1	4	15	10	37	16	26	Manchester City	34	14	3	0	46	17	6	3	8	20	20	66	37	46	1.7837
Sunderland	20	8	1	1	26	11	2	3	5	11	17	37	28	24	Aston Villa	34	11	2	4	32	15	8	2	7	31	28	63	43	42	1.4651
Birmingham City	18	7	0	2	20	9	4	1	4	13	12	33	21	23	Sunderland	34	11	3	3	37	19	5	5	7	23	25	60	44	40	1.3636
Aston Villa	21	7	2	3	20	11	3	1	5	16	17	36	28	23	Sheffield United	34	13	0	4	39	20	6	2	9	25	36	64	56	40	1.1428
1905/06																														
Liverpool	21	8	2	1	29	9	5	0	5	19	22	48	31	28	Liverpool	38	14	3	2	49	15	9	2	8	30	31	79	46	51	1.7173
Aston Villa	22	10	1	2	36	10	2	2	5	6	13	42	23	27	Preston North End	38	12	5	2	36	15	5	8	6	18	24	54	39	47	1.3846
Sheffield Wed.	22	8	1	2	23	10	4	2	5	11	15	34	25	27	Sheffield Wed.	38	12	5	2	40	20	6	3	10	23	32	63	52	44	1.2115
Preston North End	21	7	4	1	22	10	1	5	3	9	13	31	23	25	Newcastle United	38	12	4	3	49	23	6	3	10	25	25	74	48	43	1.5416
Newcastle United	21	7	3	3	31	18	3	1	4	15	13	46	31	24	Manchester City	38	11	2	6	46	23	8	3	8	27	31	73	54	43	1.3518
Birmingham City	21	8	1	0	27	3	2	3	7	9	25	36	28	24	Bolton Wanderers	38	13	1	5	51	22	4	6	9	30	45	81	67	41	1.2089
1906/07																														
Everton	22	10	1	1	36	8	4	1	5	12	15	48	23	30	Newcastle United	38	18	1	0	51	12	4	6	9	23	34	74	46	51	1.6086
Newcastle United	20	8	0	0	24	7	4	4	4	17	17	41	24	28	Bristol City	38	12	3	4	37	18	8	5	6	29	29	66	47	48	1.4042
Arsenal	20	8	1	1	21	8	4	2	4	19	20	40	28	27	Everton	38	16	2	1	50	10	4	3	12	20	36	70	46	45	1.5217
Aston Villa	22	8	2	1	29	12	4	1	6	15	20	44	32	27	Sheffield United	38	13	4	2	36	17	4	7	8	21	38	57	55	45	1.0363
Bristol City	21	6	2	2	21	10	3	4	4	16	19	37	29	24	Aston Villa	38	13	4	2	51	19	6	2	11	27	33	78	52	44	1.5000
Sheffield Wed.	20	6	3	2	24	14	2	5	2	10	13	34	27	24	Bolton Wanderers	38	10	4	5	35	18	8	4	7	24	29	59	47	44	1.2553
1907/08																														
Manchester United	20	10	0	0	29	11	6	2	2	27	13	56	24	34	Manchester United	38	15	1	3	43	19	8	5	6	38	29	81	48	52	1.6875
Sheffield Wed.	21	9	0	3	35	17	3	2	4	13	14	48	31	26	Aston Villa	38	9	6	4	47	24	8	3	8	30	35	77	59	43	1.3050
Newcastle United	21	6	2	2	25	12	4	3	4	19	18	44	30	25	Manchester City	38	12	5	2	36	19	4	6	9	26	35	62	54	43	1.1481
Bury	21	5	2	2	15	10	4	4	4	21	22	36	32	24	Newcastle United	38	11	4	4	41	24	4	8	7	24	30	65	54	42	1.2037
Bristol City	21	5	4	1	17	11	3	3	5	21	25	38	36	23	Sheffield Wed.	38	14	0	5	50	25	5	4	10	23	39	73	64	42	1.1406
Everton	20	5	3	1	21	12	4	1	6	18	20	39	32	22	Middlesbrough	38	12	2	5	32	16	5	5	9	22	29	54	45	41	1.2000
1908/09																														
Everton	20	6	1	3	25	15	7	3	0	23	8	48	23	30	Newcastle United	38	14	1	4	32	20	10	4	5	33	21	65	41	53	1.5853
Newcastle United	20	9	0	2	18	14	3	3	3	13	11	31	25	27	Everton	38	11	3	5	51	28	7	7	5	31	29	82	57	46	1.4385
Manchester United	19	8	1	1	25	13	4	1	4	16	18	41	31	26	Sunderland	38	14	0	5	41	23	7	2	10	37	40	78	63	44	1.2380
Sheffield Wed.	20	9	0	1	26	11	1	5	4	12	17	38	28	25	Blackburn Rovers	38	6	6	7	29	26	8	7	4	32	24	61	50	41	1.2200
Bristol City	20	4	3	2	11	10	4	3	4	12	15	23	25	22	Sheffield Wed.	38	15	0	4	48	24	2	6	11	19	37	67	61	40	1.0983
Aston Villa	19	3	6	1	14	10	4	1	4	13	13	27	23	21	Woolwich Arsenal	38	9	3	7	24	18	5	7	7	28	31	52	49	38	1.0612
1909/10																														
Bradford City	19	8	0	1	23	7	4	3	3	20	15	43	22	27	Aston Villa	38	17	2	0	62	19	6	5	8	22	23	84	42	53	2.0000
Sheffield United	21	6	3	2	28	12	5	2	3	15	12	43	24	27	Liverpool	38	13	3	3	47	23	8	3	8	31	34	78	57	48	1.3684
Blackburn Rovers	20	7	3	0	28	9	4	2	4	18	17	46	26	27	Blackburn Rovers	38	13	6	0	47	17	5	3	11	26	38	73	55	45	1.3272
Notts County	22	7	3	1	25	13	3	3	5	17	19	42	32	26	Newcastle United	38	11	3	5	33	22	8	4	7	37	34	70	56	45	1.2500
Aston Villa	19	8	2	0	25	9	3	1	5	10	12	35	21	25	Manchester United	38	14	2	3	41	20	5	5	9	28	41	69	61	45	1.1311
Liverpool	20	6	2	1	23	15	5	1	5	18	19	41	34	25	Sheffield United	38	10	5	4	42	19	6	5	8	20	22	62	41	42	1.5121
1910/11																														
Aston Villa	20	7	3	0	26	10	5	1	4	13	14	39	24	28	Manchester United	38	14	4	1	47	18	8	4	7	25	22	72	40	52	1.8000
Manchester United	21	7	1	1	21	9	6	1	5	16	14	37	23	28	Aston Villa	38	15	3	1	50	18	7	4	8	19	23	69	41	51	1.6829
Everton	21	9	0	3	22	8	3	2	4	7	10	29	18	26	Sunderland	38	10	6	3	44	22	5	9	5	23	26	67	48	45	1.3958
Sunderland	20	6	3	2	23	13	3	5	1	11	9	34	22	26	Everton	38	12	3	4	34	17	7	4	8	16	19	50	36	45	1.3888
Bradford City	20	7	1	3	21	12	4	2	3	12	16	33	28	25	Bradford City	38	13	1	5	33	16	7	4	8	18	26	51	42	45	1.2142
Middlesbrough	20	7	2	0	19	6	2	5	4	11	21	30	27	25	Sheffield Wed.	38	10	5	4	24	15	7	3	9	23	33	47	48	42	0.9791
1911/12																														
Newcastle United	21	7	2	2	28	17	6	1	3	15	12	43	29	29	Blackburn Rovers	38	13	6	0	35	10	7	3	9	25	33	60	43	49	1.3953
Blackburn Rovers	21	6	4	0	18	6	4	1	6	12	19	30	25	25	Everton	38	13	5	1	29	12	7	1	11	17	30	46	42	46	1.0952
Everton	21	7	2	0	12	4	4	1	7	10	16	22	20	25	Newcastle United	38	10	4	5	37	25	8	4	7	27	25	64	50	44	1.2800
Manchester United	20	5	3	3	17	12	4	3	2	12	10	29	22	24	Bolton Wanderers	38	14	2	3	35	15	6	1	12	19	28	54	43	43	1.2558
Bradford City	21	7	0	2	16	7	3	4	5	11	16	27	23	24	Sheffield Wed.	38	11	3	5	44	17	5	6	8	25	32	69	49	41	1.4081
Middlesbrough	20	7	4	0	23	11	2	1	6	10	14	33	25	23	Aston Villa	38	12	2	5	48	22	5	5	9	28	41	76	63	41	1.2063

1912/13

West Bromwich Alb.	20	6	2	3	19	12	5	3	1	19	11	38	23	27
Sheffield Wed.	20	8	1	2	22	10	4	2	3	13	18	35	28	27
Aston Villa	21	8	1	1	41	12	2	5	4	16	18	57	30	26
Derby County	20	5	1	4	21	16	6	2	2	16	14	37	30	25
Oldham Athletic	19	7	2	0	20	4	2	5	3	10	21	30	25	25
Bolton Wanderers	20	6	2	1	16	8	5	1	5	14	19	30	27	25

Sunderland	38	14	2	3	47	17	11	2	6	39	26	86	43	54	2.0000
Aston Villa	38	13	4	2	57	21	6	8	5	29	31	86	52	50	1.6538
Sheffield Wed.	38	12	4	3	44	23	9	3	7	31	32	75	55	49	1.3636
Manchester United	38	13	3	3	41	14	6	5	8	28	29	69	43	46	1.6046
Blackburn Rovers	38	10	5	4	54	21	6	8	5	25	22	79	43	45	1.8372
Manchester City	38	12	3	4	34	15	6	5	8	19	22	53	37	44	1.4324

1913/14

Blackburn Rovers	21	8	1	1	35	7	4	4	3	21	17	56	24	29
Sunderland	21	4	3	2	12	8	6	3	3	26	17	38	25	26
Manchester United	20	6	2	3	22	11	6	0	3	12	12	34	23	26
Oldham Athletic	20	5	2	3	17	10	5	2	3	14	16	31	26	24
Bradford City	20	5	3	2	14	8	2	6	2	9	9	23	17	23
West Bromwich Alb.	20	4	5	0	14	7	3	4	4	9	12	23	19	23

Blackburn Rovers	38	14	4	1	51	15	6	7	6	27	27	78	42	51	1.8571
Aston Villa	38	11	3	5	36	21	8	3	8	29	29	65	50	44	1.3000
Middlesbrough	38	14	2	3	55	20	5	3	11	22	40	77	60	43	1.2833
Oldham Athletic	38	11	5	3	34	16	6	4	9	21	29	55	45	43	1.2222
West Bromwich Alb.	38	11	7	1	30	16	4	6	9	16	26	46	42	43	1.0952
Bolton Wanderers	38	13	4	2	41	14	3	6	10	24	38	65	52	42	1.2500

1914/15

Oldham Athletic	19	7	2	0	32	13	5	3	2	16	16	48	29	29
Manchester City	19	5	4	1	15	9	5	2	2	11	8	26	17	26
Everton	20	5	2	2	25	13	5	3	3	15	7	40	20	25
Blackburn Rovers	20	6	1	3	27	15	5	2	3	19	14	46	29	25
Sheffield Wed.	20	6	2	2	26	16	4	3	3	13	16	39	32	25
Bradford City	20	6	3	1	26	11	2	4	4	13	16	39	27	23

Everton	38	8	5	6	44	29	11	3	5	32	18	76	47	46	1.6170
Oldham Athletic	38	11	5	3	46	25	6	6	7	24	31	70	56	45	1.2500
Blackburn Rovers	38	11	4	4	51	27	7	3	9	32	34	83	61	43	1.3606
Burnley	38	12	1	6	38	18	6	6	7	23	29	61	47	43	1.2978
Manchester City	38	9	7	3	29	15	6	6	7	20	24	49	39	43	1.2564
Sheffield United	38	11	5	3	28	13	4	8	7	21	28	49	41	43	1.1951

1919/20

West Bromwich Alb.	21	9	0	2	37	11	7	0	3	24	14	61	25	32
Burnley	23	6	3	3	25	23	7	2	2	12	7	37	30	31
Newcastle United	22	7	3	2	20	8	4	2	4	9	12	29	20	27
Sunderland	22	8	1	1	21	10	4	1	7	17	21	38	31	26
Chelsea	22	8	1	2	19	4	3	2	6	14	23	33	27	25
Bolton Wanderers	23	5	3	3	22	14	4	4	4	20	21	42	35	25

West Bromwich Alb.	42	17	1	3	65	21	11	3	7	39	26	104	47	60	2.2127
Burnley	42	13	5	3	43	27	8	4	9	22	32	65	59	51	1.1016
Chelsea	42	15	3	3	33	10	7	2	12	23	41	56	51	49	1.0980
Liverpool	42	12	5	4	35	18	7	5	9	24	26	59	44	48	1.3409
Sunderland	42	17	2	2	45	16	5	2	14	27	43	72	59	48	1.2203
Bolton Wanderers	42	11	3	7	35	29	8	6	7	37	36	72	65	47	1.1076

1920/21

Burnley	21	10	0	1	32	7	3	5	2	11	10	43	17	31
Bolton Wanderers	22	9	2	0	34	9	1	5	5	10	19	44	28	27
Liverpool	21	6	3	2	24	10	4	3	3	14	11	38	21	26
Newcastle United	21	7	2	1	24	9	4	2	5	12	13	36	22	26
Manchester City	21	8	2	0	23	7	3	2	6	12	20	35	27	26
Middlesbrough	21	7	2	1	17	6	4	2	5	16	21	33	27	26

Burnley	42	17	3	1	56	16	6	10	5	23	20	79	36	59	2.1944
Manchester City	42	19	2	0	50	13	5	4	12	20	37	70	50	54	1.4000
Bolton Wanderers	42	15	6	0	53	17	4	8	9	24	36	77	53	52	1.4528
Liverpool	42	11	7	3	41	17	7	8	6	22	18	63	35	51	1.8000
Newcastle United	42	14	3	4	43	18	6	7	8	23	27	66	45	50	1.4666
Tottenham Hotspur	42	15	2	4	46	16	4	7	10	24	32	70	48	47	1.4583

1921/22

Liverpool	23	8	4	0	24	8	3	6	2	8	10	32	18	32
Burnley	23	11	1	0	32	9	4	1	6	16	19	48	28	32
Aston Villa	24	9	2	1	34	12	4	0	8	15	22	49	34	28
Bolton Wanderers	22	5	3	2	20	11	5	3	4	16	18	36	29	26
Tottenham Hotspur	23	6	3	3	25	13	4	2	5	12	9	37	22	25
Huddersfield Town	23	7	1	3	16	6	3	4	5	14	17	30	23	25

Liverpool	42	15	4	2	43	15	7	9	5	20	21	63	36	57	1.7500
Tottenham Hotspur	42	15	3	3	43	17	6	6	9	22	22	65	39	51	1.6666
Burnley	42	16	3	2	49	18	6	2	13	23	36	72	54	49	1.3333
Cardiff City	42	13	2	6	40	26	6	8	7	21	27	61	53	48	1.1509
Aston Villa	42	16	3	2	50	19	6	0	15	24	36	74	55	47	1.3454
Bolton Wanderers	42	12	4	5	40	24	8	3	10	28	35	68	59	47	1.1525

1922/23

Liverpool	23	9	1	1	33	11	7	1	4	15	11	48	22	34
Sunderland	22	8	3	0	29	15	4	4	3	17	17	46	32	31
Huddersfield Town	23	7	1	3	18	7	4	6	2	16	11	34	18	29
Middlesbrough	23	8	4	0	29	13	2	5	4	10	16	39	29	29
Manchester City	23	9	2	1	27	14	2	4	5	6	15	33	29	28
Sheffield United	24	7	5	1	22	11	3	2	6	12	19	34	30	27

Liverpool	42	17	3	1	50	13	9	5	7	20	18	70	31	60	2.2580
Sunderland	42	15	5	1	50	25	7	5	9	22	29	72	54	54	1.3333
Huddersfield Town	42	14	2	5	35	15	7	9	5	25	17	60	32	53	1.8750
Newcastle United	42	13	6	2	31	11	5	6	10	14	26	45	37	48	1.2162
Everton	42	14	4	3	41	20	6	3	12	22	39	63	59	47	1.0677
Aston Villa	42	15	3	3	42	11	3	7	11	22	40	64	51	46	1.2549

1923/24

Cardiff City	23	8	3	0	22	8	5	5	2	19	13	41	21	34
Bolton Wanderers	25	8	3	1	30	10	3	7	3	15	9	45	19	32
Huddersfield Town	23	9	2	0	23	5	4	2	6	15	16	38	21	30
Aston Villa	25	4	9	0	18	7	5	2	5	11	13	29	20	29
Sunderland	23	7	4	1	24	14	5	1	5	17	17	41	31	29
Blackburn Rovers	23	9	1	2	24	7	2	4	5	13	21	37	28	27

Huddersfield Town	42	15	5	1	35	9	8	6	7	25	24	60	33	57	1.8181
Cardiff City	42	14	5	2	35	13	8	8	5	26	21	61	34	57	1.7941
Sunderland	42	12	7	2	38	20	10	2	9	33	34	71	54	53	1.3148
Bolton Wanderers	42	13	6	2	45	13	5	8	8	23	21	68	34	50	2.0000
Sheffield United	42	12	5	4	39	16	7	7	7	30	33	69	49	50	1.4081
Aston Villa	42	10	10	1	33	11	8	3	10	19	26	52	37	49	1.4054

1924/25

West Bromwich Alb.	23	8	2	1	25	9	6	2	4	11	8	36	17	32
Huddersfield Town	23	6	3	2	17	4	5	5	2	19	11	36	15	30
Bolton Wanderers	22	8	2	1	29	10	2	6	3	11	14	40	24	28
Birmingham City	23	7	3	2	17	11	4	3	4	9	15	26	26	28
Newcastle United	24	5	5	2	24	12	2	7	3	9	12	33	24	26
Liverpool	22	7	3	2	25	14	3	3	4	11	15	36	29	26

Huddersfield Town	42	10	8	3	31	10	11	8	2	38	18	69	28	58	2.4642
West Bromwich Alb.	42	13	6	2	40	17	10	4	7	18	17	58	34	56	1.7058
Bolton Wanderers	42	18	2	1	61	13	4	9	8	15	21	76	34	55	2.2352
Liverpool	42	13	5	3	43	20	7	5	9	20	35	63	55	50	1.1454
Bury	42	13	4	4	35	20	4	11	6	19	31	54	51	49	1.0588
Newcastle United	42	11	6	4	43	18	5	10	6	18	24	61	42	48	1.4523

1925/26

Arsenal	23	8	2	2	33	12	5	2	4	19	24	52	36	30
Sunderland	23	10	1	0	39	14	2	4	6	15	26	54	40	29
Huddersfield Town	21	5	6	1	20	11	5	2	2	23	22	43	33	28
Manchester United	22	7	2	2	23	10	4	2	5	16	21	39	31	26
Tottenham Hotspur	23	7	2	2	30	22	4	2	6	15	25	45	47	26
West Bromwich Alb.	22	8	3	1	42	17	2	2	6	8	20	50	37	25

Huddersfield Town	42	14	6	1	50	17	9	5	7	42	43	92	60	57	1.5333
Arsenal	42	16	2	3	57	19	6	6	9	30	44	87	63	52	1.3809
Sunderland	42	17	2	2	67	30	4	4	13	29	50	96	80	48	1.2000
Bury	42	12	4	5	55	34	8	3	10	30	43	85	77	47	1.1038
Sheffield United	42	15	3	3	72	29	4	5	12	30	53	102	82	46	1.2439
Aston Villa	42	12	7	2	56	25	4	5	12	30	51	86	76	44	1.1315

1926/27

Burnley	23	9	3	0	35	14	3	3	5	23	23	58	37	30
Newcastle United	22	9	1	1	36	12	3	4	4	20	20	56	32	29
Sunderland	24	9	2	0	35	9	3	3	7	20	30	55	39	29
Huddersfield Town	22	7	3	1	28	13	1	8	2	17	21	45	34	27
Leicester City	22	7	2	2	35	19	3	4	4	18	23	53	42	26
Bolton Wanderers	22	8	3	0	27	9	2	2	7	18	22	45	31	25

Newcastle United	42	19	1	1	64	20	6	5	10	32	38	96	58	56	1.6551
Huddersfield Town	42	13	6	2	41	19	4	11	6	35	41	76	60	51	1.2666
Sunderland	42	15	3	3	70	28	6	4	11	28	42	98	70	49	1.4000
Bolton Wanderers	42	15	5	1	54	19	4	5	12	30	43	84	62	48	1.3548
Burnley	42	15	4	2	55	30	4	5	12	36	50	91	80	47	1.1375
West Ham United	42	9	6	6	50	36	10	2	9	36	34	86	70	46	1.2285

1927/28

Everton	23	7	4	1	39	13	6	2	3	24	19	63	32	32
Huddersfield Town	22	8	1	1	26	11	4	3	5	27	24	53	35	28
Leicester City	24	8	3	1	38	15	3	3	6	15	25	53	40	28
Arsenal	21	7	2	1	30	14	3	3	5	15	26	45	40	25
Cardiff City	23	6	4	1	21	13	3	3	6	20	29	41	42	25
Blackburn Rovers	23	6	5	0	19	8	2	4	6	13	27	32	35	25

Everton	42	11	8	2	60	28	9	5	7	42	38	102	66	53	1.5454
Huddersfield Town	42	15	1	5	57	31	7	6	8	34	37	91	68	51	1.3382
Leicester City	42	14	5	2	66	25	4	7	10	30	47	96	72	48	1.3333
Derby County	42	12	4	5	59	30	5	6	10	37	53	96	83	44	1.1566
Bury	42	13	1	7	53	35	7	3	11	27	45	80	80	44	1.0000
Cardiff City	42	12	7	2	44	27	5	3	13	26	53	70	80	44	0.8750

1928/29

Sheffield Wed.	23	11	1	0	31	10	3	4	4	18	21	49	31	33	Sheffield Wed.	42	18	3	0	55	16	3	7	11	31	46	86	62	52	1.3870
Blackburn Rovers	23	9	3	1	30	10	3	2	5	16	20	46	30	29	Leicester City	42	16	5	0	67	22	5	4	12	29	45	96	67	51	1.4328
Derby County	23	8	2	2	37	11	4	1	6	14	23	51	34	27	Aston Villa	42	16	2	3	62	30	7	2	12	36	51	98	81	50	1.2098
Sunderland	23	8	1	2	37	18	3	3	6	16	22	53	40	26	Sunderland	42	16	2	3	67	30	4	5	12	26	45	93	75	47	1.2400
Leicester City	23	8	4	0	42	15	2	2	7	14	29	56	44	26	Liverpool	42	11	4	6	53	28	6	8	7	37	36	90	64	46	1.4062
Aston Villa	22	8	2	2	30	15	4	0	6	21	28	51	43	26	Derby County	42	12	5	4	56	24	6	5	10	30	47	86	71	46	1.2112

1929/30

Sheffield Wed.	21	7	2	2	28	10	6	2	2	25	14	53	24	30	Sheffield Wed.	42	15	4	2	56	20	11	4	6	49	37	105	57	60	1.8421
Manchester City	22	7	2	1	25	12	6	2	4	29	25	54	37	30	Derby County	42	16	4	1	61	32	5	4	12	29	50	90	82	50	1.0975
Aston Villa	23	8	1	3	31	17	4	3	4	18	24	49	41	28	Manchester City	42	12	5	4	51	33	7	4	10	40	48	91	81	47	1.1234
Derby County	23	9	1	1	32	17	3	3	6	13	23	45	40	28	Aston Villa	42	13	1	7	54	33	8	4	9	38	50	92	83	47	1.1084
Leeds United	23	10	0	2	30	11	2	2	7	13	22	43	33	26	Leeds United	42	15	2	4	52	22	5	4	12	27	41	79	63	46	1.2539
Liverpool	23	8	2	3	24	17	3	2	5	15	26	39	43	26	Blackburn Rovers	42	15	2	4	65	36	4	5	12	34	57	99	93	45	1.0645

1930/31

Arsenal	22	7	2	1	33	15	8	3	1	35	17	68	32	35	Arsenal	42	14	5	2	67	27	14	5	2	60	32	127	59	66	2.1525
Sheffield Wed.	23	7	2	1	35	11	7	3	3	28	25	63	36	33	Aston Villa	42	17	3	1	86	34	8	6	7	42	44	128	78	59	1.6410
Aston Villa	23	8	3	1	46	21	4	3	4	21	26	67	47	30	Sheffield Wed.	42	14	3	4	65	32	8	5	8	37	43	102	75	52	1.3600
Derby County	23	7	5	1	31	15	4	2	4	22	21	53	36	29	Portsmouth	42	11	7	3	46	26	7	6	8	38	41	84	67	49	1.2537
Portsmouth	23	5	5	1	25	15	5	3	4	28	25	53	40	28	Huddersfield Town	42	10	8	3	45	27	8	4	9	36	38	81	65	48	1.2461
West Ham United	23	9	2	1	38	17	2	3	6	13	29	51	46	27	Derby County	42	12	6	3	56	31	6	4	11	38	48	94	79	46	1.1898

1931/32

Everton	22	9	0	1	51	15	6	1	5	27	24	78	39	31	Everton	42	18	0	3	84	30	8	4	9	32	34	116	64	56	1.8125
West Bromwich Alb.	23	6	3	2	24	7	5	2	5	19	17	43	24	27	Arsenal	42	14	5	2	52	16	8	5	8	38	32	90	48	54	1.8750
Aston Villa	21	9	0	2	40	17	2	4	4	19	20	59	37	26	Sheffield Wed.	42	14	4	3	60	28	8	2	11	36	54	96	82	50	1.1707
Arsenal	22	4	4	2	21	12	6	2	4	29	21	50	33	26	Huddersfield Town	42	11	8	2	47	21	8	2	11	33	42	80	63	48	1.2698
Sheffield United	22	7	1	3	30	17	5	1	5	23	21	53	38	26	Aston Villa	42	15	1	5	64	28	4	7	10	40	44	104	72	46	1.4444
Newcastle United	21	8	1	1	28	12	4	1	6	17	26	45	38	26	West Bromwich Alb.	42	12	4	5	46	21	8	2	11	31	34	77	55	46	1.4000

1932/33

Arsenal	23	9	1	2	45	18	8	2	1	27	15	72	33	37	Arsenal	42	14	3	4	70	27	11	5	5	48	34	118	61	58	1.9344
Aston Villa	23	10	0	2	40	19	3	6	2	18	17	58	36	32	Aston Villa	42	16	2	3	60	29	7	6	8	32	38	92	67	54	1.3731
Sheffield Wed.	23	10	2	0	30	12	4	2	5	23	23	53	35	32	Sheffield Wed.	42	15	5	1	46	20	6	4	11	34	48	80	68	51	1.1764
Newcastle United	22	8	2	2	27	16	5	1	4	16	11	43	27	29	West Bromwich Alb.	42	16	1	4	50	23	4	8	9	33	47	83	70	49	1.1857
Derby County	23	7	4	1	31	15	4	3	4	21	23	52	38	29	Newcastle United	42	15	2	4	44	24	7	3	11	27	39	71	63	49	1.1269
Leeds United	23	6	5	1	20	13	4	4	3	12	15	32	28	29	Huddersfield Town	42	11	6	4	32	17	7	5	9	34	36	66	53	47	1.2452

1933/34

Arsenal	23	8	3	0	26	6	6	3	3	15	14	41	20	34	Arsenal	42	15	4	2	45	19	10	5	6	30	28	75	47	59	1.5957
Derby County	22	8	3	0	29	9	4	3	4	14	14	43	23	30	Huddersfield Town	42	16	3	2	53	19	7	7	7	37	42	90	61	56	1.4754
Huddersfield Town	23	8	3	1	31	11	3	5	3	21	24	52	35	30	Tottenham Hotspur	42	14	3	4	51	24	7	4	10	28	32	79	56	49	1.4107
Tottenham Hotspur	23	8	1	3	30	16	4	3	4	12	10	42	26	28	Derby County	42	11	8	2	45	22	6	3	12	23	32	68	54	45	1.2592
Manchester City	23	7	2	2	21	11	3	5	4	11	22	32	33	27	Manchester City	42	14	4	3	50	29	3	7	11	15	43	65	72	45	0.9027
Portsmouth	23	6	4	2	15	8	3	3	5	14	16	29	24	25	Sunderland	42	14	6	1	57	17	2	6	13	24	39	81	56	44	1.4464

1934/35

Sunderland	23	7	1	4	33	16	6	4	1	23	14	56	30	31	Arsenal	42	15	4	2	74	17	8	8	5	41	29	115	46	58	2.5000
Manchester City	23	8	2	1	25	10	6	1	5	22	25	47	35	31	Sunderland	42	13	4	4	57	24	6	12	3	33	27	90	51	54	1.7647
Arsenal	23	10	1	1	53	12	1	6	4	17	20	70	32	29	Sheffield Wed.	42	14	7	0	42	17	4	6	11	28	47	70	64	49	1.0937
Stoke City	23	7	2	2	29	13	6	0	6	20	21	49	34	28	Manchester City	42	13	5	3	53	25	7	3	11	29	42	82	67	48	1.2238
Liverpool	22	8	2	1	29	15	4	1	6	16	33	45	48	27	Grimsby Town	42	13	6	2	49	25	4	5	12	29	35	78	60	45	1.3000
Grimsby Town	23	8	4	0	29	11	2	2	7	17	21	46	32	26	Derby County	42	10	4	7	44	28	8	5	8	37	38	81	66	45	1.2272

1935/36

Sunderland	22	11	0	0	45	15	5	2	4	23	20	68	35	34	Sunderland	42	17	2	2	71	33	8	4	9	38	41	109	74	56	1.4729
Derby County	23	9	3	0	28	10	1	4	6	5	15	33	25	27	Derby County	42	13	5	3	43	23	5	7	9	18	29	61	52	48	1.1730
Huddersfield Town	22	7	3	0	15	3	4	2	6	18	29	33	32	27	Huddersfield Town	42	12	7	2	32	15	6	5	10	27	41	59	56	48	1.0535
Arsenal	22	6	2	2	28	11	4	4	4	22	14	50	25	26	Stoke City	42	13	3	5	35	24	7	4	10	22	33	57	57	47	1.0000
Birmingham City	23	6	4	1	22	14	3	3	6	12	19	34	33	25	Brentford	42	11	5	5	48	25	6	7	8	33	35	81	60	46	1.3500
Stoke City	23	6	2	3	18	11	5	1	6	17	23	35	34	25	Arsenal	42	9	9	3	44	22	6	6	9	34	26	78	48	45	1.6250

1936/37

Arsenal	22	6	4	1	29	16	5	2	4	19	14	48	30	28	Manchester City	42	15	5	1	56	22	7	8	6	51	39	107	61	57	1.7540
Sunderland	22	11	0	0	33	9	2	2	7	16	29	49	38	28	Charlton Athletic	42	15	5	1	37	13	6	7	8	21	36	58	49	54	1.1836
Brentford	22	10	2	0	33	13	2	2	6	11	22	44	35	28	Arsenal	42	10	10	1	43	20	8	6	7	37	29	80	49	52	1.6326
Charlton Athletic	23	7	3	1	18	8	3	5	4	11	18	29	26	28	Derby County	42	13	3	5	58	39	8	4	9	38	51	96	90	49	1.0666
Derby County	23	7	1	4	31	22	4	3	4	20	25	51	47	26	Wolverhampton Wan.	42	16	2	3	63	24	5	3	13	21	43	84	67	47	1.2537
Huddersfield Town	23	9	2	1	30	9	0	5	6	13	22	43	31	25	Brentford	42	14	5	2	58	32	4	5	12	24	46	82	78	46	1.0512

1937/38

Brentford	23	7	2	2	25	15	5	3	4	14	16	39	31	29	Arsenal	42	15	4	2	52	16	6	6	9	25	28	77	44	52	1.7500
Leeds United	22	8	3	1	24	13	1	5	4	13	20	37	33	26	Wolverhampton Wan.	42	11	8	2	47	21	9	3	9	25	28	72	49	51	1.4693
Arsenal	22	7	2	1	25	9	3	3	6	16	17	41	26	25	Preston North End	42	9	9	3	34	21	7	8	6	30	23	64	44	49	1.4545
Wolverhampton Wan.	20	6	4	0	22	6	3	2	5	10	17	32	23	24	Charlton Athletic	42	14	5	2	43	14	2	9	10	22	37	65	51	46	1.2745
Preston North End	22	6	5	1	21	10	2	3	5	15	16	36	26	24	Middlesbrough	42	12	4	5	40	26	7	4	10	32	39	72	65	46	1.1076
Charlton Athletic	20	6	3	2	20	11	2	5	2	10	13	30	24	24	Brentford	42	10	6	5	44	27	8	3	10	25	32	69	59	45	1.1694

1938/39

Derby County	24	9	2	1	28	12	6	3	3	18	15	46	27	35	Everton	42	17	3	1	60	18	10	2	9	28	34	88	52	59	1.6923
Everton	23	10	1	1	35	10	4	1	6	11	16	46	26	30	Wolverhampton Wan.	42	14	6	1	55	12	8	5	8	33	27	88	39	55	2.2564
Wolverhampton Wan.	23	5	5	1	20	6	5	2	5	18	12	38	18	27	Charlton Athletic	42	16	3	2	49	24	6	3	12	26	35	75	59	50	1.2711
Liverpool	23	9	3	0	26	10	1	4	6	15	24	41	34	27	Middlesbrough	42	13	6	2	64	27	7	3	11	29	47	93	74	49	1.2567
Middlesbrough	23	7	4	1	35	14	3	2	6	16	23	51	37	26	Arsenal	42	14	3	4	34	14	5	6	10	21	27	55	41	47	1.3414
Charlton Athletic	22	8	2	1	21	13	3	2	6	11	15	32	28	26	Derby County	42	12	3	6	39	22	7	5	9	27	33	66	55	46	1.2000

1946/47

Wolverhampton Wan.	24	9	0	3	35	15	7	3	2	22	12	57	27	35	Liverpool	42	13	3	5	42	24	12	4	5	42	28	84	52	57	1.6153
Liverpool	23	7	2	3	26	16	6	2	3	27	17	53	33	30	Manchester United	42	17	3	1	61	19	5	9	7	34	35	95	54	56	1.7592
Blackpool	24	10	0	2	25	18	4	2	6	17	23	42	41	30	Wolverhampton Wan.	42	15	1	5	66	31	10	5	6	32	25	98	56	56	1.7500
Middlesbrough	22	7	2	2	28	17	5	3	3	20	13	48	30	29	Stoke City	42	14	5	2	52	21	10	2	9	38	32	90	53	55	1.6981
Preston North End	22	7	2	3	26	17	5	3	2	20	17	46	34	29	Blackpool	42	14	1	6	38	32	8	5	8	33	38	71	70	50	1.0142
Manchester United	22	8	2	1	29	12	2	5	4	18	18	47	30	27	Sheffield United	42	12	4	5	51	32	9	3	9	38	43	89	75	49	1.1866

1947/48

Arsenal	23	8	3	1	24	7	6	4	1	17	7	41	14	35	Arsenal	42	15	3	3	56	15	8	10	3	25	17	81	32	59	2.5312
Burnley	23	7	3	2	17	7	5	5	1	17	11	34	18	32	Manchester United	42	11	7	3	50	27	8	7	6	31	21	81	48	52	1.6875
Preston North End	24	8	3	1	27	18	5	1	6	14	19	41	37	30	Burnley	42	12	5	4	31	12	8	7	6	25	31	56	43	52	1.3023
Derby County	24	6	5	1	21	10	4	3	5	23	22	44	32	28	Derby County	42	11	6	4	38	24	8	6	7	39	33	77	57	50	1.3508
Wolverhampton Wan.	23	7	1	4	29	18	4	4	3	22	20	51	38	27	Wolverhampton Wan.	42	12	4	5	45	29	7	5	9	38	41	83	70	47	1.1857
Manchester United	23	5	4	2	26	18	3	6	3	21	14	47	32	26	Aston Villa	42	13	5	3	42	22	6	4	11	23	35	65	57	47	1.1403

1948/49

Portsmouth	24	10	3	0	31	8	3	5	3	14	13	45	21	34	Portsmouth	42	18	3	0	52	12	7	5	9	32	30	84	42	58	2.0000
Newcastle United	24	7	3	2	22	17	6	4	2	24	14	46	31	33	Manchester United	42	11	7	3	40	20	10	4	7	37	24	77	44	53	1.7500
Derby County	24	10	1	1	26	11	3	6	3	15	18	41	29	33	Derby County	42	17	2	2	48	22	5	7	9	26	33	74	55	53	1.3454
Manchester United	24	5	4	2	21	11	6	4	3	28	15	49	26	30	Newcastle United	42	12	5	4	35	29	8	7	6	35	27	70	56	52	1.2500
Stoke City	24	10	1	1	28	13	2	4	6	16	22	44	35	29	Arsenal	42	13	5	3	51	18	5	8	8	23	26	74	44	49	1.6818
Charlton Athletic	24	7	5	1	26	15	2	5	4	18	24	44	39	28	Wolverhampton Wan.	42	13	5	3	48	19	4	7	10	31	47	79	66	46	1.1969

1949/50

Liverpool	25	7	6	0	29	14	5	5	2	16	12	45	26	35	Portsmouth	42	12	7	2	44	15	10	2	9	30	23	74	38	53	1.9473
Manchester United	25	7	3	2	26	11	5	6	2	16	10	42	21	33	Wolverhampton Wan.	42	11	8	2	47	21	9	5	7	29	28	76	49	53	1.5510
Blackpool	24	7	5	1	22	10	4	4	3	11	10	33	20	31	Sunderland	42	14	6	1	50	23	7	4	10	33	39	83	62	52	1.3387
Wolverhampton Wan.	25	5	6	1	25	13	6	3	4	20	20	45	33	31	Manchester United	42	11	5	5	42	20	7	9	5	27	24	69	44	50	1.5681
Portsmouth	25	5	7	1	22	11	6	1	5	22	15	44	26	30	Newcastle United	42	14	4	3	49	23	5	8	8	28	32	77	55	50	1.4000
Burnley	26	6	5	2	17	10	5	3	5	10	15	27	25	30	Arsenal	42	12	4	5	48	24	7	7	7	31	31	79	55	49	1.4363

1950/51

Tottenham Hotspur	25	9	2	1	33	13	6	4	3	23	17	56	30	36	Tottenham Hotspur	42	17	2	2	54	21	8	8	5	28	23	82	44	60	1.8636
Middlesbrough	25	9	4	1	42	18	5	4	2	19	16	61	34	36	Manchester United	42	14	4	3	42	16	10	4	7	32	24	74	40	56	1.8500
Arsenal	26	8	3	2	36	16	6	2	5	15	13	51	29	33	Blackpool	42	12	6	3	43	19	8	4	9	36	34	79	53	50	1.4905
Wolverhampton Wan.	24	8	2	3	31	15	5	3	3	20	15	51	30	31	Newcastle United	42	10	6	5	36	22	8	7	6	26	31	62	53	49	1.1698
Newcastle United	24	7	3	1	28	13	5	4	4	15	21	43	34	31	Arsenal	42	11	5	5	47	28	8	4	9	26	28	73	56	47	1.3035
Burnley	25	6	6	1	20	8	3	4	5	13	18	33	26	28	Middlesbrough	42	12	7	2	51	25	6	4	11	25	40	76	65	47	1.1692

1951/52

Manchester United	26	9	1	3	30	17	5	5	3	28	22	58	39	34	Manchester United	42	15	3	3	55	21	8	8	5	40	31	95	52	57	1.8269
Portsmouth	25	8	2	3	26	18	6	3	3	19	18	45	36	33	Tottenham Hotspur	42	16	1	4	45	20	6	8	7	31	31	76	51	53	1.4901
Arsenal	26	8	4	1	33	19	5	2	6	18	18	51	37	32	Arsenal	42	13	7	1	54	30	8	4	9	26	31	80	61	53	1.3114
Preston North End	25	7	1	4	23	12	6	4	3	27	18	50	30	31	Portsmouth	42	13	3	5	42	25	7	5	9	26	33	68	58	48	1.1724
Newcastle United	25	7	3	2	35	13	5	3	5	29	31	64	44	30	Bolton Wanderers	42	11	7	3	35	26	8	3	10	30	35	65	61	48	1.0655
Tottenham Hotspur	26	9	1	3	28	17	4	3	6	21	24	49	41	30	Aston Villa	42	13	3	5	49	28	6	6	9	30	42	79	70	47	1.1285

1952/53

Wolverhampton Wan.	24	6	4	2	28	19	5	4	3	18	18	46	37	30	Arsenal	42	15	3	3	60	30	6	9	6	37	34	97	64	54	1.5156
West Bromwich Alb.	23	7	1	4	17	10	6	2	3	19	16	36	26	29	Preston North End	42	15	3	3	46	25	6	9	6	39	35	85	60	54	1.4166
Sunderland	23	8	2	1	21	12	4	3	5	19	24	40	36	29	Wolverhampton Wan.	42	13	5	3	54	27	6	8	7	32	36	86	63	51	1.3650
Arsenal	21	7	1	2	25	14	4	5	2	21	16	46	30	28	West Bromwich Alb.	42	13	3	5	35	19	8	5	8	31	41	66	60	50	1.1000
Burnley	23	6	4	2	17	12	4	4	3	17	15	34	27	28	Charlton Athletic	42	12	8	1	47	22	7	3	11	30	41	77	63	49	1.2222
Blackpool	23	7	3	2	29	15	4	2	5	19	24	48	39	27	Burnley	42	11	6	4	36	20	7	6	8	31	32	67	52	48	1.2884

1953/54

Wolverhampton Wan.	25	10	0	2	34	14	6	5	2	27	21	61	35	37	Wolverhampton Wan.	42	16	1	4	61	25	9	6	6	35	31	96	56	57	1.7142
West Bromwich Alb.	25	9	2	2	38	15	7	2	3	28	19	66	34	36	West Bromwich Alb.	42	13	5	3	51	24	9	4	8	35	39	86	63	53	1.3650
Huddersfield Town	25	9	4	0	30	10	4	3	5	15	17	45	27	33	Huddersfield Town	42	13	6	2	45	24	7	5	9	33	37	78	61	51	1.2786
Burnley	25	11	0	2	34	16	5	0	7	21	26	55	42	32	Manchester United	42	11	6	4	41	27	7	6	8	32	31	73	58	48	1.2586
Manchester United	25	6	5	2	27	17	3	5	4	19	18	46	35	28	Bolton Wanderers	42	14	6	1	45	20	4	6	11	30	40	75	60	48	1.2500
Bolton Wanderers	24	8	4	0	26	11	2	4	6	16	23	42	34	28	Blackpool	42	13	6	2	43	19	6	4	11	37	50	80	69	48	1.1594

1954/55

Sunderland	24	5	7	0	24	15	4	5	3	17	16	41	31	30	Chelsea	42	11	5	5	43	29	9	7	5	38	28	81	57	52	1.4210
Wolverhampton Wan.	24	8	2	3	36	19	3	5	3	18	18	54	37	29	Wolverhampton Wan.	42	13	5	3	58	30	6	5	10	31	40	89	70	48	1.2714
Charlton Athletic	24	7	1	4	30	19	6	2	4	24	20	54	39	29	Portsmouth	42	13	5	3	44	21	5	7	9	30	41	74	62	48	1.1935
Portsmouth	24	8	3	1	32	12	3	3	6	14	19	46	31	28	Sunderland	42	8	11	2	39	27	7	7	7	25	27	64	54	48	1.1851
Chelsea	25	6	3	4	28	21	4	5	3	18	16	46	37	28	Manchester United	42	12	4	5	44	30	8	3	10	40	44	84	74	47	1.1351
Huddersfield Town	24	6	2	3	18	12	4	6	3	25	24	43	36	28	Aston Villa	42	11	3	7	38	31	9	4	8	34	42	72	73	47	0.9863

1955/56

Manchester United	26	11	2	0	35	15	3	4	6	18	23	53	38	34	Manchester United	42	18	3	0	51	20	7	7	7	32	31	83	51	60	1.6274
Blackpool	25	9	2	2	36	19	3	4	5	15	21	51	40	30	Blackpool	42	13	4	4	56	27	7	5	9	30	35	86	62	49	1.3870
Luton Town	25	9	2	1	33	14	3	3	7	15	20	48	34	29	Wolverhampton Wan.	42	15	2	4	51	27	5	7	9	38	38	89	65	49	1.3692
Burnley	25	8	2	3	23	11	3	5	4	16	20	39	31	29	Manchester City	42	11	5	5	40	27	7	5	9	42	42	82	69	46	1.1884
Charlton Athletic	26	9	1	3	35	17	3	3	7	21	34	56	51	28	Arsenal	42	13	4	4	38	22	5	6	10	22	39	60	61	46	0.9836
Portsmouth	24	6	5	2	29	26	5	0	6	20	25	49	51	27	Birmingham City	42	12	4	5	51	26	6	5	10	24	31	75	57	45	1.3157

1956/57

Manchester United	23	9	1	1	32	16	7	3	2	25	18	57	34	36	Manchester United	42	14	4	3	55	25	14	4	3	48	29	103	54	64	1.9074
Tottenham Hotspur	24	9	3	0	42	10	5	3	4	23	22	65	32	34	Tottenham Hotspur	42	15	4	2	70	24	7	8	6	34	32	104	56	56	1.8571
Arsenal	26	8	2	3	30	12	6	2	5	26	31	56	43	32	Preston North End	42	15	4	2	50	19	8	6	7	34	37	84	56	56	1.5000
Leeds United	25	8	3	1	32	11	3	5	5	16	23	48	34	30	Blackpool	42	14	3	4	55	26	8	6	7	38	39	93	65	53	1.4307
Birmingham City	24	10	3	0	36	10	2	2	7	10	24	46	34	29	Arsenal	42	12	5	4	45	21	9	3	9	40	48	85	69	50	1.2318
Preston North End	25	7	3	2	30	15	4	4	5	22	28	52	43	29	Wolverhampton Wan.	42	17	2	2	70	29	3	6	12	24	41	94	70	48	1.3428

1957/58

Wolverhampton Wan.	25	11	1	0	36	10	6	4	3	24	18	60	28	39	Wolverhampton Wan.	42	17	3	1	60	21	11	5	5	43	26	103	47	64	2.1914
West Bromwich Alb.	25	8	4	1	38	17	3	7	2	22	24	60	41	33	Preston North End	42	18	2	1	63	14	8	5	8	37	37	100	51	59	1.9607
Preston North End	25	10	1	1	34	9	4	3	6	21	26	55	35	32	Tottenham Hotspur	42	13	4	4	58	33	8	5	8	35	44	93	77	51	1.2077
Manchester United	25	9	0	4	34	15	4	5	3	26	25	60	40	31	West Bromwich Alb.	42	14	4	3	59	29	4	10	7	33	41	92	70	50	1.3142
Manchester City	25	9	2	1	39	19	5	0	8	27	42	66	61	30	Manchester City	42	14	4	3	58	33	8	1	12	46	67	104	100	49	1.0400
Luton Town	25	9	2	2	29	12	4	1	7	12	24	41	36	29	Burnley	42	16	2	3	52	21	5	3	13	28	53	80	74	47	1.0810

1958/59

Wolverhampton Wan.	24	9	1	2	33	8	6	1	5	21	20	54	28	32	Wolverhampton Wan.	42	15	3	3	68	19	13	2	6	42	30	110	49	61	2.2448
West Bromwich Alb.	23	4	3	4	22	19	7	4	1	32	15	54	34	29	Manchester United	42	14	4	3	58	27	10	3	8	45	39	103	66	55	1.5606
Arsenal	25	9	1	3	36	19	4	2	6	22	22	58	41	29	Arsenal	42	14	3	4	53	29	7	5	9	35	39	88	68	50	1.2941
Manchester United	25	6	3	3	29	18	6	2	5	28	26	57	44	29	Bolton Wanderers	42	14	3	4	56	30	6	7	8	23	36	79	66	50	1.1969
Bolton Wanderers	24	8	1	3	29	16	3	6	3	15	19	44	35	29	West Bromwich Alb.	42	8	7	6	41	33	10	6	5	47	35	88	68	49	1.2941
Blackpool	24	5	7	0	19	8	4	3	5	17	18	36	26	28	West Ham United	42	15	3	3	59	29	6	3	12	26	41	85	70	48	1.2142

1959/60

Tottenham Hotspur	24	6	4	2	27	15	6	4	2	26	15	53	30	32	Burnley	42	15	2	4	52	28	9	5	7	33	33	85	61	55	1.3934
Preston North End	24	6	4	2	22	18	6	3	3	27	21	49	39	31	Wolverhampton Wan.	42	15	3	3	63	28	9	3	9	43	39	106	67	54	1.5820
Burnley	24	8	0	4	35	21	5	3	4	20	19	55	40	29	Tottenham Hotspur	42	10	6	5	43	24	11	5	5	43	26	86	50	53	1.7200
Blackburn Rovers	24	9	2	1	29	15	4	1	7	15	20	44	35	29	West Bromwich Alb.	42	12	4	5	48	25	7	7	7	35	32	83	57	49	1.4561
West Ham United	24	9	0	2	29	12	4	3	6	18	30	47	42	29	Sheffield Wed.	42	12	7	2	48	20	7	4	10	32	39	80	59	49	1.3559
Wolverhampton Wan.	24	9	1	2	34	14	4	1	7	25	31	59	45	28	Bolton Wanderers	42	12	5	4	37	27	8	3	10	22	24	59	51	48	1.1568

1960/61

Tottenham Hotspur	25	10	2	0	44	15	12	0	1	37	13	81	28	46	Tottenham Hotspur	42	15	3	3	65	28	16	1	4	50	27	115	55	66	2.0909
Wolverhampton Wan.	25	10	2	1	39	21	6	2	4	27	27	66	48	36	Sheffield Wed.	42	15	4	2	45	17	8	8	5	33	30	78	47	58	1.6595
Burnley	24	8	0	4	37	24	8	1	3	35	21	72	45	33	Wolverhampton Wan.	42	17	2	2	61	32	8	5	8	42	43	103	75	57	1.3733
Sheffield Wed.	24	11	1	1	29	10	2	6	3	14	18	43	28	33	Burnley	42	11	4	6	58	40	11	3	7	44	37	102	77	51	1.3246
Everton	25	8	2	2	30	14	6	2	5	29	30	59	44	32	Everton	42	13	4	4	47	23	9	2	10	40	46	87	69	50	1.2608
Aston Villa	25	10	1	2	33	18	3	2	7	21	32	54	50	29	Leicester City	42	12	4	5	54	31	6	5	10	33	39	87	70	45	1.2428

1961/62

Burnley	22	9	1	1	30	14	6	1	4	35	27	65	41	32	Ipswich Town	42	17	2	2	58	28	7	6	8	35	39	93	67	56	1.3880
Tottenham Hotspur	24	10	1	1	35	18	4	2	6	15	18	50	36	31	Burnley	42	14	4	3	57	26	7	7	7	44	41	101	67	53	1.5074
Everton	24	11	0	2	34	11	2	4	5	12	15	46	26	30	Tottenham Hotspur	42	14	4	3	59	34	7	6	8	29	35	88	69	52	1.2753
Ipswich Town	24	10	0	2	36	20	3	3	6	19	24	55	44	29	Everton	42	17	2	2	64	21	3	9	9	24	33	88	54	51	1.6296
West Ham United	24	8	3	2	31	21	4	2	5	23	26	54	47	29	Sheffield United	42	13	5	3	37	23	6	4	11	24	46	61	69	47	0.8840
Arsenal	24	7	4	1	26	15	3	3	6	15	23	41	38	27	Sheffield Wed.	42	14	4	3	47	23	6	2	13	25	35	72	58	46	1.2413

1962/63

Everton	23	9	3	0	35	12	5	3	3	17	14	52	26	34	Everton	42	14	7	0	48	17	11	4	6	36	25	84	42	61	2.0000
Tottenham Hotspur	24	8	4	1	49	20	6	1	4	24	14	73	34	33	Tottenham Hotspur	42	14	6	1	72	28	9	3	9	39	34	111	62	55	1.7903
Burnley	23	9	2	1	26	9	4	3	4	22	24	48	33	31	Burnley	42	14	4	3	41	17	8	6	7	37	40	78	57	54	1.3684
Leicester City	23	8	4	1	34	16	3	3	4	13	15	47	31	29	Leicester City	42	14	6	1	53	23	6	6	9	26	30	79	53	52	1.4905
Liverpool	23	8	1	2	24	10	3	3	6	16	20	40	30	26	Wolverhampton Wan.	42	11	6	4	51	25	9	4	8	42	40	93	65	50	1.4307
Aston Villa	22	8	1	2	25	11	2	5	4	17	22	42	33	26	Sheffield Wed.	42	10	5	6	38	26	9	5	7	39	37	77	63	48	1.2222

1963/64

Blackburn Rovers	26	7	3	3	30	15	7	3	3	31	19	61	34	34	Liverpool	42	16	0	5	60	18	10	5	6	32	27	92	45	57	2.0444
Tottenham Hotspur	24	8	2	1	31	13	6	3	4	34	32	65	45	33	Manchester United	42	15	3	3	54	19	8	4	9	36	43	90	62	53	1.4516
Liverpool	23	8	0	5	31	14	7	2	1	15	9	46	23	32	Everton	42	14	4	3	53	26	7	6	8	31	38	84	64	52	1.3125
Arsenal	26	9	3	2	46	24	4	2	6	23	29	69	53	31	Tottenham Hotspur	42	13	3	5	54	31	9	4	8	43	50	97	81	51	1.1975
Manchester United	25	9	1	2	33	11	4	3	6	19	28	52	39	30	Chelsea	42	12	3	6	36	24	8	7	6	36	32	72	56	50	1.2857
Sheffield Wed.	25	10	1	1	31	9	2	4	7	17	28	48	37	29	Sheffield Wed.	42	15	3	3	50	24	4	8	9	34	43	84	67	49	1.2537

1964/65

Manchester United	25	8	3	1	28	8	7	4	2	24	17	52	25	37	Manchester United	42	16	4	1	52	13	10	5	6	37	26	89	39	61	2.2820
Leeds United	25	10	2	1	33	15	7	1	4	16	17	49	32	37	Leeds United	42	16	3	2	53	23	10	6	5	30	29	83	52	61	1.5961
Chelsea	24	9	1	3	27	12	6	4	1	25	13	52	25	35	Chelsea	42	15	2	4	48	19	9	6	6	41	35	89	54	56	1.6481
Tottenham Hotspur	25	11	2	0	36	9	1	4	7	17	31	53	40	30	Everton	42	9	10	2	37	22	8	5	8	32	38	69	60	49	1.1500
West Ham United	24	8	2	2	28	12	4	2	6	23	23	51	35	28	Nottingham Forest	42	10	7	4	45	33	7	6	8	26	34	71	67	47	1.0597
Nottingham Forest	25	6	3	3	31	25	5	3	5	18	21	49	46	28	Tottenham Hotspur	42	18	3	0	65	20	1	4	16	22	51	87	71	45	1.2253

1965/66

Liverpool	24	9	1	2	33	10	6	3	3	16	11	49	21	34	Liverpool	42	17	2	2	52	15	9	7	5	27	19	79	34	61	2.3235
Burnley	23	9	2	1	32	14	5	2	4	21	15	53	29	32	Leeds United	42	14	4	3	49	15	9	5	7	30	23	79	38	55	2.0789
Manchester United	22	7	6	0	27	9	4	1	4	18	21	45	30	29	Burnley	42	15	3	3	45	20	9	4	8	34	27	79	47	55	1.6808
Tottenham Hotspur	23	9	2	1	34	16	3	3	5	14	18	48	34	29	Manchester United	42	12	8	1	50	20	6	7	8	34	39	84	59	51	1.4237
Leeds United	20	8	2	1	25	6	3	3	3	11	10	36	16	27	Chelsea	42	11	4	6	30	21	11	3	7	35	32	65	53	51	1.2264
Stoke City	22	6	4	1	20	11	3	4	4	14	20	34	31	26	West Bromwich Alb.	42	11	6	4	58	34	8	6	7	33	35	91	69	50	1.3188

1966/67

Manchester United	24	9	3	0	29	9	6	0	6	20	24	49	33	33	Manchester United	42	17	4	0	51	13	7	8	6	33	32	84	45	60	1.8666
Liverpool	23	7	4	0	25	10	5	3	4	18	18	43	28	31	Nottingham Forest	42	16	4	1	41	13	7	6	8	23	28	64	41	56	1.5609
Nottingham Forest	24	9	3	1	25	10	3	3	5	11	19	36	29	30	Tottenham Hotspur	42	15	3	3	44	21	9	5	7	27	27	71	48	56	1.4791
Stoke City	24	7	3	3	27	13	6	0	5	16	17	43	30	29	Leeds United	42	15	4	2	41	17	7	7	7	21	25	62	42	55	1.4761
Chelsea	24	3	6	3	21	20	6	4	2	25	17	46	37	28	Liverpool	42	12	7	2	36	17	7	6	8	28	30	64	47	51	1.3617
Leeds United	23	8	3	1	26	12	2	5	4	7	17	33	29	28	Everton	42	11	4	6	39	22	8	6	7	26	24	65	46	48	1.4130

1967/68

Manchester United	24	9	2	0	25	8	5	5	3	22	19	47	27	35	Manchester City	42	17	2	2	52	16	9	4	8	34	27	86	43	58	2.0000
Liverpool	24	10	1	1	25	7	2	7	3	10	11	35	18	32	Manchester United	42	15	2	4	49	21	9	6	6	40	34	89	55	56	1.6181
Leeds United	24	10	2	0	29	9	3	3	6	7	12	36	21	31	Liverpool	42	17	2	2	51	17	5	9	7	20	23	71	40	55	1.7750
Manchester City	24	10	1	2	35	13	3	3	5	17	18	52	31	30	Leeds United	42	17	3	1	49	14	5	6	10	22	27	71	41	53	1.7317
West Bromwich Alb.	23	7	2	3	26	12	4	3	4	19	20	45	32	27	Everton	42	18	1	2	43	13	5	5	11	24	27	67	40	52	1.6750
Newcastle United	24	9	3	0	27	10	0	6	6	10	27	37	37	27	Chelsea	42	11	7	3	34	25	7	5	9	28	43	62	68	48	0.9117

1968/69

Liverpool	26	12	2	0	28	7	5	3	4	17	8	45	15	39	Leeds United	42	18	3	0	41	9	9	10	2	25	17	66	26	67	2.5384
Leeds United	24	10	3	0	26	6	5	4	2	14	14	40	20	37	Liverpool	42	16	4	1	36	10	9	7	5	27	14	63	24	61	2.6250
Arsenal	24	8	4	1	21	6	6	3	2	11	7	32	13	35	Everton	42	14	5	2	43	10	7	10	4	34	26	77	36	57	2.1388
Everton	25	10	1	1	30	5	4	6	3	23	18	53	23	35	Arsenal	42	12	6	3	31	12	10	6	5	25	15	56	27	56	2.0740
Chelsea	25	5	6	1	21	12	6	2	5	25	16	46	28	30	Chelsea	42	11	7	3	40	24	9	3	9	33	29	73	53	50	1.3773
West Ham United	25	7	4	1	33	12	2	6	5	13	19	46	31	28	Tottenham Hotspur	42	10	8	3	39	22	4	9	8	22	29	61	51	45	1.1960

1969/70

Everton	26	12	0	1	30	13	7	3	3	17	11	47	24	41	Everton	42	17	3	1	46	19	12	5	4	26	15	72	34	66	2.1176
Leeds United	27	11	4	0	36	10	4	6	2	18	14	54	24	40	Leeds United	42	15	4	2	50	19	6	11	4	34	30	84	49	57	1.7142
Chelsea	26	7	5	0	21	8	5	5	4	20	18	41	26	34	Chelsea	42	13	7	1	36	18	8	6	7	34	32	70	50	55	1.4000
Liverpool	25	7	4	2	25	15	5	4	3	21	14	46	29	32	Derby County	42	15	3	3	45	14	7	6	8	19	23	64	37	53	1.7297
Derby County	27	9	2	3	27	8	4	3	6	9	16	36	24	31	Liverpool	42	10	7	4	34	20	10	4	7	31	22	65	42	51	1.5476
Stoke City	26	8	4	1	21	11	3	5	5	18	22	39	33	31	Coventry City	42	9	6	6	35	28	10	5	6	23	20	58	48	49	1.2083

1970/71

Leeds United	24	10	2	0	25	6	6	5	1	16	9	41	15	39	Arsenal	42	18	3	0	41	6	11	4	6	30	23	71	29	65	2.4482
Arsenal	23	9	3	0	28	4	6	3	2	16	13	44	17	36	Leeds United	42	16	2	3	40	12	11	8	2	32	18	72	30	64	2.4000
Chelsea	22	6	4	1	18	14	4	5	2	13	11	31	25	29	Tottenham Hotspur	42	11	5	5	33	19	8	9	4	21	14	54	33	52	1.6363
Tottenham Hotspur	22	6	3	2	19	8	4	5	2	14	9	33	17	28	Wolverhampton Wan.	42	13	3	5	33	22	9	5	7	31	32	64	54	52	1.1851
Manchester City	22	5	5	1	18	8	5	2	4	14	11	32	19	27	Liverpool	42	11	10	0	30	10	6	7	8	12	14	42	24	51	1.7500
Wolverhampton Wan.	23	7	1	3	22	17	4	4	4	19	22	41	39	27	Chelsea	42	12	6	3	34	21	6	9	6	18	21	52	42	51	1.2380

1971/72																														
Manchester United	23	9	1	1	25	12	5	6	1	24	15	49	27	35	Derby County	42	16	4	1	43	10	8	6	7	26	23	69	33	58	2.0909
Manchester City	23	9	2	1	29	7	4	4	3	16	15	45	22	32	Leeds United	42	17	4	0	54	10	7	5	9	19	21	73	31	57	2.3548
Leeds United	23	9	3	0	24	5	4	2	5	10	13	34	18	31	Liverpool	42	17	3	1	48	16	7	6	8	16	14	64	30	57	2.1333
Sheffield United	23	7	4	1	28	11	6	0	5	14	19	42	30	30	Manchester City	42	16	3	2	48	15	7	8	6	29	30	77	45	57	1.7111
Derby County	23	7	4	0	25	8	4	3	5	14	14	39	22	29	Arsenal	42	15	2	4	36	13	7	6	8	22	27	58	40	52	1.4500
Liverpool	23	8	3	0	21	11	3	3	6	9	12	30	23	28	Tottenham Hotspur	42	16	3	2	45	13	3	10	8	18	29	63	42	51	1.5000
1972/73																														
Liverpool	25	12	0	0	32	11	4	6	3	17	15	49	26	38	Liverpool	42	17	3	1	45	19	8	7	6	27	23	72	42	60	1.7142
Arsenal	26	10	3	1	20	7	4	4	4	14	17	34	24	35	Arsenal	42	14	5	2	31	14	9	6	6	26	29	57	43	57	1.3255
Leeds United	24	10	2	1	29	8	3	5	3	16	17	45	25	33	Leeds United	42	15	4	2	45	13	6	7	8	26	32	71	45	53	1.5777
Ipswich Town	25	6	4	2	20	11	5	5	3	15	15	35	26	31	Ipswich Town	42	10	7	4	34	20	7	7	7	21	25	55	45	48	1.2222
Newcastle United	24	8	2	2	23	12	3	3	6	17	20	40	32	27	Wolverhampton Wan.	42	13	3	5	43	23	5	8	8	23	31	66	54	47	1.2222
Derby County	25	9	2	1	24	10	2	3	8	8	27	32	37	27	West Ham United	42	12	5	4	45	25	5	7	9	22	28	67	53	46	1.2641
1973/74																														
Leeds United	23	7	3	0	22	6	9	4	0	20	6	42	12	39	Leeds United	42	12	8	1	38	18	12	6	3	28	13	66	31	62	2.1290
Liverpool	23	10	0	0	18	5	3	5	5	11	13	29	18	31	Liverpool	42	18	2	1	34	11	4	11	6	18	20	52	31	57	1.6774
Burnley	22	7	6	0	18	9	4	1	4	12	12	30	21	29	Derby County	42	13	7	1	40	16	4	7	10	12	26	52	42	48	1.2380
Everton	23	7	5	1	16	7	3	2	5	11	14	27	21	27	Ipswich Town	42	10	7	4	38	21	8	4	9	29	37	67	58	47	1.1551
Leicester City	23	6	4	2	17	9	3	4	4	13	15	30	24	26	Stoke City	42	13	6	2	39	15	2	10	9	15	27	54	42	46	1.2857
Derby County	23	7	3	1	20	9	2	4	6	5	13	25	22	25	Burnley	42	10	9	2	29	16	6	5	10	27	37	56	53	46	1.0566
1974/75																														
Ipswich Town	25	9	2	1	24	4	5	0	8	10	15	34	19	30	Derby County	42	14	4	3	41	18	7	7	7	26	31	67	49	53	1.3673
Middlesbrough	25	6	4	2	22	12	5	4	4	15	16	37	28	30	Liverpool	42	14	5	2	44	17	6	6	9	16	22	60	39	51	1.5384
Liverpool	23	8	2	2	25	11	4	3	4	9	9	34	20	29	Ipswich Town	42	17	2	2	47	14	6	3	12	19	30	66	44	51	1.5000
Everton	24	5	7	1	19	12	3	6	2	14	13	33	25	29	Everton	42	10	9	2	33	19	6	9	6	23	23	56	42	50	1.3333
Stoke City	25	8	4	1	23	12	3	3	6	16	21	39	33	29	Stoke City	42	12	7	2	40	18	5	8	8	24	30	64	48	49	1.3333
West Ham United	25	7	3	2	28	13	3	5	5	14	20	42	33	28	Sheffield United	42	12	7	2	35	20	6	6	9	23	31	58	51	49	1.1372
1975/76																														
Liverpool	24	8	4	1	25	13	4	5	2	12	7	37	20	33	Liverpool	42	14	5	2	41	21	9	9	3	25	10	66	31	60	2.1290
Manchester United	24	9	2	0	20	6	5	3	5	18	16	38	22	33	Queen's Park Rgs.	42	17	4	0	42	13	7	7	7	25	20	67	33	59	2.0303
Leeds United	23	9	1	2	26	9	5	3	3	16	13	42	22	32	Manchester United	42	16	4	1	40	13	7	6	8	28	29	68	42	56	1.6190
Derby County	24	11	0	1	27	17	2	6	4	10	13	37	30	32	Derby County	42	15	3	3	45	30	6	8	7	30	28	75	58	53	1.2931
Queen's Park Rgs.	24	9	4	0	20	5	1	6	4	11	13	31	18	30	Leeds United	42	13	3	5	37	19	8	6	7	28	27	65	46	51	1.4130
West Ham United	23	9	1	2	19	10	3	3	5	16	20	35	30	28	Ipswich Town	42	11	6	4	36	23	5	8	8	18	25	54	48	46	1.1250
1976/77																														
Liverpool	22	9	1	0	26	5	4	3	5	11	16	37	21	30	Liverpool	42	18	3	0	47	11	5	8	8	15	22	62	33	57	29
Ipswich Town	19	6	4	0	21	6	5	2	2	16	12	37	18	28	Manchester City	42	15	5	1	38	13	6	9	6	22	21	60	34	56	26
Manchester City	21	6	4	1	16	9	3	6	1	12	7	28	16	28	Ipswich Town	42	15	4	2	41	11	7	4	10	25	28	66	39	52	27
Aston Villa	20	8	1	1	32	12	3	2	5	11	14	43	26	25	Aston Villa	42	17	3	1	55	17	5	4	12	21	33	76	50	51	26
Newcastle United	19	7	3	0	19	7	2	3	4	13	15	32	22	24	Newcastle United	42	14	6	1	40	15	4	7	10	24	34	64	49	49	15
Arsenal	19	6	2	1	21	9	3	3	4	15	20	36	29	23	Manchester United	42	12	6	3	41	22	6	5	10	30	40	71	62	47	9
1977/78																														
Nottingham Forest	23	8	3	0	22	5	8	1	3	22	9	44	14	36	Nottingham Forest	42	15	6	0	37	8	10	8	3	32	16	69	24	64	45
Everton	23	7	3	2	28	16	5	4	2	19	11	47	27	31	Liverpool	42	15	4	2	37	11	9	5	7	28	23	65	34	57	31
Liverpool	23	8	2	1	16	3	4	4	4	14	13	30	16	30	Everton	42	14	4	3	47	22	8	7	6	29	23	76	45	55	31
Arsenal	23	6	4	1	17	7	6	1	5	14	12	31	19	29	Manchester City	42	14	4	3	46	21	6	8	7	28	30	74	51	52	23
Manchester City	23	9	1	2	31	10	3	3	5	13	14	44	24	28	Arsenal	42	14	5	2	38	12	7	5	9	22	25	60	37	52	23
Coventry City	23	7	3	2	28	17	4	3	4	14	19	42	36	28	West Bromwich Alb.	42	13	5	3	35	18	5	9	7	27	35	62	53	50	9
1978/79																														
Liverpool	21	9	1	0	26	2	6	2	3	21	7	47	9	33	Liverpool	42	19	2	0	51	4	11	6	4	34	12	85	16	68	69
Everton	22	8	3	0	17	5	4	6	1	15	11	32	16	33	Nottingham Forest	42	11	10	0	34	10	10	8	3	27	16	61	26	60	35
West Bromwich Alb.	20	5	3	1	20	7	8	2	1	23	11	43	18	31	West Bromwich Alb.	42	13	5	3	38	15	11	6	4	34	20	72	35	59	37
Arsenal	22	7	4	1	24	11	4	3	3	15	9	39	20	29	Everton	42	12	7	2	32	17	5	10	6	20	23	52	40	51	12
Nottingham Forest	20	4	6	0	11	6	4	5	1	10	6	21	12	27	Leeds United	42	11	4	6	41	25	7	10	4	29	27	70	52	50	18
Leeds United	23	6	1	4	24	12	3	7	2	20	18	44	30	26	Ipswich Town	42	11	4	6	34	21	9	5	7	29	28	63	49	49	14
1979/80																														
Liverpool	22	8	3	0	27	4	6	3	2	22	10	49	14	34	Liverpool	42	15	6	0	46	8	10	4	7	35	22	81	30	60	51
Manchester United	23	10	2	0	26	3	3	4	4	10	13	36	16	32	Manchester United	42	17	3	1	43	8	7	7	7	22	27	65	35	58	30
Southampton	23	8	1	2	30	13	3	3	6	6	15	36	28	26	Ipswich Town	42	14	4	3	43	13	8	5	8	25	26	68	39	53	29
Arsenal	23	5	5	2	14	7	3	5	3	13	12	27	19	26	Arsenal	42	8	10	3	24	12	10	6	5	28	24	52	36	52	16
Aston Villa	22	5	3	3	14	11	3	6	2	13	11	27	22	25	Nottingham Forest	42	16	4	1	44	11	4	4	13	19	32	63	43	48	20
Middlesbrough	22	7	4	1	16	6	3	1	6	8	13	24	19	25	Wolverhampton Wan.	42	9	6	6	29	20	10	3	8	29	27	58	47	47	11
1980/81																														
Liverpool	25	9	4	0	28	9	2	8	2	18	18	46	27	34	Aston Villa	42	16	3	2	40	13	10	5	6	32	27	72	40	60	32
Aston Villa	25	9	2	1	23	6	5	4	4	19	17	42	23	34	Ipswich Town	42	15	4	2	45	14	8	6	7	32	29	77	43	56	34
Ipswich Town	23	6	4	0	17	4	6	5	2	23	17	40	21	33	Arsenal	42	13	8	0	36	17	6	7	8	25	28	61	45	53	16
Arsenal	25	8	5	0	22	10	2	5	5	15	18	37	28	30	West Bromwich Alb.	42	15	4	2	40	15	5	8	8	20	27	60	42	52	18
Nottingham Forest	25	9	1	3	31	16	2	6	4	9	11	40	27	29	Liverpool	42	13	5	3	38	15	4	12	5	24	27	62	42	51	20
West Bromwich Alb.	24	7	3	2	20	8	3	6	3	11	16	31	24	29	Southampton	42	15	4	2	47	22	5	6	10	29	34	76	56	50	20
1981/82																														
Manchester City	20	6	3	2	19	9	4	1	4	10	13	29	22	34	Liverpool	42	14	3	4	39	14	12	6	3	41	18	80	32	87	48
Southampton	19	8	0	2	25	12	2	3	4	10	16	35	28	33	Ipswich Town	42	17	1	3	47	25	9	4	8	28	28	75	53	83	22
Swansea City	20	7	2	1	18	7	3	1	6	13	24	31	31	33	Manchester United	42	12	6	3	27	9	10	6	5	32	20	59	29	78	30
Manchester United	18	6	2	1	14	4	3	3	3	14	11	28	15	32	Tottenham Hotspur	42	12	4	5	41	26	8	7	6	26	22	67	48	71	19
Ipswich Town	16	6	1	1	15	8	4	1	3	13	11	28	19	32	Arsenal	42	13	5	3	27	15	7	6	8	21	22	48	37	71	11
Tottenham Hotspur	17	4	0	5	14	13	5	2	1	12	6	26	19	29	Swansea City	42	13	3	5	34	16	8	3	10	24	35	58	51	69	7
1982/83																														
Liverpool	21	8	2	0	32	10	5	3	3	18	9	50	19	44	Liverpool	42	16	4	1	55	16	8	6	7	32	21	87	37	82	50
Nottingham Forest	21	8	1	1	22	8	4	1	6	16	22	38	30	38	Watford	42	16	2	3	49	20	6	3	12	25	37	74	57	71	17
Watford	21	8	2	1	26	7	3	1	6	13	17	39	24	36	Manchester United	42	14	7	0	39	10	5	6	10	17	28	56	38	70	18
Manchester United	21	7	3	0	19	4	3	3	5	9	13	28	17	36	Tottenham Hotspur	42	15	4	2	50	15	5	5	11	15	35	65	50	69	15
West Ham United	21	7	1	2	23	11	4	0	7	14	21	37	32	34	Nottingham Forest	42	12	5	4	34	18	8	4	9	28	32	62	50	69	12
Coventry City	22	9	2	1	21	7	1	2	7	9	21	30	28	34	Aston Villa	42	17	2	2	47	15	4	3	14	15	35	62	50	68	12

1983/84																														
Liverpool	21	7	2	1	22	5	6	3	2	14	11	36	16	44	Liverpool	42	14	5	2	50	12	8	9	4	23	20	73	32	80	41
Manchester United	21	8	1	3	26	12	4	4	1	13	11	39	23	41	Southampton	42	15	4	2	44	17	7	7	7	22	21	66	38	77	28
West Ham United	21	7	2	2	26	11	5	1	4	9	8	35	19	39	Nottingham Forest	42	14	4	3	47	17	8	4	9	29	28	76	45	74	31
Southampton	21	8	1	1	15	6	3	4	4	9	10	24	16	38	Manchester United	42	14	3	4	43	18	6	11	4	28	23	71	41	74	30
Nottingham Forest	21	8	2	2	26	11	3	1	5	12	16	38	27	36	Queen's Park Rgs.	42	14	4	3	37	12	8	3	10	30	25	67	37	73	30
Luton Town	21	5	2	3	21	14	6	0	5	15	16	36	30	35	Arsenal	42	10	5	6	41	29	8	4	9	33	31	74	60	63	14
1984/85																														
Tottenham Hotspur	22	7	3	1	29	12	6	1	4	16	10	45	22	43	Everton	42	16	3	2	58	17	12	3	6	30	26	88	43	90	45
Everton	22	6	3	2	29	14	7	1	3	18	14	47	28	43	Liverpool	42	12	4	5	36	19	10	7	4	32	16	68	35	77	33
Manchester United	22	8	3	0	28	6	4	2	5	17	21	45	27	41	Tottenham Hotspur	42	11	3	7	46	31	12	5	4	32	20	78	51	77	27
Arsenal	22	8	3	0	24	7	4	0	7	18	21	42	28	39	Manchester United	42	13	6	2	47	13	9	4	8	30	34	77	47	76	30
Nottingham Forest	22	8	1	2	23	13	3	2	6	13	20	36	33	36	Southampton	42	13	4	4	29	18	6	7	8	27	29	56	47	68	9
Sheffield Wed.	22	6	4	1	23	13	3	4	4	12	10	35	23	35	Chelsea	42	13	3	5	38	20	5	9	7	25	28	63	48	66	15
1985/86																														
Manchester United	23	8	3	1	20	3	7	1	3	21	13	41	16	49	Liverpool	42	16	4	1	58	14	10	6	5	31	23	89	37	88	52
Chelsea	23	10	0	1	23	8	4	5	3	15	15	38	23	47	Everton	42	16	3	2	54	18	10	5	6	33	23	87	41	86	46
Everton	24	8	2	2	31	12	6	2	4	23	18	54	30	46	West Ham United	42	17	2	2	48	16	9	4	8	26	24	74	40	84	34
Liverpool	24	10	2	0	30	7	3	5	4	17	16	47	23	46	Manchester United	42	12	5	4	35	12	10	5	6	35	24	70	36	76	34
West Ham United	23	8	2	1	26	9	5	4	3	12	11	38	20	45	Sheffield Wed.	42	13	6	2	36	23	8	4	9	27	31	63	54	73	9
Sheffield Wed.	24	7	4	1	22	19	5	2	5	16	18	38	37	42	Chelsea	42	12	4	5	32	27	8	7	6	25	29	57	56	71	1
1986/87																														
Arsenal	22	8	3	0	19	3	5	3	3	17	8	36	11	45	Everton	42	16	4	1	49	11	10	4	7	27	20	76	31	86	45
Everton	22	7	3	1	25	8	5	2	4	18	12	43	20	41	Liverpool	42	15	3	3	43	16	8	5	8	29	26	72	42	77	30
Liverpool	22	6	3	2	23	9	5	2	4	17	14	40	23	38	Tottenham Hotspur	42	14	3	4	40	14	7	5	9	28	29	68	43	71	25
Nottingham Forest	22	7	4	0	24	8	4	0	7	21	23	45	31	37	Arsenal	42	12	5	4	31	12	8	5	8	27	23	58	35	70	23
Norwich City	22	7	3	1	18	12	3	4	4	13	19	31	31	37	Norwich City	42	9	10	2	27	20	8	7	6	26	31	53	51	68	2
Tottenham Hotspur	22	5	3	3	16	11	5	2	4	19	16	35	27	35	Wimbledon	42	11	5	5	32	22	8	4	9	25	28	57	50	66	7
1987/88																														
Liverpool	21	10	1	0	30	3	6	4	0	21	8	51	11	53	Liverpool	40	15	5	0	49	9	11	7	2	38	15	87	24	90	63
Nottingham Forest	20	6	2	1	23	5	7	2	2	21	11	44	16	43	Manchester United	40	14	5	1	41	17	9	7	4	30	21	71	38	81	33
Arsenal	22	7	1	3	22	9	5	3	3	13	11	35	20	40	Nottingham Forest	40	11	7	2	40	17	9	6	5	27	22	67	39	73	28
Manchester United	21	6	4	0	18	9	4	4	3	17	13	35	22	38	Everton	40	14	4	2	34	11	5	9	6	19	16	53	27	70	26
Everton	22	8	2	1	22	5	2	5	4	10	10	32	15	37	Queen's Park Rgs.	40	12	4	4	30	14	7	6	7	18	24	48	38	67	10
Queen's Park Rgs.	22	6	3	2	16	10	4	3	4	11	17	27	27	36	Arsenal	40	11	4	5	35	16	7	8	5	23	23	58	39	66	19
1988/89																														
Arsenal	18	4	2	1	14	8	7	2	2	26	12	40	20	37	Arsenal	38	10	6	3	35	19	12	4	3	38	17	73	36	76	37
Norwich City	19	4	6	1	15	12	6	1	1	13	7	28	19	37	Liverpool	38	11	5	3	33	11	11	5	3	32	17	65	28	76	37
Millwall	18	6	1	1	16	7	2	5	3	13	14	29	21	30	Nottingham Forest	38	8	7	4	31	16	9	6	4	33	27	64	43	64	21
Everton	18	5	3	1	17	8	3	3	3	8	9	25	17	30	Norwich City	38	8	7	4	23	20	9	4	6	25	25	48	45	62	3
Liverpool	18	2	5	2	9	7	5	2	2	13	6	22	13	28	Derby County	38	9	3	7	23	18	8	4	7	17	20	40	38	58	2
Coventry City	19	4	2	3	11	9	3	4	3	11	11	22	20	27	Tottenham Hotspur	38	8	6	5	31	24	7	6	6	29	22	60	46	57	14
1989/90																														
Liverpool	21	6	3	1	19	5	6	2	3	23	16	42	21	41	Liverpool	38	13	5	1	38	15	10	5	4	40	22	78	37	79	41
Aston Villa	20	8	2	1	25	11	3	2	4	8	9	33	20	37	Aston Villa	38	13	3	3	36	20	8	4	7	21	18	57	38	70	19
Arsenal	20	8	2	0	24	6	3	1	6	9	16	33	22	36	Tottenham Hotspur	38	12	1	6	35	24	7	5	7	24	23	59	47	63	12
Southampton	20	5	4	1	22	14	3	3	4	16	18	38	32	31	Arsenal	38	14	3	2	38	11	4	5	10	16	27	54	38	62	16
Chelsea	20	3	5	2	19	16	5	2	3	14	12	33	28	31	Chelsea	38	8	7	4	31	24	8	5	6	27	26	58	50	60	8
Norwich City	20	4	6	0	15	9	4	1	5	10	11	25	20	31	Everton	38	14	3	2	40	16	3	5	11	17	30	57	46	59	11
1990/91																														
Arsenal	20	8	2	0	25	5	5	5	0	15	5	40	10	46	Arsenal	38	15	4	0	51	10	9	9	1	23	8	74	18	83	56
Liverpool	19	8	1	0	23	5	6	2	2	15	11	38	16	45	Liverpool	38	14	3	2	42	13	9	4	6	35	27	77	40	76	37
Crystal Palace	20	7	3	0	16	9	5	3	2	15	9	31	18	42	Crystal Palace	38	11	6	2	26	17	9	3	7	24	24	50	41	69	9
Leeds United	20	7	2	2	24	10	4	4	1	12	8	36	18	39	Leeds United	38	12	2	5	46	23	7	5	7	19	24	65	47	64	18
Tottenham Hotspur	20	7	2	1	25	13	2	4	4	8	12	33	25	33	Manchester City	38	12	3	4	35	25	5	8	6	29	28	64	53	62	11
Manchester United	20	6	2	3	19	10	3	4	2	11	12	30	22	33	Manchester United	38	11	4	4	34	17	5	8	6	24	28	58	45	59	13
1991/92																														
Manchester United	21	7	3	0	21	3	7	3	1	21	11	42	14	48	Leeds United	42	13	8	0	38	13	9	8	4	36	24	74	37	82	37
Leeds United	23	7	5	0	21	11	5	5	1	18	7	39	18	46	Manchester United	42	12	7	2	34	13	9	8	4	29	20	63	33	78	30
Sheffield Wed.	22	8	2	1	25	10	3	4	4	11	13	36	23	39	Sheffield Wed.	42	13	5	3	39	24	8	7	6	23	25	62	49	75	13
Manchester City	23	6	3	3	16	13	5	3	3	16	14	32	27	39	Arsenal	42	12	7	2	51	22	7	8	6	30	24	81	46	72	35
Aston Villa	22	8	1	3	22	12	3	2	5	11	15	33	27	36	Manchester City	42	13	4	4	32	14	7	6	8	29	34	61	48	70	13
Liverpool	22	6	3	1	16	9	2	8	2	9	9	25	18	35	Liverpool	42	13	5	3	34	17	3	11	7	13	23	47	40	64	7
1992/93																														
Norwich City	22	7	3	1	15	9	5	2	4	19	25	34	34	41	Manchester United	42	14	5	2	39	14	10	7	4	28	17	67	31	84	36
Manchester United	22	6	3	2	17	8	4	5	2	13	9	30	17	38	Aston Villa	42	13	5	3	36	16	8	6	7	21	24	57	40	74	17
Aston Villa	22	6	3	2	18	11	4	5	2	14	13	32	24	38	Norwich City	42	13	6	2	31	19	8	3	10	30	46	61	65	72	-4
Blackburn Rovers	22	8	1	2	22	8	2	6	3	12	12	34	20	37	Blackburn Rovers	42	13	4	4	38	18	7	7	7	30	28	68	46	71	22
Ipswich Town	22	5	6	0	18	11	3	6	2	13	12	31	23	36	Queen's Park Rgs.	42	11	5	5	41	32	6	7	8	22	23	63	55	63	8
Chelsea	22	4	5	2	13	10	5	3	3	15	12	28	22	35	Liverpool	42	13	4	4	41	18	3	7	11	21	37	62	55	59	7
1993/94																														
Manchester United	23	8	4	0	25	10	9	1	1	24	10	49	20	56	Manchester United	42	14	6	1	39	13	13	5	3	41	25	80	38	92	42
Blackburn Rovers	22	7	3	2	16	8	5	3	2	15	10	31	18	42	Blackburn Rovers	42	14	5	2	31	11	11	4	6	32	25	63	36	84	27
Leeds United	23	8	2	1	24	13	3	6	3	14	13	38	26	41	Newcastle United	42	14	4	3	51	14	9	4	8	31	27	82	41	77	41
Arsenal	23	7	3	2	17	8	4	4	3	10	5	27	13	40	Arsenal	42	10	8	3	25	15	8	9	4	28	13	53	28	71	25
Newcastle United	22	6	3	2	22	8	4	3	4	16	13	38	21	36	Leeds United	42	13	6	2	37	18	5	10	6	28	21	65	39	70	26
Queen's Park Rgs.	22	6	3	1	21	11	4	2	6	16	18	37	29	35	Wimbledon	42	12	5	4	35	21	6	6	9	21	32	56	53	65	3
1994/95																														
Blackburn Rovers	21	8	0	1	27	9	7	4	1	18	7	45	16	49	Blackburn Rovers	42	17	2	2	54	21	10	6	5	26	18	80	39	89	41
Manchester United	22	9	1	1	23	3	5	3	3	19	16	42	19	46	Manchester United	42	16	4	1	42	4	10	6	5	35	24	77	28	88	49
Liverpool	22	7	3	0	20	5	5	3	4	20	14	40	19	42	Nottingham Forest	42	12	6	3	36	18	10	5	6	36	25	72	43	77	29
Newcastle United	21	6	3	0	23	9	5	3	4	17	15	40	24	39	Liverpool	42	13	5	3	38	13	8	6	7	27	24	65	37	74	28
Nottingham Forest	22	6	3	2	19	11	5	3	3	16	12	35	23	39	Leeds United	42	13	5	3	35	15	7	8	6	24	23	59	38	73	21
Tottenham Hotspur	22	4	3	4	18	17	5	3	3	20	17	38	34	33	Newcastle United	42	14	6	1	46	20	6	6	9	21	27	67	47	72	20

1995/96																														
Newcastle United	20	10	0	0	24	5	4	3	3	16	13	40	18	45	Manchester United	38	15	4	0	36	9	10	3	6	37	26	73	35	82	38
Manchester United	21	8	3	0	24	9	4	2	4	16	14	40	23	41	Newcastle United	38	17	1	1	38	9	7	5	7	28	28	66	37	78	29
Liverpool	20	7	2	1	23	6	3	3	4	13	12	36	18	35	Liverpool	38	14	4	1	46	13	6	7	6	24	21	70	34	71	36
Tottenham Hotspur	21	4	3	3	12	11	5	5	1	15	10	27	21	35	Aston Villa	38	11	5	3	32	15	7	4	8	20	20	52	35	63	17
Arsenal	21	6	4	1	19	10	3	3	4	9	8	28	18	34	Arsenal	38	10	7	2	30	16	7	5	7	19	16	49	32	63	17
Nottingham Forest	20	6	4	0	18	8	2	6	2	12	19	30	27	34	Everton	38	10	5	4	35	19	7	5	7	29	25	64	44	61	20
1996/97																														
Liverpool	21	6	4	1	23	10	6	2	2	15	9	38	19	42	Manchester United	38	12	5	2	38	17	9	7	3	38	27	76	44	75	32
Manchester United	20	7	2	1	22	8	3	5	2	20	17	42	25	37	Newcastle United	38	13	3	3	54	20	6	8	5	19	20	73	40	68	33
Arsenal	20	6	4	0	24	10	4	3	3	13	10	37	20	37	Arsenal	38	10	5	4	36	18	9	6	4	26	14	62	32	68	30
Wimbledon	19	6	2	1	18	10	5	2	3	15	13	33	23	37	Liverpool	38	10	6	3	38	19	9	5	5	24	18	62	37	68	25
Newcastle United	20	6	2	2	27	12	4	2	4	8	10	35	22	34	Aston Villa	38	11	5	3	27	13	6	5	8	20	21	47	34	61	13
Aston Villa	20	6	2	2	16	7	4	2	4	13	12	29	19	34	Chelsea	38	9	8	2	33	22	7	3	9	25	33	58	55	59	3
1997/98																														
Manchester United	21	9	1	0	30	4	5	3	3	19	12	49	16	46	Arsenal	38	15	2	2	43	10	8	7	4	25	23	68	33	78	35
Blackburn Rovers	21	7	3	1	25	12	4	5	1	13	9	38	21	41	Manchester United	38	13	4	2	42	9	10	4	5	31	17	73	26	77	47
Chelsea	21	6	2	1	17	7	6	1	5	29	14	46	21	39	Liverpool	38	13	2	4	42	16	5	9	5	26	26	68	42	65	26
Liverpool	20	7	0	3	23	10	4	4	2	13	9	36	19	37	Chelsea	38	13	2	4	37	14	7	1	11	34	29	71	43	63	28
Leeds United	21	5	3	3	16	12	5	2	3	14	11	30	23	35	Leeds United	38	9	5	5	31	21	8	3	8	26	25	57	46	59	11
Arsenal	20	6	2	2	21	8	3	5	2	14	15	35	23	34	Blackburn Rovers	38	11	4	4	40	26	5	6	8	17	26	57	52	58	5
1998/99																														
Aston Villa	20	7	2	1	19	12	4	4	2	12	8	31	20	39	Manchester United	38	14	4	1	45	18	8	9	2	35	19	80	37	79	43
Chelsea	20	6	4	0	15	5	3	6	1	16	12	31	17	37	Arsenal	38	14	5	0	34	5	8	7	4	25	12	59	17	78	42
Manchester United	20	7	3	1	27	12	2	5	2	12	11	39	23	35	Chelsea	38	12	6	1	29	13	8	9	2	28	17	57	30	75	27
Arsenal	20	6	4	0	15	4	3	4	3	7	7	22	11	35	Leeds United	38	12	5	2	32	9	6	8	5	30	25	62	34	67	28
Leeds United	20	6	3	1	18	5	2	6	2	16	14	34	19	33	West Ham United	38	11	3	5	32	26	5	6	8	14	27	46	53	57	-7
West Ham United	20	6	3	1	16	10	3	2	5	8	13	24	23	32	Aston Villa	38	10	3	6	33	28	5	7	7	18	18	51	46	55	5
1999/2000																														
Leeds United	20	8	1	1	16	7	6	1	3	18	15	34	22	44	Manchester United	38	15	4	0	59	16	13	3	3	38	29	97	45	91	52
Manchester United	19	8	2	0	33	7	5	2	2	17	18	50	25	43	Arsenal	38	14	3	2	42	17	8	4	7	31	26	73	43	73	30
Arsenal	20	8	2	1	23	8	4	1	4	13	12	36	20	39	Leeds United	38	12	2	5	29	18	9	4	6	29	25	58	43	69	15
Sunderland	20	7	3	1	18	8	4	2	3	17	16	35	24	38	Liverpool	38	11	4	4	28	13	8	6	5	23	17	51	30	67	21
Liverpool	20	8	0	3	20	8	3	4	2	11	9	31	17	37	Chelsea	38	12	5	2	35	12	6	6	7	18	22	53	34	65	19
Tottenham Hotspur	19	6	1	2	21	12	3	3	4	10	11	31	23	31	Aston Villa	38	8	8	3	23	12	7	5	7	23	23	46	35	58	11
2000/01																														
Manchester United	21	8	1	1	28	5	6	4	1	20	10	48	15	47	Manchester United	38	15	2	2	49	12	9	6	4	30	19	79	31	80	48
Arsenal	21	9	2	0	30	7	2	4	4	8	14	38	21	39	Arsenal	38	15	3	1	45	13	5	7	7	18	25	63	38	70	25
Ipswich Town	21	5	4	2	17	10	6	0	4	15	12	32	22	37	Liverpool	38	13	4	2	40	14	7	5	7	31	25	71	39	69	32
Sunderland	21	7	3	0	12	4	3	3	5	13	17	25	21	36	Leeds United	38	11	3	5	36	21	9	5	5	28	22	64	43	68	21
Leicester City	20	6	3	1	15	10	4	2	4	8	11	23	21	35	Ipswich Town	38	11	5	3	31	15	9	1	9	26	27	57	42	66	15
Liverpool	20	8	1	1	23	7	2	2	6	14	18	37	25	33	Chelsea	38	13	3	3	44	20	4	7	8	24	25	68	45	61	23
2001/02																														
Arsenal	20	5	2	3	22	18	6	4	0	19	6	41	24	39	Arsenal	38	12	4	3	42	25	14	5	0	37	11	79	36	87	43
Newcastle United	20	6	1	3	16	11	6	2	2	22	14	38	25	39	Liverpool	38	12	5	2	33	14	12	3	4	34	16	67	30	80	37
Leeds United	20	4	4	1	16	10	6	4	1	14	7	30	17	38	Manchester United	38	11	2	6	40	17	13	3	3	47	28	87	45	77	42
Liverpool	19	5	2	2	12	8	6	2	2	17	11	29	19	37	Newcastle United	38	12	3	4	40	23	9	5	5	34	29	74	52	71	22
Manchester United	20	6	1	3	26	11	5	2	3	22	19	48	30	36	Leeds United	38	9	6	4	31	21	9	6	4	22	16	53	37	66	16
Chelsea	20	4	4	1	17	7	4	5	2	14	9	31	16	33	Chelsea	38	11	4	4	43	21	6	9	4	23	17	66	38	64	28
2002/03																														
Arsenal	21	9	1	1	25	9	4	3	3	17	13	42	22	43	Manchester United	38	16	2	1	42	12	9	6	4	32	22	74	34	83	40
Chelsea	21	6	3	1	19	6	4	5	2	15	11	34	17	38	Arsenal	38	15	2	2	47	20	8	7	4	38	22	85	42	78	43
Manchester United	21	9	1	1	21	6	2	4	4	12	15	33	21	38	Newcastle United	38	15	2	2	36	17	6	4	9	27	31	63	48	69	15
Newcastle United	20	9	0	1	20	7	2	2	6	14	22	34	29	35	Chelsea	38	12	5	2	41	15	7	5	7	27	23	68	38	67	30
Everton	21	6	3	1	14	9	4	2	5	9	13	23	22	35	Liverpool	38	9	8	2	30	16	9	2	8	31	25	61	41	64	20
Liverpool	21	5	5	1	16	8	4	2	4	14	13	30	21	34	Blackburn Rovers	38	9	7	3	24	15	7	5	7	28	28	52	43	60	9
2003/04																														
Manchester United	19	8	1	1	24	7	7	0	2	14	6	38	13	46	Arsenal	38	15	4	0	40	14	11	8	0	33	12	73	26	90	47
Arsenal	19	7	2	0	16	6	6	4	0	19	6	35	12	45	Chelsea	38	12	4	3	34	13	12	3	4	33	17	67	30	79	37
Chelsea	19	7	1	1	20	7	6	2	2	16	9	36	16	42	Manchester United	38	12	4	3	37	15	11	2	6	27	20	64	35	75	29
Charlton Athletic	19	3	3	3	13	14	5	3	2	14	8	27	22	30	Liverpool	38	10	4	5	29	15	6	8	5	26	22	55	37	60	18
Fulham	19	5	2	3	16	11	3	2	4	14	15	30	26	28	Newcastle United	38	11	5	3	33	14	2	12	5	19	26	52	40	56	12
Liverpool	18	4	1	4	15	12	3	4	2	13	9	28	21	26	Aston Villa	38	9	6	4	24	19	6	5	8	24	25	48	44	56	4
2004/05																														
Chelsea	20	8	2	0	20	3	7	2	1	20	5	40	8	49	Chelsea	38	14	5	0	35	6	15	3	1	37	9	72	15	95	57
Arsenal	20	6	4	0	27	11	7	1	2	21	11	48	22	44	Arsenal	38	13	5	1	54	19	12	3	4	33	17	87	36	83	51
Manchester United	20	7	3	0	19	5	4	4	2	12	8	31	13	40	Manchester United	38	12	6	1	31	12	10	5	4	27	14	58	26	77	32
Everton	20	7	1	2	13	10	5	3	2	10	7	23	17	40	Everton	38	12	2	5	24	15	6	5	8	21	31	45	46	61	-1
Middlesbrough	20	6	3	1	18	9	4	2	4	16	15	34	24	35	Liverpool	38	12	4	3	31	15	5	3	11	21	26	52	41	58	11
Liverpool	20	8	1	1	20	7	2	3	5	14	13	34	20	34	Bolton Wanderers	38	9	5	5	25	18	7	5	7	24	26	49	44	58	5
2005/06																														
Chelsea	20	11	0	0	28	6	7	1	1	15	3	43	9	55	Chelsea	38	18	1	0	47	9	11	3	5	25	13	72	22	91	50
Manchester United	20	6	3	1	20	6	7	2	1	20	11	40	17	44	Manchester United	38	13	5	1	37	8	12	3	4	35	26	72	34	83	38
Liverpool	18	8	1	1	16	4	4	3	1	10	5	26	9	40	Liverpool	38	15	3	1	32	8	10	4	5	25	17	57	25	82	32
Tottenham Hotspur	20	7	3	1	17	7	3	4	2	12	11	29	18	37	Arsenal	38	14	3	2	48	13	6	4	9	20	18	68	31	67	37
Wigan Athletic	20	6	1	4	16	14	5	0	4	9	10	25	24	34	Tottenham Hotspur	38	12	5	2	31	16	6	6	7	22	22	53	38	65	15
Arsenal	19	8	0	1	20	4	2	3	5	7	11	27	15	33	Blackburn Rovers	38	13	3	3	31	17	6	3	10	20	25	51	42	63	9
2006/07																														
Manchester United	21	9	1	1	26	7	8	1	1	21	6	47	13	53	Manchester United	38	15	2	2	46	12	13	3	3	37	15	83	27	89	56
Chelsea	21	7	4	0	20	8	7	1	2	17	9	37	17	47	Chelsea	38	12	7	0	37	11	12	4	3	27	13	64	24	83	40
Bolton Wanderers	21	7	1	3	17	10	5	2	3	10	8	27	18	39	Liverpool	38	14	4	1	39	7	6	4	9	18	20	57	27	68	30
Liverpool	21	8	2	0	20	3	3	2	6	9	13	29	16	37	Arsenal	38	12	6	1	43	16	7	5	7	20	19	63	35	68	28
Arsenal	21	5	5	0	24	8	5	1	5	13	11	37	19	36	Tottenham Hotspur	38	12	3	4	34	22	5	6	8	23	32	57	54	60	3
Portsmouth	21	7	2	1	19	7	3	3	5	13	14	32	21	35	Everton	38	11	4	4	33	17	4	9	6	19	19	52	36	58	16

YOUR AUTHOR

My father was a Birkenhead man, working on aircraft repair and maintenance at Feltham and Redhill during the war, when business matters brought him to Tollerton, near Nottingham. A meeting with my mother at the local Palais de Dance led to their marriage in 1942 and my arrival in 1944. Life was not particularly easy for anyone in the 1940s, but after a few years living with my grandparents, my parents were able to buy a house of their own in Nottingham.

My father took me to my first match at the City Ground in 1955. I don't remember him going to many games, though he always kept an eye on Tranmere Rovers' results. My grandfather Wilfred Blythe was a regular on the terraces of Meadow Lane and the City Ground but late in life he found the match-day crowds crossing Trent Bridge difficult to contend with and settled for the games at the County Ground, since it was the nearer of the two. When I started cycling or walking the three miles to the grounds on my own, I followed grandfather's example and would watch County one week and Forest the next. I believe many other people also supported both clubs in those days; I don't think there were as many one-club-only supporters as there are today.

With Forest's rise and County's decline in the late 1950s I found myself at the City Ground most of the time. I saw many of the games in Forest's 1959 FA Cup run; luckily my school was not far away for catching the last few minutes of mid-week afternoon replay action! My four entries in the club's ballot for Wembley tickets were unsuccessful, but luckily a friend in the Scouts was a cousin of Forest reserve winger John Rowlands and tickets were eventually acquired for both of us. Here we are at Victoria Station, about to catch our 12/6d special to the match. I'm in the middle, waving a rattle, which is still up in the attic somewhere. Do they allow them in grounds these days, or are they classed as offensive weapons?

My efforts at playing the game were not of the highest standards – I usually played at full-back, where my height and weight might have been effective if it wasn't for the fact that short sight made it difficult for me to see the rest of the players. My only claim to fame is appearing once in the same Mundella school team as the young David Pleat, later the manager of Luton Town, Spurs and Leicester City. As far as I know, I'm not related to Tony Brown of West Bromwich Albion and England fame.

I had something of a culture shock in 1962 when I left the bright lights and heady heights of Nottingham and Division One football for university in Bangor, North Wales. However, adjustments were soon made and I was able to enjoy the delights of Cheshire League football. Most clubs in this league had a star player on their books, usually well past their best, but still able to show flashes of former skills. In Bangor City's case, it was Tommy Banks, once of Bolton Wanderers. Tommy was by then as wide as he was tall; since many opposing right-wingers were callow youths of 17 or so, I expect Tommy took great delight in shepherding them into touch (or the stands) every now and then.

Armed with degrees in Physics and Pure Mathematics I went south to London in 1966 to join a new computer programming team set up by International Computers and Tabulators, later ICL. In London I was fortunate to see the Chelsea team of Osgood, Cooke and others, playing the sort of football that I believe Mr Abramovich is looking for today. My football watching declined to a few games a year in the next decade, as marriage, young children and life in Dorking took priority. There was short-lived excitement in the Surrey town when Guildford City arrived to play as Guildford and Dorking United. Great ambitions for the new club soon turned to dust.

In 1981 I was still at ICL, working in office automation, a business area we now call information technology. The opportunity arose to move back to Nottingham and work in the same field for a telecoms company, Plessey. It seemed a good idea for all sorts of reasons, personal as well as professional. Living down south, I hadn't seen much of Forest's great European Cup years under Brian Clough, but he was still the man in charge when I returned to Nottingham. I was able to persuade my eldest son that he was not really a Liverpool fan and we settled back into a City Ground much changed in appearance since I was a boy. Annual visits to Wembley became the norm. Watching Des Walker and Stuart Pearce in their pomp was a real treat.

By the early 1990s, Plessey had become part of Lord Weinstock's GEC and their dreams of cracking the IT market had faded. Redundancy followed, though my severance terms were so miserly that they only just covered the costs of a short holiday for my partner and me. I needed a regular income; however 50 counts as old age in computing companies and the litany of "you are not too old to work here, Mr Brown" meant just the opposite. I grew tired of the interview rounds and tried to work out if I could survive self-employed.

A digression. My background in software meant that when a benchmark was needed for a new computer at Plessey, I thought something football-orientated might be suitable. A benchmark is a set of routines that are run repeatedly to test some aspect of the hardware. On this occasion we needed to test the low-level disc handling routines, so I typed in a season's worth of Division One results and wrote a program to calculate the league table. We timed the calculation program and used it as the benchmark; when we needed more data I added a few more seasons. Later on, the data acquisition bug really caught hold of me and I finished off what I imagine was the first complete database of Football League results.

1998: Yours truly gets to grips with two trophies. Notts County were Third Division champions that year and Nottingham Forest won the First Division.

After the lack of success in finding what my family would call 'a proper job' I set out to see if I could make a living from a business based on the football databases. There was some initial success with licensing them to media groups but it rapidly became apparent that the business could not survive on data sales alone. The databases represent a valuable business asset and I knew they could help in producing books. At the time I was working closely with the Association of Football Statisticians; as a first step into publishing I took over production of their Annuals for the 1930s. The next step was to publish complete record books. Breedon Books had been pioneers in this field but had more or less run out of steam by then, leaving Dave Twydell's Yore Publications as the most active publisher of such titles. At that time (the mid-1990s) there were still a couple of dozen League clubs without a complete record, so I started the 'definitive' series to try to fill in the remaining gaps.

The business today is far more active in book publishing than I envisaged at the start. Nevertheless, I have maintained a focus on the databases and the range and content of them continues to expand. The next big step for the data is to compile 'the ultimate database' of English football, which will contain every result, attendance, and line-up since 1888. The raw data is already on the computer, but the task of turning into a usable product and making it available on the internet remains only a plan at this stage. As for my publications, the "Match by Match" series of season-by-season results and line-ups books has reached 1962/63. With 1969/70 planned as the final edition (to overlap the first Rothmans Yearbook) I have a few year's work left on them, and some gaps to fill between 1893 and 1939. There are plans for more definitives and my catalogue of general books on football continues to increase.

The fact you are reading this paragraph probably means I owe you my thanks for buying the book. Many others have been helpful in supporting my efforts over the years. If you don't get a mention below and feel you deserve one, you will have to excuse my fading memory! Don Starr and Ray Spiller were supportive of my early efforts to get underway. Phil Heady and more than a hundred others helped the major project to document the qualifying rounds of the FA Cup and were thanked in the book that followed. Among the 400 regular customers on the mailing list, a dozen of you seem to have bought nearly every title. I won't embarrass you here by naming you, but thanks! Fred Lee, Eddie Stubbings and others keep me entertained on the phone from time to time. Fellow publishers Dave Twydell and John Robinson are quick to offer advice and support. Thanks go to all my authors, with apologies if I caused you extra work. John Nagle at the Football League asks me odd questions but I seem able to answer most of them. Keith Warsop proffers advice when I need it. Kit Bartlett spends time at Colindale for me. John Brodie must find my coffee to his taste and I drink Ken Smales' tea. Michael Joyce's player database is a work of art and I am fortunate to have the use of it. Thanks of course to my immediate family of Claire, Duncan, Helen, Hilary, Howard, Jenny, Jessica, Terri and Tabitha, all of whom have to put up with the slightly unconventional me. Finally, I must not forget to say thanks to my father Alec, still going strong at 91, and still enquiring after Tranmere Rovers.

Tony Brown
October 2007

SOCCERDATA PUBLICATIONS

Listed in order of ISBN. Some titles are out of print.

ISBN	Title	Year	Author
978-1-899468-00-3	FL & Premiership Results and Dates	2006	Tony Brown
978-1-899468-01-0	Definitive Rochdale	1995	Steve Phillipps
978-1-899468-02-7	Definitive Northampton Town	1996	Frank Grande
978-1-899468-03-4	Definitive Chesterfield (1st ed.)	1996	Stuart Basson
978-1-899468-04-1	Definitive Portsmouth	1996	Mick Cooper
978-1-899468-05-8	Definitive Barnsley	1996	Brian Dennis
978-1-899468-06-5	Definitive QPR	1996	Gordon Macey
978-1-899468-07-2	Definitive Scunthorpe United	1996	Michael Norton
978-1-899468-08-9	Definitive Aldershot	1997	Mark Elliott
978-1-899468-09-6	Definitive Torquay United	1997	Leigh Edwards
978-1-899468-10-2	Definitive Luton Town	1997	Steve Bailey/Brian Ellis/Alan Shury
978-1-899468-11-9	Definitive Reading	1998	Leigh Edwards/David Downs
978-1-899468-12-6	Definitive Hartlepool United	1998	Gordon Small
978-1-899468-13-3	Definitive Hull City	1999	Mike Peterson
978-1-899468-14-0	Definitive Barrow	2000	Michael Gardner
978-1-899468-15-7	Definitive Darlington	2000	Frank Tweddle
978-1-899468-16-4	Definitive Newton Heath	2002	Alan Shury/Brian Landamore
978-1-899468-17-1	Definitive Cardiff City	2002	Richard Shepherd
978-1-899468-18-8	Definitive Bournemouth	2003	Leigh Edwards/John Treleven
978-1-899468-19-5	Definitive West Ham United	2003	John Northcutt
978-1-899468-20-1	Definitive Gillingham	2003	Tony Brown/Roger Triggs
978-1-899468-21-8	All About Avenue, the Definitive Bradford PA	2004	Malcolm Hartley/Tim Clapham
978-1-899468-22-5	Iron in the Blood; Thames Ironworks	2005	John Powles
978-1-899468-23-2	Definitive Workingtor	2005	Tom Allen
978-1-899468-24-9	Definitive Halifax Town	2005	Johnny Meynell
978-1-899468-25-6	Match by Match 24/25	2002	Tony Brown
978-1-899468-26-3	Match by Match 25/26	2003	Tony Brown
978-1-899468-27-0	Match by Match 26/27	2003	Tony Brown
978-1-899468-28-7	Match by Match 27/28	2004	Tony Brown
978-1-899468-29-4	Match by Match 28/29	2004	Tony Brown
978-1-899468-30-0	Match by Match 29/30	2005	Tony Brown
978-1-899468-31-7	Match by Match 30/31	2005	Tony Brown
978-1-899468-32-4	Match by Match 31/32	2006	Tony Brown
978-1-899468-33-1	Match by Match 32/33	2007	Tony Brown
978-1-899468-34-8	AFS Annual 34	1996	Tony Brown
978-1-899468-35-5	AFS Annual 35	1997	Tony Brown
978-1-899468-36-2	AFS Annual 36	1997	Tony Brown
978-1-899468-37-9	AFS Annual 37	1998	Tony Brown
978-1-899468-38-6	AFS Annual 38	1998	Tony Brown
978-1-899468-39-3	AFS Annual 39	1999	Tony Brown
978-1-899468-40-9	Match by Match 1919/20 & 1920/21	2005	Tony Brown
978-1-899468-41-6	Match by Match 1921/22	2005	Tony Brown
978-1-899468-42-3	Match by Match 1922/23	2005	Tony Brown
978-1-899468-43-0	Match by Match 1923/24	2005	Tony Brown
978-1-899468-44-7	Match by Match 1888/89 to 1892/93	2007	Tony Brown
978-1-899468-47-8	Match by Match 46/47	2002	Tony Brown
978-1-899468-48-5	Match by Match 47/48	2002	Tony Brown
978-1-899468-49-2	Match by Match 48/49	2002	Tony Brown
978-1-899468-50-8	Match by Match 49/50	2002	Tony Brown
978-1-899468-51-5	Match by Match 50/51	2002	Tony Brown
978-1-899468-52-2	Match by Match 51/52	2003	Tony Brown
978-1-899468-53-9	Match by Match 52/53	2003	Tony Brown
978-1-899468-54-6	Match by Match 53/54	2004	Tony Brown
978-1-899468-55-3	Match by Match 54/55	2004	Tony Brown
978-1-899468-56-0	Match by Match 55/56	2005	Tony Brown
978-1-899468-57-7	Match by Match 56/57	2005	Tony Brown
978-1-899468-58-4	Match by Match 57/58	2005	Tony Brown
978-1-899468-59-1	Beezer League Yearbook 95/96	1996	Leigh Edwards/Alan Platt
978-1-899468-60-7	Unibond League Yearbook 95/96	1996	Leigh Edwards/Alan Platt
978-1-899468-61-4	Tommy Lawton - Match by Match	2000	Tony Brown/Keith Warsop
978-1-899468-62-1	Special & Intermediate Internationals	2002	Keith Warsop
978-1-899468-63-8	Football League Players' Records (1st ed.)	2002	Michael Joyce
978-1-899468-64-5	Scots Players' Records 1976-2000	2002	Steve Emms/Derek Gray
978-1-899468-65-2	Scots Players' Records 1946-1975	2004	Steve Emms/Richard Beal
978-1-899468-66-9	Scots Players' Records 1890-39	2007	Steve Emms/Richard Wells
978-1-899468-67-6	Football League Players' Records (2nd ed.)	2004	Michael Joyce
978-1-899468-68-3	Premiership and FL Referees 1888-2005	2005	Gilbert Upton
978-1-899468-69-0	FA Trophy Complete Results	2005	Tony Brown
978-1-899468-70-6	FA Vase Complete Results	2005	Tony Brown
978-1-899468-71-3	FA Cup Complete Results (2nd ed.)	2006	Tony Brown
978-1-899468-72-0	FA Cup Complete Results (1st ed.)	1999	Tony Brown
978-1-899468-73-7	Red Missed (sendings-off 1979/80 to 2000/01)	2001	Tony Brown
978-1-899468-74-4	FL Results and Dates Vol 1	2002	Tony Brown
978-1-899468-75-1	FL Results and Dates Vol 2	2002	Tony Brown
978-1-899468-76-8	FL Results and Dates Vol 3	2002	Tony Brown
978-1-899468-77-5	FL Results and Dates Vol 4	2002	Tony Brown
978-1-899468-78-2	Early FA Cup Finals & the Southern Amateurs	2004	Keith Warsop
978-1-899468-79-9	Soccerdata Form Guide 2004/05	2005	Tony Brown
978-1-899468-80-5	Hamilton Academicals Who's Who	1997	Peter McLeish

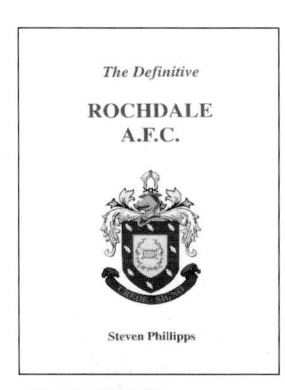

SOCCERDATA PUBLICATIONS: CONTINUED

ISBN	Title	Year	Author
978-1-899468-81-2	Crewe Alexandra Match by Match	1997	Marco Crisp
978-1-899468-82-9	Definitive Chesterfield (2nd ed.)	1997	Stuart Basson
978-1-899468-83-6	Shooting Stars - Blackburn Olympic	2007	Graham Phythian
978-1-899468-84-3	Football in Europe 2002/03	2003	Graeme Riley
978-1-899468-85-0	Football in Europe 2003/04	2004	Graeme Riley
978-1-899468-86-7	The Forgotten FA Cup (of 1945/46)	2007	Jack Rollin/Tony Brown
978-1-899468-87-4	Soccerdata Form Guide 2005/06	2005	Tony Brown
978-1-899468-88-1	Football in Europe 2004/05	2005	Graeme Riley
978-1-899468-89-8	Football League Cup Complete Results	2007	Tony Brown
978-1-899468-90-4	The Wembley Way - Halesowen Town	2006	John Woodhouse
978-1-899468-91-1	The Lads of '23	2006	Brian Belton
978-1-899468-92-8	Match by Match 58/59	2006	Tony Brown
978-1-899468-93-5	Match by Match 59/60	2006	Tony Brown
978-1-899468-94-2	Match by Match 60/61	2007	Tony Brown
978-1-899468-95-9	Soccerdata Form Guide 2006/07	2006	Tony Brown
978-1-899468-96-6	Football in Europe 2005/06	2006	Graeme Riley
978-1-899468-97-3	Match by Match 61/62	2007	Tony Brown
978-1-899468-98-0	Football in Europe 2006/07	2007	Graeme Riley
978-1-899468-99-7	Definitive Notts County	2007	Keith Warsop/Tony Brown
978-1-905891-00-9	Soccerdata Form Guide 2007/08	2007	Tony Brown
978-1-905891-01-6	Up the Avenue - Bradford PA Centenary Book	2007	Malcolm Hartley/Tim Clapham
978-1-905891-02-3	Champions All!	2007	Tony Brown
978-1-905891-03-0	Match by Match 1962/63	2007	Tony Brown

The first title to carry the SoccerData imprint was Definitive Luton Town in 1997.

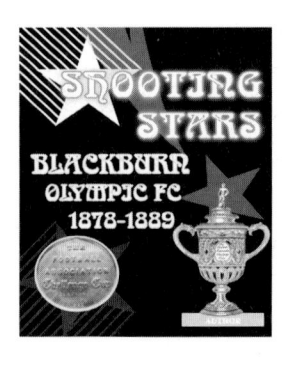

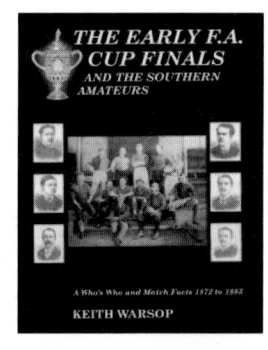

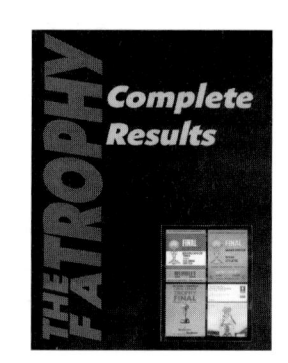

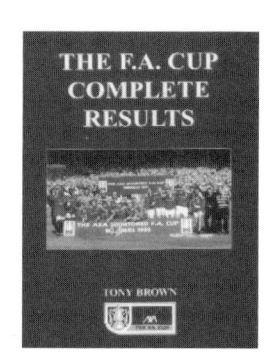

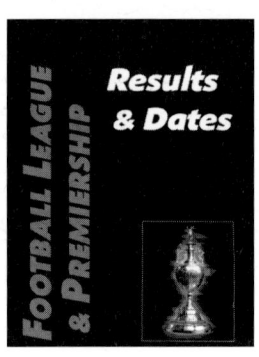

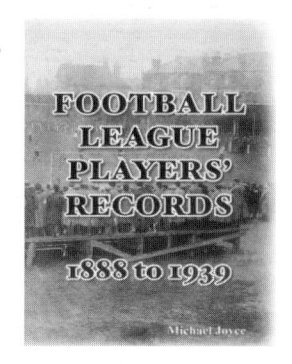